ECONOMIC PRINCIPLES
AND PUBLIC ISSUES

Other Rinehart books on economic principles and policies

RICHARD H. LEFTWICH *The Price System and Resource Allocation*
ALFRED R. OXENFELDT *Economic Systems in Action*
RAYMOND P. KENT *Money and Banking*
HENRY H. VILLARD *Economic Development*

Rinehart books for intermediate and advanced courses in economics

JACK N. BEHRMAN AND *International Economics: Theory, Practice,*
WILSON E. SCHMIDT *Policy*
GEORGE N. HALM *Economic Systems: A Comparative Analysis*
ALFRED KUHN *Labor: Institutions and Economics*
HARVEY J. LEVIN *Business Organization and Public Policy: A Book of Readings*
KENYON E. POOLE *Public Finance and Economic Welfare*
GERHARD TINTNER *Mathematics and Statistics for Economists*
EMORY TROXEL *Economics of Public Utilities*
Economics of Transport

ECONOMIC PRINCIPLES AND PUBLIC ISSUES

Alfred R. Oxenfeldt

Graduate School of Business
Columbia University

WITH THE ASSISTANCE OF
Charles Hoffmann
Department of Economics
Queens College

RINEHART & COMPANY, INC., NEW YORK

*To Joan Beth
and Alice Ellen*

Preface

This book develops the basic analytical tools of economic theory in considerable depth, while by-passing those parts of economic analysis which require far more effort than they warrant. Only the key analytical concepts that contribute to an understanding and solution of major public issues are developed in detail; minor ones are passed over with a reference to sources where they are discussed fully.

In deciding what materials to include and the emphasis and space to attach to them, I have been guided by the following principles:

1. An economics text should build upon the existence of widespread interest in public economic issues.

2. It should devote no greater attention—but certainly no less—to economic principles than is required to understand the most pressing issues of the present day.

3. Economic principles should not be taught as an end in themselves.

4. An economics text should treat public issues with explicit reference to the moral, political, and social problems that they present. It should not be cut short by arbitrary subject-matter boundaries.

5. The author should take a clear and unequivocal stand on public-policy matters where he holds strong convictions.

6. Difficult materials of minor importance should not be "proved" at the expense of long and tedious digressions and the omission of more important subjects. (Instead, they should be set forth as conclusions held by most economists, and reference should be made to publications where proof can be found.)

7. Considerable attention should be paid to possible measures that might be enacted to improve defective conditions.

8. A basic text should provide fairly extensive and annotated bibliog-

raphies to stimulate student interest in the major contributions to the subject.[1]

This book is a lineal descendant of *Economics for the Citizen* in its devotion to these principles. It differs in that much more space is devoted to the development of the basic concepts and "tools" of economic analysis.

The economy has undergone a gradual, but dramatic, change since World War II. An economy of abundance is replacing an economy that was characterized by scarcity and extreme inequality. The basic forces operating in a prosperous, relatively stable, and mildly inflationary economy are not yet clear and may not even be new. One must, however, be prepared to find the forces that now dominate economic activity are substantively different from any that we have known and that economists who acquired their fundamental viewpoints during the depressed 1930's may not be able to interpret the changes that are under way. We may have to wait for the postwar generation of economists to mature, for we may need their help to see clearly what is blurred to this generation.

Subjects of economic study that are appropriate for an economy of extreme scarcity may have little interest in an economy like ours. For example, emphasis on production and scarcity seems less warranted than, say, emphasis on the nature of consumers' choices. Also, the enormous gulf—judged in terms both of the resources involved and the moral problems posed—between the end of the production line and final purchase will require far more discussion than it has received up to now, for conventional economics texts describe an economy in which the producer sells directly and costlessly to the ultimate consumer. The entire problem of resource allocation, which seeks a neat and delicate balance in the output of individual products, ceases to be crucial in a world where business, labor, and government are concerned with idle resources and the need to sell more, rather than with overcoming shortages. Similarly, the performance of an economy is changed very substantially when business decisions are made by individuals with little direct ownership interest in the firms they serve and when the time perspective of their decisions is extremely long-run and also heavily colored by regard for public relations.

I have not attempted to write a principles of economics for the new American economy that may be emerging. On the other hand, I have tried to shift the emphasis in the discussion of established economic principles toward issues of current importance. This shift has given greater weight to some areas of analysis that have had less relevance to the world

---

[1] The bibliographies are found at the end of each part, rather than at the end of each chapter.

of affairs in the past and has greatly reduced the attention that is devoted to some traditionally central subjects.

I have received help from many persons in the course of writing this book, and it is my pleasure to acknowledge and express my thanks for their assistance. My greatest debt is to Dr. Charles Hoffmann of Queens College, who has prepared the annotated bibliographies, has actually written some passages of the text itself, has criticized the entire manuscript, and has taken major responsibility for the illustrations, the proofreading, and the preparation of the index. This book would probably have remained stillborn if I had not received his help and if it had not been given so cheerfully and conscientiously.

The following persons made detailed suggestions for the whole book that were of enormous value: Professor Harlan M. Smith, University of Minnesota; Professor Elliot Zupnick, City College of New York; Mrs. Robert L. West, Yale University; Professor Melvin Eggers, Syracuse University; Dr. Lawrence Ritter, the New York Federal Reserve Bank; Professor Leland E. Traywick, Michigan State University, Professor Bryce J. Jones, St. Joseph's College (Indiana); and Professor Donald A. Moore, Los Angeles State College. Valuable suggestions for key portions of the manuscript were received from Professor Harvey J. Levin, Hofstra College; Dr. Morris Mendelsohn, the National Bureau of Economic Research; Professor Helen Potter, Loyola University (Chicago); and Professor John Perry Miller, Yale University. My sincere thanks go to all of these persons. Finally, I wish to express my gratitude to the editorial staff of the College Department of Rinehart & Company for many valuable suggestions and for assistance of many kinds.

Of course, I am responsible for all of the errors and failings of this book; their number would be far greater and their magnitude more grievous were it not for the assistance of the many persons I have named.

A. R. O.

New York, N. Y.
February, 1959

Contents

PART SIX: MUST THE ECONOMY OF THE UNITED STATES SUFFER UPS AND DOWNS?

Part

1 How Do Economists Analyze Problems?

1 Economics and Citizenship

"It does not matter for whom you vote; just be sure to vote." Statements such as this abound at election time. But surely it is more valid to state, "It does not matter whether you vote unless you make sensible use of your vote." Voting is not simply a ritual that blesses everyone who performs the act.

We know of several major countries in which the right to vote does not carry the power to change economic and social conditions but is simply an empty privilege. Such nations offer their citizens democracy in name only. Similarly, when voters do not exercise their power to vote, or when they vote in ignorance, or on the basis of unquestioned preconceptions or prejudice, much of the substance of democracy is lacking. Unless most citizens use their vote to enact policies that reflect their carefully considered wishes, their political system is more a *potential* or *formal* democracy than a *functioning* or *substantive* democracy. Unless the term "democracy" is defined to vary in proportion to the activity, interest, information, and intelligence, as well as to the formal right of voters, it will describe equally well the political system of the United States and that of the Soviet Union.

While the importance of voting is generally described in lofty, almost lyrical, terms, relatively little is done to equip the average citizen to make the best use of his voting power. With little or no preparation, he is expected to decide and participate intelligently in issues concerning such involved matters as international trade, monetary policy, and remedies for depression and inflation. Small wonder that voters find most public issues so baffling. And, when issues bewilder the voters, they are likely to stay home on Election Day.

Discussions of voting and citizenship are technically out of place in an economics book; they ordinarily are confined to books dealing with government and political science. The existing division between economics and political science and government may explain why voters receive so little help. Economists, on the whole, devote themselves to subjects that are highly technical and seemingly quite remote from the issues that the electorate must decide; moreover, they write in a jargon that even other economists sometimes find difficult to understand. Specialists in political science and government, for their part, seem concerned primarily with the forms and procedures of government. As a consequence, most discussion of public policy in the United States is conducted by non-specialists who earn their livelihood generally as journalists, radio commentators, public officials, and paid spokesmen for special interests.

Actually, economists have a great deal to contribute to a better understanding of the issues with which the average intelligent voter is concerned. Many of the subjects discussed when members of families meet at the dinner table, or in the chitchat of neighbors, once the subject of the weather has been dispatched, have been studied for generations by specialists in economics, whose writings are too difficult for most persons to understand. Accordingly, it is the object of this book to interpret these writings and to apply them to the main issues of the present day.

It should soon appear that, apart from its usefulness in voting, economics can be fun and challenging in itself. Part of the fun comes from finding that what seems to be plain common sense proves to be sheer nonsense. Some pleasure comes from facing squarely many questions about which we have deep anxieties and doubts or about which we hold uneasy conclusions—by getting directly to the heart of the matter and by profiting from the information collected on such problems by those who have long studied them scientifically.

Unfortunately, the author can promise the reader fun and excitement more confidently than he can promise a set of unassailable conclusions about today's pressing economic issues. Problems remain controversial issues largely because the right is not all on one side. Even though it is possible to confuse issues and to mislead people, problems that have a demonstrable solution get solved in time and disappear from popular discussion. Consequently, readers must reconcile themselves to learning the arguments, old and new, on both sides of most issues. They will find that many widely held opinions are based on invalid arguments, but they will also learn that these opinions often can be supported by valid arguments.

If readers desire pat answers, they will be disappointed. When they feel frustrated as more questions are raised than answered in the pages that follow, let them remember that the author's purpose is to present the basic principles derived by economists and to show how they can be applied to problems of the present day—rather than to provide what the author believes to be "correct" solutions for the public issues discussed here. Most readers probably have learned the unhappy fact that there are no completely certain answers to the most pressing problems of life—whether the problem be the selection of a career, a mate, a vacation spot, or even a course in economics. We must ponder and examine evidence and at some point make conjectures; we can never know most things *for certain.* ("Certain" is not used in the philosophical sense here, but more in the judicial sense of knowing "beyond a reasonable doubt.")

Readers are entitled to know that economics is a peculiar subject in some ways—not at all what people expect who study the social sciences for the first time. (Even among the social sciences, economics is quite distinctive in some of the aspects singled out here for discussion—though the differences are of degree rather than of kind.) The most striking peculiarities of the subject will be explained briefly at the outset, even though they cannot be understood thoroughly until one has become familiar with the subject itself. The three most distinctive and unusual features of economics singled out for discussion here are (1) the "viewpoint" adopted, (2) the "method of analysis" employed, and (3) the "timelessness" of its generalizations.

The economist adopts a *viewpoint* that is unfamiliar to many. He views all problems from the standpoint of mankind as a whole, rather than from the position of his own or some other single group. He tries to discover what would be in the interest of the greatest number of people, and to balance objectively the needs and desires of competing groups. For example, he may conclude that the groups whose taxes should be increased most are the middle- and upper-middle-income groups—even though he belongs to one of these groups.

The viewpoint of the economist—and of other social scientists—comes very close to what we expect of devoted and selfless civil servants. In colloquial terms, government officials are expected to do "what is best for the country." Some men who have entered government service from other occupations have failed because they have not been able to adopt this "social viewpoint." Some readers doubtless will find it difficult at the beginning to rise above their personal economic interest. With effort, though, they will learn to project themselves into the position of someone who regards all groups and segments of the population as equally deserving.

In no respect is economics so peculiar and difficult to fathom as in the *method of analysis employed.* Economists are far from agreement about the nature of their methods; in fact, some of the most violent criticisms of economists' methods come from members of the profession. Some economists would take exception to what is said here on this subject, it should be noted.

Almost everyone would agree that economics employs a method of analysis that differs considerably from that employed by most other social sciences. Although economics includes a description of economic institutions, a tracing of their development and the like—similar to the descriptive and historical aspects of the other social sciences—economics is distinguished by the extent to which it employs the "theoretical method." The controversy concerning method centers about the core of economics, which is ordinarily known as "economic theory." (Some economists restrict the term "economics" to include *only* economic theory.)

We can best understand the method of analysis underlying economic theory if we understand why economists have not used the more orthodox methods of scientific inquiry—in particular, observation, experimentation, and the formulation and testing of hypotheses. The two main reasons are, first, that economists analyze situations in which many factors operate simultaneously and in combination; and, second, that economists are seldom able to conduct controlled experiments.

In the main, a scientist tries to isolate and explain the forces at work, so that mankind can forecast and control these forces. In particular, he seeks to account for the operations of each factor separately. Let us take a concrete example from economics. Economists may desire to explain the behavior of prices in general, in order to enable people to explain and control each individual price. A full understanding of prices requires at least the following: first, an identification of all factors influencing prices; second, a determination of the direction in which price is affected by changes in each factor (for example, one would conclude that a product's price changes in the same direction as its costs—if all other influences on price remain unchanged); third, an explanation of the circumstances that determine the effect that each factor exerts on price (for example, an increase in costs has little effect on price if the product's output is not affected by the increase—some agricultural prices fall in this category); fourth, an indication of the relative importance of each factor.

Physical scientists seek answers to similar questions about subjects primarily by observing things as they occur "naturally" and by conducting controlled experiments. Sometimes, as in the field of astronomy, they cannot experiment, but in the fields of biology, chemistry, and physics, laboratory experiments are possible for most areas of study. By this means, it is possible to hold all factors constant except one and thereby to isolate the effect of that one factor. Consequently, by sheer diligence and effort, one can obtain a great deal of information about the nature of many physical phenomena.

Unfortunately, experimentation is rarely possible in economic matters. Often the whole nation would be affected by both the impact and outcome of an experiment, and national leaders are understandably disinclined to run the risks that experimentation would involve. A change in popular attitude might make it possible to experiment far more than would be acceptable at present. Certainly, if more economic experimentation would yield the same understanding and control over economic affairs that we now command over physical forces, extensive economic experimentation would be advisable. Even so, the difficulties of setting up economic experiments and the costs involved are so huge that experimentation would have to be kept at a low level, whatever the popular attitude might be.

The inability to conduct experiments has placed the economist under severe handicaps. To make headway in understanding economic forces, he was compelled to devise a method of study that made maximum use of "common knowledge" and scraps of historical and statistical information; in particular, he began to rely very heavily upon pure logic. He has developed a method of analysis—largely by accident and slowly over a long period of time—that is sometimes described as "model building." (Interestingly, model building has become rather extensively applied in recent years to the solution of military and business problems with the development of the field of "operations research.") Let us then try to get some idea of what is involved in economic theory in general and model building in particular.

Economic theory may be described as the application of logical reasoning to a few simple propositions about human motivation and behavior, and about the natural forces involved in production. With respect to the first, economists accept the view that individuals, in their activities as consumers, seek to obtain maximum satisfaction from their money outlays. When individuals function as businessmen, economists assume they will endeavor to obtain maximum profit. These propositions about human motivations rest upon so-called common knowledge and personal observation rather than upon scientific findings, and there is considerable question about their validity. However, by this method and despite the shakiness of the foregoing assumptions about motivations of individuals, economists have been able to make some sense out of the bewildering complexity of economic life.

In attempting to account for the operation of natural forces involved in production, economists have derived the famous, and generally misunderstood, "law of diminishing returns." (See Chapter 4, for example.) This principle, which is the hub around which most economic reasoning about physical forces revolves, explains that beyond some point a person begins to exhaust the productivity of any piece of land, or machine, or building, or worker as he attempts to use it more intensively. Interestingly, this principle, derived well over a century ago, remains a central proposition in present-day economic thinking.

Thus, with these few propositions as their starting point, economists have been able to analyze many different economic situations. Their analysis is conducted by applying rigorous logic to an assumed set of circumstances (for example, that the costs of producing some product have increased) and by drawing upon the propositions already described about human motivation and upon the law of diminishing returns. Obviously, the reader cannot understand clearly all that such an analysis means until he himself has worked through one, but it will help him to know about this unusual method of study before he finds himself right in the middle of it.

As economists worked through more and more problems, they developed methods of translating them into a form that permits the use of mathematics and geometry. (For most students, the geometry used by economists represents simple sketches which state more clearly and simply what otherwise must be stated at great length in words.) Ultimately, economists developed "models" of various economic situations which describe the main forces at work and the relation among these forces. For example, the famous law of supply and demand is a simplified model of the forces that determine price; it can be described in very simple diagrammatic terms to give added clarity and precision.

The models constructed by economists are almost always gross simplifications—even as are most of the generalizations of the physical sciences. These models consciously exclude many of the forces at work in most realistic situations—even as the physical generalization that a falling body accelerates at the rate of 32 feet per second applies only in a vacuum. The fact that disturbing forces are excluded from these models does not mean that these forces are ignored or unrecognized. By such simplification, the scientist is able to explain phenomena which he might otherwise not be able to understand. The economist has been particularly benefited by the study of simplified models; it has enabled him to employ "intellectual experiments" in the absence of laboratory experiments. He is able to inject, one by one, different forces into his simple model and to analyze intellectually the effect of each force separately. Also, he can explore their interactions and to some degree analyze their effects in combination. Thus, by his method of theorizing and model building, the economist has been able to achieve in some measure what other scientists can accomplish more directly and reliably by means of controlled laboratory experiments.

Although the central core of economics consists of economic theory of the type we have been discussing, economics is not composed of economic theory alone. Few economists have stuck rigidly to their simple assumptions and refused to incorporate, in some fashion, whatever reliable factual information is available to them. Consequently, economics has grown by a combination of refinements and elaborations of theoretical models and by the incorporation of additional factual information. Despite the fairly rapid growth of factual evidence about economic phenomena in recent years, however, economics remains heavily dependent upon the theoretical method.

Thus we see that economists have been driven to the development of an unfamiliar type of analysis by conditions beyond their control. But a person makes a serious error if he thinks that economists are oblivious to what goes on in the world of affairs, or that they would much rather spin fine theories than face up to the facts of life. (No doubt there are some economists of whom this is true—and we probably benefit from the fact that some people specialize in the refinement of theory while others concentrate primarily on empirical investigations.)

Economics as we find it today embodies the contributions of hundreds of great minds and the work of thousands of researchers and investigators who have devoted their lives to a further understanding of economic phenomena; that economists employ the unusual method of analysis is to be explained by the fact that this method alone permitted them to make headway with the extremely complicated problems they tried to solve.

We have seen that economic theory is not chiefly a factual and experimental discipline but instead rests heavily upon the reasoning of men. Consequently, if they are to achieve validity, any conclusions reached in this manner must be confirmed by experience. Most of the conclusions of economic theory fall into either of two categories: first, they can be taken as correct conclusions about what would occur if the assumed conditions existed; or, second, they can be regarded as the "best" general conclusions one can draw under the circumstances. *In the absence of verification from actual experience they cannot be regarded as reliable descriptions of reality.* However, if they are the most valid conclusions that can be drawn under the circumstances—that makes them valuable enough.

The third distinctive quality of economic generalizations is their *timelessness*. Utilization of the theoretical method yields generalizations that have a nonhistorical quality. As stated, economic principles seem to claim for themselves the timeless quality of, say, the law of gravity. This timeless quality has made economic theory vulnerable to sharp criticism. One can readily concede that the forces of nature operate in the same way now as when the pyramids were built. But it is offensive to common sense, and inconsistent with certain simple historical facts known to everyone, to assume that all factors governing the behavior of individuals and firms in their money-making activities have remained fundamentally the same over even the last century. One is therefore almost instinctively suspicious of economic principles expressed in a manner that suggests they are eternal verities. On the other hand, many who have studied economic theory marvel at the extent to which some long-established economic principles help us to understand economic processes in the present economy, which is so very different from the one prevailing when the conclusions were reached originally. In other words, for certain kinds of problems, economic theory does single out and explain helpfully the fundamental economic forces—forces which apparently operate in economies that are outwardly very different. The trick, as in all sciences, is to apply the right principle to the right problem, whether the principle is old or new.

The apparent timeless quality of many economic principles re-enforces a fairly common misapprehension, especially prevalent among persons in their late 'teens and twenties. Reference is made to the unconscious assumption that conditions always were much as they are now and will remain essentially the same throughout our lifetime. (One common variation of this view holds properly that conditions were very different when one's parents were "young" but mistakenly assumes that all of the changes are over.) Things just don't stand still! Everyone must expect to live, when he is in his fifties, in a world very different from that of his 'teens. We must expect change and try to understand it—rather than concern ourselves exclusively with how existing arrangements work. In other words, we need some economic principles that include or explain change itself.

More important, we may want to influence the direction in which things change. Most developments don't just happen; they occur as a result of the actions of people. All too often, changes occur because of the unplanned actions of people who are unconcerned with or unaware of the consequences of their own behavior. But there are developments of a highly beneficial sort that can be traced to the constructive efforts of individuals who wanted to improve the state of affairs. Many men have made economics their life's career simply because they hoped to discover ways of improving existing economic arrangements. Although such things are rarely publicized, there have been innumerable economic "ideas" (one might call them "inventions"), some of which are large and most of which are tiny, that have contributed to the well-being of all. The inventions may have been in ways of linking wage rates to changes in the cost of living, or in ways of imposing taxes so that they would be paid by those best able to bear them, or in monetary arrangements that made it possible for everyone to use paper money or bank deposits with almost complete confidence.

The opportunity to make such inventions has not passed. Our nation still needs them, for many facets of our economic system could stand improvement. Consequently, one can see in the certainty of change in the future a challenge rather than a threat; an opportunity to shape the world of tomorrow rather than a compulsion to adapt to the unexpected. In this connection, one must note that most economists have not done much until very recently—and very little even then—to account for the way that economic systems change over time. Even the process by which nations develop from a primitive state where living standards are extremely low, where individuals produce for themselves most of what they consume, where productive skills and machinery are scarce, into a developed state such as the one in which the United States finds itself, is not well understood. It should be observed, however, that the Great Depression of the 1930's prompted many economists to consider relatively short-term fluctuations in business conditions, usually called the business cycle. The competition between capitalism, democratic socialism, and communism since World War II, moreover, has inspired new interest in long-term (or secular) growth and development.

This unhistorical quality of most economics—resulting from the timeless quality of its generalizations and its frequent failure to account for the process of economic change—is, if anything, exaggerated in this book. The reason is that this book concentrates upon the problems of the present day in order to develop understanding of them and to suggest possible solutions. As a consequence, the author has little occasion to dwell on conditions in earlier times. On the other hand, Part Two of this book is concerned largely with long-term economic development; Part Six analyzes "ups and downs" in the economy of the United States; and every chapter recognizes the inevitability of change.

Up to this point, we have discussed the social viewpoint adopted by economists, their use of the theoretical method, and the timeless quality of their principles. The diverse purposes that economic writings seek to achieve call for a final comment. Partly because it adopts the social viewpoint, a great deal of economics is concerned with how things "should be"; indeed, one branch of the subject, commonly described as "normative economics," deals with an ideal state of affairs. Its purpose is to explore the nature of conditions that would serve society best, as a basis for suggesting improvements in existing arrangements. Another branch of economics may be called "descriptive economics," for its purpose is to make clear how things are at present. A third branch—possibly one would describe it as "interpretive economics"—has as its purpose to explain why things happen as they do. Whatever one names them, there are these three related, but in many ways distinct, purposes that economists have in mind: to explain how things should be, to describe the way they are, and to explain why things happen as they do. This book divides its emphasis about equally among these different purposes, and the reader would be wise to make sure that he knows whether the author is discussing how things are or why, or how he believes they should be.

It is unlikely that a few introductory pages will prepare many readers to place their first systematic discussion of economic subjects within the broad frame of the world of knowledge and the needs of citizenship. As he proceeds, the reader will become accustomed to the point of view and method of analysis. However, there will doubtless be many times when he will wonder "what is going on"; at such times he may want to turn back to these introductory pages, which try to explain in what ways and for what reasons economics is both a vital and a peculiar subject.

As this chapter has implied, the economist—as economist—does not pass judgment on people's moral, esthetic, and political choices. On the other hand, in analyzing economic issues, the economist frequently must take account of such noneconomic choices. Finally, economic analysis can be of great help to the citizen who wants to make responsible choices among conflicting political solutions to public issues with economic aspects. In today's world almost all public issues involve economics.

SELECTED READINGS FOR PART 1

Boulding, Kenneth E. *The Skills of the Economist.* Cleveland: Howard Allen, Inc., 1958. Pp. vii, 189. The author discusses the contribution of the economist to our culture vis-à-vis the scientists in the biological and physical areas. Also dealt with are the problems peculiar to the social scientist.

Chase, Stuart. *Democracy under Pressure.* New York: Twentieth Century Fund, 1945. P. 142. This book, one in a series by the author, is a popular portrayal of the role of pressure groups in our society and how they stand in the way of the public interest. The pressures of big business, labor, agriculture, and government itself are analyzed, and ways of counteracting them are outlined.

Downs, Anthony. *An Economic Theory of Democracy.* New York: Harper & Brothers, 1957. P. 310. This is an extremely interesting effort to set forth a model of democracy not inconsistent with theories of private economic action. By setting up an ideal democratic state, the author organizes political science into a formal theoretical system. Basic economic concepts such as costs, uncertainty, and the like are adapted to political uses.

Fortune. *The Changing American Market.* New York: Hanover House–Garden City Books, 1955. P. 304. This book is a reprinting of 12 articles from *Fortune* which deal with different aspects of the American market: population, consumption patterns, income changes, transformations in urban living patterns, etc.

Heilbroner, Robert L. *Worldly Philosophers: The Lives, Times, and Ideas of the Great Economic Thinkers.* New York: Simon & Schuster, Inc., 1953. P. 342. An interesting and well-written presentation of the work and lives of a number of economists whose thought had an important political impact on societies. Included in the presentation are Adam Smith, Malthus, Ricardo, Marx, Mill, George, Veblen, and Keynes.

Robertson, Dennis H. *Lectures on Economic Principles.* London: Staples & Staples, Ltd., 1957, Vol. 1. P. 172. This is the first of a series on economic principles by an outstanding British economist. The material was originally delivered as lectures at the University of Cambridge. The author deals with the basic questions of economics, the theory of value, the productive factors, monopolistic competition, etc.

Robinson, Marshall A., Herbert C. Morton, and James D. Calderwood. *An Introduction to Economic Reasoning.* Washington, D.C.: Brookings Institution, 1956. Pp. xi, 335. This is a valuable popular examination of the basic principles of economic theory and their relation to current economic problems. In nontechnical terms, the authors present the layman with the tools of the economist.

Schumpeter, Joseph A. *History of Economic Analysis.* New York: Oxford University Press, 1954. Pp. xxv, 1260. A monumental treatment of scientific economic analysis from Greco-Roman times to the present in the context of social and political history. Although the book is oriented to economic analysis it also deals with the other social sciences.

Solo, Robert (ed.). *Economics and the Public Interest.* New Brunswick, N.J.: Rutgers University Press, 1955. Pp. xiv, 318. A group of essays arranged according to the methods of economics, economics and social policy, problems of economic growth, etc., and ranging widely over the subject area of economics. Many different viewpoints are reflected in this useful work.

Part

2 Can Poverty Be Eliminated?

2 The Meaning
and Measurement
of Economic Welfare

I. INTRODUCTION

Practically no one is as well off as he would like to be. All persons and nations want more than they now have. But very few things that people want are available in unlimited quantities; the things we desire are "scarce"—though to a greater or lesser degree from time to time and from place to place. Accordingly, almost everyone, however reluctantly, "goes to work" to increase his supply of goods and services.

Even the panhandler has to make some effort and put up with considerable embarrassment and harassment (at least at the start) to get his daily bread. Similarly, those who work hard and skillfully often find that they have fewer goods than they desire. So, despite the exercise of intelligence and diligence, nearly everyone and certainly every nation suffers a relative lack of things.

Enormous differences exist among individuals and nations in the degree of their poorness. Some persons feel they lack many things, but they only want a great deal.[1] We are rather less concerned with their plight than with that of the hundreds of millions who lack even the fundamental, biological essentials to sustain life on a level that can be considered "human."

Poverty—especially in other countries than one's own—is something that previous generations just took for granted, to the extent they were aware of its existence. Prosperous people found their own way of closing their eyes to the miseries of the very poor. The cleverest rationalizers discovered in poverty a character builder or evidence of divine punishment

---

[1] A study of executives in the $25,000-a-year class found that most of them were compelled to live beyond their income to keep up with their colleagues and to keep themselves in the running for promotions higher up the executive ladder.

for sins. Most persons somehow learned to shift their thoughts and eyes to other subjects when they came into contact with fellow men who, for whatever reason, were abjectly poor.

It is no longer possible for either individuals or public officials, in the United States or in other prosperous nations, to ignore the existence of poverty in the world. Perhaps reluctantly, the prosperous nations are becoming increasingly aware of poverty and are even beginning to feel responsible for reducing it. They are being pushed into awareness by the poorer countries, who demand at least a minimum of assistance, for which they generally wish to pay, within the limits of their capacity. The awakened concern of the prosperous nations results from a combination of political and humanitarian motives. Also, recent technological advances hold forth the hope, possibly for the first time, that the elimination of poverty is an attainable goal.

The evils resulting from poverty—social and political unrest, disease, crime, painful ignorance, and sometimes starvation—are contagious and often spread across national boundaries. Social revolution and war that sometimes result, directly or indirectly, from poverty, tend to spread. *Moreover, poverty reduces considerably a nation's ability to trade, and in this way restricts the total amount of goods available to the rest of the world;* history shows that prosperous countries gain from trade with all nations—whether rich or poor.

At present, prosperous nations are helping the poor primarily for political reasons. The Western countries are competing with the Communist bloc for the support of countries uncommitted in the international political struggle, by offering to help them alleviate the worst pangs of their poverty. Apart from political considerations of self-interest, efforts to aid poorer peoples can be traced partly to an awakening of social conscience.

Their often painful experience with "colonialism" has led many poor nations to conclude that they have suffered exploitation, and no doubt some have. The leaders of many such countries maintain that their poverty is partly the fault of nations that are now well-off. (They claim, moreover, that the prosperity of colonial powers is in no small degree due to their exploitation of their colonies.) Accordingly, they expect assistance from prosperous nations as a "right."

This section of the book discusses the extent, causes, and general remedies for poverty and retarded economic development. Lest the American reader assume that poverty is strictly a "foreign" problem, he will be shown that sizable areas of the United States can also be considered "underdeveloped" and "poor," and that during periods of depression a fairly large number of impoverished persons may be found here.

II. THE MEANING AND MEASUREMENT OF POVERTY

There are many kinds of poverty; some unfortunates are afflicted with almost all of them. One can be poor in "spirit," in mental or physical health, in the "enduring virtues," in the grace of God, in prestige, and in friendship, as well as in worldly goods. Various types of poverty often go together. On the other hand, as the Bible suggests, material riches may be associated with spiritual poverty. In discussing poverty, we must therefore take great pains to assign it a clear and precise meaning. Poverty is defined here in material terms, as is most appropriate in a book on economics. Economists understandably prefer to have specialists in other fields deal with other types of impoverishment.

A. *Meaning of Economic Welfare*

When dealing with unfamiliar and vague notions like "economic welfare," one is wise to think in terms of familiar examples. We want to know how to judge the economic condition of individuals and entire nations; for the words "economic welfare," we can substitute the words "how well-off." Since certain occupational groups have received extended treatment in novels, movies, and over radio and TV, we can use them for illustrative purposes. We shall contrast the material well-being of a successful business executive, college professor, and white-collar criminal. Let us first attempt a thumbnail sketch of each.

Our business executive works very long hours under severe pressure, feels threatened by some of his associates, is always required to show "progress," and lives in an environment requiring him to consume fairly lavishly to convey the aura of "success." He sometimes is forced to discharge associates of long standing "for the good of the company." Occasionally, to obtain advancement, he must edge associates aside by not altogether admirable means. Note that this executive cannot get, say, two thirds of his present income and be relieved of one third of his present burdens; he does either the whole job or none of it. If he were to take another job, he generally would have to work at least as hard and might receive smaller rewards for his efforts. We can place him in "middle management" in a large corporation with a salary of $25,000 per year and state that he must spend almost all he makes if he hopes to keep his position and remain in the running for promotion.

Our second man is a teacher at a large university who receives an annual salary of $7,000 and holds the rank of associate professor. He teaches about thirty-two weeks a year and is in class about twelve hours a week. His rank entitles him to "tenure" (almost complete security of position), and he lives in an academic community in which his salary is well above the average. Our professor is under moral obligation to contribute to the advancement of his profession and to set a good example for his students and associates. On the whole, he is able to work largely at his own pace on a schedule that is mainly of his own making.

Our third man is a very successful criminal whose income has averaged $100,000 over the previous five years, all obtained from illegal activities. Although no paragon of civic virtue, this man essentially dislikes what he is doing (though he dislikes holding a menial job at a very low salary far more), mistrusts many of his associates, and is constantly fearful that he will be apprehended and his family disgraced.

These three types admittedly are extreme and bare caricatures; in themselves they prove nothing. Nevertheless, a comparison of their material well-being can illuminate what enters into a measurement of economic welfare. Most persons who are asked which of the three enjoy the best economic situation find it difficult to choose between the first two; almost no one selects the criminal. There is no single correct answer to the question raised here. Still, the question makes clear that *economic welfare involves much more than the amount of money a person earns.* Let us then turn to a more general discussion of the ingredients of economic welfare—both for individuals and for nations.

From the *conceptual* viewpoint, *economic welfare should be defined in terms of three attributes: (1) the quantity of goods and services consumed; (2) the sacrifice and effort put forth to acquire goods and services; and (3) the desire for goods and services.* That is, we shall consider people to be poor in a material sense if they have very little in the way of goods and services, if they must undergo great physical or mental suffering to meet their material needs, and if their desires for goods are stimulated to the point where they suffer shame or embarrassment because of lack of goods—even though they may have a great many more things than people in other countries have.

From a *practical* viewpoint, however, most of what follows—and especially comparisons of relative prosperity in different countries and at different times—deals with only the first—quantities of goods and services. Although the other two factors are also discussed, they are difficult to assess even subjectively, let alone to use for precise measurement. Even the following discussion of the first attribute will not be simple, because great complexities are faced in measuring quantities of goods and services.

Before undertaking a discussion of methods of measuring material prosperity, one general conclusion must be emphasized—especially for those embarking upon a study of economics: *Man does not live by bread alone! Human dissatisfaction can be great despite material plenty, as almost everyone can readily observe among prosperous families of his acquaintance.* Conversely, some persons of limited means lead full and, in every other sense, rich lives. The same condition may hold for entire nations as well as for individuals and families.

B. *Measurement of Poverty*

At the outset we must guard against confusing poor countries with poor individuals. Some of the world's richest individuals are to be found in one of the world's poorest countries—India. Conversely, in a prosperous nation such as New Zealand there are few really wealthy persons. The poverty of nations as a whole must be distinguished from poverty resulting from unequal distribution of an otherwise adequate national income. The causes and cures of each are somewhat different.

A nation is called poor if its *national income or national product— both defined as the total output of goods and services produced for sale within the nation's boundaries, after proper allowance is made for the amount of resources used up in the course of production,* when equally distributed, cannot provide for each citizen a level of living that meets prevailing domestic minimum standards of nutrition, health, clothing, shelter, and rudimentary education (the sacrifices incurred in the production of these goods and services being taken into account). It is not suggested that income *should be* divided equally, because, as will be explained, equality of income may have unfortunate consequences; however, if the total output *could* provide a minimum standard of living for all, the nation is not termed poor, even if it actually has a large proportion of *poor individuals.* Our concept of national poverty is therefore on a per capita basis.

This definition is not altogether free from complications, since some differences of individual income are needed to provide work incentives and to maintain a healthy economy. Consequently, the bare-minimum level under this definition would leave at least a few individuals below "standard." Nevertheless, this definition provides at least a useful working standard that is unambiguous.

1. WHAT WE SHOULD LIKE TO MEASURE

How can we describe the total amount of goods and services produced by a nation? Approached directly, this task requires the compilation of an incredibly long list of items produced during some period—say, a year. The list for the United States would include upward of a million different products; the Sears-Roebuck catalogue alone includes almost half this number—and it includes no services. Few could find the time even to read such a list, let alone retain and fully comprehend its contents. And it would be impractical, sometimes impossible, to compare lists of output at different times and for different nations. There would always be some items on a list from one country that are absent from the list of another country, and for the same country the list varies from time to time. How could one tell with any exactness whether one list represents a greater or lesser output than another list? Still more troublesome is the problem of including services, like concerts, ball games, shoeshines, auto repairs, etc., which certainly make up a large part of output.

If we look at the problem from the opposite side, it certainly would be convenient if a nation's output could be described by a single all-inclusive number, for such a number would make it simple to compare output at different times and different places. Yet if a single number were used to describe something so vast and heterogeneous as the total output of goods and services, many compromises would be required. No single number could begin to convey all the desired information from a full listing.

If total output is to be summarized in a single number, it must be measured in money. *Money is the only common denominator that can be applied to goods and services alike.* Other measures, such as weight, number of units, size, and the like, give wholly unwarranted importance to some goods at the expense of others. And services would be virtually impossible to pin down by this kind of physical measure. But if production is to be measured with money, how much money value should we assign to each good or service? Should we pick an arbitrary amount, the market amount, some variation of the market amount, or what?

In order to answer this question, we must be entirely clear about what we want to measure. It is very easy to get so involved in the details of measurement that we lose sight of our objective. What we seek is a single all-inclusive figure, capable also of being broken down into a few subtotals, that measures the material well-being of a nation as it is affected by the nation's output. Our aim is therefore not simply to get a total list or sum of output, but to get an indication of the contribution of this output to well-being. We might say that we are trying to measure the material welfare of nations.

But, if the contribution of products to total output is to be reckoned by their usefulness or intrinsic value, who is to estimate the contribution to material welfare of individual products? What basis could he use?

Clearly, *the "value" of a product is not the same for all people.* The very thing that some people cherish is hated by others. Even within the framework of any religious creed or narrow cultural grouping, there are great differences in the valuation that individuals place on almost every product. Consequently, we are driven to the conclusion that the "value" of a product is essentially a matter of personal opinion and that the opinions of people about specific products vary widely.

However, our object is not to place a value on national output that measures the "value" of a product to any one person. *Our goal is to determine the contribution of output to the material welfare of the people who consume that output.* In other words, we seek a unit of measure that reflects intrinsic value and the ability to satisfy the human wants of those who consume the products. It is essential that this unit of measure be independent of any individual's subjective judgment; it must reflect the judgment of *all* consumers.

a. Prices paid as a measure of material welfare

The best indicator available for this purpose is the price paid for products and services by persons who consume them. Prices paid represent the minimum amount that purchases are worth to the persons who buy them. While people often err in purchasing, by and large they have a fair amount of knowledge and experience with nearly all the things they buy. What they buy and what they pay tells us, therefore, approximately the relative value of these objects to these people.

Recognize that this measure is not advanced as something highly reliable and accurate; the only claim made for it is that it is by far the best available. Let us, therefore, examine this unit of measure as an indicator of material welfare. Is it, for example, reasonable to say that if one product is purchased for $10 and another for $1 that the first is ten times more valuable in terms of national welfare than the second?

The justification for using price as a measure of welfare is far from simple. In technical language it is to be explained by the *principle of utility maximization by equalizing all marginal utilities.* This principle defines how individuals should spend their funds and, to a considerable extent, describes how people actually do spend their incomes. There is no need for the reader to master this principle in all its ramifications. The following three of its elements are particularly relevant to the problem under consideration:

1. The more of anything you consume, the less the value to you (welfare) of consuming still more of it. This relation between the quantity of a thing people have and its value to them is known as the *principle of diminishing marginal utility.* It may be understood best by imagining how you would react to having a fifth banana split at one sitting. If that prospect is not immediately repulsive, imagine the reaction to having the tenth, and compare it with the first.

2. As a result of the fact that the added pleasure a person derives from things drops as he consumes more and more of them within a short period, it is impossible to consider any product—except in the abstract—more valuable than another. Bread is considered a necessity by most, but a third loaf a day might be of less value to a family than a bow for a child's hair.

3. A consumer tries to get as much satisfaction from his expenditures as possible. To do so, he must divide his outlays in such a manner that he

gets an equal amount of satisfaction[2] from the last dollar he spends in each use that he makes of his money. If he did otherwise, he would be spending too much on some things and too little on others. Only when all uses he makes of his funds give equal satisfaction for the "final" dollar spent does he get the greatest possible total. (This conclusion really is simple arithmetic. As long as one use gives more satisfaction than any other, the total satisfaction to be obtained would grow by shifting from another use to the preferred use. Only when the return from all uses is equal is the possibility of increasing the total by shifting one's purchases eliminated.)

Thus, in a restricted sense, everything a person buys may be considered equally valuable to him, per dollar of cost; and, every dollar's worth of purchase represents roughly an equal contribution to his material welfare. There is, therefore, considerable logic in using buyers' payments for goods and services as indicators of the relative contribution to material welfare of these goods and services.

b. Qualifications to prices paid as a measure of material welfare

The foregoing line of argument must not be pushed too far. It explains why prices paid *may* measure the relative contribution to material welfare of the *last* unit of products consumed; it does less well as an indicator of *total* or *average* contribution of a product per dollar spent on it. The satisfaction obtained from the last dollar spent on all goods and services may be equal, but *the average value of all units bought of any particular product is almost certain to be greater than the amount figured from the "final" dollar spent on it.* As we saw in the banana-split example, the first one is very delicious, while the fifth and especially the tenth within an hour will prove downright disagreeable; practically no one, however great his liking for them, would be willing to pay what it would cost to eat so many at a single sitting. Yet, in the ordinary situation, it is obvious that the average value to a consumer of all the units of any product he buys is greater than is reflected in the price he pays. Since the buyer pays the same price for every unit, we can conclude that the value of each unit—including the very last and least volume to him—is at least equal to price. If it were not, he would not have bought it.

If we could assume that this phenomenon of diminishing utility operated equally for all products, then dollar amounts paid by buyers would measure the relative value to each buyer of everything he purchased. And, since prices paid are essentially the same for everyone in a

---

[2] The author admits that he cannot define to his own satisfaction the words "pleasure," "satisfaction," "value," "fun," and "contribution to material welfare." Generally speaking, they designate any and all things that persons consider desirable—no matter what their reasons.

country, one could say that the relative value of all products actually purchased was the same for all persons. (That is, Mr. Jones and Mr. Brown both value the last unit of a product costing $10 ten times as much as the last unit of another product for which they paid $1.) This result comes about despite differences in consumers' needs and tastes because of the manner in which each person will arrange his purchases in the light of existing prices. The relative value of all "last units" would be "made" the same by individuals buying different amounts of the product.

Economists rely on money prices paid for output (final expenditures) to measure its welfare significance only for short periods of time—when consumers purchase things that remain essentially the same. As years to be compared are farther and farther apart in time, the comparison becomes less and less realistic: tastes change, needs alter, and the whole complexion of the economy and the basic values of buyers undergo constant evolution over the years. *The more dynamic is the economy, the greater the likelihood of error in using dollar value of purchases as a measure of relative welfare.*

There are some other less critical qualifications that must be made to the use of prices paid by buyers as a measure of material welfare. First, some purchases are erroneous in that the buyer finds, after making the purchase, that it is not worth what it cost, and he does not repeat the purchase. In such situations the prices paid for goods and services will exaggerate the "final" value that buyers actually derive from them. We can imagine that this result might occur frequently when purchases are made by children and by highly impulsive persons.

Another qualification (actually, it is not a qualification, but a point that might be overlooked) is that the same product need not be equally valuable to all persons who buy it—even though they may have the same tastes and pay the same price. We are here facing up to the fact that big differences in income may make unreliable the use of prices paid as a measure of material welfare. For example, one would suppose that a poor man gets far more satisfaction from a loaf of bread or a pound of potatoes than does a prosperous man who can buy them in great quantity; yet we count equally the expenditures of the rich and poor in our computations of national output.

In other words, the use of final expenditures to measure the welfare contribution of output is affected by the existence of large differences in personal incomes—unless the proportions of the population that are in each income class remain fairly stable. The rich man spends more than the poor man because he has more money. As explained by the *principle of diminishing marginal utility* (which readers might find easier to remember as the banana-split principle), he gets less pleasure from the "final" dollar spent on things that he buys—and also gets less average satisfaction per dollar of over-all expenditure than does the poor man. Of course, the

poor man rightly is not greatly comforted to find that the *average* satisfaction he gets per dollar spent is higher than that of the rich man; since
he has far fewer dollars to spend, his *total* material satisfaction will be a
lot less.

2. ECONOMIC ACCOUNTING AND THE MEASUREMENT OF NATIONAL OUTPUT

The foregoing pages explained why the prices that buyers pay for
goods and services are the best available measure of the contribution of
material output to welfare; and they discussed some of the qualifications
to this measure. We shall now consider the techniques that have been
developed for measuring the total output of nations—techniques that permit comparisons of welfare at different times and in different places.

During the 1930's, largely through the personal efforts of Professor
Simon Kuznets, a branch of economics was developed that is sometimes
called "economic accounting." The main result has been a technique
which describes the state of the economy, much as ordinary accounting
methods describe the state of an individual business. *Thus it is possible
to measure, though not precisely, changes in the output of goods and
services within any country over the years; and, within rather wide limits,
we can now compare the level of material prosperity in different countries at the same time.*

Economic accounting has various uses. Here we are concerned only
with its use in measuring the material welfare of nations. Consequently,
it is not necessary for the reader to become an economic accountant.
There are, however, a few general propositions he should master for our
purposes, and, almost as important, there are assumptions and limitations
to these propositions that he should learn.

Economic accounting permits us to estimate with rough accuracy the
amount of all goods and services produced at the prices paid for them
by those who are going to consume them—called "final consumers." In
addition, it divides the output of goods and services into categories that
shed considerable light on their contributions to national welfare. For
example, it indicates what proportion of output went to consumers for
their use and what proportion took the form of plant and equipment. It
shows the share of output that consists of *durable consumer goods*, like
automobiles, refrigerators, washing machines, etc.; the share that is *semi-
durable*, like clothing and shoes; and the share that is *nondurable*, like
processed food, eggs, and so on; it also shows what proportion of output
takes the form of *services*, like transport, laundering, haircuts, movies,
higher education, and so on.

Economic-accounting techniques also divide total output according
to the sums paid to the groups that have a claim against output. That is,
one can now determine how much of what was produced was income

earned from the efforts of labor, how much was earned by proprietors, how much by professionals, government employees, etc.

Clearly, *total output stated in terms of the price of productive factors that brought it into being should match total output stated in terms of the prices of goods and services produced.* Such is the case, and each measurement serves as a check on the accuracy of the other.

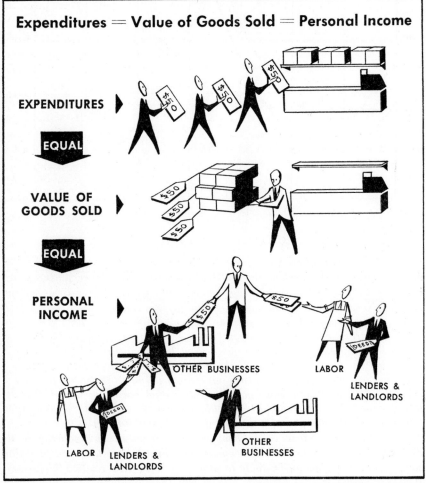

GRAPHICS INSTITUTE, N. Y. C.

National income is best visualized as a pile of goods and services valued at market price. Since the value of goods sold is equal to expenditures (for they are opposite sides of the same shield) and to personal incomes received (for all funds received by sellers ultimately become income to someone), national income can be measured by expenditures and personal income, as well as by value of goods sold.

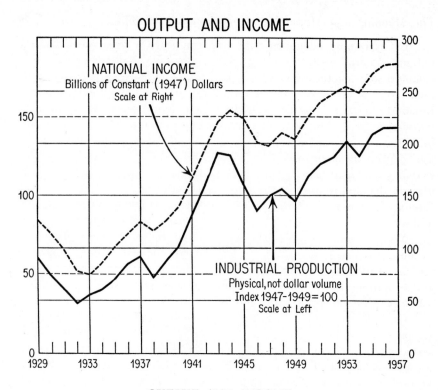

OUTPUT AND INCOME

OUTPUT AND INCOME

Various measures are used to describe changes in total output. Among the most widely used are National Income and Industrial Production. As this chart indicates, they do not mean the same thing, and therefore are not necessarily parallel. National Income measures output of everything during a specified period; Industrial Production excludes such vital spheres of activity as agriculture, distribution, and the service trades. In addition, National Income excludes the output of goods that replace what has been used up in the course of production. That is, the value of machinery, buildings, and natural resources that were consumed in order to turn out current output is deducted from total output. Industrial Production simply measures total output of manufacturing, mining, and construction industries without reference to whether the output is a net addition or simply replaces what was used up in production.

Divergent movements of National Income and Industrial Production, such as those depicted in this chart, are explained by the fact that not all major segments of the economy fluctuate together, nor does their relative importance remain the same over long periods. Specifically, there has been a steady increase in the relative importance of the service and distributive trades for over a half century, and agricultural output has declined relative to the total. During the shorter period covered by this chart, the divergence between National Income and Industrial Production resulted from the sharp rise in military goods output during World War II. During wartime, manufacturing, mining, and construction expand relatively more than other lines of activity. Consequently, Industrial Production rises more than National Income during such periods.

By examining economic data, one can learn a great deal about a nation's material welfare. And in later sections we shall have occasion to examine some of the detailed breakdowns of activity in particular segments of the economy. At this point we are mainly interested in the broadest, and perhaps the crudest, single figure—a measure of *total national output.*[3] The concept that best meets our needs is what economists term *Gross National Product,* which *is the sum of the amounts that final consumers spent for finished goods and services produced during the period (usually a year).* Thus it is the kind of figure which we have already decided represents the best single indicator of the material welfare of a nation, to the extent that it is determined by the output of goods and services.

National product (which is exactly equal in size to national income, because it is simply another way of measuring the same thing) translates the incredibly huge and complex output of goods and services into a single number. Since this single figure attempts to do such an ambitious job, it must be interpreted with caution.

One of the main deficiencies of *national product* as a measure of national material welfare results from the omission of certain goods and services produced for use and not for sale. Important services not included are those of housewives and mothers, and of husbands who are "handy" around the house. Some important kinds of goods are difficult to include accurately in measurements of national product; houses in which owners live, food produced and consumed by farmers, food preparation and household care within the household, and the like, must be estimated without the benefit of a market price to determine their value.

Failure to include output produced for use rather than sale complicates—and sometimes invalidates—comparisons of output in the same country over relatively short periods of time. For example, as larger numbers of mothers have taken employment—a trend characteristic of industrialized countries—national income totals have become exaggerated. They have risen more than the output which they aspire to measure, because they include services produced for working mothers which formerly were produced by these mothers themselves for "use" and were therefore omitted from measurements of national product. (This discussion of the effects on welfare measurements of an increased employment of mothers is purely economic. Many imponderables are involved in the effect of mothers taking employment in increasing numbers; these imponderables, however, have to do more with the effect of such employment on national welfare than with the effect on output. However, these effects cannot be measured by economic accounting.)

---

[3] Actually, this figure must be adjusted for the difference between the claims of foreign residents against domestic output and the claims of native residents against output in other countries.

DIFFERENT MEASURES OF TOTAL OUTPUT
(Illustrated by 1957 data)

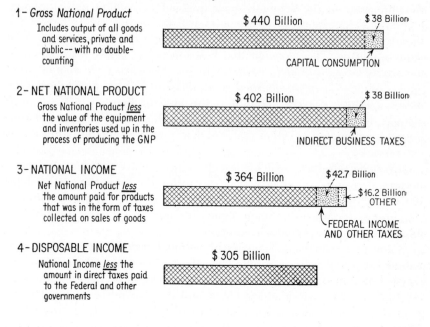

1 – Gross National Product

Includes output of all goods and services, private and public -- with no double-counting

$ 440 Billion $ 38 Billion

CAPITAL CONSUMPTION

2 – NET NATIONAL PRODUCT

Gross National Product _less_ the value of the equipment and inventories used up in the process of producing the GNP

$ 402 Billion $ 38 Billion

INDIRECT BUSINESS TAXES

3 – NATIONAL INCOME

Net National Product _less_ the amount paid for products that was in the form of taxes collected on sales of goods

$ 364 Billion $ 42.7 Billion

$ 16.2 Billion OTHER

FEDERAL INCOME AND OTHER TAXES

4 – DISPOSABLE INCOME

National Income _less_ the amount in direct taxes paid to the Federal and other governments

$ 305 Billion

This figure summarizes, in simplified form, the relationships between four different measures of national income. Gross National Product—the total value of all goods and services produced—is reduced to Net National Product by subtracting from it the capital used up during the period of production. (Capital consumption includes depreciation charges, accumulated damage to fixed capital, and capital outlays charged to current expense.) The next measure, National Income, is derived mainly by subtracting indirect business taxes from Net National Product. Actually business transfer payments (such as contributions to charity) are also subtracted from, and government subsidies less current surplus of government enterprise are added to, Net National Product to obtain the National Income figure. The last measure, Disposable Income, is gotten by a series of complicated additions to and subtractions from National Income, the most important of which is income taxes paid the federal government by individuals and corporations. Additions to National Income include government and business transfer payments and net interest paid by government. Subtractions from National Income include personal and corporate taxes, contributions made for social insurance (such as Old-Age and Survivors Insurance), undistributed corporate profits and corporate inventory valuation adjustments, and the excess of wage accruals over disbursements. Disposable Income, thus, is what people receive in money income to be used either to buy consumer goods and services or to save.

Comparisons of material welfare in different countries are especially hazardous. Unequal values are given to similar things in different countries. Identical houses or quantities of similar foods will count for a good deal more in one country than in another, because of different price relations. For example, house rent is subject to strong government control in many countries. The effect of such control is to depress the value of housing in the economic account below what it ought to be if it is to be strictly comparable with the treatment of housing in other countries. The effects of subsidies, tariffs, price supports, and the like all tend to distort comparisons of output in different countries and even in the same country at different times.

Moreover, some items which are included in national income (wholly apart from harmful goods) ought to be omitted or treated differently. An important example of this is personal transportation. A significant amount of time and money is expended in the United States and other highly industrialized countries, in getting to and from work. Few people live close to their places of work; consequently, one of their costs of holding employment is the outlay required to cover the cost of commuting to and from work. These expenditures ought to be included as production costs —little different in kind from the cost of carrying raw materials and finished products to market, or the cost of elevator service in a tall building. Furthermore, time is consumed in getting to and from work; possibly some portion of this time should be included as "time on the job." Consequently, when output in the United States is compared with that of the past, or with that of nations where transportation to work is far less costly and time-consuming, we tend to exaggerate the margin of its advantage over other periods and other nations.

As implied earlier, national-product computations take no account of the distribution of income within nations. The small nation of Kuwait, for example, has a per capita national income from its oil wells—after accounting for profits taken by the Anglo-Iranian Oil Company—which is virtually the same as per capita income in the United States. Yet income is distributed so unequally that a large proportion of the population is extremely poor; however, the nation itself is very prosperous, if we employ as our yardstick a measure of total national product.

Similarly, in some small countries, profit taking by foreign firms and other types of foreign exploitation substantially reduce the share of income which the local populace receives. Consequently, national product does not accurately indicate national welfare. Especially in considering the material welfare of colonial countries in Africa and the Middle East does this factor require heavy weight.

Similarly, figures describing total national product do not take into account the widely different populations (and age distribution of populations) in various countries. In 1949, for example, the small country of Belgium had a total national income of $5 billion, and the large country of Brazil had an income of $5.5 billion; but their respective *per capita* incomes were $580 and $110. While total output has some, though only modest, significance for determining military prowess and, in this respect, influence on international trade, *economic welfare must be measured in terms of per capita incomes.*

What has been said thus far only scratches the surface of economic accounting and the measurement of the relation between output of goods and services and material welfare. The reader should, however, by now realize that the problem is vital and complicated; he should also have made a start toward understanding the most vital ideas and concepts involved, and the outstanding issues involved. For the moment, we must be satisfied with this much.

3. MEASUREMENTS OF SACRIFICES IN PRODUCTION

Economic welfare cannot be measured by goods and services alone. Those who must work so hard, or at such unpleasant or dangerous occupations that their lives are shortened, or made into an agony of shame, tension, fear, or excess fatigue must be considered poor, if they have no alternative method of obtaining a tolerable level of living.

Unfortunately, effort and sacrifice in production can be discussed only in the most general terms. Measurement is almost out of the question, except for such factors as the number of hours worked, and the proportion of the working force that consists of children, wives, mothers, and the aged. Effort and sacrifice are only crudely indicated by these factors. Other elements in productive sacrifice, namely, the suffering from monotony, insecurity of position, from doing work the final usefulness of which is unclear or remote, from subjection to the unscrupulous direction of others whose whims must be humored, cannot be reduced to statistical totals. All we can hope to do is to raise some important questions about economic welfare in individual countries.

Recognition of these elements of poverty has practical implications. Any nation could increase its output somewhat if it were to increase the exertions of its population. If the population were already working very hard, such a course would not cure poverty; it would merely change its form or make it worse.

Let us take two extreme economies and contrast their sacrifices in production. Compare an African tribesman with an American workman. The former is usually engaged in subsistence agriculture, ordinarily in the form of shifting cultivation. (That is, he moves from one tract of land to another as the land loses fertility, rather than continues to cultivate the same land.) He generally uses simple tools and has no draft animals to assist him.[4] Sometimes subsistence agriculture is combined with keeping cattle, though in forest and tsetse-fly-infested areas this is not possible. In these areas cattle are generally not used for consumption or as an aid in production, but serve primarily as money. Society is organized along tribal lines, but the precise character of tribal organization varies widely.[5] Usually it is a highly autocratic arrangement in which individuals are subject to the arbitrary rule of chieftains. Diet is unvaried, simple, and often lacking in elements required for health and vigor. Sanitation is poor, with disease very common. Life expectancy is about one half that in the United States.

Contrast with the foregoing, the situation of most American workers, with which most of us are sufficiently familiar for the purpose at hand. Although conditions vary widely, it is nevertheless easily seen that the contrast between the two groups is extreme at almost every point.

Note, however, that this contrast merely describes; it does not condone or criticize. Individuals' reactions to all activities depend upon what they expect, what they are familiar with, and the general attitudes prevalent in their community. It can be said, with considerable supporting evidence, that the African tribesman would regard an eight-hour work day in one place, day in and day out (even if only five days in the week), as a Western type of cruelty. On the other hand, the average American worker probably would consider it a horrible punishment simply to remain in the typical African community, because of the climate, the dullness of the life, and the exposure to disease and superstition.

The foregoing comparison should make clear the impossibility of saying anything precise about the amount of sacrifice in production, at least in different countries. Nevertheless, it would be a serious mistake to ignore these sacrifices as an element in economic welfare simply because we cannot measure them accurately. Where they exist, we must take into account factors like monotony of work, independence from direction by others, security, ability to work at will, exposure to disease, education, disruption of home life and child rearing (in the employment of mothers), and so on.

4. MEASUREMENT OF NEED FOR OUTPUT

In addition to the supply of goods available and the sacrifices entailed in production, the level of prosperity depends upon what people "need." A moment's reflection will make clear that *prosperity is partly a relative concept*. The enormously wealthy potentates of earlier times lacked many

---

[4] United Nations, Economic and Social Council, *Review of Economic Conditions in Africa*, Department #/1910/ad. 1; 5 February, 1951, p. 3. (Issued as a section of the preliminary version of the *World Economic Report*, 1949-50.)

[5] *Ibid.*, p. 13.

things that Americans consider commonplace today. Anesthetics, automobiles, radio, television, electric lighting and electrical household appliances, plumbing, expert dental and medical care, and air conditioning were not available to even the richest classes in 1870. If it were possible to measure economic riches accurately, it might turn out that King Henry VIII was poorer than the average government clerk today. Similarly, today's rich may be considered poor by later generations.

As a nation grows more prosperous and the average level of living rises, more things come to be regarded as necessities. Indoor plumbing is not considered a necessity in most of the world today, though United States government statistics classify houses without indoor plumbing as "substandard." Almost every American considers indoor plumbing a necessity. Similarly, a high school education is widely regarded as a necessity in the United States today, whereas a hundred years ago less than 5 per cent of the people had one, and even though today almost half the population of the world cannot even read or write.

Although it is difficult for Americans to understand, there are places in the world where people believe that beyond physical necessities, leisure is superior to anything that money can buy—where there are no "needs" for our type of essentials. For example, an expert in labor problems was sent to Italian Somaliland in 1951 to discover why it was so difficult for employers (mostly agricultural) to secure a stable supply of labor. He concluded:

It appears that the important factor in deciding firstly whether any work should be done on a particular day, and secondly the amount or duration of the work performed, is largely the necessity of eating. *Work is done simply to get enough to eat for the day* (italics mine). Desire for other things may sometimes inspire the worker to longer and more sustained efforts, but there is as yet no general or consistent willingness to work in order to acquire articles of such value as would demand sustained effort over a long period.[6]

The lack of interest of the people of Italian Somaliland in material things may easily be illustrated. There exists a "practice on the Juba River of setting night lines to catch fish. If in the morning on the way to work a native finds a good fish on his line, he will return home immediately, food having been assured for the day."[7]

---

[6] *Conditions in the Trust Territory of Somaliland under Italian Administration,* Document T/935, 3 August, 1951, p. 13. (Report of the Mission of Somaliland and Transmitted to the Secretary-General by the International Labor Office, 17 July, 1951.)

[7] The Mission to Italian Somaliland suggested that "Education of women will be a spur to demands for better housing, clothes and household utensils, leading to more work by their husbands—and possibly by themselves as well." The suggestion that education will be the indirect means to get husbands to work harder is a new argument in favor of free education, though hardly likely to gain male votes. *Ibid.,* p. 31.

Italian Somaliland is not the only place in the world where people work only to obtain basic necessities and where they believe that beyond physical necessities leisure is superior to anything that money can buy. Much of Africa varies only in degree from Italian Somaliland. Similar attitudes can be found in most of the world outside the United States, and even in some parts of this country. Persons with as great a "need" for material goods as ours probably constitute a small minority of the world's population.

How can we define "needs" if they vary so widely from time to time and from place to place? One definition is that they are those things necessary for mere survival, which is to say that anyone who is alive and stays alive is not poor. A definition of needs that is more liberal but also based on biological considerations would include anything required to maintain a person in good health and at high working efficiency.

A definition of needs in biological terms is useful for some purposes, but in the main it helps very little. Most needs are "conventional." That is, they are dictated by prevalent attitudes rather than by biological necessity. Perhaps we could agree that all goods most people possess, and that almost everyone will make strenuous efforts to acquire, should be considered necessities.

Conventions vary over time, between countries, and even among groups and individuals. A person of moderate means in the United States probably would be considered extremely wealthy if he were to have the same income in Yugoslavia. Although the biological necessities for survival are much the same everywhere (except for needs that vary with climate), conventional necessities vary enormously. Accordingly, *poverty will be considered a state of acute unhappiness due to a lack of material things or to inordinate sacrifices in production.* Poverty so great that lives are shortened or productivity impaired is an extreme form.

If needs are defined in conventional rather than in biological terms, two conclusions are apparent. First, differences in level of true prosperity from time to time and country to country are probably much smaller than differences in the output of goods, since where output is consistently low, conventional needs are usually small. Second, the elimination of poverty becomes an endless undertaking. As the average person obtains more goods, the minimum amount of goods he may have and still be considered poor increases. It has been suggested that wants keep pace with the means of satisfying them.[8] If so, all nations will suffer from being "poor," no matter how much they possess. While it seems difficult to believe that people are not better off when they get electricity, vacuum cleaners, automobiles, electric refrigerators, radios, and so on—simply

---

[8] G. Stigler, *Five Lectures on Economic Problems* (New York: The Macmillan Company, 1950), p. 6.

because everyone else has them—psychic states cannot be measured accurately, and we therefore cannot determine whether persons are happier or less happy and by how much, because of a change in their possessions. There is risk in comparing the well-being of widely different societies.

In the absence of any evidence that will resolve the issue, let us nevertheless contrast different national levels of living and try to judge whether economic welfare is as different as the big differences in output per person would suggest. Consider the poorest countries of Africa or Asia. Can we conclude that they are poor because almost everyone in these countries lacks material things?

First, we find that these people lack even biological necessities. The average length of life of the native inhabitants of some African countries is approximately one half that in the United States. In addition, the physical vigor and productivity is far lower than that in countries where a more adequate diet and level of medical care exist, so that they work relatively hard in comparison with what they get by way of material reward. We learn that their "happiness" is in large measure a reflection of their physical well-being. Those with aches and pains question the hypothesis that "life can be beautiful."

Second, people in most parts of the world know a good deal about the luxuries widely consumed in the richest countries. The wealthy classes in each country obtain luxuries from the rest of the world. Moreover, some groups in poor countries, often to gain political advantage, stress the differences in living levels between underdeveloped and highly industrialized countries. If anything, these groups will paint glowing pictures of the things that the population might obtain for itself by the political or economic change they advocated. Such measures tend to raise the populace's *standard* of material welfare only.

Thus, although the peoples of Africa or Asia regard their conventional needs to be much smaller than, say, Americans do, they must be considered poor. Not only do they lack some biological necessities, but they have also been encouraged to want many things that they lack. In short, these people now regard many things as "necessities" that are possessed by few persons in their countries. Thus a general lack of most goods that are commonplace in other countries may well intensify the dissatisfaction of people in poor countries. Some of their present distress over being without our conventional necessities can be traced to a feeling of inferiority, to an obvious inability to conform to the consumption standards of the rest of the world community as they imagine that community.

In all societies, no matter what the general level of conventional needs, it is desirable to distinguish two broad types of need. One, here termed "positive needs," is the conventional and biological kind, the fulfillment of which brings satisfaction whether or not others acquire the same things.[9] Things desired positively are usually consumed privately, rather than in the company of those with whom one competes for social status. It is difficult to list desires that are "purely" positive, inasmuch as almost all consumption is sometimes public, or can be made so by the telling. One would think of the pleasures enjoyed by the "cultivated mind," the satisfaction from leisure, the relief obtained from expert medical care, as fundamentally "positive"; however, possession of a cultivated mind [10] also carries social prestige in most societies; individuals seek position by taking long vacations from their work; and medical care—especially operations—become common topics of conversation in which the narrator sometimes seeks distinction on grounds of having employed an expensive physician. Even though no clear and sharp line can be drawn to separate positive needs from those of other types, the essential character of this type is clear enough: they consist of things wanted for their own sake, rather than for the social prestige that may attach to their possession.

The second major type of need may be termed "competitive desires." These things may also be conventional necessities, even though their value to those possessing them stems partly from the social position or status attaching to their possession. These wants are fundamentally self-defeating, for if satisfied by all people, no one would feel better off.[11] When one person gains gratification from the acquisition of something that his associates lack, his pleasure is offset, and possibly more than offset, by the added discomfort of his associates. Included among "competitive desires" are all those things termed by Thorstein Veblen "objects of conspicuous consumption." Included primarily among these objects are articles of attire, like clothing or jewelry (both rarely purchased primarily for comfort, warmth, or intrinsic beauty). Most of the things we buy are consumed in the presence of others and therefore are conspicuous to some degree. Cadillac automobiles would be less valuable if cars were driven only in the dark of the night.

As a matter of fact, most desires contain both positive and competitive elements. The proportions vary from product to product, of course. Considering the components of a basic or subsistence standard of living,

[9] It is primarily to this type of want that Professor F. H. Knight refers when he writes, "The chief thing which the common-sense individual actually wants is not satisfactions for the wants he has, but more, and better wants." See F. H. Knight, *Ethics of Competition* (New York: Harper & Brothers, 1935), p. 22.

[10] Dr. Hans Singer points out that education, in and of itself, represents a large increase in the level of living. Moreover, it is a relatively inexpensive substitute for other types of economic output, which do not give comparable satisfaction in the long run. See "The Economic Case for Educational Advance," *Pilot Papers* (London: Pilot Press, Ltd., 1945).

[11] Professor Stigler's conclusion that people are no better off when all their possessions increase together presumes that all desires and wants are of the competitive type.

we find that the basic need could probably be satisfied at lower economic cost, *if* the social position associated with it were disregarded. To dress solely for warmth and comfort would surely call for coverings for female limbs that were much less costly, yet far less attractive, than sheer stockings; but in our society such coverings would carry a social stigma. Men's attire would hardly include ornamentation like neckties or hats that give little protection against the elements, if mere physical utility were the reason for their purchase.

The proportion of "positive" and "competitive" elements in any subsistence budget probably varies from country to country, and from time to time. Prosperous countries seem to be moving in the direction of higher "competitive" desires. In these countries a major industry has developed which aims primarily to increase wants. One of the principal devices employed in advertising is to imply a loss of social position if one does not keep pace with other people. An advertising slogan that aroused a torrent of complaint, though it differs only in degree from the usual type, urged parents to purchase television sets and thus spare their children the embarrassment of being compelled to see television in a neighbor's house.

A fundamental fact that must not be overlooked or taken lightly in considering economic welfare is the extent to which an economic system creates wants of either the positive or the competitive type. The stimulation of positive wants contributes to welfare; the second probably lowers it, on balance. All who cannot satisfy their artificially created wants feel mostly pain and deprivation, perhaps mixed with a little pleasant anticipation of the pleasures they are told will await them when they do fill these wants. And if they cannot afford articles that their close associates possess, their pain probably becomes fairly acute, not so much because they must get along without the product, but because they have been relegated to a slightly inferior social position.

To create a desire for things that do give satisfaction—such as improved sanitation, literature, music, leisure, athletic activity, and the like —contributes to a fuller life. Not only the anticipation but the realization are fundamentally pleasant for everyone. Accordingly, a nation whose population, out of ignorance, does not aspire to certain material things should be charged with a higher level of real need than is felt by the average member.

If we define poverty by the relations between the average output of consumers' goods and the minimum cost of a "decent" level of living *in that place* (sacrifices in production do not enter into our calculations because they defy quantitative measurement), we must measure degrees of economic welfare in the following manner: *for each country, or each point in time, we must compute a ratio between the average output of consumers' goods and services per person and the per capita cost of, say, a minimum decent level of living.* By this measure the most prosperous countries in the world might not have the greatest per capita welfare.

Many will object to this method of measuring prosperity because they tend to take their own conception of "needs" for granted. In measuring prosperity, the ratio of output to cost of a decent level of living places as much weight on peoples' desires for goods as upon the supplies of goods. There is strong psychological support for the conclusion that "happiness" or "adjustment" is increased quite as much by a scaling down of desires as by greater means of satisfying wants. This ratio conforms closely to our definition of poverty *as acute unhappiness due to lack of material things.*

However, if prosperity is to be measured by a ratio of per capita output to "needs," some reliable measure of "needs" would have to be found. Can we define a "decent" standard of living so that calculations of "need" for different times or different places will be strictly comparable? Probably not. To estimate the cost of a minimum decent level of living requires a measurement of psychic states. In effect, we want to discover the cost of that quantity of goods that will give equal "satisfaction" or "pleasure" in different countries or in the same country at different times. Since psychic states cannot be measured accurately, estimated costs of minimum decent living standards will necessarily vary.[12] Second, can we obtain calculations of the minimum cost of a decent level of living, whether directly comparable or not, for many countries? If we are willing to accept local standards, and combine with them as completely as possible certain well-defined biological factors, we can establish a reasonable estimate of cost. This will not allow us to compare one society with another, or precisely to determine the ranking of any particular individual in the welfare structure of a society. At least, however, a rule of thumb is possible. Unfortunately, very little statistical work has been done along this line.

III.CONCLUSION

In summary, it will be recalled that a nation is here termed poor when its per capita output is insufficient to provide a decent level of living for all its citizens, taking into account the sacrifices involved in production. Note that the notion of a decent level of living varies from country to country. Our definition therefore takes into account different nations' concepts of what is needed to provide such a standard.

Two of the elements of economic welfare—the degree of sacrifice

---

[12] Indeed, the measurement of the minimum cost of a decent level of living for one time and for one place also implies a measurement of psychic states. Even the cost of minimum *biological* needs can be computed only roughly at best.

involved in production and the need for output—are matters that are practically impossible to measure, even roughly. They remain, nevertheless, significant aspects of welfare. Accordingly, the following chapter will discuss variations in economic welfare from country to country, with due consideration for these two immeasurables.

DISCUSSION QUESTIONS

1. How well off is your family? If you were to move to a more exclusive neighborhood, would you become better off if your income remained the same?

2. By what standards would you judge a person's material prosperity? How accurately do you believe you can measure it? What elements of material prosperity are most difficult to measure?

3. Compare the material prosperity of a college professor having an income of $7,000 a year with a doctor whose annual income is $16,000.

4. Under what conditions would a person with a $25,000 income feel poor?

5. What measurements of an entire economy indicate whether or not that country is "poor"? What important elements relating to economic welfare are omitted from these over-all measures of material welfare?

6. In comparing the economic welfare of different countries, what measures are helpful?

7. If you were to draw a picture of the national output or gross national product, what would it look like?

8. What are the major sacrifices in production in present-day United States?

9. If the alternative to conditions in India were the squalid industrial towns and exploitation of child labor characteristic of the early industrial revolution, would India be better off after the change?

10. Explain why it would be misleading to define material prosperity without reference to sacrifices incurred in production and level of need.

Chapter

3 Economic Welfare from Country to Country

The preceding chapter indicated the conceptual difficulties involved in determining how well off people are in any country. Even if welfare is defined to embrace only material matters, it is enormously difficult to measure differences from time to time and from place to place. At best, existing methods of measuring the major elements of material welfare are crude, and even these have not been applied to many countries. As a result, a reliable comparison of levels of living for some countries is not possible.

Even though available measures of economic conditions leave much to be desired, they are immensely better than no information at all. Moreover, by supplementing statistical evidence with some qualitative information, it is possible to piece together a suggestive picture of variations in economic welfare among the nations of the world.

I. INTERNATIONAL COMPARISONS

A. *Comparison of Money Income*

Output varies greatly from country to country. At one extreme are such countries as Burma and Uganda, whose per capita product in 1952-1954 "equivalent" dollars was $50, while at the other extreme is the United States, whose per capita product was $1,870—more than 37 times as great. There is great variation in the output of even the richest countries. Canada, with the second largest average output, was less than three quarters as prosperous as the United States. The most prosperous industrialized countries averaged incomes about half that in the United States.

Apart from these huge differences among individual nations, per capita output varies considerably from continent to continent. Africa and Asia, the latter including the Middle East, averaged incomes about 5 to 7 per cent of those in North America. Even Oceania (composed of Australia and New Zealand primarily) had average incomes little more than one half those in North America.

Table 1. National and Per Capita Product of Various Countries, 1952-1954 Average*

(Grouped by continent)

Continent and Country	Population, 1953 (thousands)	National products in U.S. dollars † Amount (millions)	Per capita
Africa			
Belgian Congo	12,154	$ 850	70
Egypt	22,062	2,650	120
Kenya	5,851	330	60
Rhodesia and Nyasaland	6,708	670	100
Uganda	5,343	270	50
Union of South Africa	13,153	3,950	300
America			
Argentina	18,393	8,460	460
Brazil	55,772	12,830	230
Canada	14,781	19,360	1,310
Chile	6,437	2,320	360
Colombia	12,111	3,030	250
Cuba	5,807	1,800	310
Dominican Republic	2,291	360	160
Ecuador	3,464	520	150
Guatemala	3,049	490	160
Honduras	1,564	230	150
Jamaica (1952)	1,457	260	180
Mexico	28,056	6,170	220
Panama	863	220	250
Paraguay	1,496	210	140
Peru	9,035	1,080	120
Puerto Rico	2,213	950	430
United States	159,643	298,530	1,870
Venezuela (1952–1953)	5,440	2,940	540
Asia			
Burma	19,045	950	50
Ceylon	8,155	890	110
India	372,000	22,320	60
Israel	1,650	770	470
Japan	86,700	16,470	190

* Arithmetic average of annual aggregate and per capita product.
† Net national product at factor cost.
SOURCE: United Nations, Statistical Office, *Per Capita National Product of Fifty-five Countries, 1952-1954* (New York, 1957), Series E, No. 4, pp. 8-9.

Continent and Country	Population, 1953 (thousands)	National products in U.S. dollars †	
		Amount (millions)	Per capita
Korea (South)	21,376	$ 1,500	70
Lebanon	1,353	350	260
Malaya (1952–1953)	5,706	1,770	310
Pakistan	79,330	5,550	70
Philippines	21,039	3,150	150
Thailand (1952–1953)	19,556	1,560	80
Turkey	22,461	4,720	210
Europe			
Austria	6,954	2,570	370
Belgium	8,778	7,020	800
Denmark	4,369	3,280	750
Finland	4,141	2,770	670
France	42,860	31,720	740
Germany (Western)	48,994	24,990	510
Greece	7,824	1,720	220
Iceland	151	120	780
Ireland	2,945	1,210	410
Italy	47,551	14,740	310
Luxembourg	304	270	890
Netherlands	10,493	5,250	500
Norway	3,359	2,490	740
Portugal	7,990	1,600	200
Sweden	7,171	6,810	950
Switzerland	4,877	4,930	1,010
United Kingdom	50,611	39,480	780
Oceania			
Australia	8,815	8,400	950
New Zealand	2,047	2,050	1,000
Total of 55 countries	1,325,684	$590,120	445

Tables 1 and 2 describe national production. Included are such things as the output of military goods, capital goods, and worthless and actually harmful goods—as well as goods and services that contribute to material welfare. In the world's poorest nations, the share of the national income devoted to uses other than direct consumption is very small. Their poverty does not permit them the luxury of a strong military defense and forbids their appropriating large sums to investment in improved methods of production. On the other hand, the wealthiest nations take a substantial proportion of their national output in the form of military goods and capital goods. (Moreover, since so large a proportion of what is produced does not serve any basic physiological need, one would suppose that there would be many purchases made that were later regretted.) Consequently, the difference in material welfare in the richest and poorest nations is much less than the figures in these tables suggest.

Table 2. Approximate Per Capita Incomes of Continental Divisions of the World, 1949

(In equivalent American dollars)

Africa	$ 75
North America	1,100
South America	170
Asia	50
Europe	380
U.S.S.R.	310
Oceania	560
World total	$ 230

SOURCE: United Nations, Economic and Social Council, *Volume and Distribution of National Income in Under-Developed Countries,* Report by the Secretary-General, Series E, No. 3, 28 June, 1951, Table 3, p. 15.

The main reason why the figures in Tables 1 and 2 exaggerate the differences in material welfare in the rich and poor nations of the world is that they measure (with only minor exceptions) only output produced for sale. It happens that the poorest countries are primarily populated by subsistence homesteads in which families produce almost everything they consume. Consequently, most of the output in such countries does not affect measures of national product. We gain some insight into the magnitude of the omission when we attempt to visualize what a person could buy in the United States with $50 per year. He could not have survived on that size of per capita income, in 1952-1954, but Burmese did so. (And, in view of the fact that the figures in Table 1 represent averages, presumably almost half had incomes below $50.) For these reasons, United Nations' statisticians who have compiled the computations of national product state that measurements of output for many underdeveloped countries tend "to be understated." [1]

As previously indicated, the proportion of total output consisting of goods not used directly by the population varies widely from country to country. Table 3 suggests the wide variation in the kinds of goods produced in various countries. It shows that countries with the highest per capita income usually derived the smallest proportion of their total output from agriculture. For example, in the United States, 4 per cent of the

[1] United Nations, Statistical Office, *Per Capita National Product of Fifty-five Countries, 1952-1954* (New York, 1957), Series E, No. 4, p. 4.

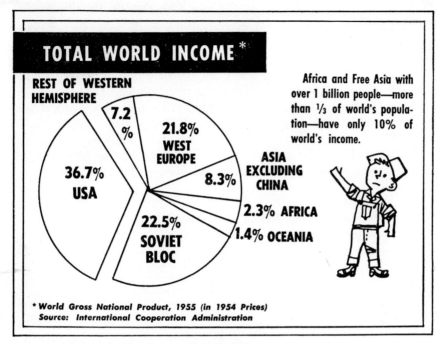

TOTAL WORLD INCOME *

REST OF WESTERN HEMISPHERE

Africa and Free Asia with over 1 billion people—more than ⅓ of world's population—have only 10% of world's income.

7.2%

21.8% **WEST EUROPE**

36.7% **USA**

8.3% **ASIA EXCLUDING CHINA**

22.5% **SOVIET BLOC**

2.3% **AFRICA**

1.4% **OCEANIA**

*World Gross National Product, 1955 (in 1954 Prices)
Source: International Cooperation Administration*

SOURCE: Department of Research, AFL-CIO.

WORLD OWNERSHIP OF RADIOS, TELEPHONES, AUTOMOBILES, AND TV SETS IN 1957

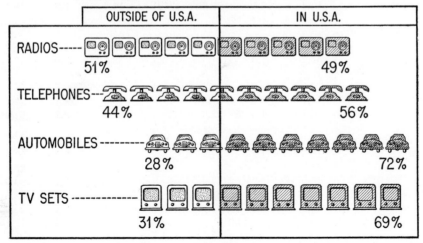

	OUTSIDE OF U.S.A.	IN U.S.A.
RADIOS-----	51%	49%
TELEPHONES---	44%	56%
AUTOMOBILES--------	28%	72%
TV SETS------------	31%	69%

With only about 6 per cent of the world's population, and an even smaller proportion of the world's area, the United States contains about half or more of many products associated with a high level of living.

national income was produced in agriculture; in Canada, 10 per cent. The poorer countries usually obtained a much larger proportion of their total output in the form of agricultural products.

Table 3 also indicates that a few of the poor countries derived a considerable share of their national income from mining. These countries (Belgian Congo and Peru, in the table) have rich mineral deposits, a fact that accounts for their major industry—producing goods for sale. In these and similar countries, a substantial proportion of the total domestic output is paid to residents who are foreigners. Most of the income produced for domestic consumption, even in these countries, comes from subsistence farming.

Table 3. Percentage Distribution of National Product by Major Branches of Industry, 1956*

Continent and Country	Agri-culture	Mining	Manu-facturing	Construction, transport. & communi-cation	Com-merce	Dwellings	Others
Africa							
Belgian Congo	26.5	24.0	12.4	16.9	8.1	5.0	7.1
Egypt (1954)	35.2	0.8	10.6	9.5	9.8	7.1	17.0
Kenya	38.6	1.2	13.1	12.9	15.5	3.3	15.4
Morocco (1954)	37.2	5.1	14.4	7.3	17.1	...	18.9
Tunisia (1953)	33.1	5.7	9.9	8.5	23.9	...	13.2
Union of South Africa	14.4	13.5	23.5	7.9	16.4	2.5	21.8
America, North							
Canada	10.1	4.4	28.5	16.0	18.2	4.8	18.0
Honduras	52.2	1.0	11.3	9.5	13.6	7.0	5.4
Jamaica (1955)	18.9	4.8	13.8	15.9	21.0	4.4	21.2
Panama (1954)	33.8	0.2	8.8	5.2	16.6	12.8	22.6
Puerto Rico	14.7	0.2	21.8	11.1	18.0	11.1	23.1
United States	4.1	1.6	28.6	10.6	21.6	2.1	31.4
America, South							
Argentina	18.8	1.2	22.2	5.3	25.9	7.1	19.5
Brazil (1955)	31.5	19.4		8.3	16.4	3.8	20.6
Chile (1954)	15.0	4.7	17.9	10.9	19.2	8.7	23.6
Colombia (1955)	38.5	2.8	15.4	8.2	10.6	9.2	15.3
Ecuador (1955)	35.8	2.4	15.7	8.1	14.4	7.7	15.9
Paraguay	50.9	14.0		6.9	10.7	5.4	12.1
Peru (1955)	28.3	13.2	15.1	5.1	19.6	...	18.7

* Unless otherwise indicated, figures between two columns are for combined branches.

SOURCE: United Nations, *Yearbook of National Accounts Statistics, 1957* (New York, 1958).

Continent and Country	Agriculture	Mining	Manufacturing	Construction, transport. & communication	Commerce	Dwellings	Others
Asia							
Burma	41.4	1.5	10.6	5.1	25.4	3.9	12.1
Ceylon	48.7	0.1	4.7	17.1	7.2	2.2	20.0
China, Taiwan	32.7	2.2	18.3	9.7	17.5	. . .	19.6
Cyprus	24.8	14.4	15.7	6.3	10.7	. . .	28.1
India (1955)	43.7	1.0	18.3	19.2		4.7	23.1
Indonesia (1952)	56.4	2.3	8.2	4.2	13.4	6.5	9.0
Israel	13.2	20.5		13.8	20.4		32.1
Japan	19.1	2.1	25.8	14.0	22.0		17.0
Philippines	39.9	1.7	14.4	6.6	11.4	. . .	26.0
Thailand (1955)	45.2	1.6	12.7	8.1	21.0		11.4
Turkey	41.0	1.3	14.5	12.0	14.3	3.3	13.6
Europe							
Austria	13.2	44.3		11.5	9.6	. . .	21.4
Denmark	19.9	0.2	27.7	16.4	16.3	4.1	15.4
Finland	22.3	31.9		17.2	11.9	4.0	12.7
France (1952)	16.2	32.6		13.5	14.8	0.8	22.1
Germany, West	8.4	42.3		14.4	12.7	2.5	19.7
Greece	33.9	1.2	18.9	10.3	14.2	7.0	14.5
Ireland	31.1	28.1		15.4		1.8	23.6
Italy	22.0	1.4	31.8	13.4	12.7	2.0	16.7
Netherlands	10.9	43.6		8.9	14.5	5.0	17.1
Norway	14.0	1.7	26.5	26.1	13.9	3.1	14.7
Portugal	27.8	0.8	36.1	5.2	10.6	4.0	15.5
Spain (1953)	35.2	2.1	26.4	6.8	9.9	2.5	17.1
United Kingdom	4.4	3.7	38.5	14.5	14.8	3.2	20.9
Oceania							
New Zealand (1952)	23.7	0.9	21.1	16.0	17.3	4.6	12.8

Most of the people in the world derive their livelihoods from working on the land. Each person produces most of the things he himself consumes—and consumes nearly all that he produces. Many are tenants, and a few own their land. As a rule, they obtain little more for their labors than enough food to sustain themselves with a minimum of home-fabricated clothing and primitive shelter.

One great difficulty arises in translating the output of many nations into a single currency for purpose of comparison. The statistician employs foreign exchange rates for this purpose. For a variety of technical reasons, this procedure is rough and, sometimes extremely misleading. Nevertheless, the data presented here, based on extremely painstaking efforts on the part of highly skilled statisticians, represent the best information now available on this subject.

B. Nonmonetary Indicators of Consumption Levels in Different Nations

The relative availability of consumers' goods in various countries can be shown most dramatically by comparing the consumption of individual goods and services directly. An ingenious and laborious comparison of this type has been made by Professor M. K. Bennett for the years 1934-1938 for 31 countries embracing 85 per cent of the world's population.[2] Although Dr. Bennett's data are now quite out of date, his general conclusions still apply broadly. His calculations, which rest upon a combination of 19 indicators of consumption levels, show differences of about 6 to 1 between the most prosperous (United States) and the least prosperous (French West Africa). The richest and poorest nations are even farther apart now than they were then.

Considerable information, which had not been compiled when Professor Bennett made his analysis,[3] is now available on the consumption of individual goods and services. Table 4 brings together figures which describe consumption of diverse products and services. It makes clear one very significant fact: *differences in the consumption of basic necessities are far smaller than differences in the consumption of other products.* For example, when one compares calories per person per day, the difference between the highest and lowest is little more than 2 to 1; a similar relation holds for total protein grams per person per day. On the other hand, differences in telephones and motor vehicles owned between the richest and poorest are on the order of 250 to 1.

C. International Comparisons of Sacrifices in Production

Except for the less important aspects, such as the number of hours worked, sacrifices in production defy quantitative measurement. Still, we should no more ignore the more important elements involved in productive sacrifice than those involved in other immeasurables.

We shall deal more specifically with sacrifices in production in the United States later in the chapter. As for an international comparison, there can be little doubt that the *sacrifice does vary greatly from country to country, though probably not so much as the output of goods.* It is important that we keep in mind that sacrifice in production is one of the means by which we gauge the poverty of a nation, and that *if conditions*

---

[2] M. K. Bennett, "Disparities in Consumption Levels," *American Economic Review,* September, 1951, Table III, p. 648.

[3] The data presented, although the best available, are far from wholly reliable. Moreover, they are not always strictly comparable. Nevertheless, they are thoroughly satisfactory for the use made of them here.

in poor countries are to be corrected, all types of sacrifice—slavery, inhumanity to workers, personal abuse, dangerous and unhealthy conditions of work—need to be remedied fully as much as does lack of output. We should realize that improvements in the conditions of production would increase personal well-being quite apart from the increases in material output that often accompany them.

For instance, accidents in African, South American, and in east and west European mines and factories are generally high relative to those in the United States today. Ignorance and superstition in African communities, centering largely around their economic life, result in terrible fears and primitive practices. Sickness resulting from a scarcity of medical services takes a heavy toll. Apartheid, or racial isolation and discrimination in the South African economy, contributes to the native African's low sense of his personal worth. The rigid economic and social systems in India and in Moslem countries tend to instill in the individual a fatalism and despair that not only stifle efforts to raise productivity but also eliminate hope of betterment in this world.

D. Costs of a "Minimum Budget" in Various Countries

Finally, in comparing levels of prosperity from country to country, account must be taken of variations in the national conception of "need." Estimates of minimum needs apparently have not been made in any country[4] other than the United States, and were made here for the first time only in 1947 and have not been continued regularly since 1952. However, in Australia some judicial investigations into the matter have provided information that will suffice to indicate a striking conclusion. Whereas the output of goods and services in the United States (national income) per person in 1949 was 2.1 times that in Australia, when the accepted needs for income are considered, the average Australian was found to be better off than the average American. Let us examine the basis for this conclusion.

Australia employs a "basic wage" in arbitration proceedings. This wage was declared in 1941 to be adequate for a family unit of three persons "on our accepted standards of living, looking at it from the needs point of view only."[5] On November 1, 1949, the basic wage for 30 towns and 6 capital cities in Australia was 129 shillings.[6] In 1948-1949, the per capita income of Australia was 240 pounds (Australian) annually;[7] for

---

[4] The author made an effort to obtain such estimates. Extensive correspondence has unearthed only the evidence about Australia presented here.

[5] *Commonwealth Official Yearbook of Australia, 1949*, p. 428.

[6] *Ibid.*, p. 429.

[7] Computed from United Nations, *National and per Capita Incomes of Seventy Countries—1949* (New York, October, 1950), Table 1, p. 14.

Table 4. Nonmonetary Indicators of Relative National Consumption Levels

Country	Calories per person per day *	Total protein grams per person per day *	Textile consumption †
United States	3,100	93	17.1
New Zealand	3,350	104	9.8
Switzerland	3,150	93	10.1
Sweden	2,970	79	10.4
United Kingdom	3,270	84	12.0
France	2,810	99	8.9
Italy	2,570	75	4.7
U.S.S.R.	3,020	97	6.6
Czechoslovakia	2,690	82	...
Latin America			
Argentina	2,950	104	8.3
Cuba	2,740	68	2.7
Uruguay	2,810	92	7.3
Chile	2,490	77	4.6
Brazil	2,350	57	4.7
Colombia	2,370	55	3.9
Mexico	2,050	56	4.0
North Africa			
Tunisia	2,517	75	2.3
Morocco	1,852	62	2.4
Algeria	1,421	43	2.1
Libya	...	...	2.6
Ghana	...	...	4.6
Middle East			
Turkey	2,670	87	4.9
Cyprus	2,590	68	3.9
Egypt	2,560	73	3.8
Israel	2,860	89	5.9
Iraq	1,930	60	5.0
Iran	1,820	58	1.6

* For the most recent year available, generally in mid-1950's, although 1946-1949 averages are included. SOURCES: United Nations, *Statistical Yearbook, 1957*, Table 127; Food and Agricultural Organization, *Second World Food Survey*, 1952, Appendix IV; and FAO, *World Outlook and State of Food and Agriculture*, 1950, Table A.

† Kilograms per capita of apparel fibers (cotton, wool, rayon, and synthetic), 1955-1956 average. SOURCE: FAO, *Monthly Bulletin of Agricultural Economics and Statistics*, November, 1957, pp. 4-5.

Telephones (per 1,000 population)‡	Inhabitants per physician‡	Elementary school teachers (per 1,000 of population)‡	Motor vehicles (per 1,000 of population)‡	Illiterate population (% illiterate)§
358	790	4.11	388	4.3
261	700	5.05	239	. . .
257	700	3.74	18	. . .
316	1,300	5.88	27	0.1
139	. . .	3.46	100	. . .
76	980	1.86	112	3.3
51	820	3.70	30	21.6
. . .	610	. . .	. . .	. . .
27	680	. . .	. . .	4.1
59	760	5.63	31	13.3
24	1,000	3.16	25	23.6
46	860	3.15	32	. . .
22	1,900	. . .	14	19.4
14	2,500	2.46	12	51.4
15	2,900	2.49	12	38.5
13	2,200	2.84	18	51.6
9	6,600	1.77	14	. . .
12	9,000	. . .	19	. . .
15	5,000	1.33	17	94.0
7	10,000	2.30	11	. . .
3	22,000	3.66	5.5	. . .
6	3,400	1.51	2.9	65.4
25	1,500	3.54	40	35.7
8	3,500	1.93	4.1	74.5
40	450	6.50	20	6.9
9	5,900	2.29	7.8	. . .
3	8,800	1.56	2.8	. . .

‡ SOURCES: United Nations, *Statistical Yearbook, 1957*, Tables 1, 139, 149, 179, and 181. Telephone data are for 1956 (Cuba and Czechoslovakia, 1953); data on physicians are for various years from 1952 through 1957; teachers are the number in various years from 1952 through 1956 (sometimes only public school teachers are reported); motor vehicles mainly refer to 1956, but 1952 through 1955 are also included where necessary.

§ From population census data; in advanced countries 1930's or 1946, other countries 1940 through 1954. SOURCES: United Nations, *Statistical Yearbook, 1957*, Table 180; 1949/1950, Table 163.

Table 4 (cont.) Nonmonetary Indicators of Relative National Consumption Levels

Country	Calories per person per day *	Total protein grams per person per day *	Textile consumption †
Other Asia			
Japan	2,270	64	7.4
China, Mainland	. . .	. . .	1.3
Vietnam	. . .	. . .	0.7
China, Taiwan	. . .	. . .	3.5
Pakistan	1,990	47	2.1
Thailand	2,020	53	2.0
Burma	1,990	68	1.4
Ceylon	1,940	47	1.8
Philippines	1,890	49	1.3
India	1,880	51	2.3
Indonesia	1,880	42	1.4

a family of three, output averaged 276 shillings weekly. This sum more than doubles the average basic wage, which was declared to be adequate for a family of three.

Similar computations for the United States in the same year show the following. The annual cost of a minimum budget for an urban family of four in 1949 was between $3,295 and $3,773 (see Table 6). The per capita national income that year was $1,440, or $5,760 for a family of four—significantly less than twice the cost of a minimum budget for four persons.

The foregoing crude comparisons are reinforced by statements made by former residents of Australia. Those to whom the author has spoken estimate that the Australian is just about as well off, in a material sense, as the average American. New Zealanders are convinced that material prosperity is higher in their country than in the United States. To a large extent the difference between the apparent level of prosperity and the output of goods and services is accounted for by differences in conventional needs. There is no doubt that, on the average, Americans have (and "need") a larger quantity of goods than people in other countries.

II. LEVEL OF PROSPERITY IN THE UNITED STATES

Up to this point we have primarily defined economic prosperity and discussed its measurement. To crystallize the problems involved in definition and measurement, the discussion has been oriented around interna-

Telephones (per 1,000 population)‡	Inhabitants per physician‡	Elementary school teachers (per 1,000 of population)‡	Motor vehicles (per 1,000 of population)‡	Illiterate population (% illiterate)§
39	940	3.91	5.7	...
...	...	...	...	...
0.5	61,000	0.45	1.7	...
5	2,300	2.90	1.4	...
0.6	15,000	...	0.6	...
0.6	6,800	4.00	2.5	46.3
0.4	8,400	1.34	1.5	42.7
3	5,100	...	9	42.0
3	...	...	6	37.8
0.7	5,500	1.61	10	82.1
0.9	71,000	1.35	1.6	...

tional comparisons of prosperity. We are now in a position to review evidence describing the level of material prosperity in the United States.

A. Output in the United States

In our international comparisons of economic prosperity, we relied heavily on data describing national product. Only this type of information permitted us to compare *total* output in a large number of countries. As indicated, national product estimates include the output of such items as military and capital goods, which, while essential in the present-day world, do not directly satisfy personal material needs. In examining the level of economic prosperity in the United States, it will be possible to use a measure of total output that is more relevant than national income to calculations of material prosperity. That measure is *"disposable personal income,"* which *computes the amount of money that all individuals possess after paying direct personal taxes (that is, mainly income taxes).* This income can be spent in any way the owner chooses; he also has the option of saving it. Given our definition of economic prosperity, disposable personal income comes close to measuring the quantity in which we are interested. However, it does exclude the value of some services provided by government to consumers, like roads, public health services, schools (in part), and social insurance.

Table 5 describes total disposable income for the years 1929 to 1958 in *"current dollars."* The latter phrase *designates the number of dollars actually received by consumers, without regard to possible changes in the value of money.* These figures may be misleading unless they are adjusted

HOW MUCH BETTER OFF WERE WE
IN 1958 THAN IN 1929 ?

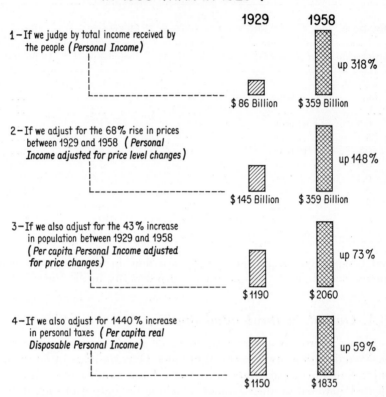

1929   1958

1 – If we judge by total income received by
the people (*Personal Income*)

up 318%

$ 86 Billion $ 359 Billion

2 – If we adjust for the 68% rise in prices
between 1929 and 1958 (*Personal
Income adjusted for price level changes*)

up 148%

$ 145 Billion $ 359 Billion

3 – If we also adjust for the 43% increase
in population between 1929 and 1958
(*Per capita Personal Income adjusted
for price changes*)

up 73%

$ 1190 $ 2060

4 – If we also adjust for 1440% increase
in personal taxes (*Per capita real
Disposable Personal Income*)

up 59%

$ 1150 $ 1835

Although national income more than quadrupled between 1929 and 1958, a rise in prices of almost 70 per cent, an increase in population of almost 45 per cent, and a tremendous jump in federal income taxes (over 1,440 per cent) left us with real per capita disposable income 59 per cent higher than in 1929. In other words, we were better off in 1958 to the extent of providing people with enough money to buy 59 per cent more goods and services per person than in 1929.

for at least two circumstances. First, account must be taken of the rise in population—which was about 43 per cent between 1929 and 1958. Second, the figures must be made comparable *in real terms* (that is, in terms of real goods and services rather than units of money) by adjusting them for changes in the value of money. Since 1929 the amount of goods that a dollar would buy has varied greatly. For example, it would buy about twice as many consumers' goods in 1938 as in 1957. This fact is indicated by the figures in column 5, which show the price index of consumers' goods in 1933 to have been 46, and 100 in 1957. (The index of consumers' prices measures the changing cost of an unchanging variety of goods from year to year.)

Table 5. Is the United States Prosperous or Poor?

(1)	(2)	(3)	(4)	(5)	(6)	(7)	(8)
		Total	Disposable		Disposable income per	Con- sumption per	Savings per
		disposable	income	Consumer's	person	person	person
	Population	income	per	price index	(1957	(1957	(1957
Year	(millions)	(billions)	person	(1957=100)	dollars)	dollars)	dollars)
1929	121.8	$ 83.1	$ 682	61.0	$1,118	$1,063	$ 55
1930	123.2	74.4	604	59.4	1,017	970	47
1931	124.1	63.8	514	54.1	950	913	37
1932	124.9	48.7	390	48.6	802	812	—10
1933	125.7	45.7	364	46.0	790	803	—13
1934	126.5	52.0	411	47.6	863	862	1
1935	127.4	58.3	458	48.8	938	906	32
1936	128.2	66.2	516	49.3	1,048	991	57
1937	129.0	71.0	550	51.1	1,077	1,021	56
1938	130.0	65.7	505	50.2	1,007	990	17
1939	131.0	70.4	537	49.4	1,088	1,044	44
1940	132.1	76.1	576	49.8	1,157	1,093	64
1941	133.4	93.0	697	52.3	1,333	1,174	159
1942	134.9	117.5	871	58.0	1,502	1,147	355
1943	136.7	133.5	977	61.6	1,585	1,193	392
1944	138.4	146.8	1,061	62.6	1,694	1,267	427
1945	139.9	150.4	1,075	64.0	1,680	1,360	320
1946	141.4	160.6	1,136	69.4	1,636	1,499	137
1947	144.1	170.1	1,180	79.5	1,485	1,443	42
1948	146.6	189.3	1,291	85.5	1,510	1,422	88
1949	149.2	189.7	1,271	84.7	1,501	1,434	67
1950	151.7	207.7	1,369	85.5	1,601	1,504	97
1951	154.4	227.5	1,473	92.3	1,597	1,472	125
1952	157.0	238.7	1,520	94.4	1,611	1,483	128
1953	159.6	252.5	1,582	95.2	1,662	1,531	131
1954	162.4	256.9	1,582	95.5	1,656	1,534	122
1955	165.3	274.4	1,660	95.3	1,742	1,631	111
1956	168.2	290.5	1,727	96.7	1,786	1,656	130
1957	171.2	305.1	1,782	100.0	1,782	1,661	121
1958	174.1	306.2°	1,759	102.5†	1,716	1,609	107

° Seasonally adjusted average for the first half of 1958.

† January-June average.

SOURCES: Population, U.S. Department of Commerce, Bureau of the Census; midperiod estimates of total population, including armed forces overseas. Total disposable income: U.S. Department of Commerce, Office of Business Economics, Consumers Price Index; U.S. Department of Labor, Bureau of Labor Statistics.

To adjust for changes in population and in the value of money, the following computations have been made. Total disposable income has first been divided by the population in each year to obtain the disposable income per person—in current dollars (column 4). Thereupon the result was divided by an index of consumers' prices to arrive at the estimated disposable income per person in 1957 dollars (column 6). A similar calculation was made for consumer expenditures, and placed in column 7. The difference between column 6 and column 7 is savings per capita in 1957 dollars. The consumption data give us the better idea of current welfare.

Disposable income per person—what is left for each individual to spend or save after payment of all taxes—tripled over the period. That this increase is smaller than the quadrupling of product-per-person is due to the fact that taxes per person became higher on the average. Disposable income per family also rose, but not by the same percentage because the number of persons per family has declined.

SOURCE: *Economic Growth in the United States: Its Past and Future* (New York: Committee for Economic Development, February, 1958), p, 28.

An illustration will clarify the meaning of Table 5. Take the years 1933 and 1957. Disposable income in 1957 was $305.1 billion; in 1933, it was $45.7 billion. These figures alone suggest that economic prosperity was almost seven times as great in 1957 as in 1933. We find, however, that after disposable income is adjusted for changes in the population, the difference is narrowed to $1,782 and $364 per person—still a ratio of 5 to 1. Moreover, when account is taken of the fact that the index of prices in 1933 was 46, or less than half as high as in 1957, the difference in the level of material prosperity is found to narrow down to $790 versus

$1,782, in 1957 dollars. That is, the average American consumer had $1,782 to spend in 1957. In 1933 he had only $790 in money of 1957 purchasing power. Thus, after the adjustments mentioned, an *apparent* difference in material prosperity of almost 7 to 1 is reduced to a little more than 2 to 1. The relative rise in both income and prices is shown in the above chart, in which it is clear that income outstripped price rises but not by nearly as much as we might have supposed.

These computations show United States output in 1933, and several other depression years, to be insufficient to provide the average family with its essential physical and conventional needs. If income had been evenly divided (it was not), a family of four could have bought in 1933 what $3,160 would have bought in 1957; the estimated cost of an "adequate" budget for urban families in 1957 varied between $4,135 and $4,815.[8] Even if we allow for an increase in the standard of living, that is, in the amount of "need," during the period, it is still obvious that average income was below average requirements.

Accordingly, columns 6 and 7 of Table 5 measure two elements of material prosperity—the total goods *available* to the average individual, and the total goods *consumed* by the average consumer (the reader should understand that the negative savings in the years 1932 and 1933 indicate that plant and equipment were permitted to deteriorate).

Two further elements must be considered in measuring material well-being in the United States: the amount of sacrifice entailed in production and the cost of a minimum decent level of living.

Before those factors are taken into account, some implications of Table 5 will be set forth. Its results show great variation in disposable income in current dollars from year to year. Even though most of this variation arises from changes in prices, and in part from population growth, substantial variations from year to year are also shown in the amount of consumers' goods at the disposal of the average American consumer. For example, between 1929 and 1933 the total amount of goods produced per American dropped 28 per cent; in money terms, the drop was more than 40 per cent. The actual amount of goods consumed fell on the average by 25 per cent. (Part of the goods consumed represented a drop in goods held in inventory.)

Table 5 also shows that output varies less than the dollar value of the goods produced. Prices tend to rise at the same time that output increases, and they ordinarily fall when output declines. Accordingly, from prosperity to depression, changes in the physical quantity of goods produced are smaller than the changes in value of output.

Even in as short a period as that covered by Table 5, the rise in income per person becomes clear. If we compare two years of full employ-

---

[8] See Table 6 of this chapter.

ment, 1929 and 1956, we find total income per person increased from $1,118 to $1,786 in dollars of 1957 purchasing power. This rise amounted to 60 per cent over a twenty-seven-year period, a rise averaging about 1.8 per cent per year, compounded.

Because population tripled over the period, the rise in product-per-person was naturally less than the rise in total product. The product-per-person in 1956 was four times as much as in 1880. This covered not only the income earners but everybody in the population, from day-old infants to nonagenarians.

SOURCE: *Economic Growth in the United States: Its Past and Future* (New York: Committee for Economic Development, February, 1958), p. 27.

B. Sacrifices in Production in the United States

Have the sacrifices made in production increased or fallen much since 1929? Sacrifices in production include at least the following elements: conditions of work (light, air, physical safety, and such), steadiness of employment, personal prestige, security against personal abuse and insult, appeal of the work, opportunities for advancement, duration of work (whether it is to the point of excessive fatigue or acute tedium), the employment of housewives and mothers (thereby denying husband, wife, and children some elements of a stable home life).

It has already been stressed that most sacrifices in production defy accurate measurement. However, changes in productive sacrifice since 1929 are fairly apparent. For example, there is little dispute that physical conditions of work have improved since 1920—partly as a result of more rigorous enforcement of already existing laws under governments sympathetic to labor, and because of the greatly increased strength of labor unions since 1933. Similarly, security of employment against being discharged on personal grounds has grown as unions have won the right to require cause for dismissals, administrative machinery to give an employee a hearing in the event of doubt, and as the proportion of the work force made up of civil servants has risen. Personal abuse and insult also have lost their terror for members of strong unions that combat abusive foremen and managements to the limit of their strength. In most respects workers have improved the conditions of work, and labor has become a more highly regarded calling, with increased prestige. In addition to opportunities for advancement on the job, laborers now have an opportunity to advance within the officialdom of labor unions to positions of high income and prestige.

The length of the work week can be measured fairly accurately. In the United States it has declined steadily. In 1909, for example, hours[9] worked in manufacturing industries averaged fifty-one per week. At present they average about forty. More significant than the number of hours actually worked is the number required in the basic work week. From a six-day week of more than eight hours per day, the conventional work week has become five eight-hour days or slightly less. Furthermore, vacations with pay have increased from a week per year to two and, for senior workers, to three weeks a year in most industries. Provisions for paid sick leave and for paid holidays have increased considerably.

On only one important score can it possibly be argued that sacrifices in production have increased. There has been a steady increase in the proportion of wives and mothers employed in industry. If one considers all women, without respect to marital status, it appears that between 1900 and 1957 they increased from 18.4 to 34.8 per cent of the total labor force.[10] In March, 1957, 12.7 million married women—29.6 per cent of all married women—were working or actively looking for jobs, more than 4 million more than held jobs during the peak of World War II.[11] Even a considerable proportion of mothers, and a substantial number with children of school age, held jobs. About 18 per cent of all women with children of preschool age were in the labor force in March, 1957.[12]

Sometimes the employment of wives and mothers is the result of the husband's inability to earn enough to support the family adequately; in part, however, it results from the desire of some women to pursue their

[9] U.S. Department of Labor, Bureau of Labor Statistics, *Monthly Labor Review*, 71, No. 1 (July, 1950), p. 39.

[10] U.S. Department of Commerce, Bureau of the Census, *Current Population Reports*, "Marital Status of Workers: March, 1957," Series P-50. No. 76, November, 1957, p. 7.

[11] *Ibid.*, p. 2.

[12] *Current Population Reports*, Series P-50, March, 1958.

careers or to escape household duties for which they may have little taste or talent. When the desire to work arises from the quest for more pleasant activity rather than for additional income, the employment of women presumably means a reduction rather than a rise in sacrifice. On the whole, employment of women seems to include more of the first group than the second; however, the proportion of women who are compelled to accept employment in order to supplement their husbands' income seems to be falling. Consequently, like the other forms of sacrifice in production, this one seems to be declining.

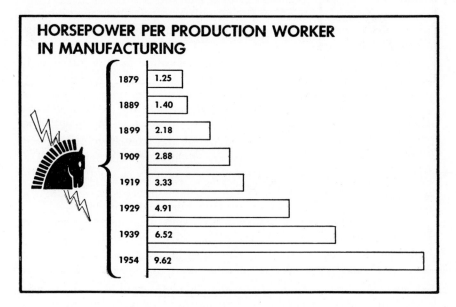

High among the causes explaining ever-rising output per man-hour has been the increase in the amount of capital goods standing behind the average worker. One indication of the increase in capital is the steady advance in the horsepower available in manufacturing establishments for each production worker employed. All kinds of capital goods, however, including those provided by governmental investment, have assisted in raising output per man-hour.

SOURCE: *Economic Growth in the United States: Its Past and Future* (New York: Committee for Economic Development, February, 1958), p. 32.

We can conclude that the economic well-being of Americans has probably increased steadily because of a decline in their sacrifices in production. But though output per person has risen, and sacrifices in production have declined, economic prosperity has not necessarily increased, because, possibly, the rise in conventional necessities has outrun the increase in output and the reduction in sacrifices.

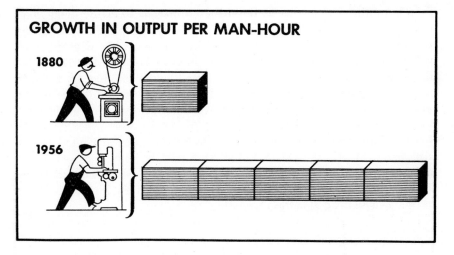

GROWTH IN OUTPUT PER MAN-HOUR

1880

1956

Our society now produces five times as much in each hour worked as it did in 1880. This central development in the panorama of growth was made possible by many interacting factors: advancing technology, an increasing quantity of capital goods, improvements in the skills of labor and of business management, larger markets, increasing specialization—all operating within a society of great mobility, and having political, economic, and social institutions favorable to growth.

SOURCE: *Economic Growth in the United States: Its Past and Future* (New York: Committee for Economic Development, February, 1958), p. 31.

C. Cost of a Minimum Budget in the United States

Many different levels of living have been defined. One author has separated eight of them. They are "poverty," "bare subsistence," "minimum for health and efficiency," "minimum comfort," "comfort," "moderately well-to-do," "well-to-do," and "liberal." [13] Other terms have been used to describe different levels of living. Among these have been "emergency budgets," which indicate the minimum amount on which a family might survive for a few months under the harshest necessity; "adequate" budgets, which measure the cost of a level of living according to prevailing United States standards of the needs for health, efficiency, nurture of children, and participation in community activities. Other levels of living have been termed "subsistence" and "minimum health and decency."

---

[13] This distinction was first used by Paul Nystrom, and was more recently employed by P. D. Converse in a tabular analysis entitled "The Leveling Off of Incomes." The analysis is obtainable from Professor Converse at the University of Illinois.

These phrases and words do suggest different levels of living, but probably do not connote the same things to all people. "Lower living standards shade into higher standards by imperceptible degrees, and where one sets the poverty line depends on one's beliefs about how people should be entitled to live." [14] Common understanding of what is meant by any level of living is possible, if at all, by examining the list of products consumers obtain, and whatever specifications are given concerning their quality.

The most widely used estimate of living costs in the United States is prepared by the Bureau of Labor Statistics. It estimates the annual dollar cost of a worker's family budget in 34 large cities. The items included represent a compromise between what workers actually purchase and their needs as defined by "scientific" standards for housing, nutrition, and such. The budget is neither a "subsistence" nor a "luxury" budget. It provides a modest and adequate American standard of living based upon the kinds and quantities of goods and services that workers actually select.[15] The budget estimates the cost for a four-person family living in a separate house or apartment. The family consists of an employed father, aged thirty-eight years, a housewife of thirty-six, not gainfully employed, a boy of thirteen in high school, and a girl of eight in grade school.

The items included and missing from this budget suggest the level of living it affords. The cost of a college education is not included, since neither child is of college age. No home telephone service is allowed, but three calls per week for the entire family from public booths is included. A ratio of 7 autos for 10 families was used in all except the very largest cities, where 4 cars per 10 families was used as the basis for calculation. Each member of the family was allowed four doctor's calls a year, and a serious illness or accident about once in four years. In clothing, the husband gets an overcoat once in seven years; the wife a coat once in four. The home is equipped with such conveniences as mechanical refrigerator and washing machine, electric or gas stove, and the wife is expected to do all cooking, cleaning, and laundry. The budget allows for some miscellaneous items like newspaper, one monthly magazine, tobacco, some treats, gifts, church and club money. No liquor allowance is included, but it does cover the cost of one bottle of beer a week and two bottles of soft drinks for the entire family.[16] Of course, no savings are provided for in this budget.

---

[14] L. Reynolds, *Labor Economics and Labor Relations* (Englewood Cliffs, N.J.: Prentice-Hall, Inc., 1949), p. 469.

[15] U.S. Department of Labor, Bureau of Labor Statistics, *Handbook of Labor Statistics, 1947*, p. 123.

[16] U.S. Department of Labor, Bureau of Labor Statistics, *Workers' Budgets in the United States: City Families and Single Persons, 1946 and 1947* (Washington, D.C.: Government Printing Office, 1948), p. 5.

Whatever one calls the foregoing budget, it clearly provides far less than that which we are told constitutes the average American "standard of living." A family restricted to that budget will not suffer acute unhappiness for lack of material goods; nevertheless, it will almost certainly have a strong desire for additional goods.

This budget has been computed for only a relatively brief period (specifically, since June, 1947). Moreover, it applies to a nontypical group. Only 9 per cent of the labor force consists of a family of four with one wage earner. Nevertheless, this budget represents the single best yardstick available for the measurment of minimum conventional needs in the United States.

Table 6 indicates the cost of such a budget for the years 1947 to 1957. Against this cost are set the per capita disposable income of the

Table 6. Family Incomes and the Cost of a Minimum Family Budget, 1947-1957

(Incomes and budget cost put on basis of a family of four)

Year	Average family income *	Median family income	Cost of minimum family budget	
			Low	High †
1947	$4,720	$3,033	$3,092	$3,546
1948	5,164	3,190	n.a.	n.a.
1949	5,084	3,107	3,295	3,773
1950	5,476	3,319	3,453	3,933
1951	5,892	3,714	3,812	4,454
1952	6,080	3,889	3,900	4,565
1953	6,328	4,233	3,930	5,595
1954	6,328	4,167	3,950	4,615
1955	6,640	4,420	3,940	4,605
1956	6,908	4,787	3,985	4,650
1957	7,128	n.a.	4,135	4,815

* Represents per capita disposable income times 4 to make it comparable with the four-person family for which living costs were calculated.

† Represents annual cost of a "modest but adequate" level of living for a four-person urban family. No national average is reported. The figures here presented represent the highest and lowest cost in the 34 cities for which such information is compiled.

The 1947 figure is for June, the others are for October.

SOURCES: Median Family Income, from U.S. Department of Commerce, Bureau of the Census, *Current Population Reports,* Series P-60, Consumer Income.

Budget cost, from U.S. Department of Labor, Bureau of Labor Statistics, *City Workers' Family Budget,* reported in the *Monthly Labor Review.* Budget figures from 1952 on are estimated roughly on the basis of changes in Consumer Price Index.

Average family income derived from Department of Commerce data on disposable personal income.

average American for the same years and the median family income in the United States. These figures indicate, albeit roughly, the level of living that the output of the United States economy would afford if evenly divided when operating near full capacity.

As Table 6 shows, during the years 1947 to 1957 the total output was more than sufficient to provide the items included in the "minimum budget." Indeed, the total disposable income, if evenly divided, would have given each family of four about one and one-half times as much as would be required to obtain the minimum budget. Nevertheless, the total disposable income would not have been sufficient to provide the average family of four with all the goods and services that Americans have been taught to believe are part of the average standard of living. For example, the average family of four could not, without drawing upon savings, send its children to college out of town and would find it very difficult to run a modest home, keep a car, obtain full medical and dental care, and take an annual vacation.

We see, moreover, that even during highly prosperous years such as 1947 to 1957, about half the American families receive income below the amount needed for the minimum decent level of living estimated by the Bureau of Labor Statistics. (The column, in Table 6, of median incomes, shows the income above and below which fell half of all income recipients.) Thus, when account is taken of the fact that *incomes are not equally distributed,* we find that many Americans are "poor" by a fairly austere standard of "needs."

III. CONCLUSION

The United States economy is capable of producing substantially more than is needed to provide everyone with minimum conventional needs. However, during years when the economy fell far short of full employment the total output would not permit satisfaction of even minimum conventional needs. Moreover, when account is taken of the inequality of personal incomes, *at least part of which is nevertheless required if the same level of total output is to be achieved,* it appears that half of all families cannot afford the conventional necessities—even during periods of full employment.

Thus, in comparison with the rest of the world, the United States has a large output of material goods. Its level of sacrifice is not significantly greater, and probably is less, than that in other developed countries. But when compared with the level of need felt by Americans, the nation is not especially prosperous. When the economy departs significantly from full employment, the country can be considered actually poor in terms of what Americans feel is a minimum income.

DISCUSSION QUESTIONS

1. What difficulties arise in comparisons of the quantity of goods available per person in different countries?

2. Which are the poorest sections of the world? Which are the poorest sections of the United States? What do they have in common?

3. Compare the material prosperity of the people of the United States with that of people in any other country you know through travel or study. How can the differences between them in material prosperity be measured?

4. How great are the differences in supplies of goods per person between the richest and the poorest countries? Why do you suppose they are far smaller when one takes relative supplies of particular products than when one considers national income?

5. How would you compare the amount of goods available in the United States, on the average, in two different years? Make such a comparison by referring to Table 5, for the years 1933 and 1941.

6. What items do you believe should be included in a "minimum family budget"? Comment specifically on the following: comic books, presents for relatives, school supplies (for example, notebooks, pencils, and so forth), alcoholic beverages to serve guests, cost of admission to zoos, museums, and horseraces, and Christmas presents for the mailman and the garbage collector.

7. Are people better off than others with an equal amount of goods, simply because their desires for goods may be smaller? Illustrate your answer with references to desires for particular things.

Chapter

4   Causes of

National Poverty

Enormous variation was shown to exist among nations in the level of
material prosperity. Even the United States, apparently the richest country in the world, frequently provides its citizens *as a whole* with fewer
material possessions than they believe are "necessary." As yet nothing
has been said about the many instances of individual poverty resulting
from the fact that income is not equally distributed in any country. The
causes and effects of income inequality will be discussed in Part Three.
In this chapter the major reasons why total national output may be insufficient to provide for the material needs of a nation as a whole will be
explored.

I.   CAUSES FOR LOW OUTPUT

The major cause for national poverty where it exists is an inability
to produce large quantities of useful goods and services. While productive
sacrifices and high desires may aggravate a condition of low output, these
are only rarely the primary causes of national poverty. It will quickly
emerge from the discussion to follow that a wide variety of factors not
ordinarily considered economic strongly influence the quantity of goods
and services available to a population.

A. *Stinginess of Nature*

You cannot get blood out of a turnip, and it is equally difficult to get
food out of rocky soil. Some countries have been favored by excellent
climate, fertile soil, rich mineral deposits, convenient water-power sites,
and rivers for navigation. Others have few of these natural gifts.

Even countries where nature has been least generous cannot blame
their low output on small resources alone. As a committee of United Na-

tions experts from five countries concluded in an excellent analysis of the causes of, and remedies for, low economic development, ". . . whatever their resources may be, all countries are currently in a position where their national incomes could be greatly increased by better utilization of what they have." [1]

The limit set by natural resources upon the potential development of an area is very elastic. A nation need not have many rich mineral deposits or favorable conditions for agriculture and the like. In this era of national as well as personal specialization, *a nation can be prosperous if it is richly endowed for the production of only a few products.* By means of trade with other countries—richly endowed with other resources—its many needs could be filled. Thus a nation need not have a balanced supply of all resources to enjoy high prosperity.

An interesting, and exceptional, example in point is the country of Kuwait. This tiny country, lying between Saudi Arabia and Iraq, has a population of 100,000 natives, mainly Arabs. It is extremely rich in oil deposits but is otherwise an arid wasteland. If the nation received no income from its oil deposits, the population would barely eke out a minimal living. As it happens, the income from oil makes this country the richest in the world; that is, taking the total value of output—the national income, or even total disposable personal income—and dividing it by the population, the result is higher than the per capita national or disposable personal income in the United States. Of course, such a per capita income figure must be interpreted with care, and especially in the light of the manner in which income is distributed.

To be specific, in 1951 an agreement was concluded between the Anglo-Iranian Oil Company, the Gulf Oil Company, and the native ruler of Kuwait, Sheikh Abdullah de Salim de Sabah. By this agreement, the Sheikh received $140 million annually. Divided among the population of 100,000, this alone amounted to a per capita personal income of $1,400. The sum roughly matches the per capita disposable income in the United States in the year the agreement was concluded. Of course, other incomes from the oil industry, as well as incomes from other pursuits, swell the total. Especially if the income of the British and American companies produced in Kuwait—properly considered part of its national income—is added, the total greatly exceeds the per capita output of the United States. [2]

---

[1] United Nations, *Measures for the Economic Development of Under-Developed Countries,* Report by a Group of Experts appointed by the Secretary-General, May, 1951, p. 4.

[2] The facts presented here are drawn from a story in "The News of the Week in Review," *New York Times,* December 9, 1951, p. 2. By 1956, the output of oil producd in Kuwait had risen to more than 1,200,000 barrels a day and yielded more than $280 million annually in revenue to the Sheikhdom. See *New York Times,* April 2, 1957, p. ME 6.

B. The Inefficiency of the Economic System

With equal natural resources, some nations probably could produce a larger output than others could. Ability to turn natural resources and manpower into material goods varies from country to country. Although it is extremely difficult to evaluate whole economic systems—problems of value judgment complicate the task tremendously—there are almost certainly substantial differences in the efficiency of alternative economic systems.

The officials of the world's poorest nations apparently recognize that something is wrong with their economy, but they may not correctly diagnose the difficulty. As might be expected, they tend to blame circumstances for which they are not personally responsible, particularly a shortage of capital.

Two aspects of economic systems should be singled out for particular emphasis: their ability to generate incentives for individuals to put forth strong productive efforts and to invest in productive enterprises; and the ability to provide employment for all productive resources offered for employment.

If individuals cannot secure the fruit of their own efforts, they are not likely to exert themselves to the utmost. In most societies, the opportunity to better one's lot in material ways is a strong motive for action.

In some nations this incentive is blunted by economic arrangements. Americans and British especially have heard many allegations that high income taxes are "killing incentive." Economic incentive in underdeveloped countries is blunted in ways that are unfamiliar to Westerners. Among the more prevalent discouragements to maximum economic effort are (1) property laws, which in many countries require that pasture and agricultural land be used in common, or laws that do not protect tenant farmers from eviction from their property, thereby discouraging them from improving the land; (2) custom or law, according to which, in some countries, certain productive methods are prohibited by religious doctrine, and those who adopt new methods are considered to commit sacrilege; (3) laws binding people to the soil, and laws or customs that restrict individuals to particular "castes" from which advancement is virtually impossible; (4) inefficient and corrupt governments, which prey on the individuals who are successful and, in effect, rob them of their achievements.

Laws and conditions such as these cannot everywhere be easily eliminated. They do not represent simply the misguided notions of men who do not know better. As the experts called together by the United Nations to study the causes of underdevelopment concluded:[3]

---

[3] United Nations, *Measures for the Economic Development of Under-Developed Countries,* pp. 15-16. Hereafter this source will be referred to as "United Nations Experts."

In our judgment, there are a number of under-developed countries where the concentration of economic and political power in the hands of a small class, whose main interest is the preservation of its own wealth and privileges, rules out the prospect of much economic progress until a social revolution has effected a shift in the distribution of income and power.

Failure of an economic system to utilize its available productive resources can create poverty in the midst of potential prosperity. As already indicated, the United States was a poor country during years when the economic system could not provide a high level of employment.[4]

The United Nations experts concluded that the poor nations of the world do not generate depressions or unemployment themselves; where those conditions do occur, they are generated by the industrial countries with which they trade.[5] The economic systems of underdeveloped countries, however, are generally afflicted with "underemployment." This is a situation wherein far more workers are engaged in an occupation—a condition most characteristic of agriculture—than are required to produce the current output. Underemployment arises mainly when a supply of arable land is too small to engage fully those employed on the land. Failure to direct surplus labor to occupations where it could be fully employed may be attributed to the economic system, and it is therefore responsible for underemployment.

C. Inefficient Production Methods

Production techniques vary widely. In some parts of the Middle East agricultural techniques are no better today than they were in the times of the Pharaohs. In the field of irrigation, present techniques there are inferior to those of ancient times.[6] Other nations constantly improve their techniques so that in nearly every generation technology in some major industries is revolutionized.

1. CONDITIONS IN AGRICULTURE

Most of the world's population is engaged in agriculture. Accordingly, national prosperity in most countries depends primarily upon the productivity of agriculture.

Labor productivity in agriculture is very uneven. North and Central American agriculture is about 20 times as productive as African agricul-

---

[4] It is not suggested that unemployment and depression are inevitable under capitalism. At a later point, arrangements that almost certainly would prevent depression will be indicated. Until they are adopted, and they have not yet been adopted in full, even such relatively prosperous countries as the United States, the United Kingdom, France, Belgium, and Holland, among others, face the threat of poverty because of failure of the economic system.

[5] United Nations Experts, *op. cit.*, p. 5.

[6] *Ibid.*, p. 28.

ture, nearly 12 times as efficient as agriculture in Asia, and more than 5 times as efficient as South American agriculture (Table 1). Output per hectare (which in the metric system equals 2.47 acres) is much more equal the world over than output per worker (Table 1, column 2). Typically, countries with low farm output per worker suffer from "underemployment"; that is, people's productive efforts are not fully utilized, for there is not enough work for them to do. In other words, low productivity is closely associated with overpopulation. Hence the land in underdeveloped countries is intensively, even though inefficiently, cultivated.[7]

Table 1. Productivity of the Agricultural Population by Continents and for the World,* 1947-1948

Continent (1)	Yield per hectare 1947–1948 (Metric tons) (2)	Yield per person in agriculture 1947–1948 (Metric tons) (3)
World average	1.30	0.42
North and Central America	1.50	2.57
South America	1.39	0.48
Europe	1.34	0.88
Oceania	1.20	2.38
Asia	1.20	0.22
Africa	0.73	0.12

* Excluding the Union of Soviet Socialist Republics.

SOURCE: Food and Agriculture Organization of the United Nations, *Monthly Bulletin of Food and Agricultural Statistics*, Vol. 2, No. 9, September, 1949; arranged in order of yield per hectare in 1947-1948.

2. CAUSES FOR INEFFICIENT PRODUCTION

Inefficiency in agriculture will be explained first. Apart from the great differences in the quantity and quality of arable land from nation to nation, the major causes for low farm output in some countries are

1. The excessively small size of the average farm holding, which is insufficient to provide a subsistence minimum for those tilling the soil, and to provide an opportunity for full utilization of the farmer's equipment;[8] (one may express the same point as a condition of excessive population).

2. The splitting up of individual farm holdings into different plots

---

[7] These conclusions rest upon data that are very inexact. However, they probably are not very wide of the mark as indicators of the degree of difference in productivity of agriculture from country to country.

[8] Most of this discussion is based on United Nations Experts, *op. cit.*, pp. 11-20.

that are widely scattered, which wastes time and effort in moving from one field to another, and discourages the use of equipment.

3. Inability and unwillingness to learn improved techniques and insufficient capital to put them to use.

Most of the causes of production inefficiency are the same for agriculture, industry, mining, and distribution. Some of these causes are greatly underestimated. For example, the level of education and literacy strongly influences production methods. In some countries personnel is lacking even to copy the methods used in other countries. This statement applies not only to imitating the methods used by the more complicated industries like steel making or petroleum refining, but to agriculture as well. "The first major obstacle to the general advance in technology in underdeveloped countries is therefore the lack of an educational and administrative structure through which the producers can learn the new technology." [9]

The "outlook" of the people obstructs the improvement of productive methods in many poor countries. The scientific tradition, which carries with it a spirit of exploration, discovery, and experimentation, and the conception of natural regularities that can be discovered and adapted to human betterment are lacking. If religious views or custom dictate that past methods be continued, and punish by social ostracism or worse those who improve productive methods, technical advances will be slow, if they occur at all.

Even among countries with a scientific tradition and a high level of education and literacy, there are wide differences in productive efficiency. Part of this difference is traceable to the amount of effort devoted to research. Countries that rely on individuals to get "bright ideas," and neglect organized methodical research will be left in the lurch. Another part of the difference is attributable to the amount of pressure under which businessmen operate to improve their techniques. Businessmen, facing intense competition, typically strive to cut costs and to improve their product. If, on the other hand, they operate together as a team, through some secret or public understanding or organization, new methods of production may improve only slowly. Patent laws, which influence the profit to the man who develops or puts to use new ideas, vary from country to country and probably affect the level of productive efficiency.

Greatest attention has been drawn to the availability of capital as the determinant of output. A nation's *capital is the accumulation of factories, equipment, machinery, stocks of unfinished and finished goods, and the like, all of which are used to make possible the production of other goods and services.* Countries unable to purchase equipment that embodies the latest techniques suffer in comparison with those able to

---

[9] United Nations Experts, *op. cit.*, p. 29.

do so. However, the shortage of capital is more complicated than is ordinarily supposed.

First, it should be recognized that most machinery is designed to do things that many underdeveloped and poor countries do not need done—that is, to save labor. Most underdeveloped countries have an excess of labor. They need equipment that either will save other equipment—that is, cheap machines to do the work now done by expensive machines—or will, with the same amount of labor, contribute toward greater total output. In certain fields, notably agriculture and mining, machinery may not be able to increase total output at all, because it is limited by natural and other circumstances.

Second, the capital shortage in most poor countries exists more in the form of inadequate trained personnel to administer and establish business enterprises than in shortages of machinery. Human capital is most scarce in poor countries. Without the necessary personal skills to use it correctly, machinery of the latest design is not efficient.

Third, some countries have a domestic supply of capital, but it is owned by persons or businesses that do not desire to invest it in productive enterprises. Those with capital who may not want to invest it in enterprises that would increase total output offer numerous arguments, two of which are most important: one, they regard the domestic political situation as unstable or the government as corrupt, and are not certain that they would be permitted to enjoy the profits of their undertakings; two, they find that the most profitable fields for them—though not for the country as a whole—are speculation in real estate, basic commodities, or mercantile enterprises of various sorts. As a result, the development of modern farms or factories is passed by for less arduous and more profitable undertakings.

Fourth, a shortage of capital is a result as well as a cause of poverty. To obtain factories and machinery, a country, much as an individual, must save. That is, it must give up the chance to consume goods in order to devote resources that could otherwise go for consumption into the production of machinery and factories. Capital goods do not immediately yield things that individuals can use; consequently, to acquire them involves the sacrifice of goods today in anticipation of more goods tomorrow. However, countries that are already poor are not able to reduce their output of consumers' goods greatly, even to get valuable machinery, schools, laboratories, etc. As a result, they lack the capital equipment needed to raise their output substantially. If their output were somehow to rise sharply, even for a brief period, their ability to spare resources for investment in plant and machinery would rise also, and a favorable circle of events might come about. But, being poor, they are trapped by a vicious circle. Because they cannot afford to invest in efficient productive arrangements, they are likely to remain too poor ever to afford them.

D. Foreign Exploitation

If judged by their total output relative to their population, some countries are prosperous. However, if the proportion of domestic output belonging to foreigners is deducted, these countries become significantly poorer. In some underdeveloped countries the major industries producing for the market (hence responsible for a large proportion of the nation's income) are not owned by natives. If the profits in these industries are high, as they often are, foreigners obtain a significant proportion of domestic national income, while the natives are left with a correspondingly smaller share.

Some evidence suggests the extent to which foreigners receive income in the world's poorest countries. In the unusual case of Kuwait, the proportion was almost 50 per cent of gross income; in Northern Rhodesia, 27 per cent; in Venezuela the proportion was 17 per cent; in Iran 13 per cent of the national income went to foreigners.[10]

Foreign ownership of domestic enterprises need not be harmful to the native inhabitants. On the contrary, as will be indicated in Part Seven, both creditor and debtor countries ordinarily gain from *free foreign loans*. Foreign ownership does not arise exclusively from free loans, however. By force and chicanery some nations have appropriated to themselves what belongs to others, and thereby have contributed to poverty in certain countries. The world has undergone a fairly ruthless period of imperialism during which this type of exploitation took place. The results of imperialism are still found in foreign ownership of some enterprises that yield large returns to foreigners. A new, and not altogether clear, form of exploitation of the present day is the domination of so-called satellite countries by the U.S.S.R., the most outspoken foe of earlier types of imperialism.

For example, in several African countries the tiny proportion of the population that is non-African takes a very large proportion of total income. In Northern Rhodesia in 1946, 45.3 per cent of total personal income was obtained by the non-African population, which represented only 1.4 per cent of the total population. In Southern Rhodesia, in the same year, 65.3 per cent went to non-Africans, who represented 5 per cent of the population. In Kenya, in 1949, non-Africans, representing 2.9 per cent of the population, obtained 50.9 per cent of total personal income.[11]

Taken alone, these figures cannot be considered proof that the native

---

[10] United Nations, Economic and Social Council, *Volume and Distribution of National Income in Under-Developed Countries,* Report by the Secretary-General, Series E, No. 3, 1951, p. 10. On Kuwait, see "The News of the Week in Review," *New York Times,* December 9, 1951, p. 2.

[11] United Nations, *Volume and Distribution of National Income in Under-Developed Countries,* p. 19.

population was injured by the non-Africans. The income of the natives might possibly be even lower if it were not for the presence of foreigners, though this possibility is made to seem unlikely by the many efforts that non-Africans employ to repress natives—suggesting that their relations are not free and not based on mutual economic advantage. Moreover, when the per capita income of natives in Northern Rhodesia, for example, is found to average 5 pounds in 1946 (maybe the equivalent of $20), it is difficult to believe that they were benefited by non-Africans.

The presence of a foreign population that is resident and exercises control over the governmental machinery in its own interest could influence the total national income as well as its distribution. By keeping natives in subjection, by limiting educational facilities and thereby denying natives opportunities to develop their potential productive abilities, by suppressing their leaders, and so on, these persons may increase their own incomes, while lowering the total income of the nation. On the other hand, enlightened and conscientious foreign leadership might raise the living levels of indigenous populations.

E. Restrictionism

The output of goods in many nations, including the United States, is checked by many types of restriction on production. Restrictions on output result from strong market power possessed by industrial firms and labor organizations, and from barriers against imports. Each of these will be described briefly.

There is no such thing as a *complete* monopoly; some degree of rivalry is to be found everywhere. Many sellers can significantly alter the *total* supply of their product that is offered for sale, and can thereby directly influence its price. The means by which some firms obtain power to control output and price vary; the power can arise from patent monopolies, control over the supply of suitable natural resources, agreements with actual or potential competitors, and the like. Some firms can set a price for their products and refuse to sell at a lower figure, with the assurance that no other firms will offer enough of the product for sale to drive the price down. As would be expected, firms with strong market power tend to set relatively high prices for the things they sell, in an effort to make as much profit as they can. At the high prices they charge, their sales are less than they would have been at lower prices. Consequently, by setting high prices these firms limit sales, and, since production tends to keep pace with sales, market power tends to reduce output of particular goods.[12]

---

[12] The effect of market power on *total* national income is not always the same. This question is discussed later. See Chapter 14.

Powerful industrial firms limit output in other ways. There are forms of industrial "feather-bedding" that limit total output. Ordinarily, industrial feather-bedding takes the form of setting unnecessarily high standards for products, requiring that more material and labor be devoted to these products than is needed. For example, the building codes in some communities allegedly incorporate unreasonable standards for plumbing and electrical work, greatly increasing the cost of the house without adding much, if anything, to the service the owner gets. Organizations of independent artisans, often in collaboration with unions, have been successful in securing the enactment of such requirements and in policing them.

Some labor organizations control such a large proportion of the labor supply needed to produce a particular product that they can greatly raise wage rates and win other benefits for their members. Sometimes they exert their power in restrictive ways. First, they tend to raise the price of the thing they sell—labor—and thereby may reduce the amount of it that will be purchased, with resultant unemployment and lower output. Second, powerful labor organizations generally limit the length of the work week. Fewer goods can be produced by a worker in, say, thirty-five hours than in forty-four hours per week; if laborers work all year around, they will turn out more goods in the longer work week. Third, strong labor unions sometimes compel feather-bedding. While feather-bedding is difficult to define rigidly, it essentially means a compulsion to use more labor than is really needed for the job in question. The clearest types of feather-bedding call for workers to be employed who do absolutely nothing. An extreme case is the "stand-by" musicians who must be employed by theaters or radio stations that elect to use recorded music, though they will not play at all. To tie up labor in such unproductive activities will, of course, reduce the output of goods and services.

Restrictions on imports are another factor tending to reduce the standard of living. For a whole host of reasons, some nations are able to produce some things far more cheaply than others. Purchase of things abroad at lower prices than would be possible at home would permit each individual (and the nation as a whole) to obtain more goods than by producing those goods for themselves. Nevertheless, most nations hinder the importation of goods and thereby deny their people the opportunity to increase their living standards. The reasons for the enactment of restrictions on imports need not be elaborated here; they will be discussed later. It might simply be noted that domestic producers wish to be protected from the competition of foreign producers and to secure the enactment of tariffs that compel consumers to subsidize their relative inefficiency.

F. War Damage

Some nations are poor because of heavy war damage. War generally results in the destruction of factories, railroad lines, shipping, and productive manpower. In addition, during wartime vital types of repair and maintenance of plant and equipment, and the usual production of new machinery and the like, are postponed. Consequently, total output is likely to be hard hit. Nations that have frequently served as battlefields—like France, Belgium, Poland, and Russia in both World War I and World War II—may suffer poverty almost entirely because of war damage.

II. CAUSES FOR EXCESSIVE SACRIFICE

The discussion of causes of poverty thus far has dealt with factors limiting output. We must now consider influences that create poverty through excessive sacrifices in production. We shall deal, though very briefly, with two main factors: (1) slavery and near slavery, and (2) economic insecurity.

A. Slavery and Near Slavery

There is no scarcity of examples of man's inhumanity to man. Slavery, or its equivalent, still exists in many parts of the world today. As we shall see, it is difficult to draw a line between slavery and freedom. Certainly no person is completely free, and even slaves have some liberty.

To be subject to the orders and whims of another person is among the greatest hardships free men can imagine. Even to persons accustomed to it, slavery often is a hateful state. Between full slavery, wherein a man is legally entitled to treat certain other human beings as he wishes without restraint from the authorities—and would even receive help from law-enforcement authorities to ensure that his orders were obeyed—and a situation where each individual can do whatever he wishes short of interfering with the rights of others, are an infinite number of combinations of coercion and liberty. Individuals will surely draw the line at different places in separating slavery from freedom. Yet there can be little argument that some conditions contain so much coercion and opportunity for personal abuse that such conditions are the source of economic poverty. Therefore, even if slavery could increase physical output, the net welfare of society would diminish because of the great sacrifices of the slaves.

Symptomatic of what we here term slavery or near slavery are such conditions as the following: a required workday far longer than individuals wish to work at the same hourly pay; compulsory residence in "compounds" or other areas, separated from home and family; inability to change employment; lack of access to training for advance on the job; lack of any constituted authority to which one could bring complaint in the event of underpayment of wages, personal injury, and such, with the expectation of fair treatment.

B. Economic Insecurity

Many present-day societies—especially those that are tribal—ensure individuals against economic want beyond that jointly suffered by the entire group. All members of the tribe recognize a mutual responsibility to assist those who suffer misfortune. During the feudal period, the forebearers of present-day Europeans and Americans likewise were assured of support at some specified "station in life." In the advanced industrialized countries, a person's economic condition has become much more uncertain than it was under feudalism. Generally speaking, individuals receive income only if they can obtain gainful employment and if they can hold such employment against the competition of others.

Uncertainty of income, if one is protected against extreme want, may be a source of interest and excitement. However typically, loss of income for a brief period threatens a man and his family with privation, loss of social position, personal embarrassment, and the like. Economic insecurity is acutely painful in our society. In many countries, and especially in lines of business where employment is particularly unstable from year to year, many individuals suffer high productive sacrifices simply from economic insecurity.

Apart from insecurity of income caused by general depression or low productivity, insecurity results from changes in production techniques and from "overage." The introduction of new techniques can turn a valuable labor skill into one for which there is no market. Employers are generally reluctant to take on employees who have passed the peak of their vigor. They have different notions about the age beyond which workers should not be hired. When workers have passed the age at which some employers will not hire them, except in periods of acute labor scarcity, they experience an additional insecurity. To lose one's job then takes on a new complexion and seriousness.

There are other possible sources of excessive sacrifice. The wrong choice of a job—especially if it results from lack of freedom to choose—can compel workers to continue at tasks that are peculiarly painful for them. Undue specialization of work, which is difficult to define but is increasingly likely since specialization is on the increase, can also make work hours sheer misery to those who require variety and novelty almost as much as they need food and air. Another possible source of excessive sacrifice in production is the lack of personal contacts in one's·work—with the resultant feeling that one is regarded, not as an individual, but as a cog in production. Some jobs call for work in isolation—the night watchman is an extreme example. Most jobs in large-scale industry divorce the individual from the owners of the business, and the immediate supervisor has anomalous status. He does not take the place of the owner, except in the negative aspects of personifying authority, discipline, and the threat of dismissal. In addition, many workers suffer if their connection with the final product is so remote that they do not feel they are making any productive contribution. This outgrowth of great specialization is characteristic of the most mechanized industries; it deprives workers of the feeling of social contribution and gives rise to misgivings about their "purpose" and importance in society.

The possible sources of excessive sacrifice listed do not apply to everyone. Some people welcome a routine that they can master fully and thereby free their minds for pleasant daydreams or for conversation "on the job"; some workers are not plagued by thoughts about their social contribution, and have no need for personal contact with their employers. Some workers tend to gravitate toward those jobs that suit their psychological needs most, though when jobs are scarce this tendency is very weak. Others tend to become accustomed to their situation and are finally inured to some aspects of it that were painful at the outset.

III. CAUSES FOR INORDINATE NEED

Increased output, even without increased sacrifices in production, need not raise the level of material prosperity. If population keeps pace with output, then output per person will remain the same. Similarly, if the strength of desire for goods keeps pace with the supply of goods, then material welfare may, according to how one views the matter, not increase even when output per person expands greatly. Two major causes for inordinate need—overpopulation and stimulation of excessive desire for material possessions—will be discussed in turn.

A. Overpopulation

Double output and double population at the same time, and the amount of goods available for each person, on the average, will remain the same. As stated, this proposition is simple arithmetic. Nevertheless, it is highly significant, for in large parts of the world population does, in fact, keep pace with output.

The arithmetic of population growth leads to startling prospects, if we look ahead several centuries. Given the current rate of increase the world over, population doubles about every thirty years. In a century it would be 8 times its present size; in two centuries it would be 64 times as large as it is now. It seems unlikely that the output of goods and services can *permanently* increase faster than the current rate of population increase. Viewed in this broad perspective, poverty is inevitable for the whole world unless population growth is checked.

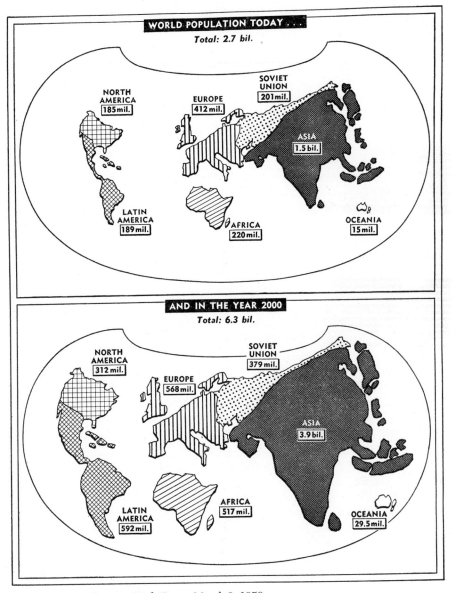

SOURCE: *The New York Times,* March 9, 1958.

The ability of modern man to increase his numbers must be included among his most startling and dubious accomplishments. In the year 1500, world population was a little short of one-half billion. Not until 1800 was this figure doubled. The 1800 world population was doubled in 1930. Population growth in recent decades is presented in Table 2, which shows an increase of more than 40 per cent in thirty-six years.

Table 2. World Population, 1920-1956

Year	World population (millions)
1920	1,890
1930	2,013
1940	2,246
1950	2,495
1955	2,691
1956	2,737

SOURCE: United Nations, *Statistical Yearbook, 1956* and *1957*, Table 1A.

Population growth, like the level of personal income, is extremely uneven. In some nations, population is growing at staggering rates. For example, in Ceylon and Malaya, the birth rate is about 40 per thousand; with a death rate of 10.4 and 12.2, respectively, the net population growth is extremely rapid, amounting to a doubling in 25 years. On the other hand, most of Western Europe and Scandinavia have almost stable populations. *As a rough rule, population growth is most rapid in nations with the lowest level of living.*[13]

Put more precisely, population has tended to pass through four stages. (See Chart 1.) In the first stage, both birth and death rates are high and roughly equal. Few countries are in this stage, though some African areas may fit the pattern. In the second stage, the birth rate remains high while the death rate falls, with the result that there is a rapid growth in population. Most of the underdeveloped nations of the world are in this stage. The third stage is characterized by a decline in both birth and death rate, with the decline in births exceeding the drop in deaths. Accordingly, population grows more slowly during the third than the second stage. The fourth stage is one of low and nearly equal

---

[13] An interesting qualification of this has been the experience of the United States and Canada in the past decade, where population growth has been at a very rapid pace. With the birth rate approximately 25 per thousand in the United States and 28.5 per thousand in Canada, and the death rate about 9.5 per thousand in the United States and about 8 per thousand in Canada, population growth in these two advanced and prosperous countries is comparable with the rapid population growth in underdeveloped countries. See Metropolitan Life Insurance Company, *Statistical Bulletin,* December, 1957, pp. 1-3.

birth and death rates. England, France, Belgium, and the Scandinavian
countries have reached stage four. It took them from one to three centuries to pass through the full cycle.

We would not be justified in assuming that all nations will pass
through these four stages. The present underdeveloped nations might
follow a different pattern. And developed countries might add a fifth
stage, possibly characterized by substantially higher birth rates such as
we find in the United States and Canada currently.

THE NATIONAL POPULATION CYCLE

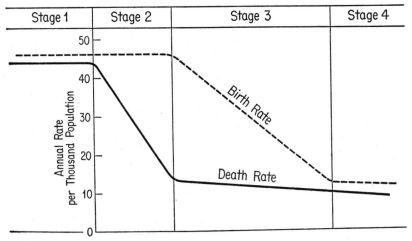

CHART 1

Our concern here is with nations whose living levels are low and
whose population grows more or less apace with increases in *total* output. One may say that these nations are using their greater output of
goods to support a larger population at bare subsistence levels.

The close connection between population growth and national poverty was pointed out very dramatically about 150 years ago by Thomas
Malthus, an English clergyman and economist. His views are largely responsible for the study of economics having received the name of "the
dismal science." Malthus held that there is a natural tendency for population to grow in a geometric progression—that is, 1, 2, 4, 8, 16, and so
forth. In other words, periodically population would double itself unless
held back by natural forces or preventive measures. Malthus minimized
the possibility that preventive measures might be effective: he ruled out
birth control on religious grounds and did not view the postponement of
marriage as likely to become a widespread pattern of behavior. Thus he
focused attention on the natural forces, and in particular on what he
considered an inherent inability of the economy to produce food in quan-

tities sufficiently large to keep up with the tendency for population to grow geometrically. Other natural forces, he explained, such as war, epidemics, floods, and the like, also would keep population from growing at a geometric rate.

Thus any tendency for a country to add to its well-being would be held in check by the natural tendency for population to grow very rapidly. The specter raised by Malthus, in other words, was that increases in output would not raise living levels but would be turned into larger populations whose members lived on the brink of starvation—a prospect dismal in the extreme. Unfortunately, Malthus' theory proved quite accurate for a large part of the world up to the present day.

The connection between output and population is fairly direct. Increased supplies of goods—particularly food—reduce the number of deaths directly and indirectly resulting from malnutrition. As a result, as output rises the death rate falls, leaving a larger population. The tendency for population to keep pace with output has made many persons pessimistic about raising living levels in countries where birth-control measures are not generally known and practiced.

The Secretariat of the United Nations has estimated the rate of population growth in areas having the lowest levels of living (Table 3). These estimates indicate the rate of increase in output that must be achieved if the prevailing low levels of living are merely to be maintained. If living levels are to be raised, the growth in population must be exceeded. For example, the population of Latin America is growing at the rate of more than 2.0 per cent annually. This figure gains meaning when compared with the rise in output in the United States during the period of rapid growth in productivity and population. Between 1879 and 1938 total output in the United States increased at an annual rate of 3.5 per cent.[14] (The rise in per capita income was approximately 2.2 per cent annually.) Thus, if Latin America is to increase significantly its *current* per capita income, it must increase its total output as rapidly as the United States did during the period of its most rapid expansion.

Population growth in poor countries can be expected to continue even if output does not keep pace. The death rate now "first and foremost depends upon the extent to which medical knowledge is made available to the people."[15] Both medical knowledge and its dissemination are increasing the world over, largely because of the activities of the World Health Organization.[16]

---

[14] Simon S. Kuznets, *Uses of National Income in Peace and War*, National Bureau of Economic Research, Occasional Paper, No. 6 (New York, 1942), p. 30.

[15] United Nations Experts, *op. cit.*, p. 46.

[16] A summary of the development of rural health services in various regions is presented in the United Nations General Assembly Document entitled *Organization of Rural Health Services*, A/AC., 35/L.42 10 August, 1951.

Population growth affects living standards in two separate ways. First, as indicated, it increases the need for output. Consequently, increases in population require a proportional rise in total output if living levels are not to fall. Second, increases in population seem sometimes to lower average output. This second effect is not simple arithmetic and needs further discussion.

Table 3. Recent Population Growth

Area	Population mid-1956 (millions)	Per cent of growth per annum 1950–1956
World total	2,737	1.6
Africa	220	1.7
Northern Africa	72	1.7
Tropical and Southern Africa	148	1.8
America	374	2.1
Central America	60	2.7
South America	129	2.4
Asia, excluding U.S.S.R.	1,514	1.6
South West Asia	73	2.5
South Central Asia	506	1.4
South East Asia	190	1.8
East Asia	745	1.6

SOURCE: United Nations, *Statistical Yearbook, 1957,* Table 1A.

If all productive resources—*defined as the various economic inputs such as land, labor, machinery, factories, water-power sites, deposits of natural resources, and the like which are combined to produce goods and services*—were increased in equal proportion, and technology and methods of organization remained the same, output would keep pace with the population. That is, if the quantity of land, other natural resources, machinery and factories were to double whenever population doubled, average output would not be affected by the rise in population. Double everything exactly that goes into production, and everything that comes out will double!

In fact, however, when population rises, some productive resources will not increase proportionally. These resources are sometimes termed "natural capital," and consist of fertile land and natural resource deposits, water-power sites, and the like, which are fixed in quantity and limited to what nature has provided. Consequently, as population grows, the amount of fertile land per worker (or per consumer) declines. Unless the supply of other resources increases more than population and thereby offsets the decline in natural resources per person, or unless the organization of production is improved, output per person should decline. Equal output per worker cannot be expected when the amount of soil tilled per worker declines. (If the amount of land per worker did not matter, we should logically expect to be able to feed the whole world out of a flowerpot.)

Of course, improvements in agricultural technique—better seed, use of fertilizer, crop rotation, equipment, and the like—might offset or more than offset the drop in natural capital per person. However, one has no solid basis for assuming that this adjustment will always take place. In any event, a drop in natural capital per person would tend to make living levels lower than they otherwise would be.

The famous, but generally misused, *law of diminishing returns* states what has been said in the preceding paragraphs. Specifically, it *provides that as* added *quantities of some productive factor are applied to a* fixed *quantity of one factor, total output will increase less than proportionally after some point.* This principle, which has been verified experimentally, reflects the fact that when you vary the proportions of productive resources you have less of some resource relative to the others. You cannot expect to get as much output with few resources as with many.

Thus we can see that in the Malthusian theory of population growth a basic assumption is the law of diminishing returns. The rate of population growth cannot be paralleled by a similar rate of growth in the output of food, since as more productive factors are applied to fixed quantities of land the output of land must increase less proportionally than the increase in productive factors.

The twin tendencies for the death rate to fall as output rises and for output per person to fall as population grows, makes the outlook for many nations extremely dark. Even if the efforts to expand output and greatly speed the rate of economic development were highly successful, countries showing these tendencies seem doomed to continue at essentially the present levels of living.

This dark outlook may be brightened from two possible sources. The first is that, as in North America, Scandinavia, and Europe, population growth will be checked by family planning; the second is that technological improvements will become so great and rapid that output will outrun an unchecked growth of population. (Obviously, a rapid increase in output combined with a check to population growth would permit an even greater increase in living levels.) After all, there is an upper limit to the decline in death rate—though man may make surprising strides in the direction of immortality—and, it is unlikely that in nations where population is unchecked at present, birth rates will rise further.

Of these two possible sources[17] of hope for an end to the persistent bare-subsistence life in much of the world, the more promising is a check in population. Family planning has, in fact, been practiced successfully in the more highly developed nations of the world. Moreover, the substantial strides that have been made recently in the field of birth control have produced methods likely to overcome many of the aesthetic scruples which have discouraged the adoption of birth-control techniques heretofore.

Attempts to encourage family planning during the last decade or so have had mixed results. On one hand, the speed with which people have accepted the principle of birth control has been much more rapid than most observers had anticipated. On the other hand, the problem of instructing people in birth-control methods and of providing devices has turned out to be far more difficult than had been assumed. Birth control, it turns out, implies a level of education that has not been attained in many parts of the underdeveloped world; even the simplest new ideas cannot be disseminated rapidly among illiterate people.

As for the prospect that the growth in output will outstep unchecked population increases, there is little basis for optimism. Even nations that have made strenuous efforts to speed economic development have realized only extremely meager increases in output. These small increases do not even remotely approach a figure which would outweigh and more than offset the potential population growth.

Up to this point, we have discussed population as a potential source of national poverty when it takes the form of overpopulation. A nation may also be impoverished because of underpopulation. If natural capital is great and the population is relatively small, then the exploitation of natural resources may be inefficient because of inadequate labor. In order to make full use of the potential benefits of labor specialization and the use of specialized equipment, it is necessary to produce a large total quantity. Production for a small domestic population has a limited market. It may be too small to justify full specialization, because a high degree of specialization allocates a small function to each individual. If everyone is to perform a small function and yet remain fully occupied, the total output produced must be large.

It appears that underpopulation is not a common condition. The United Nations experts guessed that "not many parts of the under-

---

[17] A third possible, partial solution to the population problem is emigration. Ideally, if areas with excess populations were able to channel people into the more sparsely peopled countries, the pressure of population on resources would be eased. Obviously, the practical obstacles, mostly of a political nature, make this solution almost a hypothetical one.

developed world would benefit from having a larger population." [18] That is, in their opinion, overpopulation was a far graver problem. They did suggest that some parts of Africa, Latin America, and some of the islands of southeast Asia and parts of the Middle East might gain from a larger population.[19]

Even though population is tending to become stabilized in some industrialized countries and occasionally has actually declined, these countries have not approached a condition of underpopulation. Although many of them have taken measures to encourage large families—by giving special tax exemptions or actual children's allowances—the purpose of encouraging larger families has not been to raise the general standard of living. The motives have been military or political.

B. Stimulation of Desire for Material Possessions

To want things that cannot be obtained is painful. *To create a desire for things that one cannot obtain therefore tends to make material welfare worse.* In the ordinary course of selling goods, sellers stimulate buyer desire. Their motives and their means vary, but the results are much the same. Some individuals who cannot immediately or in the foreseeable future obtain goods are stimulated to desire them.

The indiscriminate creation of a desire for goods—as by wholesale advertising, which is intruded on the thoughts of persons of all incomes almost without discrimination—is almost certain to cause the pain of unsatisfied desires. Beyond premeditated efforts by vendors to create a desire for their wares, sometimes a culture will communicate standards that foster material desires. In direct contrast to the situation in Italian Somaliland already alluded to, where the natives strive only enough to provide themselves with their daily food, in the United States, social position largely, if not overwhelmingly, reflects material wealth, though other factors also play some part.

To have a great deal of goods in materialistic societies therefore does not guarantee high material welfare. It may, indeed in the United States it very commonly is the case, be associated with acute dissatisfaction simply because other persons have even more possessions. Conversely, some groups (certain religious sects and tribal communities in particular) enjoy the pleasures of economic security and the feeling that their material wants are met, even though the quantity of goods they possess is not large.

An economic system that creates virtually no desires also may be objectionable. Difficult philosophical problems are raised about the merits

---

[18] United Nations Experts, *op. cit.*, p. 46.
[19] *Ibid.*

of an economy that does not even evoke a desire for sanitation and good medical care. However, one need not be a philosopher to recognize that everyone would be better off, and no one would be injured, if levels of health and sanitation were raised. Some creation of desire is therefore to be sought in an economic system. A line must be drawn—and each person is at liberty to draw it where he wishes—separating legitimate desires from inordinate desires. There can be little question that goods that are desired simply for the purpose of display and for social position probably cause those lacking them quite as much pain as they give pleasure to those who possess them.

IV. CONCLUSIONS

A long list of causes for economic poverty has been presented. It is desirable to separate those that are most pressing at the present time from those that are less important.

An extremely important cause of poverty at present, though not necessarily the most important one, is overpopulation. Thomas Malthus, who forecast that the entire world would hover close to starvation because of the tendency of population to keep pace with output, proved to be correct for large parts of the world. The places where he proved to be wrong, consisting of North America and Western Europe, Scandinavia, and Oceania, are themselves illuminating. These are places where family size is consciously restricted by most of the population.

Poverty is often attributable to low levels of output, which in turn must be explained. The vicious circle in which a poor nation often finds itself—it cannot afford to divert resources to obtain highly productive capital goods—is one major cause of poverty. Fully as important is a whole complex of social, religious, cultural, and political circumstances that fetter the minds, desires, and ambitions of many countries in the world. We shall probably learn in the years ahead, as strenuous efforts are made to help poor countries, that it is far easier to provide efficient machines for a poor country than to release the latent energy and imagination of its population.

In the most prosperous nations in the world the greatest source of poverty is the inculcation of inordinate desires for goods. Competition in the consumption of material wealth becomes ingrained, turning efforts for economic betterment into a kind of rat race that no one can win.

DISCUSSION QUESTIONS

1. What do you believe to be the major cause of poverty in India, Central Africa, and the South Sea Pacific Islands?

2. When the United States is "poor," what is usually the cause? Explain.

3. In what ways might a defective economic system make poor a country that is rich in resources?

4. As explanations of the high material prosperity of the United States, relative to most other countries, how can one separate the effects of rich natural resources, an industrious population, the form of economic system we have, and our escape from direct damage to property during recent wars?

5. What is the difference between labor-saving machinery and capital-saving machinery? Which type is needed most by underdeveloped countries? Why?

6. In what way is poverty a cause of capital shortage? In what way is it a result?

7. What forms of restriction lower output in some American industries?

8. Is it possible to give individuals economic security and still hold forth potent incentives for strong productive exertions? Discuss.

9. What forms, other than in hours spent on a job, does productive sacrifice take in present-day United States? Which do you believe to be most painful?

10. Would it be unintelligent for a husband and wife to decide to have a large number of children rather than to be able to afford more luxuries for a smaller family? Would a nation as a whole err if it elected to have a large population rather than a higher output of goods per person? Discuss.

11. Why, beyond some point, would one ordinarily expect levels of living to decline with increases in population? If one projects far ahead, say 500 years, is it conceivable that the output of goods can keep pace with a doubling of population every thirty years? Discuss.

12. Do Americans need most of the things they think they need? Discuss.

Chapter

5   Measures for Accelerating

Economic Development

The Congress of the United States holds the view that poor countries must be helped to raise their levels of living. Whether our motives be humanitarian or selfish—in this situation they could be both—financial and technical aid to such countries would seem to be advisable. On what bases can we determine whether, how much, and in what forms assistance should be extended to poor countries? Decisions on these matters probably will be called for almost annually far into the future. What, then, would be involved in reducing the poverty of the world's many poor countries?

Correct its causes, and you will end poverty. As we have seen, the major factors causing low output, great sacrifices in production, and inordinate need vary from country to country. Each country is, at least in part, a special problem. The best methods for raising the level of economic welfare will therefore vary from place to place.

Today the most extreme instances of national poverty are associated with a very low level of economic development. Some industrialized nations are poor also, but they are not the most extreme examples. Rather than attempt a discussion of remedies for all sources of poverty, this chapter will be confined to the broad subject of economic development. Certain matters will be omitted. In particular, little will be said about cures for poverty resulting from excessive sacrifices in production or from inordinate need.

Even though this chapter will deal only with economic development, it cannot cover such a vast subject thoroughly. Singled out for special attention are (1) the kinds of measures required to speed the economic development of the world's poorest nations, (2) the most promising methods by which these measures may be financed and carried out, and (3) the major efforts now under way.

I.   COSTS OF ECONOMIC DEVELOPMENT

A. *Economic Development Defined*

Before the cost of economic development can be estimated, some clear idea is required of what we mean by economic development. The term is used in many ways. We shall use it here to denote *a substantial rise in national output resulting from increased productivity.* Consequently, improvements in health and education not accompanied by greater productivity would not represent economic development. Increased productivity would constitute economic development, no matter whether its cause was a decline in population, increased mechanization, improved agricultural methods, greater exertions by individuals, or more efficient direction and regulation of the economy by the government. Economic development is not synonymous with increased economic welfare, because it takes no account of sacrifices in production or the level of need.

The foregoing definition of economic development takes us only a slight distance. Would an increase in productivity at the rate of one quarter of 1 per cent per year be considered economic development? Must we expand productivity at the rate of 10 per cent annually to achieve economic development? Any answer would be arbitrary. It should be clear that the smaller rate of increase would be so low that it could not reduce the inequality of living levels between the prosperous and the poor countries. Since prosperous countries probably will increase productivity by 2 per cent annually or more on the average, a smaller increase in underdeveloped countries would widen the gap between them and the prosperous countries.

Economic development will be defined as *a rise in productivity large enough to permit a more rapid rise in the future, and that will soon allow productivity to rise by 2 per cent annually.* This definition is not intended to imply that we should not work for a 1 per cent increase in productivity annually if that is all we can achieve. Some specific rate of improvement must be included in our definition, for otherwise it will be impossible to estimate the cost of economic development.

B. *How Much Does Economic Development Cost?*

Estimates have been made of the money cost of increasing output in the underdeveloped countries. Surveys made of individual underdeveloped countries have set down programs for economic development, sometimes including an estimate of their cost. In addition, a group of experts assembled by the United Nations estimated the sum required to achieve economic development in all of the underdeveloped countries of the world. The major aim of this program was to increase national income by 2 per cent annually, by shifting population from farm to nonfarm pursuits and by improving agricultural methods. Specifically, they estimated the cost of transferring 1 per cent of the total working population in underdeveloped countries from agriculture, and the cost of agricultural extension services, research, and farm capital on and off farms needed to raise national income by 2 per cent annually. The estimated annual cost of this program is $19,134,000,000.[1]

The purpose of this program is not to reduce agricultural output and replace it with industrial production. Rather, as we have seen, employment on farms is far greater than required. The experts hoped that the surplus population could be moved outside agriculture and that farm output could be maintained or even increased.

Although this total cost of over $19 billion annually seems great, it is modest when one realizes how many people would be helped by the expenditure. The countries whose needs were included in this estimate have populations of over 1.5 billion persons. On the average, the annual cost of the program comes to $12.50 per person.

It is "natural" to estimate the cost of economic development in money terms. Money is our usual unit of measurement, and other units are too variable and complex to be widely understood. However, money is only one of several possible requirements for increasing productivity. Productivity can be increased without any monetary outlay. To measure the cost of economic development in money terms is misleading, moreover, for it implies that somehow *financial* means must be found to carry out economic development. As will be shown, *important increases in productivity can be achieved without financial outlay.* What are the main requirements for economic development? Which of them can be provided with little or no financial outlay? For what things must financial resources be obtained?

C. Major Requirements for Economic Development

Even as the causes of national poverty vary considerably, so too do the requirements for economic development. In any specific instance, it is necessary to diagnose both the major barriers to economic progress and to assess the nation's resources that offer greatest opportunity for material advancement. Each nation represents a unique bundle of economic resources and potentialities as well as a special set of social and political arrangements which calls for an individualized attack on its own problems. Accordingly, the following discussion cannot be applied directly

---

[1] United Nations, *Measures for the Economic Development of Under-Developed Countries,* Report by a Group of Experts appointed by the Secretary-General, May, 1951, pp. 75-77. Those who prepared this estimate would be the first to admit its approximate nature.

to the solution of any one country's difficulties, though it may suggest alternative lines of attack.

If there is any single most important requirement for economic development, it must be that population growth be checked in poor nations where it now is very rapid. As already indicated, unchecked increases in population can—and indeed have for centuries—fully offset increases in total national output in many countries. A very close second requirement for economic development is the spread of literacy so that new methods and technical training can be disseminated widely and the support of the masses won for a program of increased development.

Apart from a check to population growth and broader literacy, the main requirements for economic development are essentially pedestrian in nature. They represent a large number of relatively undramatic measures for increasing output which are simply taken for granted in the world's developed nations. A very brief description of these measures follows.

1. IMPROVED KNOWLEDGE OF AGRICULTURAL METHODS

Productivity in agriculture requires mainly knowledge and application of improved techniques and information about horticulture. Included here are such things as knowledge of, and access to, improved strains of seed; awareness of the usefulness of fertilizer (including human fertilizer, one of the major sources in Japan); irrigation; recognition of the best depth to plow, and the like. Paradoxically, complex agricultural equipment really is not important for most underdeveloped countries. They already have a great surplus of workers on farms; machinery that would simply save labor would only increase the number of unemployed workers. Almost all of the needed things listed here would not involve much money outlay. They consist primarily of a dissemination of knowledge; the actions that should follow from the use of this knowledge presumably would be contributed voluntarily by individuals who would gain directly from its application.

2. IMPROVED ROADS

Roads outside the cities of underdeveloped countries generally are very poor. Consequently, it is exceedingly difficult to transport output from surplus to shortage areas. Improvement of roads would permit a development of the "household" or "putting-out" system of manufacture that would be an economical and speedy method of increasing nonfarm production. These methods utilize idle labor and obviate the need for factory space and general public services (such as housing, electricity, and the like) to serve new factories. Roads can be costly. But in most underdeveloped countries they could be constructed by inhabitants of each area by relatively primitive means. It would not even be necessary to compensate individuals for working on the roads; a tax in the form of workdays might be levied on all able-bodied adults. Or special privileges might be extended to those who worked on roads, according to the number of days worked (evidence of work performed might take the form of certificates that looked like and had some of the functions of money). Or public drives to secure voluntary participation in road building might be relied upon.

3. PLANT AND EQUIPMENT FOR DOMESTIC MANUFACTURING

When the average American and European thinks of economic development, he thinks of highly mechanized manufacturing enterprises, because he lives in a nation where labor is so scarce, relatively, that often it is profitable to reduce the use of labor by substituting machinery. *Machinery is not so vital in underdeveloped countries. Productivity in these countries could be increased greatly merely by applying the simple principle of specialization of labor.* Of course, some types of equipment would be highly useful—especially as a substitute for *skilled* labor.

The cost of plants in which manufacturing of various kinds might be carried on could be covered with small financial outlay if the governments were able to mobilize their idle resources. A surplus of labor is there; so is the necessary land; the raw materials and equipment needed to construct factories are simple and inexpensive. What is most needed is a method of getting them utilized.

4. ORGANIZATIONAL SKILL AND ABILITY TO MOBILIZE IDLE RESOURCES

Money is simply an instrument that permits its holder to acquire other kinds of resources. As indicated, most underdeveloped countries have considerable underutilized resources. They are not in need of resources from other countries; ordinarily they are not using their own to capacity. Consequently, instead of money they could use devices suited to their culture whereby underutilized resources could be put to productive use. (Certain types of cooperative enterprises have proved successful in some areas.) When the resources exist, there are almost certainly methods by which they can be put to use. It takes imagination, initiative, and organizational skill—qualities that are themselves scarce in all societies—to mobilize and unleash idle resources. However, to accomplish this goal a little organizational skill could go a long way—especially by setting a pattern to be followed.

5. NONECONOMIC REQUIREMENTS FOR ECONOMIC DEVELOPMENT

It has already been shown that some poor countries show little interest in increasing their levels of living. Others, where interest in material betterment is great, nevertheless obstruct economic development in various ways—as by land tenure systems that discourage increases in productivity.

One of the major deficiencies of underdeveloped nations is a shortage of entrepreneurial skills and the qualities of temperament and character requisite for entrepreneurship. In simple terms, the entrepreneur is the person or agency which initiates and takes responsibility for an undertaking. Applied to economic development, the entrepreneur is the source of ideas and funds, and of skills in mobilizing and organizing resources—all combined with a willingness to "take the rap" if the undertaking fails. The entrepreneurship function could be assumed by the individual, the private organization, or by the government; each has its own peculiar strengths and weaknesses. Compared with sources in developed countries, however, all sources of entrepreneurship in underdeveloped countries are in short supply and of low quality.

Closely related to the shortage of entrepreneurship is a limited supply of risk capital. Often one finds in underdeveloped countries that a few extremely rich men have the financial resources needed to carry out large, socially desirable, and quite profitable projects. However, in most underdeveloped countries, the most profitable uses of funds are in speculation on real estate. Consequently, very little money becomes available for economic development.

Such countries, of course, could accumulate surpluses for economic development by taxing persons with large fortunes. However, the balance of political forces almost always prevents this from happening.

Elimination of the legal, social, political, and educational obstacles to economic development need not involve heavy financial payments. Indeed, most of these obstacles cannot be simply bought away. If they are to be met, it will be through the exercise of intelligence and sympathetic understanding of attitudes and customs that are incomprehensible to most inhabitants of prosperous countries.

Where can underdeveloped countries obtain the financial resources, organizational skill and direction, dissemination of modern techniques, and the other things needed to speed economic development? In the simplest terms, these can be acquired either at home or abroad. We have already mentioned the possibility of organizing idle domestic resources and using native personnel to disseminate information. The kinds of aid that could possibly be obtained from outside the country are similar to those obtainable at home: financial resources, organizational skill, skilled personnel, and leaders to disseminate information and modern techniques.

II. EFFORTS UNDER WAY TO SPEED ECONOMIC DEVELOPMENT

Efforts to speed economic development in nations that are suffering most from poverty are being made currently under various auspices: the underdeveloped nations themselves, the United Nations, the developed countries of Western Europe, the United States, and the U.S.S.R. Of these, the efforts by underdeveloped countries to help themselves are by far the most important. Other nations provide resources contributing to economic development which, while relatively small in dollar amounts, nevertheless are strategic and perhaps unavailable otherwise.

The following brief discussion of aid in economic development is restricted to activities by the United Nations and the United States—though they are not, as explained, the largest or most important. Efforts by underdeveloped nations to help themselves are touched upon very briefly also.

A few words are called for about the program launched in 1955-1956 by the U.S.S.R. to assist underdeveloped countries. This program, which seemed to achieve considerable success in a very short time, apparently was aimed to embarrass the United States and to establish strong political ties with uncommitted countries—particularly in the Middle East. Some of the gains by the Soviet Union were lost because of its intervention in the Hungarian rebellion late in 1956. One must expect that the Soviet program to win allies among underdeveloped countries will be intensified to regain the ground lost as a result of the Hungarian episode.

A. United Nations' Program for Economic Development

Many UN agencies contribute to economic development in one way or another. For example, the World Health Organization (WHO) provides ideas, personnel, and medical supplies to improve health and sanitation—most particularly in poor countries. The Food and Agricultural Organization of the United Nations (FAO) similarly contributes to economic development by working on nutrition programs, the elimination of animal disease, forestry and soil conservation, food preservation, and the development of irrigation schemes. Other United Nations agencies whose activities assist underdeveloped countries include the International Labor Organization, the United Nations Economic and Social Council, the International Monetary Fund and the International Bank for Reconstruction and Development.

In addition to the work of its specialized agencies, the United Nations has established a Technical Assistance Board (TAB), which is charged exclusively with fostering economic development. Among its other responsibilities, the TAB is responsible for coordinating the work of all United Nations agencies engaged in economic development.

Table 1 describes the outlays by the United Nations in 1955 for economic-development activities. It will be noted that the "direct project cost" totaled little more than $21 million for the full year 1955. It also indicates the regions in which these expenditures were made. Almost one third went to nations in Asia and the Far East; little more than one fourth went to Latin American countries. Countries of the Middle East received 22 per cent of the total, while the balance, amounting to about one fifth, went to Africa and Europe, or was interregional.

Table 1. Distribution of United Nations Direct Project Costs by Region, 1953-1955

	1953		1954		1955	
Region	Thousands of U.S. dollars	Per cent	Thousands of U.S. dollars	Per cent	Thousands of U.S. dollars	Per cent
Africa	$ 1,497	8.4	$ 1,279	8.5	$ 1,809	8.5
Asia and the Far East	5,719	32.1	4,650	30.8	6,622	31.1
Europe	1,568	8.8	1,500	9.9	1,706	8.0
Latin America	4,793	26.9	3,921	25.9	5,631	26.4
Middle East	3,528	19.8	3,252	21.5	4,676	21.9
Interregional	713	4.0	509	3.4	866	4.1
Totals	$17,818	100.0	$15,111	100.0	$21,310	100.0

SOURCE: United Nations, *Technical Assistance Newsletter*, No. 20, June 15, 1956, p. 3; reissued by the U.N. Department of Public Information in cooperation with the Technical Assistance Board.

Table 2 indicates the form in which this assistance was given by the United Nations. Almost exactly two thirds in 1955 took the form of payments to "experts"; 22 per cent went to finance fellowships, and little more than 1 dollar in 10 was used to pay for equipment and supplies. As Table 2 indicates, payments to experts, as a percentage of the total, have been declining steadily since 1953, and the other forms of assistance have been increasing correspondingly.

The funds "obligated" to United Nations agencies involved in economic development for 1956 are greater than they were in 1955.

Under the working arrangements established by the United Nations, individual countries desirous of obtaining help send a request to the Technical Assistance Board of the United Nations, part of the Secretariat located in New York City. The request indicates the nature of the help desired. At United Nations headquarters the request of the individual government is translated into a specific project. Many requests have been for assistance in collecting statistical data in order to obtain the informational basis upon which to project a general plan for economic development. Some nations have requested technical assistance on such matters as public health, monetary arrangements, and the establishment of a major industry, such as power generation, steel production, and the like.

When a mission is dispatched by the United Nations, it prepares a report for the government that has requested assistance. Its report is not public information and in no way influences the actions taken by the United Nations. The government to which the report goes is under no compulsion to act on the recommendations made by the mission. In addition, the United Nations has established training centers to develop the personnel needed for economic development, given fellowships and internships to create the human capital needed for development, and through the World Health Organization has provided health serums, D.D.T., and drugs of all kinds.

Specific projects for development requiring outside financial help are submitted to the International Bank for Reconstruction and Development. By about 1949, this institution had completed its program of restoring war damage. Consequently, its present activities are concerned almost exclusively with economic development. This bank, technically a part of the United Nations but actually quite autonomous, behaves much like a private lending agency; it requires repayment (generally within twenty-five years) and charges interest (around 4½ per cent). In some measure it takes risks that an ordinary lender might not be willing to take. In particular, the IBRD is prepared to make longer-term loans than are ordinarily available from private banks. Also it lends for projects—such as roads—that are not themselves self-liquidating, something that private financial institutions never do.

The IBRD obtains its funds for foreign lending partly from the original capitalization provided by the member countries. (The Soviet bloc of countries does not belong.) In addition, the International Bank is authorized to raise funds by issuing its own securities—which are in effect guaranteed by countries that are members of the International Bank.[2]

Up through 1951, the IBRD made relatively few loans for economic development. It has been charged that the bank has been overzealous in appraising the credit-worthiness of applicants and not sufficiently mind-

---

[2] In 1956 the IBRD set up an affiliate, the International Finance Corporation, with capital subscriptions exceeding $78 million from 31 countries. The IFC's purpose is to promote growth of private enterprise in underdeveloped areas through investing its funds, together with amounts of private capital where such capital is available only in limited sums. This new organization also endeavors to bring together investment opportunities and private capital and to secure technical and managerial skill for such projects.

Table 2. Types and Amounts of United Nations

		1953 Cost	
Type of Assistance	Number	In thousands of U.S. dollars	Per cent
Experts	1,825	$13,585	76.2
Fellowships	1,195	2,532	14.2
Equipment and supplies	. . .	1,701	9.6
Totals		$17,818	100.0

SOURCE: United Nations, *Technical Assistance Newsletter*, No. 20, p. 3.

ful of the nonfinancial objectives it is expected to serve. Since 1952, the Bank has made more loans for economic development. Its total commitments to underdeveloped countries for developmental loans between 1947, when it first began active operations, and the end of February, 1958, amounted to $3,090 million.

B. Measures Taken by the United States

Although the activities by the United Nations in support of economic development cover an extraordinarily wide range, they are tiny in over-all magnitude. The United States, wholly apart from its contributions through the United Nations (for 1959, the United States appropriated $20 million to the United Nations Technical Assistance Administration) spends roughly twenty times as much to foster economic development in other nations as does the UN. Contributions made by the United States to economic development also embrace a wide variety of activities; many of them are on the border line between assistance in support of military defense and pure development assistance.

In the fiscal year 1959, the Congress of the United States appropriated $200 million for "special assistance." This type of assistance includes economic-aid programs designed to support the recipient nations in their own efforts to maintain economic and political independence. A "development loan fund" of $400 million was also appropriated. Countries receiving development assistance during the fiscal year 1957 were Egypt, Israel, Jordan, Lebanon, and Libya—all from the Middle East and Africa; in Asia, recipient nations were India, Ceylon, Indonesia, and Nepal; two Latin American countries received development assistance: Bolivia and Guatemala. Development assistance typically is used to provide part of the supplies, commodities, or funds needed for economic development. Wherever possible, it is rendered in the form of long-term, low-interest loans—often repayable in local currency.

In addition to the $200 million for special assistance, the Congress

Technical Assistance, 1953-1955

	1954 Cost			1955 Cost	
Number	In thousands of U.S. dollars	Per cent	Number	In thousands of U.S. dollars	Per cent
1,652	$11,194	74.1	2,108	$14,250	66.9
1,524	2,540	16.8	2,431	4,670	21.9
...	1,377	9.1	...	2,390	11.2
	$15,111	100.0		$21,310	100.0

of the United States in the fiscal year 1959 appropriated $150 million for "technical cooperation." Technical Assistance Programs are widely known also as Point Four. They involve sharing of skills, knowledge, and experience with newly developed nations and are carried out at the request of friendly governments who are making concerted efforts to foster economic development. These programs consist largely of advice, teaching, personnel training, and exchanging information; they do *not* supply capital needed for economic development. Recipients of Technical Cooperation Assistance in 1957 included 11 nations and 5 dependent territories of the Middle East and Africa; 14 Asian nations and 19 nations, plus 5 dependent territories in Latin America.

The United States' budget for the fiscal year 1959 also included $750 million for purposes described as "defense support." Among the defense-supporting activities for which assistance was granted in recent years by the United States were $81.5 million to support the development of transportation systems; approximately $93.5 million to stimulate the development of industry and mining, and some $80 million for housing, village improvements, and the development of national resources. Funds labeled "defense support" also financed the costs of some 500 United States technicians and paid for the training of more than 2,000 foreign nationals in specialties essential to the progress of newly developed countries.

It is to be doubted that technical assistance can go very far toward creating rapid economic development. Most of the nations to which the United Nations and the United States are sending experts already have small corps of experts of their own. Rather than a few experts who know the best methods of farming, for example, most countries need thousands of trained workers ". . . who would be willing to work directly with the many millions of peasants in the country." [3] "A really effective program

---

[3] R. F. Mikesell, *United States Foreign Economic Policy* (New York: McGraw-Hill Book Company, Inc., 1952), p. 226.

may need to include financial aid to local governments, as well as substantial numbers of trained personnel, to help them create the large organizations needed to educate the masses in new techniques, supply them with simple tools where needed . . . and to bring about the changes in economic organization, e.g., land reform, necessary for the adoption of the more productive methods." [4]

For these reasons, the original Point Four program has led to the creation of the Technical Assistance Corporation. In addition to technical assistance, TAC also provides underdeveloped countries with some types of equipment. Most of the effort thus far under Point Four has taken the form of pilot projects, whereby personnel and equipment are sent to underdeveloped countries to demonstrate new techniques right on the spot.

Serious doubts may be raised also about the contribution toward economic development that can be expected from increased private investment. Many large areas of necessary investment in underdeveloped countries are ". . . either not suitable to foreign private enterprise or not likely to be attractive to American private enterprise." [5]

Foreign aid extended by the United States under the so-called Marshall Plan (which was administered by the Economic Cooperation Administration) and under the International Cooperation Administration included help for the overseas territories of recipient countries. The mechanics by which aid is given to overseas territories (colonies) of Western European countries are complex and need not concern us. Suffice it to say that the United States also aided economic development under its Marshall Plan program.

C. Efforts by Underdeveloped Countries to Speed Their Economic Development

Many underdeveloped countries have a "Development Corporation." In South American countries, these are known as the "Fomento" corporations. Literally every country in South America, other than those that are already moderately well developed, has one or more such corporations. Their activities vary in vigor and scope. All of them do provide the administrative framework through which suggestions for economic development can be channeled and through which offers of assistance must pass. At the present time the Fomentos are primarily engaged in devising strategic plans for the priority of various stages in economic development. They also deal with the appropriate agencies of the United Nations to get information and assistance that will further their plans.

---

[4] *Ibid.,* p. 227.
[5] *Ibid.,* p. 228.

There can be little question that economic development will be organized and directed by the governments of underdeveloped countries. Every single country is determined to dictate the lines along which the nation is to develop, and to supervise and curb the activities of private industrial companies or investors. Economic development is to be "planned" rather than allowed to be the product of free economic forces. One unfortunate consequence of this fact is that the competence and integrity of government officials—which is not high in many underdeveloped countries—will set a ceiling on the imagination and intelligence with which economic development moves forward.

In most countries efforts have been made to keep the agencies responsible for economic development out of politics. These efforts appear to be fairly successful. Economic development is regarded in most underdeveloped countries as a technical problem that should be above, and unaffected by, changes in governments.

III. GENERAL LINES OF APPROACH TO ECONOMIC DEVELOPMENT

The cost and needs of economic development have been sketched, and the major measures under way to speed economic development have been described briefly. It is appropriate to list the particular lines along which increased material output is to be sought. Underlying the following list are the writings of economists who have concerned themselves with the general methods by which a nation's material welfare may be increased. From economic writings we can draw up the following measures that have received greatest emphasis:

1. Ensure that the goods produced are those that satisfy the population more than any other goods that could be produced with equal effort. Be sure that the quality of products is such that they give the greatest possible service relative to their cost, and that goods are turned out in the proportions that correspond to consumers' preferences.

2. Balance the production of goods with the desires of the population for leisure. That is, do not produce added goods by extending the hours of workers already highly fatigued, unless these goods are extremely precious to the community.

3. Use methods of production that involve minimum sacrifice. To do so, be sure that those who select productive techniques know alternative methods that might be employed and have strong incentives to use the most efficient.

4. Direct the population, natural resources, and so on, into activities for which they are best suited. Be certain that round pegs are not forced into square holes.

5. Ensure that all productive resources have the opportunity to be put to work. Specifically, eliminate economic fluctuations by stabilizing at a high level of resource use.

6. Distribute income in a manner that, as far as possible, provides maximum satisfaction to the population as a whole. That is, do not give almost all of it to a few while everyone else is abysmally poor. Moreover, distribute income in such a way that everyone has strong incentives to use his productive capabilities diligently and efficiently. (These objectives could conflict, and a balance must be found.)

7. Be certain that efforts are made to develop new methods of production and to introduce new products, and, in general, to keep the economic system progressive.

8. Increase the supply of productive resources as much as is practicable. Invest in human capital by making certain that all individuals have the opportunity to develop their productive capabilities. Increase the supply of capital goods as much as possible in the light of the willingness of the population to give up goods today in order to increase the output of goods in the future.

These methods for increasing output are extremely general. They nevertheless suggest the kind of measures that must be taken and point up the types of difficulty a program of economic development would entail.

For example, the foregoing list makes clear that important judgments must be made—particularly about the lines of industry that should be encouraged and the speed at which development should go forward. In addition, delicate decisions about the distribution of income and the unfreezing of social restrictions and the like are involved. Economic development clearly is not solely an undertaking for engineers and builders of big irrigation projects, machinery, ships, and so forth. It requires above all a clear conception of the goals toward which a nation's energies should be devoted. That is, a conscious choice between added goods and productive sacrifices involved in industrialization must be made. Population policy poses enormously complex issues. In short, economic development requires that nations clarify their basic goals, and then decide how best these goals can be achieved.

IV. ECONOMIC DEVELOPMENT VIEWED IN HISTORICAL PERSPECTIVE

Many people discuss economic development as if it were a wholly new problem that arose after, and possibly as a result of, World War II. National poverty is about as old as the existence of national states. All the present-day prosperous nations were much poorer not too long ago. And, a few centuries ago, they were similar in many ways to underdeveloped countries of today. Consequently, we have historical evidence that poverty can be reduced and some understanding of the forces that both contributed to and retarded economic development in Western Europe, the United States, the Scandinavian countries, Australia, New Zealand, and the U.S.S.R. Minor features of economic development varied from country to country, but in the main they were similar. In all these countries, economic development was made possible by concurrent progress along many fronts. It was necessary for literacy and education to expand as capital became more plentiful; governments had to maintain law and order more rigorously, and opportunities had to be provided for individuals to advance themselves socially and economically as a result of their efforts and accomplishments; also, a desire for more and better material things had to develop apace with opportunities to improve one's situation; and birth rates declined as levels of living improved.

Thus economic development was a process that permeated all phases of life—the very cultures and values of nations as well as the way they produced goods and services. In all probability, economic development remains an all-embracing process rather than a result that can be achieved by a concentrated effort to, say, increase the supply of machinery available in poor countries.

One should not assume that economic development in poor nations will necessarily take place or that if it occurs it will follow in the usual mold of increased economic welfare. New relations have developed among nations (and take concrete form in the United Nations and its associated agencies). The assumption by some nations of an obligation to assist the poorest countries, the development of new techniques for creating power (atomic energy), and vastly improved methods of communication—as well as greater understanding of methods for changing attitudes and providing a rudimentary education—all of these changes raise the possibility that economic development may take a very different course in the future than it has taken in the past.

Whatever form it takes, one can be certain that it will not be easy or swift. Even the most favored prosperous nations in the world today took a minimum of a century to turn a general condition of bare subsistence into one of modest "surplus." Many of the underdeveloped nations of the present day are too poorly endowed with natural resources, climate, culture, political conditions, and tradition to make much economic progress. On the other hand, there are many countries that have already produced concrete evidence of progress. So there are grounds for hope, but overoptimism can only cause early disappointment and create a temptation to stop trying.

V. CONCLUSIONS

Great obstacles lie in the path of overcoming poverty, especially where it is most severe. Only in very recent years has an organized effort been made to combat poverty in a general way throughout the world. In part this effort rests on a humanitarian basis, but at present it seems to be dictated largely by political considerations. Little progress has been made thus far beyond the establishment of agencies that can contribute to the attack on poverty. Among the most serious obstacles to the elimination of poverty are the tendency for population to keep pace with output and the existence of social, religious, and political barriers to change in the poorest countries. We must not conclude, however, that the goal is unattainable; some progress has already been made. But we must realize that the undertaking is one that will certainly occupy decades and centuries, rather than months and years.

DISCUSSION QUESTIONS

1. Can you defend our helping foreign countries as long as there are poor people in our own country? Explain.

2. Does any increase in total output represent economic development and an improvement in economic welfare? Discuss.

3. The cost of a modest rate of economic development (2 per cent annually) was estimated by international experts to be $19 billion annually. Is this sum large, viewed from the standpoint of what it is designed to accomplish? Discuss.

4. Comment on the thesis that, where underutilized or unemployed resources exist, there are almost certainly methods by which they can be put to use without the use of money.

5. Why is complex labor-saving agricultural machinery less valuable to underdeveloped countries than such things as improved seed, irrigation, and fertilizer?

6. If you were a businessman in an undeveloped country and you wanted to engage in manufacturing, would you use highly technical advanced machinery? Why or why not? What kinds of machinery would you be especially anxious to obtain?

7. In what ways does the United Nations contribute to economic development in underdeveloped countries?

8. In your opinion, which is more important, financial assistance or technical assistance, to underdeveloped countries? Explain your answer.

9. Do you believe that unrestrained free enterprise will lead to rapid economic development or that planning would be more effective? In your answer have you taken into consideration the quality of governments in underdeveloped countries?

10. Explain the thesis that the United States is highly underdeveloped.

SELECTED READINGS FOR PART 2

Bauer, P. T., and B. S. Yamey. *The Economics of Underdeveloped Countries.* London: James Nisbet & Company, Ltd., 1957. Pp. xiii, 271. This is an especially useful book for understanding the problems of underdeveloped countries and the kinds of policies that make sense under varying conditions. The authors clearly sketch the significant qualities of underdeveloped economies and outline practical government policies for hastening healthy economic development.

Bennett, M. K. *A Study of the Interrelations of World Populations, National Diets, and Food Potentials.* New York: Harper & Brothers, 1954. Pp. vi, 282. A thorough treatment of the world food problem, taking into account population, food resources and output, variations in diet, and related factors.

Buchanan, Norman S., and Howard S. Ellis. *Approaches to Economic Development.* New York: Twentieth Century Fund, 1955. Pp. xiv, 494. The problems of economic growth in underdeveloped areas are surveyed in this book. Such factors as capital formation, technology, and social institutions in their relation to economic development are dealt with. The economic growth of various industrial nations is delineated.

Burns, Arthur R. *Comparative Economic Organization.* New York: Prentice-Hall, Inc., 1955. Pp. xv, 766. This is an extremely useful comparison of economic institutions and organization in different countries over time. Different aspects of economic organization are taken up separately and viewed from the vantage points of different economies.

Clark, Colin. *The Conditions of Economic Progress* (3rd ed.). New York: St. Martin's Press, Inc., 1957. Pp. xiv, 720. This is a very valuable reference book for international economic comparisons. Real national-product data for 1950 are presented for many countries, with comparisons for earlier years. There are copious statistics on various facets of national output.

Edey, Harold C., and Alan T. Peacock. *National Income and Social Accounting.* London: Hutchinson House, 1954. Pp. viii, 224. This book explains the details and techniques involved in national-income accounting. It deals also with input-output analysis and covers thoroughly the national economic budget on a balance-sheet basis.

Kindleberger, Charles P. *Economic Development.* New York: McGraw-Hill Book Company, Inc., 1958. Pp. xiii, 325. This book is very useful for understanding the major problem of economic development. The author emphasizes the benefits of world markets that function effectively. He sketches various theories relating to how productive factors can best be used in economic development. Beside the ingredients of development, there are included general aspects of the process of growth.

Lewis, W. Arthur. *The Theory of Economic Growth.* London: George Allen & Unwin, Ltd., 1955. P. 453. This book is a valuable introduction to the area of economic growth. Both the economic and noneconomic institutional arrangements to be taken into account in dealing with economic growth are discussed.

McCleary, G. F. *The Malthusian Population Theory.* London: Faber & Faber, Ltd., 1953. P. 191. A very well-written reappraisal of Malthus and his population theory. The presentation of Malthus' theories aims at rectifying popular distortions of the theory.

Madan, B. K. (ed.). *Economic Problems of Underdeveloped Countries in Asia.* Bombay: Oxford University Press, 1953. Pp. iv, 290. The book comprises a number of essays on problems of economic development related to Asian areas. Discussion, mostly by Asian economists, deals with the problems of such countries as Burma, Indonesia, India, Thailand, Philippines.

Meier, Gerald M., and Robert E. Baldwin. *Economic Development: Theory, History, Policy.* New York: John Wiley & Sons, Inc., 1957. Pp. xix, 588. This is a very helpful introduction to the problem of economic development. Theories of development are surveyed, as well as actual facts of industrialization in the Western world. The underdeveloped areas of today are viewed in the context of the varied problems standing in the way of rapid economic growth.

Millikan, Max F., and W. W. Rostow. *A Proposal: Key to an Effective Foreign Policy.* New York: Harper & Brothers, 1957. Pp. xi, 170. The authors propose concrete suggestions on how, through foreign assistance on a long-term basis, the United States can help create the conditions necessary for the propagation of free societies. The economic development of underdeveloped areas must be so fostered for our survival in this world.

National Bureau of Economic Research. *Capital Formation and Economic Growth.* Princeton, N.J.: Princeton University Press, 1955. Pp. xiii, 677. This book is comprised of a series of essays on different facets of the problem of capital formation in underdeveloped countries, and on its international comparison. Among the contributors are outstanding economists such as Simon Kuznets, W. W. Rostow, and the like.

Nurkse, Ragnar. *Problems of Capital Formation in Underdeveloped Countries.* London: Oxford University Press, 1953. P. 163. A very well-conceived discussion of the nonmonetary and nonfinancial aspects of capital formation in underdeveloped areas. The different problems of capital formation are related to such considerations as population, capital supply, level of living, trade policy, and the size and nature of the domestic market.

Political and Economic Planning. *World Population and Resources.* London: Political and Economic Planning, 1955. Pp. xxxvii, 339. A very valuable study of the relation of world population and world resources which covers the world as a whole, as well as a number of specific areas where relations vary. One of the main values of this book is its nontechnical treatment of a most important problem.

Spengler, Joseph J., and Otis D. Duncan (eds.). *Population Theory and Policy: Selected Readings.* Glencoe, Ill.: Free Press, 1956. Pp. x, 522. This is very useful as a reference work on the subject of population. It is a compilation of articles and excerpts from books, by subject area, covering the major facets of the population problem.

Staley, Eugene. *The Future of Underdeveloped Countries.* New York: Harper & Brothers, 1954. Pp. xiv, 410. The author discusses economic development in the context of "communistic" or "democratic" ways. He points out how the interest of the United States is best served by a program of increased aid to underdeveloped areas.

United Nations. *Measures for the Development of Under-Developed Countries.* New York: United Nations, 1951. P. 108. National and international measures necessary to the growth of underdeveloped areas are outlined.

————. *Statistics of National Income and Expenditure.* New York: United Nations, 1954. P. 85. An important paper providing valuable information on 67 nations. The source, distribution, and composition of national income are given.

————. Economic Commission for Europe. *Growth and Stagnation in the European Economy.* Geneva: Economic Commission for Europe, 1954. Pp. xvi, 342. This is a comprehensive study of the growth of the European economy from 1913-1950. In addition to a short discussion of the problem of economic growth, this survey covers both industries and countries for the period indicated. It is a very valuable work for reference purposes as well as for its wealth of ideas on growth.

Viner, Jacob. *International Trade and Economic Development.* Glencoe, Ill.: Free Press, 1952. P. 154. The special problems of economic development in the context of international-trade theory and the mechanism of international payments are dealt with.

Wilson, Harold. *The War on World Poverty.* London: Victor Gollancz, Ltd., 1953. P. 232. A popular treatment of the problem of world poverty. The author reviews the efforts to provide assistance to underdeveloped areas, and projects the establishment of a "high-command," world-development authority to deal with the problem.

Part

3 Should Income Distribution Be Altered?

Chapter

6 How Unequal
Should Incomes Be?

I. INTRODUCTORY

Income distribution is many-sided, and it is difficult to obtain a fully balanced understanding of the problem. Added to its inherent complexity is the fact that it is generally discussed in an emotional and partisan manner. Apparently, there is a high concentration of nerve endings around the pocketbook. Measures that would take even small sums from someone, arouse him in ways that few things can. Money is treasured in capitalist societies because it gives its possessor more than the power to obtain worldly goods. It carries prestige, proof of success, economic security, and social and political influence. Individuals frequently doubt whether they are making progress in the pursuit of their life's goals; by accumulating wealth their progress can be reduced to simple calculation, they think. For these reasons, among others, disagreements about economic subjects become very bitter, for they generally imply conclusions about how money income should be distributed.

However income is distributed, it confronts everyone with troublesome ethical questions. In a purely egalitarian society—of which history provides very few examples—the untalented person must wonder about the legitimacy of his receiving as much as the most talented. In the societies where income is unequally distributed, most individuals require an explanation for the differences that exist. To some degree, everyone makes payments to others for their services and demands payment from others for his own services. A person's feelings about such payments depend largely upon his system of values—that is, on circumstances that he believes justify differences in payments among individuals. Because everyone buys many things from many people, thereby shifting income from himself to them, and sells his services to one or more employers, thereby shifting funds from others to himself, we inevitably develop and require standards for the distribution of income.

From time immemorial great thinkers of many societies have wrestled

111

with income distribution as a fundamental ethical problem. The most primitive societies produce a body of argument to explain how and why income is distributed as it is. For example, the Melanesians of the Southwest Pacific, as well as many other primitive peoples, distribute a great deal of their food output by making gifts during ritual ceremonies. Reciprocity thus provides all members of the society with much of their subsistence on a customary basis. The Greeks and Romans produced a variety of views on income distribution. Among the more notable are those of Plato and Cicero. Plato believed that for ethical reasons large incomes are undesirable and incompatible with the "good," while Cicero maintained that luxury and the drive to accumulate riches are not praiseworthy.

II. PROBLEMS OF INCOME DISTRIBUTION

Income distribution is to some extent a matter of personal taste. Some individuals prefer a roughly equal distribution of income. Others prefer that some people be quite wealthy; they believe that the existence of riches enhances the lives of even the poor. Neither preference can be called right or wrong, any more than individuals' preferences among ice-cream flavors. Nevertheless, individuals can be asked to consider more than their personal tastes in these matters. Apart from the strong possibility that their personal preference would be altered by careful study of the subject, they have a duty, before they take a stand on the problem, to consider the social, psychological, ethical, economic, and political implications of the manner in which income is distributed.

Most of the pages that follow discuss income inequality as an economic problem. However, before we turn to the economics of income distribution, let us raise—unfortunately, we cannot wholly settle—some of the perplexing noneconomic questions. Let us ask, first, what group in the community deserves to receive the highest incomes on ethical grounds. Second, we shall discuss how the distribution of income affects personal and social adjustment of most individuals. Third, we shall inquire into the relation between inequality and democracy.

A. Income Distribution as an Ethical Problem

Which individuals deserve to enjoy the highest level of material prosperity in the nation? Many argue that those who are talented, energetic, trained, trustworthy, and the like deserve higher compensation than those lacking these qualities. These groups are held to deserve higher compensation because they earn it; in other words, higher compensation is considered proper when it is for economic and social service rendered.

This argument can be attacked on the ground that those who are talented, skilled, conscientious, and the like may not themselves be responsible for their social virtues. Indeed, most psychologists and sociologists agree that individuals are products of their heredity and environment, and are not reflections of their own free will.

Individuals surely cannot claim that they earned the qualities they inherited at birth. Clearly, these qualities are in the form of a gift. *One might think it more fair that people be required to pay for their inherited virtues than that they receive payment for them.* Similarly, their environment is largely, and some would argue entirely, not of their own choosing or making. One does not choose his early home environment and his early associates and friends. Early environment combined with heredity is held by most sociologists and psychologists to determine the kind of things a child will do as an adult. Accidental and unforeseen things that occur throughout life will influence a person, but for these events, just as for early environment and heredity, he cannot properly be held accountable. In short, cannot an individual's actions and personal qualities be traced back entirely to his heredity and environment, over which he had no control?

Some people argue that if a person is lazy, surely it is because of his own doing. But one must ask why one individual is lazy while others are energetic. Is not this quality also related to his environment and heredity, something that an individual cannot decide for himself? Presumably, everyone wants to enjoy work. Some people seem to get as much pleasure from working as others get from leisure. Do the first deserve to be paid for doing what they enjoy, while the others deserve no pay for relaxing? By definition, the group that prefers work is not making any greater effort or sacrifice than the one that favors leisure.

If human beings are rewarded on the basis of native physical or mental ability, together with personal characteristics such as industriousness, honesty, stability, and charm, the result will be to favor those who have already been blessed by generous heredity and environment. Such a policy aggravates existing inequalities. It is perhaps easier, on the face of it, to defend an opposite policy, whereby those who have been endowed with exceptionally fine heredity or environment would be subject to special taxes. The proceeds of these special taxes might be used to give "consolation prizes" to those not equally favored through no fault of their own. Such a policy would be necessary if full equality were sought.[1]

The foregoing view does not imply that individuals' qualities cannot

---

[1] A philosophy of this kind, of course, goes far beyond inheritance taxes. In the United States, inheritance taxes are based only on material and financial (liquid) assets, since they are relatively easy to identify and measure. They are collected from people who have not earned the wealth themselves.

be altered. Unquestionably, substantial changes can be made in an individual's behavior, especially during the early years of his life. It is still argued, however, that the factors that bring such changes about are not of the individual's own making. Accordingly, it is not clear why he should be rewarded for them—on ethical grounds. As will be indicated presently, it may be expedient to do so, anyway.

B. Personal and Social Adjustment and Income Distribution

Are people happiest when they share the good things of life more or less equally? Or do the vast majority find greatest self-fulfillment, the best adjustment to their environment, and the greatest personal happiness when there are some whose condition is worse than theirs with whom they can compare themselves favorably, and when there are others who are better off whose presence gives hope of a better life in the future? Or does the presence of the rich serve as a constant irritant to poorer men, making the poorer men's achievements seem trivial and marking these persons as inferior by one of the major tests of our society —the ability to earn income? Do the richest people goad all others on to ceaseless exertions so that no one has peace until he is one of the richest? (And do any escape but the few who are not impelled to rate themselves?)

Surely our attitude toward income inequality should depend largely upon the answer to these questions. Unfortunately, they have no single and demonstrably correct answer. It does, however, seem that the effect of inequality varies from person to person. Some persons are goaded on, haunted, tortured, and driven almost to distraction whenever they are in situations that bring to their attention the greater wealth of others. On the other hand, some poor people probably do get a vicarious pleasure from merely seeing the outward manifestations of wealth that is not theirs. It is only to be hoped that most people quickly reconcile themselves to the fact that some others will always have more than they, and that it really does not matter very much.

C. Income Distribution and Democracy

Certain critics of capitalism argue that unequal distribution of income is incompatible with full political democracy. They contend that capitalism inevitably results in highly unequal personal incomes and that political democracy cannot flourish where personal incomes are markedly unequal. This argument is often heard from radicals of the left. Communist criticism of unequal distribution of income in capitalist countries is weakened by the fact that the Soviet Union distributes personal incomes very unequally. Let us explore the connection between the manner in which income is distributed and the character of the political system.

In the broadest terms, a democratic country is dedicated to the "greatest good for the greatest number." While this goal has never been precisely defined, it presumably calls for a wide division over the population of the good things of life. Concentration of wealth, income, and political power in the hands of a few is clearly the opposite of this democratic ideal. (Indeed, high concentration of income is unlikely in a nation where all adults can vote and use the franchise in their own interests. The majority could be expected to use their voting power to transfer the riches of the few to themselves, through such measures as high inheritance and income taxes, and capital levies.)

At least a moderate degree of income inequality could be justified by the goal of the greatest good for the greatest number. It can be argued that certain advantages should be given to the most talented and skilled members of the community so that they may better serve the entire community. For example, it might help the entire community if talented persons were free from routine tasks that most people must do, in order to save their time and husband their energies for the skilled tasks that they alone can perform. In this way, one might justify servants, automobiles, comfortable working and living quarters, and the like, for part of the population, for the benefit of those who themselves would not be given these things.

Democracy in a narrower, political sense means that government officials should be responsive to the wishes of the people, and should simply represent the wishes of the electorate. Does the manner in which income is distributed influence the responsiveness of government to the electorate? The media upon which the voter must rely are likely to espouse the views of the prosperous element in the community, since these media are owned by the prosperous. In Chapter 10 it will be indicated that business groups, and especially "big business," are considered by many to exert disproportionate influence over government. Big business implies— though there is no theoretical necessity that it must result in—considerable income inequality; the executives of large enterprises will, or at least do, obtain incomes far higher than workers. However, it was also argued that political democracy need not be greatly impaired by these factors. An alert, active, intelligent, and interested electorate can overcome these influences; however, they must be reckoned as examples of the way inequality of income weakens political democracy.

Political democracy is also defined by some to mean a minimum of restriction on the liberty of citizens. Except when they may injure their fellow citizens, individuals are to be permitted to follow their own inclinations, and to enjoy the consequences—good or bad—of their own actions. One would suppose a requisite of maximum freedom to be the liberty to pursue and dispose of income in any desired way. All government actions to limit income received or spent could be viewed as an abridgment of personal freedom. Consequently, if individuals obtain varying incomes when left free to their own devices, interferences with personal liberty are needed to make incomes roughly equal.

Thus the connection between income distribution and political democracy is complex. While there is no *necessary* inconsistency between income inequality and full democracy, the former does seem to make democracy harder to maintain.

D. Psychological Aspects of Income Distribution: How Much Inequality Is Desirable?

Are there reliable psychological grounds for arguing in favor of or against income inequality? We use the term "psychological" in a rather technical sense, for ultimately all of our arguments are psychological in that they refer to their effect upon individuals. For a long time economists have advanced a psychological principle known as the "principle of diminishing utility," which is pertinent to arguments about the best way to distribute income. It must be remembered that this principle has no firm acceptance among psychologists, though it has not been rejected by them.

The principle of diminishing utility states that the amount of satisfaction an individual gets from additional goods or money declines with increases in the amount he possesses. That is, each additional thousand dollars of income gives the recipient less additional satisfaction than any previously added thousand dollars of income. Carried to its logical conclusion, this principle suggests that a nation will achieve the greatest total amount of "utility," or welfare, only when incomes are roughly equal. This conclusion is reached along the following lines. If $1,000 were taken from a rich man, very likely he would scarcely notice his loss. If that amount were then given to a poor man, his situation would be very much improved. The net effect of the transfer would be to make the combined well-being of the two men much larger—though the richer man would be not quite so well off as before. The same general results should follow from redistribution of income between those whose incomes were not extremely different. Take $1,000 from a person whose income is $10,000, and give it to someone whose income is $6,000. The loss to the first man would be smaller than the gain to the second, according to the principle of diminishing utility. On similar grounds, one would be making matters better if $1,000 were taken from someone with a $10,000 income and given to another with an $8,000 income.

Few economists would apply the principle of diminishing utility in so mechanical a way. It is clear that individuals' needs and desires vary; their previously accumulated wealth will not be the same, and their reactions to changes in income will differ according to whether they are reducing or raising their living standards. (It is generally agreed, though not proved, that a person compelled to cut his standard of living by $1,000 annually will suffer considerably more than he would gain from raising it by the same amount.) There is a hard core of validity to the principle of diminishing utility, however, that makes clear that large income inequality means a loss of total human satisfaction.

The basis upon which the principle of diminishing utility rests should be considered. First, it, like all principles referring to psychic states, cannot be demonstrated, for we cannot yet measure psychic states accurately. We do not know which of two individuals is happier, by how much, or even why. However, the principle is supported to some extent by the fact that people buy many products and not one alone. If the added satisfaction we get from added quantities of a product did not decline, presumably we would buy only one product, or possibly a few, the ones we like or need most, or are easiest to buy. But of course, everyone buys many different products.

Secondly, the principle of diminishing utility can also be tested by introspection. That is, we can imagine how it would feel to obtain successive increases of income. Almost everyone would agree that a specific sum gives far greater utility when one is poor than when one is rich.

Even if the principle of diminishing utility is valid, the conclusion that a country would be better off if incomes were roughly equal follows under one condition—that the *total amount* of income is not too greatly reduced by greater equality in its distribution. If equal income distribution were to reduce the total amount of goods and services in a country, the gains from greater income equality might be offset, or more than offset, by the sacrifice following a drop in total income.

It is difficult to argue that income distribution does not affect total income. We can be fairly certain that if income were distributed equally in economically developed countries, total output would fall, because a major motive for exerting effort—the desire for material rewards—would be lost. *Advocates of capitalism, socialism, communism, and fascism all agree that equal incomes would worsen the condition of a nation as long as people retain their current attitudes.* As a result, if income distribution were equalized, two consequences would be expected. On the one hand, it would lower total output and tend to make the nation worse off thereby. On the other hand, it would add to national welfare by transferring income from those who get little satisfaction to those who would benefit a great deal. If income distribution were made exactly equal, however, it seems to be agreed that the gains would be far more than offset by the decline in total output. That is why, presumably, diverse types of economic systems continue to pay unequal incomes.

The practical issue to be faced is not whether we should distribute income equally, but how much inequality is desirable. It might be possible to make income distribution more nearly equal and still maintain total output. If so, it would seem that national welfare would be increased. Possibly income could be distributed much more equally and bring about only a slight reduction in total output. Or it might turn out that, by permitting even more unequal incomes than exist today, output would expand so much that the nation as a whole would be better off. A very large number of possible results might follow from altering the distribution of income. We should like to find the degree of inequality that would give maximum national welfare; however, there is no way to locate it without direct experimentation. And even this would be difficult to interpret.

We are now raising complex psychological problems of "incentive." While much is said on this subject, we know little about incentives; some recent studies fly in the face of notions that were generally accepted.[2] We do not know why some persons respond primarily to monetary inducements, while others do their best work in response to nonmonetary incentives. We know that many men and women willingly forego income for prestige and to make a social contribution, but we also know of people who degrade themselves in order to increase their material position. What are the most potent nonmonetary incentives that spur people on? Are they sufficient to ensure that most people would make a substantial productive contribution even if incomes were equal? If everyone were guaranteed a "minimum" income, and otherwise incomes were quite unequal, how strong would productive incentives be? Psychologists have not done much more than scratch the surface of these questions, for it is difficult to devise tests that yield reliable answers to them.

A second reason for expecting the distribution of personal income to affect the total amount of income available is its probable effect upon total personal savings and, through savings, upon the level of capital accumulation. All studies of personal savings show that the recipients of the largest incomes account for most of the total. To eliminate very high incomes thus probably would drastically lower the amount of savings available to those seeking to borrow. Foremost among borrowers are businessmen and governmental units who use the proceeds of loans in the construction of new plant, equipment, transportation and power facilities, roads, and the like. The decline in funds available for lending thus would

---

[2] For example, Professor Thomas H. Sanders was persuaded after interviews with 160 executives, representatives of banking, finance, selling, and advertising, that changes in tax rates have not affected the effort executives put forward. See his *Effects of Taxation on Executives* (Cambridge, Mass.: Harvard University Press, 1951).

lower the nation's productive capacity and thereby tend to make the total output of goods and services lower than it would have been had savings been greater. In appraising the ultimate effect of a more equal distribution of income upon capital accumulation, it should be observed that the American economy does not suffer currently from a shortage of funds for investment. Although these may not be so plentiful as they were in the middle thirties, they cannot be considered scarce. Accordingly, the risk that a modest increase in personal income equality would drastically reduce capital accumulation is small at best. (Direct taxation of corporate incomes tends to lessen corporate savings, that is, investment.)

In considering the desired degree of income inequality, we should recall the discussion of need in the previous section. It was pointed out there that men's wants usually depend upon what others have, and that wants based upon biological need and other "positive" desires are a relatively small proportion of the current American level of living. We saw that one eminent economist concluded that total well-being is not improved by increases in output because, in effect, a person's elation at obtaining more material possessions is offset by his dejection at others' also acquiring the same things. He is no more elevated relative to others than he was before he increased his material possessions.

We can speak of this tendency to measure oneself against others as a "tendency to make invidious comparisons." This tendency offers strong reason for emphasizing total income less than its distribution. For example, it suggests that if the excessive incomes of the rich were reduced and even eliminated, everyone else would feel better. It would not even matter if everyone's material possessions were reduced somewhat, as long as the gap between themselves and the most prosperous members of the community were greatly narrowed.

As with the principle of diminishing utility, the tendency for invidious comparisons has little scientific foundation. We must judge it primarily by introspection and by the expressed views and behavior of our associates. To the extent that it is valid, it clearly tells us to increase income equality—if necessary, at the expense of some reduction in total output. There does seem to be much validity in the argument that many goods are desired simply because their acquisition puts one higher than others in the social scale. Consequently, if most everyone were to be cut back in his possessions somewhat, while the wealthiest were cut back a great deal, we might all be better off.

Summing up, we may say that inequalities of income cannot be defended easily on ethical grounds, and that such inequality probably makes it difficult to achieve some of the goals of a democratic society. To what extent people gain more satisfaction from vicariously enjoying the display of wealth of the rich, than they would get from actually possessing an equal share of it cannot be determined. The tendency toward diminishing utility suggests, however, that direct enjoyment of material goods and services is enhanced for society as a whole through more equal incomes. And the tendency for people to get enjoyment from social standing based on economic rank also suggests that more nearly equal incomes, and therefore a better chance for the average man to rise on the income scale, would enhance total well-being. But a serious flaw in the arguments for more income equality, if equality is carried too far, is that inequality serves as a spur to productive effort and that total income would eventually fall off sharply if this incentive were virtually eliminated. The possibility of nonmonetary reward instead is a real one, of course, but such a reward is difficult to establish and has not been practiced to the exclusion of material reward in any society.

Rather than speculate further about the desired degree of income inequality, we shall examine the various methods that might be used to alter the distribution of income, together with their probable effect upon total output. It will appear that this effect depends upon the specific measures employed. Some offer an opportunity to make incomes more equal without affecting total output at all. In such circumstances, there would be no offset to the gains in utility that should follow from the greater equality of income distribution.

Before we discuss measures for redistributing income, the manner in which personal income is and was distributed in the United States and in some other countries will be described. Our discussion will show that many pronouncements on income distribution one usually hears are superficial and likely to be misleading. For example, statements such as, "The richest 1 per cent of the population gets 8 per cent of the national income, while the poorest 20 per cent gets only 4 per cent" need not mean what they seem to say. When interpreting data on income distribution we must take into account such things as whether the income is calculated before or after taxes, whether the figures apply to years of depression or prosperity, whether nonmoney income is taken into account, whether adjustment is made for the age and needs of individuals and the cost of living in the area where they live, and the like.

III. INCOME DISTRIBUTION IN THE UNITED STATES

In interpreting income distribution at any time, it is helpful to recognize that most persons pass through a lifelong income cycle. During the first years of their employment they receive low incomes; normally they are unmarried and live at home then, and their needs are corre-

spondingly low. As they acquire work experience, their income tends to
rise. Some occupations, such as athletics and jobs dependent upon physical beauty—models, entertainers, and the like—pay peak incomes for a
very short time. But workers usually increase their income throughout
most of their life; at some point they retire or are discharged because of
advanced age. Most persons receive their lowest income during their
youth and when they are aged. Even most of those who have been extremely prosperous during the prime of their career probably received
very small incomes in their first job, and after they are retired. Low incomes in a given year do not mean that the same people will have low
incomes in future years, or had them in previous years.

Businesses also undergo a life cycle. During their earlier stages, firms
typically show operating losses; similarly, their revenue is low just before
they discontinue operations. Moreover, even many successful businesses
will show losses during a general downturn of business. Consequently,
many business owners at any time may have low incomes—or losses—
even though their average earnings over the years are substantial.

The fact that distribution of money income is only an approximation
of level of living is easily established. Other things must be taken into
account before a full picture of the economic status and well-being of a
family can be fully appreciated. Two families with exactly the same income and exactly the same number of children may have a sharply different economic status owing to any one of a number of other factors. Owning one's house, holding stocks and bonds, receiving gifts of food and
clothing, having a member of the family seriously ill, living in a different
locale or with relatives, having to get special training for a retarded child
—any one or a variation of these factors could have a potent effect on the
over-all level of living of the family. Thus, to get a fuller measure of a
family's economic well-being, we must have information on such matters
as liquid asset holdings, age, number of dependents, living arrangement,
place of residence, fluctuations in income, illnesses or other unusual conditions necessitating extraordinary expenditures, etc.

Taking just one of these factors—age—we can see how money income may not reflect adequately the economic status of many families. In
1950, 70 per cent of all persons over 65 had incomes below the cost of a
"minimum but adequate" budget. When all economic resources, including
income, assets, etc., were evaluated, it was found that only 42 per cent of
the aged did not have enough to provide a minimum level of living. If
such information were available for all families at all income levels, a
more precise picture of economic well-being would be possible. According to the income data now available, many families whose total economic
situation is a reasonably good one are included in the "poor" category,
while families whose income is above the minimum level of living are

"poor" because of special factors which put a heavy drain on their income and leave an inadequate amount to meet basic needs.[3]

With these qualifications in mind, the results of a Bureau of Census survey in 1956 may now be summarized and interpreted. Table 1 indicates the number of families and individuals with given cash incomes in 1956. The incomes of families are shown separately from those of individuals not in families. Table 2 presents the same information, but in percentages rather than in absolute numbers.

Table 1. Numbers of Families and Individuals, by Income Group (before Taxes), United States, 1956

Earners of Income	Total	Numbers in thousands				
		Under $2,000	$2,000 to $3,000	$3,000 to $5,000	$5,000 to $10,000	$10,000 and over
Families and individuals	53,100	12,640	5,680	13,650	17,630	3,500
Families	43,440	6,690	4,430	11,900	16,990	3,430
Individuals not in families	9,660	5,890	1,240	1,820	640	70

SOURCE: U.S. Department of Commerce, Bureau of the Census, *Current Population Reports,* Series P-60, No. 27, April, 1958, p. 23. Totals will not add up precisely because of rounding.

Table 2. Proportion of Families and Individuals, by Income Group (before Taxes), United States, 1956

Earners of Income	Total	Percentage distribution				
		Under $2,000	$2,000 to $3,000	$3,000 to $5,000	$5,000 to $10,000	$10,000 and over
Families and individuals	100.0	23.8	10.7	25.7	33.2	6.6
Families	100.0	15.4	10.2	27.4	39.1	7.9
Individuals not in families	100.0	61.1	12.8	18.9	6.6	0.7

SOURCE: U.S. Department of Commerce, Bureau of the Census, *Current Population Reports,* Series P-60, No. 27, April, 1958, p. 23.

As the tables show, about 7 million families (approximately 18 million persons, and one sixth of all families in the country), received

---

[3] From a study of low-income groups, under the direction of Isador Lubin, to be published by the Franklin D. Roosevelt Foundation, New York, N.Y.

cash incomes of less than $2,000. About 3 of every 5 individuals not in families received cash incomes of less than $2,000 in 1956.

The amount of noncash income received can only be guessed. The most important source of income other than cash is food produced and consumed on the farm, and services of various types that farmers enjoy as a by-product of their operations. However, a rough measure of total income is found in statistics about the cash incomes of farm and nonfarm families (see Table 3).

Table 3. Farm, Urban, and Rural Nonfarm Families, by Income Group (before Taxes), United States, 1956

		Percentage distribution		
Residence	Total (thousands)	Under $2,000	$2,000 to $3,000	$3,000 and over
All families	43,445	15.4	10.2	74.4
Urban families	27,496	10.4	8.7	80.9
Rural nonfarm families	11,041	15.6	10.7	73.7
Rural farm families	4,908	43.1	16.9	40.0

SOURCE: U.S. Department of Commerce, Bureau of the Census, *Current Population Reports*, Series P-60, No. 27, April, 1958, p. 21.

Of the almost 7 million families with less than $2,000 of income, 4,570,000, or about 65 per cent, did not live on farms. The balance, farm families, presumably received somewhat more goods and services than their money income would indicate.

The number of low incomes that can be attributed to youth—just getting started—and to advanced age is suggested by Table 4. This table includes only family income. It shows that almost 40 per cent of the families with less than $2,000 were headed by persons who were under twenty-four years of age or were sixty-five years old or more.

Table 4. Families by Age of Head and by Income Group (before Taxes), United States, 1956

		Numbers in thousands		
Age of Family Head	Total	Under $2,000	$2,000 to $3,000	$3,000 and over
All families	43,445	6,690	4,430	32,320
Under 24 years	2,144	360	340	1,440
25 to 64 years	35,560	4,050	3,140	28,370
65 years and over	5,741	2,280	950	2,510

SOURCE: U.S. Department of Commerce, Bureau of the Census, *Current Population Reports*, Series P-60, No. 27, April, 1958, p. 23.

As would be expected, workers who are highly skilled or trained generally receive higher pay than those who are not. For example, 48 per cent of male professionals who were self-employed in March, 1957, obtained incomes of $10,000 or more in 1956. Whereas self-employed professionals averaged $9,496, the average for all employed male civilians was $3,608. The number of female professionals who were self-employed is relatively small. Nevertheless, only 15 per cent of salaried female professionals earned more than $5,000, as against about 63 per cent of salaried male professionals. Among craftsmen, foremen, and similarly skilled male workers, about 22 per cent earned $6,000 or more; but only some 10 per cent of machine operators earned more than this amount. Women in the former category were very few, and in the latter category only about 0.3 per cent earned more than $6,000. Women apparently have much less opportunity to learn and work in the more skilled occupations.

Unquestionably, some families whose incomes were less than $2,000 in 1956 are not to be considered poor. Some had small needs, for they had no dependents to support; others had substantial noncash income; some had large savings on which they could draw; others could count on some inheritance from parents or gifts and other types of assistance from family, relatives, or friends. Many of those whose incomes were low in 1956 had every reason to look forward to a prosperous life because they were launching businesses and professional careers that promised to yield incomes far above the average in the near future. Certain groups stress the fact that not all families with low incomes can be considered poor, but little emphasis has been given to the converse view, that many families with even moderate incomes may be considered poor.

It should be re-emphasized that the dividing line most frequently used to separate the poor from the bare-minimum living standard, specifically, $2,000 cash income, is very low. Even two persons would have suffered severe privations if they had had to rely on this amount in 1956. In very few communities would they have been able to afford decent housing (unless they had an apartment with a ceiling that kept rentals at or near their prewar levels). Large families, of course, would have been compelled to purchase a house or to take housing that most would consider substandard. And they would have had to forgo other elements of a minimum-comfort budget, the cost of which was estimated to be over $4,600 for a city family of four in 1956.

Some of the arguments used to eliminate families with a small income from the ranks of the "poor," work in reverse to add families with moderate income to these ranks. First, even as some families with low incomes may have small needs, those with moderate incomes—say, between $2,000 and $6,000, which include more than 50 per cent of all families—may have had unusually large needs. Surely many of them were afflicted by major illnesses that were extremely expensive. Others must have had needs that were greater than could be judged from family size. Aid to aged or sick parents is a common obligation and often a large one. For every family that has accumulated savings, moreover, there probably is another that is in debt. Unless most of these debts and the interest on them are paid when due, the family may lose possessions in which it has already invested heavily. Its home, furniture, car, and basic electrical appliances may be in danger of loss through failure to make regular payments. Similarly, it may be compelled to allow insurance to lapse. Clearly, a family of four with an income of $6,000, in which the wife has a chronic illness requiring the expenditure of money for extra household help as well as for costly medical care, and in which there are aged parents to support, should be considered poor. Minimum comfort budgets do not allow for chronic illness or for aid to parents.

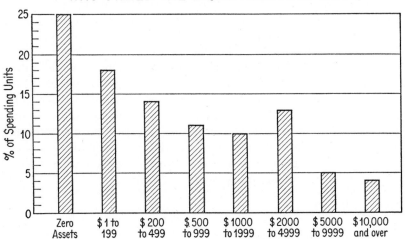

WHO OWNED THE LIQUID ASSETS IN 1957 ?

Liquid asset holdings—one dimension of wealth—like income are unequally distributed. In 1957, 25 per cent of the spending units in the United States had no liquid assets (savings accounts, checking accounts, government bonds, etc.). On the other hand, almost one third of the spending units had liquid assets of $1,000 or more, with less than 10 per cent having $5,000 and over. The remaining spending units—about 43 per cent—had liquid assets under $1,000.

Second, even as some families have noncash income, others give up income in forms other than cash. The obligations to provide housing and food to needy relatives are burdens not ordinarily taken into account in deciding whether families are well off or poor.

Third, families face risks, other than those to health, that typically are not considered in calculating minimum budget costs. Automobile and household accidents may entail heavy costs through property damage; household repairs sometimes are very costly and cannot be postponed. Almost every family loses some property—articles of clothing, writing implements, and the like—every year. All of those are costs of living that should be, but are not, reckoned in living cost.

Clearly, poverty is to be found among families with moderate as well as with small incomes. Thus the number of persons with low incomes does not set an upper limit to the number who are poor. Economists who very properly exclude some families with low incomes from the total number of the poor are obligated to add to this number all families of moderate income who actually are poor. There is no reason to assume an equality between the number of families with less than $2,000 annual income that are not poor and those with incomes above this amount who are poor. We do not know enough to estimate the numbers in each group. It must be said, however, that there are no compelling reasons to suppose that the number of poor families with incomes of more than $2,000 is smaller than the number of those who get by on less than $2,000. While we do not have the evidence needed to measure accurately the number of poor people in the country in 1956, available data are sufficient to demonstrate that a very large proportion of American families (almost certainly as many as one eighth, and perhaps one quarter) are suffering acute hardship from a lack of material goods. It should be emphasized that these estimates apply to a year of extreme prosperity; poverty is far more prevalent, of course, during periods of depression.

An analysis of families with low incomes suggests that the following factors are the most important causes of low income.

First, old age.

Second, unemployability, due to a variety of causes such as blindness, deafness, and dumbness at birth.

Third, lack of skill at any job.

Fourth, race; nonwhite families have significantly lower incomes than whites, even of the same skill.

Fifth, broken families, that is, families headed by women who are widows, divorcees, or were deserted by their husbands.

Sixth, lack of education, due in large measure to lack of opportunity to obtain schooling.

Seventh, disability; included are persons who lost their ability to hold a job because of injuries after they had once been employed.

The data presented show that a large proportion of the nation suffers more or less acutely from economic privations even during periods of unusual prosperity. If it were possible to devise ways of increasing the incomes of these families without markedly reducing total output, national welfare would be greatly improved. Not only the poor would benefit. There is every reason to believe that everyone would gain from a rise in the level of education, diminishment of delinquency and communicable diseases, and an increase in political stability. (It is not suggested that everyone would be better off in every way, or even on balance, but

Table 5. Income Received by Upper-Income Groups, 1919-1946

Year	Per capita income *		Percentage of countrywide income received by †	
	Top 1 per cent	Top 5 per cent	Top 1 per cent	Top 5 per cent
	(1)	(2)	(3)	(4)
1919	$2,978	$1,549	12.2	24.3
1920	3,110	1,650	11.8	24.0
1921	3,055	1,574	14.2	29.3
1922	3,043	1,751	14.4	29.0
1923	3,443	1,576	13.1	27.0
1924	3,460	1,657	14.3	28.7
1925	3,779	1,969	16.5	31.1
1926	4,048	1,976	16.3	30.8
1927	4,017	1,951	17.2	31.9
1928	4,002	2,032	19.1	34.1
1929	4,199	2,027	18.9	33.5
1930	3,617	1,773	15.1	30.3
1931	3,043	1,659	14.6	31.2
1932	2,280	1,300	12.3	29.6
1933	2,127	1,246	12.6	29.3
1934	2,368	1,385	12.4	27.8
1935	2,547	1,469	12.8	27.9
1936	2,871	1,582	13.8	28.4
1937	3,011	1,701	13.0	27.4
1938	2,809	1,577	12.1	27.0
1939	3,004	1,637	12.1	26.8
1940	3,050	1,752	11.4	25.4
1941	3,714	1,847	9.9	23.0
1942	4,148	2,062	7.8	19.0
1943	4,686	2,363	6.4	16.7
1944	4,729	2,124	6.6	15.8
1945	5,155	2,139	7.3	16.7
1946	5,593	2,326	7.7	17.7

* Represents lower limit in percentage band for "economic income variant." The variant includes imputed rents of owner-occupied dwellings, but no adjustment for taxes and capital gains and losses.

† Represents disposable income, including capital gains and losses and including imputed rent of owner-occupied houses.

Adapted from Simon Kuznets, *Shares of Upper Income Groups in Income and Savings* (New York: National Bureau of Economic Research, 1953), pp. 637, 643.

Table 6. Per Capita Income of High-, Medium-, and Low-Income
(Before and after federal income taxes and in current and 1939 dollars)

	Top 1%	
	1929	1948
Average income	$9,547	$11,563
Average federal income tax	813	3,602
Average income after tax	$8,733*	$7,961*
Cost of living index 1939=100	126.5	177.4
Income after tax in 1939 dollars†	$6,904	$4,488

* Details do not necessarily add to vertical totals, because of rounding.

† U.S. Department of Commerce, *Survey of Current Business,* National Income groups buy different kinds of goods whose price movements need not be identical, the

some gains should accrue to everyone.) It is difficult to look at the figures presented here and conclude that inequality of income is a trivial problem in the United States.

As the figures collected by the Bureau of the Census show, only 8 per cent of all families received incomes of $10,000 or more in 1956 (Table 2), and their combined incomes probably accounted for about 10 per cent of the total. Those with incomes over $25,000 almost certainly did not account for more than 5 per cent of total personal income.

How much the living levels of the poor could be raised by a redistribution of income can be seen by reference to income statistics of a past year. If one were to take all income of more than $25,000 received by any family, say, in 1948, the total would amount to about $10 billion; if evenly divided, this sum would have raised the income of all other persons approximately $66. If the $10 billion had been divided equally among, for example, the poorest 5 million families, each family would have been given $2,000 extra—a very big gain indeed.

In 1956, of the estimated 43.4 million families, 3.5 million, or 7.9 per cent, had incomes of more than $10,000, before federal income taxes. The 6.8 million families with cash income below $2,000 represented [4] about 15 per cent of all families. Thus almost everyone has a low or a modest income. The extremely rich and the very poor are a small proportion of the total. America is primarily composed of middle-income persons.

Up to this point, we have described only the distribution of personal income according to the latest report. No indication has been given of broad trends in income inequality.

Professor Kuznets has studied in detail [5] shifts in income among the

---

[4] U.S. Department of Commerce, Bureau of the Census, *Current Population Reports,* Series P-60, No. 27, April, 1958, p. 1.

[5] Simon Kuznets, *Shares of Upper Income Groups in Income and Savings* (New York: National Bureau of Economic Research, 1953).

Groups, 1929 and 1948

2–7% band		Lower 93%		All	
1929	1948	1929	1948	1929	1948
$1,755	$2,836	$485	$1,117	$652	$1,381
1.42	354	nil	53	8	107
$1,753*	$2,482*	$485	$1,124	$644	$ 718
126.5	177.4	126.5	177.4	126.5	177.4
$1,386	$1,399	$383	$ 633	$509	$1,274

Edition, 1951, p. 146, Table B, implicit price deflators. Because different income use of the same index for each group does not give a precise adjustment.

upper income groups. Some of his results are presented in Table 5. According to these results, the following proportions of total personal income, after federal income taxes, were received in 1946 by the richest 1 per cent and 5 per cent of the population: 7.7 and 18 per cent, respectively. (If the undistributed income for corporations were allocated to persons holding stock in those firms, the figures would be 9.9 and 20 per cent.)[6]

Professor Kuznets found that, comparing the years 1929 and 1946, income inequality has dropped very substantially. For example, in 1929 the highest 5 per cent of income recipients obtained 34 per cent of the total personal income—after taxes; by 1939 their share dropped to 27 per cent, and by 1946, to 18 per cent. A more recent estimate, for the period 1950-1955, shows a further drop to about 21 per cent. The share of the top 1 per cent group in total income was 19 per cent in 1929 and 7.7 per cent in 1946.[7] The magnitude of this shift in less than two decades is made more vivid by Table 6.

Table 6, which is based on the data collected by Professor Kuznets and further work by Geoffrey H. Moore,[8] presents a computation in dollars of constant purchasing power of the per capita incomes, after federal income taxes, of the top 1 per cent, next 6 per cent (called the "2-7 per cent band"), and the lower 93 per cent in the years 1929 and 1948. It shows that, expressed in dollars possessing the purchasing power money had in 1939, the following changes took place between 1929 and 1948

---

[6] A. F. Burns, *Looking Forward*, 31st Annual Report of National Bureau of Economic Research (New York, 1951), n 1.

[7] Kuznets, *op. cit.*, p. 637, and Selma F. Goldsmith, "Changes in the Size Distribution of Income," *American Economic Review Papers and Proceedings*, May, 1957, pp. 504-518.

[8] See Geoffrey H. Moore, "Secular Changes in the Distribution of Income," *American Economic Review*, May, 1952, pp. 527-544.

Table 7. Per Capita Income in Dollars by Source for Various Income

	Top 1%	
	1929	1948
Employee compensation	$2,643	$ 3,742
Entrepreneurial	1,900	4,123
Property (total)	5,005	3,699
Dividends	3,406	2,730
Interest	1,235	530
Rent	364	439
Total income *	9,547	11,563
Federal income tax	813	3,602
Income after the tax*	8,733	7,961

    * Details do not necessarily add to vertical totals because of rounding.

in average per capita income after federal income taxes: the top 1 per cent group dropped from about $6,900 to approximately $4,500; the 2-7 per cent band remained essentially unchanged at about $1,400; and the bottom 93 per cent improved their situation from $383 to $633.

The explanation for the change in real income of the high, middle (2-7 per cent band), and low incomes is suggested by Table 7, which describes the amount that each group obtained from the various main sources of income. (Note that this table is expressed in "then current" dollars—that is, not adjusted for changes in purchasing power.) The most interesting fact disclosed by this table is that "property income" of the 1 per cent group actually declined more than 25 per cent between 1929 and 1948; the sharpest decline occurred in interest income, which fell by 57 per cent. Table 7 also makes clear how low is the amount of property income obtained by the overwhelming majority of Americans. Specifically, the lower 93 per cent of the population received $69 of property income in 1948, of a total income of more than $1,100.

Fluctuations in the relative importance of different income sources for the high, medium, and low income recipients are shown most clearly in Table 8. It shows the percentage change in each income source for each income group between 1929 and 1948. From this table we learn that the top 1 per cent group enjoyed a large increase in "entrepreneurial income" (profits from professional practice and unincorporated businesses), and only a modest rise in salary income. Their income taxes increased greatly—but by a far smaller proportion than did the income taxes of the middle- and low-income groups. Tables 7 and 8 compress in short space a wealth of information about what happened to personal incomes between 1929 and 1948.

Whether or not the distribution of personal income will continue to become more equal in the United States is best determined by an anal-

Groups, 1929 and 1948

2–7% band		Lower 93%		All	
1929	1948	1929	1948	1929	1948
$1,018	$1,711	$360	$ 914	$423	$ 990
371	828	77	194	111	272
366	296	48	69	118	119
121	157	7	15	48	51
144	72	24	26	43	34
102	67	16	28	27	34
1,755	2,836	485	1,117	652	1,381
($1.42)	354	(nil)	53	8	107
1,753	2,482	485	1,124	644	1,274

ysis of what caused the trend toward equality in the first place. The most rapid change in income distribution took place after the onset of World War II, and it can be traced directly to the relative shortage of labor that has continued pretty much unabated since that time. Apart from this increased shortage of labor, two other factors are mainly responsible: the sharp rise in federal income taxes and a dramatic decline in interest rates. Since 1944, federal income taxes on the very highest incomes have declined considerably because of the privilege extended in 1947 to man and wife to submit joint returns (which has had the effect of making the effective tax rate equal to what it had been on an income half its size); interest rates have increased substantially; also, the shortage of labor is far less acute. Consequently, it is quite likely that the movement toward

**Table 8. Per Capita Income Percentage Change by Source
for Various Income Groups between 1929 and 1948**

	Top 1%	2–7% band	Lower 93%	All
	1929–1948	1929–1948	1929–1948	1929–1948
Employee compensation	+ 42 *	+ 68 *	+154 *	+ 134 *
Entrepreneurial	+117	+123	+152	+ 145
Property	− 26	− 19	+144	+ 1
Dividends	− 20	+ 30	+114	+ 6
Interest	− 57	− 50	+ 8	− 21
Rent	+ 21	− 34	+ 75	+ 26
Total income	+ 21	+ 62	+130	+ 112
Federal income tax	+343	+(very large)	+(very large)	+1,237
Income after the tax	− 9	+ 42	+132	+ 98
Income after the tax (adjusted by index)	− 35	+ 1	+ 65	+ 41

* All figures in this column are *percentage change* based on the 1929 figure.

greater income equality has been stopped or reversed. Certainly, a trend toward more equal personal incomes cannot simply be taken for granted.[9]

IV. INCOME DISTRIBUTION IN THE UNITED STATES AND SELECTED FOREIGN COUNTRIES COMPARED

Data on income distribution in the United States gain new meaning when they are compared with information for other countries. Table 9 describes personal income distribution for several highly dissimilar countries. Although the impression often prevails that incomes are much more unequal in the United States than in almost any other country—possibly because of the large number of very rich people who live here—the facts do not support this belief. For example, Italy's richest 10 per cent obtained a significantly larger proportion of total income than did the richest American families. (See Table 9.) A similar difference exists in Ceylon,

Table 9. Income Distribution in Various Countries

Country	Year	Before or after income tax	Per cent of income received by upper					
			10%	30%	50%	70%	90%	100%
United States	1949	before	30	57	77	91	99	100
United States	1949	after	28	56	76	91	99	100
Denmark	1948	before	29	58	77	92	99	100
Italy	1948	before	34	57	77	89	98	100
Puerto Rico	'46–'47	before	41	68	84	n.a.	n.a.	n.a.
United Kingdom *	'47–'48	before	32	n.a.	74	n.a.	n.a.	n.a.
United Kingdom *	'47–'48	after	26	n.a.	70	n.a.	n.a.	n.a.
Ceylon *	1950	before	33.3	n.a.	78.6	n.a.	n.a.	n.a.
El Salvador *	1946	before	43.6	n.a.	74	n.a.	n.a.	n.a.

* United Nations, *Preliminary Report on the World Social Situation* (New York, 1952), p. 133.

SOURCE: United Nations, Economic and Social Council, *Volume and Distribution of National Income in Under-Developed Countries,* Report of the Secretary-General, Series E, No. 3, 1951.

and an even more favorable comparison for the United States can be made with El Salvador and Puerto Rico. No country shows a very much

[9] One factor which may affect adversely the trend toward greater income equality is the pattern of population growth. If a goodly proportion of new babies is born to families in the lowest income group, greater inequality in income distribution will result from this fact alone.

more equal distribution, although the United Kingdom distributed income more equally, after taking account of income taxes.

V. CONCLUSIONS

Thus far, the moral, social, psychological, and political problems and implications of income inequality have been discussed, and some evidence describing the present and past distribution of income in the United States and elsewhere has been reviewed. Several tasks remain. First, we shall explain the size of individual incomes and in this way account for income inequality. Second, we shall examine possible methods of reducing income inequality, with special attention to their probable effects upon total output. Finally, we shall discuss the causes of friction and waste in the determination of personal incomes and the measures by which they might be ended.

DISCUSSION QUESTIONS

1. Do you believe that a lazy person "deserves" as much pay as an industrious one? Do you think it would be advisable to pay lazy people as much as industrious ones? In the course of your answer, define a lazy person.
2. In what way is your personal situation worsened by the existence of very wealthy persons around you? In what way do you believe yourself to be benefited by their existence?
3. If we believe that everyone is entitled to equal voting rights, does it not follow that they are entitled to equal income? Discuss.
4. Explain how the principle of diminishing utility leads to the conclusion that incomes should be roughly equal.
5. Would you consider the distribution of personal income in the United States very unequal, roughly equal, or fairly unequal? What standards are you applying? How would you measure the degree of income inequality? How has it changed over the last quarter century?
6. What factors besides current money income should be taken into account in deciding whether a person belongs in the low-income group?
7. List the groups that make up the nation's poor.
8. Explain, by means of an illustration, the life cycle of a business and the variations in the personal income of an individual employed by others.

7 Why People Receive
the Incomes They Do

I. DETERMINANTS OF PERSONAL INCOMES

Why do some people receive $1 an hour for their labor while others receive $10? On what factors does a person's income depend? Personal incomes will be shown to be determined primarily by the following: productivity, market power, ownership of property, access to social welfare services, and personal and political influence. Each will be discussed in turn.

A. *Influence of Productivity upon Incomes*

Most people justify large and small incomes alike by saying that "people get what they earn." The economic doctrine known as the *theory of marginal productivity* presents the same conclusion. According to this doctrine, an individual's income depends upon his *marginal value productivity*. This term, and the theory of marginal productivity, will take a little explaining.

1. MARGINAL VALUE PRODUCTIVITY DEFINED

Put simply, marginal value productivity means "what a productive factor is worth to a businessman," and can best be explained by taking each of its terms in *reverse* order. *Productivity denotes the physical quantity of output attributable to the addition of a factor of production, after deducting the output attributable to other factors of production.* By *factor of production* we mean *anything that must be hired or purchased to contribute to output, and we include land, labor, funds, machinery, and the like.* Productive factors are desired by business owners because they will increase output. For example, an additional worker may be desired by a mill owner who believes that the worker could increase his output of cotton fabric by 1,000 yards per week. He may calculate further that the added costs of the additional output, like raw cotton, electric power, clerical expense, and the like would amount to $40. Accordingly, he could say that an additional worker's productivity was 1,000 yards of fabric less $40.

Value productivity refers to physical productivity translated into dollar amounts. To calculate value productivity, the business owner must multiply physical output by the price at which it will be sold. For the moment it will be assumed that additional output would sell at the same price as the rest of the output. If the fabric sold at 15 cents a yard, the business owner could calculate the value productivity of the laborer to be $110 (1,000 times .15, less $40).

The term *marginal* has no exact synonym. Closest to it in meaning are the words "last," "additional," and "extra." Marginal is a word of wide usage in economics; indeed, formal economic theory frequently is referred to as "marginal analysis."

Marginal value productivity, then, *means the value added to output by the very last factor of production.* More specifically, *it designates the dollar amount by which the sales income (revenue) of the businessman would be increased through the employment of an additional factor of production—after adjustment for the other costs involved in its employment.*

2. WHY INCOMES ARE BELIEVED TO DEPEND ON MARGINAL VALUE PRODUCTIVITY

Once the meaning of the term is fully understood, it becomes clear why payments to a factor of production are believed to approximate marginal value productivity. An employer gains the marginal value product from the employment of a factor of production ($110 in the example of the textile-mill worker just used). If the employer pays less than the factor's marginal value product, he obtains a profit of the difference. Conversely, his net profit would be reduced by payments to production factors in excess of their marginal value product.

Assume for a moment that all textile-mill operators knew that an additional worker would add $110 to their incomes. How much would they be willing to pay for workers? Clearly, if they paid, say, $75, they would make $35 net profit for themselves, and would presumably welcome the opportunity to hire additional men. If mill owners could employ as many men as they wished at $75 a week, then wages need not rise to $110. However, the large profit they could make from employing added workers would create such a strong demand for the desired type of labor that not enough would be available. In order to obtain a part of the short supply of labor, individual mill owners presumably would try to bid away some workers from other mills by offering more than $75. Rather than allow rivals to hire a laborer for $75 whose employment would yield $35 net profit, a mill owner could be expected to offer the worker more than $75. The bidding for workers could reach, or approximate, $110, unless the owners agreed among themselves about the amount to pay.

The bidding would not exceed $110. Should an owner pay more than that, he would lower his net profit by adding an extra worker. Businessmen cannot be expected to suffer *knowingly* an avoidable reduction of profits.

The amount that a particular factor of production is worth to employers depends, among other things, on its relative scarcity. In a country that has a huge population and little factory space and machinery, an additional laborer can contribute little, as a rule, to output. Employers who do not have enough machinery and factory space cannot use all workers effectively; that is, if all workers were employed, some would be without machinery and their contribution would be very small. Consequently, pay scales would tend to be low, despite the fact that labor might receive its entire marginal-value product. Further, the paucity of income constricts the market in overpopulated countries, and sales can be expanded by lowering prices substantially, a procedure which would further reduce the *value* of the marginal product of labor. Thus both low over-all productivity and the low prices that have to be asked for goods would tend to keep wages low in nations with a relative surplus of labor.

If the supply of machinery and factory space were great and the supply of labor small, the reverse would be true. Without workers, owners of factories would be compelled to produce less than capacity, thereby foregoing their potential output. If an owner hired a worker, he would obtain even more than the high direct contribution of the employee; he would also unleash the latent and otherwise unutilized productive power of machinery already in hand. Thus wages would tend to be high.

The effect of the relative supply of productive factors upon their compensation can be illustrated clearly from two extreme cases. In India, a nation with a huge labor supply and relatively little capital, wage rates are pitifully low, while rates of interest on capital are very high. Wages in the United States are very high, for our labor supply is relatively small, while the large supply of capital makes interest rates the lowest in the world.

3. CONCLUSIONS SUPPORTED BY THE THEORY OF MARGINAL PRODUCTIVITY

The theory of marginal productivity yields conclusions that are pertinent to public policy. Primarily it shows that you cannot simply legislate higher pay. No employer will knowingly hire a productive factor at rates above the value of its output to him. Compulsory increases in wage rates—*without a rise in either the amount of goods a worker produces or the price at which it can be sold*—will leave the amount that employers are willing to pay their workers unchanged. If the law sets the mini-mum wage rate above the marginal-value productivity of the worker, other things remaining equal, he will not be employed. This conclusion holds even though the theory of marginal productivity is not generally ac-cepted as a complete explanation for the size of personal incomes.

4. CRITICISMS OF THE THEORY OF MARGINAL PRODUCTIVITY

The theory of marginal productivity has fallen into disrepute. While the logic of the principle is unassailable, it rests upon the major assump-tion that the worth of a productive factor to its employer can be estimated accurately. But it is almost impossible to measure marginal value pro-ductivity in specific instances. In the first place, it is extremely difficult to estimate the price at which additional output can be sold. Most firms already sell as much as they are able at the prevailing price. If they are to increase their sales, they must be able to offer customers inducements to increase their purchases. In most cases the most attractive inducement is a price reduction. Accordingly, in estimating marginal value produc-tivity, a firm must compute the decline in price it will have to accept in order to sell additional output, and it must allow for the fact that the additional output will lower the price it is able to obtain on its entire out-put—not only on the marginal output.

Second, some factors of production do not add to physical output but make their contribution in more indirect ways. For example, an air-conditioning system in a retail shop may not influence the business in any way but to attract more customers into the store. How could this effect be translated into physical output? How is marginal value pro-ductivity to be calculated in such situations?

Third, some factors of production are hired in fixed combinations with others, and it is logically impossible to attribute changes in output to any one of these factors. There is no calculable marginal value product for any one of the factors, but only for all combined. *At best, the theory of marginal productivity explains that the combined prices paid for the various factors will not exceed their combined output.* The proportions in which the total product of complementary productive factors is di-vided among individual factors are critically important, but go unan-swered by the theory.

The theory does not apply where individuals are able to determine their own incomes, almost without respect to their true value. The most likely illustration is the top business executive in a large corporation, who gets only a trifling share of his income from his firm's profits. Generally such men are members of the board of directors and really "control" the business. They can often "write their own ticket" when it comes to their salary.

Productive factors can raise their real income without altering their productivity. For example, most strong labor unions have increased their members' real income faster than it would have risen otherwise. (Though one cannot prove this statement absolutely, the evidence that could be used to support it includes the more rapid rise in wage rates in unionized than in nonunionized occupations; the opposition to unions by many employers; and the desire for unionization on the part of most workers.) Unions raise wage rates by the exercise of market power. They compel employers to pay higher wage rates or forgo the use of labor. Thus they greatly reduce the influence of the employer in the determination of how much labor shall be paid; the employer can decide only how many to hire. The theory of marginal productivity indicates that employers will not knowingly pay more than the marginal value product for any employee. However, in that application the theory helps only to explain the amount of a factor that will be employed, not to account for the wage rate that the union will set.

Job Evaluation—One Way of Determining Personal Income
(Point System of Evaluating Job Factors)

		Maximum
1. Elemental		250 points
2. Skill		500 points
General or special education	160	
Training time on job	40	
Memory	40	
Analytical	95	
Personal contact	35	
Dexterity	80	
Accuracy	50	
3. Responsibility		200 points
For company property	25	
For procedure	125	
Supervision	50	
4. Effort (physical factors)		50 points
Place of work	5	
Cleanliness of work	5	
Position	10	
Continuity of work	15	
Physical or mental strain	15	

SOURCE: National Office Managers Association, *Clerical Job Evaluation*, Bulletin No. 1, 1946.

Once the above point system is devised, it can easily be used to determine the actual dollar wage or salary amount to be paid the employee:

1. From each job description, make a schedule, indicating qualitatively to what extent the specific job has the various factors listed above.

2. Translate the qualitative descriptions into quantitative units by applying the measuring yardstick given for each job factor in the above point system.

3. For each job, total up the amounts for the individual factors.

4. List the jobs by rank according to the total scores obtained in the preceding procedure.

5. Determine the actual dollar value to be given to relative positions in the job ranking.

B. Influence of Group Power on Incomes

While productivity (marginal value productivity) unquestionably influences the payments any productive factor receives, other factors frequently exert greater influence. The most important is power, both market and political. As already indicated, some industrial firms possess strong market power which they use to restrict output in order to obtain high prices and large profits for their owners. Sometimes, too, the leading industry in a locality may constitute the only real demand for labor in that area, with the result that anyone seeking work must accept the wages offered by the firm or move himself and his family to another area. Such monopoly power may be used to keep wages extremely low unless labor gains sufficient collective strength to force a wage increase by striking, or unless another industry enters the locality.

Both industrial and labor organizations may also possess political influence which they use to secure legislation favorable to themselves—that is, that increases their incomes. For example, business and labor in some industries join forces to obtain tariff "protection" against foreign competitors. Or businessmen may secure the enactment of laws that prohibit sales below cost, specify minimum markups, or that permit manufacturers to set minimum retail prices (known as resale-price maintenance laws)—all measures that do or are expected to increase the businessman's income. Similarly, professional men, doctors primarily, have limited the numbers admitted to their ranks. One of the most striking examples is farm price supports.

Laborers can achieve strong market power by forming organizations that control most of the supply of some type of labor. Let us consider in some detail the elements that go to make up the market power of labor, which is by far the largest single source of personal income. First, as indicated, a laborer's income will depend upon whether he belongs to a union. With only rare exceptions, organized workers can bring greater pressure to bear on employers than individual workers can muster. Second, the characteristics of the union largely determine its power. Unions that control the entire supply of a particular type of labor are much more powerful than those composed of only a small proportion of workers in a trade. The control over the supply of any productive factor may come from obedience to a central command. That is, if almost all masons and plumbers obey the instructions of their leaders (or the decisions of the majority of the union), those who need masons and plumbers will be required to pay a sum acceptable to the collective union membership. Since the skills of masons and plumbers are possessed by few workers other than those practicing the trade, and since no machines can be used to replace them for most purposes, there would be little chance of finding others to take the place of unionized masons and plumbers. Third, unions that are strategically placed to cause employers heavy losses or to cause great inconvenience to the public gain bargaining power. Fourth, in small measure, a union's market power depends upon it financial resources, on which it would draw in the event of a strike.

In addition to the power that comes from joint action by workers, labor organizations control the supply of labor by the more or less naked use of physical violence, or the threat of its use. Specifically, workers can restrict the supply of substitute workers by using violence against them. For example, most men in the United States could drive a truck or could assist in the loading and unloading of vessels; thus the potential supply of truck drivers and stevedores is enormous. However, only a small fraction of these men belong to unions of their trades. Yet these two unions have about as much market power as any in the country. For the most part, their power results from a militancy of union members— that is, they "believe in" unions and stand by their leaders—combined with a readiness to use physical violence to achieve their objectives. They have at times used violence against both their employers and other men who would try to take their jobs.

Laborers use physical force and coercion in several ways to limit the number of competitors for their jobs. First, *picketing* is usually the mildest form of coercion used. Picketing may be defined as the posting of union members at the entrance of a firm when workers are out on strike or when the place is being boycotted. Picketing activities may include the carrying of posters, the distribution of handbills, jeering at "scabs," ostracism, threats, and at times violence against strikebreakers. The effectiveness of picketing depends upon the responsiveness of other workers, customers, and suppliers to a type of moral pressure, and upon the fear that a picket may strike or "rough up" anyone who passes the picket line. Unions fought for the right to use so many pickets that it would be impossible for anyone to squeeze through the line (known as mass picketing), but recent laws have restricted the number of pickets; now they can exert only moral rather than direct physical force.

Second, workers who do not follow the decisions of the union membership or leaders to go on strike, and nonunion workers who try to take work in a business that is on strike (known as "scabs") run a risk of physical assault. They may be attacked at or near the business or at their own homes. It is charged, and with a fair amount of supporting evidence, that the use of force in strikes sometimes seems to be organized and centrally directed. At other times violence appears to be the result of the personal idea of a worker who takes matters into his own hands.

WORKING TIME LOST BECAUSE OF WORK STOPPAGES, 1927–1958

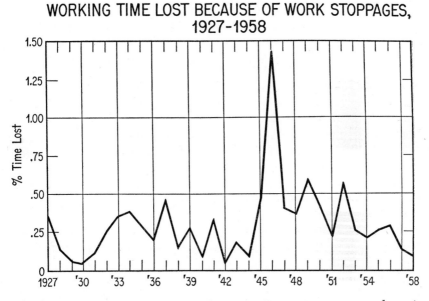

The burst of unionism during the Great Depression seems to have increased the number of strikes. The working time lost, however, represents only a drop in the bucket. In 1946, a year of many and long strikes, the loss was less than 1.5 per cent of total working time. Since then the trend has been downward.

One form of physical force used in this country some time ago, but now illegal (it still is used in some foreign nations on occasion) is the "sit-down strike." This form calls for workers to stay in a factory that is on strike and thereby make it impossible for others to work in their places. Sometimes the sit-down strike is combined with the use of force to prevent entry into the plant of other workers.

While this list of ways in which workers use physical force to increase their market power is incomplete, it will suffice to support the conclusion that market power can rest on physical violence.

Needless to say, workers have not been alone in their use of force. Many of the employer techniques commonly used prior to the passage of the National Labor Relations Act in 1935 resulted in violence, and frequently in many deaths. Industry's use of strikebreaking agencies and private police systems (and alliances with local police forces) were notable examples of management's activities. Although business firms nowadays use financial and legal, rather than physical, force to win their decisions, a long history of violence *against* labor, going back over a century, is not easily forgotten either by labor or the public.

Other factors in the use of market power by labor include laws which enable a union to become the sole bargaining agent for all the workers of a firm, and to have a *union shop*. Both the National Labor Relations (Wagner) Act of 1935 and the Labor-Management Relations (Taft-Hartley) Act of 1947 give a union bargaining rights if it can command a majority of a firm's workers.[1] And likewise, if a majority votes for a *union shop*, it can be established.[2] Previously, the Clayton Anti-Trust Law of 1914 exempted unions from antimonopoly proceedings. The effect of such laws has been to give *organized* labor a much freer hand in developing its market power. Congress intended that this should come about to offset the otherwise preponderant bargaining strength of employers. The political aspects of group power (for all groups) may therefore be related to market power.

A more subtle but often effective union weapon has been social pressure, by which a nonunion man and his family are simply ostracized until he joins the union. Workers and their wives usually react strongly to this pressure when their community and particular firm are highly unionized.

The labor market thus allows for market power on both sides of the market. Equally, businesses of various sorts and small-interest groups have a diversity of ways in which they exercise such power. The government itself, through its licensing activity, indirectly restricts the supply of various kinds of goods and services by setting minimum standards or other limiting rules.

In sum, because of differences in market and political power, factor groups often obtain substantially different payments than would be justified by their real productivity.

---

[1] However, the Taft-Hartley Act is less favorable to labor than was the older Wagner Act. In general the Taft-Hartley Act, by restraining certain labor-union practices and by guaranteeing certain employer rights, was supposed to redress the alleged favored position that labor had gained from the Wagner Act.

[2] A *union shop is one in which any worker employed by the firm must join the union within a specified period of time after being hired.* The *closed shop,* which was allowed by the Wagner Act but outlawed by the Taft-Hartley Law, *meant that a worker had to be a union member before being hired.* This gave a union great power over hiring. Recently, strong advocates of "right-to-work" laws have appeared, and a number of state legislatures have passed statutes outlawing even the *union shop.* The constitutionality of these laws has been upheld, except where they conflict with federal law (specifically, the Federal Railway Labor Act Amendment of 1951). Eighteen states had right-to-work laws in 1956, most passed shortly after the end of World War II. See *Congressional Digest,* February, 1956, for a full discussion of this issue.

C. Property Ownership and the Distribution of Income

The highest individual incomes are not obtained from labor or from the active direction of a business. A relatively small number of workers receives very high salaries for personal services. Among those receiving the highest incomes are top executives of some of the nation's largest businesses, actors and actresses, and outstanding athletes. For the most part, the highest incomes come largely from "property"—that is, as payment for the use of real estate, as interest on bonds, and as dividends on stock. To obtain a great deal of income from property one must own a large amount of it. The number of large property owners in the United States is fairly great. Recent data[3] show that, of 99,800,000 civilian adults in the United States, 10,000,000 owned shares in corporations. Although there are many stockholders with very large holdings and high incomes, 65 per cent of those owning securities of publicly held corporations earned less than $7,500 total personal income, that is, not including wholly family-owned incorporated businesses; the latter represent a considerable number of shareholdings. For the most part, the largest capital holdings in this group were inherited, for personal income taxes are so high now that accumulation of large personal fortunes is increasingly difficult. The largest holdings tend to be concentrated in the family-corporation group.

Table 1 indicates the number and major sources of the largest incomes in the United States in 1935 (the last year for which data are available). It clearly shows that only a few large incomes can be traced to high personal productivity, or to market or political power. The largest incomes are to be explained by the existence of a substantial number of personal fortunes.

The relative importance of income from property has been a matter of hot dispute and deep controversy. Many believe that a large share of the national income goes to owners of large corporations—"industrialists," in common parlance. Table 2 shows the proportion of total personal income received in the form of proprietors' and rental income from unincorporated businesses, and dividends and personal interest from incorporated business. These figures indicate that personal income from unincorporated businesses is much larger, while the dividend and interest income from incorporated firms is a relatively small proportion of the total national income, amounting to approximately 8 or 9 per cent in postwar years.

Although the information presented in Table 2 does not tell us exactly what we would like to know, it does clearly indicate the general dimensions of income from business operation. Dividends, not shown alone but combined with personal interest, accounted for 8 per cent;

---

[3] *New York Times*, July 24, 1956, p. 33.

Table 1. Number and Sources of Personal Incomes of Different Size, 1935

Net Income Class	Number of income recipients	Income primarily from personal service	Income primarily from property
All income classes	52,327,000	82.2%	17.8%
Under $5,000	51,826,885	86.4	13.6
$5,000 and over	500,115	53.0	47.0
$5,000 to $10,000	339,842	71.5	28.5
$10,000 to $25,000	123,564	55.3	44.7
$25,000 to $50,000	26,029	40.4	59.6
$50,000 to $100,000	8,033	32.4	67.6
$100,000 to $500,000	2,497	21.4	78.6
$500,000 to $1,000,000	109	5.8	94.2
$1,000,000 and over	41	1.5	98.5

SOURCE: Adapted from *T.N.E.C. Monograph No. 4, Concentration and Composition of Individual Incomes, 1918-1937*, p. 48.

Table 2. Personal Income Received in the Form of Profits, Rents, Dividends, and Interest

Year	Total personal income (billions)	Proprietors' and rental income (billions)	Per cent of proprietors' and rental income to total personal income	Dividends and personal interest income (billions)	Per cent of dividends and personal interest income to total personal income
1929	$ 85.8	$20.2	23.5	$13.2	15.4
1933	47.2	7.6	16.1	8.3	17.6
1939	72.9	14.4	19.8	9.6	13.2
1941	96.3	20.9	21.7	10.3	10.7
1947	191.6	42.0	21.9	14.7	7.7
1948	210.4	47.5	22.6	15.9	7.6
1949	208.3	43.9	21.1	16.9	8.1
1950	228.5	46.6	20.4	19.5	8.5
1951	256.7	51.8	20.2	20.3	7.9
1952	273.1	52.4	19.2	21.1	7.7
1953	288.3	51.3	17.8	22.6	7.8
1954	289.8	51.3	17.7	24.4	8.4
1955	310.2	52.8	17.0	27.0	8.7
1956	330.5	53.3	16.1	29.1	8.8
1957	347.9	54.8	15.8	31.1	8.9

SOURCE: U.S. Department of Commerce, *National Income,* A Supplement to the *Survey of Current Business,* 1954 ed., pp. 238-240; and U.S. Department of Commerce, *Survey of Current Business,* July, 1958, pp. 16-17.

alone, they may have been the source of 5 per cent of the total personal income in the years 1948 to 1957. All types of property income, which include proprietors' and rental income, dividends and personal interest, amount to 25 per cent of total personal income.[4] This sum is not inconsiderable.

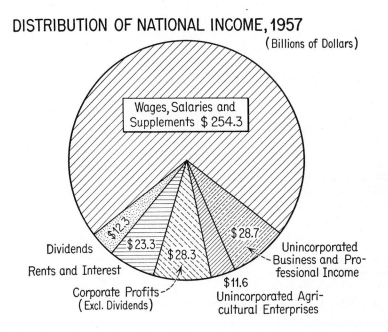

DISTRIBUTION OF NATIONAL INCOME, 1957

(Billions of Dollars)

Wages, Salaries and Supplements $ 254.3

$12.5

Dividends $ 23.3

$ 28.3

$ 28.7

$11.6

Rents and Interest

Corporate Profits
(Excl. Dividends)

Unincorporated Agricultural Enterprises

Unincorporated Business and Professional Income

More impressive than the total amount of income from property is the manner in which it is distributed. It seems to go primarily to those whose incomes are large. That is, while it does not represent a very large lump of income itself, it tends to become personal income of large lumps for relatively small numbers of people.

D. Income from Free Social Services

Some public services are free. Everyone does not share equally in these services. Although social services provided without charge have expanded greatly since the early 1930's, they still represent a small proportion of the total national income. However, for some individuals they are an important source of income.

Many social services are provided by the government. In most of

---

[4] Only part of proprietors' income can be considered property income, for payments for the proprietors' services are included. Consequently, total property income is less than 25 per cent of the total.

these all persons share more or less equally. The use of roads, education, police protection, fire protection, national defense, and the like are used by all in roughly equal proportion. However, some things are provided especially to those who need them. These include assistance for the aged, the indigent, and the unemployed.

In addition to the services provided on the basis of need by various government units, much is provided for the needy by private philanthropic agencies. Foremost among these agencies are free clinical medical care, and partly subsidized education in heavily endowed educational institutions. It is extremely difficult to estimate accurately the value of the services received by the needy from these sources; since they are not paid for directly, they cannot be measured by the ordinary yardstick of money value. Indeed, great dispute rages over the question of the medical care provided for poor people—regarding its quality, quantity, and the degree of embarrassment suffered by those who accept it.

It is impossible to calculate accurately the proportion of the national income composed of social services that are distributed fundamentally on the basis of need. There can be little question that such services are the largest source of income for members of the population who would otherwise be utterly lacking in material support. The author estimates that the total of these services combined constitutes less than 4 per cent of the national income. In addition to the money income received from their employers or their customers, Americans receive free or at low-cost goods and services equivalent to additional income. Perhaps the most important of these come through the program of social insurance. Under the three major types of social insurance—workmen's compensation, unemployment compensation, and old-age and survivors insurance—people receive valuable benefits without being required, by the "means" test, to prove that they absolutely need it.

Workmen's-compensation laws forcing employers to insure their employees against accidents on the job have been enacted by all states. The insurance itself may be held with the state or a private company, which pays the injured employee a part (usually less than half) of the wages lost plus medical expenses, in most cases.

Unemployment insurance was inaugurated on a national scale by the passage of the Social Security Act of 1935. This act levied a tax of 3 per cent on the payrolls of employers, but specified that in states where a satisfactory unemployment insurance program was established, any amount of this tax, up to a maximum of 2.7 per cent of payrolls, could be paid, instead, into the state unemployment insurance program. Since this provision meant that any state could set up a program costing up to 2.7 per cent of payrolls without increasing the cost to the employer, the states rapidly enacted laws, so that by 1938 all states had schemes that met the standards of the federal law.

Benefits under the unemployment-compensation laws vary from state to state, but a typical plan provides for a payment to the unemployed person of considerably less than half the employee's weekly income while employed, and provides that this payment continue for a maximum of twenty-six weeks a year. All states require a waiting period, usually two weeks, before the employee is eligible for benefits.

The *net* cost of unemployment insurance must not be measured only by the amount of benefits paid. One way or another, a family whose income is cut off by unemployment must cover the cost of its minimum needs. That is, in the absence of formal unemployment insurance, people must in effect insure themselves or obtain money from others. Self-insurance has its costs. Savings may be drawn, property may be sold (also durable goods like autos, TV sets, and the like), relatives may be requested to help, personal loans may be taken out, and often charity or relief are resorted to; these are some of the ways in which living expenses may be met. Through unemployment insurance, the cost of unemployment is borne by the community as a whole as well as by the unemployed. The net costs resulting from unemployment are not necessarily higher under a formal insurance program. From a welfare point of view, they may actually be lower, owing to wider coverage.

Naturally, there have been some abuses of the unemployment insurance system. By various means, people have obtained benefits to which they were not entitled. The number of these abuses and their cost have been greatly exaggerated, however. Abuses take the form of certifying for benefits persons who are not eligible; it is doubtful that this practice will ever be completely eliminated. However, the amount of funds disbursed in unemployment benefits during years of high employment has been far less than the contributions to the unemployment funds. Some of the stories that have been circulated suggest that many, perhaps most, workers prefer not to work—just live off unemployment benefits.[5] It would be more nearly correct to say that the overwhelming majority of workers would take overtime work to increase their income, rather than cut their pay drastically in order to avoid work.

The Old-Age and Survivors Insurance, also enacted in the Social Security Act of 1935, pays annuities to retired workers over sixty-five years old, or to the worker's survivors. These benefits are financed by payroll taxes of equal amount on the employer and employee, or, for the self-employed, entirely by the self-employed person. Under recent amend-

---

[5] An indication of the maximum amount of cheating can be derived from the following figures. In March, 1952, 1.8 million persons, of a labor force of almost 60 million, were unemployed; of these, fewer than 1.2 million received unemployment compensation. Recipients of compensation represented fewer than 1 in 50 in the labor force. The proportion of fraudulent cases was, at most, only a small fraction of the smaller total.

ments to the act, disability insurance benefits for workers of fifty years of age or older have been included, as has the payment of reduced benefits to women who elect to retire at the age of sixty-two. The payroll tax rates go up gradually in steps every three years from 2½ per cent starting January 1, 1959, to a maximum of 4½ per cent by 1969. For self-employed persons the maximum in 1969 is to be 6¾ per cent. These tax rates are levied on the first $4,800 of income, with both employees and employers paying a like amount and self-employed persons paying the steeper rate.

Annuities are based on average monthly income and range from a minimum of $33 per month for a single worker whose monthly income averaged $50 to a maximum of $127 per month for a single worker with a monthly income averaging $400. The payments for a husband and wife range from a minimum of $49 to a maximum of $190 per month. If the worker dies, his family receives a lump sum, plus monthly payments for the surviving children until they reach the age of eighteen. A single survivor gets monthly benefits ranging from $33 to $95. A widow and two children would receive monthly benefits ranging from $53 to $254.

The major groups exempted from this provision of the Social Security Act are federal government employees who are subject to another federal retirement system, some state employees who are covered under a retirement system, and self-employed physicians. Certain groups, such as employees of nonprofit organizations, may be voluntarily covered. With the increased coverage provided by the amendment of 1956, it is estimated that more than 90 per cent of the labor force is now covered by a retirement system sponsored by the government.

In addition to the unemployment, old-age, and disability insurance programs, there exists a wide variety of welfare programs which give benefits to large numbers of needy persons. Apart from the extensive and costly programs for veterans' education and training, and hospital and medical care, the federal government gives direct public assistance, provides work and direct relief, promotes public health, gives aid to education, and to library and research activity, carries an elaborate program for assistance to farmers, and conducts a labor placement service. Of increasing size and scope among federal welfare activities is the public housing program under which the federal government subsidizes the construction of relatively low-cost housing for poor and middle-income families.   .

The welfare programs undertaken by the federal government represent a small and a fairly recent beginning in spheres with which most Western European countries have had considerable earlier experience. In the United States they are considered to be controversial issues, though they have been "accepted" by an increasing proportion of the population with the passage of time. Apart from their potential psychological contribution to a feeling of ease and security, these programs could conceivably—they are far from that point now—weaken productive incentives.

E. *Political and Family Influence*

Many Americans believe that a majority of those who achieve outstanding economic success nowadays do so primarily on the basis of "pull." That is, their success is directly or indirectly due to help they receive from friends and relatives—and particularly from their parents—on the basis of personal and family ties rather than merit.

There can be little question that parents help their offspring to material success in many ways. A large number of youths enter successful businesses controlled by their parents or other close relatives. Or individuals who are in debt for past favors or who hope to gain something in the future will help children of influential parents. We must also recognize the effect of intangible qualities—manner of dress, speech, value system, habits, lineage, and the like—on an individual's chances for success. The attitudes and habits which make a successful businessman are best learned in the home of such a man, and there is often a close relationship between the success of the father and that of the son. This fact has been amply demonstrated by studies of the backgrounds of top business leaders. In Table 3 we find compared the principal occupations of the fathers of the top business leaders of the years 1870, 1900, and 1950.[6] (Similar results are to be expected for other fields.)

Table 3. Occupational Distribution of Business Leaders' Fathers, 1870, 1900, 1950

Father's Main Occupation in Business Leader's Youth	Business leaders in the years		
	1870	1900	1950
Businessman	47%	50%	57%
Professional man	16	25	14
Public official or politician	3	5	1
Farmer	26	16	15
Wage or office worker	8	4	12
	100%	100%	100%

While the opportunity for sons of businessmen to become business leaders appears to be increasing steadily, this increase has lately been accompanied by a decline in the proportion of sons of professional men and "public servants" who became business leaders. The opportunity for

---

[6] Suzanne I. Keller, Doctoral dissertation (Columbia University, Business Library).

sons of farmers, which declined up to the turn of the century, has been stabilized since then, and being born into a wage earner's family has become less of a handicap. But the distribution of success in the business field is still heavily in favor of the "business family." This is strikingly evident in the Table 4[7] where the main occupations of the paternal *grandfathers* of 1950's business leaders is contrasted with the over-all occupational distribution prevailing in the year 1870.

Table 4. Occupational Distribution of Business Leaders' Grandfathers, 1870 and 1950

Paternal Grandfather's Occupation	Per cent of paternal grandfathers of 1950's business leaders	All males in 1870, per cent
Businessman	42	6
Professional man	12	3
Farmer or planter	33	32
Wage or office worker	8	57
Other	5	2
	100	100

Some persons, without assistance from their own family, win the loyalty and aid of influential people. They may become the favorites of a strong political party "machine" or simply the good friend of prosperous and powerful men. While such persons win their influence by their own efforts, nevertheless their rewards may not be commensurate with their contribution on the job.

It will be indicated in later chapters that some groups have been able to raise their incomes by exerting disproportionate political influence. Various groups secure the passage of preferential legislation (like tariffs, subsidies, exemptions from the antitrust laws, and so on). Possibly some are able to use their influence to avoid the full impact of regulations and taxes that those less influential must pay.

Taken altogether, there are many ways in which family and political influence alters the distribution of income. The number of those who gain advantage from these sources can only be conjectured, though it does seem that the proportion of those who owe their success to special influence and favor is substantial.

II. CONCLUSIONS

Payments to individuals in the United States depend upon many factors: their productivity, market power, their holdings of property, their

---

[7] *Ibid.*

income from free social services, and political, personal and family influence. It should be clear that *no single factor accounts for the distribution of personal income*, although many individual incomes are influenced disproportionally by one factor. For example, some incomes are so strongly affected by market power that they may bear little relation to productivity.

DISCUSSION QUESTIONS

1. How would you measure the marginal value productivity of your economics instructor? Of your father to his employer or business?

2. Would you expect the marginal value productivity of labor to be higher in China or France? Why?

3. Will the marginal value productivity of capital be high or low in a country like the United States, where the supply of savings is relatively great? Why? Would your answer be different if the population were very great?

4. Do you believe that productivity is the major determinant of individual incomes? Defend your answer.

5. In what way does the power exerted by laborers through unionization differ from that of employers who form large firms?

6. Do most people who receive very large incomes get them for services rendered or from the ownership of property? Explain your answer.

7. Has the United States become a "welfare state"? Discuss in terms of the amount of social security provided for the average American family.

8. To what extent is someone born to poor parents in the United States doomed to remain poor himself? Explain factors facilitating movement into a more prosperous group, and those hindering such movement.

9. To what extent is the bargaining power exerted by labor unions based upon the use of economic force? To what extent on physical force?

10. What are some of the techniques used by labor unions to increase their members' security? What restrictions are placed on these union techniques by the government?

Chapter

8   Can Income Distribution

Be Improved?

We have seen how incomes are distributed and why some are large and others small. It is now appropriate to ask whether there is anything that we want to do about it, and what, if anything, can be done.

We find two diametrically opposed attitudes on these questions. On one hand, there is frequently an attitude of resignation. Those with this attitude consider income inequality to be inevitable in approximately its present degree. (Those holding this view often seem to believe that it is desirable.) On the other hand, many believe that inequality is remediable.

Those in the first group point to differences in the character, skill, and desire for income among individuals. Some of them emphasize the apparent inevitability of laziness and improvidence side by side with industriousness and thrift. They say that in all and any societies the first group will have less material wealth than the second group; hence, they say, "if all income and wealth were equally divided at noon, by dusk many people would be poor and many would be rich."

Those who believe that income inequality can be greatly reduced argue that the distribution of income is not determined by the laws of nature but by man-made laws. They point to the substantial reduction in inequality already achieved, and take it as proof that man has the power to distribute income in whatever way he chooses. Many holding this view emphasize that inequality results from the use of force (political, physical, and economic) by some who use it to enrich themselves at the expense of others, and from superior opportunity to get ahead. These circumstances may be changed, they argue.

Let us examine methods that have been and may be employed to alter income distribution. Only in this way can we judge reliably whether we must resign ourselves to existing inequality or can change it.

I.   METHODS OF REDUCING INCOME
INEQUALITY

In studying measures to reduce the inequality of income, it is important to ask three questions. First, whose income will be increased? We must be sure to define this group very specifically; for example, laws that increase the powers of labor unions will increase the income of workers in unions and of those who will join them, and not those excluded from unions or unlikely to join them. Second, from whom will the income be taken that is to be given to the poor group? Here, too, we must try to be very specific. Much is gained simply from recognizing that income given to one group must come from another group unless total income is sufficiently increased in the process. The third question is, What effect will the measure have on total output?

Many measures redistribute income, and it will not be feasible to discuss all of them. The most important will be taken up, however, and we shall consider in some detail the following: taxes, minimum-wage legislation, encouragement to unions, and equalized economic opportunities.

A. Taxes

The most direct way of redistributing income in the United States is through tax policy. This is a particularly effective device where the government expends a significant proportion of the national income.

1. CLASSES OF TAXES

Taxes are generally divided into two broad types: regressive and progressive. In tax matters these words are almost synonymous with "bad" and "good," "unfair" and "fair." These terms describe the incidence of the tax—that is, who *ultimately* pays the tax. In rough terms, if the tax is paid mostly by rich people, it is considered progressive; if it falls heavily upon the poor, it is termed regressive. However, these terms can and must be made more precise. (A third type of tax may be distinguished from the other two. It is the proportional tax, and really represents the dividing line between regressive and progressive taxes.)

Regressive taxes are precisely defined as those that take a larger *proportion* of income from people of low income than from those in the higher brackets. Progressive taxes take a higher percentage from high incomes than from low. The reason for the distinction between progressive and regressive taxes is to be found in the doctrine of "ability to pay." This doctrine expresses an ethical judgment as to which persons should pay taxes and how much. It has no very exact meaning, but essentially holds that rich people should not only pay more in taxes than poor people but also pay a *larger proportion* of their incomes. (Even if everyone paid the same proportion of his income in taxes, the rich man would pay more dollars than the poor man.) The distinction between progressive and regressive taxes is very crude, for it leaves almost an infinite variety of possible tax rates that are progressive (and regressive). It gives no clue to the manner of administering progressive taxes in accordance with ability to pay. The goal of a "fair" tax, we are told, is that it should "hurt" everyone equally—that is, everyone should contribute "equally" to the common cause. This objective is so vague that wide disagreements arise concerning tax rates that give these results.

2. THE INCIDENCE OF TAXES

Most taxes are borne by persons other than those who pay them directly to the government. The effects of many taxes are so complex that we cannot be sure of their full burden and cannot tell for certain who ultimately pays a particular tax. Let us illustrate with a few examples.

Sales and excise[1] taxes are paid directly by retailers; however, they are passed on to the customer, who understands that the price he is asked does not include the sales tax. Yet we must not conclude that the entire burden of the tax falls on the consumer. The retailer feels it in the form of reduced sales, for it affects individuals' purchases, and the retailer's total sales volume and net profits presumably suffer. The extent of the burden felt by the retailer cannot be estimated exactly, because his purchases decline, with a resultant effect on his suppliers and on the workers of all firms producing and selling his product.

In the United States graduated income taxes are a relatively recent and significant development.[2] Many states still do not raise revenue by this means. Personal income taxes provided about 52 per cent of all federal revenues and about 6 per cent of state tax revenues in 1958.

Although the incidence of the corporate profits tax—a form of income tax—is not clear, it is generally agreed that personal income taxes are borne mainly by those who pay the tax.[3] The personal income tax is thus considered a very effective instrument for placing the burden of taxation on specific income groups and for enabling money collected to be redistributed in goods and services to other groups.

---

[1] The difference between "sales" and "excise" taxes is simply that the former are a percentage of all prices, whereas the latter are a percentage of the prices of specific goods, for example, cosmetics.

[2] The federal government got undisputed power to tax personal income from all sources only with the enactment of the Sixteenth Amendment in 1913.

[3] In some instances increased income tax rates may induce groups such as organized workers to press for more income. This may be one way in which the tax is "passed on."

Business property taxes are a very important type of local tax. Superficially, they are paid by businessmen; they are not passed along to consumers as obviously as are sales taxes. However, property taxes are part of the cost to business of operations, such as wages, salaries, interest, and the like. They really constitute part of the rental cost of business, which must be paid if it is to continue in operation. Thus these taxes become counted in with other costs that businesses calculate in deciding whether and what to produce and how much to charge. To the extent that they enter into the final price, they are similar in their incidence to sales taxes.

However, this view of the matter is too simple, for we know that moderate increases in business property taxes have sometimes had no perceptible effect on prices. In such situations we can say that the tax is borne by the owner of property or those who rent it from him.

Full understanding of the incidence of business property taxes requires that we analyze the impact of the tax according to the incomes of those who pay it. For example, poor people buy relatively more material goods and *fewer* personal services (like the services of shoe-shine boys, delivery men, barbers, laundries, dry cleaners, taxis, airlines, hotels, night clubs, as well as those of maids, gardeners, chauffeurs, tutors, cooks, nurses, watchmen, butlers, and so on) than do the wealthy. The things they buy generally involve the use of property in both production and sale. On the other hand, the wealthy members of the community make a fairly large proportion of their total purchases in the form of personal services, which involve little or no property in production or sale. Accordingly, one can conclude that property taxes that are passed along to customers take a larger proportion of the income of the poor than of the rich.

The foregoing discussion has been quite superficial. Some important matters pertaining to the subject were deliberately omitted. However, it should be amply clear that *the ultimate resting place of taxes frequently is far from the person who pays them directly to the government*, and that we cannot measure the full incidence of any tax exactly. Experts, however, are agreed, with one possible exception—corporate profits taxes— about which kinds of taxes are progressive and which regressive, though they may hold different views about the degree of progressiveness of each one.

In general terms, sales, excise, and business property taxes are regressive (though excise taxes on luxuries purchased almost exclusively by the wealthy are progressive; so are personal property taxes based on possessions of the wealthy). The most progressive is a graduated personal income tax; business profits taxes are also considered a progressive tax by most economists, though the matter is disputed.

Some studies have been made with the purpose of determining the effect of all taxes combined upon the distribution of income in the United

States. Unfortunately, these are out of date. However, they do give information that helps to emphasize the fact that taxes take a much larger proportion of income than the average person realizes. Moreover, these studies put into numerical terms the estimated incidence of taxes so that the relative regressiveness of various taxes can be judged. The most detailed description of the tax burden borne by different income groups is the one prepared for the Temporary National Economic Committee for the year 1938-1939. (Government finances are recorded on a fiscal year that begins and ends at the middle of the year.) Although this study offers results that are recorded even to decimal places, one must recognize that they are simply intelligent estimates.

This study divides taxes into three groups. The first is termed "personal taxes," and includes poll taxes, income, inheritance and gift taxes, and nonbusiness personal property taxes. Second are excise taxes on specific products, like tobacco, liquor, gasoline, tires, automobiles, appliances, and "luxury taxes." Finally, there are business taxes, which include the following: payroll and sales taxes, business excise taxes, corporate profits taxes, and business property taxes.

The relative importance of each of these groups in 1938-1939 is shown in Table 1. The size of the various taxes is expressed as a percentage of income for income recipients who have been divided into 10

**Table 1. Relative Importance of Personal, Excise, and
Business Taxes, 1938-1939**
(In percentages of income)

Income Classes	Personal taxes		Excise taxes		Business taxes		All taxes		
	Federal	State & local	Federal	State & local	Federal	State & local	Federal	State & local	Federal state & local
Under $500	1.1	0.2	3.0	4.3	3.8	9.5	7.9	14.0	21.9
$500 to $1,000	.7	.2	2.9	3.5	3.0	7.7	6.6	11.4	18.0
$1,000 to $1,500	.7	.3	2.8	3.6	2.8	7.0	6.4	10.9	17.3
$1,500 to $2,000	1.0	.5	2.8	3.9	2.8	6.9	6.6	11.2	17.8
$2,000 to $3,000	1.0	.5	2.7	4.0	2.6	6.6	6.4	11.1	17.5
$3,000 to $5,000	2.3	1.1	2.4	3.7	2.3	5.8	7.0	10.6	17.6
$5,000 to $10,000	4.8	1.8	1.9	3.1	1.8	4.6	8.4	9.5	17.9
$10,000 to $15,000	12.1	4.5	1.5	2.7	1.4	3.4	14.9	10.6	25.5
$15,000 to $20,000	17.3	6.6	1.3	2.3	1.2	2.9	19.8	11.9	31.7
Over $20,000	25.5	7.0	.8	1.6	.8	2.0	27.2	10.6	37.8
All classes	4.3	1.4	2.4	3.6	2.5	6.0	9.2	11.0	20.2

SOURCE: Compiled from *T.N.E.C. Monograph No. 3, Who Pays the Taxes?* pp. 6, 13.

income classes. Thus we can see how large a proportion of the incomes of the poorest members of the community went in taxes—it was 22 per cent in that year—and how much was paid by more prosperous groups. We see, for example, that everyone taken together paid 20 per cent in taxes of all sorts, which is lower than the proportion paid by those with incomes below $500 a year. Table 1 also divides taxes according to whether they were federal or state and local.

Note that in 1938-1939 state and local taxes were more important than federal taxes (11.0 per cent vs. 9.2 per cent). Yet all state and local taxes taken together showed no progression and were appreciably regressive on incomes under $500. This condition resulted from the fact that personal income taxes that are progressive were relatively unimportant and were completely offset by the regressiveness of excise and business taxes among low- and medium-income groups.

Even for the federal government, taxes were not effectively progressive on incomes under $10,000. If all taxes are considered together, the percentage taken by taxes was remarkably constant for incomes between $500 and $10,000; the per cent in taxes was *higher* for incomes under $500, and became appreciably progressive only for those larger than $10,000.

Thus, in 1938-1939 progressive income taxes had caused progressive taxation only of incomes larger than $10,000. For the 80 per cent of total

Table 2. Tax Burden by Income Groups, 1946-1947 and 1948

Consumer Income	Taxes, as per cent of income ‡	
	1946–47 *	1948 †
Under $1,000	19.6%	23.6%
$1,000–$2,000	15.1	20.3
$2,000–$3,000	17.3	21.6
$3,000–$4,000	17.7	21.8
$4,000–$5,000	22.9	21.7
$5,000–$7,500	24.2	23.1
$7,500 and over	36.3	31.7
Total	24.2	24.7

* John Adler, "The Fiscal System, the Distribution of Income and Public Welfare," in K. E. Poole (ed.), *Fiscal Policies and the American Economy* (Englewood Cliffs, N.J.: Prentice-Hall, Inc., 1951).

† R. A. Musgrave, J. J. Carroll, L. D. Cook, and L. Frane, "Distribution of Tax Payments by Income Groups: A Case Study for 1948," *National Tax Journal*, March, 1951, p. 47.

‡ The difference between these two studies probably results from the fact that Musgrave *et al* assume that business profits taxes are shifted, while Adler does not.

personal income received by those with incomes between $500 and $10,000, the tax burden was proportional to income, becoming regressive for incomes below $500. It is clear that, except for a small amount of income received by the rich, taxes had not been used up to 1938-1939 to bring about an effective change in the distribution of incomes.

Table 3. Federal Income Tax Burden by Income Groups, 1952-1954

Family Income (before income taxes)	Tax as a per cent of income		
	1952	1953	1954
Under $1,000	0	0	0
$1,000–$1,999	2.9	2.9	2.6
$2,000–$2,999	5.2	5.2	4.6
$3,000–$3,999	6.1	6.1	5.4
$4,000–$4,999	6.9	6.9	6.0
$5,000–$5,999	8.6	8.5	7.5
$6,000–$7,499	9.9	9.9	8.7
$7,500–$9,999	10.5	10.3	9.0
$10,000–$14,999	11.8	11.5	10.1
$15,000–$19,999	15.2		
$20,000–$24,999	18.0		
$25,000–$49,999	24.3	24.0	21.3
$50,000 and over	40.9		
Totals	10.8	10.9	9.5

SOURCE: U.S. Department of Commerce, *Income Distribution in the United States,* a Supplement to the *Survey of Current Business,* 1953, p. 85; and *Survey of Current Business,* June, 1956, pp. 13-15.

The incidence of taxes in the postwar period apparently is similar to that in the prewar period. In 1948 American families with incomes below $1,000 paid about 24 per cent of their incomes in taxes to federal, state, and local governments; all families with $3,000 or less—representing 53 per cent of the entire population—paid an average of 21.8 per cent. The 42 per cent of all spending units with incomes between $3,000 and $7,500 paid an average of 22.2 per cent—almost exactly the same as poorer people, but not so much as the poorest single group. Thus, taken altogether, our tax system apparently does not fall more heavily upon the middle-income group than on the poor. However, the recipients of the highest incomes do pay a substantially larger portion of their incomes in taxes than does any other group. The incidence of *all* taxes by individual income group, according to two studies for the years 1946-1948 is presented in Table 2. The recent incidence of federal income taxes is presented in Table 3.

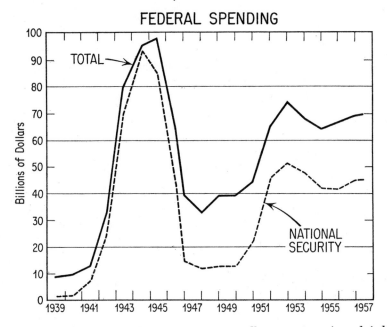

Although military spending was a very small proportion of total federal expenditure in 1939, it has accounted for half or more of the total in recent years.

3. GOVERNMENT EXPENDITURES

To examine only those who pay the taxes is to see but half of the effect of taxes. To understand their full effect, it is necessary to examine the use made of the tax proceeds. It is essential to realize that someone receives and something is obtained for the taxpayers' money. All tax proceeds are used in some way. Except for the rare occasion when they are used to accumulate bank balances, the proceeds of taxes will be respent, and will augment the income of persons who receive them. The manner in which their governments spend their revenues determines whether they will supplement high or low incomes primarily.

Table 4 indicates the major uses for which tax revenues were spent in 1957 and 1958. In effect, the tax system takes funds in the manner described by Table 2 and transfers them to those whose identity is suggested by Table 4.

As Table 4 clearly indicates, the government today spends most of its tax proceeds for armaments and the maintenance of its armed forces. A relatively small proportion pays for the conduct of the ordinary affairs of government. If the government is to effect savings through greater efficiency, it must hope to do so primarily by increasing the efficiency of its military establishment—or of its diplomatic measures to maintain peace.

Table 4. Analysis of Government Expenditures, Years Ending June 30, 1957, and 1958

| | 1957 | | 1958 * | |
Function	Total (millions)	Per cent of total	Total (millions)	Per cent of total
Major national security	$44,414	63.97	$44,871	61.65
International affairs and finance	832	1.20	1,468	2.02
Commerce, transportation, and industry	1,404	2.02	1,795	2.47
Natural resources	1,296	1.87	1,457	2.00
Agriculture and agricultural resources	4,582	6.60	4,924	6.76
Labor	400	0.58	411	0.56
Housing and community development	49	0.07	351	0.48
Education and general research	361	0.52	433	0.59
Social security, welfare, and health	2,205	3.18	2,599	3.57
Veterans' services and benefits	4,793	6.90	5,034	6.92
General government	1,789	2.58	1,377	1.89
Interest	7,308	10.53	7,867	10.81
Reserve for contingencies	—	—	200	0.27
Total budget expenditures	$69,433	100.00	$72,788	100.00

* Estimate from President's Budget message.

SOURCE: U.S. Treasury Department, Bureau of the Budget, *The Federal Budget in Brief* (Washington, D.C.: Government Printing Office, 1958), pp. 52-53.

Although all of the government's income is spent, and therefore gets into the hands of someone, it may not be spent wisely. An inefficient and corrupt government will give its taxpayers very little for their money. On the other hand, a government that studies the nation's needs and plans intelligently for their satisfaction gives taxpayers full value. At a later point we shall inquire into the efficiency with which government performs its functions.

4. HOW TAXES COULD REDUCE INCOME INEQUALITY

If taxes are going to be used to make income distribution more equal, personal income taxes must be the instrument employed, for these taxes

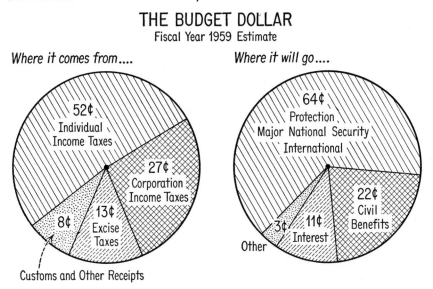

THE BUDGET DOLLAR
Fiscal Year 1959 Estimate

Where it comes from....

52¢
Individual
Income Taxes

27¢
Corporation
Income Taxes

13¢
Excise
Taxes

8¢

Customs and Other Receipts

Where it will go....

64¢
Protection
Major National Security
International

22¢
Civil
Benefits

11¢
Interest

3¢

Other

are potentially the most progressive type. The procedure in the use of income taxes to redistribute income is simple: tax the high income recipients heavily and spend the proceeds to provide services for those with lower incomes. These services could consist of "national defense"—something valued by rich and poor alike. Or they could consist of free medical services, free school lunches, or national roads, parks, public housing, old-age pensions, unemployment insurance, and the like. *When the poor benefit from government services in greater proportion than they pay for those services, income has been redistributed in their favor.* For example, if income taxes were used to provide free medical care to everyone, the poorest families, who pay no income taxes, would nevertheless get medical services. Their real income would thus be increased. The people who paid income taxes would be defraying the costs of the medical services obtained by the poor as well as by themselves.

5. HOW PROGRESSIVE INCOME TAXES INFLUENCE TOTAL OUTPUT

What is the effect on total output of our present personal income taxes? Would a decrease in rates on the higher-bracket incomes induce those with high incomes to work longer hours, or more diligently, or to shift to occupations where they add more than they do now to total output? Or would it be possible to increase income taxes on all groups without tending to cause workers to be on the job fewer hours, to become less conscientious in their work, or to shift to occupations in which they were less productive? Should the taxes on low income groups be reduced?

Much has been said and written about the effect of high income taxes on the incentive to work, but little information has been presented. Some revealing figures now available should be studied carefully. In most of the industrialized countries of the world, income taxes have been collected for many years, and in general there has been a steady increase in tax rates in most countries. What have been the observed effects on incentive? Is there any evidence that higher income taxes have reduced total output? While it is necessary to recognize the existence of influences on total output other than tax rates, certain facts in the American experience stand out.

National output was higher during recent years when income tax rates were higher than in years when they were lower. This fact does not support the conclusion that total output increased *because of* rising income tax rates. What it does show is that *the higher tax rates did not prevent a large rise in national income.* British experience following World War II with higher tax rates than ours was similar.[4]

To understand the influence of increases in income tax rates upon total output, the concept of "economic surplus" is useful. Economic surplus may be defined as the amount of income that could be taken away from an individual, without lowering his productive contribution by causing him either to shift to an occupation in which he would be less productive, or to work fewer hours. One can determine how much economic surplus an individual receives only by observing his response to a change in tax rates. To judge by past experience, most people receive more income than they must be paid to induce them to continue to work with the same intensity for the same number of hours in their present occupation. Large increases in income tax rates enacted in recent years have not induced many persons to work fewer hours or to move to other occupations. One study concluded that top executives did not perceptibly reduce their efforts because of the greatly increased income taxes.[5]

Failure of individuals to change their economic activities because their net compensation has changed results from various causes. Reluctance to look for another job, unwillingness to move to another community, or even to risk developing new associations at work, the inability to keep one's job and yet reduce the number of hours or days worked weekly, and the like, tend to hold workers in their current employment. Moreover, the pressure within a firm to earn the respect of one's subordinates, colleagues, and superiors militates against a relaxation of effort. As a consequence of these circumstances, even employees whose subjective incentives to work may have been weakened may nevertheless continue to work as hard and as long at the same job.

---

[4] Findley Weaver, "Taxation and Redistribution in the United Kingdom," *Review of Economics and Statistics,* August, 1950, pp. 201-213.

[5] Thomas H. Sanders, *Effects of Taxation on Executives* (Boston: Harvard University Bureau of Business Research, 1951).

It is obvious, however, that if tax rates were to increase greatly so that they took, say, 80 per cent of an individual's income, he might decide to work fewer hours. *A very high rate of income tax reduces the price of leisure.* That is, when taxes rise, one gives up less income in using his time as leisure. At the lower "price," people could be expected to "buy" more of it.

The reasons why increases in income tax rates have not induced many persons to retire or to shift to other occupations probably include the following: First, men and women work for reasons other than money returns, especially those in the very high brackets, who probably have accumulated enough to enable them to retire on a modest income. They work primarily because they would not know what else to do with their time, or because they enjoy their work more than they would enjoy complete leisure—partly because their work allows them considerable freedom to use their time as they wish and because they prize most highly the "power," prestige, or opportunity for public service that their work affords. Second, if these individuals were to transfer to other occupations, in which they might be less productive, they would be exposed to the high tax rate there also. Consequently, a shift to a less remunerative (which we will assume is also likely to be a less productive) occupation would involve a double loss of income—a drop in pay added to the rise in tax rates.

One type of occupational shift is likely to be induced by substantial increases in income tax rates. Those occupied in work where incomes are very uncertain (that is, you might make a great deal of money or lose a great deal) would have strong economic incentive to shift to occupations where income is more stable. Typical of these are song writers and composers, artists, sculptors, and novelists and playwrights, who may produce a work over a two- or three-year period and yet receive all income from it in one year—a big success would be largely wiped out by regular graduated taxes. Risky businesses of all kinds become unattractive if one must bear the entire burden of losses himself, and yet lose in taxes most of his profits. Allowance of "carry backs" and "carry forwards" in calculating tax liabilities, that is, the right almost to average income over a period of several years for income tax purposes, weakens the incentive to shift to less risky occupations.

To sum up, then, considerable evidence suggests that almost all individuals have received considerable economic surplus in the past. Consequently, it has been possible to increase income tax rates without reducing most persons' productive contribution. It is impossible to estimate how much economic surplus remains at current tax rates; that information can be obtained only by experimentation with higher rates.

Further tax increases might reduce incentives to work to the point where total output suffers significantly; however, past experience with tax increases in this country suggests that such an effect is far from certain.

Indeed, the reverse seems equally likely. Increases in income taxes might add to rather than reduce total output. Most individuals seem determined to maintain at least the level of living that they enjoy currently. With a rise in tax rates, most individuals would be required to work longer hours or to enter more lucrative fields to obtain the net income needed to maintain their conventional levels of living. Moreover, high income tax rates probably lengthen the average number of years that men work before retiring. Those who would have retired had they been able to save the money they paid in income taxes have had to continue working to maintain living levels and have thereby increased total output.

Taxes that take the economic surplus of the wealthy and transfer it to the poor would contribute toward more equal income distribution (which, as we have seen already, would tend to increase national well-being) without sacrificing any output. Since in all probability the amount of economic surplus varies considerably from individual to individual, it would be rather difficult to devise taxes that would fall only on those who receive economic surplus. Increases in income taxes are likely to induce at least a few workers to retire, to work fewer hours, or to shift to an occupation paying less. On the other hand, some would almost certainly work harder as a result of higher tax rates. *As a practical matter, the effects of higher tax rates can be determined only by trying them out.*

High taxes give rise to many effects beyond those intended by the legislatures that enact them. They underline the vital fact that in considering legislation careful thought must be given to many such unintended effects; some of these might be windfall and unexpected advantages; however, some serious evils may arise. High taxes on personal incomes and profits cause certain individuals to lose almost all interest in increasing their incomes; for the increase will go almost entirely to the government in higher taxes. Similarly, corporations paying the very highest tax rates are relatively willing to spend their income; for if they did not spend it, almost all of it would have to be paid to the government. The following kinds of things happen as a result of the high tax rates. First, businesses and individuals have less reluctance to make gifts to charity and to other philanthropic institutions. Second, individuals have an incentive to establish "foundations" at least ostensibly to do some "good work," and at least partly to retain income in the family. Institutional advertising and technical research are fostered by very high tax rates, for businesses would rather spend funds in building up their reputation and consumer appeal than in paying most of the income to the government.

In addition, one feature of American tax law gives rise to many odd and distorted types of expenditure and investment. This feature is known as the "capital gains tax," which taxes profits on the sale of assets held six months or more, at a far lower rate than other types of income. It thereby creates a strong incentive for recipients of high income to seek ways of obtaining income through capital gains rather than as ordinary income. One effect is to encourage receivers of high income to take on risky investments and to buy assets whose value appreciates substantially over time, even though initial losses are involved. For example, the capital-gains feature of the tax law encourages purchases of orchards, animal breeding farms, and the like, which initially involve losses, and when sold, give income in the form of capital gains, taxable at relatively low rates.

The manifest opportunity to shift taxes, and their uncertain resting place, limit the value of taxation as an instrument for redistributing income. Even the tax with the clearest impact—the personal income tax—seems to be shifted in part. When taxes on workers are increased, for example, workers feel stronger pressures to obtain a wage increase and accordingly will make greater efforts to do so. It is to be expected that their efforts bear some fruit and result in higher wage rates. In turn, prices tend to rise, reflecting higher labor costs and, as already explained in connection with excise taxes, the tax will affect producers, sellers, and buyers. There is considerable evidence that changes in personal income tax rates also lead to corresponding changes in the rewards of those who receive the highest incomes in the community, such as top business executives, professionals, and outstanding entertainers.

Thus taxes are a weapon that is always fired at a moving target. Generally, when it is aimed at one group, another group also ends up with less money in its pocket.

B. Minimum Wages

One measure for reducing income inequality that is widely favored, and indeed has been enacted into law, is the legal prohibition of wages below a prescribed minimum in designated occupations. At the present time, the minimum wage is $1, and approximately 22 million workers are engaged in the occupations subject to the amendment to the Fair Labor Standards Act that went into effect March, 1956. We must inquire whether minimum-wage legislation reduces inequality of income, from whom it takes the funds that are transferred to low-income recipients, and what are its effects on total output.

As already indicated, employers will not knowingly pay a worker more than his marginal-value productivity. In the event that the wage set by law exceeded the marginal-value productivity, workers would presumably be discharged, since their continued employment would impose a loss on the employer. However, there is no information indicating that such unemployment has in fact resulted either from the imposition or the raising of the minimum wage.

Clearly, if minimum-wage legislation causes some workers to be discharged, it would increase rather than reduce inequality of income. It reduces some workers whose incomes were low to a complete lack of income. This effect is more or less offset by the increase in the incomes of those who are not discharged. The *net* effect of minimum-wage laws upon inequality requires a detailed measurement of their many effects. There is no reliable method of determining in advance what effect will be uppermost in any occupation. Such an estimate will depend upon a host of factors, among which the following are likely to be most important. First is the extent to which workers were being paid less than their marginal-value productivity. Workers who have little bargaining power, or who are unskillful or misled in the exercise of the power they do possess, may be paid far less than they add to the value of their employer's output. When workers are being "underpaid," the minimum-wage laws will simply transfer income from the employers to workers receiving very low pay.

Second, the effect of minimum-wage legislation depends upon the possibility of substituting machinery for labor in each occupation. Some occupations cannot mechanize their operations and consequently must use labor, no matter what its cost. Other trades may be pushed by minimum-wage legislation to adopt machinery that would not have yielded savings at the former low wage.

Third, to raise minimum-wage rates may directly influence worker marginal-value productivity. If worker productivity rises when minimum-wage rates are increased, unemployment need not result at all. Clearly, minimum wages raise the incomes of those who suffer most from inadequate diet, housing, and medical care. Moreover, workers receiving less than the minimum prescribed by law are likely to be the least "satisfied" workers. Increases in incomes of the lowest paid workers might increase their productivity by allowing them to obtain more adequate food, housing, and medical care. In addition, their "morale" might be improved, so that they exert greater efforts in their employers' behalf. If the effect of minimum-wage legislation were to increase labor productivity more than labor costs, employment might actually increase. Like many other problems with which we deal, this is one concerning which we cannot make abstract pronouncements. We must experiment to determine its effect.

Fourth, if the higher labor costs due to minimum-wage legislation could be passed along to customers, the effects of the laws would depend upon the relative incomes of customers and workers. As seems most likely, if the customers' personal incomes were higher than those of workers whose incomes had been below the legal minimum, the laws would make for more equal income distribution. If customers' incomes were lower than those of the workers, the incomes would actually be more unequal. It is difficult to name a single product whose customers average lower incomes than are received by workers whose pay is below the legal minimum. Accordingly, a transfer of income from consumers to workers with low wages would almost always make income more equal.

Fifth, if managements are alert, the effect of minimum wages may inspire them to do whatever they can to increase productivity, and thereby to benefit all workers and consumers.

Thus, minimum-wage legislation could actually reduce the incomes of workers who could not obtain employment at the minimum wage specified by law. On the other hand, it would help those who retained their jobs after the law went into effect. Minimum-wage laws could increase equality of income by raising the productivity of the lowest paid part of the population, and thereby enable them to command higher incomes.

C. Labor Unions

In a highly competitive, fully employed economy, a laborer's wage rate would be determined primarily by productivity. Not only would there be no need for minimum-wage laws or labor unions, but such attempts as these to raise wages would be positively harmful. If, for example, a labor union demanded an increase in wage rates, the employer could grant the raise only by paying the workers more than the value of what they produce for him. He could be expected to respond to such a situation by laying off some workers. A higher income for some of the laborers would thus be possible only at the expense of unemployment of others. Or, if labor alone were highly organized, inflation might result when there also is an "easy money" policy in government. This would partially or wholly offset initial gains in real wages.

This argument has been used often in the past in answer to the demands of unions for higher wages. However, even a superficial examination of the assumptions of the argument—perfectly competitive markets, with a speedy movement of workers to the highest paying employments, reasonably full employment—reveals the weakness of the argument that higher wages mean unemployment. Because of the lack of full competition in the economy, the inability of workers to move themselves and their families from one geographical area to another, and inadequate measures of cost, it is quite possible for workers to receive less (and, on rare occasions, more) than their marginal-value product, and for this condition to persist for long periods of time. Since the marginal productivity would be impossible to measure in most situations, one could never say with any assurance that the marginal product and the wage were equated, anyway.

Workers are understandably reluctant to accept an explanation of their income which leaves them the alternatives of either accepting the going wage rate, however low, or contributing to unemployment. Through their unions, labor has argued that its concerted demands for wage boosts have not only failed to cause unemployment and to lower total labor income, but have actually helped to increase employment. Laborers make this claim on the ground that they redistribute income in favor of poor people who spend their entire funds, at the expense of prosperous persons who might save part of theirs. If this argument were valid, total spending might rise as a result of union action and more would be produced and more persons would be employed. Thus members of labor unions view their organizations as instruments for raising total national income as well as a device for redistributing income in their favor. Economists are not agreed as to the validity of this view.

Our nation has had considerable experience with unions. Can we determine from actual experience what has been the effect of unionization upon the distribution of personal income?

1. THE EFFECTS OF UNIONS UPON THE DISTRIBUTION OF PERSONAL INCOME

The effect of unions upon labor income is unclear. It is not even obvious how their effect might be measured. One method would be to compare the share of the national income that goes to labor with the growth of unionism. One difficulty in applying this criterion is that it does not take account of changes in the size and skills of the labor force. For example, if workers grew as a proportion of the population, or increased their skills and productivity more than the rest of the population, one would expect labor to obtain a larger proportion of total output, quite apart from any effects of unionization. Only part of this difficulty would be removed by measuring labor's share of the national income on a per capita basis.

In addition, information describing the share of the national income going to labor does not fully meet our needs, because it includes salary income. Thus in "labor" income are included the earnings of top business executives, and supervisory and professional employees whose incomes have not been to any great extent affected by unionization.

Despite the shortcomings of the data, the available information describing labor's share of all personal income is presented in the accompanying chart. It shows that the proportion of national income going to wage and salary recipients has varied moderately from year to year, but that there has been no steady rise in labor's share during the period of union growth. In considerable measure, variations in labor's share of total personal income seem to be the result of changes in general business conditions. Whatever variations have occurred seem to be largely the result of factors other than changes in the strength of unions.

LABOR'S SHARE OF NATIONAL INCOME

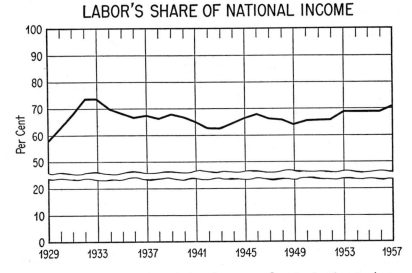

How can the apparent failure of increased unionization to increase substantially labor's share of the national income be explained? We should remind ourselves of the fact that the poor quality of the evidence available may actually conceal substantial increases in labor's share of total income. If this possibility is set aside, what other explanations can be offered for the failure of the manifest growth in union strength to increase the share of all income that went to labor? First, it is possible that the increased strength of unions forestalled a decline in labor's share of the national income that would have occurred otherwise. Second, the failure of unions to increase the share of the national income going to labor as a whole can be attributed in part to the fact that they redistribute income *among laborers*. When strongly unionized workers succeed in winning higher wage rates—or even a higher total wage income—they may do so by pushing up the prices of the things they produce. The higher prices may simply be paid by other workers, as well as farmers, white-collar workers, and such, whose real incomes are reduced commensurate with the rise in income of the unionized workers. There can be little question that highly unionized workers have won their gains at least in part at the expense of nonunionized workers. Most union leaders are quick to acknowledge this fact. They say that the remedy for the situation is more and not less unionization. In their view, what is required for a redistribution of income between labor and nonlabor groups is universal unionization of roughly equal strength. Third, unions may have given labor its gains primarily in the form of fewer hours of work for equal total pay.

It is possible to measure the effect of unionization upon the real income of workers by another means—measuring changes in output per man-hour from decade to decade and determining what proportion of increases in productivity was paid over to labor, and then relating this proportion to variations in union strength. This method is also subject to many of the pitfalls met in measuring labor's share of total national income.

Data available permit the calculation of the total output of goods and services between the years 1900 and 1949, and its division by the number of man-hours worked in each year to determine how much was produced per man-hour. This result can be adjusted for changes in prices to measure output per man-hour in 1949 (constant) dollars. These calculations show, for example, that output per man-hour in 1949 dollars increased from 51 cents in 1900 to $1.83 in 1949, a rise in per hour productivity of well over 300 per cent during this half century.

Output per man-hour can be compared with earnings per man-hour, also stated in 1949 dollars. Earnings per man-hour are calculated by taking total compensation of wage and salary earners and dividing by the number of man-hours worked, and adjusting for changes in price level.

By these calculations we can compare changes in output with changes in employee earnings. The relation between the two can be related to degree of unionization to determine whether workers obtained a larger or smaller proportion of their added income before or after unionization made great strides. Such a comparison is presented in Table 5.

The results show that during 1929-1939, the period of most rapid union advance,[6] the full rise in output per man-hour of 25 cents was matched by wage and salary increases. Prior to that time—and thereafter also—output rose substantially faster than earnings. (One should expect output to rise faster than labor's earnings, for part of a rise in output surely is attributable to the contributions of owners, investors, and owners of land.) In contrast to the decade 1929-1939, between 1920 and 1929 output per man-hour increased by 29 cents, while earnings per hour increased 14 cents. Between 1900 and 1920 output increased by 32 cents, while worker income rose only 19 cents. To complete the story, while output per man-hour increased 46 cents between 1939 and 1949, earnings per man-hour rose by 33 cents. Between 1949 and 1957 output per man-hour rose by 52 cents; earnings per man-hour rose by 55 cents. One must qualify this comparison, however, by noting that the years 1929-1939 were depression years, and not strictly comparable with the boom times of the other three periods. Increased productivity in part arose from the fact that the least efficient plants and processes were abandoned. Hence higher productivity would be expected. But this effect alone would not account for the wage increase associated with the depression era.

---

[6] A brief but highly competent review of the ebb and flow of union strength is presented by Nathan P. Feinsinger and Edwin E. Witte, "Labor Legislation and the Role of Government," *Monthly Labor Review*, July, 1950, pp. 48-61.

The foregoing comparison suggests two conclusions. First, with the growth in unionism, labor was able to command a larger share of increases in productivity for itself. Even the period 1939-1949, when union power probably waned somewhat, was one in which labor obtained a larger

Table 5. Output and Earnings per Man-Hour Compared with Strength of Unions

Year	Output per man-hour (in 1949)	Earnings per man-hour (in 1949)	Number of union members (thousands)	Rise in earnings * —————— Rise in output
1900	$0.51	$0.43	791	. . .
1920	.83	.62	5,034	59%
1929	1.12	.76	3,625	48%
1939	1.37	1.01	8,980 *	100%
1949	1.83	1.34	14,000–16,000 †	72%
1957	2.35	1.89	18,363 †	41%

* The rise in earnings and output is measured from the preceding year listed in the table.

† Includes Canadian members of Labor Unions with headquarters in the U.S. This totaled 712,598 in 1949; about 1 million in 1957.

SOURCES: Based on *How to Raise Real Wages*, a statement on national policy by the research and policy committee of the Committee for Economic Development, Table 1, of the statistical appendix prepared by Dr. Sumner H. Slichter, p. 31. A detailed description of the sources used by Professor Slichter is included in his appendix.

U.S. Department of Labor, Bureau of Labor Statistics, *Handbook of Labor Statistics, 1950*, p. 139.

National Industrial Conference Board, *Management Record*, December, 1957.

share of productivity increases than it had prior to 1929. Second, when the comparison of labor income is made on a per-hour basis rather than in totals, the influence of unions seems to be quite clear. Thus, it would appear that *the major effect of increased unionization has been to reduce the work week without reducing, and possibly even slightly increasing, worker real income.*

2. OTHER EFFECTS OF UNIONS

Labor unions have aimed to do much more than increase labor's share of the national income. Recently the larger unions have followed a new wage policy, the object of which has been to eliminate the changes in labor's income resulting from fluctuations in the cost of living. Accordingly, they have tied their wage rates to the prices of goods purchased by workers' families (specifically, to the Consumers Price Index compiled by the Bureau of Labor Statistics). As a result of this policy, many workers have been able to prevent declines in their real income due to price rises, but there can be no doubt that there has been a resulting inflationary effect as well.

Labor unions are trying also to stabilize worker income by winning guaranteed annual wages (GAW) or supplemental unemployment benefits (SUB) in direct negotiation with employers. Both GAW and SUB put a relatively high floor under workers' income which would prevent a great drop even during a period of widespread unemployment. GAW and SUB are highly flexible arrangements, permitting different definitions of the workers who will be protected by the plan, and allowing variations in the proportion of regular wages that will be insured and in the length of time that the guarantee is in effect.

For example, in 1956 the United Steelworkers union reached an agreement with steel companies which provided for Supplementary Unemployment Benefits. The SUB proviso stipulated that all workers with two years' seniority were entitled to 65 per cent of their take-home pay for a period not exceeding fifty-two weeks. Under this agreement, the steel companies would supplement the eligible workers' unemployment compensation payments with an amount of money necessary to make the total payment equal to 65 per cent of their take-home pay. Thus the unemployed steelworker covered by the SUB proviso would collect unemployment compensation from the state (he would also pay the regular premium to the unemployment insurance system), as well as a supplementary payment from his employer. In this way, the burden of unemployment on workers would be substantially reduced—though far from eliminated altogether. Limitations of both SUB and GAW arrangements from labor's standpoint are that many workers are not covered, and that the coverage is substantially less than 100 per cent of wages and does not extend beyond a year.

The Guaranteed Annual Wage goes considerably farther than supplementary unemployment benefits to insure worker income against a sharp decline during a depression, though the difference between them is essentially one of degree. Guaranteed Annual Wage plans have been in operation in some firms for many years. Perhaps the most famous are the Hormel Company plan and the one in operation in Proctor and Gamble. The earliest known plan was instituted in the wallpaper industry before 1900. Each plan adopted or proposed has contained some unique features which make generalization about their provisions and effects impossible. Although the old American Federation of Labor unions are still cool toward the GAW and SUB, the demand for them will undoubtedly be heard more and more in years ahead.

In addition to getting more income for workers and negotiating fixed-income plans for periods of unemployment, labor unions have bargained successfully for "fringe benefits." Such benefits cover a wide range of items, including employer contributions to union health and welfare funds (many of which provide sickness benefits and comprehensive medical and pension coverage), additional paid holidays, paid birthday-anniversary holidays, discount-purchasing privileges, improvements in working conditions, more safety measures, and the like.

A recent union demand by Walter Reuther, President of the United Automobile Workers' Union, for profit sharing by automobile manufacturers on all profits above a certain level not only attracted widespread public interest but also raised the critical question of "management prerogatives"—that is, the right of management to autonomy in making decisions affecting output, prices, profit distribution, etc. This issue is more and more likely to emerge in the United States, as it has in European countries, when labor unions find it difficult to push wage and hour demands beyond certain limits. In such circumstances, union leaders are strongly motivated to explore other areas of collective bargaining in order to get more for their members and thus to maintain their positions of leadership.

During the past two or three decades unions have become a new and important political force in the American economy. As representatives of about 16 million workers and their families, labor unions constitute the largest economic group now attempting to exert pressure on the composition and activities of legislative bodies. The political strength of the unions is most obvious in their campaigns for measures that aid their members directly, such as expanded welfare expenditures, social insurance, and minimum-wage laws.[7] But increasingly the unions have voiced their opinions on much broader issues—the causes and remedies for unemployment, for example, or the effects of a high-tariff policy, or loans to foreign countries. Labor places strong emphasis on obtaining a more favorable political and legislative climate in which to carry on collective bargaining. It is clear that in addition to their direct attempts to influence income distribution, labor unions try to exercise political power, in order to obtain legislation that will, directly or indirectly, increase labor's income.

An excellent example of labor's interest in political strength as a means to forward its ends is the AFL-CIO merger which took place on December 5, 1955. Not only did the two great unions agree to refrain from competition between the AFL and CIO unions and locals, but they also decided to push for special legislation in health and welfare, for a higher minimum wage, and for repeal or modification of the Taft-Hartley Law. They agreed to push the labor press vigorously and emphasized its importance to them. Specific plans were formulated for political education

---

[7] Despite the large numbers of workers represented in the AFL-CIO, labor has often failed to achieve major political ends. For example, on the national level the goal of repealing the Taft-Hartley Act has been frustrated at each congressional session. On the state level, the spreading number of state right-to-work laws, which outlaw closed and union shops, attests to another major failure.

and action. In other words, the joining, at the highest levels, of America's two large labor affiliations had a political as well as an organizational meaning.[8]

In addition to the foregoing effects of unions upon the distribution of money income, there are other influences that warrant at least passing mention. Perhaps, above all else, unions have given many workers a feeling that they are no longer powerless before their employer. (Unfortunately, some workers have simply replaced their employer with an equally powerful and no more beneficent union leader.) Many workers feel that they need not cringe before their foreman, for their fellow workers will stand by them if they are given discriminatory treatment. Thus, union members gain new self-respect and a feeling of security and power that surely is of great satisfaction to them, and a gain to a free society. As a result, worker morale and productivity are possibly improved, though it is sometimes argued that output is adversely affected by increased independence of the workers. Unions also affect their members directly through such activities as union welfare funds, educational services, camps, clinics, housing projects, recreation services, and many other operations involving member participation and benefits. Membership in labor unions has increased rapidly during this period. From a peak membership in 1920 of more than 5 million persons, the unions lost ground during the twenties and early thirties, when they claimed only 3 million members. Thereafter, with a change in the environment provided by a favorable national administration, organized labor gained in strength until at present about 18 million persons belong to various unions.

By abusing their position, union leaders can sometimes enrich themselves. A vigorous and cohesive union can cause great difficulty for employers, who may therefore try to bribe union leaders to betray the union membership, and under conditions of undemocratic internal control there is very little that rank-and-file members can do. Union leaders sometimes have "sold out their men" for personal profit. Moreover, these leaders can sometimes supplement their personal incomes by selling favors to members—favoring some workers over others in job placement, distributing "rights" to gambling concessions, personal lending privileges, and the like. Because of the high monetary value of union leadership, there has been some invasion of the labor-union field by racketeers, aided and abetted by businessmen who hope to gain from racketeer control over unions. It is impossible to give an exact measure of the proportion of unions subject to racketeer control, but it clearly is a small fraction of the total.

---

[8] While the AFL-CIO unsuccessfully supported Stevenson in the 1956 presidential election, some success was achieved in certain areas of the country. See *New York Times,* December 3, 1956, p. 1.

3. FORMULATING A POLICY TOWARD LABOR UNIONS

Until fairly recently, a person's economic philosophy could be described largely in terms of his attitude toward labor. He was either "pro-labor" or "antilabor." Such a division of opinion was always superficial, but it almost sufficed for a period when a prominent characteristic of our economy was low pay and insecurity for labor.

The principle of labor unions has been accepted by many groups, even some of the most conservative. However, the appropriate scope, responsibility, and behavior of unions and their leaders are in great dispute. Much of the debate is conducted in fairly lofty terms like "democracy in unions," "responsibility of unions," "communism in unions," "freedom to work without being compelled to join any organization,"[9] "labor monopolies," and the like. However, there is essentially only one point at issue: Will a particular regulation increase union strength, and thereby raise the wages of union labor, or will it weaken unions and tend to lower the income of their members? In appraising the conflicting arguments about labor legislation, one is wise to look behind the principles allegedly involved and ask how the distribution of personal income would be affected. (This suggestion is not a counsel to ignore matters of principle. Rather it is a caution that principles espoused by both sides are largely window dressing covering their desire for increased bargaining power.)

How can an impartial person decide where he stands on issues involving labor and labor unions? An answer frequently offered is that he should favor measures that would make bargaining power equal. This is no answer, for no guide exists that shows when bargaining power is equal. A little reflection makes it obvious that relative bargaining power must be defined by the distribution of income to which its gives rise. More specifically, if one believes that the pay of labor is too low, the very probable conclusion is that its bargaining power is too weak. Conversely, only those who believe wages are too high will argue that the bargaining power of management is less than that of labor.

Those formulating their attitude toward labor unions cannot evade the necessity of deciding whether workers should be paid more than they receive at present.[10] This decision cannot be made on scientific grounds. It must rest on personal values. For this reason, the dispute between those for and those against labor's causes has continued to rage and can be expected to go on and on.

---

[9] This is the intent of the states' "right-to-work laws"; see discussion in Chapter 7.

[10] An equally significant question is whether real wages *can* be raised. Specifically, would a rise in money wages be accompanied by an equivalent increase in prices, leaving real wages unchanged?

D. Measures to Equalize Economic Opportunity

The most desirable way to equalize personal incomes would be through equalized productivity. More particularly, if the earning capacity of the lowest-income recipients could be raised, the distribution of personal income would tend to equalize automatically, provided obstacles to payment according to productivity were small. Greater income equality achieved in this way would have the advantage of increasing total output of goods and services, through enhanced productivity, rather than merely redistributing current levels of output.

An indeterminate, but certainly a large, proportion of the population has no opportunity to develop its latent productivity. A major obstacle to the full development of productive potentialities is the inability to afford training or education. Not only do job training and education usually require direct outlays, but they force an individual to give up the maximum income that he might have obtained as an unskilled or uneducated worker. A substantial number of the most promising graduates of high school are unable to afford further education.[11] It might be possible to protect children from the necessity of supporting sick parents before the children have had a chance to develop their productive capabilities, for example. Accordingly, extensive health and accident insurance for parents would greatly contribute toward the increased economic opportunity of their children.

Full equality of opportunity is impossible; one can only hope to make it more nearly equal. One of the more important influences on an individual's productivity is his parental guidance and inspiration, and it is beyond the power of the nation to equalize this. While there are high school graduates who would like to go on to college but cannot afford to do so, there are also perfectly capable graduates who, despite having the wherewithal, do not place any particular value on a higher education or even on special job training. Then, too, there are those unfortunate persons who, by reason of chronic illness or mental deficiency, can never contribute more than nominally to their own support (the number of these is generally larger than most people realize).

On the whole, however, greater equality of access to job training and higher education would contribute substantially toward income equality and higher total national output.

---

[11] For a brief summary of several factual surveys, see Joint Committee on the Economic Report, *Low Income Families and Economic Stability* (Washington, D.C.: Government Printing Office, 1949), pp. 16-19.

E. Other Measures

A variety of measures other than those mentioned here may be employed to equalize income. Among them are higher inheritance taxes; retraining and relocation of persons who are employed in declining industries or in depressed areas; and price supports such as those currently employed in agriculture. Perhaps the most direct and immediate method to reduce inequality is to increase government expenditures that provide goods and services directly to the needy—such as money supplements to low incomes to bring them up to a prescribed minimum, family allowances (payments to parents of large families according to the number of the children); housing subsidies and public housing; stamp plan and similar devices for providing necessities to the poor at extremely low prices; and public sickness insurance, free medical care, and enlarged old-age benefits.

II. FRICTION IN THE DETERMINATION OF INCOME

As indicated at the beginning of this chapter, friction—in the form of strikes, lockouts, boycotts, interrupted production in nonaffected industries, and interruption of supplies for consumers—frequently arises in the process of determining how much income individuals shall receive. Income determination has always involved some friction; however, its impact and its costliness have grown with the interdependence of all industry. An understanding of the causes and cures for this friction is one of the most urgent problems of present-day America. Indeed, some students of the problem have concluded that this friction is almost certain to increase and to make our type of economic system intolerable, and ultimately will force us to change to another type of system. (Some have attributed the rise of fascism in Germany and Italy to this very problem.)

It is not surprising that considerable disagreement is generated in the process of determining the size of incomes. In developed industrialized countries, the average person's desire for income is quite intense—enough to persuade him to do work that is generally irksome most of his waking time. It is to be expected that each person will seek as large a share of what is available for distribution as he can get. Since increases in any one person's share will usually reduce the income of someone else, deep disagreements are likely to arise.

Note that most people in the United States work for others. This fact holds, even though a large majority of the agricultural population is self-employed. The income of those who work for others is determined by a process ordinarily termed "bargaining." For the most part, up to

1933, wage bargains were arrived at between individual firms and individual employees. In effect, a firm offered a wage, and workers either accepted it or looked elsewhere for work. That process has changed into a negotiation procedure wherein spokesmen for labor and management, through discussion and argument (often profane and abusive), try to arrive at a satisfactory bargain. Almost always this negotiation procedure works. For every negotiation that fails to reach a mutually satisfactory agreement, thousands do end amicably. In view of the intense feeling on the part of both the workers and management about the matter, this high proportion of successes is striking. However, the failures are sufficiently numerous to cause the losses to society already alluded to, and there is reason to fear that these losses will mount in areas where the public is most immediately affected and where the social costs are greatest.

This gloomy forecast arises from what may be called the "stalemate" theory of labor strife. This theory holds that as the bargaining power of both sides in a negotiation process becomes more nearly equal, the difficulties of reaching mutually satisfactory agreement multiply, and disputes grow. The underlying basis for this view is that when both contestants are roughly equal in power, each is likely to misjudge his strength relative to the other. As a result, both sides demand more than the other side feels it must give, and deadlock ensues.[12]

In industries where the public would be severely injured by work stoppages, workers' bargaining power tends to be strong. At least, workers are encouraged to hold out for good terms in the certainty that strong measures will be taken by public officials to secure a speedy settlement; in practice this bargaining power usually results in the public's tendency to meet their demands. Similarly, industry is assured that it can afford to hold firm to its terms because the union will suffer adverse public relations in the event of a strike that greatly inconveniences the public.

Aside from these considerations, there has been a great growth in union strength, especially in industries where the public is most affected by a work stoppage—in transportation, steel, coal, freight loading, telephone, and even in such public services as garbage collection, and the like. In these industries, bargaining power is much more nearly equal than ever before. Neither side can present terms on a "take it or leave it" basis. The issues must be discussed and mutually agreeable terms reached, and this process does not always result in agreement.

There are, moreover, pressures within unions themselves that tend to foster strikes. These take the form of a general feeling that the workers never get enough and the "bosses" do not deserve what they get. In large measure this feeling rests upon the long history of labor relations in

---

[12] The protracted negotiations over the Korean armistice—the longest in military history—are an interesting parallel. Neither side was decisively beaten.

which most laborers were powerless and when incomes were relatively far more unequal than they are today (see Table 5). Past abuses are still fresh in the minds of most older members of a union, and they do not let their memories die. They are rehashed and probably exaggerated, so that even the younger men share the resentment of the older ones. The net result of this situation is that in almost every union some members will feel that the workers still do not get enough. They are likely to charge their union leadership with being too weak or ineffectual—or, sometimes, with being disloyal to the union. To weaken the appeal of this group—which threatens to displace incumbent leaders with others—union officers are sometimes forced into making demands and adopting aggressive tactics that they do not themselves approve.

III. SUMMARY AND CONCLUSIONS

It has been shown that the redistribution of income involves more than deciding from whom one wants to take it and to whom to give it. A free-enterprise system depends primarily upon monetary incentives to induce workers to put forth their greatest productive efforts. To tamper with personal incomes in certain ways might well reduce total output by dampening incentives. However, even under the stress of heavy personal income taxes, it seems that individuals continue to put forth as much effort as they did with lower rates. At some point the redistribution of income might so reduce the financial rewards of some persons that they would refuse to make efforts or take risks that serve all society.

It appears that considerable redistribution of personal income has taken place. The relative contribution toward this redistribution made by progressive taxes, minimum wages, and labor unions is not susceptible to measurement. Graduated income taxes and property taxes have clearly taken income from the rich and in that way have contributed toward greater equality; minimum-wage legislation has raised the incomes of the lowest paid workers (and possibly has caused some of them to be unemployed); labor unions probably have raised the share of income going to workers in unionized industries. Of the three, taxes would seem to have been most influential in redistributing income.

Has this redistribution gone as far as it should? The author thinks that the inequality of income in the United States, while considerable, no longer represents one of the foremost shortcomings of our economy. The redistribution since 1913 has led, after accounting for price changes but excluding income taxes, to a significant *decline* in the per capita real income of the top 1 per cent group, while the other 99 per cent have *gained* by 60 per cent of their 1913 level of living; the over-all share of the lower 95 per cent group rose from 74 per cent of the total income in

1920 to about 80 per cent in 1948. Further redistribution would be valuable, nonetheless. Perhaps the method of redistributing income in the future should be in ways that are especially helpful to the poorest people —more free education and training, free medical care, greater social insurance benefits and wider coverage, nondiscrimination based on race or religion, and the like. While equalization of opportunity is a method that all Americans can endorse in principle, many are reluctant to endorse the expenditures needed to put this principle into practice.

Profound changes have taken place in the American economy even since the major depression that started in 1929. Unions have become numerically large, financially strong, and politically effective. The progressive income tax has made deep inroads into the incomes of the wealthy. A political and economic philosophy adopted before, say, 1940, may not fit today's conditions. Economic betterment today calls primarily for increasing the total output of goods and services in which the whole population may share. Now the "liberal" must seek increased productivity rather than outright income redistribution.

On the matter of labor unions, where does the man who was strongly "prolabor" in the 1930's stand under existing conditions?

Strong unions sometimes seem merely to redistribute income among laborers, taking from those who are not unionized and therefore relatively weak and poorly paid. While the great growth in union strength since 1933 probably has made labor's share of the national income larger than it would have been otherwise, it seems also to have increased the inequality of income among workers themselves. All in all, the dramatic change in our economy since the major depression requires a revamping of positions taken on many economic issues before the changes occurred.

DISCUSSION QUESTIONS

1. In what ways can the government spend funds that benefit the poor primarily? What types of government expenditure benefit the prosperous primarily?

2. What type of tax is most likely to rest on the most wealthy members of the community? Which ones bear most heavily on the poor? Explain your answers.

3. What types of taxes are most likely to reduce total output? How?

4. Explain how high personal income tax rates may result in higher total output.

5. Can you think of any way of deciding how progressive personal income taxes should be?

6. Do you believe that the poorest people in the community should pay any taxes? Explain. Would you oppose any and all taxes that would be paid by very poor people?

7. Under what circumstances should a government not rely exclusively on personal income taxes? Why should it, otherwise, rely on that type alone?

8. Must laws that raise minimum wages reduce employment? Under what circumstances might they result in increased employment?

9. Does the relative stability of the share of income paid to labor prove that labor unions have not affected average real wages? Explain.

10. Can you provide measurable criteria of the balance of bargaining power? What criteria do you use in deciding whether "labor has become too strong" or "capital is too strong"?

11. Do you believe the contribution of unions to labor to be primarily financial? Indicate their major nonfinancial contributions.

12. What are the major barriers to advancement on the part of talented individuals in this country? By what measures could economic opportunity be made more equal?

13. How could you tell which party to a dispute was responsible? In what ways can management cause strikes?

14. If strikes are prohibited in industries vital to the national interest, whose bargaining power is curbed most, that of labor or management? How might the effect of such a ban on strikes be made to bear equally on both sides?

15. Do you believe that workers and management in industries vital to the national interest should be compelled to abide by compulsory arbitration? If you were part of management, would you favor compulsory arbitration? As a worker would you favor it? As an official of a labor union?

16. To what extent have labor unions widened the scope of their economic demands? List some of the newest demands in labor's collective bargaining arsenal.

SELECTED READINGS FOR PART 3

Burns, Eveline M. *Social Security and Public Policy.* New York: McGraw-Hill Book Company, Inc., 1956. Pp. xvi, 291. This book is a comprehensive study of the problems of social security. It deals with financial, administrative, and economic facets of social security and refers to various countries for comparative purposes.

Chamberlain, Neil W. *Labor.* New York: McGraw-Hill Book Company, Inc., 1958. Pp. viii, 625. An outstanding text on the economics of labor. The author deals with the historical, structural, collective-bargaining, and price aspects of labor in the United States.

Cochrane, Willard W., and Carolyn S. Bell. *The Economics of Consumption.* New York: McGraw-Hill Book Company, Inc., 1956. Pp. viii, 481. A very useful textbook on consumer behavior and problems concerning it. Expenditure patterns and similar considerations are dealt with, and valuable statistical material related to these subjects is presented.

Colm, Gerhard, and Theodore Geiger. *The Economy of the American People: Progress, Problems, Prospects.* Washington, D.C.: National Planning Association, 1958. Pp. viii, 167. This is a very helpful and informative explanation of the most significant factors which have helped to increase the productivity of the United States economy. The authors also discuss some of the most important economic problems besetting the economy today and the prospects for their solution.

Dahlberg, Arthur O. *National Income Visualized.* New York: Columbia University Press, 1956. P. 117. The author effectively puts into visual form such difficult concepts as the different segments of national-income accounting. The logic of the system of national income used today is made clear through diagrammatic techniques.

Kuhn, Alfred. *Labor: Institutions and Economics.* New York: Rinehart & Company, Inc., 1956. P. 616. Using collective bargaining as a unifying theme, the author treats the institutional and economic aspects of the history, methods, goals, and accomplishments of organized labor—and of management's responses.

Kyrk, Hazel. *The Family in the American Economy.* Chicago: University of Chicago Press, 1953. P. 424. A treatment of the economic function of the family as a social and economic institution. Deals mainly with the economic aspects of the family in the United States and presents many significant insights into the economic role of the family.

Lauterbach, Albert. *Man, Motives, and Money.* Ithaca, N.Y.: Cornell University Press, 1954. Pp. xiv, 366. The author deals with the psychological frontiers of economics, presenting an analysis of motivation in business which includes decision making, effects of government intervention, and social pressures. Relating personality and the social forces shaping it to economic motive, he qualifies greatly the concept of "economic man."

Miller, Herman P. *Income of the American People.* New York: John Wiley & Sons, Inc., 1955. Pp. xii, 187. This is an excellent treatment of the distribution of income in the United States by occupational groups, as well as along other functional lines. The 1950 and 1940 data, derived from the census, are compared. A wealth of statistics is presented.

Oliver, Henry M., Jr. *A Critique of Socioeconomic Goals.* Bloomington: Indiana University Press, 1954. Pp. vii, 191. A review of the basic assumptions of different social goals and their implications regarding the role of the state. Such basic views as welfare economics, the classical theory, and the like are dealt with and related to state intervention.

Sanders, Thomas H. *Effects of Taxation on Executives.* Boston, Mass.: Division of Research, Graduate School of Business Administration, Harvard University, 1951. Pp. xiii, 229. In this study the author presents the results of interviews of executives in different areas of business (banking, advertising, retailing, etc.) aimed at ascertaining the incentive function of taxes. His conclusion is that changes in tax rates have not affected executives' efforts in their jobs.

Strachey, John. *Contemporary Capitalism.* New York: Random House, Inc., 1956. Pp. viii, 374. This work by one of the spokesmen of British socialism takes a fresh look at the problems of contemporary economic institutions. The implications and effects of nationalization, income redistribution, etc. are viewed against the background of the British postwar experience.

United States Congress, Joint Committee on the Economic Report. *Character-*

istics of the Low-Income Population and Related Federal Programs. Washington, D.C.: Government Printing Office, 1955. Pp. xii, 240. This is an extremely important study of American low-income families, their work status, their income distribution, their size, etc. Government programs aimed at aiding such families are reviewed.

United States Department of Commerce. *National Income: 1954 Edition.* Washington, D.C.: Government Printing Office, 1954. Pp. v, 249. The revised edition of the Department of Commerce's analysis of the national-income accounts of the United States, indicating the source, methods, and actual series for the period 1929-1953. A most valuable basic work in national-income accounting.

United States Department of Labor, Bureau of Labor Statistics. *Brief History of the American Labor Movement* (rev. ed.). Washington, D.C.: Government Printing Office, 1957. Pp. vi, 85. This very useful popular sketch of the history of organized labor in the United States up to 1957 traces the main events from the beginnings of organized labor in the eighteenth century. In a concise manner the book effectively emphasizes the most significant facts and factors in the evolution of organized labor.

Wermel, Michael T., and Geraldine M. Beideman. *Supplemental Unemployment Benefit Plans: Their Economic and Industrial Relations Implications.* Pasadena: Industrial Relations Section, California Institute of Technology, 1957. P. 51. The reasoning for and against supplemental unemployment benefit plans is presented in a balanced manner. The authors give invaluable information on this new fringe benefit of collective bargaining.

Part

4 Is Big Business Too Big?

Chapter

9   Size and Growth

of American Business

I. INTRODUCTORY

Big business sometimes claims to be persecuted by the government. Government officials protest that they do not object to bigness as such, but seek only to eliminate monopoly, which is not always associated with bigness. The regulatory agencies of the government have declined to debate the merits of bigness in business *in itself*.

Many persons condemn bigness in business in and of itself. Part of the objection seems to be emotional and traditional. However, some sober criticisms have also been advanced. The defenders of big business, even outside its ranks, are more numerous than its critics.[1] They, too, base their praises largely on emotional grounds, but are able to advance strong arguments to support their conclusions. Whether big business is "good" or "evil" is one of the most heated public issues of the present day.

Popular consideration of bigness in business has suffered badly because of two errors. First, many persons have taken bigness to be synonymous with monopoly. Second, most people have considered the problem of bigness to be exclusively economic and have neglected other and equally important aspects of bigness.

II. BIGNESS DEFINED

Bigness, whether in business, labor, agriculture, government, education, or elsewhere, should be defined primarily in administrative terms. That is, bigness exists whenever many persons belong to an organization whose activities are determined by a few at its head. When bigness exists,

---

[1] An elaborate poll of a national sample of 1,227 persons to learn their attitudes toward big business was conducted by the Survey Research Center of the University of Michigan, and the results are reported in *Big Business As the People See It*, by B. R. Fisher and S. B. Withey.

many individuals must subordinate themselves to the directions of others and carry out the orders set down for them. Moreover, most persons in big organizations must work according to rules that are substituted for the personal direction of the few at the top of the organization. In addition, almost all employees in very large organizations are responsible for narrowly specialized tasks, and are divorced from contact with the final product or service provided by the organization. These conditions are associated with bigness in all types of organization. They exist whether the organization is a monopoly or faces rigorous competition from other large organizations.

A hypothetical example will crystallize the distinction between bigness and monopoly. Imagine that 200 huge business enterprises, each producing *all* possible goods and services and keenly contending with one another for markets, are the only firms in existence. Such a situation would, by definition, be competitive, but would also exemplify extreme bigness in business. To fill out the picture of extreme bigness without monopoly, we could imagine that there were 200 huge labor unions that represented the employees of each firm, and a strong central government that regulated the activities of both the business firms and labor unions. The condition depicted is one of extreme bigness without monopoly; in the view of many, the American way of life would be completely altered if such a condition were even remotely approached.

This section is rigorously confined to the problems of bigness and does not deal with the monopoly problem—despite the fact that bigness often results in monopoly. Part Five deals with the problems of competition and monopoly; to the extent that monopoly results from bigness, it is treated there. By treating bigness and monopoly separately, one both simplifies the problem of understanding them and makes clear that they often are unrelated. On the other hand, their interrelations are dealt with quite explicitly where they are relevant.

It should be emphasized that financial power (and the political power it sometimes is associated with) can give rise to monopoly in several ways. It can be used to win favors from government in the form of excluding foreign rivals through quotas and tariffs; it can be used to exclude newcomers from trades by requiring special licenses and the like. Thus a separation of bigness and monopoly is at least partly artificial. Although such a separation is made in this book, every attempt will be made to insure adequate treatment of this important connection between financial power and monopoly, or market power.

What Bigness Means to the Individual

FROM FAMILY HEAD TO HIRED HAND

HOW MANY PROMOTIONS BEFORE I'M A V.P. ?

I CAN'T SEE HOW I HELPED MAKE THIS

INFLEXIBILITY CUTS MY EFFICIENCY

GRAPHICS INSTITUTE, N. Y. C.

III.THE EXTENT OF BIGNESS IN
AMERICAN INDUSTRY

If we define bigness as a condition wherein many persons are part of organizations in which their activities are directed by a few with whom they have virtually no contact, how can we determine its extent? One might suppose that it would be simple to define and measure the size of business firms. Unfortunately, such is not true. Business size can be measured by at least ten different yardsticks,[2] and firms that are very large by one may be less impressive by another. From the standpoint of determining how many people are subordinated to the direction of a few remote top executives, it is best to measure business size by the number of employees in each firm. Equally common measures of business size are their total assets, income generation, sales volume, and net profits. None of these measures, including the number of employees in business firms, measures the property of "bigness" exactly. It is a condition that can be directly determined only by examining the internal structure of each enterprise and studying the relations between top management and individual employees and the managerial procedures employed.

Some problems arise even in the measurement of the employee size of American business. It is possible to attach different meanings to the word "business." Some definitions would include subsidiaries of a parent concern as part of the business, while others would exclude them. Some would include exclusive dealers and agents of a firm, while other definitions would not. Some would include government enterprises, philanthropic organizations, labor organizations, and financial concerns, while other definitions would not count them as business. As a practical matter, these problems create only slight difficulty for the student of this problem. He must accept the data that are available—and they unfortunately were not prepared with his purposes in view.

The most recent information describing employee size of business was compiled by the United States Department of Commerce. It is based upon the reports of individual businesses under the Old-Age and Survivors Insurance System, which requires reports from businesses on many matters, including the number of their employees. (Under this social insurance system, firms with fewer than four employees need not submit reports; consequently, information for the smallest firms is an estimate made by the Department of Commerce Office of Business Economics.)

Table 1 describes the employee size of the more than 4 million American businesses operating on January 1, 1951, outside the fields of agri-

---

[2] E. B. George, "How Big Is Big Business?" *Dun's Review,* March, 1939, p. 19.

Table 1. Per Cent Distribution of Firms and Employment within Industry

(Division by size of firm, 1951)

Industry Division	Number of employees							
	0 to 3	4 to 7	8 to 19	20 to 49	50 to 99	100 to 499	500 to 999	1,000 or more
Firms (January 1, 1951)								
All industries	74.7	12.6	7.7	3.1	1.0	0.7	0.1	0.1
Mining and quarrying	60.4	14.2	12.9	6.8	2.6	2.4	0.3	0.3
Contract construction	70.2	15.2	9.3	3.5	1.0	0.6	*	*
Manufacturing	42.5	16.1	17.8	12.0	5.4	5.0	0.6	0.6
Metals and metal products	37.5	14.7	18.3	13.3	6.4	7.1	1.1	1.2
Other manufacturing	43.9	16.4	17.6	11.7	5.1	4.5	0.5	0.4
Transportation, communication, and other public utilities	77.1	9.9	7.1	3.3	1.1	1.1	0.2	0.2
Wholesale trade	63.0	16.6	13.0	5.2	1.4	0.7	*	*
Retail trade	78.9	12.8	6.1	1.7	0.4	0.2	*	*
Finance, insurance, and real estate	80.9	10.5	5.7	1.8	0.6	0.5	*	0.1
Service industries	82.7	9.3	5.1	1.9	0.6	0.3	*	*
Paid employment (mid-March 1951)								
All industries	6.3	7.0	9.8	9.9	7.3	15.7	6.0	37.9
Mining and quarrying	2.1	3.5	7.2	9.2	7.9	22.0	8.6	39.5
Contract construction	10.1	12.9	17.6	16.7	11.4	18.2	4.6	8.6
Manufacturing	0.9	1.7	4.3	7.2	7.2	19.7	8.4	50.6
Metals and metal products	0.4	0.8	2.2	4.0	4.3	14.0	7.0	67.4
Other manufacturing	1.2	2.4	5.9	9.6	9.3	23.8	9.5	38.1
Transportation, communication, and other public utilities	2.0	2.3	3.8	4.4	3.5	10.1	5.2	68.7
Wholesale trade	7.3	10.7	19.3	18.9	11.8	16.0	4.1	12.1
Retail trade	14.8	16.3	17.5	12.1	6.0	8.2	2.7	22.5
Finance, insurance, and real estate	13.2	9.2	11.5	9.2	6.9	16.2	5.9	28.1
Service industries	15.8	13.5	17.1	15.8	10.5	15.9	3.6	7.8

* Less than 0.05 per cent.

SOURCE: U.S. Department of Commerce, *Survey of Current Business,* May, 1954, pp. 18, 23-24.

culture and the professional service. As this table indicates, only one business in 1,000 employs 1,000 or more employees. However, this tiny proportion of all businesses accounted for 38 per cent of all industrial employment.

The line between bigness and nonbigness in business can be drawn at any place. Since our definition of bigness runs in terms of subordination of individuals to remote executive direction, the line should hardly be drawn at less than 100 employees, and scarcely above 1,000. There is no need to be arbitrary on this point, however. We can determine the number of firms of various sizes.

Table 1 indicates that the overwhelming proportion of American businesses are very small. Three of every four had fewer than four employees, and seven of every eight employed fewer than eight persons. If information for agriculture and the professions were added, the proportions of small firms would be even greater. Nevertheless, Table 1 also makes it quite clear that most business in the United States is done by very large firms and that a large proportion of the labor force—a majority if one uses as his dividing line businesses with 100 employees or more—is employed in large concerns.

Bigness in business varies enormously from one sector of industry to another. The largest firms are to be found in manufacturing. This sector of industry is probably the most "strategic," for manufacturers seem to be able to influence strongly the firms from which they buy and through which they sell their output. However, manufacturing accounts for less than one quarter of all gainfully employed persons.

In 1951, more than 320,000 manufacturing firms were in operation. Of these, six firms in every thousand employed more than 1,000 workers, and these together accounted for half of all employment in manufacturing. Even in manufacturing, however, the average firm was small. More than 58 per cent of all manufacturing concerns had fewer than eight employees. They accounted for only 2.6 per cent of all employment in manufacturing, however. To examine the largest manufacturing firms closely, on January 1, 1958, the 25 largest manufacturing corporations possessed total assets of $60 billion.[3] In 1957, 39 manufacturing concerns had annual sales in excess of $1 billion.[4] Unfortunately, there are no convenient data describing the employee size of the nation's largest manufacturing firms.

It will be impossible, and it is unnecessary for our purposes, to summarize the very large body of available information describing the size of businesses. Instead of such a summary, the salient conclusions supported by the available evidence are set forth:

---

[3] Calculated from table in First National City Bank, *Monthly Letter*, September, 1958, p. 105.

[4] *Business Week*, April 26, 1958, p. 174.

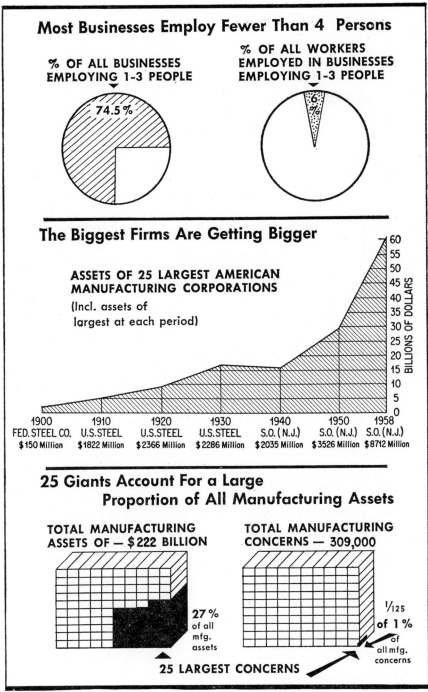

Most Businesses Employ Fewer Than 4 Persons

% OF ALL BUSINESSES EMPLOYING 1-3 PEOPLE

74.5%

% OF ALL WORKERS EMPLOYED IN BUSINESSES EMPLOYING 1-3 PEOPLE

6%

The Biggest Firms Are Getting Bigger

ASSETS OF 25 LARGEST AMERICAN MANUFACTURING CORPORATIONS

(Incl. assets of largest at each period)

BILLIONS OF DOLLARS

60 55 50 45 40 35 30 25 20 15 10 5 0

1900	1910	1920	1930	1940	1950	1958
FED. STEEL CO.	U.S.STEEL	U.S.STEEL	U.S.STEEL	S.O.(N.J.)	S.O.(N.J.)	S.O.(N.J.)
$150 Million	$1822 Million	$2366 Million	$2286 Million	$2035 Million	$3526 Million	$8712 Million

25 Giants Account For a Large Proportion of All Manufacturing Assets

TOTAL MANUFACTURING ASSETS OF — $222 BILLION

27% of all mfg. assets

TOTAL MANUFACTURING CONCERNS — 309,000

1/125 of 1% of all mfg. concerns

25 LARGEST CONCERNS

GRAPHICS INSTITUTE, N. Y. C.

1. A relatively small number of very large firms employ a large fraction of the nation's labor force.

2. The largest firms in the country now are far larger than they were even fifteen years ago.

3. The number of *small* firms in the country is far larger than at any time before World War II.

4. A substantial proportion of the labor force is engaged in agriculture, where the predominant production unit is the single-family farm, and in the professions, where the average business unit is also very small. The evidence upon which these four conclusions rest can be set forth very briefly. Table 1 supports the first conclusion, that a large proportion of the labor force is employed in firms with total employees of 50 or more. If we take 500 employees as the dividing line between big and small business, we find that 44 per cent of the industrial labor force is accounted for by large firms.

The great growth in the size of the largest business firms in the last fifty years is shown by Table 2, which describes the asset size of the 25 largest manufacturing firms in the nation in selected years since 1900. Unfortunately, similar compilations were made for firms outside manufacturing only in 1958.

The total number of concerns operating in December, 1957, exceeded 4.3 million. This figure should be compared with a total of 3.7 million in 1940 and 3 million in 1943. Almost the entire rise was accounted for by small firms. As we have seen, 7 of every 8 businesses employ fewer than eight persons. It thus appears that more than 3.7 million businesses operating in 1957 had fewer than eight employees.

No accurate measure is available of the number of firms operating in the United States over a very long period. The best information available suggests a steady rise since the depth of the depression, save for the effects of the war. Thus, even while the nation's largest firms were growing in size, the number of small firms was also expanding. (See Table 1.)

In appraising the prevalence of big business, it is important to take account of the occupational shifts in the population of the United States. Apart from the information presented in Table 1, which describes business size by industry divisions, it must be noted that a large proportion of the population is nonindustrial, and that the small unit is the dominant one in those occupations. Specifically, 9.6 per cent of the labor force was engaged in agriculture in 1957, and 10 per cent was in the professions.[5] The one-man or one-family unit is the most prevalent type in those fields.

It therefore is clear that business in the United States is not solely in the hands of huge business enterprises. Probably more than half the

---

[5] U.S. Department of Commerce, Bureau of the Census, *Current Population Reports*, P-50, No. 85, June, 1958, pp. 3, 36.

population is engaged in enterprises that have fewer than 100 employees. However, the number (though not necessarily the proportion) of employees in huge business enterprises has grown rapidly even in the last two decades.

There is no clear evidence that the proportion of total business or total employment accounted for by very large firms has increased. Measurements of bigness in business made in recent years reflect opposite movements. The over-all pattern seems to indicate an increase in concentration. The proportion of value added by manufacture accounted for by the 200 largest manufacturing concerns—one measure of bigness—rose from 30 per cent of the total in 1947 to 37 per cent of the total in 1954.[6] Other evidence shows that in some industries, such as beet-sugar refining and synthetic fibers, the growth of concentration was quite marked, while in other industries, such as manufacturing of motorcycles and typewriters, there was a decline in concentration.[7] Thus industrial concentration seems to have remained much the same over the last few decades. As one observer put it, "The extent of concentration shows no tendency to grow, and it may possibly be declining. Any tendency either way, if it does exist, must be at the pace of a glacial drift."[8]

There is no inconsistency between the conclusion that the size of the largest businesses has grown while industrial concentration has not. Concentration concerns the *proportion of total business or employment* accounted for by the largest firms; it does not depend directly upon the size of the largest businesses. If total employment rises faster than employment in large firms, concentration declines. Concentration can therefore fall while the size of the largest firms increases.

The foregoing review of evidence describing the prevalence of big business units does not in itself tell whether bigness in business is a major problem. It is conceivable that the existence of a few huge businesses could give rise to serious problems if in some way they were able to affect markedly all other firms (for example, if large firms acted as "leaders" or "policemen" and thereby determined what all firms did). Conversely, the existence of a large number of big businesses would be no ground for worry, because if the large number of firms checked one another, abuses arising would necessarily be short-lived. Accordingly, before the magnitude of the problems of big business can be assessed, it will

---

[6] See U.S. Senate. Committee on Judiciary. Subcommittee on Antitrust and Monopoly. 85 Congress. 1st Session. *Report* (Washington, D.C.: Government Printing Office, 1957).

[7] See U.S. Federal Trade Commission, *Report . . . on Changes in Concentration in Manufacturing, 1935 to 1947 and 1950* (Washington, D.C.: Government Printing Office, 1954).

[8] M. A. Adelman, "The Measurement of Industrial Concentration," *Review of Economics and Statistics*, November, 1951, p. 295.

be necessary to account for their effects. These will be discussed in the
following chapter.

**Table 2. Twenty-five Largest American Manufacturing
Corporations, Based on Reported Total Assets at
Beginning of Years 1900-1958**
(In millions)

1900		1910	
Federal Steel Co.	$ 150	U.S. Steel Corp.	$ 1,822
U.S. Leather Co.	137	Standard Oil Co. (1906)	372
Am. Steel & W. Co. of N.J.	106	American Tobacco Co.	286
Amer. Sugar Ref. Co.	102	Inter. Harvester Co.	173
Continental Tob. Co.	100	Amalgamated Corp. Co.	170
National Tube Co.	94	Central Leather Co.	138
American Tobacco Co.	77	Pullman Company	131
Am. Smelt. & Ref. Co.	74	Armour & Co.	125
National Steel Co.	73	Amer. Sugar Ref. Co.	124
Amer. Car & Fdy. Co.	69	U.S. Rubber Co.	121
American Woolen Co.	62	Am. Smelt. & Ref. Co.	119
National Biscuit Co.	58	Swift & Co.	113
Internat. Paper Co.	56	General Electric Co.	102
Republic In. & St. Co.	51	Corn. Prod. Ref. Co.	97
Amer. Tin Plate Co.	51	Amer. Car & Fdy. Co.	91
Glucose Sugar Ref. Co.	42	American Can Co.	90
Amer. Writ. Paper Co.	41	Lackawanna Steel Co.	88
Amer. Steel Hoop Co.	38	American Woolen Co.	86
Am. Hide & Lea. Co.	36	West. Elec. & Mfg. Co.	85
Swift & Co.	34	E. I. duPont Powd. Co.	75
Ten. C., I. & R. R. Co.	34	Republic In. & St. Co.	73
National Lead Co.	31	Va.-Car. Chem. Co.	72
General Electric Co.	30	Internat. Paper Co.	71
Union Bag & Pap. Co.	28	Bethlehem Steel Corp.	69
Rubber Goods Mfg. Co.	27	Amer. Locomotive Co.	69
Total	$ 1,601	Total	$ 4,762

1920		1930	
U.S. Steel Corp.	$ 2,366	U.S. Steel Corp.	$ 2,286
Stand. Oil Co. (N.J.)	853	Stand. Oil Co. (N.J.)	1,767
Armour & Co.	491	General Motors Corp.	1,325
Swift & Co.	490	Bethlehem Steel Corp.	802
General Motors Corp.	447	Anaconda Cop. Min. Co.	764
Bethlehem Steel Corp.	357	Ford Motor Co.	761
Ford Motor Co.	333	Stand. Oil Co. of N.Y.	708
U.S. Rubber Co.	320	Stand. Oil Co. (Ind.)	697
Stand. Oil Co. of N.Y.	300	Gulf Oil Corp.	687

1920		1930	
Midvale Steel & Ord. Co.	280	Shell Union Oil Corp.	662
General Elec. Co.	277	Texas Corp.	610
Inter. Harvester Co.	267	Stand. Oil Co. of Calif.	605
Sinclair Con. Oil Corp.	265	E. I. duPont deN. & Co.	542
Texas Company	261	General Electric Co.	516
Anaconda Cop. Min. Co.	254	Armour & Co.	452
Phelps Dodge Corp.	247	Sinclair Con. Oil Corp.	401
E. I. duPont deN. & Co.	241	Allied Chem. & Dye Corp.	388
Gulf Oil Corp.	218	Inter. Harvester Co.	384
Am. Smelt. & Ref. Co.	215	Western Electric Co.	373
American Tobacco Co.	206	Union Oil Co. of Calif.	370
Transcont. Oil Co.	198	Un. Carb. & Car. Corp.	354
Magnolia Petrol. Co.	182	Swift & Company	351
B. F. Goodrich Co.	176	Kennecott Cop. Corp.	338
Stand. Oil Co. of Calif.	174	Inter. Paper Co.	333
Pullman Company	171	Pullman, Inc.	316
Total	$ 9,589	Total	$16,792

1940		1949	
Stand. Oil Co. (N.J.)	$ 2,035	Stand. Oil Co. (N.J.)	$ 3,526
U.S. Steel Corp.	1,769	General Motors Corp.	2,958
General Motors Corp.	1,707	U.S. Steel Corp.	2,535
Socony-Vac. Oil Co.	930	E. I. duPont deN. & Co.	1,585
E. I. duPont deN. & Co.	858	Stand. Oil Co. (Ind.)	1,500
Bethlehem Steel Corp.	733	Socony-Vac. Oil Co.	1,443
Standard Oil Co. (Ind.)	723	Texas Company	1,277
Ford Motor Co.	692	Gulf Oil Corp.	1,191
Texas Corp.	661	General Electric Co.	1,177
Stand. Oil Co. of Calif.	629	Stand. Oil Co. of Calif.	1,075
Anaconda Cop. Min. Co.	588	Bethlehem Steel Corp.	1,029
Gulf Oil Corp.	523	Ford Motor Co. (1948)	1,026
Allied Chem. & Dye Corp.	405	Cities Service Co.	992
Inter. Harvester Co.	402	Western Electric Co.	786
Shell Union Oil Corp.	401	Un. Carbide & Car. Corp.	723
General Electric Co.	392	Sinclair Oil Corp.	710
Republic Steel Corp.	365	Westinghouse Elec. Corp.	694
Kennecott Cop. Corp.	361	American Tobacco Co.	687
Consolidated Oil Corp.	358	Inter. Harvester Co.	672
Un. Carbide & Car. Corp.	337	Anaconda Cop. Min. Co.	660
Swift & Co.	312	Shell Union Oil Corp.	641
Armour & Co.	303	Allied Chem. & Dye Corp.	597
American Tobacco Co.	291	Phillips Petroleum Co.	579
Western Electric Co.	288	Kennecott Cop. Corp.	575
Aluminum Co. of Am.	251	Chrysler Corporation	541
Total	$16,314	Total	$29,179

1958			
Standard Oil Co. (N.J.)	$ 8,712	Chrysler Corporation	1,497
General Motors Corp.	6,826	Sinclair Oil Corp.	1,481
U.S. Steel Corp.	4,074	Union Carbide Corp.	1,456
Gulf Oil Corp.	3,241	Westinghouse Elec. Corp.	1,401
Ford Motor Co.	3,114	Shell Oil Co.	1,385
Socony Mobil Oil Co.	3,105	Western Electric Co.	1,329
Texas Company	2,729	Aluminum Co. of Amer.	1,316
Standard Oil Co. (Ind.)	2,535	Cities Service Co.	1,279
E. I. duPont deN. & Co.	2,519	Inter. Bus. Mach. Corp.	1,087
General Electric Co.	2,361	Anaconda Co.	1,030
Bethlehem Steel Corp.	2,260	Inter. Harvester Co.	1,021
Stand. Oil Co. of Calif.	2,246	Republic Steel Corp.	930
Phillips Petroleum Co.	1,520	Total	$60,454

SOURCE: National City Bank, *Monthly Letter,* June, 1949, p. 70, and First National City Bank, *Monthly Letter,* September, 1958, p. 105.

Before we turn to an evaluation of big business, we shall explain the means by which the nation's largest firms attained their great size. In part we shall try to discover whether bigness in business is inevitable; in part we shall inquire whether it is the result of efficiency and superior contribution to the nation.

IV. FACTORS CONTRIBUTING TO THE GROWTH OF LARGE BUSINESSES

Our purpose is not to account for the size of all firms, but simply to explain by what methods the very largest firms in the country attained their size. Large firms have come into being by two primary methods: first, by combining with or acquiring other firms; second, by internal growth. These two broad methods of increasing business size can be carried out by a variety of specific means, which will be described briefly.

Growth of business size, whether through combination or internal growth, has been facilitated enormously by the corporate form of business organization. Without it, businesses would hardly have reached their present huge size. Accordingly, before discussing business growth through combination and internal growth, the contribution of the corporate form of organization to the creation of large businesses will be explained.

A. Contribution of the Corporate Form to the Growth of Big Businesses

The corporation is a form of enterprise created by law. It may be considered a legal invention produced primarily to meet the need for increased financial resources in business. Up to 1811, when New York passed the first general incorporation law, each corporation had to obtain the privilege to operate by special act of a state legislature. At present, and in almost every state since 1850, private business corporations come into existence by complying with conditions laid down in a general incorporation law. It has become extraordinarily simple to obtain a corporate charter, largely because of competition among states for the lucrative business of granting charters. Several states, Nevada and Delaware particularly, make incorporation essentially a matter of paying a specified fee.[9]

The contribution of the corporate form to the growth of large firms is best understood if corporations are contrasted with the "common law," or older, forms of business organization, for example, the individual proprietorship and partnership. The latter two forms imposed severe financial risks on those interested in a business. They had to put their entire personal fortunes in jeopardy if they became principals in a business undertaking. Under the corporate form, owners could not lose more than the funds they directly invested through the purchase of stock; their property outside the business could not be touched by creditors of the corporation. The corporation therefore provided an instrument whereby those who were interested only in investing in an enterprise, but not in taking responsibility for its direction, could do so without inordinate risk. It is this feature of "limited liability" that represents the big contribution of the corporate form. Other features, such as continuous life of the business even beyond the life of its principals, are far less significant.

In the eyes of the law, corporations are distinct and separate entities. They are controlled by those of its owners who own voting stock. Stock certificates are documents that give evidence of ownership. (They should not be confused with bonds, which are evidence of debt.) There are various types of stock certificates which carry different privileges. Beyond variations in the voting privileges, they also convey different rights to share in the profits of the corporation. The most important classes of stock are "common stock" and "preferred stock," though there are important subclasses of each type. Typically, owners of common stock have a right to vote; preferred stockholders customarily do not have the voting privilege. As owners, neither type of stockholder is "guaranteed" or "owed" any profits. If the firm makes profits, the preferred stockholders are the first to share in them, but their share generally is limited to a fixed sum. That is, owners of preferred stock may be entitled to receive 6 per cent of the face value of their stock before any funds can be paid to holders of common stock. However, if the profits earned by the corporation are large, the common stockholders may obtain payments without any upper limit.

---

[9] For an extensive discussion of the background of the corporation, see D. F. Pegrum, *The Regulation of Industry* (Homewood, Ill.: Richard D. Irwin, Inc., 1949), pp. 54-72.

As is true of political states, corporations are managed by a system of representative government. Holders of voting stock elect a board that sets down the broad policies under which appointed executives operate the enterprise. The voting privilege is not equal; individuals can vote once for every share of voting stock they own. Periodically there are elections of members of the board of directors. At such times the corporation's officials mail an announcement of the election to all owners of voting stock. They enclose a "proxy," which is a slip of paper that permits the stockholder, simply by affixing his signature, to transfer his voting power to persons designated on the form. Only a trifling proportion of all stockholders vote their stock in person in large corporations. Ordinarily, more than half the stock in large corporations is voted by proxy.

As a general rule, the top executives "control" large corporations through their ability to mail proxy forms to the stockholders at the corporation's expense. Their power of control is due to the inertia of small stockholders and their hesitation to transfer their voting privilege to persons who are unknown to them. Whatever the reasons, most stockholders as a matter of routine return their proxies and give the incumbent management the power to elect the members of the board of directors.

It should be clear from the foregoing description of the corporate form of organization that it is a potent instrument for the creation of large firms. It greatly enhances the attractiveness of investment in business by removing the huge risk attaching to investment in other forms of business. Great power is put in the hands of a few persons who control the corporation. High among the powers of these persons is the ability to increase the firm's stock issue and to use the new stock to purchase almost anything they wish. As a matter of record, persons in control of very large corporations have not infrequently issued stock to pay for other businesses. In other words, corporations that are successful have the power to create something—additional stock in their business—that is almost the equivalent to money, and frequently this stock has been used to purchase other firms.

The corporation has given rise to some abuses, most of which are caused by the fact that many investors in corporations have little influence over their direction. Sometimes those who control a corporation seek to enrich themselves at the expense of other owners. One particular abuse, which is related particularly to the growth in business size, is the practice on the part of "promoters" of reorganizing corporations and fostering mergers and acquisitions in order to "earn" themselves a profit.[10] Usually

---

[10] One student of mergers, Jesse W. Markham, asserts that the most important motive for mergers during the height of merger movements has been promotional profits. See Universities-National Bureau Committee for Economic Research, *Business Concentration and Price Policy* (Princeton, N.J.: Princeton University Press, 1955), pp. 180-182.

large corporate mergers have been accompanied by a big payment to the persons who engineered them. (These persons are generally called "promoters.") Sometimes the payments were so great that they could be interpreted only as excessive fees paid with the approval of the top executives who presumably shared in them. The ability to reward oneself richly for engineering a merger gave rise to mergers in large numbers. Rewards for the promoters rather than greater operating efficiency or increased profitability for owners was the major motive for many mergers or acquisitions. Of course, there were other reasons for merger, like the desire to eliminate troublesome rivals, to diversify the firm's product line, to acquire properties and personnel more inexpensively than by constructing a new plant, and to achieve some operating economies.

It should therefore be clear that the invention and extension of the corporate form of business organization greatly fostered the growth of business enterprises. Beyond the effects already mentioned, it will be shown that a particular form of corporation—the holding company—added a new and ingenious means for increasing the size of business firms.

B. Growth through Combining with or Acquiring Rivals

Combination of established firms can be effected by three major methods: direct acquisition, merger, and formation of holding companies. The distinction between acquisition and merger is not sharp. Acquisition means the purchase of the assets or controlling stock of one firm by another with the intention of operating both under common ownership and direction. Where acquisition occurs, the acquiring firm takes the initiative in bringing the two firms together, and it determines how the new firm is to be operated, and its name remains and applies to the new larger unit. The top management of a firm that has been acquired loses its independent status, and often is not incorporated into the larger firm.

Merger represents an agreement among independent firms to form a new firm of which they will form a part. Typically, the large firm will bear a new name, and the component firms pool their executives according to a prearranged plan to direct the new enterprise.

One can distinguish between different types of combinations.[11] Some combinations are of firms in the same line of business that perform the same productive operations. These are termed "horizontal combinations." Others bring together firms in different stages of the same industry—such as a combination of firms manufacturing, wholesaling, and retailing

---

[11] For an analysis of recent mergers and their impact on market structure, see J. W. Markham, "Merger Policy under the New Section 7: A Six Year Appraisal," *Virginia Law Review,* May, 1957, pp. 489-528.

shoes. These are called "vertical combinations." Still other combinations of firms in different industries are called "conglomerate combinations." The most numerous type has been the horizontal combination.

Acquisition and merger have been the chief methods whereby the nation's largest firms have grown. Growth by merger and acquisition occurs every year, but it has been concentrated in several periods. The first and most important is generally dated 1897-1903; the second, between 1925 and 1929; the third between 1940 and 1947; and the last since 1948.

The contribution of mergers and acquisitions to the formation of the nation's largest businesses might be measured by the number and assets of the firms that disappeared in the process, or by listing the names of very large firms that grew by bringing together many small or moderate-sized firms. Unfortunately, detailed and reliable information on the number of firms disappearing through merger and acquisition is available only since 1919; data on the amount of assets held by the firms that disappeared and by those that acquired them is available only since 1940. For the first merger period, we must rely on the names of the large firms that were formed by combination. The available information yields the following description of the four merger periods.

1. During the early period, 1897 to 1903, 234 of the 318 firms that one authority listed as trusts in 1903 were formed by merger during this period.[12] The industries chiefly affected by mergers during the period of 1897 to 1903 were petroleum, iron and steel, copper, lead, sugar, paper, linseed oil, starch, salt, powder, cans, whiskey, cottonseed oil, and coal.[13]

2. The number of concerns in manufacturing and mining alone, that disappeared between 1925 and 1929, was 4,583.

3. Between 1940 and 1947, more than 2,450 formerly independent manufacturing and mining companies disappeared through merger and acquisition. The assets of these firms totaled $5.2 billion, equal to more than 5 per cent of the total assets of all manufacturing and mining corporations in the country.[14]

4. From 1948 to 1954, more than 1,770 firms in the mining and manufacturing industries were absorbed through merger and acquisition, and from 1951 through 1956 the total in all areas was 4,686.[15]

---

[12] *T.N.E.C. Monograph No. 27*, p. 231. The authority was Moody, and the list of trusts is presented in his book, *The Truth about the Trusts* (New York: Moody Publishing Company, 1904).

[13] V. Mund, *Government and Business* (New York: Harper & Brothers, 1950), p. 96.

[14] Federal Trade Commission, *Summary of the Report on the Merger Movement* (Washington, D.C.: U.S. Government Printing Office, 1948).

[15] Federal Trade Commission, *Report on Corporate Mergers and Acquisitions* (Washington, D.C.: Government Printing Office, 1955), and National Industrial Conference Board, *Business Record*, May, 1957, p. 216. From 1919 to 1956 more than 13,800 mergers and acquisitions occurred in mining and manufacturing. See Markham, *loc. cit.*, p. 527.

As has been indicated, new firms can be acquired and mergers can be effected without raising any new funds. Firms can be paid for by an exchange of newly issued stock in the acquiring firm for the assets of the firm that is acquired. Similarly, mergers can be carried out, and usually are, by exchanging stock in the new firm for the securities of the component firms out of which it will be formed. It thus appears that successful corporations have the ability to create the purchasing power they need in acquiring other businesses.

C. Growth by Means of Holding-Company Formations

The holding company has played a notable role in the formation of some of the nation's largest firms. Among the best-known holding companies are The American Telephone and Telegraph Company; the United States Steel Corporation; Sears, Roebuck and Company; the Standard Oil Company of New Jersey; and the National Dairy Products Corporation. In 1936, 70 per cent of the 475 largest industrial corporations controlled at least one other firm through ownership of its securities.[16] Holding companies have been especially prominent in the formation of large public-utility systems; in 1929, three holding companies controlled 45 per cent of the total energy generated by the public utilities.[17]

A holding company is itself a corporation. Its assets include enough shares of voting stock of other businesses to control them. Holding companies are formed, like other businesses, for the profit of their owners. When competing firms are combined, the owners may profit primarily from the control over price that their holdings give them. Not infrequently, holding companies have sought to profit by selling goods and services at excessive prices. Their control over operating companies permits them to dictate from whom they shall make purchases.

The holding company contributed to the growth of big business for two major reasons. First, it provided a relatively inexpensive way of acquiring control over businesses. Second, it offered a way of unifying rivals just at the time when the antitrust laws outlawed certain other important methods that were being used to bring rival firms together under single control.

Control of many firms can be acquired inexpensively by means of a pyramid of holding companies; that is, by forming holding companies that control other holding companies. A simple hypothetical example will show how this would work.

Assume that 12 rivals operate in one industry and that a group of men agree to eliminate competition in the industry by obtaining control

---

[16] H. G. Guthmann and H. E. Dougall, *Corporate Financial Policy* (New York, Prentice-Hall, Inc., 1940), pp. 618-619.

[17] The Twentieth Century Fund, *Electric Power and Government Policy* (New York: The Twentieth Century Fund, Inc., 1948), p. 31.

over all of them. Their financial resources might not permit them to purchase all 12 operating companies outright. If each of the 12 corporations had *voting* stock outstanding that sold for $10 million, the group would have to spend about $5 million to gain control over each one—or $60 million for all 12.

Instead of acquiring the stock in the 12 companies directly, a company could be established to acquire enough stock to control in the 12 companies, which we saw would cost $60 million. The group need only acquire a controlling interest in the company holding the stock—which would cost a maximum of $30 million—in order to control the 12 operating companies. (The other $30 million needed to acquire the controlling interest in the 12 operating companies would be provided by persons who would be induced to purchase stock in the holding company.) Thus, with $30 million, the group could acquire control of 12 operating companies with voting stock of $120 million. This sum could be further reduced by forming two layers of holding companies.

Instead of a single holding company, four holding companies could first be formed, each holding a controlling proportion of the voting stock of three operating companies. In our example, each holding company would hold $15 million of voting stock ($5 million of each company). Each holding company would, in turn, issue stock worth $15 million (with which it would acquire a controlling amount of the voting stock of the operating companies). This stock in turn could be purchased by other holding companies. Say, two holding companies were formed, each to acquire over two of the four holding companies.

These two holding companies need acquire only 50 per cent of the voting stock of two holding companies, at a maximum cost of $15 million in our example. Control of these two holding companies could be gained by acquiring half their voting stock—that is, a maximum of $15 million of stock. In turn, the necessary investment to control the 12 operating companies could be cut in half by setting up a single holding company to acquire the two holding companies, which owned a controlling interest in the four holding companies that in turn controlled the 12 competing operating companies. Thus control over operating companies with voting stock of $120 million could be acquired with an outlay of $7.5 million.

How this pyramid operates is depicted visually in the diagram below.

Holding companies that control operating companies, that is, companies that actually produce products or services, are called "first-degree" holding companies. Those that control other holding companies, which control operating companies, are called holding companies of second degree, and so on. In our illustration, we had a holding company of the third degree.

A HYPOTHETICAL HOLDING COMPANY PYRAMID

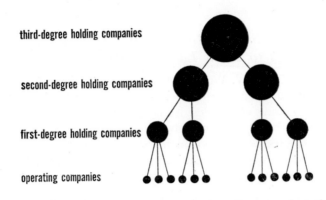

third-degree holding companies

second-degree holding companies

first-degree holding companies

operating companies

The example given was extreme on several scores, but the under-lying principle illustrated holds nevertheless. In practice, not all stock in corporations carries the voting privilege, so that to gain control of a corporation could involve ownership of only a tiny proportion of all out-standing stock. Moreover, holding companies could raise most of their funds by selling bonds that likewise do not carry the voting privilege. Furthermore, it rarely is necessary to hold 50 per cent of a corporation's voting stock to control it. In large corporations 15 to 20 per cent is gen-erally sufficient, because a large proportion of stockholders do not exer-cise their voting power, or, if they do, they serve completely as a rubber stamp for the incumbent management. For these reasons, a pyramid of holding companies can achieve control over far more assets per dollar of investment than has been illustrated here. And it must not be forgot-ten that control over both operating and holding companies can be ef-fected by exchanging stock in a "higher" holding company, that is, one farther removed from the operating companies. The potentialities of the pyramiding of holding companies is illustrated by the achievement of Howard Hopson, who gained control over a public utility empire with assets of 1 billion dollars by holding only $100,000 of voting stock.

Holding companies are found in all branches of industry. They are numerically most important, and pyramiding was carried farthest in the public utility field.

The holding company assisted the growth of large firms in a manner beyond and above the economy it permits in acquiring control over other firms. It provided a substitute for the "trust" device, which was the favorite means for combining rival firms, before the trust was outlawed by several state legislatures. At that time New Jersey granted permission to form holding companies, and trusts were reformed in holding-company form, and further "trustification" was carried out through this handy substitute. Almost certainly, industrial enterprises would be substantially smaller than they are today if the holding company had not been legalized.

D. Motives for the Merger and Acquisition of Business to Form Larger Units

Professor Myron W. Watkins, in his analysis of the factors causing industrial consolidation, attributes relatively little weight to the desire to achieve operating economies. As he properly points out, the method of consolidation by combining firms of small or medium size affords only slight technological advantage. In his view, the main factors were not technical economies but financial and strategic advantages. The financial motive had many facets.

It included along with promoter's profits and prospective underwriting fees some genuine economic advantages in the way of access to the capital market and a certain flexibility resulting from the diversification of corporate securities. But it is hard to escape the conclusion that the major "financial" advantage sought and secured by corporate consolidation was the opportunity afforded, through the dispersion of ownership interests and through the erection of intricate, pyramided, labyrinthine, corporate structures for the manipulation of corporate funds, corporate policies and corporate accounts by "insiders," or irresponsible "outsiders," to their own enrichment and without regard to the interests of the enterprise, the workers, the stockholders, or, least of all, the consumers.[18]

No one would deny that some mergers and acquisitions were effected in order to create a more efficient organization. At best, there must be some disagreement about the relative importance of the various motives underlying merger and acquisition. Yet it seems manifest that strong motives other than economic efficiency were involved; it would be unwarranted to assume that mergers or acquisitions contributed either to economic efficiency or to greater profitability for investors. Such studies as have been made of the financial experience of consolidated firms show that they were not clearly either more or less profitable than firms that had not been consolidated.

---

[18] *T.N.E.C. Monograph No. 13, Relative Efficiency of Large, Medium-Sized and Small Business* (Washington, D.C.: Government Printing Office, 1941), p. 135. Jesse Markham contends that relatively few mergers in the twentieth century have had market monopolization as their direct goal. Rather, the most important goal has been promotion profits. Although this statement may be true, other students of the problem emphasize that, regardless of the motive, the effects have been a significant amount of concentration in economic power. See Universities-National Bureau Committee for Economic Research, *Business Concentration and Price Policy*, pp. 180-182, for Markham's position, and pp. 182-212 for different positions by Walter Adams and George W. Stocking.

E. Internal Growth

Very few of the nation's largest firms achieved their present stature without combining with many formerly independent firms. Among the nation's largest firms, only the Ford Motor Company, Goodyear, Firestone, the Singer Sewing Machine Company, and the Aluminum Company of America expanded primarily by means of internal growth. In other large firms, combinations of all types have figured prominently in the expansion of size.

Some internal growth will occur in every successful enterprise. And much of the growth in business size indicated by Table 2 between 1930 and 1956 is attributable almost entirely to internal growth. The consolidation movement of post-World War II was confined largely to business of medium size, and not the very largest in the country.

Internal growth at least superficially seems to be closely connected with operating efficiency. On the face of things, businesses that expand simply respond to consumer preference for their goods over those offered by rivals, or to a better price. No doubt considerable internal growth comes in response to exactly this kind of pressure. However, even in financing internal growth, promoters have played a big part, especially during the 1920's, when there was a large market for corporate securities. Executives in control of some large corporations were persuaded to float new security issues by investment banks which could make a handsome profit on their distribution. It may be assumed that corporation executives shared, in one way or another, in these profits.

Especially since the end of World War II, internal growth of corporations has been financed without public security issues. More than half the large corporate profits after taxes were retained and used to finance expansion. A combination of high and fairly secure demand generated by the war, the defense program following World War II, and high profits gave rise to rapid internal growth of corporations.

F. Miscellaneous Factors Influencing Business Expansion

Motives other than the direct pursuit of profit account for the persistent growth of businesses that are already large. Much of the increased average size of business units has resulted from the addition to the firms' offerings of new, and frequently dissimilar, products. In part, such growth may result from the desire to increase the firm's security of income, through greater diversification of risk. (Frequently diversification of product offerings results from the attempt to effect production economies also.) Sometimes a firm expands by adding a new product because the research department turned it up in the course of seeking something else.

In addition, there doubtless are many subtle pressures and vague motives that encourage the expansion of large businesses.[19] Growth of a business is, in and of itself, accepted as evidence of success. Moreover, the larger the business, the greater the power of executives to hand out contracts and to give employment. These activities generally give personal satisfaction and a feeling of power; they also may create obligations to those who hand out these favors that may rebound to the financial advantage of the executives of an expanding corporation. To undertake an expansion may transform a job that has become fairly routine into an exciting and significant activity.

From the foregoing account of the means by which the largest firms attained their great size, several conclusions emerge. First, the growth of business size was only in part a response to the desire to gain increased operating economies; second, the desire to obtain profits by promoting mergers and acquisitions, and from the sale of newly authorized securities, was a potent motive for growth which may have caused expansions in the face of diseconomies; third, in recent years, internal growth seems to be the most common form of growth among the largest firms.

V. SUMMARY AND CONCLUSIONS

We have seen that some huge businesses operate in the United States; all combined, the largest firms in the country account for a significant proportion of total employment. However, a substantial majority of the population is employed in firms with fewer than 100 employees. Enterprises with less than eight employees account for about 87 per cent of total businesses, but for only a small proportion of industrial employment (13 per cent).

There is no evidence that the *proportion* of the population employed in huge enterprises has increased over the last two decades or more. However, the absolute size of business firms has increased at a rapid rate; the big firms are considerably bigger now than they were in, say, 1929. As we define "bigness," which is the subordination of many individuals in an organization to the direction of a few, with remoteness of the individual from the final output of the organization, it seems to be on the increase. It is difficult to discern any tendencies under way that will reduce the employee size of the nation's largest firms.

The increase in bigness has not been accompanied by a decline in the number of small one-family businesses. At least since World War II, the number of small firms has risen sharply. Thus we find no terrifying trend

---

[19] One interesting analysis of the growth of firms focuses attention on an inherent predisposition to expansion found in the very nature of business firms. See Edith Penrose, "Limits to the Growth and Size of Firms," *Papers and Proceedings of the American Economic Association,* May, 1955, pp. 531-543.

toward a concentration of all industry in the hands of a few monster businesses, even though the largest firms are growing even larger.

Most of the largest firms became large partly by combining with other firms. The corporate form, and in particular the holding company, contributed significantly to the growth of the firms in operation today. Almost all huge firms also grew considerably on their own, primarily through the reinvestment of profits.

The growth of large businesses cannot be explained, for the most part, as either efforts to achieve economies, or as a response to past operating success. Financial motives, whereby promoters enriched themselves through high promotional fees, were important in accounting for the several periods of feverish merger and consolidation of business. In part, consolidations were due to efforts to gain control over a market, rather than to achieve operating economies. The bigness of a business most emphatically cannot be taken as proof that it is efficient.

DISCUSSION QUESTIONS

1. How would you distinguish between bigness and monopoly? Why is the distinction important?

2. If you were the top executive of a large corporation with an annual salary of $250,000, would you desire to have the corporation expand? Explain your answer.

3. If a law were passed which made it illegal for large corporations (above a particular size) to expand their sales volume, would such corporations be subject to pressures to produce efficiently and give good consumer service? If so, what are these pressures?

4. In what way did the legalization of the holding company contribute to the growth of very large firms?

5. If you were starting a new small business, would you start a corporation or an individual enterprise? Why? Would the opportunity to pool large numbers of small pools of capital be a significant advantage to you? Explain.

6. Do you have personal knowledge of any business acquisitions? Do you know, or can you guess, the motives of the acquiring firm? Of the acquired firm? What happened to the management of the acquired firm?

7. Would you generalize about the difference in motive and consequences between business growth through combination and that through internal growth?

8. What measure of business size do you consider most appropriate for a discussion of "bigness"? Explain several alternatives and indicate the reasons for your preference.

10 Results of Bigness
in Business

Is bigness in business a good or a bad thing? Does it threaten our very way of life? Unfortunately, these questions cannot be answered directly by empirical studies. Many of the effects or alleged effects of bigness are of a type that are not amenable to factual study. In addition, bigness raises important issues of personal preference, and these cannot be settled by any type of evidence.

Accordingly, we shall limit ourselves to an examination of the major arguments favoring and opposing big business. As far as possible, evidence will be adduced to judge the validity of these arguments. This review of both sides of the question will clear the ground so that everyone can make his own evaluation of the major merits and demerits of bigness.

I.   ARGUMENTS IN FAVOR OF BIG BUSINESS

One argument in favor of big business overshadows all others. It holds that big businesses are more efficient than smaller firms and consequently can produce at a lower cost and sell at a lower price. We shall examine this argument closely, for it is widely held, despite considerable evidence to the contrary. In addition to the allegation that very large firms are most efficient, it is also contended that they offer the following advantages: they are more scrupulous in observing the law than are smaller firms, they simplify the mobilization of industry for war, and they facilitate economic controls during such emergencies as depression and inflation.

The following analysis of the consequences of big business will not contrast them with those of small business; they will be compared with those of all other sizes of firms. The question under discussion is, in part, What is gained by having huge firms such as General Motors and United States Steel, rather than those no larger than Studebaker and Inland Steel?

A. Are the Largest Firms the Most Efficient?

Before we can hope to know whether the largest firms are the most efficient, we must make clear what we mean by "efficient." The word is used in two senses. First, the business with the lowest unit cost of production can be adjudged the most efficient, no matter why its costs were low. Second, only firms that use a minimum of all factors of production to turn out a unit of output would be considered most efficient. While firms efficient in the first sense might also be efficient in the second, they need not be so. To illustrate, a firm might incur exceedingly low unit costs simply because it acquired its plant and equipment at an extremely low price from a bankrupt concern. This firm might use more labor, raw materials, and the like per unit than others in the industry with similar equipment, and still have the lowest unit costs. Should we consider the firm efficient or inefficient? Clearly, it was "efficient" or "wise" to buy its plant and equipment when it did, but the firm is not being run efficiently at present. Since it was using more factors of production than were needed, it could be charged with a waste of resources. Some of these resources could have been transferred to other employments where they would have added valuable goods and services to national output.

Consider a situation where the difference in efficiency judged by money costs and by quantities of productive resources is more directly related to size of firm. Take two companies that are equally efficient in the sense that they use equal quantities of productive factors to turn out a unit of output. Assume that the large one possesses great buying power and purchases its supplies at half the price paid by smaller firms, so that its money costs are substantially lower than those of the smaller one. Would it be correct to say that the larger firm was the more efficient? The larger one did not reduce the amount of productive resources that it or other firms required to turn out the final product; it merely lowered the price it paid to other firms for supplies and parts. In effect, the large concern reduced the proportion of its income paid to other firms and increased the proportion it retained for itself. It used its bargaining power to redistribute income between itself and its suppliers in its own favor. It did not, however, increase the total output of goods that could be produced with a given quantity of resources.

From the community's point of view there is an enormous difference between lowering money costs by exerting bargaining power and by smaller use of productive resources for each unit of output. The first does not add to the total quantity of goods that the community will possess; the second does. It takes only a moment's reflection to recognize that if we do not improve the use made of the productive factors, we cannot hope to increase their output, no matter how much one firm pays another for its supplies. Accordingly, it is imperative to distinguish these two types of efficiency. The first will be called "bargaining-power advantages"; the second will be termed "real advantages." To the individual businessman, of course, both types are equally real, and he is likely to resent the distinction. To the economist, the distinction is significant, and yet empirically he has great difficulty in keeping the two distinct.

What "real advantages" do very large firms possess over those of smaller size? Very large concerns generally are credited with ability to use complex machinery and to subdivide productive tasks until they yield the full possible benefits of specialization. That is, the advantages of large firms are ordinarily conceived to be advantages *in production,* rather than in selling, management, financing, research, and the like. Do the largest firms in an industry, in fact, produce on a larger scale than those of medium size in the same industry?

At first this question may seem ridiculous, for it appears to ask whether big firms are bigger than medium-size firms. What is meant by "produce on a large scale"? It means something other than to produce a large quantity under a single ownership. It means to produce a large amount *within a single plant.* For example, take two companies producing petroleum products. Say one has *total* production that is 10 times as great as that of the other. Assume also that the first operates 50 refineries and the second operates 5, and that all 55 refineries are of the same size. We would say that both companies produced on the same scale. The larger would not be able to use more complex machinery and subdivide its production tasks more finely than the second. *Advantages of size in production are all obtained within a single plant.* Large businesses need not produce on a larger scale than small ones. The reverse is quite possible; for example, United States Steel, the largest producer of steel, actually produces less in each of its plants than some of the smaller steel companies.

Examine any of the industries where the largest firms in the nation are to be found, and you will find that they usually operate many plants to perform similar operations. The ownership of many plants that do the same things cannot be attributed to "benefits of large-scale production." Perhaps other benefits are realizable from producing a large total output.

To understand how unit costs are affected by the size of the firm, economists divide the total costs of any business into their functional components and then analyze each one separately. Specifically, total costs are divided into production (or technological), managerial, marketing (buying and selling), financing, and miscellaneous costs. *There is no necessary reason why these different types of cost should be influenced in the same way by increasing total output.* Indeed, we should expect that minimum unit costs for some functions might be achieved on quite a small scale, whereas other services are most economically performed on a far larger scale. The best scale of output for the company as a whole would then be a compromise among the levels of output that give lowest unit costs for each function. The influence of changes in total output upon each of these types of cost will be examined in turn.

1. HOW UNIT PRODUCTION COSTS VARY WITH OUTPUT

As already indicated, by increasing output a firm can afford to use complex and specialized machinery that would not be fully utilized if it were to produce less. Accordingly, the machinery costs per unit of the small concern would be substantially larger than those of one that could keep its machinery occupied all the time. Similarly, large firms can divide each productive operation down into its simplest possible tasks and in that way use unskilled labor, and also capitalize on the proficiency that comes from the constant repetition of simple tasks. The ability to use complex machinery and to achieve the full possible gains from specialization are the major benefits enjoyed by the large firm, and they also apply outside the field of production.

The size a firm must reach to achieve the full benefits of specialization and mechanization will surely vary according to what it produces. A product that is simple to produce offers to a large firm few opportunities for specialization that a smaller one cannot also enjoy. The gains from the use of machines depend upon the type of machines commercially produced and the possibility that small firms can keep them fully occupied. Many large factories represent a collection of a large number of the same types of machines. Large spinning and weaving plants differ from small ones, not in the kinds of machines they use, only in their number. Accordingly, small firms in these industries can fully enjoy the benefits of mechanization on a small scale. What has been said about mechanization applies also to specialization. Simple products offer fewer opportunities than complex ones do, for subdivision of tasks, and in their production small firms may subdivide tasks as finely as large ones.

2. HOW MANAGERIAL COSTS VARY WITH OUTPUT

Production costs per unit are fairly easy to calculate, but it is almost impossible to measure managerial costs accurately. Specifically, management costs per unit might be measured by dividing managerial salary and equipment costs by total output. This would be an erroneous way of measuring managerial costs. A firm could easily assure itself of low-unit managerial costs figured in terms of managerial salaries and equipment. But unless this management made correct decisions, all other costs would be excessive. These excessive costs are properly chargeable against management. In specific cases it is not possible to know the minimum possible level of nonmanagement costs. Therefore full managerial costs cannot be measured accurately. Nevertheless, conceptually, these include direct payments to managers and for equipment used in management, plus unnecessary costs due to imperfections in management.

Up to some size, larger firms ordinarily enjoy advantages over small firms in their managerial costs. Management is one form of labor, and up to some point its unit costs fall, with increases in output as full division of labor is achieved. Small firms require that each executive perform many diverse managerial tasks. Large firms can afford a separate person for each job.

The decline in unit managerial costs following increased output is not without limit. Beyond some size, firms become unwieldy. Managers of some of the nation's largest enterprises have confessed to a lack of coordination among the many policies by which their firms are governed, to a slowness in making decisions, and to a conflict of internal policies. It is generally conceded that the severest limitation on the size of a firm is set by the difficulty of maintaining high-quality management beyond some point. As would be expected, the size of the company where this occurs will vary widely from industry to industry, according to the complexity of the tasks that management must perform.

A study completed in 1952 by the American Management Association casts some light on the alleged superior efficiency of large corporations. A staff of management specialists talked with officials of 40 big and small companies. These companies were picked because they have made a conscious attempt to study organization objectively and scientifically. Approximately 150 other companies were spot-checked on specific questions. The results of this study strongly suggest that small rather than large units possess an advantage in management.[1]

This study found that decentralization of authority is probably the goal of most organization changes. The young president of a big United States company said, "The greatest contribution to effective organization would be the reduction of our plants to a maximum size of 2,500 men."

As indicated, large organizations operate largely according to general rule, rather than on the basis of individual judgments to meet specific problems. The director of the study for the American Management Association, Ernest Dale, concluded, "Uniformity of company practices may give way to rational irrationality." Dale also concluded that the big corporation of the future may become ". . . merely management advisory bodies—with an umbrella of mass research, financing and the like—for small, almost autonomous units. Initiative will revert to the small manager, instead of to a hydra-headed bureaucracy."

3. HOW MARKETING COSTS VARY WITH OUTPUT

Marketing includes both buying and selling activities. In assessing marketing costs, two elements must be considered: first, the costs of

---

[1] This discussion is based upon a prepublication discussion of the book, *Planning and Developing the Company Organization Structure,* American Management Association, April, 1952, in *Business Week,* April 12, 1952, p. 42.

performing the operations involved in buying and selling; second, the prices paid for things purchased and the prices obtained for things sold.

a. Buying

Buying involves the following activities, among others: alternative sources of supply must be sought out; the quality of goods offered by alternative suppliers must be evaluated; contracts must be placed; fulfillment of contracts, as to quantity, quality, and timing, must be supervised; and payment must be made. In the performance of many of these functions, specialization offers opportunities for reductions in cost. Some large purchasing departments are also able to mechanize their testing for quality and their record keeping, and consequently enjoy lower unit costs than smaller firms enjoy. As in productive operations, however, there doubtless are limits to the gains achieved from specialization and mechanization.

Some small businesses apparently obtain many of the gains of large-scale purchasing by employing organizations that specialize in buying for others. These organizations are generally large and enjoy the economies of large-scale operations. Competition among these firms and the threat that the individual firm will do its own purchasing probably keep their charges fairly close to the costs involved in making purchases. Consequently, small firms need not spend much more than large firms when they have access to competing purchasing concerns.

An expert buyer knows thoroughly the conditions in all markets where things he purchases are sold. Use of his expert knowledge permits him to buy from those who will accept the lowest price, who will give greatest quality and service, and the like. Differences in the skill of buyers generally will result in a difference in the prices they pay. Large firms can afford specialized purchasing agents and can, for the same unit cost as a small firm, pay their purchasing agents a larger salary, and should therefore be able to hire men of greater skill. Consequently, they should enjoy an advantage over smaller firms in the buying function.

The idea of the gains of large-scale buying usually implies what we have called *bargaining-power advantages*. As already indicated, these advantages accrue to individuals and not to society as a whole. Indeed, the possession of strong bargaining power might well be considered brute force that a firm can use to arrogate income to itself without any ethical justification.

b. Selling costs

The foregoing discussion of buying applies almost directly to selling: selling calls for contact with customers, a study of their needs (and ability and willingness to pay), communication with them concerning the availability of supplies and prices charged, measures to determine whether they are satisfied, and the development of close personal relations so that they will favor one source over others for personal reasons.

Specialization of personnel should yield gains that give the large concerns real advantages over small ones. Moreover, a large firm has a higher geographical concentration of customers, thus increasing the number of readers of its advertisements in national advertising media, and achieving a higher ratio of customers to be visited by each salesman for each mile of travel.

But there are also limits to the unit-cost reductions that are caused by increased sales volume. Most firms probably have some customers who are attached particularly to their specific product. The attachment may rest on geographical proximity, a personal friendship for the seller, a real or imagined superiority of the product, and the like. To sell to more buyers, a firm must attract customers who have little or no reason to favor it over other sellers; to increase its sales greatly, the firm must win over customers who start with an attachment for some competitor—and in extreme instances, who have a positive objection to the product sold. Consequently, to increase sales beyond some point, a firm will ordinarily be required to exert increased sales effort per dollar of sales.

By virtue of strong bargaining power, some concerns can command higher prices than smaller concerns in the same industry can. This form of advantage yields gains to the seller without corresponding benefits for society. On the contrary, this power ordinarily is used to take larger sums from customers, reducing their real incomes, to increase the incomes of the sellers.

4. FINANCING COSTS

Available information makes it clear that large firms are able to borrow at lower rates than smaller firms.[2] This advantage results partly from the lower cost of investigating the soundness of a loan per dollar of loan as the size of the loan increases. Also, large borrowers ordinarily are better known to the investing public than small borrowers are, and therefore find a readier market for their securities. Even the largest firms apparently have not reached a size beyond which their costs of borrowing increase.

5. MISCELLANEOUS COSTS

Businesses have costs other than those of production, top management, buying, selling, and financing. Some not discussed are research, legal, and "risk" costs. These miscellaneous items are generally only a very small percentage of costs, and the manner in which they are affected

---

[2] See J. L. Nicholson, "The Fallacy of Easy Money," *Harvard Business Review,* Summer, 1938; and George Stigler, *The Theory of Price* (New York: The Macmillan Company, 1946), p. 205.

by changes in scale of operations will not be discussed here. It should be recognized, however, that these costs probably are affected by a firm's size and that they may be a large item of cost for some industries.

6. COST AND OUTPUT

The foregoing general discussion showed that very large size can be both a cost advantage and a cost disadvantage. No conclusions could, however, be drawn about the *net* effect on unit costs of increased size of output; indeed, one must doubt that any conclusion would apply to a large majority of—let alone all—cases. Only by examining concrete facts about operating costs of firms in a given industry of different size can a net assessment be made for that particular case. Unfortunately, available data leave much to be desired in accuracy, in coverage, and in currency. Much more information than now exists must be gathered before the influence of size of business on costs of operations can be settled. Even to make use of available information requires an analysis of costs in different terms than were employed in the preceding discussion.

Rather than break costs down by "function," as was done before, most analyses of costs lump costs together and distinguish them according to whether they vary or remain unchanged as output increases. The first are appropriately termed "variable costs" and the second "fixed costs." Variable costs include such items as wages, raw materials, and power; fixed costs include primarily items like rent, depreciation and obsolescence, interest on indebtedness, and general administrative expenses. (Note that these divisions of costs into fixed and variable cut across functional lines; that is to say, some technological costs—like depreciation and obsolescence—are fixed, while others, like production labor, are variable.)

Fixed and variable costs can be described in terms of "units." That is, they can be expressed first as a total—all expenditures incurred to produce some output; then as an average per unit of output—expenditures divided by the number of units produced. We can measure total costs by adding together total variable and total fixed costs, or we can measure total unit costs by summing unit-variable and unit-fixed costs.

The economist, employing only armchair reasoning and some common knowledge, has been able to reach several significant conclusions about the effect that increased output has on costs of all types. In the first place, he knows that business size, rather than being a matter of chance, generally is planned with considerable care, and that the plant and equipment possessed by a firm will have been acquired with some particular scale of operations in view. That scale, which might be termed "physical capacity," represents the amount that those planning the firm's acquisitions of productive instruments had in mind and, presumably, that will be the level at which the firm would attain its minimum *unit* costs. In virtually every situation, it would be possible for the firm to produce more than that amount, but additions to output would involve higher costs—higher variable costs and often higher average costs. The notion of an output at which the firm will operate at maximum efficiency—that is, at minimum unit cost—is one that is met in various phases of economics; it should be mastered once and for all. This level of output is described as "capacity" in the economic sense.

In the second place, the economist knows that a firm set up to produce most efficiently at an output of, say, 100,000 units daily will have relatively high *fixed* costs—both as a total and on a per unit basis, when it is turning out only 1,000 units each day, for these heavy fixed charges would be allocated to a relatively small number of units. Similarly, he knows that the greater the output—even beyond 100,000 units—produced, the lower will be the per unit fixed costs incurred. Consequently, simple arithmetic will prove that increases in output will reduce average (per unit) fixed costs.

In the third place, the economist recognizes that the most complicated types of cost, and by far the most important, are variable costs. Just how these are affected by output cannot be resolved by reference to simple arithmetic—or by using UNIVAC either. The effect of increased output on variable costs will vary according to a variety of circumstances that will differ from industry to industry. In the foregoing discussion of individual costs defined by function we got some notion of the factors influencing variable costs. As a broad general rule—to which there are many exceptions—one can expect that variable costs will remain fairly uniform until roughly the point at which "capacity" is reached; at that point, variable costs will rise rapidly. The reason may be given that "the engineers planned it that way," in that they set up the facilities to be most efficient at capacity.

To help clarify and sharpen important areas of their subject, economists make extensive use of diagrams. They find diagrams especially helpful in explaining some of the cost relations we have just been discussing. For this reason, the student is wise to appropriate a few minutes to developing a modest proficiency in the use of simple graphs. The author assures him that, unless he is an exception to the general rule, he will quickly develop the required proficiency and even find it fun. The ability to read and construct graphs can be extremely helpful in this and other connections.

As used here, lines become a language and a tool by which many ideas may be expressed. They permit both the person stating his ideas, and his audience to use a potent sense that is largely dormant when expression is attempted by words alone; that is, he calls the eye into use.

There are relatively few "words" in "line language." Lines can go in relatively few directions and at varying "speeds"; they can slope upward

or downward; their slope can be gradual or steep—or somewhere in between. Each type of line conveys a different message. Let us take a few
concrete examples:

Chart 1 is labeled "average cost curves." The left-hand axis is labeled
"Cost in Dollars" and the bottom axis is termed "Quantity." If we were to
draw a horizontal line, line 1, it would state that the average cost of producing the product was the same—here $—no matter how large or small
a quantity was produced. Line 2 makes a different statement about average cost; its gradual downward slope states that the greater the quantity
produced by the firm the lower the unit cost. Line 3 makes a more complicated statement; it says that up to the output *OQ* average costs decline; beyond that point they rise.

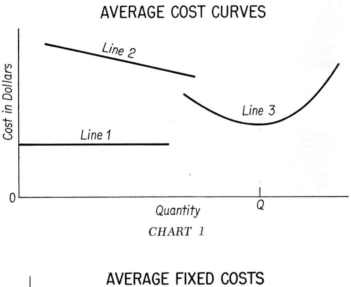

CHART 1

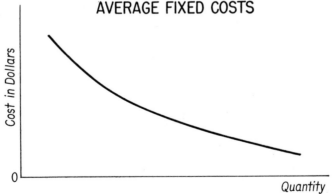

CHART 2

What has been said on the preceding pages about the influence of increased output on unit-variable and fixed costs can now be stated diagrammatically. Chart 2 shows, by a simple declining line, how a fixed amount—fixed costs—would decline when spread over a larger number of units; Chart 3 shows variable costs conforming to the pattern of remaining steady up to an output, defined as "capacity," and then beginning to rise rather rapidly. Chart 4 combines these two lines into a statement of total unit costs—sometimes termed "average costs." This line has a saucerlike appearance and sometimes is described as a "U-shaped" curve. Unless there are reasons to expect an industry to be unique in some regard, one is entitled to assume that the costs of each firm are described by a "U-shaped" average cost curve.

The question of how costs are affected by size, or which size of firm is the most efficient, revolves around the location of the lowest possible point on *any* cost curve. More specifically, if engineers were free to de-

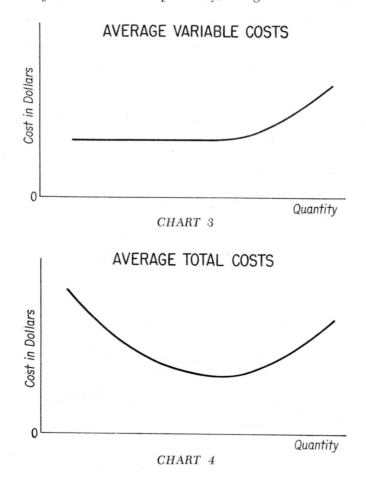

CHART 3

CHART 4

sign plant and equipment without regard to the ability of the firm to sell its output, would they find that average costs could be made lower by making the plant larger and larger? Would there be no point beyond which costs would not decline by increasing the "capacity" of the firm? And, even if technological costs were to decline indefinitely with increased capacity, could the same be said of marketing and management costs? Almost certainly, there is some limit beyond which increased size means increased average cost. (If such were not the case, then one must expect that a single firm would prevail in each industry, it being able to drive all smaller firms to the wall by virtue of its greater efficiency.)

7. EMPIRICAL MATERIALS DESCRIBING EFFECT OF SIZE ON UNIT COSTS

a. Wheat flour milling and bread baking

The Federal Trade Commission studied costs of producing wheat flour during 1913 and 1922. In 1913, the two companies classified as large both had average costs moderately below the median of the group. In 1922, however, the costs of the three largest producers exceeded the median. Individual companies in the smallest size group had both the highest and lowest average costs in both years.[3]

Analysis of costs of bread baking in the five years between 1920 and 1924 showed those of the three largest companies to be only slightly lower than average. In only one of the five years studied did one of the three very large firms have the lowest unit costs (General Baking Corporation in 1922). While two of the three large firms consistently were among the most efficient half of all producers, the other (Ward Baking Corporation) frequently was not.[4]

A detailed unit-cost study of 283 baking plants in all sections of the country was made during the months of March and September, 1945. A comparison of these costs in five sizes of companies showed the next to the largest bakeries to be the lowest-cost producers, with the "Big Four" next. The small and smallest were the highest-cost producers in both periods.[5]

b. Rubber tires

Data for 14 producers of natural and synthetic rubber tires show that the four largest firms combined incurred substantially higher costs than the other 10 firms combined. The percentage by which the costs of

---

[3] *T.N.E.C. Monograph No. 13*, Table 65, p. 62, and Table 72, p. 67.

[4] *Ibid.*, p. 69.

[5] John M. Blair, "Technology and Size," *Papers and Proceedings of the American Economic Association*, May, 1948, p. 147.

the Big Four exceeded those of the 10 smaller companies is shown in Table 1.

Table 1. Per Cent by Which Total Unit Costs of Big-Four Tire Producers Exceeded Those of Smaller Companies

	Natural rubber (Nov., 1941)	Synthetic rubber (Aug., 1943)
600 by 16 4-ply passenger	10%	6%
600 by 16 6-ply truck	8	9
700–20/32 by 6 10-ply truck	7	10
750–20/34 by 7 10-ply truck	14	21

SOURCE: John M. Blair, "Technology and Size," *Papers and Proceedings of the American Economic Association,* May, 1948, pp. 149-150.

Apparently the Big Four suffered the greatest disadvantage in producing the largest tires and were relatively less efficient in producing synthetic tires than in producing natural-rubber tires.

Unfortunately, the 10 small firms were not subdivided into smaller groups; therefore the size of the lowest-cost firms cannot be determined. From the data made available, it is impossible to know whether the medium-sized or the smallest firms had the lowest unit costs. Finally, it is not clear whether the differences in cost of individual tire sizes could result from differences in the way large and small firms allocated their fixed charges among the individual sizes of tires.

c. Fertilizer[6]

Results similar to those found in the wholesale bread and rubber-tire industries were found among producers of bulk superphosphate fertilizer. The very largest firms were not the least costly producers, but second in cost to the large producers. The difference in cost between the two groups was slightly more than 2 per cent. As in the wholesale bread industry, the smallest firms incurred substantially higher costs than did the largest firms (see Table 2).

Producers of mixed fertilizer showed a slightly different cost experience. As in the other examples, the largest firms were the second most efficient producers, and the smallest suffered the highest costs. However, the lowest-cost producers were the next to the smallest group (see Table 2).

d. Cement[7]

A study of the costs in 1929 of 45 cement companies presents more detailed information than do the studies already summarized. The costs

---

[6] *Ibid.*, p. 150.

[7] *T.N.E.C. Monograph No. 13*, p. 23.

Table 2. Total Unit Production Costs in the Fertilizer Industry, 1941-1942 Average

Company Size Group*	Mixed fertilizer (per ton)	Bulk superphosphate (per ton)
Over $10,000,000	$16.41	$ 8.30
$1,000,000–$10,000,000	17.09	8.12
$500,000–$1,000,000	15.96	9.49
Under $500,000	17.52	10.78
Average	16.68	8.45

* In terms of annual sales.

SOURCE: John M. Blair, "Technology and Size," *Papers and Proceedings of the American Economic Association*, May, 1948, p. 150.

of each company are shown individually according to four size groups. The results of the study may be summarized as follows:

1. Both the least costly and most costly producing companies were very small—costs per barrel ranged from $0.91 to $2.17.

2. The most efficient of the three largest companies was eleventh of the 45 companies studied when they were ranked, in order of increasing cost, with costs of $1.18.

3. All of the 10 most costly producers were very small.

The costs of individual companies are combined, and arithmetic averages and medians for four size groups presented in Table 3. These results show relatively little difference among the various groups taken as a whole. No matter which type of average is used, the largest firms were not the least costly producers.

Table 3. Unit Costs per Barrel of Forty-five Cement Companies, 1929

(Unit costs per barrel for four size groups)

	Median costs per barrel	Average costs per barrel
Large	119.0¢	123¢
Medium	118.5	123
Small	123.5	121
Very small	128.5	137

e. Steel

A study of costs in the steel industry during December-February, 1918, was made by the Federal Trade Commission. From these results it has been possible to calculate the median costs of producing "basic pig iron" and Bessemer pig iron separately for companies of three different sizes. These averages (medians) and the entire size comparison are grievously weakened by the small number of firms studied. The results cover 14 and nine integrated firms, respectively. Moreover, almost the entire period studied was wartime, a fact which might make the results unrepresentative of ordinary conditions. The results conform to those of the other studies reviewed.[8] For both types of pig iron the most costly producer was very large; a medium-sized company was the least costly producer.

f. Farm machinery[9]

The costs of producing many types of farm machinery in 1935 and 1936 were studied by the Federal Trade Commission. In the production of none of the seven types of equipment did International Harvester have the lowest costs. Usually the best performance was turned in by a medium-sized company (either Deere & Co., Allis-Chalmers, or J. I. Case).

g. Petroleum[10]

The U.S. Tariff Commission studied the costs of producing crude petroleum in each of the four years from 1927 to 1930, inclusive. In every year the medium-sized companies, the middle of five size groups, had the lowest costs. The smallest companies had the highest costs in every year, while the largest had next to the highest every year but one.

Other studies show that similar cost patterns obtain in different industries.[11] Sometimes, however, this general pattern does not prevail.[12]

8. SUMMARY OF STATISTICAL EVIDENCE

The limitations of the foregoing data have already been stressed. Such as it is, the available evidence indicates that the very largest firms are very rarely the least costly producers in their industry. Most often, as a group, they are second to the medium-sized concerns. The very smallest firms as a group ordinarily are the least efficient, though frequently individual concerns among them have the very lowest costs in the industry.

Failure of the largest firms to have the lowest costs can be explained in several ways. These companies sometimes represent a combination

---

[8] *Ibid.*, p. 29.

[9] *Ibid.*, pp. 30-37.

[10] *Ibid.*, p. 40.

[11] *Ibid.*, pp. 46, 48-49, and 52-63.

[12] For a discussion of some evidence not presented here, see A. D. H. Kaplan, *Small Business: Its Place and Problems* (New York: McGraw-Hill Book Company, Inc., 1948), Chap. V; Conference on Price Research, *Cost Behavior and Price Policy* (New York: National Bureau of Economic Research, 1943), pp. 243-263; and Universities-National Bureau Committee for Economic Research, *Business Concentration and Price Policy* (Princeton, N.J.: Princeton University Press, 1955), pp. 213-230, where Caleb A. Smith reviews empirical studies.

of a large number of relatively inefficient concerns which was effected to afford large promotional profits to the men who engineered the merger, but not to achieve low costs. Or they may represent the combination of relatively efficient concerns that were saddled with heavy fixed charges caused by high promotional expenses. Moreover, businessmen probably regard growth in the size of their business as an earmark of success and might overlook or minimize the possibility of an increase in unit costs as they expand. Also, even if it were known that unit costs would rise, a firm might be willing to expand, for total profits can increase despite higher unit costs.

Frequently individual small firms have the lowest unit costs in an industry, but one cannot confidently attribute that condition to the advantages of small size. Very possibly the small firm would have even lower unit costs if it were to expand. Moreover, a truly efficient small firm is almost a paradox, inasmuch as the owners and management in most businesses desire to grow larger and more profitable (at least in total amount if not in percentage terms). Small firms clearly are not efficient in realizing this objective.

Costs of production of operating firms do not provide a reliable explanation for the influence of size on unit costs for the following reason: costs data measure the combined influence of many factors which can hardly be disentangled. If a comparison could be made of a very large number of firms of all different sizes, all factors other than size might "cancel themselves out." Most industries, however, have relatively few firms of any size, and their costs and profits would probably be influenced by such factors as location (that is, some firms may have acquired convenient locations, raw-material deposits, or efficient laborers, at relatively low cost; in such circumstances their costs will be lowered without any relation to their size); time the business was formed (which would influence the technological efficiency and book cost of plant and equipment); managerial efficiency, which often is surely the most important determinant of a firm's profitability and economy of operations (since payment for management is not necessarily proportional to efficiency, either large or small firms may be very profitable because by accident they hired exceptionally talented management); existence of bargaining power, economies of purchase or sale, which can be measured only with great difficulty, if at all; *self-exploitation by entrepreneurs* (who may secure low costs and high profits by virtue of overworking themselves without charging the business fully for their efforts; this factor would presumably work in the direction of making small firms seem relatively more efficient than they really are); *inclusion of excessive costs* (like very high managerial salaries and bonuses that are out of line with productivity, excessive expenses for promotional, legal, advertising services, and such, as a result of managerial neglect or desire to increase personal income at the expense of the firm). Some of these factors may be partly correlated with the size of firm, but there is no necessary correlation between them. Consequently, it is almost always impossible to tell what firm has the lowest unit costs *because of size.*

As a practical matter, both an economist looking in from the outside for reasons of public policy and the businessman who is considering entry into an industry can only speculate concerning the most efficient scale of operations and the degree of influence that scale of operations exerts upon cost. Neither can avoid the question simply because of its difficulty. The businessman must make concrete decisions and act on them; the economist, in his recommendations on the advisability of dissolving large enterprises, must make similar judgments.

Perhaps the most significant and unquestionable fact is that in almost every industry there are firms of very different sizes that seem able to survive and flourish. It is impossible to think of an industry in which all firms are of almost the same size. General Motors is many times as large as Studebaker, but both seem to be successful; United States Steel towers over Jones and Laughlin, but neither one seems unadapted to the industry; even many corner groceries seem securely entrenched despite the enormous difference between their size and that of the A & P. While superficially it would seem that either large or small firms must be more efficient, possibly those of widely different size are equally efficient.

Perhaps we err in considering the A & P and an independent corner grocer, General Motors and Studebaker, and so on to be in the same industry; certainly they sell different lines of goods, in different locations to different kinds of customers, so that technically they cannot be said to operate in the same "market." Some apparent paradoxes can probably be traced to a loose definition of "industry."

No matter what this definition may be, there appears to be a wide zone of firm sizes at which production is more or less equally efficient. Size would exert little influence on unit costs within this zone, but might exert an important effect on costs *at the extremes.* Despite big differences in business size within the same industry, there are unmistakable differences in the typical size of firms *among* industries, suggesting that scale of output does strongly influence costs—within limits. Suggestive of these differences are the following data indicating the average number of wage earners *per establishment* in a selected group of industries (in 1937).[13]

Printing and other publishing—book, music, and job	13 workers
Bread and other bakers' products	14 "
Steel-works and rolling-mill products	1,169 "
Motor vehicles, not including motorcyles	1,485 "

---

[13] *T.N.E.C. Monograph No. 27, The Structure of Industry,* p. 15.

The general arguments and evidence presented do not demonstrate that huge businesses are needed for productive efficiency. On the contrary, it appears that very large firms are often less efficient than those of medium size. There are limits to the gains a business can enjoy by expanding its scale of operations.

B. *Large Firms Are Civic-minded and Law-abiding*

A second advantage claimed for big business is that it is responsive to social pressure and is scrupulous in observing the law. Paradoxically, one of the major reasons for the passage of the antitrust laws that were partly aimed against bigness in business was the "public be damned" attitude of some big businesses, and the prevalence of predatory practices by which large firms abused their smaller rivals. Among the opponents of big business today are some who still consider this attitude immoral and abusive. Others hold exactly the opposite view.

The excesses of the large firms generally are illustrated from the activities of such firms as the Standard Oil Company, the National Cash Register Company, and the tobacco trust. The objectionable activities of the firms cited here date back to before 1920, and some of them to before 1900. To find proved examples of abuse of rivals or of the public by large firms, it is not necessary to reach back into the fairly distant past, but the number of current cases is very small. Apparently the behavior of big business has changed. This change may simply reflect a growing concern for "good public relations," rather than a sincere penitence and reform of character. It is also possible that this reformed behavior can be traced to the fact that government regulatory agencies have become more vigilant, and find it relatively easy to maintain surveillance over the largest business in the land. Whatever the reason, the behavior of big business seems to have improved.

Nowadays, large companies rarely are indicted by the Federal Trade Commission for unfair competition against small or medium-sized firms. Disparagement and injury of rivals seem to be much more common among small firms than among large. Men in government agencies responsible for administering wartime regulations apparently were in almost complete agreement that large firms rarely violated the regulations, while many small firms were guilty of this offense. In this regard, the difference in behavior of large and small firms seems to be most closely related to cost and convenience of enforcing regulations. It is not clear, however, that very large firms were more diligent in observing wartime regulations than medium-sized firms in the same industry.

C. Large Firms Are Main Sources of Research Effort and Technical Development

Another advantage often attributed to big business is that it contributes more to the progressiveness of the economy than do small firms. Greater advances in research and technology and more effective innovations in production and marketing are claimed for larger firms. The argument is made that "because development is costly, it follows that it can be carried on only by a firm that has the resources which are associated with considerable size. Moreover, unless a firm has a substantial share of the market it has no strong incentive to undertake a large expenditure on development. . . ."[14]

Under these conditions big business has an important role in stimulating economic progress. With more and more funds being funneled into research and development, the economy's capacity to produce greater quantities of goods more efficiently is being extended by the growth of big business. Economic growth is thus presumably greater than it would be if small firms had a more predominant role.[15]

D. Large Firms Facilitate Government Regulation during Periods of Emergency, like War, Inflation, and Depression

The existence of very large firms undoubtedly simplified the task of the procurement agencies during World War II. The armed forces were able to contract for more than half their armament needs through less than 100 firms.[16] Consequently, the mechanics of negotiating prices, working out specifications, making inspections, assuring uniformity of the product, and the like, were expedited.[17] Some people have even attributed the victory of World War II to this feature of big business.

Owing to the large concentration of American industry, the activities of only a small group of firms are of strategic national importance. The

---

[14] J. K. Galbraith, *American Capitalism,* rev. ed. (Boston: Houghton Mifflin Company, 1956), p. 87. For similar views of the role of big business in research and technical development, see A. D. H. Kaplan, *Big Enterprise in a Competitive System* (Washington, D.C.: Brookings Institution, 1954), pp. 187-194, and David E. Lilienthal, *Big Business: A New Era* (New York: Harper & Brothers, 1953), pp. 68-72, 109-113.

[15] The relation of big business and economic progress is dealt with further in connection with the problem of monopoly in Chapter 14.

[16] Report of the Smaller War Plants Corporation, *Economic Concentration and World War II,* 1946.

[17] Critics of this position point out that big business, big labor, and big agriculture may intensify nonmonetary pressures on the price level and that big business and big labor may join hands at the expense of the unorganized consumer.

actions of these firms, especially if coordinated, could do the economy great good or great harm.

Since very large firms are few, it is feasible for high government officials to make direct personal appeals to their top executives. Government representatives can rely on fear on the part of business that refusal to negotiate with government officials, and rejection of direct personal appeals to adopt a policy involving slight sacrifice for the benefit of the nation, would injure any firm's public relations. High industrial concentration should therefore make it possible to induce top executives of the largest firms to take quick action in forestalling an economic crisis, without relying upon the slow legislative machinery to achieve the same result. Businessmen should be more willing to adopt similar policies designed for national benefit from mutual awareness that other firms, together accounting for most industrial output, would do the same. Examples of the kinds of action that might be made possible by industrial concentration are agreements by top executives of large firms not to retrench during early depression; to expand plant and equipment facilities during depression; to pool their industrial facilities during wartime; to curtail expansion plans during inflation, and the like. In assessing this advantage from bigness in business, one should only recognize that it remains potential; it has never been realized.

E. Miscellaneous Advantages Claimed for Big Business

A variety of lesser advantages is claimed for big business. Among them are the claims that big firms are largely responsible for industrial research, that they pay employees higher wages and give them greater job security, that they provide more equal opportunities for employees to get ahead because nepotism (the hiring of relatives) does not influence the hiring of a large proportion of all employees in very large organizations. These advantages are possibly demonstrable when large firms are compared with very small firms, but are debatable when very large firms are compared with those whose employees are numbered in thousands, but not in the hundreds of thousands.

II. ARGUMENTS AGAINST BIG BUSINESS

Three grievances against big business are uppermost. First, it is said to exercise disproportionate influence over government and thereby to make the government less democratic. Second, big firms allegedly drive small firms out of business. Third, big business is accused of interfering with a happy adjustment by many individuals to their environment. These grievances will be discussed briefly. (We leave for later a discussion of monopoly, a sin with which big business is often charged. As indicated, bigness and monopoly are distinctly different conditions, and great confusion results from grouping them together.)

A. *Big Business Exerts Disproportionate Influence over Government*

In a democracy, only individuals possess voting power. Business, labor, agricultural, and fraternal organizations cannot vote. However, most economic groups organize to further their interests by influencing legislation in their own behalf. Big business is not different in either its objectives or its methods; it is believed, however, to be far more successful than other groups in getting its wishes written into law.

It is impossible to measure accurately the political influence of any group. The effect on legislators' decisions of letters from constituents, visits from affluent political supporters, the platform of the political party, and activities of lobbyists can only be guessed in specific situations. Possibly each legislator would have voted exactly as he did in the absence of pressures upon him. Legislators themselves probably do not know the relative influence of each kind of pressure upon their decisions. Accordingly, the following discussion is best considered the expression of a point of view—probably the dominant viewpoint among social scientists—rather than a summary of solid empirical evidence.

Analysts of pressure groups are almost unanimous in holding that big business exerts great political power, even though it commands few votes directly.[18] Authorities also agree on the whole that prior to the election of Franklin D. Roosevelt to the Presidency in 1933, local, state, and federal legislators and executives represented primarily the interests of business groups, and big business in particular. With a few brief and notable exceptions, labor and agriculture were relatively puny political forces in the United States during the late nineteenth and twentieth centuries up to 1933. Business groups, in which big businesses played a dominant role, had things pretty much their own way. Authorities also are agreed that the influence of business interests has always been greater on local and state government officials and legislators than on federal officials.

Strong evidence that business groups lost some of their political influence is the continued election between 1932 and 1948 of Presidents who were opposed by spokesmen for big business. Franklin D. Roosevelt and Harry S Truman were violently denounced by most top execu-

---

[18] See, in particular, Donald E. Blaisdell, *Economic Power and Political Pressures* (Washington, D.C.: Government Printing Office, 1941), *T.N.E.C. Monograph No. 26;* note the statement (p. 187) by Senator O'Mahoney of Wyoming that ". . . organized business has no right . . . to control the government." See also Stuart Chase, *Democracy under Pressure* (New York: The Twentieth Century Fund, Inc., 1945).

tives of big business and by organizations that depend upon them for financial support. These two presidents in no sense of the word were defenders or representatives of big business—even their critics on the left grant them that much.

It is not clear, however, that the legislation enacted during Roosevelt's and Truman's administrations was predominantly opposed by, and counter to the interest of, big business. As was already indicated, the absolute size of the nation's largest firms is substantially greater today than it was when Franklin D. Roosevelt took office, and industrial concentration apparently has not declined. Consequently, if the administrations opposed by big business were intent upon harming it, they were not successful.

Evidence that the decline in political influence of big business has been reversed since World War II consists in a review of legislation enacted after 1945, in the elections of Dwight Eisenhower to the Presidency in 1952 and 1956, and in the high concentration of big business executives represented in his cabinet.

As already stated, it would be impossible to prove the accuracy of the author's conclusion that big business exerts disproportionate influence over government. It is even difficult to define "disproportionate political influence." The best basis for judging the political power of any group probably is the legislation that is enacted. In using this basis of judgment, one judges by results rather than by general discussion. If most new laws were supported by the group in question and opposed by many other groups, it must be considered powerful. While this test would be unreliable if applied to a few isolated laws, it is fairly reliable when applied to most legislation. Unfortunately, no careful analysis of major legislation during, say, the years following World War II has been made in these terms. Rather than attempt such an analysis here, only some major laws enacted since 1945 will be listed as examples of measures that were opposed by numerically large groups but were passed largely because of the support of big business groups. The order in which the laws appear in the following list has no special significance: repeal of the excess-profits tax following World War II; repeal of price control; enactment of the Taft-Hartley Act; revision and reduction of personal income taxes in 1948; and the so-called anticommunist legislation (particularly the McCarran Act of 1950).

It is not difficult to uncover the alignment of the political pressure groups on each of these issues. Most of these measures were openly supported by big business and opposed by labor, with agricultural groups either divided or silent. Inasmuch as these laws were enacted during President Truman's administration, they have special significance. Business groups seem to have got what they wished in many matters, despite the fact that their interest opposed the party in power. Presumably, it would have obtained more, or would have had less of a struggle, under an administration sympathetic to big business.

If it is true that big business exerts very strong influence over legislation, then legislation does not represent the interests of the majority of the people, and the quality of democracy suffers. Big business, including those who obtain most of their income from large firms either as executives or stockholders, is composed of a tiny fraction of all voters. The general dimensions of the stockholding group are suggested by the fact that fewer than 75,000 persons received one half of all dividends received by individuals in 1937. Half of all stockholders in that year, a year of relatively high dividend payments, received less than $100 in dividends.[19] Thus the number of those who obtain a substantial proportion of their income as dividends from large firms is insignificant.

If so small a group can overrule the wishes of such groups as labor and agriculture, then it is inaccurate to argue that all persons have equal political power, as is postulated by democracy. Disproportionate political power in the hands of one group has consequences similar to the disenfranchisement of members of other groups. The existence of big business seems to have brought about a departure from the desired conditions and consequences of pure democracy. Some authorities consider the concentration of industry a threat to the democratic foundations of our nation.

The methods by which big business exerts great political power, despite the extremely small number of those whose economic interest can be identified with it, will be listed briefly. It will be noted that most of these methods are directly or indirectly related to the ability of big firms to spend large sums of money—or to hire men at large salaries. Groups that compete with big business for political influence, even though they directly command far more votes, lack such great financial resources.

The political influence of big businesses can be traced to the following factors. First, they are the major source of financial support for media of public communication—the radio, newspapers, and magazines—and indeed, these media are for the most part owned by big business. Accordingly, big business is able to reach a huge audience with its views. Second, big businesses devote considerable resources to exert political pressure—in the form of lobbying. Third, big business representatives can hold out as bait the prospect of rewarding their friends with remunerative employment. Fourth, big businesses are sufficiently few and cohesive to permit effective cooperative action, and their efforts can be coordinated so that they will achieve large returns for their efforts and expenditure. Fifth, big businesses are the source from which men are frequently selected to fill administrative posts in government, and they tend to befriend their former associates. Although many government administrators and legislators

---

[19] *T.N.E.C. Monograph No. 29*, p. 13.

do not come directly from the ranks of big business, they are frequently lawyers and other professionals who either have, or hope to obtain, clients from this source. Sixth, partly by their heavy contributions to the media of communication and to academic institutions, men from big business have succeeded in coloring the political and economic philosophy of most of the population; therefore many whose economic interests conflict with those of big business nevertheless are predisposed to sympathize with the big-business point of view. Finally, big business is such a large purchaser of goods and services that a major segment of the population is directly or indirectly dependent upon its patronage. These people ordinarily believe that their interests are best served by measures favorable to big business.[20]

B. Big Businesses Drive Small Firms Out of Business

Big business frequently is charged with driving smaller firms out of existence. Indeed, the efforts to spark legislation to curb monopoly and big business can be traced to organizations of small businessmen, who seem to think they are engaged in a battle for survival against large firms.

Part of this belief apparently stems from the rapid rise of chain stores and supermarkets in food distribution. Most consumers know more about the retailing of food than about any other business, and are able to observe the shift away from the independent local grocer. They tend to build on this fact and make it into a trend for all business that will end with the extinction of most, if not all, small firms. To settle this issue, we shall examine the information available to determine whether small firms are indeed becoming extinct.

We should also try to explain why small firms fail, in order to see whether the failure can be traced to actions by large firms, and we should explore the probable consequences of a reduction in the number of small firms—if it were ever to occur. However, time and space limitations compel us to skip over these interesting and important questions.

Approximately 4.3 million nonfarm businesses operated in the United States in 1957 (Table 4). Prior to the war, the number was significantly less—about 15 per cent smaller. Of this large number of firms, as has already been indicated, all but a trivial proportion are relatively small. It will be recalled that 99 of every 100 firms have fewer than 100 employees. Thus it is clear that almost all of the 4.3 million firms operating are small or medium-small.

It should also be apparent that, rather than extinction, small firms seem to face the hardships of overpopulation. More specifically, the num-

---

[20] For a balanced view and brief description, see Corwin D. Edwards, "The Conglomerate Enterprise," presented before the Conference on Business Concentration and Price Policy, Princeton University, June, 1952, pp. 34-40.

ber of small firms in the nation as a whole is near its all-time peak. To judge by the total number of small firms, there is no immediate threat of extinction for the small businessman.

Table 4. Number of Nonfarm Businesses in the United States, Selected Years 1900-1957
(In thousands)

Year	Number of firms	Year	Number of firms
1900	1,174	1944	2,917
1905	1,357	1945	3,114
1910	1,515	1946	3,487
1914	1,655	1947	3,783
1919	1,711	1948	3,948
1921	1,927	1949	4,000
1925	2,113	1950	4,051
1929	3,029	1951	4,109
1933	2,782	1952	4,167
1935	2,992	1953	4,196
1939	3,222	1954	4,193
1940	3,291	1955	4,239
1941	3,270	1956	4,292
1942	3,186	1957	4,323
1943	2,905		

SOURCE: Data for years 1900-1928 from Dun & Bradstreet, Inc., and for other years from the Department of Commerce, U.S. Office of Business Economics.

How, then, in the face of these data, can it be argued that large firms drive small firms out of existence? Several answers may be offered. First, there may be several important fields in which small businesses are losing ground to large ones, and the outcry against large firms may be explainable by efforts of small firms in these industries to prevent further retrogression. Second, the growth in number of small firms may be temporary—owing to the war and the postwar inflation, and there may be strong reason to expect a decline in their numbers in the years ahead. Between September, 1948, and September, 1949, the number of firms that discontinued operations exceeded the number of new firms; consequently, the number of small firms did in fact suffer a slight decline. With the Korean military operations and the projected increase in defense spending, another increase in the number of small firms took place. (See Table 5.) This rise may turn out to be temporary again. Third, the complaint against big businesses may not really mean that they are overpowering small firms, but that they are making them far less remunerative than before. That is, large firms, such as chain and department stores, by selling at lower prices than do small firms, or by advertising far more than small stores do, may reduce the sales volumes of the small stores and lower their total profit beyond the survival point. Fourth, those making the complaint may know it is not valid, but they may hope to strengthen their position by curbing large firms.

Table 5. New Firms and Discontinuances, 1948-1957
   (In thousands)

Year	Half year (last month)	New firms	Discontinuances	Total firms
1948	June	200.3	155.2	3,944.0
	Dec.	199.1	194.7	3,948.4
1949	June	194.0	230.4	3,912.0
	Dec.	278.0	190.0	4,000.0
1950	June	221.5	176.0	4,045.5
	Dec.	181.6	176.4	4,050.7
1951	June	210.7	161.2	4,116.9
	Dec.	152.5	148.1	4,121.3
1952	June	213.0	158.8	4,175.4
	Dec.	150.9	147.5	4,178.8
1953	June	199.3	172.4	4,205.7
	Dec.	141.2	161.6	4,185.3
1954	June	189.0	177.6	4,196.7
	Dec.	145.2	153.0	4,189.0
1955	June	210.2	166.9	4,232.3
	Dec.	170.2	157.2	4,245.2
1956	June	223.9	174.9	4,294.2
	Dec.	156.9	162.1	4,289.0
1957	June	211.0	176.9	4,323.2
	Dec.	154.6	155.1	4,322.7

SOURCE: U.S. Department of Commerce, successive issues of *Survey of Current Business.*

The information available does not make clear which explanation is correct. Possibly each accounts in part for the widespread allegation that large firms drive small firms to the wall. The preponderance of evidence indicates that small firms are a large segment of the business population and that there is no prospect that their numbers will shrink greatly. Consequently, the "middle class," which in this country is largely composed of owners of small firms, shows no inclination to disappear (contrary to the prediction of Karl Marx).

C. Big Business Interferes with Happy Personal and Social Adjustment

To work in a large business is to become a small cog in a huge wheel. For everyone in a large firm who feels himself to be part of the enterprise, who feels that he knows where the firm is headed and the basic policies that underlie its activities, there are perhaps hundreds who simply do what they are told and try to hold down their job. Most employees in large firms have little contact with the final product that the enterprise produces; their contribution represents a tiny part of the whole. Individuals therefore can hardly identify themselves with a specific productive contribution. Moreover, "this depersonalization of the conduct of economic affairs has largely removed from those who are supposed to direct them, the salutary checks of personal honor and personal responsibility." [21]

It is contended, and by students and experts in the matter, that the position of a worker in a large enterprise is incompatible with a happy personal and social adjustment. Their argument is that most persons have to feel that they make a social contribution and that their life counts in the entire scheme of things. Individuals who feel that they would not be missed if they were to leave their job—and many employees in large firms do have that feeling, we are told—understandably wonder what meaning their lives have. It has been argued that Americans are fundamentally less well-adjusted to their environment than most other people and that this fact is to be explained by the large proportion of the population employed in large businesses.

Connected with the loss of identification on the part of the worker with the thing he produces is the feeling that he is "lost in the shuffle." Each worker in a very large firm is one among very many, and most of them have contact with supervisors who have relatively little more influence than they. Those in this situation must regard all top executive posts in the organization as utterly beyond their reach. The person whom they might impress with their ability has little opportunity—and even less incentive—to help them to advance. Accordingly, most employees in large firms must look forward to a life of labor that is a continuation of their present work. There are, of course, some exceptions; those who enter a large firm in an executive training program, or who work even as clerks in the offices of top executives, have an opportunity, however slight, to gain recognition and advancement. These employees represent a small proportion of the total work force of a large firm, however.

There has been considerable debate about the impact upon the individual worker of highly routinized and repetitive work. Most of those who discuss this subject try to project themselves into the position of a person who constantly repeats a minor productive operation. They imagine the worker's position to be unbearable. However, it must not be forgotten that individuals react differently to similar situations. The greater numbers of those who find repetitive work intolerable pursue occupations of a different type. Moreover, most individuals tend to adjust to their situation and in time cease to be irked by what they first thought would be unen-

---

[21] M. W. Watkins, *T.N.E.C. Monograph No. 13*, p. 137.

durable. The best opinion on this matter at present seems to be that the high degree of specialization in large-scale firms does not—in itself and apart from separation from a finished product—result in personal maladjustment.

To some extent trade unionism has appealed to many workers as a means of gaining psychic rewards. These may come on the job, through giving the worker a feeling of some power over decisions affecting his working conditions, or in the union itself, where the worker's involvement may meet needs of ego satisfaction that the job cannot.

A more recent complaint against big business is that the bureaucratization of big business has forced the individual into a mold of conformity and dullness. It is charged that individual creativity and self-expression on the job have been sacrificed to the dictates of the "organization." The "organization man" must be liked by others; he must not upset the group's smooth functioning with unorthodoxy of thought or action. In a word, in dress, demeanor, appearance, outlook, and way of life, he must conform to the demands of big business if he is to enjoy the material fruits of success.[22]

D. Miscellaneous Allegations against Big Business

Big business has been charged with responsibility for creating "big labor" and "big government." According to this view, unionization was stimulated by the development of large firms, primarily as a defensive measure. In turn, the multiplication of governmental functions has been attributed to the necessity of curbing the large and powerful business, and now labor, organizations.[23]

The following additional criticisms have been submitted. Big business is charged with not permitting men to reach the top on the basis of merit and fair competition; with suppressing inventions; with being "heartless," and with being so motivated by desire for profits that it will not hesitate to enter into agreements that would weaken the country in the event of war. Probably more important than these is the allegation against big business that it sets examples—especially with respect to prices and

---

[22] See William H. Whyte, Jr., *The Organization Man* (New York: Simon & Schuster, Inc., 1956), for one expression of this theme. Other writers have dwelt on variations of this view as well as developed other aspects of the individual's problems in a corporate body of great size. Daniel Bell, *Work and Its Discontents* (Boston: Beacon Press, 1956); A. A. Berle, Jr., *The 20th Century Capitalist Revolution* (New York: Harcourt Brace & Company, 1954); and C. Wright Mills, *The Power Elite* (New York: Oxford University Press, 1956).

[23] For a sophisticated version of this thesis, see J. K. Galbraith, *American Capitalism* (Boston: Houghton Mifflin Company, 1952), pp. 115-139. For a critique of Galbraith's thesis, see W. Adams, "Competition, Monopoly and Countervailing Power," *Quarterly Journal of Economics*, November, 1953, pp. 469-492.

wages—that are followed, either voluntarily or because of fear, by smaller firms. This allegation will be discussed in the next section.

III. NET EVALUATION OF BIGNESS IN BUSINESS

An attempt might be made to strike a balance between the benefits and evils of big business, but much more to the point would be suggestions whereby the benefits associated with bigness might be achieved without our suffering the evils to which it sometimes gives rise. Specifically, we need methods of discovering where bigness does give economic efficiency and for insuring that this advantage is used to benefit society as a whole, rather than a few persons.

In assessing the effects of bigness, one final caution deserves emphasis. There is a common tendency to place gains in economic efficiency above all others. That is, many persons seem to be resigned to the evils of bigness, as they see them, if big firms are demonstrably more efficient than smaller ones. Surely it makes little sense to argue that political democracy should be weakened, personal and social adjustment worsened, and that big labor and big government should be fostered to achieve minor cost reductions. Economic gains do not necessarily take precedence over other kinds of benefits—especially in a nation that is already the most prosperous in the world. There consequently is no easy escape from the difficult task of weighing and balancing all likely benefits and evils, whether political, social, or economic, of bigness in business.

IV. SUMMARY AND CONCLUSIONS

It is easy to understand why bigness in business remains a highly controversial and highly emotional subject. Strong arguments for and against bigness can be given strong support; some of the claims and attacks take on almost religious fervor both when big business is found to be the major cause of American prosperity and victory in World War II, and when it is charged with corrupting democracy and wiping out the small businessman.

The claim—indeed, it is almost a universal creed in this country—that very large firms are indispensable for productive efficiency was examined in great detail. Even the very concept of efficiency was found to be complex, consisting of a monetary and a "real" meaning. Both a theoretical examination of the consequences of increased business size and a review of available evidence suggest strongly that there is a limit to the gains from bigness in business. In many industries the very largest companies apparently have lost rather than gained from their great size. Nevertheless, it is also clear that in many major industries the one-man or even the hundred-man business has little chance of survival.

Other claims for big business to the effect that they are civic-minded and law-abiding, and that they facilitate government regulation, were examined rather briefly and found to have considerable merit. Some alleged lesser advantages were also listed.

The major charge against big business is that it exerts disproportionate influence over government and weakens democracy. Evidence that can be adduced on this allegation is weak at best, for the very subject at issue defies quantitative measurement. The author believes that big business does exert disproportionate political power, recognizing that he may be mistaken, for he must rely upon shaky evidence. Rather than this condition being the result of evil motive and corrupt practice, however, it seems to be primarily a consequence of the apathy of individual voters and their ignorance concerning public issues.

The argument that large firms are driving small ones out of existence was shown to be sadly lacking in factual basis. However, the charge that big business interferes with happy personal and social adjustment was shown to have more merit. Here, again, solid empirical evidence is lacking because of the very nature of the subject matter at issue.

In our discussion of bigness in business, we have been careful to consider it wholly apart from monopoly. As will be discussed later, monopoly is not exclusively enjoyed by large firms, and many of the latter face extremely intensive competition from equally large rivals. It should nevertheless be quite clear that bigness is a major social problem, wholly apart from any possible connection with monopoly. The intelligent voter must decide where he stands on this issue.

DISCUSSION QUESTIONS

1. What is the meaning of "efficiency" in economic terms? Why is its clear definition important?

2. What is the essential point of difference between bargaining-power economies and real economies? Give illustrations of both.

3. If all bargaining-power economies could be eliminated, how would the size of the national income be affected? Would your answer hold for real economies? Explain.

4. Take any American industry as an illustration of predominance of large firms; do you believe the major gains to firms in that industry to be in the form of economies in production or other types of economies? Explain what conditions seem most conducive to production economies from large-scale operations.

5. When a firm has many very similar production units (plants, stores,

and the like), what can one deduce concerning the relative importance of production and other types of economies? Explain.

6. Summarize the evidence presented here about the relative costs of very large, large, medium-sized, and small business—on the average, and as individual firms.

7. What circumstances tend to make firms become less efficient beyond some point?

8. How do you account for the differences in costs of firms in the same industry?

9. In what ways are costs related to output? How are costs affected by the size of the plant or the firm?

10. On what grounds has it been argued that large firms are more law-abiding than small firms?

11. For what reasons are large firms said to be the main source of research effort and technical development? How good an argument is this?

12. Do you believe that small firms are being driven out of existence by large firms? Do you think that in certain industries this is happening? Explain.

13. Discuss the ways in which big-business groups exert their political power. Contrast these methods with those used by labor unions, farm groups.

Chapter

11   Can the Evils

of Big Business

Be Corrected?

In several earlier chapters measures were suggested for overcoming defects in the economy. Nothing was said there about the difficulties that arise when government tries to improve economic and social conditions. A discussion of these difficulties is especially pertinent when measures to correct evils due to bigness in business are being considered. Accordingly, before contemplating what can and should be done about bigness, the nature and hazards of government intervention in economic and social matters will be explored briefly.

I.   THE BASIS FOR GOVERNMENT INTERVENTION

Viewed simply, the federal government is the ultimate source of physical power in the United States. It controls the nation's military forces and the federal police force; it can use them to fine, imprison, tax, and even to kill people. Government power can be used either to compel men to do certain things or to prevent them from doing proscribed things.

Whereas the government possesses ultimate power which can be used over individuals in the ways described, the people in turn hold the ultimate power over a democratic government. (Even in a dictatorship, the populace may be able to throw out its government forcibly and to replace it with another.) In a democracy, the power to replace one group of leaders with another and to change the laws under which government operates is lodged with a majority of voters.

When conditions are not to a people's liking, they will, or can be expected to try, to change them. Rather than take matters into their own hands and use force, in a democracy they will employ the powerful instrument of government, which is available. That is, they will legislate against objectionable conditions. The truth of this observation is attested by the very large number of laws both introduced and adopted in all democratic countries.

At this point we are not concerned with what type of law should be enacted to deal with our specific problem—bigness in business. That question will be dealt with a little later. Before turning to that, let us probe the hazards involved in employing government intervention to correct a defect in our economic or social situation. We shall assume that we have decided what condition is objectionable and have selected a method to correct it. What hazards arise between that stage and the successful execution of the program to eliminate the objectionable condition?

II. POSSIBLE SLIPS BETWEEN A LAW AND ITS ULTIMATE GOAL

First, laws may be enacted in a form that may hinder or even prevent the attainment of their objectives. Those who draft legislation may incorporate booby traps consciously to frustrate the voters' intentions, while ostensibly the law was passed to carry out the electorate's wishes. At best, the drafting of legislation is difficult even when the purpose and underlying conception of the law are clear. However, in practice, representatives of various economic groups participate in writing important pieces of legislation, and not all have the same end in view. Each group seeks to escape the restrictive effects of a law while gaining for itself maximum benefits. Loopholes through which particular groups may escape from a law probably are more often put there for that very purpose than by accident.

Second, after a law, whether with or without loopholes, has been enacted, there are various means of frustrating its provisions. The personnel appointed to the task of administering it may be selected because they exhibit little enthusiasm for vigorous enforcement. Sometimes administrators are selected primarily because they are inefficient or not expected to be conscientious in carrying out their duties. For example, the Federal Trade Commission for some time was made up of members who came close to being opposed to the legislation they were called upon to administer.

Third, the provisions and the administrators of a law can be checked by insufficient appropriations. With regard to the antitrust laws, Congress enacted a fairly potent piece of legislation, and men were appointed to the job of administering it who showed energy and imagination, but they were held to small achievements by the tiny appropriations made for their agency. All too often the electorate, even if it has been aroused over an issue, will be satisfied once a law has been put on the statute books which purports to do what they desire. They lose interest before the details of the law are hammered out; they scarcely pay attention to the personnel entrusted to administer it, and do not even know whether an appropriation was made to pay for the execution of the law.

Fourth, by harassing and intimidating government personnel, Congress can cripple the administration of a law. It can require the top officials of a very busy agency to appear at hearings day in and day out so that they cannot do their jobs. (It has been charged that Leon Henderson's constant summons to appear before Congressional committees when he was administrator of the O.P.A. were so motivated.) Or the personnel can be abused, insulted, and even threatened by Congressional committees so that they voluntarily elect to leave their job. One form of intimidation employed to influence an administrative agency is a subtle but commonplace type of blackmail. A congressman, especially one on the appropriations committee of either legislative body, might call the top official of an administrative agency, explaining why he believes some particular action should be taken. The administrator often will feel that if that action is not taken, his agency's appropriations will be cut.

It is not suggested that Congress usually does not desire to carry out the policies it ostensibly enacts into legislation. However, it is prudent to take account of the realities of politics. Sometimes congressmen believe it would cost them many votes if they opposed some measure that they find objectionable—it does not matter for what reason. Some of the means of preventing a policy from being carried out without actually voting against it have been indicated; it cannot be accurately determined how frequently such measures are employed, but no one will deny their existence. Indeed, any experienced Washington newspaper reporter could expand the list and give many examples of each.

Another hazard in enacting legislation to correct economic and social conditions lies along another line. A desirable law, well drafted, efficiently administered, with adequate appropriations and free from harassment, may linger beyond the time it is needed. Almost every law is drawn to remedy a defect in a particular situation. As long as the contextual situation continues, the law may be desirable. When the general situation changes, the law may do more harm than good. Consequently, whenever a law is enacted, there is the risk that it may be applied under conditions to which it is unsuited. This danger may be averted by placing a time limit on legislation so that Congress must reconsider its suitability to the then current situation.

Clearly, it no simple matter to carry through the enactment of a law, from the determination to employ the power of government to correct an objectionable condition, to constructive action. The many methods of defeating attempts to legislate a better economic situation that have been listed here may seem insurmountable. However, they are trifling compared to the difficulty of deciding what situations should be changed and in selecting the best means for bringing about the desired change. A law may do more damage than the situation it was designed to correct. When a law is passed, even after thorough analysis, more often than not it will prove to have unintended objectionable effects. It seems to be impossible to foresee accurately all the consequences of any law. For example, an ordinance may be enacted requiring inspection of barbershops to insure their cleanliness. It is likely to turn out in practice that someone influential in the barber trade will be made the chief inspector and will use his office to compel all barbers to adhere to a price agreed upon by the barber association. Anyone who cuts price would be inspected, with the certainty of being pronounced unsanitary and incurring a fine. Thus, a measure ostensibly aimed at protection of the public health can be turned into a raid upon the public purse.

The upshot of this discussion is not that all laws are bad or undesirable. As will appear, the author endorses legislation on many subjects. He has little patience with those who pronounce the words, "The government should keep its hands out of business," as if they were one of the Ten Commandments. However, the reader is forewarned that he invites disillusionment if he reacts to every situation that seems defective by demanding that "there ought to be a law against it." Legislation is not only complicated, requiring considerable knowledge and intelligence; it is the profession of hardheaded, experienced, and ingenious men. While their motives may be pure, they seldom are simple; their methods are clever and devious. Anyone who advances a scheme to make things better should have more to recommend it than his good intentions. Otherwise his effort to do good may be turned into a pretext for enacting legislation that makes matters worse.

Let us now turn back to our discussion of possible remedies for the evils of big business. The foregoing discussion should serve as a cold shower for those who argue that "the government should do something about big business." Moreover, if anyone concludes that a sure-fire cure for any evil from bigness is listed here, he is urged to reread the first part of this chapter. At best, the following discussion presents possible lines of approach. The author is not certain that any of them would work. These suggestions are presented simply to convey the idea—a deep conviction of the author—that many, if not all, objectionable situations can be improved with sufficient thought and effort.

Unfortunately, the branch of social science that is concerned with devising measures for improvement is as yet quite new and undeveloped. Before long, far better remedies than those listed here are almost certain to be brought forward. It will, however, serve our purpose to discuss briefly the few measures set forth below.

III. LINES OF ATTACK ON THE EVILS OF BIGNESS

Cure is generally far more difficult than prevention.[1] The elimination of business empires already in existence, some of which employ hundreds of thousands of men and women, would call for enormous change in existing arrangements. Before such profound change is undertaken, it is essential to calculate carefully both the cost and the gain.

Perhaps the most fundamental question is how much would be gained by reducing the number of employees in a firm from, say, 200,000 to 30,000. Would such a change significantly alter the relation of an individual to the final product—would it offer sufficient opportunities for personal advancement and escape from tedium to warrant great disruption of existing arrangements? While superficially it appears that if bigness is bad, then substantial reduction in size is desirable, this conclusion may not follow. Probably little gain is achieved unless the size of individual enterprises is brought down below, say, 1,000. (Note that here we are not considering problems of monopoly; where bigness is associated with monopoly, a separate remedy must be applied.)

The author concludes that a program to break up all large enterprises today is inadvisable, since the evils sometimes associated with bigness can be mitigated through other measures. Let us consider the major objections to large firms and see whether they might be removed even when large firms are retained. First, what might be done to abridge the political power of large businesses?

A. *Possible Remedies for Excessive Political Power of Large Businesses*

The great political power of big business is better described as weakness of the individual voter. Big business obtains strong political power because individual voters fail to exert theirs. Would not an awakening of active voter interest and participation end the excessive political influence of big business? If so, is it a feasible solution?

In the opening section we discussed the difficulties besetting voters

---

[1] For an analysis of antitrust policy supporting this position, see Donald Dewey, "Romance and Realism in Antitrust Policy," *Journal of Political Economy*, April, 1955, pp. 93-102.

in a modern complex society. Vigorous democracy was shown to involve many difficult requirements. While substantial improvement in the vigor of American democracy is altogether possible, the progress that can be anticipated realistically makes this solution both slow and uncertain.

Other means might be employed to curtail excessive political power of big businesses. However, if these are to be effective, sufficient political influence must be achieved for their enactment, because big business groups can be expected to try to preserve conditions that allow them disproportionate political influence. Among the various means of curtailment available are reduction in the number of political appointees by an extension of civil service rules to most employees of government; a substantial increase in civil service salaries to reduce the vulnerability of government employees to enticements from businessmen seeking government's favors; strict penalties for various actions that tend to intimidate government employees and legislative representatives; the creation of committees of public figures to investigate violations of the spirit of democracy and to use publicity to punish those who exert disproportionate political influence; extension of public information about the operations of government, so that what is "common knowledge" among Washington reporters is made known to the electorate; strict regulation and limitation on the activity of lobbies, and the like.

Essentially, the many proposals listed depend upon the wide dissemination of information. As a result, their success rests upon wholehearted cooperation from the press. If this were not forthcoming, a government-sponsored and financed newspaper for spreading this information might be created. (While government control over the press clearly would be an anathema, the prospect of a self-supporting government newspaper in competition with the private press is at least an intriguing proposal.)

B. Possible Remedies for Regimentation in Big Business

The social and psychological effects of bigness were indicated to be perhaps the most serious. Can anything be done to give workers a feeling of active and meaningful participation in the affairs of a very large firm? Can we eliminate the feeling that one is "lost" under dozens of layers in a huge and impenetrable hierarchy with little chance of obtaining recognition?

Some efforts taken by unions and by large corporations suggest that indoctrination programs can go far to mitigate these conditions. Most hopeful in this regard is the similarity of interest between employer and employee. If worker *esprit* can be bettered, the firm will gain in improved morale, which usually increases output and reduces work stoppages. The worker, on the other hand, would gain from the feeling that his work served some socially useful purpose and from the larger volume of output in which he could share.

Organized arrangements for training employees so that they may be promoted to more skilled jobs is another method of adding to the attractiveness of working in large corporations. Attendance at meetings addressed by the top executives has sometimes helped to bring the worker a feeling that he is not an isolated and insignificant zero who could disappear without being missed.

Other devices could partly offset the objectionable social and psychological effects of bigness. Among them are efforts to obtain suggestions from employees on methods of improving productive efficiency; clearly defined grievance machinery so that workers could be assured an opportunity of being heard if they believe themselves to be unjustly treated; and clearly defined conditions of status, with explicit regulations governing dismissal, promotion, and pay increases.

Decentralization within a large enterprise might also help to mitigate the social and psychological evils of bigness in business. A large organization can treat its component parts very much as separate units, even giving them a separate name. Management of each component might be made quite autonomous, save for coordination at the highest level. In this way, the size of the enterprise that the individual *feels* he is working for might be greatly reduced. Other advantages might ensue to the firm itself from such an arrangement.[2]

C. Protection of Small Firms against Abuse from Large Firms

It has been shown that the charge against big firms that they abuse small ones and drive them out of business is difficult to substantiate. Many inefficient businessmen attribute their failure in business to their small size rather than to their incompetence. However, big firms do possess some advantages—unrelated to real merit—that allow them to injure small competitors. The greatest of these is "bargaining power" that may be used in making purchases. Especially during periods of poor business, but at other times as well, large customers are highly prized by suppliers. To keep their patronage, sellers are made to feel that they must offer them preferential prices. As a result, small firms are required to pay higher prices than are demanded of the large firms. Since such discounts often are kept secret, it is difficult to determine how frequently large firms enjoy this advantage and how much preference they receive in price.

---

[2] For a discussion of the gains achievable from decentralization, see M. E. Dimock, *Free Enterprise and the Administrative State* (University: University of Alabama Press, 1951), pp. 77-124.

The Robinson-Patman Act was passed in 1936 to prohibit discriminatory prices; if a large firm receives a lower price than small firms do, it (and the seller as well) must be able to justify the difference by differences in cost of handling their businesses. Unfortunately, it is extremely difficult to calculate costs of production and distribution, regardless of effort and expense. Apart from practical difficulties in calculating costs, there are basic conceptual problems that make it unlikely that everyone will arrive at the same results. Just how much secret price cutting in favor of large buyers goes on despite the Robinson-Patman Act can only be conjectured. Most authorities believe that the legislation has greatly reduced the practice.

Protection of small businesses can serve society best if it strengthens them rather than weakens the large. Measures to facilitate group buying on behalf of small concerns, cooperative research facilities, joint advertising arrangements and collection of information about market conditions would enable small firms to enjoy most of the advantages of large firms.

IV. SUMMARY AND CONCLUSIONS

It appears unfeasible, even if it were desirable, to break up all very large firms. (If they were monopolies in addition to being large, it might be necessary to break them up.) There also would seem to be little gained and much lost from limiting the *internal growth* of firms that are now very large, though some purpose might be served by prohibiting merger or consolidation with firms that are already large. The most fruitful lines of approach to this problem consist of finding antidotes for the evils of bigness, while leaving existing business structure intact. Opportunities for further growth of large firms is essential if they are to possess strong incentive to compete, because, basically, businesses compete in an effort to increase their share of the market.

Some lines of approach have been suggested. None of the suggestions is more than a possibility. None has been tested. All pose administrative and legislative difficulties that might prove insurmountable. Just the same, bigness in business is certainly more than a problem one wants to learn about. It is one that we should try to *do* something about.

DISCUSSION QUESTIONS

1. Explain how sometimes the best way to prevent regulation of an industry is to pass a law that ostensibly regulates it.

2. By what means can a piece of legislation be so drafted that it is virtually certain to fail in the objectives of many of its supporters?

3. List the various hazards to a law between its introduction and its successful execution.

4. Do you believe that the largest firms in the nation (lacking any monopoly power) should be broken up? Explain.

5. Is it necessary to break up large businesses to end their disproportionate political power? By what means might this goal be achieved?

6. Would you favor special assistance to small firms, say, in the form of subsidies, legislation outlawing price cutting, and such, so that they could not be driven out of business by large firms?

7. How small must a firm be before a worker can achieve a feeling of being an important cog in the operation and feel that special merit will be recognized and rewarded?

SELECTED READINGS FOR PART 4

Bain, Joe S. *Barriers to New Competition*. Cambridge, Mass.: Harvard University Press, 1956. P. 329. Dealing with one of the most important aspects of a competitive market—freedom of entry, the author attempts to evaluate barriers to entry in twenty manufacturing industries. The main barriers are product differentiation, absolute cost advantages of existing producers, and the economies of scale. These barriers are related mainly to the techniques of production, the market situation, and consumer preference.

Berle, A. A., Jr. *The 20th Century Capitalist Revolution*. New York: Harcourt Brace & Company, Inc., 1954. P. 192. The author views the corporation as a chief revolutionary instrument in twentieth-century capitalism. Corporate planning for increased output on a mass scale, and corporate social responsibility for the repercussions of its policies, are emphasized as major elements in the economy's progress. Competition in the twentieth century is more political than economic, with supply being equated to demand by corporate decision making based on considerations of public opinion.

Bowen, Howard R. *Social Responsibilities of the Businessman*. New York: Harper & Brothers, 1953. P. 259. A general discussion of the social responsibilities of leaders of large-scale enterprise. Ethical standards of the leaders in a capitalist system governed by the profit motive are dealt with, together with the many problems which arise in decision making.

Crum, William L. *The Age Structure of the Corporate System*. Berkeley: University of California Press, 1953. P. 181. Deals with the age distribution of corporations by size, by industry, and by degree of profit. Also provides important statistical information on mergers and the birth and death of corporations.

Dimock, M. E. *Free Enterprise and the Administrative State*. University: University of Alabama Press, 1951. Pp. x, 179. This book, an institutional view of the free-enterprise system in the United States, examines the organization and management of the system. The author places major emphasis on the role which administration plays in the system, and administrative theory is examined thoroughly.

Drucker, Peter F. *America's Next Twenty Years*. New York: Harper & Brothers,

1957. P. 114. This critical examination of the most important economic events of the recent past shows how they are likely to shape the form of the future. Within this framework the author discusses the labor force, the problem of automation, the new industrial leaders, etc.

Quinn, Theodore K. *Giant Business: Threat to Democracy; the Autobiography of an Insider.* New York: Exposition Press, 1953. P. 321. An attack on bigness of business enterprise by one who has been connected with big business. Large corporations are viewed as iniquitous wielders of power against competitors and small business.

Shuchman, Abraham. *Codetermination: Labor's Middle Way in Germany.* Washington, D.C.: Public Affairs Press, 1957. P. 247. The system of co-determination—wherein labor has representatives on the boards of directors of corporations—is explained and analyzed in an extremely interesting book. The lessons and experiences of codetermination are scrutinized for their pertinence in dealing with labor problems.

Stelzer, Irwin M. *Selected Anti-Trust Cases.* Homewood, Ill.: Richard D. Irwin, Inc., 1955. Pp. x, 210. This is a very useful book of significant antitrust cases which illustrate some of the principles reflected in the courts' disposition of major problems concerning business behavior. The cases selected deal with proprietary consolidations and monopoly, loose-knit federations, trade practices, legal monopolies under federal antitrust, and foreign commerce and international arguments.

United States Congress, Select Committee on Small Business. *Congress and the Monopoly Problem . . . 1900-1956.* Washington, D.C.: U.S. Government Printing Office, 1956. Pp. x, 662. A catalogue of important antitrust legislation and legislative proposals, as well as a summary and analysis of all antitrust laws now in operation.

United States, Federal Trade Commission. *Report on Corporate Mergers and Acquisitions.* Washington, D.C.: Government Printing Office, 1955. Pp. v, 201. This is an invaluable document bringing up to date the available statistics on mergers in mining and manufacturing for the period 1948-1954. Results are compared with an earlier study showing mergers for 1947 and earlier years. The extent to which mergers are distributed by industry and size of firm is shown.

————. *Report of the F.T.C. on Changes in Concentration in Manufacturing, 1935 to 1947 and 1950.* Washington, D.C.: Government Printing Office, 1954. Pp. v, 153. This is a follow-up to an earlier FTC report on concentration in 1947. The report measures the changes that have occurred in the degree of concentration and the factors involved in these changes.

Universities-National Bureau Committee for Economic Research. *Business Concentration and Price Policy.* Princeton, N.J.: Princeton University Press, 1955. Pp. x, 514. Revised versions of papers delivered at the Conference on Business Concentration and Price Policy held at Princeton University, June 17-19, 1952. Economists contributing include Joe S. Bain, George W. Stocking, Corwin Edwards, Fritz Machlup, Milton Friedman. Papers covered a wide range of subjects relating to concentration, such as economic theory and measurement of concentration, empirical evidence on economies of scale, and costs and prices.

Weston, Fred J. *The Role of Mergers in the Growth of Large Firms.* Berkeley: University of California Press, 1953. P. 156. An analysis of factors of importance in the merger process. Significance of mergers in growth is minimized, and factors determining external and internal growth of firms are considered.

Whyte, William H. *The Organization Man.* New York: Simon & Schuster, Inc., 1956. P. 429. This provocative book raises many important questions about the bureaucratization of our society in general and business activity in particular. The author, a former editor of *Fortune,* bewails the mediocrity of mind being shaped by corporate enterprise and comes out squarely for the individual and his need to fight the organization in order to preserve his autonomy.

Chapter

12 Resource Allocation
and the Price System

The work a modern economic system must perform is fantastically complicated: stated simply, it is to decide what shall be produced, in what quantity, by whom, and by what means. Stated this way, these functions convey very little feeling of either their complexity or their importance.

A person might get a clue to an economy's functions by recalling his last picnic. Very likely, the needs of some members of the group were overlooked so that one who suffered from an ulcer found himself without his precious milk and had to choose between water and Coke—the first probably tepid and unpleasantly flavored, the second of wholly acceptable temperature and taste but certain to cause discomfort, if not pain. Some in the group may have objected to the fare of hamburgers and frankfurters because of life-long prejudices. (We pass over the inevitable person who cannot understand why you did not buy steaks or lobster tails.) Also, almost every picnic is marred by some oversight. The woman assigned the job of looking after the coffee may have neglected to bring anything along to drink it from; or no one thought to bring napkins along or to weigh down the paper plates and cups when the wind started to blow.

When we conduct a post mortem on a picnic we often find ourselves saying something like "we should have been able to do better with $20 to feed eight people." Picnic managers generally conclude that they could have used their funds more wisely; even then, one rarely finds complete agreement on just what they should have done. The picnic does not exist where the amount of money available is sufficient to buy *all* the things that everyone would like to buy. This brief reminder of the tribulations of picnic planning may make more vivid and believable the following discussion of the functions an economic system must perform, though one might say that "running an economic system is no picnic."

I. THE CENTRAL ECONOMIC PROBLEM: RESOURCE ALLOCATION

Like picnickers, no nation has everything its people want. Indeed, it is not clear that even the rich people in any country can afford to buy everything for which they have the slightest desire. People with imagination and intelligence may acquire wants faster than very large incomes can satisfy them. Whether or not rich people can purchase anything they wish, there can be little dispute that almost everyone wants far more than he can have.

The layman uses scarcity of money to explain why people cannot get whatever they desire. From his personal standpoint, this explanation is correct; if he had all of the money he desired, he could buy everything he wanted. Even a doubling of the money supply *in a nation*, however, would not increase the quantity of things its population could purchase; they would be able to buy just about as much as they could when they had half as much money.

The reason that people cannot have nearly as many things as they would like is that productive resources are scarce. Output is limited by the supply of labor, natural resources, organizational ability, machinery, fertile land, and the like, rather than by the ability of a government to create money. Accordingly, we must do without many things we desire because the combined efforts of all people in the United States, even using the latest methods of production, would still far from satisfy all our material wants. In short, we must resign ourselves to a chronic condition of scarcity, inasmuch as human wants exceed greatly the means for satisfying them.

Because nobody can have all he wants, individuals, as consumers, businessmen, laborers, and owners of land and investible funds, must make choices. They select what they want most, and are willing to pay for, among the main goods and services available, and forego the rest. By doing so, they carry out a basic function of the economic system: their selections determine what use will be made of productive resources. A nation with rich natural resources and a highly skilled labor force would still suffer great privation if these were devoted to the production of goods that failed to satisfy basic needs. By making the things people want most, a nation keeps the unfilled wants of its population to a minimum. In this way, their welfare is maximized.

But the production of the most urgently needed goods and services is not enough. A potentially prosperous country might be kept in relative poverty if production methods were inefficient. There are many ways of producing the same article, and some methods are far more costly of productive resources than others are. Thus another major function of an economic system is to combine productive resources in the most efficient manner, in order to maximize the output of desired goods and services. These functions of satisfying most urgent needs and making efficient use of available resources generally are called "allocation of resources"; every economic system performs this function, but some do it much more effectively than others.

In the United States, we employ a system of "free enterprise" (sometimes called a "competitive system," a "price system," a "profit system," or a "market economy") to allocate resources. Our system is distinguished primarily by its emphasis on decentralization; i.e., upon allowing very large numbers of people to make economic decisions. On the other hand, socialist countries use a system in which relatively few planners decide how to allocate the nation's resources. The free-enterprise system is comparatively new; during medieval times "economic planning" was done after a fashion by special groups, like the Church, local guilds, and city councils.

No economic system has ever been a completely pure type. The American economy, for example, does not rely wholly on free enterprise or competition. Some of our industries are controlled by legal and regulated monopolies (public utilities, holders of patents, etc.); some are directly owned and operated by the government (the post office; municipal electric, gas, and water companies; public schools; fire and police protection; and the like); some activities are suppressed outright (vice, rackets, gambling, etc.); some are competitive but are controlled and regulated anyway (banking, the stock exchanges, for instance). The rest of the economy is subject to laws whose object is to ensure rigorous and "fair" competition. Nevertheless, in the United States most decisions affecting resource allocation are made by millions of private individuals. In the Soviet Union, which has the most thoroughly planned economy in the world, isolated parts of the economy resemble a free-enterprise system. But, despite these exceptions, resource allocation in the U.S.S.R. is largely the responsibility of a relatively small number of government officials.

The key point here is that "economizing"—the efficient allocation of scarce resources—is an inescapable function of every economic system, regardless of how the job is done. In the remainder of this chapter and in the next, we shall see how a price system works in theory. In order to clarify what is said at several points, examples will be drawn from the economy of the United States. The reader should not allow himself to be confused by these examples; our interest in this chapter is with a "pure model" of a free-enterprise system, rather than with existing conditions.

II. LOGIC OF A FREE-ENTERPRISE ECONOMY

A. *How It Works*

"Consumer and producer sovereignty" is the basic allocating principle of the free-enterprise economy. In oversimple terms, buyers decide *what* items shall be produced by their purchases; producers decide *how* these items shall be produced. Businessmen presumably offer for sale what they believe their customers want and faithfully do their customers' bidding (within the bounds imposed by the cost and availability of productive resources), under threat of financial penalty.

A free-enterprise system relies upon individual businessmen to select methods of production, and it offers them strong financial incentives to find the most efficient production methods. Since businessmen risk their private property in enterprises devoted to production for sale, they are automatically penalized if they use resources clumsily; inefficiencies in production raise costs, thus reducing income and possibly causing actual losses. Owing to such pressures, economic resources tend not to be used unless they are absolutely needed.

In the logic of a free-enterprise economy, things produced go to those who can afford to buy them. Businessmen respond only to customers' preferences that are backed by the ability to pay. Money income is distributed to individuals according to their productive contribution.[1] Thus the most productive members of the community and their personal dependents obtain the highest rewards, and their desires for goods have the greatest weight in deciding what shall be produced.

The foregoing discussion is brief and incomplete in many respects. Further ramifications of the capitalistic system will be taken up in later chapters. Now it is appropriate to show why a free-enterprise system must also be highly competitive if it is to serve society efficiently.[2]

B. The Necessity for Competition

The decentralized economic system described here works well only to the extent that there is competition among producers and consumers and in resource markets. Competition means rivalry, and efforts to advance in a struggle with others. It will be shown that a competitive economy in which consumers and businessmen know all they need to know to safeguard and advance their own interests needs no central plans or rules to ensure that the right things are produced in the correct proportions and by the most efficient methods.

Given competition, producers who fail to offer consumers what they

---

[1] See Chapter 7 for a discussion of the factors determining personal incomes in the United States. It is shown that in practice many factors other than productive contribution influence the size of personal incomes.

[2] Some readers may have read or seen reference to the very interesting thesis of "countervailing power" introduced by Professor J. K. Galbraith. Expressed oversimply, this thesis holds that monopoly breeds countermonopoly, which greatly reduces the rewards of the original monopoly. It should be remarked that "countervailing power" does not represent a substitute for competition but only a force leading to a sharing of the spoils of monopoly. For a lucid and interesting development of this concept by the man who originated it, see J. K. Galbraith, *American Capitalism* (Boston: Houghton Mifflin Company, 1952).

want will lose out to producers who do. If some businessmen by agreement among themselves tried to compel consumers to take what they were offered rather than what they wanted, new producers would come along and take the dissatisfied customers away. Businessmen, under competition, cater to and try to anticipate the preferences of consumers. Unwanted goods go unsold.

Moreover, competition among producers drives out of business those who cannot produce efficiently. Buyers will not pay any more for their purchases than they have to pay; they will seek out the sellers charging the lowest price. These sellers grow in number and take away business from those trying to charge more, and thus they compel all sellers to charge the same price. Inefficient producers cannot endure in the face of rigorous price competition, because their costs eventually exceed prices. Competition thus imposes heavy pressure upon businessmen to learn alternative methods of production and to employ the most efficient.

One can easily show that if competition were absent, the allocation of resources might be highly imperfect; for example, let us consider the effects of having uninformed buyers, a condition which would represent a departure from competition defined in the technical sense. Buyers, lacking knowledge of the relative quality and price of alternate brands of the same product, might pay much more or get much less than necessary. Businessmen would not be under compulsion to produce efficiently in order to survive. By ingenious salesmanship some might persuade consumers to favor their product over better brands. In the absence of competition, a very substantial waste of resources becomes possible through inefficient production and the production of low-quality merchandise; also, it becomes possible that consumers will be offered a variety of goods and services that does not correspond to their wants. In short, *a free-enterprise economy loses its underlying rationale if it is not competitive.* It could not reasonably be expected that the economy would serve society well if forces counter to competition were strong.

III. THE USES OF PRICE THEORY

The presentation of *price theory* here and in the following chapter is intended to serve two functions. First, it constructs simplified hypothetical problems that contain the essential elements of real problems. By solving these simplified cases, we learn to understand the far more complicated problems of the real world. Theory simplifies reality in the interest of greater understanding. This review will also indicate the questions we should ask about real-life situations and will suggest interrelations among various factors at work that otherwise might be overlooked.

A second function performed by price theory is to describe the fundamental forces operating in our economy. Although the description of reality presented by price theory is general and may not account exactly for any actual situation, it does show major tendencies that operate in almost every situation. Failure to achieve full accuracy of description is due to the fact that, as in other sciences, economic theory studies the operation of only the most important forces at work in concrete situations. Thus, although economic theory may not describe reality exactly, or from month to month, it does help to explain broad developments over longer periods.

IV. HOW RESOURCES ARE ALLOCATED

Three main factors determine how resources are allocated: (1) the amount that people are willing to pay for a product, termed "demand"; (2) the amount that producers must be paid to make the product available, termed "supply"; and (3) the conditions under which the product is sold, referred to as "market circumstances." It is almost self-evident that demand and supply determine a product's price. And it will be explained presently how price influences the allocation of resources.

A price is set between buyers and sellers. The upper limit of a product's price will be what the potential customers who are most eager to buy it, are willing to pay. Conversely, the lower limit to price is the minimum amount that would be acceptable to producers whose production costs are lowest and who are most anxious to sell their output. These two limits generally are very far apart, and price can settle anywhere between these two extremes. The precise point at which price will ultimately settle depends, as shall be explained, on the market circumstances under which it is offered for sale.

The concepts of demand, supply, and market circumstances are quite complicated. In order to understand these concepts thoroughly we must master the use of diagrams similar to those introduced when we discussed the effect of business size on costs of production (see the cost curves in Chapter 10). We shall also discuss the meaning of demand, supply, and market circumstances in nondiagrammatic terms.

Accordingly, the next few pages will contain a fairly concentrated dose of definitions, diagrams, and rather close reasoning. Although this discussion is likely to prove somewhat painful, diligent application by the reader at this point will pay off later in deeper and more facile understanding. Once one masters the concepts, the definitions, and the diagrams, the study of resource allocation and pricing generally becomes a gratifying experience.

Before proceeding to an analysis of demand, supply, and market circumstances, let us examine an illuminating example of supply and demand in action. The so-called specialists on the New York Stock Exchange provide a sharp illustration of the meaning of "supply" and "demand" and also indicate how these two combine to determine where price will settle.

V. AN ILLUSTRATION OF SUPPLY AND DEMAND CONDITIONS: THE STOCK MARKET

Stockbrokers[3] handle orders for almost every publicly held security—of which there are a large number. To watch each order that requires discretionary action on some particular stock would be impossible. Consequently, brokers have delegated some of their duties to "specialists" on the floor of the exchange. Acting as agents for brokers, specialists carry out their orders to buy and sell for a commission. There are various kinds of specialists, some handling several different stocks, some a few or only one; sometimes three or four handle the same highly active stock.

The specialist's basic record is his "book," in which he lists his buy (demand) and sell (supply) orders chronologically; he is required to handle them, depending on the going prices, in that order. The first order to buy a stock at a given price will be carried out when that price is offered on the exchange floor. Then the second order to buy at that price will be taken up, and so on. This procedure continues until all orders to buy a particular stock at the going price are filled, or until the price goes up (or until no more shares are offered at that price). The specialist himself may buy shares on his own account, at a given price, only after he has handled all his clients' orders.

Thus a specialist, both as an agent and as a purchaser and seller of stocks on his own account, is located at the juncture of supply and demand. He therefore knows the prices which persons "in the market" are willing to pay and to accept for a particular stock or group of stocks, as well as the number of shares available.

Suppose that all buy and sell orders for stock "A" at 56¼ had been executed on the exchange floor. A specialist in stock "A" is likely to have *sell* orders for 56⅜, 56½, 56⅝, and perhaps for other prices. On the other hand, maybe his *buy* side would show orders at 56⅛, 56, 55⅞, 55½, and other prices. (Special circumstances surrounding certain orders, e.g. "stop-loss notations,"[4] would be duly noted by him.) A broker wanting to

---

[3] A stockbroker is someone who makes his living as a middleman; he buys and sells stocks on behalf of his customers and at their direction.

[4] A "stop-loss" order directs the broker to sell the stock if the price falls below a specified minimum figure. The purpose of such an order is to limit the loss that the security owner can sustain in a rapidly declining market. It should be emphasized, however, that the broker places the order to sell only when the price of the security reaches that figure; he may not be able to sell it unless he accepts a lower price.

buy some shares of "A" stock would find none up for sale at the old price, 56¼. He would say "How's 'A'?" and the specialist would answer, "One eighth—three eighths,"[5] which means that he holds some orders to buy at 56⅛ and to sell at 56⅜; these are known as "bid and asked" quotations. All lower and higher prices are unmentioned.

The specialist's order book contains the best available information describing the supply and demand situation for his security and tells much more than a broker gets when he asks for "market and size" information. That book tells how many shares will be offered for sale and how many will be purchased *at a variety of prices*. Let us examine a hypothetical specialist's order book and see how we might arrange its contents in a manner that explains most simply how conditions of supply and demand influence the price that will prevail for a security.

On his "buy" page, the specialist may find—apart from the large number of lines crossed out to show that he had carried out those purchases—something like the following:

Buy Orders

Price	Number of Shares		Broker	Remarks
56¼	800		Jones	
	600		Brown	
	500		Smith	
	100	(2,000)	Arthur	
56⅛	1,400		Smith	
	900		Jones	
	400		Arthur	
	300	(3,000)	Brown	
56	2,300		Brown	
	2,000		Arthur	
	1,200		Smith	
	700	(6,200)	Jones	
55⅞	3,500		Arthur	
	3,200		Smith	
	2,200		Jones	
	1,400	(10,300)	Brown	

This information can be summarized in a simpler table as follows:

---

[5] Typically, the spread between these figures is kept down to ½ or ¼ point by the specialist's offering to buy and sell on his own account when he has no bids that would narrow the gap between bid and asked prices. In this way, the specialist contributes to continuous and smooth trading in his security.

Demand for Security A

	Shares
at 56¼	2,000
56⅛	3,000
56	6,200
55⅞	10,300

In turn, one can present the contents of the foregoing table in simple diagrammatic form and designated "demand schedule" as follows:

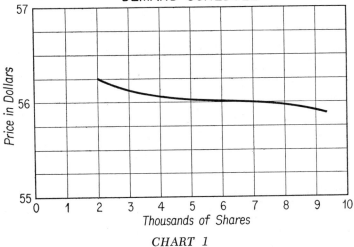

CHART 1

This simple diagram bears an extremely close relation to what is known as a "demand schedule" of the type we shall examine later in Chart 3.

The "sell orders" on the books of the specialist can be handled in a similar manner. (Sell orders represent instructions received by the specialist which specify the price at which the security, in specified quantities, is to be sold.) The listings below present a hypothetical "sell" page for the specialist, which is depicted in diagrammatic form on Chart 2 and designated "supply schedule," where it can be studied in connection with the "demand schedule."

Note that the two lines do not overlap for price. All the transactions at the prevailing price (taken to be 56⅞) and above will have been executed. What remain on the order books are unexecuted orders—to buy at prices below the current market and to sell at higher than market prices.

On the New York stock market, each specialist will receive buy-and-sell orders from many hundreds of registered brokers. They, in turn, act

Sell Orders

Price	Number of Shares	Broker	Remarks
56½	700	Brown	
	900	Smith	
	300	Jones	
	200 (2,100)	Arthur	
56⅝	1,200	Smith	
	800	Jones	
	800	Arthur	
	700 (3,500)	Brown	
56¾	2,500	Jones	
	2,000	Brown	
	1,500	Arthur	
	1,000 (7,000)	Smith	
56⅞	3,000	Brown	
	2,500	Smith	
	2,000	Arthur	
	500 (8,000)	Jones	

This information can be summarized in a more simple table as follows:

Supply of Security A

	Shares
at 56½	2,100
56⅝	3,500
56¾	7,000
56⅞	8,000

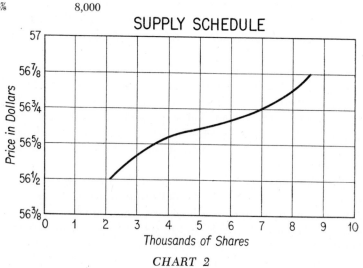

CHART 2

on behalf of literally millions of individuals and business firms that are "in the market." Thus the decisions of very large numbers of persons about the value of a single security meet at one point—in the person, or the "book," of the specialist.

The reader should recognize that stock exchanges are not typical of most markets for goods and services. They differ in several respects but most notably in the fact that a firm's corporate securities are essentially limited in supply and do not involve costs of production. Nevertheless, the clarity with which one can study conditions of supply and demand on the stock market makes it an illuminating and convenient starting place for a detailed examination of the technical meaning of "supply" and "demand" when applied to goods and services. To this we now turn.

VI. PRINCIPLES OF SUPPLY AND DEMAND

A. Demand

Demand in the general sense describes the desires of all persons to purchase a particular product for any and all reasons. These desires may be foolish and ephemeral or may reflect enlightened choices and basic needs. They may reflect a need for the product or the idea that it would make an appropriate gift. They may reflect a wish to display it in order to achieve recognition or prestige. They may reflect obscure psychological tensions which are released by making a purchase (as in the case of so-called "impulse purchases").

The desire for a product becomes economically significant and represents "demand" in the technical sense when it is combined with the ability and willingness to pay for the good. It is possible that some people may desire a product very strongly but are prevented from buying it by prejudice or fear. On the other hand, some desires of only modest intensity may be accompanied by offers of substantial prices because people are accustomed to paying those prices or for some other reasons. Thus the amounts that people are willing to pay for products may not fully and accurately reflect the relative intensity of their desires. Yet one can judge consumers' desires only by the actions they are willing to take in response to the prices of products. For this reason economists ordinarily take consumers' demands, that is, the price they will pay, as a measure of their relative desires.

Defined precisely, the demand for a commodity describes the number of units that would be bought in a particular market, during a stated time period, *at all possible prices.* Even though we may know that 100,000 units of a product are being sold monthly at a price of $1 per unit at present, we still lack the crucial information we require to know its demand. We also must know how many units would be sold if the price were 90 cents, 80 cents, 70 cents, $1.10, $1.20, etc. If we were told only the amount of sales at a price of $1, we should possess very little information about the desires of consumers for the product. And we could not separate the product in question from others whose sales at $1 might be the same but which would be sold in far larger or smaller quantities at prices of, say, 90 cents.

When we use the term "demand," we must recognize furthermore that the sale of a product is influenced by many factors other than price. Among the most important of these are the level of national income (that is, the general state of business), and the amount of selling effort—such as advertising and personal selling—that are devoted to creating sales for the product.

Used in its most precise sense, *demand designates the number of units of a product that would be sold per period of time at a series of prices, assuming no change takes place in such circumstances as sales-promotion efforts and general business conditions.*

Simple straight lines can be used to depict graphically the combined demands of all consumers for a product at a particular moment. The lines in Chart 3 represent different conditions of demand. Line 1, which is vertical, states that buyers will take the same amount of the product, regardless of the price (at least between the prices $11 and no cost— limits covered by the axis on the left). Line 2, which slopes gradually downward toward the right, states that as price declines, buyers will take more off the market. Line 3, which slopes gradually upward toward the right, describes an improbable situation in which the higher the price the more the buyers will take. Line 4, which is horizontal, states that

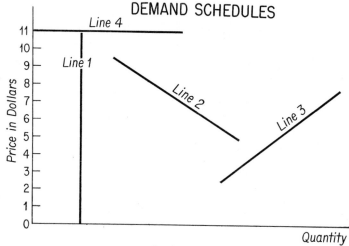

CHART 3

buyers will take as much as is offered for sale, at a given price, up to the amount covered by the bottom axis.

Table 1 below states facts about hypothetical buyers that can be translated into a diagram representing "demand." It states that they will buy 100,000 units of the product if the price is $14; 120,000 at $13; 150,000 at $12; 200,000 at $11; 280,000 at $10; and 350,000 at $9. We are here assuming that more of a product will be purchased, at any given time, at a low price than at a high one. This assumption, highly realistic, is known as "*the Law of Demand.*" (Line 2 in Chart 3 depicts the Law of Demand graphically.) More of a product will be purchased at lower prices—all other circumstances remaining the same—because (1) buyers can afford to buy more at lower prices; (2) buyers will try to substitute the lower-priced product for other products whose prices did not decline.

Table 1. Hypothetical Supply-and-Demand Conditions

Price	Supply (Quantity that would be offered for sale)	Demand (Quantity that would be purchased)
$15.00	all that would be bought	0
14.00	" " " " "	100,000
13.00	" " " " "	120,000
12.00	" " " " "	150,000
11.00	" " " " "	200,000
10.00	0	280,000
9.00	0	350,000

The shape of a demand schedule varies, among other things, according to how strongly consumers want the product in question. If the product has a ready substitute and if their need for it is not great, then as price rises they will buy much less. On the other hand, if a product is urgently needed and has no ready substitute, its sales will not fall off much even if the price rises. Responsiveness of unit sales to changes in price is called "elasticity of demand." [6] If a rise in price is accompanied by a drop in sales that is more than proportionate, the demand is considered "elastic." On the other hand, if sales increase less than proportionately when prices are reduced, the demand is termed "inelastic." [7]

To apply this concept of elasticity to a specific instance, let us determine whether the demand expressed in Table 1 is elastic or inelastic.

---

[6] Economists measure different degrees of sensitivity of unit-sales responses to changes in price by a "coefficient of price elasticity."

[7] Also, if a fall in price leads to an increase in sales that is more than proportionate, the demand is considered "elastic," and if a rise in price is accompanied by a less than proportionate decrease in sales, then the demand is termed "inelastic."

At $14, 120,000 units will be bought, while at $13, 150,000 will be purchased. In other words, when the price goes down about 7 per cent, the quantity purchased rises by 25 per cent. We conclude then that the demand is elastic at a price between $13 and $14. Similar comparisons show that the entire demand schedule from $14 down to $9 is very elastic.

Line 1 in Chart 4 reproduces the information about demand in Table 1. (It is nothing more than a curved-line variation of line 2 in Chart 3.) Line 1 represents the different amounts of the product which consumers will buy at different prices.

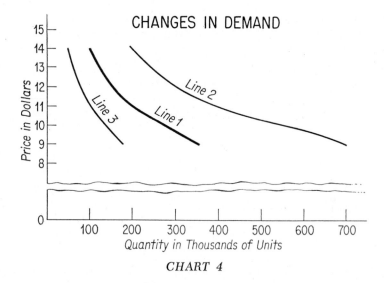

CHART 4

Changes in demand occasioned by changes in consumers' tastes or income, or in the prices of other products or any combination of these, can also be represented readily on our diagram. If all buyers combined offered to buy double the amounts indicated in Table 1 at the same prices, the increased demand would be represented by line 2 to the right of line 1. On the other hand, if buyers suddenly offered to buy only half the amounts shown in Table 1 at the same prices, the reduced demand would become line 3 in Chart 4—to the left of the original demand schedule represented by line 1. In other words, an increase in demand is represented by a shifting *of the entire demand line* to the right, while a decline in demand would result in a shift of the line to the left.

Thus we find that demand reflects many and complex conditions. And differences in the demand, as will be shown, have a significant bearing on what the price is going to be and how much is going to be produced.

B. Supply

"Supply" is defined as the number of units of a product that would be offered for sale per period of time at a series of prices. As in the situation of demand, we receive an incomplete description of supply if we know only how many units would be offered for sale at a single price. (We speak of such information as "point supply" because it describes only one point on the supply schedule.) When we define supply we must make clear, as we did in defining demand, what period of time we are discussing. The purpose of the following pages is to explain the main factors determining the supply of most goods and services and to indicate their influence upon the allocation of productive resources.

The factors determining the supply of individual products are more complex than those shaping demand. Foremost among them are costs of production, numbers of firms engaged in production, and the speed with which additional firms could enter the industry and those engaged could leave it. Accordingly, let us discuss first the effect of cost conditions upon the amount of any product that would be offered for sale.

1. COSTS OF PRODUCTION AND CONDITIONS OF SUPPLY

Clearly, the amount buyers must pay sellers to part with their output is related to what costs must be borne to produce the product. At times, sellers must accept far less than their costs because of a sudden drop in demand that makes it impossible to recover their costs, or because their merchandise is of poor style and quality and the like. Such special circumstances explain why the amount sellers obtain for their merchandise is not necessarily at or above the costs they incurred to acquire it.

On the other hand, costs are a floor below which goods ordinarily would not be produced for future sale. A firm may already possess merchandise which it must sell at whatever price it will fetch and may therefore accept less than cost; however, it does have power over what it produces and presumably would not knowingly produce for sale at a price below cost.

Although we have used the term "cost" several times without defining it, we shall soon discover that costs are among the most complicated notions in all of economics and that there are many different cost concepts. We have already met a functional division of costs which divides costs according to the general purpose for which they were incurred and includes such elements as technological costs, management costs, marketing costs, financing costs, and the like. (See Chapter 10.) We saw, too, that costs can be grouped into two types according to whether they vary as a firm increases or reduces its output; some costs rise with increases in output ("variable costs"), while others remain unchanged ("fixed costs").

When we speak of the costs that sellers must obtain to be willing to produce a particular item for sale, we have still another and a vital cost concept in mind: so-called "marginal costs." *Marginal costs* may be defined as *the additional outlays that must be made to create additional output*. The key word in this definition is "additional," because the outlays required to increase output will vary according to the level of output already achieved. For example, a firm that operates well below the level for which it was originally designed probably could increase its output at relatively low added cost. On the other hand, if the firm is "pushing capacity" [8]—that is, is producing at or above the level for which its plant was designed, it generally will incur quite high additional costs to expand output further.

It may surprise readers because homespun economics have told them that costs decline with increases in output, to learn that "marginal costs" may rise with increases in output. Especially when we are speaking of an established business with fixed plant and equipment, we can be sure that a point will be reached where efficiency of production declines and costs rise. To take a particularly simple example, at some point in expanding output a producer will incur overtime-pay obligations.

Now that we have defined marginal costs, let us return to the notion that producers will not knowingly incur costs above the price they can obtain for output. Which concept of costs should we apply in such a connection? It is no accident that the answer is "marginal costs," because otherwise we should not have taken the trouble to discuss them at this point. In effect, we have said that a firm will not be established to make a product—or will not produce an additional unit of what it is already turning out—unless the revenue it expects is at least as high as the added expenses it must incur to produce it. This conclusion is easily defended. If a firm gets more for a product, or for more units of it, than it must add to its costs to produce the product, its profits increase. On the other hand, if it were to turn out added units of a product whose costs were greater than the revenue the firm will receive from the sale of the units, its profits would be reduced in the process.

---

[8] There are several concepts of capacity: "physical capacity," "designed capacity," and "optimum output." The first represents the maximum amount that could be produced with the use of existing facilities; "designed capacity" is the volume of output for which the plant was designed; and optimum output is the level of output at which unit costs are at a minimum. The last two concepts are fairly similar, for presumably engineers design facilities to realize minimum costs at the volume they are told the plant is to produce. Physical capacity will always exceed the other two, sometimes by a great amount.

What is particularly tricky about the concept of "marginal costs" is the fact that they are easily confused with average costs, even though they are quite different. "Average costs" are all costs lumped together and then divided by the number of units produced; "marginal costs" contain only certain elements of costs—those that must be increased if one is to add to output; moreover, marginal costs can be assigned to *additions to output* and can be computed directly rather than divided over all units produced.

It is impossible to generalize about the nature of cost conditions for all firms. Products are about as different as people, and cost conditions vary widely from industry to industry. Some firms very quickly reach a point where the cost of producing additional output begins to rise; others do not reach this point until they are producing a very large quantity; a few rare firms may actually find that their unit costs decline indefinitely as they expand output. (Actually this last type of case is very difficult to imagine because beyond some point the facilities presumably would be operated at a higher level than the engineers had in mind when they designed them; inefficiencies presumably would occur that would cause marginal costs to rise, ultimately exceeding average costs.) Whatever the specific cost situation, however, the generalization holds that sellers' offerings should equal the amount they can produce at a marginal cost below the added revenue they get from selling that output. (As shall be explained later, the amount producers get from selling added output should not be confused with the price they are paid, for sometimes additional sales can be made only if a manufacturer reduces price on his entire output.)

To return to the connection between the amount that producers will offer for sale and costs of production, we can state that each firm would offer the largest output on which it could obtain added revenue in excess of original cost. Similarly, to determine what total supply[9] of a product would be offered for sale by an entire industry, we should simply total up the offerings of all individual firms—computed in the following manner.

Let us now describe, step by step, how one would construct the supply schedule for a product. Chart 5 presents several diagrams which start with the cost condition of an individual firm and end with the construction of a supply schedule for an entire industry.

The first diagram on Chart 5 shows the average and marginal costs of a hypothetical firm. Note that the average cost curve possesses the

---

[9] Used to mean the quantity that is actually produced and offered for sale, "supply" has a precise meaning only under conditions of zero or great market power. In other markets, it is necessary to distinguish between the amount firms will produce and the amount they would be willing to sell if they could obtain orders.

U shape that is to be expected in the ordinary situation, and that the marginal cost curve rises quite rapidly when output reaches "optimum capacity"—that level at which average costs are at a minimum. (The reader is urged to take a little practice in interpreting—one might call it "reading"—the marginal cost curve. At any point on the curve marked MC, he will learn what additional expenditure the firm would incur—to be found by looking at the scale on the left—if it were to produce the additional unit indicated by the scale at the bottom. For example, at the point marked, one learns that the firm would have to incur avoidable costs of $5 to produce the 11th unit if it had already been producing 10.)

The second diagram in Chart 5 indicates cost conditions for three firms making the same product. In the interest of realism, the cost conditions of each firm are assumed to be different.

Let us now assume some market price at which producers can confidently expect to sell their output after they have turned it out. Say we take a price of $6 and ask how much all of the firms in the industry would offer for sale at that price. The third diagram in Chart 5 enables us to answer this question, for it includes the marginal cost curves for all the firms in our hypothetical industry and also indicates the price that will prevail when the goods reach the market. We are able to determine the output that each firm will offer by finding the point at which the firm's marginal costs equal the expected price. For the first firm, the output would be a quantity of OQ. For the other three firms, it would be the quantities designated OQ_1 and OQ_2.

(To be sure we understand what has been said thus far, let us explain why the first firm would do best if it were to offer a quantity of OQ, in the assumed circumstances. First, if it were to offer a smaller quantity than OQ for sale, it would forgo profits. Each added unit it sold up to OQ would fetch a price higher than the added cost to produce it; on the other hand, to offer more than OQ units would reduce profits, for each added unit would cost more than the firm would get for it.)

The third diagram indicates how to determine the amount each firm would offer for sale at a particular price; to construct a full supply schedule requires that the process be repeated for every price—within reason. The fourth diagram accordingly shows, geometrically, how this process is carried out for three other assumed prices.

The fifth diagram in Chart 5 indicates how the industry supply schedule might be constructed more simply. It plots on a single diagram the marginal cost curves of all individual firms; instead of plotting them "from scratch"—starting at zero—each one is added to the others. Accordingly, S_1 represents the marginal cost curve of firm 1, plus the marginal cost curve of firm 2, and indicates the marginal costs of the two firms combined to produce corresponding levels of output. Similarly, S designates the combined marginal costs of all three firms to produce corre-

HOW TO DERIVE A SUPPLY SCHEDULE
FROM INDIVIDUAL FIRM'S COST CURVES

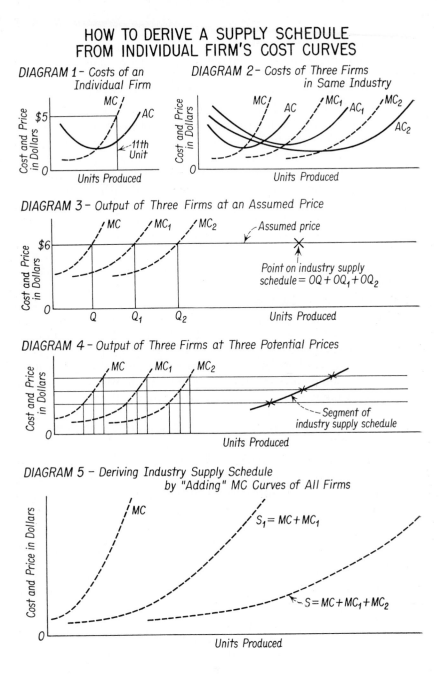

DIAGRAM 1 – Costs of an Individual Firm

DIAGRAM 2 – Costs of Three Firms in Same Industry

DIAGRAM 3 – Output of Three Firms at an Assumed Price

DIAGRAM 4 – Output of Three Firms at Three Potential Prices

DIAGRAM 5 – Deriving Industry Supply Schedule by "Adding" MC Curves of All Firms

CHART 5

sponding levels of output. A little reflection tells us that this line represents the quantity that would be offered for sale at corresponding prices.[10]

2. NUMBERS OF FIRMS IN OPERATION AND SUPPLY

Up to this point, we have explored the influence of costs of production on the quantity of any product that would be offered for sale at different prices. Other factors influence supply; among the most important is the number of firms in operation.

The point being made here may be reduced to simple arithmetic: the more firms of any size there are, the more goods will be offered for sale. To return to our discussion of the way to construct a supply schedule for an industry, if we had assumed there were 10 firms instead of the four we used for illustrative purposes, the quantity offered for sale would have been increased.

Actually, this view of the matter is oversimple. Possibly an increase in the number of firms in operation would cause the size of established firms to shrink, for as new firms entered a market they would encroach on the sales of other firms and induce them to reduce their capacity. The manner in which established firms react to the advent of new firms is fairly complicated; it need not concern us farther at this point. Suffice to say that in considering how large a quantity of product will be offered for sale, we must examine more than costs of production; we must also take into account the number of firms established to produce the product.

3. EASE WITH WHICH PRODUCTIVE FACILITIES CAN BE EXPANDED AND CONTRACTED

There is yet a third factor which influences the supply of a product: the ease with which productive facilities can be expanded and contracted. Expansion can come about either by the advent of new firms or, in established firms, by the increase of facilities. Similarly, contraction of productive facilities can be accomplished by having some firms close their doors or by having all firms continue to operate but fail to replace their facilities as they are "used up."

We shall not discuss the conditions which determine the ease with which facilities can be expanded or contracted; that is quite a compli-

---

[10] Some readers may be puzzled because the supply curve for the entire industry does not possess the U shape of the individual firm's average cost curves. As explained, it is the marginal rather than the average cost curve that determines the amount of goods a firm will offer for sale. What we have found is that the level of marginal costs at low levels of output does not influence output; only marginal costs approximating the level of output, where firms generally are operating, influence an industry's offerings of a product. With this qualification, there is a close parallel between the marginal cost curves of individual firms and the supply curve for the industry of which they are a part.

cated subject in itself. We need only record the well-established fact that conditions vary widely in this respect from industry to industry. In some, where expansion is difficult, the *"long-run supply"* of the product, beyond the point where it can be produced by established firms, can be termed "inelastic." That is, even large increases in price will not bring forth great expansions in output. Conversely, if a moderate increase in price leads to a very great expansion of capacity, one can state that the product's *long-run-supply* situation is highly elastic.

Note that we have introduced a new concept of supply here—"long-run supply." By means of this concept we distinguish two types of adjustment in supply: the first takes place by changes in output on the part of established firms using facilities already in place; the second occurs after sufficient time has elapsed for facilities either to expand or to contract. It is possible that some industries will be quick to expand output to the extent that it can be done with existing facilities, but very sluggish to do so beyond this point. And some industries may expand facilities very rapidly but not greatly increase output from established plants.

4. ELASTICITY OF SUPPLY

The concept of demand elasticity was introduced a few pages back; the related concept of supply elasticity can now be mastered quickly. The elasticity of supply indicates the responsiveness of sellers to change in the prevailing price. Specifically, if increases in price lead to proportionately greater increase in quantity offered for sale, we say that supply is elastic; conversely, if a 10 per cent increase in price were to result in a smaller than 10 per cent increase in quantity offered for sale, supply would be termed inelastic. (In a like manner, if a decline in price of 10 per cent resulted in more than a 10 per cent decline in quantity offered for sale, the supply would be termed inelastic; and if the decline in offerings were less than 10 per cent, supply would be inelastic.)

Even as we distinguished between short-run and long-run changes in physical supply, there is reason to distinguish between short- and long-run elasticities of supply. We must never lose sight of the fact that some adjustments in physical supply can be made swiftly, while larger adjustments may require a long time. A full understanding of supply conditions requires that both types be considered.

5. CHANGES IN SUPPLY

As we saw before, increases or decreases in demand are represented by shifts in the demand-schedule line to the right and left, respectively; the same is true of changes in supply. As sellers' costs change so that they can offer more or less at the same prices, the supply schedule moves in the diagram. Line 1 in Chart 6 represents the supply (cost) conditions of diagram 5 in Chart 5. Line 2 represents an increase in supply and is therefore to the right of line 1. Line 3 indicates a decrease in supply and is found to the left of line 1. If we are given the demand schedule as represented in Chart 6, an increase in supply means that more of the product will be sold, while a decrease in supply indicates that fewer units are being sold.

CHANGES IN SUPPLY

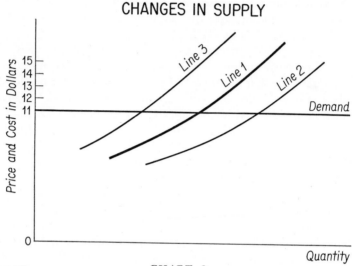

CHART 6

6. A HYPOTHETICAL SUPPLY SCHEDULE

How then, if at all, should we construct a supply schedule for a particular *real* product? Great problems arise when we attempt to determine the marginal costs of even a single firm at a particular time; these problems multiply when we attempt to learn costs at different levels of output—some of which might never have been reached by the firm. And of course it is even more complicated to determine when firms would enter and leave an industry. However, our objective is not to explain what happens in specific firms but rather to understand the forces at work in the allocation of resources. At this point, we need only recognize that the supply of a product is governed primarily by cost conditions, the number of sellers, and the speed with which facilities for production will be expanded and contracted.

Accordingly, let us construct a supply schedule for our imaginary product; in so doing we shall seek to clarify what has been said in the preceding paragraphs. Such a schedule is presented in Table 2, where the original demand schedule from Table 1 is repeated. Note that, unlike Table 1, it shows that a larger quantity would be offered for sale as price increases, and a smaller amount as price decreases. As the foregoing paragraphs explain, beyond some limit of output the additional costs to increase output rise, owing to factors described by the principle of diminishing returns, and firms require a higher price to induce them to expand their output. Let us now see how this basic concept can be expressed diagrammatically.

Table 2. Hypothetical Cost and Demand Conditions

Price	Demand (Quantity that could be sold)	Supply (Quantity that would be offered for sale)
$15	0	600,000
14	100,000	500,000
13	120,000	400,000
12	150,000	300,000
11	200,000	200,000
10	280,000	0
9	350,000	0

C. Market Circumstances

We have just seen how demand and supply are derived and what factors determine the particular shape they take. To complete our understanding of how price is determined and how resources are allocated, our attention now must be concentrated on market circumstances. After we have explained the role of market circumstances, we will, in the next chapter, examine the conditions of zero market power. Then, in the following chapter, we will explore two other types of market circumstances: (1) where market power is very great, and (2) the "conventional" market.

An exhaustive examination of market circumstances would reveal that many aspects of markets influence the level of output, methods of production, and the level of price. The nature of the product, the kinds and numbers of buyers and sellers, the problems involved in going into and out of business, the methods of promoting sales, the techniques employed to set prices, the absence or use of advertising—these are some of the many conditions which have an important bearing, together with the supply and demand, on where price settles and on how resources are allocated.

Although market circumstances encompass very many conditions affecting market transactions, economists have concentrated their attention on only a few. To classify meaningfully the types of markets through which the products of different industries reach consumers, they have singled out as most crucial aspects of the market the numbers of producers and buyers and the degree of product similarity. They have reasoned that even where the conditions of supply and demand are similar, price and allocation of resources will be different if either the number of sellers varies significantly or the product is so differentiated that consumers regard it as another product.

The discussion in the next two chapters accepts the importance of these two distinguishing qualities of market circumstances. Another quality of market behavior will be emphasized here—the routines by which management reaches decisions about what to charge and how much to produce. In today's complex markets where corporate managers have to consider many market variables, no simple formula for setting prices and output can be assumed.[11] Cost-plus, standard markups, price leadership, etc.—all these are techniques whose application strongly affects price; accordingly, they are included in what we have called market circumstances.

VII. SUMMARY AND CONCLUSIONS

We have seen that an economic system's main task is to decide what and how much is to be produced and by whom, or, in other words, how to allocate its relatively scarce resources among alternative uses. In a free-enterprise system, such resource use is supposed to be determined by the exercise of consumer and producer "sovereignty" in competitive market situations. Buyers' dollars reward producers who sell the goods and services that consumers want, and income is thus distributed to individuals (producers, workers, lenders) according to their contribution to such output. Buyers and sellers are prevented from distorting efficient resource use by competition, which forces them to buy and sell in amounts and at prices consistent with efficiency, or otherwise to suffer financial penalties.

Price theory helps us to understand how efficiently resources are used. The particular price at which a commodity or service is sold reflects resource allocation in that market. Such resource use is determined by three main factors—demand, supply, and market circumstances. Demand indicates the various quantities which buyers are willing to purchase at different prices in given market and economic circumstances. Supply, on the other hand, refers to the different quantities which sellers offer at various prices; it reflects the underlying cost conditions in production. Market circumstances include many conditions, but two of these have assumed great importance in understanding resource allocation—the numbers of producers and buyers, and the degree of product similarity. A full understanding of how demand, supply, and market circumstances

---

[11] See *Business Week*, June 15, 1957, pp. 188-198.

operate to determine price is thus essential before the degree of efficiency of an economic system can be gauged.

It is no secret that economists disagree quite a bit—though probably far less than is rumored. On few economic subjects is there as much disagreement and dissatisfaction as on this matter of price theory.

Let us make it very clear that two quite different subjects are dealt with in price theory: the first is resource allocation in a free-enterprise economy; the second is "price determination"—or how prices get to be what they are. It is quite important to recognize that these subjects are different, though related and overlapping.

In our discussion of resource allocation we were looking for an account of the forces that cause certain things rather than others to be produced; that cause far greater resources to be devoted to some products than to others; and that would explain, in a general way, by what means goods are produced. In these connections, we saw that the prime movers of resources can be reduced to three main factors, each of which reflects several factors on its own. Specifically, they are (1) demand—reflecting personal desires and money incomes; (2) supply—reflecting costs of production and the number of firms in the industry; and (3) market structure (which reflects the number of rivals), methods used to reach price and output decisions, and similarity of products sold by different firms. Also, it was seen that where market power is absent, we can anticipate that output will respond directly to consumers' demands and will be sufficient to meet the desires of all consumers who are ready to defray the minimum cost required to make the product available.

The discussion of resource allocation could easily be mistaken for an explanation for how prices are set. This confusion, of which some economists have been guilty, should be carefully avoided. Price theory is not offered as a description of how prices actually are set, but as an explanation of the manner in which scarce resources are and might be allocated among alternative uses to gratify the unlimited wants of consumers to a maximum. (There is great controversy over whether price theory does account for the level toward which price gravitates, but we need not involve ourselves in that controversy.)

DISCUSSION QUESTIONS

1. What is the major economic problem that a modern economic system must solve? What are the limits to a solution of the problem?

2. How does a "free-enterprise" economy such as we have in the United States go about allocating resources? What are the roles of the consumer and the producer in this function? How does such a system of resource allocation differ in principle from other types of economic systems?

3. In what ways does competition affect the allocation of resources?

4. List the various forms that competition takes between businesses, between laborers, between business and labor, between businesses in one country and another; between business and government?

5. How does the price mechanism in a free enterprise economy get resources allocated?

6. What would happen in an industry for a substantial period if prices were below costs? If prices were substantially above costs?

7. Why should you expect more of a product to be sold at a low than at a high price? What law expresses this relation?

8. What factors determine the demand for a product?

9. In what circumstances does a seller in an industry where sellers have no market power cut prices below the market price? In what circumstances would he ask more?

10. What are we assuming about the total output of individual sellers when we say that "they sell all they wish to at the prevailing price"?

11. What factors determine the supply of a product on the market?

12. How might sellers, or some of them, possess market power if the product they sold was not standardized?

13 Resource Use under Conditions of Pure Competition and Monopoly

Now that we have examined the concepts of demand, supply, and market circumstances in connection with the problem of making efficient use of our resources, we are in a better position to study the use of resources in some detail and in specific situations. There are very many different market conditions, but as already stated, we will focus attention on three: (1) pure competition, (2) monopoly, and (3) the conventional market. These market types will be examined closely, because they can then serve as convenient points of comparison. The three types of market differ in number of sellers, similarity of product offered by rival firms, and the routines by which management decisions on price and output are reached. In this chapter we shall deal exclusively with the first two market types—pure competition and monopoly.

I. THE MEANING OF "COMPETITION" AND "MARKET POWER"

In general usage, as we have noted, "to compete" means to contend for some valued object. This lay definition of "competition," however, differs greatly from the technical meanings that have been assigned to it by economists and lawyers.

The following discussion will use the words "market power" as well as "competition" or "monopoly." [1] *"Market power" is the ability to alter prices to one's own advantage by any means.* For example, sellers who can raise price, and profit through collusion with their rivals, have consider-

---

[1] A similar terminology has been employed by J. K. Galbraith, *American Capitalism* (Boston: Houghton Mifflin Company, 1952), Chapter V.

able market power. On the other hand, sellers who are so weak and numerous that individually they can do nothing to alter the price of the things they sell have no market power. Similarly, buyers who can depress the prices they pay have market power, while those who cannot influence the prevailing price have none.

Market power varies in degree. It is even difficult to separate buyers who have market power from those who do not. Such a distinction is so crude that an arbitrary line is required to separate characteristics that, in fact, vary only by imperceptible degrees. *Unfortunately, reliable methods for measuring degrees of market power do not exist.*

Despite the fact that market power rarely is wholly absent or unregulated and great, we shall start our analysis of resource allocation in a free-enterprise economy by examining opposing extremes. First, we shall investigate theoretically how resources are allocated when sellers have no market power whatsoever—a condition termed "pure competition." Thereupon resource allocation under conditions of complete and unrestrained monopoly will be analyzed. After these extremes have been discussed, an intermediate situation will be examined in the following chapter.

Let us, accordingly, now examine *a purely competitive market—a situation where market power is altogether absent.* To begin, let us select a real situation that closely approximates pure competition so that we can easily visualize what we are talking about.

II. AGRICULTURE—AN ILLUSTRATION OF PURE COMPETITION

Agriculture offers good illustrations of markets where sellers lack power to influence price. Let us therefore look briefly at the market for a farm staple.

Each farmer raising staples is literally one among millions who produce the same thing. Compared with the total supply, his output is one drop in a huge bucket. If he were to produce nothing, no one would notice the difference. When he sells his output, he therefore vies with millions of others who offer the same product. Buyers will not pay him more than they must pay other sellers. Consequently, to make any sales whatsoever, each farmer is compelled to accept the price at which other farmers are selling.

The farmer can do relatively little to improve his position. Advertising will not help, for his product is standardized; that is, buyers know that it is the same as that of many others. He cannot "get together" with all other farmers to restrict output or to set price, because farmers are far too numerous to organize themselves for such joint action.[2] He cannot gain market power by merging with competitors, because, even if he joined with hundreds of others, their combined output would not be great enough to exert a perceptible influence over price.

The individual farmer can directly influence three major circumstances relating to his business. First, he can decide what crops to raise and in what proportions to raise them. Second, he can choose the methods by which to raise them. (That is, he determines how much and which of the various kinds of fertilizer and machinery to use, whether or not to irrigate his farm, what kinds of seed to plant, when to plant, how deeply to plow, and so on.) Third, he is free to sell his output whenever he wishes, meaning that he can elect to hold stocks of his product for later sale.[3] The manner in which he decides these three matters strongly influences his own income but does not affect the price of the things he sells.

Once the farmer has sent his crop to market, he must accept the prevailing price, because, as already indicated, he cannot influence price. If he decides not to sell after his product has been shipped, he incurs storage and handling costs that almost invariably would exceed the benefits reasonably expected from holding his product longer. The price of the product will not be affected by his decision about when to sell.

Although the prices of farm staples cannot be influenced by the actions of any single farmer, they are determined largely by those of all farmers combined. The combined physical quantity of a product that will be offered for sale by all farmers does strongly influence its price. The larger the output offered for sale, the lower the price that will prevail; conversely, the smaller the amount put on the market, the higher the price. Let us see why this is so.

As the quantity offered for sale increases, sellers must find more buyers, and the hunt for buyers becomes more intensive. Sellers will try to turn those who are reluctant to buy at all into willing purchasers by giving price inducements, and will try to attract buyers away from other sellers of the same product by lowering price. On the other hand, the smaller the quantity for sale, the easier it is for sellers to find customers, and the

---

[2] There are exceptions to this generalization. Dairy farmers have been able to band together with the cooperation of government agencies to influence the price of milk. Other farm groups have formed associations of growers that have been able to raise price for their crop substantially—at least during short periods—by agreeing on a price below which they will not sell and threatening to picket any farmer who offers his crop at a lower price. For two examples in the field of potato growing, see *New York Times*, September 11, 1956, p. 39.

[3] Farmers can also exert political influence to secure special government assistance.

less the reason to offer concessions. When the amount offered for sale is relatively small, the pressure would fall upon buyers, who must make efforts to get part of the available supply. To induce sellers to give part of the supply to them rather than to others, buyers will tend to raise their price offers.

The characteristics of markets where sellers have no market power may be summarized in the form of a list:

1. Many sellers, none very large, contend for buyers.

2. All sellers offer products that customers believe to be equally desirable.

3. Buyers and sellers are aware of the prices that are asked and offered by others in the market.

III.A SIMPLIFIED ILLUSTRATION OF PURE COMPETITION

A. *Price and Output under Purely Competitive Conditions*

To account for price and output where neither buyers nor sellers possess market power, it will be convenient to imagine a hypothetical situation. From an analysis of this imaginary case, we shall be able to isolate the major factors determining resource use where market power is absent. Accordingly, we shall imagine a situation in which there are many buyers and sellers of a completely standardized product. Let us now describe hypothetical conditions of supply and demand for the product.

Table 1 presents a hypothetical set of supply and demand conditions. Let us first make clear the assumptions that we are making regarding both supply and demand. The number of people who are prepared to buy the product is very large, and none of these buyers purchases enough to affect appreciably the price that will be charged. In other words, no buyer has the slightest degree of market power. The "demand" column in Table 1 therefore shows how much all buyers together would buy at various prices. If the price is $15 a unit, for example, no one will purchase the product. As the price declines, buyers will buy increasing amounts of the product: 100,000 units at $14; 120,000 units at $13; and so on down to $9, the lowest price listed in the table, at which point 350,000 units of the product will be demanded.

As for sellers, let us assume that there are 1,000 firms, each of which has a designed or optimum output of 200 units but could produce up to 350 units, if cost were no object. (See Chapter 12, under heading, "Costs of Production and Conditions of Supply," where various concepts of capacity are defined.) For simplicity, let us say that the costs of each of the firms are the same; in other words, we are assuming that it would cost each firm the same to produce any given quantity of output.

Table 1. Hypothetical Supply and Demand Conditions

Price	Demand (Quantity that could be sold)	Supply (Quantity that would be offered)
$15	0	350,000
14	100,000	320,000
13	120,000	290,000
12	150,000	250,000
11	200,000	200,000
10	280,000	110,000
9	350,000	0

Thus the supply column in Table 1 tells us just how much the industry as a whole is ready to sell at different prices. At $9, no firm is willing to offer any amount of the product for sale, presumably because a price of $9 does not cover its costs. As price rises above $9, each firm is prepared to offer more of the product for sale, because, as the price goes up, marginal costs can be covered on a larger output. Table 1 indicates that if the price were $10, sellers would offer 110,000 units for sale; at $11, the amount would be 200,000; and so on to 350,000 units, at a price of $15. Thus sellers offer more for sale as price rises, whereas buyers purchase less.

The demand and supply schedules represented in Table 1 can be illustrated diagrammatically along the lines used in Chapter 12. Chart 1 depicts these schedules with the demand "curve" rising from the right to the left and measuring the different amounts that buyers would purchase at different prices. The supply curve represents the amounts of output listed in the supply column of Table 1. This curve rises from the left to the right, illustrating that as price rises sellers will offer more for sale.

The supply curve, as we saw in Chapter 12, is derived from the cost curves of the firms in the industry, meaning that the industry supply curve is obtained by adding together the individual marginal-cost curves of the 1,000 firms producing the product. Chart 2 shows the cost curve of any one of the 1,000 firms at the left and the supply curve for the product—the total of 1,000 cost curves of all the firms—at the right. Each firm's marginal cost curve (see diagram 5 in Chart 5 of Chapter 12) is parallel to the supply curve from the point where the average cost curve (at its minimum) intersects the marginal-cost curve.

Looking at Chart 1, we see that sellers would be prepared to sell

varying amounts if prices were above $10 and that buyers would be will-
ing to purchase different amounts if price did not exceed $14. In this
situation, therefore, price would necessarily settle somewhere between
$10 and $14, and the amount sold would fall between 110,000 and 320,-
000 units. Buyers would not pay more than $14, and sellers would not
accept less than $10. Where would price settle? Should we rely on a
common hunch that most things are "somewhere in the middle"? What
would happen if the price started at $14, for example?

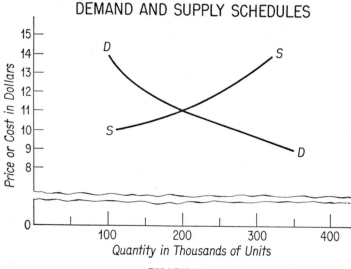

DEMAND AND SUPPLY SCHEDULES

CHART 1

At a price of $14, each of the 1,000 sellers would be willing to offer
320 units. Thus all of them together would be willing to sell more than
three times as much as the 100,000 units that buyers would be willing
to buy at a price of $14. In such circumstances, it is clear that price could
not remain for long at $14, because sellers would initiate price reduc-
tions. Inasmuch as they would be willing to accept a price as low as $11
if they were producing and selling 200 units, one must expect that each
seller would offer to sell for less than $14 in an effort to increase his sales.
Each seller would realize that he could increase his sales by lowering
price, partly by winning customers away from rivals who had not
reduced price and partly because buyers would be willing to increase
their total purchases at a lower price. In terms of Table 1, sellers would
realize that the quantity purchased would rise as prices declined, and
by reducing price they would get a share of the extra sales that would be
made.

Let us examine the reasoning of each seller in our hypothetical situation more closely, because in it we find the essential feature of a market

in which sellers lack influence over price. Recall that we assumed price to be $14 and found that an individual seller would not be able to sell all he would have liked to sell at this price. In considering what effect a price reduction on his part would have, he would recognize that he was only a very tiny factor in the total market and reason that no other seller would be concerned with what he did. From his standpoint, price reduction offers an opportunity to win customers away from other sellers and to induce customers, who would not buy at a higher price, to make purchases; as he would view the matter, his price reduction would not precipitate a drop in price throughout the entire market, because he is "too small to matter." And, if he alone were to reduce price, this view of the matter would be valid. However, not only a single isolated seller would reason in this manner; presumably all would do so. Without caring what price was asked by any other single seller, each producer would adopt a course of action designed to give him all the business he could handle at the highest price he could get, subject only to the proviso that he would not accept a price below $10.

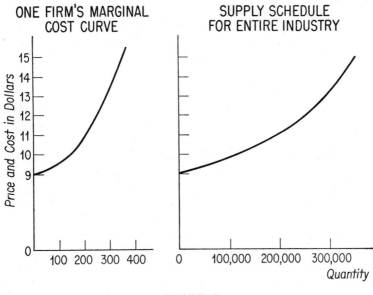

CHART 2

On their own part, some buyers would presumably not pay the first prices asked. They might surmise that sellers would accept less than $14 per unit and therefore refuse to buy at that price; their refusal would hasten the downward movement of price. If the buyers realized that sellers would meet all their requirements at $11, they presumably would refuse to buy until price had declined to that figure.

In these circumstances, price could not long remain above $11. Rivalry among sellers would lead them to lower price as long as it exceeded $11. If, for some reason, price fell to $10, which is the lowest price at which sellers would offer any quantity of the product, buyers would demand 280,000 units, and sellers, producing at levels below capacity, would be willing to sell only 110,000 units. The disparity between the amount offered for sale and the quantity demanded would be erased quickly, because sellers would soon realize that at $10 they were turning many customers away, and as many potential buyers found they could not make a purchase. Sellers would be encouraged, in such situations, to raise price, and buyers would voluntarily offer to pay more in order to get a part of the limited supply. Under the conditions assumed, price should settle at $11, because at this price producers would not want to sell more than 200,000 units and buyers would want to purchase precisely that amount. At no other price would the amount purchased just equal the quantity that sellers would make available. Thus we see that *price* would not settle somewhere in the middle. It *would settle at the point where the quantity demanded would equal the quantity offered: at this point "supply" equals "demand."*

This determination of where price will settle can be described in diagrammatic form. Chart 1, as we have seen, presents a diagram embodying line 1 of Chart 4 in Chapter 12 and a supply schedule such as was derived in diagram 5 of Chart 5 in Chapter 12. Both curves represent the price and quantity data in Table 1 of the same chapter.

The horizontal axis shows the quantity offered and the quantity demanded during some convenient period of, say, a month or a year. The vertical axis designates the prices asked by sellers and offered by buyers for the corresponding quantities of goods or services. A particular point, at the intersection of the supply and demand schedules, indicates the price and quantity of goods at which supply and demand are equal and in balance, and gives us, geometrically, the $11 price and 200,000 units that our analysis above yielded.

Our example has shown us that the price would settle at a point where output for the industry is at the optimum or designed level—200 units of output for each firm. In other words, industry would produce at its most efficient level, and resources, labor, and capital would be used in their most desirable combination. Thus, under purely competitive conditions or where market power is absent, the price mechanism would put workers, materials, and equipment to most effective uses.

Changes in costs or demand conditions (or both) would usually alter resource use. To understand how the disposition of productive resources would be affected by a change in demand, let us explore what would happen in the hypothetical example we have discussed if demand were to rise.

With such an increase in demand, the demand column in Table 1 would show that larger quantities would be purchased at each price; the demand curve in Chart 1 would move over to the right. With buyers offering to buy more at each price, the price for the product would be forced to rise, and sellers would produce above their designed (optimum) capacity—200 units. But production at points above designed capacity would involve costs above the minimum. Nevertheless, the 1,000 firms in the industry would increase output beyond capacity in response to the higher price and would realize greater profits.

Increased profits to be made in the industry would attract new firms; since we have not assumed any change in cost conditions, the new firms presumably would be of a size that would permit minimum cost (and maximum efficiency) at an output of 200 units—like those that were already operating. As more firms came into the industry, the amount of the product offered for sale at each price would increase, because the new firms would behave just as the old and add their output to what the old firms would offer. Consequently, the higher price brought about initially by the increased demand would call forth larger offerings, which would have the effect of intensifying the competition among sellers for customers. The effect of the advent of new producers would be to lower price. Ultimately, it can be shown, price would again settle at $11; put more generally, under conditions of zero market power, price would settle at the very lowest figure at which sellers could make the desired quantity of product available.

To sum up, increases in demand would first bring about a rise in price before newcomers could enter the field; at the higher price, operations would become profitable enough to attract other firms which would expand supply, thus causing price to fall. Price would return to the point which permitted sellers barely to cover minimum average costs (in our hypothetical case, $11), because any higher price would offer an opportunity for new firms to obtain enough profit to make it worth their while to enter; any lower price would fail to cover costs and the result would be that some firms would leave the industry, thereby reducing supply and causing price to rise again. Only when price is at the point which just covers minimum average cost would there be no tendency for new firms to enter or for established firms to leave the industry.

Let us reflect now on the effect of an increase in demand upon the allocation of resources. We saw that the initial effect of a rise in demand was an expansion of output by established firms; this expansion, however, required them to employ resources relatively inefficiently—attested by the fact that their production costs increased. However, the higher prices would attract newcomers into the industry; with their contribution to total output, it would be possible to produce at minimum average costs by using resources with utmost efficiency. As the new firms produced goods and caused prices to decline, the established firms would contract their output, because the lower price would not cover their marginal costs at current levels. This process of increased output from new firms and curtailed output by old firms would continue until all were producing just the amount that made minimum average costs possible. Thus the outcome appears extremely favorable: *resources flow into an industry in response to an increased desire for its output;* and *these resources are combined in proportions which keep costs to their very minimum.*[4]

Thus far, we have examined the manner in which resources are allocated in purely competitive industries—that is, where sellers possess no market power—and explored the effects on resource allocation of an increase in demand. One special feature of purely competitive markets deserves emphasis. In such markets, sellers have no incentive to advertise their product or to engage in costly sales promotion of any kind. Buyers recognize the product sold by all to be equal in quality and will not pay one seller more than the others. That is to say, they purchase solely on the basis of price. Owing to the absence of any sales-promotion activity, the amount of the product purchased would reflect the desires for the product, unaffected by outside pressures imposed by the seller. Sellers would provide consumers with exactly as much of the product as they were willing to purchase at a price just covering its cost. *Production would thus be, in effect, directed by the wishes of buyers as reflected in their willingness to buy the product.*

Let us now sum up the foregoing discussion by listing the conditions that markets must meet to be purely competitive, and then recapitulate the main consequences of such markets.

B. Conditions That Create Pure Competition

1. There are numerous sellers and buyers, all so small that the actions of no one of them can significantly influence the quantity offered or purchased.

2. All buyers believe units of the product to be equally desirable.

3. All buyers and sellers know the prices offered and asked by other buyers and sellers.

4. Easy entry into the industry, so that if profits were supernormal new firms would soon arise.

---

[4] A similar line of analysis might be employed to explore the effect of a change in cost caused by, say, the depletion of an important natural resource. Such an analysis would show that less of the product would be sold and that to some extent other factors of production would be substituted for the one that was depleted.

C. Consequences of Purely Competitive Markets

1. Price equals the minimum cost at which the product can be made available.

2. Costs do not include any expenditure for advertising or other forms of sales promotion.[5]

3. Profits are eliminated, save for "normal profits."

4. The amount of the product made available is responsive to consumers' desires, and equals the amount that consumers will purchase at a price covering the product's full costs.

An examination of these characteristics should make clear the reasons why pure competition is considered desirable. Indeed, economists ordinarily use pure competition as a standard of what is ideally desirable, and as a goal toward which to strive.

IV. A SIMPLIFIED CASE OF MONOPOLY: HOW RESOURCES ARE ALLOCATED UNDER CONDITIONS OF MONOPOLY

Up to this point we have explored the workings of markets where sellers lack market power, and we have seen that many benefits accrue in such circumstances. We are now ready to examine monopoly, which is at the opposite extreme. Pure competition, we found, generally serves as a model of the way markets should be organized; markets where sellers possess great market power are taken as examples of cardinal economic sin. Let us, then, study how resources are allocated in extremely simple cases where sellers—or a single seller—possess a monopoly.

Market power and monopoly are relative terms. *Complete* market power is difficult to imagine, while conditions of pure competition are almost as rare. Almost every sale of goods or services involves some elements of both market power and competition. While market power can be defined in various ways, it essentially means an ability to influence price in one's favor. This power may be great or small; it may be exercised in a manner that is antisocial, or it may be used in the public interest; it may be long-lasting or temporary; it may pertain to products or to markets where factors of production are exchanged; it may be in the hands of a private business or a government agency. Thus market power is an extremely complicated concept that requires a fairly long string of adjectives to convey full and clear meaning.

---

[5] There may, however, be cooperative industry advertising in such markets to promote the product rather than any brand.

A. Meaning and Basis of Market Power

Power over price arises in various ways. Basically, it is derived from "control" over the "supply" or "demand" of a "particular product or service." Since we have already examined supply and demand in Chapter 12, we can explain the other two terms and then see how power over price is exercised.

What does the economist mean by the term "particular product or service"? Like articles are the same "product" only if most consumers would be quite willing to substitute one for any other. If most buyers believe Chevrolets, Fords, and Plymouths to be more or less equally desirable, they represent different brands of the same product in the economic sense. If many prefer one brand of these cars to the other enough to pay considerably more for it than for the others, they represent different products in the economic sense. Thus, product is defined with reference to consumers' attitudes toward different articles.

On the other hand, some articles are identical physically but nevertheless are different products in the economic sense. Some radios that are sold under widely advertised brand names are identical with others whose name is unknown. Even though both radios may carry similar guarantees they will be different products in the economic sense, because most consumers will believe the widely advertised brand to be greatly superior to the other, and would not be willing to substitute it for the unknown one. The term "product" thus emphatically does not refer only to things that are identical in physical form. Indeed, products that are different in physical properties are the same product in the economic sense if consumers do not recognize their differences but value them equally.

We said that great power market consists in "control" over either demand or supply. What does the term "control" mean in this connection? To control something is to have the power to decide what shall be done with it; it is the power to influence the outcome according to one's own wish. To "control" demand thus would mean *to determine what price will be offered by most buyers for a product.* To illustrate, if there were only one buyer of raw tobacco, sellers would have to sell at the price he offered or hold on to their tobacco. (One must not conclude from this statement that the buyer could make his purchases at whatever price he wished, because sellers would refuse to sell their products at a loss for long.) Control usually is not so great as in the case illustrated. In another case, one firm that ordinarily purchased 40 per cent of all tobacco sold would also exercise some control over demand. If that company refused to pay as much as the other buyers paid, some sellers of tobacco would find themselves faced with the choice of holding their tobacco in the hope of selling it later at a higher price, or accepting the lower price. Undoubtedly, some would accept the lower price. Thus the large buyer would be able to influence the price at which tobacco was sold. However, to illustrate the absence of control, if a buyer who accounted for only a tiny fraction of all tobacco purchases were to offer less than the prevailing price, sellers would prefer to sell, and presumably would be able to sell, to buyers offering higher prices.

To "control" supply is to determine the quantity of a product offered for sale or the price that will be asked for it. Conceivably, a single firm could have this power. Ordinarily, there are at least several firms that produce the same product, or "nearby" products—that is, articles that consumers could be induced to substitute for it if its prices were too high. If a single firm produced most of the total output of a product (including all close substitutes), most potential buyers would be compelled to pay its price or go without the product. Even control of one third of a product's output gives one firm the power to raise price by withholding its output, for such action would intensify the rivalry among buyers for the limited supply of the product.

To control supply, therefore, it is necessary to be able to determine the available quantity or asking price of a significant proportion of all articles that consumers believe will serve similar purposes.

Now that the concept of "control over the supply or demand of a particular product or service" has been explained, the meaning of market power may be reasonably clear. The foregoing discussion was vague in that no sharp lines were drawn between strong and weak control over supply and demand. Also, the concept of "substitutes" is relative, and the closeness of substitutes may be debated in specific cases. Nothing is gained by glossing over the essential complexities of the problem. Unfortunately, little more can be said here about market power in the abstract.

B. Monopoly Defined

It is almost impossible to imagine, and certainly one cannot find, a state of "complete" market power. Such a situation would require that a single firm sell a unique product (that is, no one sells anything remotely like it); and that it sell to many small buyers, each of whom is unable to influence price in the slightest; and that no new firms could possibly enter upon the production of a similar item. The impossibility of such a situation stems primarily from the requirement that the product be "unique." It is difficult to find a unique quality in any product, because all of them have in common the ability to satisfy human wants or whims. If one product—very different from the others in physical form or in function—were to be priced at a level so high that its purchase involved inordinate sacrifice, then consumers would seek their satisfactions elsewhere, or they might decide to save the funds they otherwise would have spent for the item. One might say that in the latter circumstance, the consumers substituted savings for the product. In the sense, then, that there are other ways of making expenditures that yield satisfaction and consumers have the opportunity to save, one must recognize that all products have substitutes—however remote. In that sense, no product is unique, and the seller of no product can compel buyers to pay whatever price he may demand. He may have the power to set his price at any level he may choose, but his power is blunted by the reciprocal power of buyers to refuse to buy at that price. For this reason, one must recognize that *market power can never be complete and that it varies in degree*. On the other hand, we can imagine a situation in which a seller would have great power to influence price in his own favor. That situation, as indicated, would prevail if his product were very different from others that were available, if buyers were many and small, and if no newcomers could set up to produce something similar to what he is offering.

C. What Happens in Situations Where Market Power Is Great?

If a seller possesses great market power, what would happen to price? Would it be set at a level that compelled efficient production? Would high profits endure? Would considerable resources be dissipated in sales-promotion expenditure? Would the seller be immediately responsive to changes in consumer demand? These questions will be studied first by examining a simplified hypothetical example. We shall not base our conclusions upon the results of an analysis of a hypothetical case alone. The study of a simplified case will facilitate our analysis of the more complex situations faced in the real world.

Let us begin by comparing what would happen under great market power with the reverse situation. That is, let us assume the same cost and demand conditions we assumed when discussing zero market power in the preceding chapter and see how a market where a seller had complete power would operate. Table 2 presents one set of conditions assumed in Table 1 of Chapter 12. The amount purchased varies inversely with price in the manner described in that table. (It takes costs to be $11 per unit regardless of the quantity produced.)

In explaining price where market power is great, we will assume that the single seller seeks to make as much money as he can and that no law prevents his doing so. We shall assume also that he knows both his cost conditions and the conditions of demand. (At this point, it does not matter whether these assumptions are wholly realistic. We have constructed and are analyzing a logical problem to shed light on the empirical problems of the real world.)

Given our assumptions, the monopolist would set a price that would yield him maximum profit in the circumstances. In the circumstances set forth in Table 2, he would charge $14. At that price, he would sell 100,000 units and would make $300,000 net profit. Under identical conditions of cost and demand but where pure competition existed, price would have settled at $11, as we found in the preceding chapter.

**Table 2. Hypothetical Conditions of Demand,
Total Revenue, and Total Cost**

Price	Quantity that would be sold	Total costs (unit cost)	Total revenue	Net profit
$15.00	0	—	—	
14.00	100,000	$1,100,000	$1,400,000	$300,000
13.00	120,000	1,320,000	1,560,000	240,000
12.00	150,000	1,650,000	1,800,000	150,000
11.00	200,000	2,200,000	2,200,000	0
10.00	280,000	3,080,000	2,800,000	−280,000
9.00	350,000	3,850,000	3,150,000	−700,000

Let us now consider a more complicated case, where the producer's unit costs vary with output. Again, let us try to parallel our earlier example used for purely competitive market situations. In the earlier case, we assumed only one fact about unit costs—that they were at their minimum at an output of 200,000 units for the industry as a whole at a figure of $11. Nothing was said about how much they would have been at larger or smaller outputs. In the purely competitive case, it would not have mattered, because prices would have tended to reach the minimum point of $11 in any event.

When we deal with a producer possessing market power, especially if incomplete market power, another complication is introduced by the matter of selling cost. Not only will sellers not selling obviously identical products inflate their costs by sales-promotion expenditure; they will presumably alter the demand for their output. The effects of sales promotion are discussed later.[6] For simplicity, we shall ignore sales-promotion expenditure and assume that the producer with great market power has minimum unit costs of $11 if he produces 200,000 units. Also, his costs are assumed to conform to a U shape and will be assumed to be as follows: if 100,000 units are produced, costs will average $13; 120,000 units involve average costs of $12; if 150,000 are produced, costs will average $11.50; if 280,000 units are produced, costs will rise to $12; and for 350,000 units, they will reach $14. These figures are given in Table 3, which also indicates total costs and total revenues at various levels of

---

[6] See pp. 312-313 and 347-348. Sometimes the entire output of a product that is sold can be produced under conditions where costs decline as output expands. In such circumstances, great market power is likely to develop.

price; these data, in turn, provide the basis for the computation of net profits shown in the last column.

Table 3. Hypothetical Market Conditions

Price	Quantity that would be sold	Unit cost	Total cost	Total revenue	Net profit
$15.00	......	.....	....	....	....
14.00	100,000	$13.00	$1,300,000	$1,400,000	$100,000
13.00	120,000	12.00	1,440,000	1,560,000	120,000
12.00	150,000	11.50	1,725,000	1,800,000	75,000
11.00	200,000	11.00	2,200,000	2,200,000	0
10.00	280,000	12.00	3,360,000	2,800,000	− 560,000
9.00	350,000	14.00	4,900,000	3,150,000	−1,750,000

Under these conditions, the seller with great market power would charge $13. At that price he would sell 120,000 units and obtain a net profit of $120,000. In the preceding chapter it was shown that if sellers lacked market power entirely, price would settle at $11 under identical conditions of cost and demand.

Whether we assume constant costs of $11 or assume that unit costs vary with output we find the following differences in the behavior of purely competitive and monopoly markets. First, price was higher than would have prevailed in a market lacking any market power. Second, the seller would have obtained substantial profits. Third, production would have been carried on at a level that did not permit minimum production cost. Fourth, the single seller would have shut some consumers out of the market by charging prices above costs.

It should be emphasized that the preceding examples were purely imaginary. The cost and demand conditions were what we assumed them to be. We could have changed the outcomes by altering these assumed conditions. However, the different relations between price, output, profits, and such, under purely competitive and monopoly-market situations, were not solely the result of our assumptions. They reflect a necessary difference in outcome caused by different market situations.

If we so desire, we can "solve" the monopoly problem discussed above in diagrammatic form. Following the general procedures used earlier, we can express the critical information contained in Table 3 in geometric terms (see Chart 3). The determination of what to charge follows from a comparison of total costs and total revenues associated with different prices. Put more simply, at any price the seller might set, there is a particular quantity that would be sold; for that quantity of product, one can compute total production costs and total revenues (the latter is determined by multiplying unit price by the number of units that would be sold); a subtraction of total cost from total revenue would reveal the price—and output—yielding the maximum net profit. Accordingly, one can construct a chart that shows total costs and total revenue[7] at corresponding levels of price or quantity of goods that would be sold. By relating total costs to total revenue we can obtain a solution to the complete market-power price. In Chart 3, total costs (*TC*) and total revenues (*TR*) at different levels of price have been used; they show that net profit is greatest (the distance between the total cost and the total revenue lines) at a price of $13.

TOTAL COST AND TOTAL REVENUE

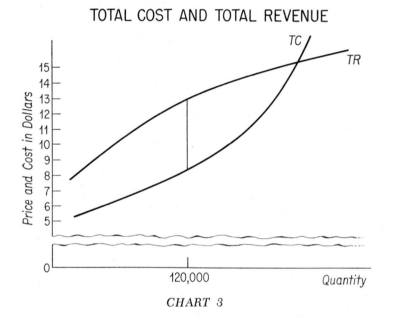

CHART 3

A solution of the monopoly problem that is more precise but substantially more complicated is possible, but it requires the introduction of a concept that has been introduced into economics only relatively recently: the concept of "marginal revenue." It is a first cousin to the marginal-cost curve already discussed (see Chart 2 earlier in this chapter) but is a good bit harder to grasp. It represents the change in total revenue that results from selling added units, taking account of the reduction in price that must be made to induce customers to purchase the added units. In the hypothetical case just discussed, to increase sales from 100,000 to 120,000 units, it was necessary to reduce price from $14 to $13; thus, to sell 20,000 more units it would be necessary to accept $1 less per unit on the 100,000 units that could have been sold at $14. (One cannot, either legally or as a matter of "good business," charge some

---

[7] A business term known to the layman is the "break-even point." It is the point at which total revenue and total cost are equal and no profit is made.

customers more than other customers similarly situated.) As a result, the
added revenue that would accrue to the firm from selling 20,000 additional units at a price of $13 would *not* be $260,000 (20,000 units times $13)
but $160,000; one must deduct from the $260,000 figure the $100,000 re-
duction in income that must be suffered on the 100,000 units that could
have been sold at $14. Another way of computing marginal revenue is by
comparing total revenue at different prices. We see that, at a price of $14,
the monopolist would obtain total revenue of $1,400,000; at a price of
$13, he would receive $1,560,000 total revenue—a difference of $160,000,
as explained above.

A comparison of marginal cost (which, it should be recalled, represents the added cost incurred to turn out additional units) with marginal
revenue will enable a producer with great market power to determine
whether or not he would gain from the sale of these additional units. If
his marginal revenue exceeded his marginal cost, his net profit would have
been increased by the sale; if marginal cost was greater than marginal
revenue, he would have lost out by the transaction. Once a person understands clearly what is meant by marginal revenue and marginal cost, he
must recognize that this conclusion is a matter of simple arithmetic.

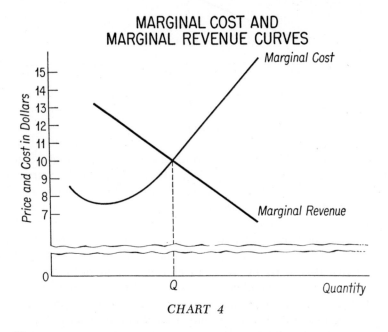

CHART 4

Chart 4 presents the marginal-cost and marginal-revenue curves that
apply to the monopoly situation described by Table 3. (As implied above,
the marginal cost and marginal revenue figures have been derived from
total costs and total revenue, representing the difference between total

costs at successive levels of output and between total revenues at successive levels of sales.) That output at which marginal revenue just exceeds marginal cost is the amount the producer with great market power must sell to obtain maximum total net profits.

To determine both the output and the price that would yield the producer maximum net profit, it is necessary to combine on one diagram a barrage of curves: average cost (*AC*), marginal cost (*MC*), average revenue (*AR*), and marginal revenue (*MR*). Such a chart has been constructed (Chart 5); it shows that a price of $13 would cause that output to be sold on which all units involve marginal costs below marginal revenue and consequently contribute to net profit; and it shows that at that price (*P*), 120,000 units would be sold.

DETERMINATION OF MONOPOLY PRICE

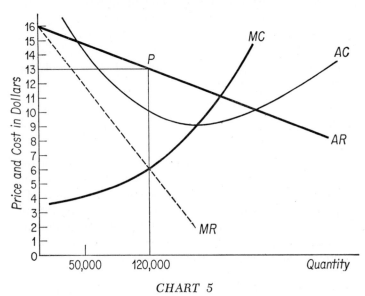

CHART 5

The best way of "proving out" this result is to examine what would happen to costs and revenues at both higher and lower prices. If it can be shown—and it can—that the hypothetical firm would make less profit at any smaller or any larger level of output, one is entitled to conclude that the price of $13 and sales of 120,000 offer the best solution to the firm with great market power. What would happen at higher prices than $13? To find the answer, look at the diagram to the left of the point marked 120,000 along the bottom axis. When you do this, you will find that on outputs below 120,000 units, the firm would obtain additions to revenue (indicated by the *MR* line) that are above additions to cost (indicated by MC); consequently, failure to produce any units up to 120,000 would cause them to forego some profit they could make. The converse situation holds beyond an output of 120,000 units. This amount would require that the firm incur additional costs which exceed the increases in their revenues. Consequently, their profits would decline by producing anything above 120,000 units. As it were by default, 120,000 units becomes the output at which profits would be at a maximum.

Let us step back for a moment and examine what we have found that bears upon the efficiency with which resources are employed in markets where sellers possess great power to influence price. Most important, we have seen that output takes place at a level below the one that would afford the minimum average costs of production. In that sense, production is less efficient than it could be. Second, we see that the firm would be obtaining some profits—in our illustration, considerable profits.

Much more will be said in the following chapter about the consequences of markets where sellers possess monopoly power. We can interrupt the analysis at this point to explore the implications of an intermediate case between purely competitive and monopoly markets. After that, we shall return to pull together all that has been said about the manner in which resources are utilized in markets of various types.

V. CONCLUSIONS

A purely competitive market, or a condition close to it, yields efficient use of productive resources. The major requirements for pure competition are many buyers and sellers informed about price and quality of product, a standardized product sold by all suppliers, and easy entry into the industry. Under such conditions, prices ultimately settle at minimum cost, no resources are expended on sales promotion, businessmen are limited to "normal profits," and output is responsive to consumers' desires. These consequences are clearly desirable.

A monopoly, or conditions similar to it, tend to result in inefficient use of productive resources. Under such conditions, output ordinarily takes place at levels below those at which costs would be at a minimum, and sellers are able to exploit their market power to obtain profits simply because they possess that power.

Readers are cautioned against applying the conclusions drawn thus far to concrete situations in the real world. We have been analyzing simplified hypothetical situations which may have few or no exact counterparts.

DISCUSSION QUESTIONS

1. Describe the characteristics of a purely competitive market. How is the absence of market power safeguarded in such a market?

2. How is price determined in a purely competitive market? Where does price settle? Why? Why is this desirable?

3. How do changes in costs or demand conditions affect resource allocation under conditions of pure competition?

4. List the consequences of purely competitive markets. Explain the significance of each one in terms of the function of an economic system.

5. What is the best example of complete market power you can think of? From what source does this power stem?

6. Do you believe that complete market power is "good for the country"? Explain. If you were a businessman would you try to attain complete market power? Explain.

7. Can you think of any ways in which your neighborhood grocer is a monopoly? In what ways does he face competition?

14 Resource Use Where Sellers Have Moderate Amounts of Market Power

The consequences of hypothetical markets on which firms have great market power or none at all have already been explored. We saw that pure competition gives highly desirable—even ideal—results. Monopoly, on the other hand, leads to results that are objectionable in several respects.

Let us now analyze the results of one—of many possible—intermediate situations. We shall set forth here one type of market to be called a "conventional" market. Like pure competition and monopoly, this is a theoretical type. It possesses the essence of many realistic situations, even though it probably corresponds exactly to few or no actual markets.

I. THE CONVENTIONAL MARKET

A. A Conventional Market Described

Conventional markets have more than one seller but far fewer than exist in markets where sellers have no market power. The number may vary somewhere between, say, four and 20 within the area (neighborhood or product-type or both) which buyers ordinarily canvass in making purchases. Described in essential character rather than in specific number, *the number of sellers in a particular conventional market is so small that each seller recognizes his interdependence with some or all of the others.* Specifically, each seller realizes that if he were to increase his sales at the expense of the others, they would make strenuous and effective efforts to regain their customers. That is, if one seller were to lower price and win many customers away from his rivals, they would respond in a protective manner—by matching the price cut or by increasing their sales efforts in other ways. We must therefore expect sellers to recognize that a price and marketing policy that won many customers from rivals would almost certainly provoke retaliatory action. As a result, each seller would be discouraged from actions which, after rivals had retaliated, left him no better, and possibly much worse, off than before. For this reason, in conventional markets each businessman hesitates to reduce his prices or step up his promotional effort, for fear that in the end he will sell little more than before and at a lower price (or higher cost) and decreased profit. (In technical parlance, this situation is known as "oligopoly," from the Greek words meaning "fewness of sellers.")

Another important characteristic of conventional markets is the nature of the goods and-or services offered for sale. Buyers prefer to patronize particular sellers, and many are willing to pay such sellers more than any other seller for things like convenience and service, the pleasure of dealing with someone of long acquaintance, credit accommodation in time of special need, the opportunity to get advice from the seller, and the "feeling," however unwarranted, that the seller's product is better than rival products.

Before explaining how a conventional market operates, let us compare it with markets of zero and great power. Clearly, the conventional market contains important elements of both types, because restrictions on market power exist side by side with opportunities to exert market power. Restriction on market power arises from two sources: first, the fact that several or many independent firms are seeking maximum profit for themselves and will seize any promising opportunity to gain at the expense of the others; second, newcomers are free to enter the market. The opportunity to exert market power stems, first, from the fact that, as relatively few firms are in active rivalry, they cannot ignore the effects of their actions on the actions of their competitors; and, second, from the real or imagined differences between their offerings. Where such differences exist, a firm may be said to have a "little monopoly." Put in technical parlance, conventional markets combine elements of "oligopoly" and "product differentiation." Many economists have analyzed thoroughly markets where oligopoly and product differentiation exist, and we can summarize their main conclusions briefly; they will assist us in understanding and appraising conventional markets.

There is no single definitive conclusion that can be drawn about either type of market; the outcome will vary from market to market, depending upon the intelligence, motives, market information of top executives, tradition in the industry, and business practices. Where oligopoly exists, businessmen have a choice among various alternative courses of conduct. It is impossible to generalize about their choices in all situations. Consequently, we must conclude that wherever oligopoly and differentiation exist, the outcome is indeterminate.

Some general tendencies apply particularly to markets that are

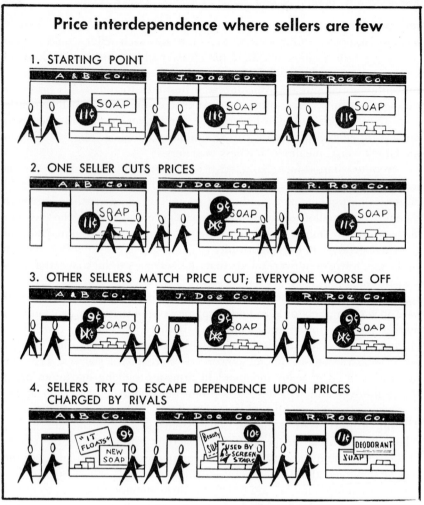

Price interdependence where sellers are few

1. STARTING POINT

2. ONE SELLER CUTS PRICES

3. OTHER SELLERS MATCH PRICE CUT; EVERYONE WORSE OFF

4. SELLERS TRY TO ESCAPE DEPENDENCE UPON PRICES CHARGED BY RIVALS

Chart by GRAPHICS INSTITUTE

SHIFT FROM PRICE TO NONPRICE COMPETITION

In markets where there are very few sellers, the price anyone can charge is strongly influenced by the prices asked by his rivals. If buyers believe the product to be identical, sellers must charge the same price. The first three illustrations show how a shift from identical prices results in a return to identical prices at a lower level, leaving all sellers worse off. The final illustration shows that sellers will try to differentiate their product, ordinarily by advertising, to avoid such close dependence upon their rivals' price decisions. When the product has been differentiated, sellers can charge different prices, though major price changes by rivals will compel them to follow suit.

oligopolistic and characterized by product differentiation. First, there is *an opportunity for* profits to be made. Both oligopolistic markets and markets where firms sell differentiated products could—at least for a while—earn a return higher than the amount required to keep firms in the industry, and sufficiently high to attract others into the business. A rate of profits which attracts newcomers into an industry is termed "supernormal," and this concept points up the vital economic relation between rates of profit and numbers of firms operating in an industry, which has already been discussed.

A second characteristic observed in oligopolistic and "differentiated" markets is the tendency to develop excessive capacity. That is to say, plant and equipment tend to operate at a level below the one for which they were designed. Excess capacity typically is the outgrowth of the supernormal profits. The typical sequence is that some or all firms in these markets obtain a high level of profits by virtue of the small number of producers (oligopoly) or the particular attractions that some customers find in their offerings (differentiation). Thereupon newcomers are attracted into the industry, encroaching upon the markets of the highly profitable firms. As a consequence, the established firms sell less than previously, reducing their output below the original level—presumably the output for which plant and facilities have been designed.

The entry of new firms into a profitable market becomes much clearer when expressed in geometric language. Let us draw a hypothetical demand curve (or schedule) for a firm operating in a conventional

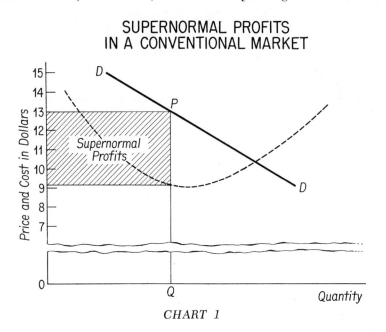

CHART 1

market, *DD* in Chart 1. On the same diagram a dotted line has been drawn to show the average costs of the firm, which, it can be seen, lie below the demand curve by a considerable amount at some levels of operation. From this fact, we can conclude that the firm, if it were aware of the demand schedule, which we assume to be so, could charge a price that would yield substantial (supernormal) profits. (For example, at the price $13 the firm would obtain supernormal profits equal to the shaded area.) As a result, new firms would be induced to enter the business—or to add this particular line to an already established business. The consequence of new entries into the business would be a reduction in the demand for the output of established firms. This effect is depicted in Chart 2, which shows the original demand curve drawn in Chart 1 and a series of lower demand schedules. Each schedule may be taken to represent what happened to the demand for this firm's product as new rivals entered the market. Chart 2 indicates one possible outcome of the entry of new firms—that new firms continue to enter up to the point where profits are depressed to "normal."

EFFECTS OF NEW FIRMS ON A MARKET

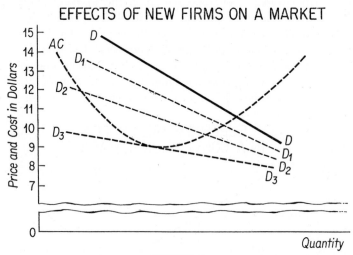

CHART 2

The foregoing discussion of the connection between profits and the entry of firms implies a vital conclusion. With the exception of some barriers to the entry of new firms, there is a fairly strong tendency for high rates of profit to be "knocked down" by the attempts of outsiders to share in the profitable market. Accordingly, when we speak of the profitability of a market type, we must be careful to specify whether the profits are temporary or persistent. *The distinguishing characteristic of situations where market power is great is that newcomers are not able to enter and profits can endure for a long time.* In oligopolistic and differentiated markets, profits may not last long. Indeed, in many lines of business—the chemical and medicinal businesses perhaps being the best examples—a firm must continually introduce new products but must expect its rivals to imitate its innovations and quickly end its extraordinary level of profits. In other words, a seller in these industries can anticipate a high level of profits only if he can create a constant stream of new products. One important new development would result in supernormal profits only for a brief period, after which the business would soon be again obtaining only a low rate of return.

Let us now turn from a discussion of oligopoly and differentiation in general to a particular type of market—the "conventional market"—which contains both elements, and where businessmen typically employ two essential market practices. First, production is adjusted to the amount of goods sold; accordingly, when sales decline, the seller will cut his output—even though his costs may be substantially below the prevailing price. (In this respect, sellers in conventional markets are different from farmers and some others, because the latter groups continue to produce as much as they can at costs below the prevailing price; they do this in the knowledge that they can sell all they wish, since they produce only a drop in the bucket individually.)

Second, each seller will arrive at price by adding a margin that does not vary over time and is not changed with variations in level of sales to a convenient base cost. If he is a distributor—wholesaler or retailer—he will almost always use the amount paid for the merchandise as his base cost. Manufacturers, on the other hand, add their margins to an average cost calculated specifically for this purpose.[1] Once the seller has determined his base cost, the matter of price is simple arithmetic. He merely adds his margin. It is difficult to explain the size of the margin that the seller adds to the base cost, however. We know only that these margins vary considerably in amount from product to product.

B. Resemblance of Conventional Markets to Realistic Cases

The conventional market should be considered a theoretical model that is not entirely realistic. However, a brief digression here will explain why this theoretical model bears a strong resemblance to many industrial markets.

Considerable evidence shows that in most lines of business certain

---

[1] No general rule will hold for the base costs of most manufacturers that use this method of setting price. Typically, they will exclude most overhead costs and will include the major cost components like labor and raw material. For convenience, we will discuss conventional markets in terms of retailing. In retailing, base costs are almost always the invoice cost of merchandise to the seller.

margins are accepted as "fair," and are more or less taken for granted by those in the trade. However, we do not know why particular margins rather than others are regarded as fair. Businessmen who are asked about this do not answer that the margin either originally or now leads to the most profitable price. They stress the ethics rather than the lucrativeness of setting price on the basis of customary markups.[2]

About the size of the margin, we shall raise one major question: How does it compare with the costs that are not included in base cost? For example, the distributor's cost other than that of merchandise may average 10 per cent of his sales price. If his margin were in excess of 10 per cent, we could conclude that it allowed for some profit. To put the matter in this way, however, is only a start, for we must decide what items should be included in cost, and for what level of operations we are calculating cost.

We need not settle all technical questions here; it suffices for our purpose to note that costs include, as before, all money payments and some "paper costs." Among them are the amount that a business owner could obtain for his labor services (including his managerial talents), capital and other property if he sold them to others, and the value of the property used up in production—depreciation. Included, too, is what we call "normal profit," which represents a sum just large enough to induce the businessman to remain in business. If he gets less than this amount, he will wind up his enterprise.

As for the level of output we have in mind when we measure costs not included in the base, it is "optimum" output. *Optimum is that level of output at which unit costs are at a minimum.* It emphatically is *not* the maximum quantity that could be turned out.

Thus, if we say that nonbase costs are 10 per cent of total costs, we will mean that the direct money outlays of the business, plus the value of the labor services and property contributed by the owner, plus the amount the owner must be paid to persuade him to remain in business— all combined, equal 10 per cent of total costs at optimum output. This notion can be made clearer by a specific example. Assume that a business incurred minimum unit costs at an output of 200,000 units, and that its nonbase costs (including all three elements) were $100,000, which amounts to 50 cents per unit at optimum output. Base costs equal $900,000 and total costs $1 million. Thus the nonbase costs of $100,000 equal 10 per cent of total costs at optimum output. It is with these nonbase costs that we shall compare the traditional margins added by sellers in conventional markets.

[2] The basis of this statement and a general discussion of this type of pricing is found in A. R. Oxenfeldt, *Industrial Pricing and Market Practices* (Englewood Cliffs, N.J.: Prentice-Hall, Inc., 1951), pp. 156-176.

These margins are almost invariably considerably larger than non-base costs at optimum output. Support for this conclusion consists in the following evidence: excess capacity almost certainly exists in most retailing trades where sellers price by adding a constant markup. The continued survival of most retailers shows that their markups are enough to cover all their costs—base and nonbase—at less than optimum output. If actual margins just equaled nonbase costs at that output, only firms operating at optimum output would be able to survive. In other words, firms pricing by the cost-plus method typically make substantial profits during periods of active business. Since they do not depart from their usual markups during such periods, their profitability results from the fact that they operate closer to capacity.

Little is known about the origin of margins in actual situations. They seem to be part of the culture and tradition of a business. Apparently they persist despite substantial changes in general business conditions, wage rates, taxes, and the like. These margins are supposed to allow businessmen a "decent" rate of return at the operating levels they usually attain. Few businesses operate at optimum output; thus the margins are expected to yield a decent return at less than that level. Moreover, few businessmen would regard what we here call "normal profits" as a "decent rate of return." Recall that when profits are just normal, businessmen will seriously consider leaving the business and will just barely decide against doing so. Another reason for expecting the margin to exceed nonbase costs at optimum output is the fact that margins represent a seller's goal; it is something to which he aspires. Sellers would scarcely pursue so puny an objective as one that yielded normal profits *at best* (that is, if the firm attained optimum output).

Perhaps the clearest examples of conventional markets are those in which "fair trade," better called "resale price maintenance," exists. Under resale price-maintenance legislation, manufacturers of branded products are permitted to designate the lowest figure at which their product can be resold. In effect, manufacturers set margins that all retailers must add to invoice costs if they wish to sell their merchandise. These margins are similar for all sellers and are relatively stable over long periods of time. Usually, they simply reflect the traditional margins in the industry before resale-price maintenance was legalized.

C. How a Conventional Market Operates

It would be possible to explore the outcome of a conventional market in which cost and demand conditions were the same as those assumed in our earlier discussion of markets where market power was either wholly absent or very great. However, there is no need to burden the reader with the details of such a comparison, which has been made elsewhere.[3] As one might expect, such a market produces results somewhere between the other two types of market.

How, then, do conventional markets compare with those in which sellers have great market power or in which they have none at all?[4] Our conclusions will be presented in the form of a list.

II. LONG-RUN RESULTS OF THREE MARKET TYPES

A. Prices, Costs, Sales Volume, and Profits Compared

1. WITH REFERENCE TO PRICES CHARGED

Prices would be lowest where market power was absent and highest where it was great.

2. WITH REFERENCE TO COSTS OF PRODUCTION[5]

Firms with no market power will operate on a scale involving minimum unit cost. Those with great market power generally will incur unit costs above the minimum because they are unlikely to produce capacity output. Unit costs of firms in conventional markets will usually be the highest of the three market types.[6] The cost relations described would result from differences in level of output relative to the optimum rather than from unequal technical skill and productive efficiency.

3. WITH REFERENCE TO TOTAL SALES

To the extent that sales depend exclusively upon price,[7] unit sales and output will be greatest in markets where sellers have no market power, and will be lowest where market power is great. To the extent

---

[3] See Alfred R. Oxenfeldt, *Economics for the Citizen* (New York: Rinehart & Company, Inc., 1953), pp. 292-295.

[4] The validity of these conclusions does not depend upon the particular cost-and-demand conditions we have assumed; they would apply in all except certain "freak" situations. However, the degree of difference in price and output among the various markets does depend upon the particular numerical illustration we used.

[5] Up to this point, selling costs have been ignored. They are discussed in the next section.

[6] This conclusion cannot be proved—at least by this author—but it represents his best guess.

[7] Actually, sales are influenced by many factors in addition to price, including amount and quality of advertising, the convenience and attractiveness of the outlets through which the product is offered, the number and skill of salesmen, the "product mix" with which the particular product is offered, etc.

that advertising, product differentiation, and sales-promotion activities influence sales, sellers possessing market power may achieve sales volumes greater than sellers wholly lacking market power.

4. WITH REFERENCE TO PROFITS

As long as new firms are free to enter an industry, profits will be driven down close to normal. Typically, where market power is absent, new firms can enter the industry freely—though this situation is not inevitable. Firms with great market power would not be challenged by new firms; if they were, their market power would no longer be great. Profits in conventional markets would be depressed by the advent of new firms, but there is no reason to assume that entry would be so free that profits would be driven down to normal.[8]

B. *Other Consequences of Differences in Market Structure*

Up to this point, the consequences of the three types of markets under consideration have been discussed in a rather narrow frame. We have explored only the relation between price and minimum possible production costs, the volume of profits, and the level of excess capacity. Other implications of market structure are equally important. Among those that require investigation are expenditures on sales promotion in different markets, the progressiveness of different types of markets, the effects of market power upon the distribution of personal income; the influence of market power upon the over-all allocation of productive resources; and the effect of market power on the level of total output. (Expression will be simplified by designating as "monopoly" all substantial departures from zero market power.)

Before this discussion is undertaken, it is essential that we be quite clear about what we are doing. In particular, we run the danger to which many economists have succumbed of drawing conclusions about the real world on the basis of an analysis of abstract, hypothetical, and unrealistic situations. We must recognize that, thus far, we have explored the operation of only three "pure" and admittedly extreme types of market structure. Probably no actual market is described exactly by any of the foregoing types; and it is not even clear that many bear these types a close

---

[8] Those who have studied economic theory will have no difficulty in seeing a close connection in their ultimate "solution," though not in the market conditions—between what are here called "conventional" markets and "monopolistically competitive" markets. The final outcome of both types depends largely upon the degree of freedom of entry. For a diagrammatic discussion of a conventional market, and a comparison with monopolistically competitive markets, see Oxenfeldt, *Industrial Pricing and Market Practices,* pp. 173-176.

resemblance. How, then, can the results of our foregoing discussion be applied to the world of reality?

The truth must be faced squarely: economists are not in a position to demonstrate conclusively the effects and implications of different types of market circumstances. Very likely they will never be able to do so. Although their tentative conclusions may be discarded, revised, or confirmed some day, they are of great interest because they represent the concensus of present-day informed opinion. These conclusions are summarized in the following pages.

We must recognize that what will be said rests largely upon an analysis of hypothetical rather than real, live-market situations, and therefore these conclusions may not apply to the real world. On the other hand, they have been checked by many economists against realistic market situations with which they are familiar; as a result, improbable conclusions have been modified or abandoned. Consequently, what follows must be considered a blend of theorizing about "pure" market types and observations of concrete market situations.

1. SALES COSTS IN THREE DIFFERENT TYPES OF MARKET

One feature of modern markets that has been widely attacked is their alleged tendency to dissipate large amounts of valuable resources in sales promotion. The type of sales promotion most widely attacked is that of "competitive advertising," which has as its purpose the diversion of patronage from other sellers to one's self. Although such advertising may prove highly profitable for the individual who is successful in its exercise, it is not clear that the economy has done anything except shift business from the bad advertisers to the good—a change which is of dubious social value. Is there likely to be a significant difference in the amount of wasteful sales effort in the three different types of market we investigated?

There is strong reason to suppose that selling expenses would be far greater in conventional markets than in the other two types. All sellers without market power, a group which includes primarily farmers, offer products that are recognizably identical. Buyers are therefore not going to be influenced by promotional efforts, which have as their principal goal the persuasion of buyers that one seller's product is better than that of the others. Sellers with great market power would have some incentive to "puff their wares" through advertising. However, they need not indulge in "competitive" sales effort. That is, they will not try to take customers away from firms selling closely related products—which in turn would try to take some of their own customers away. Their advertising would be aimed at increasing purchases either by reducing buyers' savings, or by having buyers give up altogether unrelated products. One would expect that in conventional markets, on the other hand, sales-promotion expenditures typically would be considerable. As we indicated, sellers would fear retaliation to price cuts. Efforts of sellers to expand their sales are therefore pushed into nonprice channels. Rivalry in advertising campaigns also is, no doubt, somewhat dampened by fear of retaliation. However, complete retaliation is almost impossible in advertising. A rival might increase sales-promotion expenditures equally, but the quality of the sales effort and its effect would almost certainly be different. When exact duplication is impossible, sellers who believe that they can outdo their rivals are likely to undertake actions designed to increase their share of the market. Accordingly, one would expect—and indeed experience supports this expectation—considerable "competitive" advertising in conventional markets.

2. PROGRESSIVENESS OF THE THREE MARKET TYPES

The foregoing discussion does not consider possible differences in cost that would arise from variations in the "progressiveness" of firms in different market types. The analysis proceeded on the implicit assumption that the shape and level of costs curves would be the same, regardless of the nature of the market; this assumption is unrealistic and can now be relaxed.

One would expect differences in the progressiveness of firms in various types of market. To assess the probable difference, two conflicting tendencies must be balanced. On one hand, companies that make profits can afford research activities that often turn up possible improvements in the product or in methods of production. Firms that barely survive— a state that occurs when sellers have no market power—can scarcely afford much research. On the other hand, pressure to improve production techniques is greatest where sellers have no market power. A seller who makes considerable profits because he has a protected-market position will not be forced to "pinch pennies," whereas one who is barely covering costs will make every effort to eliminate inefficiencies from his operations.

No careful study has been made of the connection between market type and expenditures for research. It is the author's strong impression, based upon an unsystematic examination of American industry, that research effort is correlated with two circumstances: profitability and the opportunity to differentiate one's offerings. Markets where sellers have no power are characterized by very small or no research efforts. Certainly, few farmers undertake research; the cotton-textile industry was responsible for none until cooperative research on behalf of the entire industry was undertaken. On the other hand, industries characterized by small numbers of large and relatively profitable firms—like chemicals, electronics, synthetic fibers, rubber, and automobiles—invest substantial sums in research.

Progressiveness in industry does not depend upon formal research efforts alone; it is at least partly related to informal efforts to improve productive efficiency. Industries with many sellers have a great many persons who give almost all of their wakeful time to thinking of ways to improve operations. Since these workers are engaged directly in the business, they have experience—almost analagous to research experience—that will contribute to their success in making improvements. Thus the larger the number of independent firms, the larger the amount of non-systematic research that will go forward, and the greater the pressure to come forward with a new idea. One cannot confidently balance the conflicting forces—size of research outlays and intensity of informal efforts to improve productivity—in the abstract. No one of the three types of market situation would necessarily excel in this respect everywhere. In the author's opinion, conventional markets—and markets containing some degree of market power—are the most progressive as a general rule.

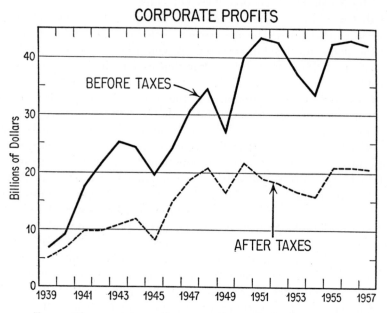

CORPORATE PROFITS

Even with corporate profits at an all-time high, due to war, inflation, and cold war, they represent a relatively small proportion of our total national income.

3. MARKET POWER AND THE DISTRIBUTION OF PERSONAL INCOME

As already indicated in another connection, the power to influence price is used in their own favor by those who possess it. They will ordinarily try to set prices high enough to obtain maximum profits for themselves. Although profits are sometimes largest when sellers charge moderate prices and sell a large quantity, a firm with power to influence price will almost invariably charge more than one lacking that power. After all, no special power is required to ask and obtain a lower price. By charging higher prices than would prevail in the absence of power over price, sellers transfer income from their customers to themselves. Buyers therefore will obtain a smaller quantity of goods with a given money income, and sellers will acquire larger personal incomes than they otherwise would.

Monopoly profits are no doubt quite large in particular instances; however, over-all they are far smaller than most people suppose. This conclusion can be supported by indirect evidence. Let us first determine the total amount of profits earned by business. (Limitations of data dictate that we study only corporate business.) As would be expected, this amount varies widely from prosperity to depression, being actually negative in deep depression. Let us take an average of three postwar years which were, on the whole, very prosperous—1947-1949. In those years, corporate profits—*before taxes*—averaged about $31 billions. From this total the profits that do not result from monopoly should be deducted. The largest deduction should be for the "interest element." That is, business owners are entitled to receive at least what they could have obtained as interest by lending funds to businesses similar to those in which they own stock. While such a calculation is not easy to make, it would seem that a conservative return would be six per cent of capital invested in industry. For the years 1947-1949, the portion of corporate profits that can be considered payment for capital investment in corporations (and not for the taking of ownership risks) would come to $14.5 billions on this basis.[9] In addition, we must subtract from total profits those that arise from nonmonopolistic sources, such as inflationary price increases, and understatement of costs due to depreciation charges lower than will be required to replace the equipment. No matter what figure is subtracted for nonmonopoly profits, it will be found that the residue is quite small as a proportion of total income—3 per cent or less. This sum is further reduced by corporate profits taxes and personal income taxes on dividends.

4. MARKET POWER AND THE ALLOCATION OF RESOURCES

Second, monopoly exerts a complicated influence upon the quantity of individual goods produced. To demonstrate its effect conclusively it would be necessary to build up a fairly elaborate set of analytical tools.

---

[9] The total net worth of American corporations, as calculated from income tax returns, was $274 billion in 1947. Owing to heavy reinvestment of profits in subsequent years, it doubtless increased significantly in 1948 and 1949. Consequently, the figure used here is almost certainly an understatement.

Rather than undertake this, the answer will be sketched only in general.

It was indicated earlier that if scarcity and poverty are to be held to a minimum, the economy must produce goods and services in proportions that correspond to consumers' desires and needs, after taking into account the effort that goes into the production of each one. For example, among goods that involve equal costs (in money, or of personal sacrifices and natural resources) in production, obviously those that are desired most should be produced. Conversely, among goods that are equally desired, those involving minimum cost (or effort and natural resources) should be produced. Furthermore, some goods should not be produced at all. They are products that give their users less "satisfaction" (which is a difficult word to define precisely, and is moreover impossible to measure quantitatively) than there is "sacrifice" (the opposite of satisfaction and equally difficult to define and measure) incurred in their production. To produce these goods would make the country as a whole worse off than it had been before. *At any given time, it would be ideal if the last unit of all goods produced gave equal satisfaction relative to the sacrifice incurred to produce it.*

Given the foregoing concept of the ideal output of products, we can distinguish two kinds of departure from the ideal. First, there are goods which if produced in larger amount would add greatly to consumer satisfaction, and would add relatively little to sacrifices in production. To take a hypothetical and admittedly unrealistic example, conceivably the work of 1,000 men for a year might turn out a gadget that would air-condition half the homes in the country. If so, the country would unquestionably be far better off to employ at least a thousand men to produce the gadget and reduce the output of other things these men now produce. If, for some reason, only a dozen men were employed in the manufacture of this gadget, we should say that the product was being *"relatively underproduced,"* for the nation clearly would be better off if we were to increase its output.

Second, conceivably some goods are turned out in such quantities that the last units give little added satisfaction, while the sacrifice entailed in their production is great. The country would be worse off for having produced these units of the product which would be *"relatively overproduced."* Clearly, it would be to the advantage of the nation as a whole (though not necessarily to the advantage of every businessman) to shift resources from industries where goods are relatively overproduced to those where goods are relatively underproduced.

Now that the conditions of output that would be ideal, and the two major types of departure from ideal output, have been described, we can understand how variations in the power to influence price might make the allocation of resources worse. Expressed simply, *the greater the power over the price of a product, the greater the likelihood that it will be underproduced relative to other products.*[10] As a result, monopoly can be charged with reducing the amount of useful goods and services we obtain from our available resources.

We have now discussed two of the three major effects of monopoly: the redistribution of personal income, and the misallocation of resources among alternative products. There remains for discussion the effect of market power upon total production.

5. MARKET POWER AND TOTAL OUTPUT

It should be noted at the outset that the effect of market power on total output is one on which eminent authorities seem to disagree more than on most other subjects.

In much of the foregoing discussion and in the following paragraphs, the term "monopoly" will be used to simplify exposition. The reader must not forget that this term is used to designate control over price achieved by a wide variety of devices and possessed to different degrees. Accordingly, the effects of monopoly discussed here do not occur equally in all situations where some influence over price exists. In the main, the effects described vary directly with degree of power over price; there are exceptions to this generalization, however.

It has just been shown that monopoly power is almost invariably used to keep price above what it would otherwise have been, and consequently the sale of monopolized products is restricted. One would suppose that monopoly lowers *total output* if it lowers the output of specific products. To hold that monopoly does not reduce total output, one must explain how the output of nonmonopolized products becomes greater than it would be in the absence of monopoly.

To ask what effect monopoly has on total output is to present a problem that is unnecessarily difficult. How would we measure output? If we took dollar value of goods produced for sale, then monopoly would probably increase national output, even though it lowered physical output. Monopolies raise prices, thereby partly, wholly, or more than entirely offsetting the reduction in output they might bring about. And if we measure output in terms other than money, we meet insurmountable obstacles. If 100,000 homes went unbuilt because of monopoly, how many men's suits, face towels, shoes, and so on need be produced to compensate for their loss? If we were to base our answer on the sales prices of those things, we should again be using a yardstick, distorted by the effects of monopoly.

Instead of inquiring into the effect of monopoly on total output, we might ask the following related questions. First, how does monopoly affect the total "benefits" or "satisfaction" that the whole community

---

[10] See discussion of great market power, in Chapter 13, and especially Chart 4.

obtains from the national output of goods and services? This question has already been answered; it has been shown that monopoly imposes a loss on the community in the form of goods that are "relatively under-produced." Second, how does monopoly affect total employment? This question has not yet been answered, and it probably is what most people have in mind when they ask how monopoly affects total output. Third, how does monopoly affect the amount of investment in productive facilities—as contrasted with the volume of expenditure on consumers' goods? (Over long periods of time, total output is influenced by the amount of plant and equipment in existence.) Let us explore the last two problems.

a. Effects of monopoly on employment

Workers are shut out of a monopolized industry by its restriction of output. Are they employed elsewhere? Does monopoly provide employment opportunities for workers in nonmonopolized industries even while reducing their job opportunities in monopolized employments? There are two major ways in which monopoly might have this effect. First, monopoly increases the incomes of those who own the monopolized firms; these persons presumably would increase their purchases of a variety of products. As a result, output of the things bought by owners of monopolized firms must be expanded, and employment in industries selling to owners of monopolies will increase over what it would have been if monopoly had been absent. To take an extreme illustration, if only owners of monopolized businesses were able to afford yachts, then the entire employment in the yachting industry would be attributable to monopoly; employment in that and other industries selling to owners of monopolies would at least partly offset the reduced employment in monopolized industries. We cannot tell in the abstract whether the gain in employment in non-monopolized industries would compensate for the restriction of employment in monopolized trades. Conceivably, it might more than make up for the restriction in employment by monopoly firms; the reverse effect is even more probable.

Second, monopolies may influence wage rates in a way that would increase employment in both nonmonopolized and monopolized industries. Specifically, by restricting the employment of workers in their own firms, monopolies increase the supply of those seeking employment elsewhere and thereby intensify the competition for jobs. Intensification of competition among sellers of anything—including labor services—exerts a downward pressure upon price. At lower wage rates perhaps more workers would be employed profitably by businessmen in producing all kinds of products.

But we must also inquire whether a lower wage rate would not ultimately reduce the demand for labor because total spending by workers would almost certainly drop if wage rates declined. This question is among the most complicated that economists study. A few of the puzzling elements in the problem will be indicated. First, will the prices of nonmonopolized products be lowered to the same extent that wages are depressed because of the existence of monopoly? (Note that wage costs are only part, sometimes a small part, of the total costs of individual producers.) Second, at the lower wage rates, will businessmen substitute less machinery for labor? Third, if lower wages in all industries are due to monopoly, how are profits affected? How will the quantity of purchases by persons whose incomes come primarily from profits be influenced? Fourth, how would the quantities of goods purchased by nonwage earners be affected by the lower level of prices in nonmonopolized industries and by the higher prices in monopolized industries? Fifth, how will workers respond to the lower wage rates? May they not be more receptive to unionization and more militant in their unionism, with the result that wage rates are not permitted to fall? The answers to these questions show that monopoly has conflicting and unclear effects upon total employment. Economists do not agree on whether monopoly reduces employment.

b. Effects of monopoly on investment

The net effect of monopoly on investment depends upon a balance of opposing influences. Again, it will not be possible to do more than list the most important influences of monopoly on investment; there will be no attempt to strike a balance. In fact, economists disagree about the net effect of monopoly on investment.

First, monopoly raises price and thus lowers sales of monopolized products. Consequently, less plant and equipment is needed to produce the output of these products than would be needed if the firms charged lower prices. Second, monopoly increases the profitability of investment, whereas competitive industries are relatively unattractive to investors. Because of competition, rates of return on investment are low. One might therefore suppose that monopoly encourages investment by firms that possess power over price. Third, monopolies frequently prevent new firms from becoming established, as was already explained. In so doing they dry up an important type of new investment. Fourth, monopolies may make substantially bigger expenditures on research than do firms in competitive industries. They therefore may create opportunities for investment in productive facilities to employ new productive methods and to make altogether new products that would not exist in the absence of research financed out of monopoly profits.

It is extremely difficult to balance these factors. One may wonder, for example, whether investment in the cotton-fabric industry would be greater *now* or *throughout the life of the industry* if sellers had possessed far more market power. There is room for extreme disagreement on this point, and we must leave this question with an acknowledgment that it is complex and controversial.

6. ECONOMIC CONSEQUENCES OF MARKET POWER SUMMARIZED

Only one economic effect of monopoly is clear and noncontroversial: it redistributes income in favor of sellers. Objection to monopoly among legislators and the public at large results primarily from resentment against overcharging. We saw that, for the economy as a whole, the magnitude of "monopoly profits"—especially after corporate and personal income taxes—are tiny compared to total personal income. The effects of monopoly on the allocation of resources and total employment and investment may be far more objectionable. Inasmuch as they are complex and controversial they have not generated much public agitation.

Despite the difficulties faced in understanding the full effects of market power, departures from zero market power create the presumption of movement away from an ideal market situation. When sellers or buyers possess market power, they are freed from some of the pressure to produce at minimum cost, prices may allow for supernormal profits, improvements in technique and quality of product may slow, an excessive number of sellers may be attracted into the industry, and consumers may be frustrated in various ways. Despite the presumption that zero market power is desirable, one cannot attribute to "monopoly" responsibility for serious malfunctioning of the economy as a whole. Monopoly, however, may create ugly and offensive particular situations; certainly it could be extremely harmful if it lodged in markets providing products essential to public consumption.

The foregoing discussion of three theoretical market types cannot prove definitely anything about the real world.[11] It does, however, suggest the ways in which departures from zero market power (pure competition) result in social injury. Moreover, it helps to explain why it is important to get a reliable answer to the question, "Is the American economy efficient?"

DISCUSSION QUESTIONS

1. Can you think of any businesses that closely resemble what is here called a "conventional market"?

---

[11] The discussion here, as in all textbook treatments of the subject which present price theory only as a tool to be used in an analysis of reality, has shifted back and forth between theory and description. It would not be surprising if the reader becomes confused or is misled by some of these shifts; it would also not be surprising if the author had made some of the shifts without realizing he had done so.

2. Would you say that a conventional market was fundamentally competitive or fundamentally monopolistic?

3. Do you believe the effect of monopoly upon the distribution of personal income is to make it more or less equal?

4. Which types of industries would you expect to be most progressive, those lacking market power, those whose market power is complete, or those with conventional markets?

5. Can you think of industries that seem to be unlike any of the types of market discussed in this or the preceding chapter?

6. In what type of industry would you expect producers to come closest to the minimum unit cost at which they could possibly produce?

7. Is the net effect of monopoly to make investment in an industry greater or smaller than it would otherwise be?

Chapter

15 Distinction between Price Theory and Pricing in Practice

It was stressed earlier that one must not confuse the preceding discussion of price theory with a description of how businessmen actually set prices. The point was emphasized that price theory attempts to explain how resources are allocated rather than to account for day-to-day movements of prices in the market place. To ensure that readers will not unconsciously assume that the foregoing account of resource allocation describes how businessmen set price, a description of price setting is offered in the following pages. However, even this account falls far short of explaining how most prices are set.

Many economists and businessmen take exception to the very words "set price." They contend that the forces of supply and demand set price. In their view, the individual seller is powerless to influence price but is compelled to accept what he can get for his wares. Certainly, for the markets on which sellers possess no market power, their position is valid; however, for the overwhelming proportion of nonagricultural output, *prices do not "just happen" but are set by individuals.* Rather than a single price to which all sellers of a single, homogeneous product must conform, one finds various brands of a single product selling at different prices—and often even the same brand sells at different prices in stores located quite close to one another; and sometimes finds the same product sold in different departments of the same store at the same time at quite different prices.

Since prices are set by people, it seems reasonable to try to understand price by examining the people who set price, by trying to appreciate the situation in which they find themselves, and by studying the methods they employ to establish price. Before we turn to these matters, however, it is emphasized that conditions vary widely from industry to industry and from firm to firm. What follows is at best a description of what many firms do; undoubtedly, numerous exceptions can be found to what is said here.

322

I. WHO SETS PRICE?

In the one-man firm, all decisions are made by the owner-manager—including decisions about price. Even this obvious statement must be qualified, because there are many products for which the manufacturer dictates the price that the retailer must charge. If the retailer does not conform to the price "suggested" by the manufacturer, he may be unable to secure the firm's merchandise.

In large firms, on the other hand, it is much easier to locate the *responsibility* for price setting than the actual *performance* of the function. No one has studied systematically the organization of the pricing function in large corporations, but this much is clear: the top executives of a firm rarely are responsible for price setting. It is "middle-management" that usually sets price, though exceptional and emergency conditions generally bring the top executive into pricing deliberations.

Ordinarily the responsibility for establishing each price in a large firm is vested in an individual who is "in charge" of the product in question. For example, the individual in charge of insecticides in a chemical company will be responsible for setting prices on insecticides. Typically, he will appoint individuals to head-up particular branches of the insecticide business. One of their duties will be to recommend prices; ordinarily they are required to obtain their supervisor's approval of each price change.

Although the location of responsibility for pricing in the large firm is unclear, there is a fairly common practice with respect to the performance of the function. More commonly, apparently, price decisions are reached after group discussions. Frequently, persons are assigned to a committee whose function is to advance a pricing recommendation. Although the composition of pricing committees varies considerably, the departments represented most commonly include manufacturing, the controller's office, sales, advertising, and research. The recommendations of pricing committees carry different weights in individual corporations. In some, they become binding upon those in charge of sales; in others, they are reviewed by individuals who simply rubber-stamp them; in still other companies, they have only advisory power and can be overruled by the individual responsible for price—and indeed frequently are overruled.

Owing to the division of pricing responsibilities among many individuals, the contribution of any one to the process cannot be assessed exactly. Sometimes a few persons, by dint of outstanding ability, specialized knowledge, long experience, or dominating personality, may exercise overwhelming influence; at other times the influence of all members of the pricing committee is fairly equal. One must further expect that the person to whom the pricing committee makes its recommendation and who could overrule it is extremely hesitant to do so in the interest of maintaining the morale and conscientious effort of the pricing committee. Because of these obscure lines between responsibility and function, between power and restraints upon its exercise, and because of the unclear contributions of each member in any group, one cannot advance a clear answer to the question "Who sets price?" [1]

II. THE PRICING FUNCTION AS VIEWED BY THE EXECUTIVE ENGAGED IN PRICING

Let us project ourselves into the position of persons who are involved in pricing on behalf of large firms. We must recognize immediately that the task will ordinarily vary considerably according to whether we view ourselves as members of a large manufacturing or of a retailing firm. These two types of business ordinarily arrive at price by quite different means, as will be explained presently. In addition to the need of being clear about the line of business in which we are to imagine ourselves, it is essential to know whether our firm sells few or many different products, and whether the sales of the different products by the firm are closely interrelated—so that if you sell one to a customer you increase the likelihood of his buying other products you offer for sale.

If we are to understand how the business executive views his pricing functions, we must also be clear about his objectives and what he knows or thinks he knows about conditions of cost and demand. Let us take these matters up in turn.

Economic theory makes very explicit assumptions about both the objectives and the knowledge of those responsible for pricing (and output) decisions. As for objectives, it assumes that businessmen seek maximum money profits; on the subject of knowledge of costs and demand, price theory assumes complete and accurate knowledge.

A. *Price Setters' Objectives*

To judge by the explanation for price provided by price theory, the objective that economists attribute to businessmen would appear to be maximum *short-run* profit. However, when they discuss the objective they

---

[1] One person frequently engaged in setting price, even in large firms, is generally overlooked. He is the salesman who calls on the customer. Since he frequently is compensated by a commission, it often is in his power, though almost always contrary to company policy, to "give away part of his commission." In addition, he can fabricate a story about a competitor's low-price offer that may induce the home office to offer the customer a major price concession.

are assuming—that is, attributing to businessmen—they name maximum *long-run* profit. So much for what is assumed by price theory; let us turn to what probably *are* the objectives of the persons who participate in pricing decisions and of those who are responsible for these decisions.

First off, we must grant that we cannot be sure about executives' objectives; objectives are tricky matters no matter what the subject. Several approaches might be employed to learn what objectives executives pursue in their pricing recommendations. One method is to examine the stated objectives of the firms by which they are engaged. A second approach is to project ourselves into the position of an executive and introspect about how he reasons and behaves. A third approach would be to "ask him." Unfortunately no one of these approaches has been employed on a large scale or in a systematic manner. Accordingly, whatever is said here may prove to be incorrect when, and if, the subject is studied more thoroughly than the author has been able to study it.

The stated objectives of large firms—and not all firms have prepared an explicit statement of their objectives in general or of their pricing objectives in particular—generally include objectives above and beyond the maximization of long-term profit. To some extent, they take cognizance of what might be termed a firm's "social responsibility" to its customers. For example, one finds statements about a firm's obligations to pass along to customers any cost reductions achieved by improvements in technology. In addition, a firm's objectives will often state that management has some responsibility to employees, even at the expense of the firm's ultimate and long-run profitability. Thus, if executives are strongly influenced by their firms' stated objectives, they depart to some extent (one cannot say to how great a degree) from the assumption that firms strive to maximize money profits.

If we speculate about the motives of individuals responsible for pricing in the large firm, we run great risk of being wrong. However, in speculating we shall raise some fundamental questions of which any student of pricing should be aware. Possible motives that might inspire an executive engaged in pricing activities, other than the maximization of profit, would include (1) a desire to be inconspicuous—which would lead him to go along with the crowd; (2) a desire to recommend a safe course rather than one which might be far more profitable but involve risks; (3) the desire to "do it the easy way" rather than the "best way," when the best way would mean a lot of extra work; (4) the desire to stick with past methods and conclusions rather than admit past error or imply that an associate was in error; (5) the desire to make a showing by taking an unorthodox stand; and the like. These motives create situations in which some executives might advance their personal position at the possible expense of the firm's profitability. The foregoing list of likely motives other than the enhancement of the firm's profits is not intended to imply that the conflict of interest between individuals and the firms which employ them is deep or great. We just do not know how great it is. Certainly it could conceivably be great; on the other hand, conflict of interest may arise only rarely and be corrected by a variety of checks within the firm. In any event, we must recognize the possibility that persons engaged in pricing on a day-to-day basis are not motivated solely by a desire to obtain maximum long-run profits for the firm.

One might try to discover price setters' motives by asking them what they are. Inquiries of this type by the author always elicit replies designed to persuade him that the respondents do their job extremely intelligently, with only the welfare of their company in mind. Price setters' statements about objectives seemed to represent a mixture of truth and homespun public relations.

Almost all studies of price setting made by questioning those engaged in the process conclude that many of the persons use a formula, or a formula tempered by "common sense." Although these formulae are defended on grounds of ensuring the firm a reasonable profit, they rarely are justified as tools for obtaining maximum profit. One line of defense generally advanced for formula pricing has been that it is "fair."

B. Price Setters' Knowledge of Demand and Costs

We have devoted considerable space to the question of price setters' objectives. The purpose has been to make more vivid and concrete than it would otherwise be the position in which those concerned with price setting find themselves within large firms. Let us repeat the process, this time exploring what price setters know about conditions of cost and demand and how they learn what they believe to be the facts on that subject.

Recognize at the outset that most firms—and especially retail firms— sell a wide variety of products. As was suggested, often the sales of a firm are made in bundles rather than in isolation; that is to say, a customer who patronizes a supermarket or department store or even a corner stationery store will ordinarily buy several items rather than one when he enters the store. Similarly, many manufacturers sell most customers several items in their line rather than a single item. When such a situation obtains, one must recognize that the demand for any single product offered by the firm becomes entangled—perhaps hopelessly—with the demand for some or all other products offered for sale. Not only do we find the demands for individual items offered by a firm to be interrelated; we find that the nature of that interrelation is extremely complicated. Some executives may be sure that they know the connection between the sales of individual items in their line; all too often, however, such certainty reflects conceit rather than knowledge.

As with demand, cost data become highly confused when a firm handles many products rather than one. Many costs are incurred to produce and market several products rather than one. Although many rules of thumb are used for allocating common costs among the products in whose production and sale they were incurred, every method is arbitrary. As a result, businessmen cannot know precisely the costs of each of the products they offer for sale, if their firm handles many products.

It should be emphasized that we have been discussing the "true nature" of costs and demand rather than the businessman's view of them. Perhaps we should inquire into how businessmen arrive at the conclusions they hold about costs and demand, and then attempt to compare those notions with the probable "true nature" of costs and demand. To do so would be extremely valuable if it could be done well. However, information on this subject is lacking, and we should be likely to go far astray if we were to undertake so ambitious a project. Nevertheless, we must recognize that in attempting to take account of cost and demand, sellers must wrestle with extremely complex problems—especially if they are selling many products. From the nature of these problems, we are entitled to conclude that errors are likely to be quite common and sometimes sizable.

Thus we find that the assumptions of price theory that businessmen pursue long-run maximum profit on the basis of known demand and cost condition do not conform to the facts. However, we cannot say with confidence whether these assumptions are close approximations or gross distortions of the facts. Especially on the matter of knowing demand, the assumptions of price theory are almost certainly wide of the mark; they probably are more adequate representations of reality on the subject of objectives and knowledge of costs—though these too are far from exact.

III. PRICING STRATEGIES AND METHODS

Now that we have examined the framework in which pricing usually takes place, let us turn to the specific types of problems faced by those responsible for pricing, and examine the solutions they have adopted. As was suggested earlier, for most purposes it is important to distinguish between the pricing problems and procedures of retailers and those of manufacturers.

A. Pricing by Retailers and Manufacturers Compared

There are three main respects in which retailers' and manufacturers' pricings differ: first, retailers know their major costs more accurately than do most manufacturers; second, retailers ordinarily sell many more related items than do manufacturers; third, retailers sell directly to the

ultimate consumer, whereas manufacturers generally sell to other businessmen. Let us examine these differences more closely and see how they
influence the way retailers and manufacturers handle their pricing problems.

Retailers know their main costs fairly accurately because these costs
are relatively unaffected by changes in sales volume. By far the heaviest
cost incurred by retailers is the cost of merchandise. (There are doubtless exceptions to this as to any other statement one might make on this
subject.) This cost is known in advance of sale and remains essentially the
same regardless of how much of each item the retailer sells; generally
termed "invoice cost," it is the amount stated on the bill presented by the
supplier to the retailer. (Interestingly enough, the cost used for pricing
by retailers is the invoice cost before account is taken of any discounts
that might be allowed for such things as prompt payment or for purchases
in large quantities.) As was explained earlier, manufacturers' costs are
influenced strongly by their sales volume; consequently, manufacturers
know their costs only on hindsight. In practice, their costs are estimated
on the basis of the company's sales forecast or upon estimated costs at
some "standard" or "average" output.

By virtue of their fairly accurate knowledge of costs, retailers tend to
base their prices very heavily upon their invoice costs. As a result, there
tend to be great similarity in the pricing methods of retailers and great
uniformity of base costs. More specifically, retailers generally arrive at
price by adding a margin (recall what was said earlier on pp. 307-309
about the factors which influence the size of the margin added to arrive
at price, and the circumstances under which the margin percentage is
changed) to invoice cost; and the invoice cost to most retailers for any
given produce is likely to differ very little, if at all. (Both base costs and
pricing methods employed by manufacturers vary considerably, in contrast to the situation found at retail.)

Retailers differ widely in the number of items they sell; near one
extreme is the store specializing in infants' and children's shoes; at the
other extreme are the department store and the supermarket. The former
sells only one type of a single product; the latter sells literally thousands
of different items. The current trend apparently is toward retailers' carrying more rather than fewer items. Almost always, the items carried by
retailers are related to one another—that is, they are the kinds of things
purchased by the same type of person; or they are different items purchased for the same general use—for example, building supplies, hard-
ware, sporting goods, etc. The reason for carrying items that are related
either in type of consumer or in use—and usually in both respects—is
that many consumers who come to the store to purchase one item will
also purchase others. If we are to understand how retailers approach
their pricing problems, we must give great weight to their desire to lure

the consumer into the store to purchase one item and then entice him into buying others.

The third difference between retailers and manufacturers with respect to pricing, in addition to differences in knowledge of costs and in the number of items carried, is that the retailer deals with the ultimate consumer, whereas manufacturers sell to other businessmen. As a consequence, retailers can feel relatively secure in the knowledge that their customers do not usually make an exhaustive and intelligent search of all alternative sources of supply. They can assume that most consumers will rely upon their present and past impressions and·common gossip about the store's general level of prices *vis à vis* its competitors' prices, rather than upon careful comparison shopping. As a result, retailers need not attach great significance to price of any individual item—unless it is one that has been promoted actively by competitors; in this event it would prove embarrassing to be higher in price than the others. In contrast, many manufacturers' prices are examined by specialists in buying whose responsibility it is to search out various sources of supply and to find those offering most advantageous terms.

B. Retailers' Pricing Strategies and Methods

Most retailers consciously attempt to create a specific "personality" for their store. They try to convey an image of the store to prospective consumers (more accurately, to *particular types* of consumer—for no store can hope to be attractive to *all* potential customers) that will win their patronage. Part of this image is created by the prices charged by the store —both on the basis of how its prices compare with the prices charged by competitors carrying the identical items and with respect to whether it handles the highest quality and price lines or concentrates on medium-priced merchandise, or is strongest "at the low end." Other characteristics of a store that combine with price to establish its personality include quality and number of sales personnel, its policies with respect to making exchanges and accepting "returns," the breadth of selection it offers, and the attractiveness of its establishment and fixtures.

Apart from attempting to establish his store's personality by means of his pricing procedures, the retailer recognizes that he has two main objectives: first, to attract patrons into the store; and, second, to sell them as much as he can—including things they had not planned to buy. The result is what may be described as "team pricing." This concept is not universally understood or applied, but it is growing both in recognition and application. "Team pricing" means that stores will sometimes assign special roles to various products they sell. For example, some may be used as "promotional items," which are priced and advertised with the prime purpose of attracting customers into the store; others may be intended to "make up for the low margin obtained on promotional items." Still other items may simply yield the "target" rate of return that management set for the department. In addition to distinguishing among items on the team according to the size of the margin added to base cost, another difference in function should be recognized. Some items are carried and priced with the purpose of being "sold against." That is, the item will be included in the retailer's offerings simply to enhance the attractiveness of other items and because its presence encourages consumers to buy another item. We are referring here to what is sometimes termed "step-up selling," in which the store attracts customers by advertising a "stripped" model at a low price and then induces them to buy more costly models carrying added features. By including far more costly items, they often make it easier to persuade customers to purchase more costly items than those they had come to buy. These very expensive items make the consumer feel (at least many retailers believe so) that he has been thrifty, even though he has spent more than he had originally intended. One can well understand how a consumer's confidence in the wisdom of a purchase is strengthened immeasurably when he has been shown another item which costs more than he paid and which lacks features possessed by the item he bought.

As was indicated, "team pricing" is not necessarily the general rule in retailing, though its prevalence is increasing. Possibly of even wider prevalence is the more-or-less mechanical cost-plus pricing of the type assumed earlier when we discussed "conventional markets." The use of an unchanging original markup is certainly widespread; it is to be explained by the fact that retailers sell too many items to price each one individually. Even those who are extremely appreciative of the potency of team pricing generally select a small handful of items to which they assign special roles and price the others according to mechanical formula.

C. Manufacturers' Pricing Strategies and Methods

Since manufacturers sell relatively few different items, and to customers who are likely to be well-informed about price and quality differences, their concern with each individual price is far greater than the retailer's. (We should, however, recognize that a considerable number of manufacturers do produce a "line" of products which are sold pretty much as a package; for example, a manufacturer will sell wholesalers or retailers his entire line of kitchen equipment or electrical appliances or stationery or shoes, rather than just one item.) For that reason, a manufacturer's price must take account of a wide variety of special circumstances which the retailer ordinarily will ignore. For example, he will be mindful of the fact that a new producer is entering the business, or of the fact that one major user of his product has been investigating the advisability of producing the item for himself; or of the growing shortage of raw materials required to make the product; or of technological developments that are in prospect; or of the state of inventories at the wholesale and retail level.

Mention has already been made of the fact that manufacturers know their costs only on hindsight—after they know their volume of sales and how long their plant and equipment will prove economically serviceable. As a result, manufacturers employ rules of thumb or sales estimates to compute a base cost which they use for arriving at price. One widely employed method, known as "standard costing," consists of computing costs at an output roughly equal to the average of output during recent years; another is to estimate cost at the estimated level of sales during the period. Whichever method is used, the outcome is essentially the same: prices come to be based upon estimated costs; one might say, they are based on some *imaginary* cost base rather than upon *actual* costs. In addition, this base cost is one that includes both direct (marginal) and fixed costs. (In contrast, the retailer's base cost is his invoice cost of merchandise, which comes very close to being an accurate measure of marginal costs.) More important, the method of computing the base cost is not standard by any means; accordingly, one might find substantial differences among firms in their *estimated* costs, even though their *actual* costs are much the same.

Inasmuch as each product is likely to influence a firm's profitability to a substantial degree, the manufacturer may well have a separate strategy for many of the items he carries. On some, he may attempt to be the "Cadillac" of the industry—offering highest quality at premium prices; on others he may be the "Ford," where he gives satisfactory quality at very modest price; he may play the role of a price shader on some items while adhering religiously to market price on others. The variations from item to item presumably would reflect differences in the competitive conditions with which he must contend as well as in his forecast of developments that impend.

Specialists in industrial pricing are in general agreement that most manufacturers allow their prices to be determined primarily by costs and to only a very slight degree by demand conditions. They find that manufacturers often arrive at price by a method not very different from the mechanical cost-plus pricing already described; the only difference is that they add their "margin" to some fictitious base cost rather than to merchandise costs. There is also considerable evidence to show that the pricing methods employed by manufacturers vary considerably—far more than is found among retailers. For example, the pricing philosophy and general marketing procedures employed by General Electric and Westinghouse—both extremely large firms whose activities overlap greatly—differ greatly, according to all accounts.

One phase of manufacturer pricing deserves special mention because it applies particularly to industries where there are relatively few sellers, each of substantial size; the automobile, steel, television, refrigerator, etc., industries are examples. In such industries, most sellers take into account far more than the direct economic effects of their price actions. They also consider the effects of price changes upon customer attitudes and upon the likelihood of government antitrust action. Price increases often trigger protests to the Anti-Trust Division of the Department of Justice or to the Federal Trade Commission that result in legal action against the firm or industry making a price increase. The outcome of management concern with customer and government reactions to price changes has been a tendency to defer price changes until a "legitimate" excuse can be advanced for increasing price. By all odds the most acceptable reason for raising price—both to the public and to the government antitrust agencies—is that costs have risen. Accordingly, it has become fairly common for firms to announce price increases at the time when labor contracts providing for wage increases go into effect.

IV. CONCLUSIONS

This chapter, while very brief and general, should prevent any reader from drawing erroneous conclusions from price theory about the way pricing is conducted in practice. It should make clear that many of the assumptions of price theory do not correspond to the facts of day-to-day market realities. However, most economists would contend that price theory does deal with the most fundamental policies at work in present-day market and that it is considered to be a reasonably accurate description of what ultimately happens when the divergence between the assumption of theory and the facts of life is great.

The author is not convinced that price theory does describe, accurately enough for many purposes, how most—or the most important—markets behave. Factors not taken up by price theory seem to exert a major influence on resource allocation. That is to say, some markets apparently are affected very strongly—in what they produce and in the way they produce it—by such factors as consumer ignorance, producer fear of antitrust prosecution, nonprofit objectives, and the potency of various sales-promotion devices. Price theory, moreover, is far more adequate as a description of some types of markets than it is of others.

However, the description of pricing practices presented here emphatically was not included as a whipping boy—set up simply to be knocked down. The truth of the matter is that, whatever its imperfections, and they are many, price theory remains the best generalized description of the broad forces operating in modern markets. As such, it deserves careful study by anyone who hopes to understand the basic mechanism of free-enterprise economy. As a person learns more about economics he discovers when he can rely on the conclusions of price theory and when they are misleading.

DISCUSSION QUESTIONS

1. To what extent does the reality of price setting in large firms depart from the notions of traditional price theory?

2. What motives shape executives' price-setting decisions? How does their knowledge of demand and costs enter into their decision making?

3. In what general way does retailer pricing differ from manufacturer pricing?

4. What specific characteristics of the market determine the different strategies pursued by retailers and manufacturers in their pricing methods?

Chapter

16 Types of Market Power
Found in the United States

I. INTRODUCTORY

The foregoing chapters have described and analyzed the consequences of three illuminating but hypothetical market situations. It is appropriate that existing market conditions should now be described.

The real world is fantastically complex. Thousands of different industries operate at the present time, and each one is unique in some respect. Study of the structure and operations of individual industries has been confined to a relatively small number, and these have been hampered by inability of investigators to obtain all the information they desire. It is therefore impossible to describe all American industry.

Moreover, it is probably futile or misleading to divide it into broad categories. Several investigators have classified all American industries according to their competitiveness.[1] In this author's opinion these classifications are interesting but quite misleading. They invariably lump together industries that are widely different. The fault lies, not with those who have made these classifications, but with the enormous complexity of industrial situations.

Since it would appear futile to divide American industry into broad categories, another method of describing it will be attempted. The respects in which many industries apparently depart from a condition of zero market power will be emphasized. As far as available evidence will allow, the prevalence of departures from zero market power will be assessed. At best only a superficial sketch of the American economy can be hoped for in the space that can be accorded to it here.

---

[1] See Clair Wilcox, *T.N.E.C. Monograph No. 21, Competition and Monopoly in American Industry;* G. W. Nutter, *A Quantitative Study of the Extent of Enterprise Monopoly in the United States* (Chicago: University of Chicago Press, 1951), and George Stigler, *Five Lectures on Economic Problems* (New York: The Macmillan Company, 1950).

334

II. MAJOR DEPARTURES FROM ZERO MARKET POWER

Significant departures from zero market power occur when

1. The number of sellers is so small that they recognize their mutual interdependence and pursue policies that serve their common interest.

2. Sellers do not operate independently but cooperate or collude with rivals, or adhere to trade practices that are good substitutes for outright collusion.

3. Sellers adopt arrangements, particularly resale-price maintenance (the so-called "fair-trade" laws) that strongly influence the behavior of the market.

4. By engaging in extensive sales-promotion activities, sellers spend large sums to increase their sales or to forestall a loss of customers to rivals.

5. Buyers are not well informed about the quality of the products offered to them, and often their demands do not reflect their true interests.

6. Sellers do not offer products that buyers believe to be identical. Almost all sellers have a peculiar appeal to some buyers who are willing to pay substantially more for a particular brand than for any available substitute.

7. New firms can enter many industries only with great difficulty; even when they make the attempt, they may not be able to produce economically enough to contend successfully with their rivals. Moreover, producers are slow to leave some markets that are generally unprofitable.

8. The number of buyers may be so small, or a few may buy such large quantities, that they are able to influence price strongly in their favor.

9. There is collusion among workers in many markets where payments to labor are determined.

Each of these departures from zero market power will be described in turn.

A. Fewness of Sellers

As already indicated, when there is zero market power, there are many sellers, each so small that he is merely a "drop in the bucket" and cannot perceptibly affect the outcome in any respect. Each seller therefore must do what the fundamental market pressures require of him. Specifically, he must produce in a manner that involves minimum cost, or he will find himself unable to stay in business. He must accept the prevailing price, for he can sell nothing above that price. However, again except for farm staples, oligopoly prevails in virtually all industry. That is, the number of sellers is so small that what any one of them does strongly influences at least *some* others to the point of compelling them to retaliate.

The mutual interdependence of individual sellers strongly influences the behavior that they find advantageous. Whereas it might be to their advantage to reduce price—if no one else would notice or retaliate—it might be highly unprofitable to do so if all other sellers followed suit. As a result, when sellers are few there will be a strong tendency for them to refrain from price reductions unless they are under severe pressure. In short, fewness of sellers contributes to a downward rigidity of prices.

There are several factors making for fewness of sellers. First, technological circumstances often offer advantages to firms that produce on a substantial scale, as was explained; consequently, an entire national market for a product can sometimes be served most economically by only a few firms. Second, firms seek to expand in size in order to increase their income; by expanding, they may also hope to eliminate rivals and gain stronger market power. Third, "horizontal expansion," via merger, offers many attractions—not the least of which is the absorption of what may have been a troublesome rival.

In Chapter nine, the effect of technological conditions upon the size of businesses was discussed. Accordingly, we shall here discuss methods by which firms reduce the number of their rivals and thereby contribute to reduction in number of sellers (and buyers also). Essentially, there are two major methods. First, by eliminating existing rivals; second, by forestalling the establishment of new firms.

1. ELIMINATION OF EXISTING RIVALS

Rival firms can be eliminated by driving them out of business. A variety of methods has been used to drive competitors to the wall, including price wars (combined with possession of superior production efficiency or greater ability to withstand losses during a price war), superior productive efficiency combined with selling at a price below the rival's costs (which would best not be considered a price war); predatory practices, like disparagement of a rival's product or personal reputation. The elimination of rivals primarily by means of superior efficiency is exemplified in the automobile industry. Outstanding examples of price cutting and a wide variety of practices that would be considered unfair today occurred in the petroleum and tobacco industries up to the time of their "dissolution" in 1911, and in the cash register industry up to about 1920.

Rivals can be bought out as well as driven out of business. Although there has been a law since 1913 that prohibits the purchase of the stock of rival companies whose elimination would materially lessen competition, it was legal up to 1951 for a firm to purchase the *assets* of rivals outright.

(The right to acquire competitors by purchases of assets rather than securities was a serious loophole in the antitrust laws, and the Federal Trade Commission was not able to close it until 1951.) Sometimes two prosperous rivals will merge their enterprises into one large one and at one blow both achieve greater size and eliminate one competitor for each of them. Sometimes a firm will try to make its rival's business unprofitable in order to acquire it at a low price.

In the United States, business acquisitions and mergers have come in big bundles. By far the most far-reaching occurred between 1890 and 1904, during which period some of the nation's largest firms of the present day were created by combining many relatively small enterprises. The 1920's were another period of active merger, largely fostered by dealers in securities who sought to capitalize on the existence of a large group that was willing to purchase speculative issues; few industrial giants resulted from these mergers. Following World War II, and especially after 1950, mergers became almost an industrial "fad." Mergers during this period rarely combined direct rivals (with the notable exception of those in the automobile industry, though even these combined firms in different price classes). Some, as in the shoe industry, mainly combined manufacturing with distribution. Many mergers reflected a desire to "diversify" and brought together lines of activity that superficially had nothing in common. A substantial proportion of mergers in the 1950's can be traced to "special tax situations," which had the effect of making some businesses far more valuable—after taxes—to the purchaser than to the seller of the business.

An important method of combining with rivals has been through the formation of holding companies. This device was described in the earlier discussion of methods whereby firms grow large.

2. FORESTALLING THE ESTABLISHMENT OF NEW RIVALS

Little is to be gained from eliminating rivals if new firms are free to take their places. Firms, moreover, have little control over price if new firms can enter the business easily. If established firms set prices high enough to obtain a substantial profit for themselves, they will attract newcomers whose added output will depress prices. They therefore will not have power to raise the price of their goods beyond the level at which many new firms were induced to enter the industry. Recognizing this fact, many businessmen take measures calculated either to discourage or to prevent newcomers from entering their line of business. Of the many methods that have been used, only a few will be listed.

Probably the most important barrier to new firms is patents, which legally prevent newcomers either from using vital technology or from producing a particular product altogether. Patents are limited in duration to seventeen years from the time they are issued. By various means, however, their lives are sometimes extended much longer.[2] Patents are completely legal; indeed, occasionally monopoly has been enforced by the government, which undertakes to penalize those violating the patent monopoly. The logic behind patent monopolies, which might appear to be in sharp contradiction with our policy of maintaining competition, is that, to get the desired rate of technological advance, opportunity for inventors to receive sizable rewards is required. According to this reasoning, the price of discoveries is to be paid by users of the new product for a limited period, after which the new idea becomes common property.

In addition to patents, newcomers are sometimes beset by obstacles put in their path by established firms. For example, old firms can create such brand consciousness that new rivals cannot hope to secure many customers unless they can afford a large advertising outlay. Or, by preventing distributors of their product from handling the products of new firms, they can make it difficult for would-be rivals to obtain the services of distributors. Some businessmen have cut prices sharply when a new company has opened, in order to make it difficult for the new firm to win customers away from them. On occasion, businessmen have secured commitments from labor unions (presumably in return for some concessions) that they would not supply labor for new firms. Occasionally, firms have bought up deposits of suitable raw materials that new firms must have, to prevent them from getting started. This list is incomplete; it indicates only the more commonplace methods by which some firms secure and retain control over price by obstructing newcomers.

Thus, by various means, the number of firms selling products that are the same—that is, they are close substitutes for one another—may be kept quite small. The extent to which American industry is characterized by industries with few sellers is suggested by Table 1. It should be stressed that unless industry is narrowly defined and account is taken of whether the firms sell in the same or in different areas, such tables can be very misleading. The definition of industry that underlies this table essentially includes producers of articles that are similar but not identical, whether they are sold locally or nationally, and whether there are close substitute products included in another industry classification. Accordingly, the reader is cautioned against drawing any conclusions from it about the intensity of market rivalry in the industries described.

Table 1 indicates the proportion of the value of shipments, in each of 35 selected manufacturing industries, that were made by the largest companies in 1954 (the total value of shipments in each industry listed was over $1 billion in that year). This study shows that only a few large firms in each industry account for a large proportion of such assets, frequently more than half.

---

[2] See *T.N.E.C. Hearings*, Part 3, especially pp. 848-853.

B. Sellers Cooperate Rather Than Compete

1. WHAT COOPERATION MEANS

Firms that are powerless to influence price when they operate independently and strive to take business away from their rivals gain great power when they agree with their rivals on price.[3] Rivals can, moreover, influence price greatly by agreements about other matters as well. For example, agreements to stay out of designated areas so that, say, one firm is given the exclusive right to sell in each area would give that firm great power over price, even though the agreement did not specify the figure at which the firm was to sell. Similarly, firms might agree on the proportion of total sales each one might make, and establish a system for penalizing those who exceeded their quotas and for compensating those who fell short.

Market power can arise from a type of understanding among rivals that parallels agreement but is not the same thing. Without any written or spoken agreement, some rivals adopt a course of action in mutual awareness of one another's policies. For example, all firms might follow the price changes of one firm in the industry. After they had done so for a while, presumably all would recognize what the others were doing, and the practice of following the price leader would be taken for granted. In time, one would expect the leader firm to select its prices in recognition of this fact, and would therefore set a price quite different from the one it would have stipulated otherwise.

Where an explicit or tacit understanding exists about price, or some other closely related business matter—such as territories of sale, shares of the market, discounts, and such—the parties to the agreement collectively possess power over price. Usually, no one of them exerts much influence, except to the extent that each might wreck the price agreement by refusing to become a party to it. While relatively few individual firms can determine the prices they pay or receive, agreement among rival firms probably is a moderately important source of influence over price in modern American industry.

2. TYPES OF COOPERATIVE ARRANGEMENTS FOUND IN AMERICAN INDUSTRY

It is important to distinguish the latent market power of a firm, or a group of firms, from the manner in which this influence actually is exer-

---

[3] Price agreements among rivals are unquestionably illegal, but so too is speeding. Both types of offense seem to be quite prevalent; because of their illegality, those accused of violating the law almost invariably protest their innocence, and confessions are rare.

Table 1. Concentration in Output of Thirty-five Selected Manufacturing Industries, 1954

(Total value of shipments of each industry was over $1 billion)

Industry	Number of companies in group	Per cent of value of shipments accounted for by		
		4 largest companies	8 largest companies	20 largest companies
Motor vehicles and parts	991	75	80	87
Petroleum refining	253	33	56	84
Steel works and rolling mills	102	54	70	85
Meat-packing plants	2,228	39	51	60
Aircraft	46	47	76	96
Radios and related products	1,612	24	35	53
Fluid milk and other products	4,572	23	29	36
Aircraft engines	202	62	81	93
Bread and related products	5,470	20	31	40
Blast furnaces	34	65	82	96
Refrigeration machinery	561	36	51	69
Canned fruits and vegetables	1,461	28	39	52
Beer and ale	263	27	41	60
Tires and inner tubes	27	79	91	99+
Structural steel and ornamental metal work	2,829	18	23	31
Footwear, except rubber	970	30	36	45
Pharmaceutical preparations	1,128	25	44	68
Cigarettes	12	82	99+	100
Paints and varnishes	1,337	27	27	50
Dresses (sold per unit)	4,072	4	7	12
Motors and generators	266	50	59	75
Tin cans and other tinware	109	80	88	96
Copper rolling and drawing	64	53	71	90
Women's suits, coats and skirts	3,178	3	6	11
Synthetic fibers	20	80	97	100
Plastics materials	149	47	69	88
Tractors	141	73	88	97
Machine tools	627	19	29	52
Men's and boys' suits and coats	1,255	11	18	31
Construction and mining machinery	589	19	29	50
Wood furniture	2,731	8	13	21
Bottled soft drinks	4,334	10	14	21
Electrical control apparatus	389	48	61	75
Farm machinery (except tractors)	1,145	38	51	64
Shipbuilding and repairing	328	43	58	74

SOURCE: U.S. Congress, *Concentration in American Industry*, Report of the Sub-committee on Antitrust and Monopoly, U.S. Senate (Washington, D.C.: Government Printing Office, 1957), Table 43.

cised by them. Firms with great market power may conceivably elect to use it in a benign manner, regarding themselves as custodians of a public trust. True, these firms may exercise great power, but in a way we consider admirable. Nevertheless, this policy must be distinguished from that of firms that pursue maximum profits, mindful of nothing but their ability to "get away with it."

The business practices employed by businessmen are closely connected with their market power. On the one hand, a firm's ability to employ particular practices (say, price collusion) depends to a large extent upon its market power. On the other hand, the practices employed determine the extent to which a firm will influence the price of the things it sells. Sellers can choose a variety of price and market practices; some are more potent than others, judged according to their effect on price, ease with which they can be "policed" by an industry, facility with which violators to an agreement are detected, ability to discourage newcomers, reduction of costs, and the like. It is a mistake to assume that market policies simply reflect the market power of sellers. It is quite as valid to argue that these practices determine the degree of sellers' influence over price. Therefore it is very important to know what businessmen do, even as we want to know how "strong" they are.

a. Price leadership

As was indicated, price leadership need not rest upon explicit collusion. It may develop accidentally and then be continued in mutual awareness that all other firms will continue the practice. Whatever its origin, it consists of an accepted pattern of behavior according to which almost all firms follow the price changes of leader firms. There can be more than one leader in an industry. Price leadership should not be confused with the simple imitation of another firm's price *by a few* firms in an industry. Only when the practice is almost industry-wide can it be regarded as a significant cooperative or collusive arrangement.

In concrete instances, it is often difficult to determine whether price leadership exists. The matching of price changes can sometimes be explained by other causes. For example, we saw that in conventional markets a rise in costs would be followed by a rise in price. To the extent that all firms in an industry experience changes in costs almost simultaneously, their prices might change—in either direction—by the same amount at the same time. Despite these difficulties, one can find some fairly current examples that look like price-leadership markets. The following string of statements, which consists of quotations from the press, describes the pattern of price changes over an eleven-month period in the rubber-tire industry. They show what, at least superficially, looks like a price leadership situation.

Goodrich and U.S. Rubber have gone along, as expected, with the price cuts in tires made by Goodyear, Firestone, and other tire sellers.[4]

Price hikes on tires have now been posted by all major producers except Goodrich and Goodyear. Seiberling Rubber started the second round of 3½ per cent boosts last week.[5]

Goodrich and Goodyear finished off the second round of price boosts on tires and tubes . . . with a 3½ per cent boost last week.[6]

The United States Rubber Company today announced an increase in truck-tire prices averaging 5 per cent on April 1. The same announcement was made last week by the B. F. Goodrich Company.[7]

With prices of natural (rubber) shooting to 29¼¢ a lb., the highest in more than 20 years, U.S. Rubber announced a 2½ per cent increase in prices of its passenger tires and a 5 per cent increase on bus and truck tires.

Within a few hours, five other manufacturers followed U.S. Rubber's lead. Goodyear, Goodrich, General, Seiberling, and Mohawk all announced comparable 2½ per cent and 5 per cent price hikes effective immediately. Firestone joined in the next day.[8]

It is not always necessary to guess whether price leadership exists. Sometimes a businessman admits that his industry follows as leader. For example, Mr. H. Lee Randall, President of the Riverside Metal Company, Riverside, N.J., told the Temporary National Economic Committee, "We follow the prices set by the bigger companies and pray that we will make a profit." He said that he would follow changes in the prices asked by the large companies even if he were satisfied with the current price, ". . . because it is the custom of the industry. We have always done it." [9]

Price leadership sometimes takes a very explicit form—as in the "basing-point system." The mechanics of basing-point pricing are slightly complicated, but in principle they are simple. Each seller asks any buyer the same price—no matter where either the buyer or the seller is located. Price to any buyer is arrived at by taking a quoted price at designated locations (these are the "basing points") and by adding transportation charges calculated according to a particular book of freight charges. Every seller uses the same quoted price at the same locations as the base price and calculates freight charges by the same form of transportation from the same location. As a result, the prices asked of any buyer by all sellers

---

[4] *Business Week,* June 18, 1949.
[5] *Business Week,* December 3, 1949, p. 28.
[6] *Business Week,* December 10, 1949, p. 28.
[7] *New York Times,* March 31, 1950, p. 43.
[8] *Ibid.*
[9] *T.N.E.C. Hearings,* Part 5, pp. 2098-2099.

bidding for his business may be identical to many decimal places even for very large orders. With the decision of the Supreme Court in 1948 ruling the basing-point system illegal, this market practice has disappeared, at least temporarily. Before 1948, it probably was a moderately widespread form of price behavior in industries selling bulky products, like steel and cement.

b. Outright price collusion

The most direct form of cooperative and collusive action is an explicit agreement among rivals to charge the same price, or to establish a rigid pattern of price differentials. Although such agreements are unequivocally illegal, they have often been found to exist. This practice is reputed to be fairly common among local businesses, where agreements can be reached easily and where regulatory authorities are inactive. Probably most examples of price collusion never come to light.

Careful students of industry have concluded that ". . . there is scarcely a branch of business in which (simple agreements) do not serve to modify somewhat the stress of unbridled competition." [10] Many indictments are brought against businessmen each year by the Anti-Trust Division and the Federal Trade Commission for price agreement. [11] An interesting "confession" is contained in a pamphlet entitled "I Quit Monster Business," by T. K. Quinn, former vice-president and chairman of the sales committee of General Electric, and chairman of the board of G.E. Contracts Corporation. Mr. Quinn tells how on one occasion executives in G.E. and General Motors, concerned with pricing and marketing of refrigerators, ". . . got a little out of hand in an argument over prices and methods. We were promptly called to New York before a joint meeting of the top officials of both corporations and the rules laid down by which we thereafter abided. . . ." [12]

There is no need to present an exhaustive list of all cooperative practices that have been employed in industry. Earlier it was indicated that sellers have a strong incentive to eliminate independent pricing and to substitute for it collective action. These probably are many and subtle practices that are uniquely adapted to particular situations in industry that those outside the industry do not know about. The antitrust laws have been enacted to prevent and to eliminate cooperative pricing. However, no one would claim that these practices have been eliminated altogether.

---

[10] H. R. Seager and C. A. Gulick, *Trust and Corporation Problems* (New York: Harper & Brothers, 1929), p. 5.

[11] For a partial list, see A. R. Oxenfeldt, *Industrial Pricing and Market Practices* (Englewood Cliffs, N.J.: Prentice-Hall, Inc., 1951), pp. 306-307.

[12] Quoted from Charles E. Noyes, "Is Big Business Bad Business?," *Nation,* August 6, 1949, p. 126.

c. Trade associations

Trade associations are organizations of businessmen engaged in the same line of business. They are financed by contributions from the member firms, and the personnel entrusted with carrying on the activities of the trade association is chosen by the members. On occasion, all members come together to discuss the activities of the association. Disagreements among members ordinarily are settled by majority vote.

Trade associations have frequently contributed to an orderly and well-mannered rivalry among members of a trade, and thus have helped to keep competition from becoming unruly and mutually injurious. As a general rule, trade associations preach the golden rule in an effort to discourage individual firms from taking what they call a shortsighted view that might lead to "cutthroat competition." In some extreme situations, trade associations have been found to be the focal point of either outright collusive arrangements or something fairly close to it.[13]

Trade associations generally gather information about the business that is intended to assist their members to make decisions intelligently. Often they report on production, inventories, and sales. In addition, they sometimes suggest standardized accounting routines and reasonable margins. Most of the time, they represent their industries in dealings with the government, labor unions and the public. In all things, the associations safeguard the interests of the industry as far as possible. Thus, in practice, they foster all actions that will, within the law, tend to raise and stabilize prices.

Apart from the strictly legal activities of trade associations, in many instances these associations have knowingly been employed to bring about uniformity of price and to shut off vigorous rivalry. As a minimum, trade associations provide a meeting place where rivals can get together and conveniently discuss mutual problems. At times the temptation to discuss prices must surely become irresistible.

Some trade associations have gone to extremes to influence price. One example will be cited in some detail to indicate the extent of such efforts toward achieving cooperative pricing. This instance concerns the National Container Association, whose activities led to a government suit and a discontinuation of the practices that are described below. That this association probably was not unique is suggested by the nature of its personnel. It was managed by the firm of Stevenson, Jordan & Harrison, which, among other things, is in the business of organizing, advising, directing, and managing trade associations. In 1940, the firm conducted the affairs of more than 30 national trade associations.[14]

---

[13] For a full discussion of trade associations, see A. R. Burns, *Decline of Competition* (New York: McGraw-Hill Book Company, Inc., 1936), pp. 43-75.

[14] *T.N.E.C. Hearings,* Part 25, p. 13,339.

The indictment against this association listed the following activities which influenced price:

1. Each member of the association was exhorted to use industry-estimating manuals that contained formulas, factors, and assorted information relating to all items of cost. Instead of the costs of any manufacturer, the manual contained arbitrary figures agreed upon by members of the association. The data in the manual were to be used in establishing price, and individual firms were dissuaded from using their own costs instead of those presented in the manual.

2. Each association member submitted copies of invoices or orders giving complete details of every sale. This information was verified and analyzed to determine whether the member adhered to the formula set forth in the manual.

3. The records of members were checked by traveling auditors and engineers who called attention to prices not conforming to the formula recommended.

4. The indictment also charged that the association had a plan for the "equitable sharing of available business," and a system to limit production. When a contract was signed, information was disseminated to other members, with the understanding that they would not compete for it.

Trade associations are numerous. In 1938, about 2,000 national trade associations had offices in the United States. In addition, virtually every community has organizations of local businessmen, which bring together members of the same trade in small and medium-sized cities. It would be a serious mistake to assume that most of them resemble the National Container Association. It would probably be naive to assume that they perform only the activities that they claim to perform.

In assessing the economic consequences of cooperative and collusive pricing, it is important to distinguish between attempts that have been made to "regularize" pricing, and successes. Many forces operating within an industry lead to a breakdown of collusive pricing arrangements. To take only one such force, when rivals get together and set price, usually they will set one well over cost. Thus they leave a fair margin for someone—their competitors would call him a chiseler—to shade the price asked by the others in order to capture a larger share of the total business. In addition, parties loyal to collusive pricing arrangements are not given any excuse for failure to pay their debts. If they find financial obligations coming due that they cannot readily meet, they may be compelled to raise cash by turning inventories into funds by lowering price in an effort to increase their sales.

When cooperative and collusive pricing arrangements are successful, they turn an apparent condition of intermediate market power into one that *in its effects* is equivalent to complete market power. All sellers acting as one in the matter of price are equivalent to a single seller acting for himself. One would therefore expect collusive pricing to raise price, increase the rate of profit, and possibly to expand excess capacity.

C. Sellers Employ Market Practices That Alter the Market Substantially

Businesses are free to elect a wide variety of practices in the sale of their product. Among these are the use of "exclusive dealers"—meaning that only designated persons can carry their product and that these persons may not carry any other brands of the same product; "tying clauses," which have the effect of requiring buyers of one product to accept other products also; selling on a "long-term requirements contract," which requires the buyer to obtain all his supplies of a particular product from a single seller over the life of the contract, and the like.

Fairly recently, the date varying from state to state, a market practice was made available to most American manufacturers that probably has important consequences. This consists of allowing a manufacturer of branded items[15] to specify the minimum price at which his product can be resold; it is ordinarily known as "resale-price maintenance" or "fair trade."

In all except six states and the District of Columbia, it was legal in 1958 for manufacturers of branded merchandise to dictate the minimum price at which their products might be sold by their distributors. To the extent that it is complied with, resale-price maintenance eliminates competition among different sellers of the same brand. Moreover, it facilitates cooperative pricing on the part of manufacturers themselves, for it weakens and almost eliminates the pressure that distributors may bring to bear upon manufacturer's price. Distributors generally strive for lower price, at least partly, in order to be able to lower the price they charge and thereby increase their share of the business.

While the evidence concerning the effects of resale-price maintenance is partly conflicting, it seems to have raised prices in most medium-sized and large cities and to have reduced them in very small towns and in outlying districts. By eliminating price competition, moreover, resale-price maintenance has stimulated sellers to increase their advertising activities

---

[15] As a result of being confined to the sale of branded items, the proportion of total output affected by these laws has been limited. No accurate information exists that measures the proportion of all retail sales that are made at prices prescribed by the manufacturer. One estimate placed it as high as 20 per cent, which is about twice what this writer would estimate.

It should be noted that the ability to prescribe resale prices applies to some products—like gasoline—which cannot themselves be branded, but which may be dispensed from containers showing the brand name.

and to try to attract customers by more lavish or convenient facilities.

In this author's opinion, the preponderance of evidence shows that resale-price maintenance has raised price.[16] This conclusion is buttressed by the unmistakable fact that independent distributors as a group are still strongly in favor of it—surely not because it lowers their margins. There can be little question that, owing to these laws, buyers who ordinarily patronize stores bidding for patronage on the basis of low price have been compelled to pay higher prices. One of the major effects of these laws has been to give the small retailer an advantage over large retailers. Under these laws, small distributors frequently can get away with considerable price cutting; the large distributors are under close surveillance of manufacturers and rival retailers. Thus, the small retailer cannot be undercut by the large distributor, and he is given considerable opportunity to undercut the large distributor.

D. Sales-Promotion Expenditures

Where market power is wholly absent, sellers will not advertise because buyers are influenced to purchase only by price inducements. Advertising is pointless because of the recognized similarity of goods offered by all these sellers. Partly because individual sellers offer different products and because even when they offer those that are identical in physical form they want consumers to think they are different, advertising has become a widespread practice. Total expenditures on all types of advertising during 1957 exceeded $11 billion. Whether or not this sum is excessive can be judged only when the consequences of advertising are determined and alternative methods of providing the services it now renders are explored.

Some advertising is informative, indicating the availability of goods that consumers would otherwise not know about; or it indicates where a known good can be obtained, or tells the terms on which it can be bought. This type of information must be provided by some means in all types of economy. Goods cannot be held under wraps, and consumers cannot be asked to stalk goods much as hunters seek out game. Consequently, the provision of information is a necessary function, and its cost is not conceptually different from, or less justifiable than, the expense involved in making the product available.

However, it would appear that the proportion of advertising expenditure made to provide the consumer with information is very small. Most advertising seems to be "competitive." That is, it rarely tells the consumer

---

[16] The best studies of the effects of resale-price maintenance include Federal Trade Commission, *Resale Price Maintenance* (Washington, D.C.: Government Printing Office, 1945); and E. T. Grether, *Price Control under Fair Trade Legislation* (New York: Oxford University Press, 1939).

anything that is new but simply tries to shift the patronage of buyers from one source to another by whatever wiles the advertiser can employ. These expenditures would seem to be clear examples of waste.

Advertising has many advocates, and since it is carried by all public media, these advocates reach a wide audience. A recent and fairly novel defense of advertising—apparently even of competitive advertising—has been advanced along these lines. Any advertisement that ". . . enhances the esteem with which a product is regarded has created value which is genuine and real." Accordingly, if the advertiser can make you want a product more than you would have wanted it otherwise, it is productive.[17] The reasoning behind this thesis is that a purchaser will get more pleasure from the use of a product because the advertising increased his appreciation for it. There seems to be an element of validity in this thesis, but it overlooks one salient fact. Advertising that stimulates esteem and expectation of pleasure that is not borne out by the product when it is consumed has the reverse effect. It leads to disappointment and frustration which must be counted into the tally of the effects of advertising.

E. Buyers Are Not Well Informed about the "Value" of Alternative Products

Closely related to the question of advertising is the knowledge consumers possess about the relative merits of goods they can purchase. One major premise of the competitive system, as we have seen, is that buyers will obtain the products they desire. They, and not a centralized planning body, are the sovereigns who dictate what shall be produced. Expressed differently, money talks in a competitive system; one of the things it is able to say is that one thing shall be produced rather than another.

Buyers lack the knowledge they need in safeguarding their best interests. This lack can be attributed partly to the confusing and conflicting claims made by advertisers. It also results partly from the wide array of products offered, generally without clear and reliable markings that indicate what the product is made of or its performance characteristics. As a result, production need not respond to consumers' true needs or wants, but may simply reflect the wants that sellers have created in them.

F. Most Industries Sell Differentiated Products

Except for some agricultural products and perhaps basic raw materials and textile fabrics, virtually all products sold are differentiated. That

---

[17] For a discussion of this thesis, see Otto Kleppner, *New! New! Improved! A Basic Fallacy in the Economic Interpretation of Advertising,* a reprint of an address before the second annual Atlanta Marketing Conference, 1951, reprinted by the Kleppner Company, New York City. The quotation comes from Section VI. (The pages are unnumbered.)

is, buyers believe different brands of the same product to be sufficiently unlike to warrant some difference in price. Even when an identical brand of product is sold in different stores, many customers will favor one store over another enough to spend more for the same brand of product in that store. Consumers buy products that are physically identical (aspirin, for example) in the same store at widely different prices, because they believe the different brands to differ in quality. There can be little question that differentiation of product is the overwhelming rule—especially in products sold directly to consumers—and standard products are extreme exceptions.

The existence of differentiation has led some people to the conclusion that each seller has a form of "monopoly" over his particular brand. Actually, such a monopoly has extremely limited market power, for other sellers can offer products that buyers will be willing to substitute for the product of the seller with the monopoly if his prices diverge too much. When a monopolist is so circumscribed that a 5 per cent rise in price will cause him to lose many customers to other sellers, the word "monopoly" completely loses its usual meaning. Nevertheless, it would be correct to say that an overwhelming proportion of all industrial markets possess some element of market power or monopoly because they sell differentiated products.

G. Financial Barriers to the Entry of New Firms

Deliberate measures sometimes taken to hinder the advent of new firms have already been discussed. To this list we need add one difficulty that frequently exists without being put there by established firms. The financing of a new firm is often a serious obstacle. Initiators of new enterprises find it extremely difficult—one might say virtually impossible—to borrow funds to start a business unless it has extraordinary prospects for success, such as patent rights to a readily marketable product. Even then, those providing funds ordinarily demand a high rate of return or a large share of the firm's profits. Consequently, when a new firm needs substantial sums to enable it to achieve an efficient level of operations, raising capital constitutes an important obstacle to the establishment of the firm, even though the level of profits may be high for established firms.

H. Fewness of Buyers

Some markets have zero seller power, but buyers have an ability to alter price in their favor. Especially in the purchase of several farm products, sellers are powerless to influence price, although buyers can do so. The most notable examples have to do with tobacco, livestock, and milk. Similar situations are faced in other industries. Retailers with great buying power are able to alter price in their favor when buying from suppliers that are numerous and small.

When buyers are few and large, they can be expected to be aware of the fact that their purchases and price offers will influence the prevailing price. Accordingly, they try to buy in ways that will create the impression of weakness in the market. A few large buyers behave, in reverse, much as a few large sellers do. They refrain from raising their offers to obtain the supplies they desire, recognizing that other buyers will feel obliged to follow suit—thereby contributing to an upward rigidity of prices. They may cooperate in their pricing and purchasing practices.

The efforts of large buyers are directed toward getting supplies at the lowest possible price. Especially when those from whom they buy are afflicted with excess capacity, they are able to depress prices severely—well below the average costs of production. Sellers possessing facilities that are unutilized can be induced by skillful buyers to sell at a price that covers direct out-of-pocket costs and contributes something toward overhead—even though the price is below average cost.

I. Labor Monopolies

The departures from competition listed thus far have concerned markets for goods and for services that are rendered to the final consumer. Some economists have argued that labor unions probably represent the most important divergence from competition in the present economy. Accordingly, the term "labor monopoly" has gained currency; it conveys the notion that labor unions are similar in their economic effects to industrial monopolies. The basis for maintaining that such a similarity does hold is that labor unions are collusive arrangements whose purpose is to influence wage rates.

Basic issues of substance rarely are settled by analogies; to liken labor unions to industrial monopolies is almost certain to obscure rather than illuminate their effects. In an earlier chapter, the evils sometimes associated with unionism were touched upon; others that will be mentioned here are virtually the same as those associated with industrial monopolies and, indeed, are illegal under the antitrust laws. However, the conclusion that labor unions are the main divergence from competition in the American economy and are essentially the same in their effects as industrial monopoly is difficult to support.

Those who attack industrial monopolies while excusing collusion among workers through unions argue that unions help to create the conditions that would arise if the economy were fully competitive and operating near full employment. That is, they say that without unions real wage rates would be much lower than the competitive amount; the effect of unions is to bring rates closer to the competitive level, rather than to push them farther away. Consequently, they argue that unions help to counteract the major departure from competition arising from the disproportionate power over wage rates, formerly held by employers. Those who consider unions no less obnoxious than product monopolies deny that employers have preponderant power in setting wage rates— especially during periods of inflation. Moreover, they stress the restrictive policies of many unions—in limiting the entry of new firms, policing price agreements among employers by refusing to supply laborers to price cutters or "fly-by-nights," placing ceilings on output, opposing the intro- duction of new and improved productive devices, and the like. (The first two activities listed are illegal under the antitrust laws.)

The effects of labor unions upon the operation of the economic sys- tem are complex and numerous. In an earlier chapter they were discussed at some length. Although the entire question of labor unions and their effects was not settled by any means, it seems to the author that viewing them as monopolies would add little to understanding. They are, almost invariably, organizations of workers created to bargain with employers of labor who are similarly organized, or operate over equally broad spheres—control hiring for a plant or firm. To do a minimum of violence to the subject, it seems best to consider labor unions an instrument created over the entire industrial world to increase the proportion of the national income paid to workers. They have received the sanction of almost all governments simply because it has been generally conceded that labor's pay often was lower than it should have been in an efficiently operating competitive economy.

III. QUANTITATIVE IMPORTANCE OF DEPARTURES FROM ZERO MARKET POWER

Thus far, a descriptive list has been presented of the major depar- tures from competition in the United States economy. Their consequences were not discussed, and for good reason. The effect of each departure from competition cannot be judged in the abstract; other characteristics of an industry will condition the consequences of any deviation from competition. For example, advertising may improve the allocation of resources when the product sold is new and unknown to buyers, and be wasteful when it is a familiar product. Some departures from competition wholly or partly cancel themselves.[18] Few buyers may be an antidote for fewness of sellers. Restrictions on newcomers to a trade may partly offset practices that would otherwise give rise to excess capacity.

---

[18] A theory of "competition" in this sense has been developed by J. K. Galbraith, *American Capitalism* (Boston: Houghton Mifflin Company, 1952), Chap. 9.

It would be useful to measure the over-all quantitative importance of departures from competition in the United States at the present time. Is the economy so heavily overlaid with noncompetitive elements that it should not be considered a competitive economy at all? Is competition the exception rather than the rule? Can the departures from pure competition be translated into a loss of national income of a specific amount?

As was said earlier, it is impossible to classify all American industry into categories equivalent to competition or monopoly. Virtually all industries lie somewhere in between. The social consequences of intermediate situations cannot be judged in the abstract. Intermediate situations may sometimes be substantially more harmful to the community than complete monopoly.[19] At best, and it is not even certain then, we can determine the social consequences of particular market circumstances by studying them in great detail.

The author is nevertheless willing to record his views, qualified by the caution that the accumulation of additional evidence may lead him to reverse his position. Competition of the zero market-power type is virtually nonexistent. As will be shown in a later chapter, even agriculture, which is the clearest parallel to zero market power, does not achieve the ideal results attainable from pure competition. Most markets depart in many respects from zero market power. How much waste results over all American industry from these departures? The author's opinion is that it is substantial. To make this guess sharper, it may represent 30 to 50 per cent of the national income.[20]

Considerable excess capacity characterizes the economy in most industries. While complete utilization of capacity is an unattainable goal, and also a dubious one for reasons that need not be elaborated here, the capacity of many American industries seems clearly inordinate. Retailing is perhaps the biggest general offender, but raw-material industries such as coal mining, oil extraction, and farming are possibly as bad. In manufacturing, industries such as textile, whisky distilling, and garment manufacture stand out. The cost to the economy of excess capacity probably is not very large, and it does offer some, though probably insufficient, compensations.

The best available information on the quality of products sold shows that consumers are unable to protect their best interests. Inferior brands

---

[19] For an example of one type, see Oxenfeldt, *op. cit.,* p. 347.

[20] One student of monopoly profits estimates that the elimination of corporate profits would benefit nonowning consumers by an amount equal to about 2 per cent of the national income. He asserts that waste from consumer ignorance and costs higher than socially necessary is much greater than from monopolists' consumption. See Henry H. Villard, "The Social Cost of Corporate Monopoly Profits," *Political Science Quarterly,* September, 1957, pp. 380-387.

sometimes are the most popular. Consumers get the best value for their money largely by accident, for they lack the knowledge and facilities to make intelligent comparisons of complex products. Production and sale of goods whose quality is substantially poorer than what could be provided at equal cost are, in the author's opinion, the largest single wastes attributable to departures from competition.

In addition, the whole problem of choice is vastly distorted by heavy advertising, which often makes consumer choice an emotional rather than a rational matter. Also, large sums are wasted on advertising. About 20 per cent of advertising expenditure may be considered of some value because it contributes toward the support of media of public information. (As we saw earlier, it also contributes toward making them unreliable sources of information.)

Occasionally, collusion among rival sellers will do the public great injury. Frequently businessmen are driven to collusion when competition becomes insufferably painful; collusion thus is sometimes a protection against "excessive" competition. Business practices designed to soften competition generally are ineffectual because some departures from competition are almost certain to arise. There nevertheless should be no letup in efforts to stamp out collusive arrangements, price leadership, and obnoxious trade-association activity. However, these forms of departure seem to be less prevalent or damaging to the economy than are certain others.

Resale-price maintenance is a relatively new departure from competition, and possibly a serious one. The extent to which this practice sometimes raises some prices is revealed in the following statement by a manager of a large metropolitan package liquor store located in a high-rental district to a representative of the Federal Trade Commission: "I could make plenty of money on an 18 per cent margin. The fair-trade contracts provide a 40 per cent margin to all retailers and my company gets an additional 10 per cent on all purchases and a further 14 and 1 per cent on most of its purchases. This gives them a discount of anywhere from 50 to 65 per cent from resale prices." [21] Price increases due to resale-price maintenance no doubt are usually far smaller than in the example cited, but it may well be substantial in many instances.

Thus, in the author's opinion, it would be very worth while to root out most departures from zero market power. However, it should not be expected that even complete success in such an undertaking would enable us to satisfy our material desires with a few hours of work each day.

---

[21] Report of the Federal Trade Commission, *Resale Price Maintenance* (Washington, D.C.: Government Printing Office, 1945), p. 359.

IV. SUMMARY AND CONCLUSIONS

We have discussed several respects in which actual market situations depart from zero market power—the market in which competition works at its best. A substantial number of deviations from pure competition were noted. Usually a departure from zero market power had the effect either of increasing price or of raising costs, or both.

Nothing definitive could be said about the prevalence of the various departures from zero market power that were discussed here. The research into the nature of American industry has not gone far enough to permit confident generalizations about its character. However, enough is known to show that these occurrences are not rare exceptions. The discussion of devices whereby businessmen operate together—either from explicit agreement or trade custom—raises important questions about the extent to which the Amercian economy can be described as a system of "free enterprise." Clearly the devices described are numerically important. The number of national trade associations is in the thousands; apparently price leadership is commonplace; and virtually no industry has failed to be governed by a price agreement at some time. ". . . Clearly, the term 'free enterprise' no longer describes, if it ever did, the way industry actually operates. No two words can describe anything so complex and also so variable over time as American industry." [22]

In estimating the prevalence of departures from competition in our economy, one paradoxical view should be examined. This view holds that monopoly is the logical conclusion of competition.[23] If this were true, an economy based on competition would depart from competition so far that, in time, the fundamental nature of the system would be destroyed. Evidence to support this hypothesis is lacking. It is far from clear that the degree of market power possessed by sellers has increased significantly since, say, 1900,[24] or that there is any more recent incipient trend suggesting a pronounced rise in the market power of those who sell goods. On the other hand, the market power of those selling labor services has unquestionably risen.

Apart from the lack of factual support for the thesis that competition leads logically to monopoly, the very logic upon which it rests is open to

---

[22] Oxenfeldt, *op. cit.*, pp. 323-324.

[23] Quoted with approval by Professor George Halm from Eduard Heimann, *Sociale Theorie des Kapitalismus* (Tuebinger: J. C. B. Mohr, 1929), p. 38, in his *Economic Systems: A Comparative Analysis* (New York: Rinehart & Company, Inc., 1951), p. 88.

[24] G. Warren Nutter, *A Quantitative Study of the Extent of Enterprise Monopoly in the United States* (Chicago: University of Chicago Press, 1949). Nutter concludes that there was at most a slight increase in monopoly over the whole economy between 1899 and 1939.

attack. True, competition does not benefit those who practice it; consequently, they presumably compete reluctantly (though businessmen and their organizations vehemently oppose monopoly in words if not in deeds). One must therefore expect them to make attempts to reduce or eliminate competition. Possibly also, as some have argued, changes in production methods favor the development of large firms and predispose a market toward monopoly.[25] The tendency for competition to find its way into even carefully prepared monopolistic arrangements must be reckoned with, however.

The stronger the monopolistic arrangement, the greater the rewards to those who participate in it, and the greater the temptation to those outside to obtain a share for themselves. As a result, monopoly invites rivals and seems quite as self-destructive as competition.[26] When it is recognized that monopoly also invites the intervention of the state—being altogether inconsistent with the postulates of American capitalism—the inevitability of monopoly seems at best an unproved hypothesis.

DISCUSSION QUESTIONS

1. Of all the departures from pure competition, which appear to be the most costly to the economy? What difficulties arise in answering this question?

2. Information about the number of sellers in 26 industries was presented in this chapter. What are the pitfalls in reasoning, from this type of information, about the intensity of competition in these industries?

---

[25] John M. Blair has taken the position that recent technological developments have tended to reduce the disadvantage in production of smaller firms. See his "Technology and Size," *American Economic Review*, Papers and Proceedings, May, 1948, pp. 121-152.

[26] A thesis, called "Countervailing Power," by J. K. Galbraith, holds that wherever monopoly profits are obtained, various pressures will arise from without as well as within the industry to reduce them. According to this thesis, high profits are a kind of honey that brings bees flying from many directions to get a share. The bees in industry include suppliers (who will ask higher prices); labor unions (who will ask for higher wages); and distributors (who will demand higher markups). The effect of countervailing power is to reduce the profits that started the process. See J. K. Galbraith, *American Capitalism* (Boston: Houghton Mifflin Company, 1952).

This very interesting thesis has won wide favor, both because of its intrinsic merit and the clarity and charm with which it has been expressed. It is essential to note, however, that even if a person accepts the theory of countervailing power, he has not proved that competition or an effective substitute operates in practice. The theory of countervailing power can be adduced only to argue that the gains from monopoly are short-lived and ultimately are shared in by others than the original monopolist. Our discussion has shown that monopoly (complete market power) gives rise to other and probably greater evils than excessive profits.

The issue of monopolistic competition is also relevant, insofar as it describes market power which ends by yielding only "normal" profits.

3. If all firms in an industry charge the same price at any time, would you consider this fact proof of the absence of market power or of its presence? Would your answer be different if this identical price charged by all sellers remained the same for substantial periods, like months or years?

4. Under what circumstances would you expect price leadership or outright collusion to arise? Are these the same circumstances that give rise to trade associations?

5. If there were few sellers in an industry, would you expect their market power to be greater or smaller if they sold to only a few large buyers instead of to many small buyers?

6. To what extent does the efficacy of our economic system depend upon consumers' being able to judge the quality of products offered them?

7. In what way does advertising contribute toward the conditions you would desire in industry? In what way does it impair the attainment of the results you would desire?

8. Do you believe consumers would be better served if products were to be standardized more or less than at present? Is your answer the same for all kinds of products?

9. How significant in total are the departures from pure competition in present-day America? Comment on the estimate offered in this chapter.

10. How are new firms prevented from entering some industries?

Chapter

17   Possible Remedies for

Excessive Market Power

One cannot assume that competition is the natural state of things. The preceding chapter has pointed out major respects in which it is absent from the American economy. Special efforts must be made, therefore, if we are to attain the advantages of competition that were set forth at the outset of this section.

One would expect that a nation whose economy was based upon competition rather than central planning would prohibit significant deviations from competition; and, where competition was not attainable, would devise some substitute arrangement that would give similar results. Indeed, laws to prevent and correct departures from competition are a necessary legal basis for a free-enterprise economy. If a competitive economy is to be realized, these laws must be enforceable, and vigorous efforts must be made to enforce them. Otherwise, competition could not be expected to be keen and the economy would suffer a consequent loss of economic efficiency.

In this chapter the various means by which the United States strives to establish competition and eliminate the evils of monopoly are discussed. Also, a few additional measures that might be employed are sketched briefly.

I. MAJOR DIFFICULTIES ENCOUNTERED IN A PROGRAM OF MAINTAINING COMPETITION

Several difficulties confront all efforts to make the American economy highly competitive. First, monopolistic conditions already exist. An economy is not being built from the ground up. Existing conditions are such that a huge job of unscrambling probably would be required to attain competition in many major industries. Second, difficult conceptual problems arise in deciding exactly what situations should be changed. Pure competition—that is, a condition in which sellers have absolutely no market power—is virtually nonexistent. Consequently, a decision must be made regarding the kinds of conditions that are "workably" or "tolerably" competitive. No methods have yet been devised that indicate which industries perform in a way that is substantially competitive. A major task that must be accomplished before success can be anticipated is a clarification of what competition means in a modern economy.

Third, political difficulties can be expected if measures are taken to alter monopolistic arrangements that are profitable for some. There is little real enthusiasm among many politically influential groups for a strict program designed to increase competition. Fourth, major difficulties probably will beset any administrative agency that is entrusted with enforcing such a program. In addition to the conceptual difficulties that will plague it and the powerful groups that will oppose it, such an agency is extremely vulnerable to the corruptive forces often arising in government agencies that regulate business.

II. CURRENT MEASURES TO ACHIEVE THE BENEFITS OF COMPETITION

The United States is virtually unique among the industrialized countries of the world in its policy toward monopoly. Many practices that are wholly acceptable in some Western European countries are illegal here. The American attitude toward monopoly is unequivocably negative —though, as we have seen, this attitude has not brought with it the ability and resolve to eliminate all traces of monopoly. Nevertheless, the matter of attitude is vital, and an important asset in any program to maintain competition is the prevailing sentiment in its favor.

It should be recognized that the popular support for "competition" is support for something very vague and undefined. It would appear that the overwhelming majority of persons who extol the virtues of competition would include under its head many situations that deviate very significantly from zero market power. For example, competitive advertising is generally regarded as wholly acceptable and indeed as evidence of "competition"; differentiation is, and perhaps properly, applauded; fewness of sellers (oligopoly), when consisting of more than, say, 10 firms, is considered a wholly acceptable situation; large capital requirements in some industries are taken for granted, and so on. The general endorsement of competition is best considered in opposition to what the public considers monopoly. It appears, though this is not certain, that the common picture of monopoly is one of an extremely abusive firm that greatly overcharges and wages unfair warfare on small rivals.

It is of great importance to recognize that Congress, the public, and the courts are not opposed to all major departures from zero market power. In other words, there is a general tolerance for market conditions and practices which our earlier theoretical analysis suggested will lead to inefficient utilization of resources. It is not altogether clear whether these departures are tolerated because their possible evils are not recognized, or on the general theory that unless some conditions are "really offensive" they should be left alone in a free-enterprise economy.

If a literal view of "free enterprise" is adopted, there need be no concern with measures for improving matters. Only situations that are obviously evil require attention; all others as a matter of principle should be left alone. This view of "free enterprise" has been rejected by the American people, though no clear substitute principle has been advanced.

The standard that was applied to the problems considered earlier will be employed with reference to the preservation of competition. This standard holds that all changes should be made that would improve conditions for the community as a whole, after the costs of effecting such changes have been considered. According to this standard, conditions need not be horrible before they are improved. Indeed, even moderately efficient arrangements would be altered if they could be made significantly better. Any individual is, of course, at liberty to reject this standard, though he should be prepared to offer reasons for so doing.

The American approach to maintenance of competition consists of three parts: the first, and most important, is known as the antitrust program; the second is government regulation and control of privately owned and managed enterprises; the third, which is seldom applied, is direct government operation and control. In a sense, these three programs represent successive measures to be adopted until success is achieved. If the first brings success, it is not necessary to go further.

A. *The Antitrust Program*

Especially in view of the great importance attached to them, the federal antitrust laws are remarkably brief and simple. (Most of the space in a government publication that summarizes the antitrust laws is devoted to exemptions from the law rather than to affirmative provisions.) Congress drafted these laws on the principle that general, vague, and broad prohibitions should be set down, and that administrative agencies and the courts would give them specific and concrete content through decisions in ensuing cases.

1. PROVISIONS OF THE ANTITRUST LAWS

The essential provisions of the federal antitrust laws are contained in four phrases, which describe activities and conditions that are prohibited. In 1890, the Sherman Act prohibited *all acts and attempts to restrain and to monopolize trade.* The Federal Trade Commission Act of

1914 declared unlawful *unfair methods of competition.* Less than one month later the Clayton Act declared illegal specific practices whose effect might be to *lessen competition substantially or tend to create a monopoly.* The practices specified were price discrimination, exclusive dealing, tying clauses, interlocking stockholdings, and interlocking directorships; however, these were illegal only if they could be shown to lessen competition substantially or to tend to create a monopoly. Thus the phrases "restraint of trade," "monopoly and monopolize," "unfair competition," and "substantially lessen competition or tend to create a monopoly" are the heart of the antitrust laws. They clearly are vague and obtain whatever meaning they possess from individual decisions by the federal courts.

Most states possess antitrust laws or constitutional provisions that are similar to the federal antitrust laws. Eight states rely primarily upon the common law for correction of monopoly.[1]

Antitrust decisions by the federal courts have passed through several phases, and the meaning of the antitrust laws has changed accordingly. Their meaning, in fact, can never be known with complete certainty, for the rulings of different courts at the same time frequently conflict. Moreover, gradually and subtly, the objectives of the antitrust laws seem to be changing. At present they seem to be relied upon for more than an elimination of glaring abuses; they are more and more used as an instrument for increasing the social contribution of industrial arrangements. This shift in objective is far from complete, is not yet wholly explicit, and may be reversed.

2. CURRENT MEANING OF THE ANTITRUST LAWS

The meaning and the objectives of the antitrust laws should be interpreted in the light of their double objectives: to *prevent* objectionable conditions and practices, and to *cure* them after they arise. Both objectives are pursued by these laws.

It is possible to summarize the meaning of the antitrust laws as of 1957 without a tedious and lengthy review of court decisions. However, clarity and simplicity can be gained only at some cost in exactness and precision. The summary to be presented will be more direct and specific than the courts have been. It omits some important qualifications explicitly stated or implied by the courts. Even if a person knows by heart the summary that follows, he does not remotely qualify as an expert in antitrust law.

---

[1] For a compilation of the constitutional provisions, statutes, and relevant court decisions of the individual states dealing with antitrust problems, see Marketing Laws Survey of the Works Progress Administration, *State Anti-Trust Laws* (Washington, D.C.: U.S. Government Printing Office, 1940), Vol. I.

a. Agreements among rivals

i. All agreements directly concerning price and output among rivals, *however ineffective,* are unlawful.

ii. Agreements among rivals on practices that *even indirectly* exert a perceptible effect on price are unlawful. (Examples of such agreements are decisions not to sell to new firms, refusal to deal with dealers who cut price, and such.)

iii. To be unlawful, agreements need not be explicit and written. The courts will infer from circumstantial evidence that an agreement exists.

b. Permissible size of firm

i. No upper limit on size has been set by any court, and no firm has been held in violation of the antitrust laws on grounds of excessive absolute size alone.

ii. The proportion of a market that may be served by a single firm is limited. One court held that 90 per cent is enough to constitute a monopoly; it is doubtful whether 60 or 64 per cent would be enough; and certainly 33 per cent is not.[2]

iii. The courts hold large size "against" a defendant and are more severe in their attitude toward the very large firms than toward the medium-sized.

c. Permissible market practices

i. No practices, beyond outright agreement among rivals, are unqualifiedly illegal. Each practice is examined in its specific industrial context to determine its legality.

ii. Practices that have the taint of overt or tacit agreement to influence price perceptibly are illegal. However, the perception of courts in identifying taints of agreement seems to vary widely.

d. Status of "intent" under the antitrust laws

i. The possession of substantial market power is unlawful, even if its possessor did not consciously attempt to gain that power, *if* there is any evidence that he is likely to use it.

ii. The attempt or intent to influence price significantly is illegal, even if no perceptible market power was achieved.

iii. The courts will assume a firm's intention to make illegal use of its market power in the future if that firm has in the past used its power to raise price or to exclude rivals.

The foregoing might be summarized in turn. The antitrust laws are

---

[2] Judge Learned Hand, in *United States* v. *Aluminum Company of America,* 148 F 2d. 416 (C.C.A. 2 d, 1945), at 424.

directed against excessive market power, which the courts define as the power "to raise prices or to exclude competition when it is desired to do so." [3] Any firm possessing the forbidden degree of power, or making efforts to achieve it, is violating the antitrust laws simply if it has, or can be presumed to have, the intent to use that power.

3. ADMINISTRATION OF THE ANTITRUST LAWS

Two federal agencies are entrusted with administering the antitrust laws. Their jurisdictions overlap to a degree, but essentially the Antitrust Division of the Department of Justice is concerned with the enforcement of the Sherman Act, while the Federal Trade Commission is entrusted with enforcing the Clayton and Federal Trade Commission Acts.

Although the procedures and powers of these agencies differ, they are alike in major respects. They undertake an action on the basis of complaints, which may be brought by any member of the public (ordinarily he will be a competitor who feels that he has been injured as a result of the violation of the law); or by a request from Congress or the President, or it can be brought by the agency itself upon its own initiative. Following a complaint in an antitrust matter, an investigation is made of the facts to determine whether a violation has occurred. After this stage, both agencies can settle the matter out of court. The defendant can be offered a chance to avoid litigation if he will promise to stop the violation with which he was charged, or if, while not admitting that he was violating the law, he will agree not to do the things with which he was charged. If the matter is not settled at this point—that is, on the basis of an investigation made by the regulatory agency—antitrust actions enter the next phase, which consists of formal hearings. As for actions brought by the Federal Trade Commission, these consist of a preliminary hearing before a special trial examiner, who is a legally trained employee of the Federal Trade Commission; this hearing will be followed by an oral hearing before the commission.

The Department of Justice must bring its defendants into Court. It has the choice of equity or criminal suits. Actions in equity essentially aim to compel compliance with the law and to bring about changes in the industry's structure; criminal actions penalize violators of the law with fines or jail sentences or both. The final stage consists of carrying out the orders of the courts or of the Federal Trade Commission.

4. ACCOMPLISHMENTS OF THE ANTITRUST LAWS

We can first dismiss the effects of the state antitrust laws or constitutional provisions that are similar to antitrust laws in intent. On the basis of a survey he made in 1949, Professor Mund concluded that "Antitrust

---

[3] *American Tobacco Co.* v. *United States,* 328 U.S. 781 (1946), at 811.

enforcement activity in states other than Texas, Wisconsin and New York appears to be largely or entirely in moribund condition." [4]

The inactivity of state antitrust enforcement agencies is especially significant, for probably about half of the national income originates from activities that are essentially intrastate in character and are therefore beyond the reach of the federal antitrust laws.[5]

As already implied, the scope of industry covered by the federal antitrust laws has been progressively narrowed. For various reasons, Congress has exempted from the jurisdiction of these laws such major industries as labor, agricultural and horticultural organizations not conducted for profit; common carriers by water in interstate and foreign commerce, on the high seas, and on the Great Lakes; export trade; marine insurance; associations of producers of agricultural products; agreements among producers, processors, and associations of producers regarding the marketing of agricultural products; telegraph company mergers; railroads and other surface carriers whose agreements are approved by the Interstate Commerce Commission. In addition, a specific exemption from the laws was made for agreements stipulating the minimum prices for the resale of a branded product. There nevertheless remains the question of how effective the federal antitrust laws have been within the areas subject to their jurisdiction.

Perhaps the most important effect of these laws is, of necessity, incapable of measurement. That effect is to discourage actions that businessmen would have taken in the absence of these laws. Some businessmen doubtless desist from practices that are made illegal by the antitrust laws simply because they are illegal; others are restrained, not by ethical considerations, but by fear of detection and punishment. The numbers of persons in a position to violate the antitrust laws who are inhibited from so doing by the laws simply cannot be estimated. We can report only on the number who have been charged with violations, and report the apparent consequences of these charges. The inhibitory effects of the antitrust laws probably have been their greatest contribution.

In addition, the antitrust agencies have charged many companies with violating the antitrust laws.[6] Relatively few antitrust suits have been undertaken, however, and the reason is simple. They are fabulously slow and costly proceedings. It has been estimated that the average expense

---

[4] Vernon A. Mund, *Government and Business* (New York: Harper & Brothers, 1950), p. 426.

[5] Jesse Markham estimates that 70 per cent of the national income originated from economic activity that was essentially intrastate in character or had been placed beyond the reach of the federal antitrust laws by specific exemptions. See "The Effectiveness of the Antitrust Laws," *American Economic Review*, March, 1950, p. 158.

[6] Measured by number of actions prosecuted, by far the most frequent offense is deceit or fraud in advertising.

per case runs to $50,000 a year, and the cases often last far more than one year.[7] Since the antitrust agencies operate on very modest budgets, most of which are consumed by routine functions other than adjudication, they cannot afford to undertake many suits. For example, the Antitrust Division of the Department of Justice in 1958 had only one-fourth the appropriation of the Interstate Commerce Commission, and less than half the appropriations of each of the following: Federal Communications Commission, the National Labor Relations Board, and the Railroad Retirement Board.[8]

This information concerning the funds put at the disposal of the Antitrust Division and the high costs of its operations suggests that Congress is not resolved on vigorous enforcement of the antitrust laws. If there are other explanations for the chronic shortage of funds made available to the antitrust enforcement agencies, they are kept strictly secret. The resources of the Federal Trade Commission are greater than those of the Antitrust Division, but these cover many activities other than antimonopoly actions. The former agency also suffers from a constant shortage of funds even to carry on its exceedingly modest actions against monopolistic practices.

Thus the antitrust program of the government is limited in scope by exemptions of important business sectors from the jurisdiction of the law, and is at best a halfhearted effort to eliminate restraints of trade, because meager resources are placed at the disposal of the regulatory agencies. Nevertheless, the law of the land does prohibit many important departures from competition, and that very fact doubtless has had considerable influence. Moreover, the threat that the Antitrust Division or the Federal Trade Commission may bring one of its few actions against them doubtless keeps many businessmen in check.

Even when the antitrust agencies succeed in winning a suit, it is not clear that they often accomplish much change in the conditions they seek to correct. The major remedy upon which the regulatory agencies and the courts rely for monopoly power is dissolution (divorcement and divestiture), which means the "busting" of large firms into smaller parts. With very rare exceptions, firms found guilty of having and exercising monopoly power have escaped dissolution.[9] As will be shown, one major reason for failure to correct objectionable conditions is that even experts in the field do not seem to be agreed on what can best be done.

---

[7] Marshall E. Dimock, *Business and Government* (New York: Henry Holt & Company, Inc., 1949), p. 382.

[8] *The Budget of the United States Government, 1959* (Washington, D.C.: Government Printing Office, 1958), pp. 100-103.

[9] A recent and notable exception is the motion picture industry, which one economist calls the "government's greatest economic victory in the 60-year history of antitrust enforcement." See Walter Adams, "The Aluminum Case: Legal Victory—Economic Defeat," *American Economic Review*, December, 1951, pp. 915-916.

On balance, it is difficult to assess the claim frequently made that the essential difference between the American economy and that of most West European countries is that we have antitrust laws. When examined closely, the laws seem to have had only modest effect; the difference in the vigor of competition in the United States and in other industrialized nations seems quite as easily attributable to such factors as the rate of change in the level of productivity, which might be explained partly by remoteness from direct war damage, and to the relatively low taxes required to finance defense expenditures until very recently; the availability of rich natural resources which encourages business investment; and, probably most important, to the difference in tradition and culture associated with our fairly recent contact with a rugged frontier.

On the whole, there can be little doubt that the antitrust laws have contributed to the maintenance of a competitive economy. The size of the contribution cannot be assessed, when compared either with what would have happened if we had had no antimonopoly laws or with what would have happened under other laws that might have been adopted in their stead.

B. Government Regulation of Privately Owned Firms

The antitrust laws are intended to create efficient conditions in industry that are self-regulating. If this objective is not attained, some other regulatory force is sometimes substituted. (There doubtless are some instances where an industry is not competitive and no other regulation is imposed.) Government regulation takes many forms, of which only public-utility regulation will be discussed here in any detail. Other types will simply be listed with little or no comment.

1. PUBLIC-UTILITY REGULATION

In effect, government decrees that a part of the industrial system cannot be regulated by competition in a way that serves the public interest. The public-utility section of industry is accordingly turned into a special species of business—publicly controlled monopoly. This sphere of business is rather extensive in the United States—far more so than in any other country. Public-utility regulation is a distinctive feature of American government and the American economy.[10]

Competition fails to serve the public interest in the public-utility field primarily because it would involve extremely costly duplication of facilities. Almost everyone uses the services of a public utility, and if the services are provided to everyone by a single firm, one set of basic facilities will suffice. If competition were allowed, there might be many

---

[10] Dimock, *op. cit.*, p. 434.

electric, water, gas, and telephone lines along each street, for example. With respect to telephone service particularly, competition would lead to additional waste and inconvenience, since users of one company's service would not be able to reach those served by another company.

It is difficult to define public utilities. Strictly speaking, a business becomes a public utility when a governmental unit with legal jurisdiction declares it to be one. In general, public utilities are distinguished by two essential characteristics: first, they provide services deemed to be so essential to the welfare of the community that they are said to be "affected with a public interest"; and second, for basic reasons, the public is not safeguarded by the operation of competition.

There are four principal categories of public utility. They are transportation—including railroads, waterways, motor transport, and local transportation services; communication—telephones, telegraph, radio, television; power—electrical, gas, hydroelectric, atomic—and water supply. While these categories include industries of major importance, they clearly do not include all the important industries in the country. A "public utility" is not synonymous with a "vital industry." [11]

Public-utility regulation rests upon the assumption that these businesses are essentially private ventures and should be run by the private owners under a minimum of restraint. The government is given power only to protect citizens against abuse of monopoly power vested in the industry. The major matters over which the public utility commissions *can* exercise control are

1. Determination of whether a firm may discontinue service or expand it, and whether a new enterprise may enter the business.

2. Determination of the manner in which public utilities may raise financial resources.

3. Decision of the rates that may be charged for the service.

4. Determination of standards of satisfactory service.

The most important power of public utility commissions is the review of rates charged by public utilities. How are these rates actually determined?

Charges for services provided by public utilities are almost always set initially by the management of the company. However, the company's pricing power is shared in a devious manner with the public-utility commission. Commissions in almost all states possess the power to discontinue existing rates; any of them can deny price changes sought by the management of the utility. Sometimes a commission sets maximum rates, which in practice become the actual rates charged.

In setting charges, managers of public utilities whose services are in strong demand are restrained either by the commission directly or by

---

[11] Dimock, *op. cit.*, pp. 436-437.

their awareness of the reaction of the commission to high earnings. On the other hand, managers of public utilities that can hardly meet costs no matter what they charge generally can set their rates without supervision or advice from the public-utility commission.

The pricing of public-utility services is a form of cat-and-mouse game. Utility companies are permitted to behave much like any other business if they do not arouse the public-utility commission. A study of the commission's habits will generally indicate what things will induce it to act. Utility companies realize that their earnings are not investigated every year; a company that maintains existing and moderately "excessive" earnings may escape regulation for a very long time.

The determination of public-utility charges generally poses extremely complicated questions. Most perplexing is what is a fair rate of return for the owners. Also involved is the problem of the rates to be charged different users. In turn, this question involves problems of how to calculate the cost of serving different users. Owing to the great difficulty of determining costs exactly under usual circumstances and the highly arbitrary nature of cost calculation when many different users are served from the same facilities under dissimilar circumstances, rate determination is an extremely complicated task.

As enforced at present, public-utility regulation is relatively ineffective. In part, its weakness is due to the highly technical character of the job that must be done and the fact that the regulatory agencies are fundamentally dependent for information upon the records kept by the regulated companies. (Although many commissions specify the kinds of records that are to be kept, accounting remains a flexible technique and the aims of the commission can be frustrated to a considerable extent in this way.) More important than the complexity of the job they are called upon to do, public-utility commissions do not earn many kudos, because, like the antitrust agencies, they are kept without the funds they need for doing their job. In addition, the personnel of the commissions frequently is selected in such a way, or is given such conditions of employment, that it tends to become oversolicitous of the interests of the regulated companies and neglects its obligations to the consuming public.

There is almost universal agreement among authorities in the field of public-utility regulation that it has not been highly successful up to this time. However, most of them seem to think that the method of regulation *could* succeed if it were to receive more support from the public and from legislatures.

C. *Government Ownership and Control*

When competition fails and public-utility regulation seems inappropriate, the United States has turned to direct ownership and operation of industry. As a general rule it is safe to say that government operation is used in this country as a last resort.

Public ownership of business enterprises is far more rare in the United States than in other developed countries of the world. For example, all the principal railroad systems of the world are publicly owned, except those in the United States. Telephone and telegraph service is similarly government owned and operated almost everywhere except in the United States. Municipal ownership of electricity, gas, and local transportation is much more widespread outside the United States.[12] The United States favors public-utility regulation for many fields in which other nations have turned to public ownership.

Even though the United States employs public ownership far less than most other countries, it has not rejected it entirely. Indeed, many fields of activity are predominantly under public ownership at present, and others are increasingly passing over to it. There has been a slow but perceptible trend toward increased public ownership in the United States dating back to perhaps the middle 1920's.

Fields dominantly under public ownership at present include police protection; provision of roads, streets, harbors, and waterways; postal service; water and sewerage works; land reclamation; education and military and nuclear research; social work and institutional care; and libraries and museums. Fields with a large amount of public ownership include municipal transit, forestry, electric power, rural resettlement, housing, credit and banking, and insurance (property, income, medical, and old age and accident).[13]

Government operation of business is most common on the municipal and national levels. State governments have not engaged extensively in the direct operation of business. The greatest expansion of government ownership in recent years has occurred on the national level. The major fields into which the federal government has entered are banking and credit, insurance, public power, and atomic energy.

There seems to be far greater agreement about the merits and defects of public-utility regulation than about public ownership. At present, insufficient evidence has been collected to warrant conclusions concerning the relative merits of private ownership, public-utility regulation, and public ownership. One point, however, is clear. Public ownership has rarely been employed at the outset. Usually it has been invoked when private ownership or public-utility regulation was found unsatisfactory. Indeed, other forms had to be so manifestly unsatisfactory that the elec-

---

[12] Dimock, *op. cit.*, p. 651.

[13] For a more exhaustive list of fields now under public ownership or passing over to government ownership, see Seba Eldridge and Associates, *Development of Collective Enterprise* (Lawrence: University of Kansas Press, 1943), p. 544.

torate would legislate public ownership into effect over the active publicity campaigns carried on by the private owners or the public utilities.

One wonders why public-utility regulation is so widely employed in the United States and why this country is so opposed to public ownership —in comparison with the nations of Western Europe. As has been noted, public-utility regulation has not been highly successful, and apparently even most of the public at large is cynical about its effectiveness. Many, and probably the overwhelming majority, of economists—some of whom are very "conservative"—prefer public ownership to public-utility regulation.[14]

No doubt part of the reason for this preference is to be found in fundamental principles to which most Americans adhere. Public ownership, in the opinion of most people, is what we mean by "socialism," and that is anathema to most Americans. That many activities now are directly owned and operated by the government without undermining the economy and way of life apparently is not widely recognized. Perhaps public-utility regulation has the support of many groups because it creates the impression of public regulation without the restrictions that are really bothersome to the private owners. In contrast to such regulation, public ownership would completely displace private owners. This result is likely to be strongly opposed, and successfully for the most part, except when the industry is unprofitable. Under such circumstances, owners are delighted to be "bailed out" by the government. Not infrequently governments have purchased unprofitable businesses at prices that the owners were happy to receive.

III. MEASURES TO INCREASE THE COMPETITIVENESS OF THE AMERICAN ECONOMY

A few suggestions for increasing the competitiveness of the American economy are implicit in the foregoing discussion. Clearly, our antitrust program will fall far short of great effectiveness unless substantially greater appropriations are made for this purpose. It is little short of shocking that such small resources are placed at the command of the two agencies that are enforcing the most basic legislation in the nation. (Congress should not be permitted to take comfort in the fact that its appropriations are larger than they were in the past.)

Second, the great cost and time consumed by antitrust cases should be reduced as much as possible. One measure that would probably contribute a great deal toward this end is the establishment of specialized courts to hear cases of this sort. The highly complex character of these

---

[14] Foremost in this group are the late Henry Simons and his many disciples.

suits and the technical nature of the problems raised in them make the use of specialized courts virtually a necessity.

Third, Congress could assist in the administration of the antitrust laws by clarifying their general objectives. Does Congress desire to rectify the prevailing conditions of oligopoly? Does it feel that parallel action on the part of rivals is obnoxious? Does it want to eliminate all significant departures from pure competition—including heavy advertising expenditure? These are questions that appropriately are left to Congress to decide. At present, the courts, the Antitrust Division, and the Federal Trade Commission are enforcing laws intended to meet conditions altogether different from those now prevailing.

Many other remedies might be advanced to correct individual departures from pure competition. Only two will be mentioned here, without either detailed explanation or endorsement. The measures listed are offered simply to suggest lines of approach that have been advanced by others and to give stimulus to those interested in means of improving existing conditions.

First, consumer knowledge about the quality of products would be greatly enhanced by the promulgation of reliable and detailed information. This goal would be partly achieved by the use of grade labeling and detailed product description prominently displayed for the consumer. A rating of competing brands of products by an impartial testing agency (on the order of Consumers' Union and Consumers' Research), with the results widely publicized, would contribute mightily toward this end. Both of these measures would reduce the effectiveness of noninformational advertising, and possibly would lower expenditures for that purpose.

Second, increased information might be made available on the relative profitability of various lines of business. By this means, trades that currently are very profitable would more speedily than now find newcomers entering to intensify rivalry in the business. Conversely, such information would reduce the number of mistaken attempts to enter businesses that are already overcrowded, and would tend to reduce the high rate of business turnover.

IV. SUMMARY AND CONCLUSIONS

The United States employs three major methods to attain the benefits of competition and to eliminate the evils of monopoly. The combined effects of all three still leave numerous departures from the conditions that would be brought about by pure competition. In part, we must reconcile ourselves to departures from the ideal state of pure competition. To do so, our thinking on this subject must be revitalized and old concepts and terms discarded. We simply do not know how to measure these departures, and this need must be filled if our attempts to achieve the results of competition are to succeed.

The antitrust program, public-utility regulation, and public ownership combined do not attack all significant departures from pure competition. Advertising, save that of the more blatantly misleading types, goes unregulated; oligopoly seems to be acceptable; excess capacity is an evil that is not directly attacked by any legislation. Here, again, clarification of the aims we seek is required. The legislation under which industry is regulated and operated harks back to an earlier period when conditions were different and our understanding of industry was far poorer.

Despite the manifest shortcomings in our program for achieving the benefits of competition and avoiding the evils of monopoly, the American economy seems to get on quite well. Before we can be satisfied and pronounce it good, for it excels others, we must make certain that all opportunities for major improvements have been utilized.

DISCUSSION QUESTIONS

1. Of the several programs now in operation to achieve the benefits of competition, which would you consider most effective? Explain the defects of each.

2. What types of monopoly are legal under the antitrust laws?

3. Can you account for the relatively small appropriations made for the enforcement of the antitrust laws?

4. Distinguish between the meaning of "restraint of trade" and "monopoly." Who determines the meaning of these terms? Have their meanings changed much since the original antitrust laws were passed?

5. What kinds of business are not subject to the federal antitrust laws? Is this gap large or small?

6. Distinguish between the kind of regulation involved in public-utility regulation and the type involved in price control (OPA or OPS style).

7. Is government ownership a new development in the United States that has been associated with the New Deal? Under what circumstances do you believe government ownership to be justified?

8. Formulate a general rule by which you would determine whether a particular law should be enacted to regulate a particular industry.

9. Do you believe that the existence of monopoly in an industry is justification for workers to form a labor monopoly? Discuss.

18 What Is the "Correct" Level for Price? A Case Study of Farm Prices

I. INTRODUCTION

The preceding chapters have explained that the American economy depends upon competition rather than upon centralized plans, and have indicated why and how competition leads to highly desirable results. Markets where sellers have some power over price were discussed both as theoretical models and in terms of realistic examples. Particular stress was placed upon the respects in which actual markets deviate from zero-market-power conditions, and the likely effects, particularly on price, of these deviations.

One conclusion implied by the discussion of prices and markets up to this point is that a particular level of price is "just right." Prices higher or lower than this presumably are undesirable. It is therefore fitting to inquire by what means the correct level of price can be recognized. This chapter accordingly explores the correctness of farm prices as a case study.

Farm prices are selected for the exceptional reason that Congress decided some time ago, and persists in the decision, that these prices are too low. The appropriateness of farm prices therefore was taken under extensive consideration and debated in detail. In the end, legislation was enacted to raise them. Agriculture warrants special discussion also because it is the sector of the economy that most closely approximates zero market power.

This chapter will be organized around the question, Were farm prices too low when Congress enacted legislation to raise them? We will also inquire whether existing legislation is warranted to support the level of farm prices. In the course of answering these questions, we shall discover the effects of the most competitive—possibly of excessively competitive—markets in our economy.

II. WHAT IS THE "CORRECT" PRICE?

Most persons are uncertain whether a particular price is too high or too low. Their uncertainty could be dispelled by deciding *what we want the price to do*. Prices do something, and once we decide what this should be, we shall have criteria by which to judge the desirability of any price.

A. Functions Performed by Price

In our earlier discussions it was indicated that a price that is high relative to cost encourages increased output. It entices businessmen to enter a field they would not enter if price were lower. Conversely, if a product's price is lower than its cost, established firms generally will leave the field or reduce their output. Accordingly, when a product's output is lower than we want it to be, its price may be considered too low. When output is excessive, prices presumably are too high. (It is no simple matter, of course, to decide whether output is excessive.)

It was also indicated that prices influence the distribution of income as well as the things that are produced. High prices for a product shift income distribution in favor of those who sell it. To redistribute income in favor of buyers, prices should be lowered. Accordingly, if we believe the incomes of sellers to be too low, then the prices of the things they sell may be considered too low.

Prices also influence processes of production. The higher the price a businessman must pay for particular types of labor, machinery, or raw materials, the greater his efforts to use something else. Conversely, producers favor the use of productive factors whose prices are relatively low. Prices of productive factors therefore determine what resources will be employed. Correct prices of productive factors would lead to the use of those that are most plentiful and that involve least personal sacrifice.

Prices were shown to affect methods of production in another way. When prices of individual products are low relative to cost, businessmen are put under strong pressure to use efficient methods and to seek out better ways of doing things. Prices substantially above costs permit businessmen to relax efforts to increase efficiency. Low prices—particularly those at or below cost—on the other hand, compel businessmen to, increase efficiency or face bankruptcy.

B. *Criteria for Determining Whether Price Is "Correct"*

From this list of the main functions performed by price, we can deduce criteria of correct price. Applied specifically to farm prices, they would be

1. Do prices result in production of farm products in desirable amounts and proportions?

2. Do they lead to an equitable distribution of income between farmers and nonfarmers?

3. Do they lead to efficient methods of agricultural production?

C. *Application of These Criteria to Specific Prices*

It is difficult to apply these criteria in concrete situations. Consider, for example, the first criterion—that price leads to the production of the best amounts and proportions. One might think that price is correct only when it results in maximum production. This conclusion is surely incorrect for two major reasons. First, to produce the maximum quantity of any product would necessarily reduce the output of some other products. Maximum output of one product could be produced only by foregoing the production of others that, at least in some quantity, are more valuable. For example, a price that caused all fertile land to be devoted to, say, wheat, would be an undesirable price. We would sorely miss many other products of the soil. Clearly, maximum output cannot be our criterion for the desired output of anything.

Second, it might be better not to produce some products at all than produce them even in small quantities. Some things are not worth the effort involved. Moreover, it rarely is desirable to produce as much of all products combined as can be produced. Production is not an end in itself. It is to be carried on only when it satisfies the population more than they would be satisfied by leisure. Although the ordinary measures of economic welfare do not take account of all sacrifices in production,[1] they must be figured in any decision about how much to produce.

Can one draw a line between goods that are worth producing and those that are not? To differentiate sharply between things that vary in slight degree is always difficult. There should be consolation, however, in the fact that everyone solves similar problems many times every day. Every time an individual decides how to spend his time, he decides consciously or unconsciously what is worth while for him and what is not. He is selecting from the many alternative courses the one he considers most valuable. When he decides to sit and rest, he is also deciding that all other things he might do are not worth the trouble. Similarly, prices

---

[1] See earlier discussion in Chapter 2.

should not encourage increases in output when the added goods are not worth the trouble.

Similar complex questions arise in applying the other criteria for correct price. A person fools only himself if he thinks that he can decide whether prices are too high or too low without trying to settle such complex issues.

With regard to farm prices, the third criterion has not been made part of the issue. Consequently, nothing more will be said about it in this connection. However, in certain circumstances—especially where productive inefficiency or a lack of technological progressiveness is associated with strong market power—the third criterion might be the crucial one. Before we apply the other two criteria of desired price to agriculture, we shall examine the arguments that were advanced for raising farm prices. By doing so, we will get a picture of American agriculture, without which we should hesitate to judge the correctness of farm prices.

III. WHY LEGISLATION WAS ENACTED TO RAISE FARM PRICES

Why was Congress persuaded to raise farm prices? By what standards were farm prices judged too low? Three major arguments were advanced in support of special help for farmers. One stressed the divergent movement of farm and nonfarm prices. Another held that farm prices are determined on competitive markets, while nonfarm prices are sold on "monopolistic" markets. A third argument held that the price system worked to the farmer's disadvantage because of perverse conditions of supply and demand in agriculture. These arguments will be reviewed in some detail, even though the condition of agriculture in the late twenties and the early thirties is not our chief concern. From this analysis we shall gain insight into the manner in which one type of market—one where market power is absent—operates.[2] We shall also find an excellent opportunity to apply our criteria for the correctness of price to an actual instance where Congress decided that prices were too low.

A. The Divergent Movement of Farm and Nonfarm Prices

Farm prices generally change in the same direction as nonfarm prices, but do not run directly parallel to them. Sometimes farm prices

---

[2] It is not implied, however, that all markets where sellers lack market power behave in the same way that most agricultural markets do. Indeed, there is even considerable difference in the way individual markets for farm products operate.

have risen while other prices were falling; conversely, farm prices declined in some years while others rose. Years of divergent movement of farm and nonfarm prices between the close of World War I and 1930 were 1920, 1922, 1924, and 1928. Most of these divergent movements were in favor of the farmer. However, as is shown in Table 1, the farmer's relative price position was worse after World War I than it had been before the war. In addition, it deteriorated badly after 1929.

If farm prices fall while other prices remain steady or rise, the farmer's condition is likely to grow worse. When farm prices fall, farm incomes generally decline also; if the prices that farmers must pay remain the same, they can buy fewer goods than before. Conversely, if a city dweller's income remains the same when prices of farm products rise, his costs rise relative to income and his condition is made worse. Such a situation is sometimes described as a change in the "terms of trade" between farm and nonfarm products, because the amount of farm goods that can be obtained with a given amount of nonfarm goods will have changed.

Table 1. Prices Received and Prices Paid by Farmers, 1910-1957

Period	Prices received for farm products [*]	Retail prices paid by farmers [†]	Ratio of prices received to prices paid [‡]
1910–1914	100	100	100
1915–1919	164	151	109
1920–1924	150	161	93
1925–1929	148	155	95
1930–1934	88	122	72
1935–1939	107	124	86
1940–1944	154	148	104
1945–1949	250	219	114
1950	256	246	105
1951	302	271	111
1952	288	273	105
1953	258	262	98
1954	249	263	95
1955	236	262	90
1956	235	264	89
1957	242	273	89

[*] Prices received for farm products, 1910-1914, equals 100.

[†] Retail prices paid by farmers, 1910-1914, equals 100. Includes all commodities used in living and in production but excludes interest, taxes, and wage rates.

[‡] This is not the so-called "parity" index, but the ratio of the two indices shown here.

SOURCES: U.S. Department of Agriculture, *Agricultural Statistics;* U.S. Department of Commerce, *Survey of Current Business,* February, 1958.

Table 1 indicates that during the twenties the prices (or the terms of trade) turned against the farmer. The prices he received declined for several years while nonfarm prices remained steady. After 1929, the terms of trade shifted rapidly to the disadvantage of farmers as farm prices fell far more rapidly than nonfarm prices. Table 1 shows an index of prices[3] received by farmers, the prices paid by them and the ratio of farm to nonfarm prices for the years 1910 to 1957.

The figures describing prices received for farm products combine many dissimilar things. Not all farm prices changed in the same direction or by the same amount. (See Table 2.) In part, divergence of farm prices resulted from tricks of nature which caused some crops to be very large and others to be small. Partly, farm prices in this country reflect the size of crops in the rest of the world, which also do not always vary together. Occasionally, the prices of individual farm crops are strongly affected by demand developments, which may create either acute shortages or, in some instances, a shift to the use of synthetic substitutes. Once we examine the maze of individual agricultural prices, we learn that any discussion of the farm problem which lumps together all products can be only a starting point. Full understanding requires separate analysis of each crop's experience. (And, as shall be indicated presently, production takes place on several fairly distinctive types of farms whose income experience differs substantially.)

One must not jump, however, from *price* comparisons of the kind just made to conclusions about *net income*. The average farmer could have been better off in 1933 than he was in, say, 1925, despite the large relative decline in farm prices. This could have come about if his costs of production had declined even more than prices; or if his total sales had increased enough to compensate for any decline in his profit per unit.

The information presented in Table 3 makes it clear that such was not the situation. The average farmer was in extremely bad condition after 1930 because of a combination of declining farm prices, lower total farm income, and an increase in the number of people on the farms. Between 1921 and 1929, per capita farm income was generally high compared with all World War I years; however, farm incomes did not enjoy as great an increase as took place in nonfarm incomes between 1910-1914 and the late 1920's.

No doubt, there is a "farm problem," but it is not a problem involving all—or even most—farmers. What is generally called the "farm problem" has two main ingredients. First, and foremost, there are competent and

---

[3] A price index measures relative price changes over time, using a selected year or period as base—to which the figure 100 is assigned. Prices in other years are related to the price in the base period.

Table 2. Movements of Selected Farm Prices, 1925-1957
(Average prices received by farmers)

Year	Wheat (dollars per bushel)	Corn (dollars per bushel)	Cotton (cents per pound)	Tobacco (cents per pound)
1925	$1.437	$0.699	19.61¢	16.8¢
1926	1.217	0.745	12.47	17.9
1927	1.190	0.850	20.19	20.7
1928	0.998	0.840	17.99	20.0
1929	1.036	0.799	16.79	18.3
1930	0.671	0.596	9.46	12.8
1931	0.391	0.320	5.66	8.2
1932	0.382	0.319	6.52	10.5
1933	0.744	0.522	10.17	13.0
1934	0.848	0.815	12.36	21.3
1935	0.831	0.655	11.09	18.4
1936	1.025	1.044	12.33	23.6
1937	0.962	0.518	8.41	20.4
1938	0.562	0.487	8.60	19.7
1939	0.691	0.568	9.09	15.4
1940	0.682	0.618	9.89	16.1
1941	0.944	0.751	17.03	26.4
1942	1.10	0.917	19.05	36.9
1943	1.36	1.12	19.90	40.5
1944	1.41	1.09	20.73	42.0
1945	1.50	1.27	22.52	42.6
1946	1.91	1.56	32.64	45.1
1947	2.29	2.16	31.93	43.6
1948	1.99	1.30	30.38	48.2
1949	1.88	1.25	28.58	45.9
1950	2.00	1.53	40.07	51.7
1951	2.11	1.66	37.88	51.1
1952	2.09	1.53	34.59	49.9
1953	2.04	1.49	32.25	52.3
1954	2.12	1.43	33.61	51.1
1955	1.98	1.34	32.33	53.2
1956	1.97	1.29	31.75	53.7
1957 *	1.94	1.17	32.50	57.0

* Preliminary.

SOURCE: U.S. Department of Agriculture, *Agricultural Statistics, 1942, 1950, 1956; Statistical Abstract of the United States, 1958* (Washington, D.C.: Government Printing Office, 1958).

industrious farmers who, for various reasons, are restricted to the raising of one or several crops—all of which do not "pay well." The number of farmers in this group probably is not very large. For the most part, efficient commercial farms can produce enough income to provide an

Soybeans (dollars per bushel)	Cattle (dollars per 100 pounds)	Hogs (dollars per 100 pounds)	Sheep (dollars per 100 pounds)
$2.34	$ ...	$ ...	$ ...
2.01	...	...	...
1.81	...	...	...
1.88	...	...	...
1.88	...	...	...
1.36	7.71	8.84	4.74
0.49	5.53	5.73	3.11
0.54	4.25	3.34	2.24
0.93	3.75	3.53	2.38
0.99	4.13	4.14	2.85
0.73	6.04	8.65	3.75
1.28	5.82	9.37	3.77
0.84	7.00	9.50	4.52
0.68	6.54	7.74	3.58
0.81	7.14	6.23	3.90
0.90	7.56	5.39	3.95
1.55	8.82	9.09	5.06
1.61	10.70	13.00	5.80
1.81	11.90	13.70	6.57
2.05	10.80	13.10	6.01
2.08	12.10	14.00	6.38
2.57	14.50	17.50	7.48
3.33	18.40	24.10	8.39
2.27	22.20	23.10	9.69
2.16	19.80	18.10	9.27
2.47	23.30	18.00	11.60
2.73	28.70	20.00	16.00
2.72	24.30	17.80	10.00
2.72	16.30	21.40	6.67
2.47	16.00	21.60	6.14
2.22	15.60	15.00	5.81
2.18	14.90	14.40	5.64
2.09	n.a.	n.a.	n.a.

"acceptable" standard of living. This first group—efficient and industrious and located on high-quality land—represents what might be called the "pure farm problem" and are associated with surpluses. Second, there are many farmers located on poor land or with small tracts of land; some are unfamiliar with the latest methods of horticulture; some are illiterate, shiftless, or sickly. These farmers probably receive the lowest farm incomes. In 1957, there were 2.7 million farms which sold less than $2,500 of farm products and 1.3 million that sold

**Table 3. Farm Incomes and All Incomes Compared,
Selected Years 1910-1957**

	Average per capita net income of the		
Year	Total population	Nonfarm population	Farm population *
1910	$ 360		$147
1914	368		145
1918	567		305
1921	546		129
1922	554		158
1923	640		187
1924	624		182
1925	659		243
1926	689		220
1927	665		215
1928	676		224
1929	715		230
1930	613		166
1931	484		129
1932	345		80
1933	323		93
1934	391	$ 468†	106
1935	448	517	182
1936	502	592	156
1937	558	642	216
1938	506	589	165
1939	537	626	168
1940	588	685	174
1941	715	823	246
1942	920	1,034	379
1943	1,126	1,240	497
1944	1,211	1,328	524
1945	1,205	1,312	554
1946	1,204	1,295	644
1947	1,287	1,394	644
1948	1,433	1,534	765
1949	1,381	1,511	567
1950	1,461	1,585	626
1951	1,641	1,763	751
1952	1,712	1,849	711
1953	1,764	1,902	666
1954	1,724	1,849	660
1955	1,830	1,975	610
1956	1,903	2,056	602
1957	1,950	2,082	658

$5,000 or more of farm products. Most of the farms producing less than $2,500 are in the South, but there are concentrations in cutover areas in the Great Lakes states and in parts of the Northwest.

Perhaps it deserves emphasis that incompetence, lack of energy or industry, and operations on too small a scale to permit high productivity are not a "farm problem." It is a general problem affecting all lines of industry and commerce also, where each year hundreds of thousands of individuals dissipate their savings in vain attempts at running their own businesses. This problem, which results from allowing individuals to select their own occupations without respect to their training, experience, and native ability, should not be included as part of the farm problem—even if it should be true—and the author does not know that it is—that inefficiency, incompetence, etc. are more common sources of low income among farmers than among other kinds of entrepreneurs.

Accordingly, in our discussion of the causes and possible remedies for the farm problem we shall have in mind only the efficiently run farms located on land suitable for farming. The problem of inefficient persons operating on land that should not be cultivated is part of a broader problem which is not at all unique to agriculture; the remedy must help the nonfarmer as well as the misguided person who attempts to make his living as an independent farm operator.

Even as it is possible to use only average farm *prices* as a starting point, average farm *income* can be highly misleading. Classified from an income-earning point of view, American farms can be divided into four *main* types; full comprehension, of course, requires separate analysis of many more types to take account of regional differences, variations in size of farm, age of farmer, types of crops grown, degree of mechanization, technical skill of farmer, etc. These four main types are the so-called "giant" or "corporate" farms, comprising about 34,000 in total number in 1954 and accounting for 32 per cent of total farm-product sales. The average family income on such farms was in the vicinity of $12,000, more than 90 per cent of which was obtained from farm sources.[4] (Owing to the great seasonality of farm labor, it is typical for farmers and members of their families to take employment in commercial and industrial firms sometime during the year if such work is available. For many farmers, nonfarm income is a major source.)

---

* Farm population income includes government payments after 1933; it has also been adjusted to include income in kind consumed on the farm and the value of farm buildings as housing, excluding income from nonfarm sources.

† There is no information on the distribution of total nonagricultural net income as between the farm and nonfarm populations for years prior to 1934.

SOURCE: U.S. Department of Agriculture, Agricultural Marketing Service, *The Farm Income Situation*, July, 1958, p. 24.

[4] Conference on Economic Progress, *Full Prosperity for Agriculture*, p. 40 *nn.*

At the opposite extreme are approximately one and one-fourth million commercial farms which are substandard in both productivity and income. In mid-1955, families living on these farms had average per capita incomes *from all sources* of about $375, and average family incomes of $1,400.[5] These farms can be found in all farm areas but are concentrated mainly in the South.

Another type of farm—the noncommercial type—about one and one-half million in number, faces problems very different from those of the first two types. Families living on noncommercial farms account for roughly 2 per cent of total farm output and obtain between one fourth and one fifth of their entire income from their farm operations. From the income standpoint, they are more nonfarmers than farmers. In mid-1955, their average family income from all sources was in the neighborhood of $2,800.

FARMS CLASSIFIED BY NUMBER AND MARKETINGS IN 1957

Number of Farms   Farm Marketings

The role of the large farm in agricultural output is clearly indicated by its contribution to total farm marketings. Though only 27 per cent of all farms are large, they contribute almost 80 per cent of total farm marketings. Small and medium farms together, comprising 73 per cent of all farms, only produce 21 per cent of all farm marketings.

About 2 million American farms might be described as "standard commercial farms"—though no sharp line can be drawn between these and the substandard farms. They account for approximately 60 per cent of total farm-product sales and yield an average family income from all sources of about $4,000. These farms are large enough to employ mechanized means of horticulture, and their proprietors are acquainted with modern methods of farming. As a group, they, together with the giant farms, produce 92 per cent of the output of food and fiber.

The major components of a farmer's income are indicated by the

---

[5] *Ibid.*, p. 41.

following breakdown of the average farm family's income in 1957. In that year, the total farm cash receipts from marketings of farm products totaled $29,757 million. Nonmoney income in that year was composed of the following:

1. Value of products consumed on farms $1,763 million
2. Gross rental value of farm homes $1,794 million

      Total nonmoney income $3,557 million

Nonmoney income amounted to 12 per cent of total money income from marketings of farm products. In addition, farmers received government payments amounting to $1,016 million. These payments were unusually high compared with preceding years; in 1956 they were $554 million; in 1954 they were $257 million.[6]

The information presented in Table 2 shows far more than the precipitate decline in farm income after 1929. It shows that, throughout the period 1910 to 1957, farm incomes were far below, and also far less stable than, the incomes of the rest of the nation. For example, in 1910 and 1914, the average per capita income of the farm population was about one third that of the total population (in which total the farmers' incomes helped to pull down the average). By 1939, it was less than one quarter of the average, and in 1932, it fell to almost one fifth. Even during the highly prosperous years for agriculture immediately following World War II, the average per capita farm income was less than half that of the nonfarm population.

Reported in a different manner from a different source, the gap between farm and nonfarm incomes appears smaller. A survey of incomes of representative farm and nonfarm families in 1956 showed that urban families and individuals averaged $4,515, whereas rural farm families averaged $2,119.[7] These figures are consistent with the per capita data in Table 2. The apparent conflict between them is accounted for by the substantially larger size of farm families.

These data on farm incomes cannot tell us whether or not farm incomes were too low in the late twenties and early thirties. They show only how these incomes compare with those of earlier years. To determine their correct level, we need standards by which we decide what incomes are "just right." A comparison with other years is no substitute for such standards. Implicit in comparisons of incomes (and prices) at different times is the assumption that income was "just right" in the early period. We must beware of the temptation to select a time in the past

---

[6] All the foregoing data come from U.S. Department of Agriculture, Agricultural Marketing Service, *The Farm Income Situation*, July, 1958, pp. 28, 31.

[7] See U.S. Department of Commerce, Bureau of the Census, *Current Population Reports*, Series P-60, No. 27, p. 24.

that is vague in our recollection and refer to it as normal, assuming that things were just as they should be. Exceptional circumstances exist practically all the time.

UPS AND DOWNS ON THE FARM

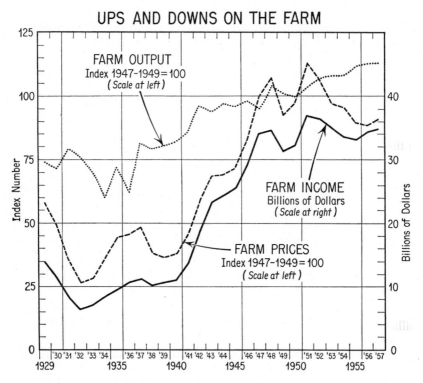

A combination of increased production and higher prices has raised the farmer's income very substantially since World War II. In 1951 farm output was about 50 per cent above prewar levels; farm income had tripled in the same period as prices increased by more than one and a half times. Since 1951, however, farmers have experienced more difficult times as prices have declined almost steadily to a level almost 20 per cent below the post-war peak and farm income has fallen by about ten per cent.

We thus see that the divergent course of farm and nonfarm prices cannot indicate reliably whether farm prices were too high or too low in the late twenties and early thirties. We cannot even prove that farm incomes have changed. And even when we find that farmers' incomes fell relative to the incomes of other members of the population,[8] we still

---

[8] Farm incomes also are far less stable than nonfarm incomes. For example, the families headed by farmers enjoyed a 40 per cent rise in income between 1949 and 1950, while all families, including farm families, experienced an increase of less than 7 per cent. See U.S. Department of Commerce, Bureau of the Census, *Current Population Reports,* Series P-60, No. 9, March 25, 1952, p. 1.

require standards by which to judge whether those incomes were too high, too low, or just right.

We need not push this discussion further. It suffices for our purpose to note that supporters of special assistance to agriculture rested their case partly on the fact that farm prices moved disadvantageously for farmers, and that their incomes also did not run parallel to the rising incomes of the nonfarm population in the years prior to 1929.

B. Farmers Bought on Monopolistic Markets and Sold on Competitive Markets

Our comparison of three market types is pertinent to the situation of the farmers. It showed that under identical conditions of cost and demand, sellers without market power—like farmers—get a lower price than those in either "conventional" markets or in markets where sellers have complete market power. The farmer can put his case for higher prices in these terms: "Give me as much as an industrial seller would get under the same conditions of cost and demand."

The farmer did not advance the equally plausible argument that prices charged by other sellers should be lowered and brought in line with his. Indeed, he could have supported his case with the argument that industrial markets waste resources through excess capacity and socially useless competitive advertising and do not serve society so well as agriculture. Perhaps the farmer showed political astuteness, for in a democracy it is highly difficult politically to lower the incomes (or prices charged) of a large group, unless this decrease can be affected by devious means. One such means is to lower that group's income by raising the prices that it must pay.

When farmers protested that they made their purchases on monopolistic markets while selling on intensely competitive markets, they had more in mind than the conventional market as we have described it. Farmers, like many others, were impressed with the high "concentration" of industry. In many lines, most of total output was produced by only a few firms—frequently only three or four.[9] Farmers suspected that sellers in at least some of these markets adopted pricing and market practices that in effect had them "acting as one." Their complaints about industrial prices were directed primarily against markets where sellers adopted cooperative and collusive practices. Some of these practices and their prevalence have been discussed in Chapter 14 of this section.

There can be little question that the farmer sold his output in markets significantly different from those in which he spent his money. Owing

---

[9] Evidence on industrial concentration and the proportion of total output of specific products contributed by the largest firms in the industry were presented in Chapter 9.

to the nature of his markets, he received lower prices than he would have obtained in conventional markets or if he had possessed complete market power. Buyers of farm staples got a "good deal" from the farmer; the prices they paid, at best, gave the farmer the minimum return that would induce him to remain in business, and they did not have to pay for unnecessary selling expenses. Thus the farmer's loss was the public's gain.

On the other hand, many, and maybe most, industrial markets—which sell the greatest amount of total output—apparently are afflicted with objectionable characteristics. They tend to generate excessive productive facilities, substantial expenditure for sales promotion, and sometimes (when established firms are able to keep newcomers out of the business) allow profits for business owners beyond a "just" payment for the services rendered.

Thus the second claim of those supporting special assistance for farmers apparently is valid, just as the first was shown to be. Let us now turn to the last major argument to justify special assistance for agriculture: it holds that conditions of cost and demand in agriculture are perverse and operate to the disadvantage of farmers. The argument implies that since the farmer performs a vital social function by raising food, he should not be compelled to suffer because of these perverse conditions. Society, which is the beneficiary of the farmer's efforts, should rightly bear the full burden involved in producing food. To supporters of the farmer's position this means that the farmer should be compensated for injury resulting from the perverse cost and demand conditions for farm products.

C. Perverse Cost and Demand Conditions in Agriculture

Do cost and demand conditions in agriculture work to the "unfair" disadvantage of the farmer? How do cost and demand conditions in agriculture differ from typical conditions in industry?

Supply and demand conditions are best described in terms of three major attributes: (1) their level; (2) their reaction to price changes—technically termed their "price elasticity"; and (3) their reaction to changes in the level of personal income—technically called "income elasticity."

When is the level of demand high or low? The answer usually is expressed as a comparison with the supply of the same product. Accordingly, one often meets statements like this: "If supply exceeds demand, price will be low, and if demand is greater than supply, prices will be high." These statements are particularly confusing because the amount of a product offered for sale always tends to equal the amount purchased. If much is produced, much will ultimately be sold, for the large supply will typically force prices down to the point where buyers will purchase all of it. When one says that supply exceeds demand, he really means that prices must fall to clear the market. Conversely, situations in which prices rise substantially are sometimes described as instances where demand exceeds supply, even though output and purchases are equal.

The major conditions of supply and demand that depress farm prices and farm incomes are the following:

1. The *output* of a few farm staples usually is excessive and is relatively unaffected by price changes.

2. *Sales* of most farm products are not responsive to price reductions. That is, even substantial reductions in individual farm prices do not greatly increase sales of farm products beyond some point. Consequently, very great price reductions are required to dispose of only modest surpluses.

3. The demand for farm output falls substantially when incomes fall during periods of depression.

1. THE TOTAL SUPPLY OF FARM PRODUCTS IS EXCESSIVE, AND FARM OUTPUT IS RELATIVELY INSENSITIVE TO PRICE CHANGES

At the root of the farm problem in the late twenties was an excessive output of farm products, a condition which, in turn, was caused by the excessive number of persons living and working on farms.[10] In terms of our first criterion for determining whether price is "correct"—that it results in an output of farm products in desirable amounts—something was clearly wrong with farm prices. By excessive farm population, we mean a number of people so large that their output could be sold only at prices below costs—but including at least a tolerable return for the farmer. (We emphatically do not mean that more food was raised than people would have consumed if food were free, or even than was needed for ideal nutrition.) In other words, agricultural output was in excess of the amount that would be purchased at constant prices. As a result, farm prices declined relatively more than industrial prices during the 1920's, as has already been shown in Table 1.

The excessive output of farm products was caused by more than overpopulation on farms. It resulted also from strides in agricultural technology, which raised farm productivity.[11] Actually, adjustment to ag-

---

[10] Farm surpluses were partly aggravated by a decline in foreign purchases of agricultural products from the United States.

[11] Farm productivity has not risen so rapidly as productivity in manufacturing industries, however. Between 1909 and 1946, on farms, the output per man increased at the rate of about 1.2 per cent annually; in manufacturing, the increase was between 3 per cent and 3½ per cent. See Morgan, *Introduction to Economics* (Englewood Cliffs, N.J.: Prentice-Hall, Inc., 1950), pp. 479, 483.

ricultural technology and rising productivity should have brought about a larger decline in farm population than actually took place. Therefore the excessive supply of farm products must be attributed to excessive numbers of the nation's farmers.

As Table 4 indicates, the number of hired farm hands, composing about 25 per cent of total farm employment, and independent farmers (who with their families represent three quarters of the total) has fallen gradually for a considerable period. However, their numbers still remain excessive to meet the demands for agricultural output at prevailing prices.

Table 4. Farm Population in the United States, 1910-1958
(In thousands)

Year	Number of persons on farms April 1 *	Year	Number of persons on farms April 1
1910	32,077	1935	32,161
1911	32,110	1936	31,737
1912	32,210	1937	31,266
1913	32,270	1938	30,980
1914	32,320	1939	30,840
1915	32,440	1940	30,547
1916	32,530	1941	30,273
1917	32,430	1942	29,234
1918	31,950	1943	26,681
1919	31,200	1944	25,495
1920	31,974	1945	25,295
1921	32,123	1946	26,483
1922	32,109	1947	27,124
1923	31,490	1948	25,903
1924	31,177	1949	25,954
1925	31,190	1950	25,058
1926	30,979	1951	24,160
1927	30,530	1952	24,283
1928	30,548	1953	22,679
1929	30,580	1954	21,890
1930	30,529	1955	22,158
1931	30,845	1956	22,257
1932	31,388	1957	20,396
1933	32,393	1958	20,827
1934	32,305		

* Estimated cooperatively by the Bureau of the Census and the Bureau of Agricultural Economics.

SOURCE: *Farm Population*, Series P-27, Nos. 16 and 25, March 9, 1953, and August 8, 1958 (Joint Series: Census–Agricultural Marketing Service).

Not only were the numbers employed on farms excessive in the late twenties, but their potential productive contribution was not fully utilized.

Even in 1950, when the farm population was significantly lower than in the late 1920's, roughly 20 to 25 per cent of potential output was lost on farms because many workers did not produce as much as the *average* worker on the medium-sized commercial family farm.[12] This loss resulted primarily from having more people working on farms than were needed to cultivate them fully. The source of lost output was *not* insufficient agricultural equipment to make cultivation efficient. Farm manpower, especially on small farms, is underemployed. Even if many people were to leave farming, total output probably would not be lower than if they were to stay. Before an exodus of people from farming would significantly affect farm output, it must be of substantial proportions—say, by one fifth or more.

The combined effect of improved farm technology and the oversupply of farm labor is shown in the output of farm products. As shown by Table 5, farm production has risen substantially since 1910. It has risen as rapidly as total population. Table 5 also depicts the productivity per farm worker and total man-hours of farm work since that time. (As Table 5 indicates, the various measures adopted since 1929 did not slow down the growth in farm output; output has increased more since 1929 than before then.)

2. SALES OF FARM PRODUCTS GENERALLY ARE NOT RESPONSIVE TO PRICE CHANGES

By 1929, it was clear that consumers of farm products would not take the available supply at prices that would give farmers a "decent" income, even during periods of peak prosperity. One cannot overemphasize the fact that the farm problem is not a result of depression; farmers did not fare too well during the twenties, which were highly prosperous years for manufacturing industry; its plight became desperate during the deep depression. Indeed, the first substantial measure to help agriculture was passed on June 15, 1929, months before the stock market crash initiated the depression that began in that year.

This situation is naturally puzzling. As Table 4 indicates, fewer persons worked on farms in the late 1920's than in the preceding decade. Total population and national income were expanding, and yet we find that the demand was inadequate to take farm output at the same prices as before. In contrast, in industry many more people were employed than before and output expanded much more than in agriculture. However, during the prosperous twenties, there were no complaints that demand for industrial output lagged behind output.

When the demand for industrial products faltered, as it sometimes

---

[12] Joint Committee on the Economic Report, *Underemployment of Rural Families* (Washington, D. C.: Government Printing Office, 1951), pp. 4-5.

did, everyone recognized the condition as temporary. On the other hand, the insufficiency of market demand for farm output was clearly one of long duration.

Table 5. Total Farm Output, Man-Hours of Farm Work, and Output per Man-Hour, United States, 1910-1957
(Index numbers (1947-1949 = 100))

Year	Farm output	Man-hours of farm work	Output per man-hour	Year	Farm output	Man-hours of farm work	Output per man-hour
1910	61	132	46	1934	60	118	51
1911	59	134	44	1935	72	123	59
1912	66	136	49	1936	65	119	55
1913	60	134	45	1937	82	129	64
1914	66	139	47	1938	79	120	66
1915	68	136	50	1939	80	121	66
1916	62	135	46	1940	83	119	70
1917	65	139	47	1941	86	117	74
1918	66	141	47	1942	96	122	79
1919	66	138	48	1943	94	121	78
1920	70	140	50	1944	97	120	81
1921	62	129	48	1945	96	112	86
1922	68	134	51	1946	98	108	91
1923	69	135	51	1947	95	103	92
1924	68	136	50	1948	104	100	104
1925	70	139	50	1949	101	97	104
1926	73	139	53	1950	100	89	112
1927	72	134	54	1951	103	91	113
1928	75	136	55	1952	107	89	120
1929	74	135	55	1953	108	88	123
1930	72	134	54	1954	108	85	127
1931	79	137	58	1955	112	85	132
1932	76	132	58	1956	113	83	136
1933	70	132	53	1957 *	113	79	143

* Preliminary.
SOURCE: U.S. Department of Agriculture, *Changes in Farm Production and Efficiency*, Statistical Bulletin No. 233, August, 1958, pp. 4, 20, and 25.

It might be thought that agriculture's plight in the 1920's was caused by the collapse of the foreign demand for American farm produce. Indeed, volume of food exports did decline during the 1920's (the over-all decline between 1921 and 1929 was about 35 per cent).[13] How-

---

[13] T. W. Schultz, *Agriculture in an Unstable Economy* (New York: McGraw-Hill Book Company, Inc., 1945), p. 141.

ever, there also was a decline in foreign sales of industrial products, which did not have similar results.

The essential difference between the demand for farm and industrial products is that increases in personal incomes bring relatively trivial increases in the demand for farm products. Also, although there is a rise in demand for these products because of population growth, it is not sufficient to create a strong market for foodstuffs.

In considering the demand for farm products, it is important to distinguish between the physical quantity of farm products purchased and the amount of money paid for them. As already indicated, the physical quantity of farm produce that will be purchased will depend upon its price; typically, the entire output will be purchased, for prices will adjust in a manner that brings this result. Therefore, we learn little when we examine only the physical quantity of purchases. Our interest must be with the amount of money farmers receive for their output, and, more particularly, the incomes of farmers after they have paid their direct out-of-pocket production costs. We examined such figures earlier when we studied the course of farm incomes. We found that, even during highly prosperous years for the nation as a whole, farmers' incomes declined.

The best evidence indicates that individuals spend a relatively small proportion of any increase in their incomes on farm products. To be specific, it is estimated, that when the average family income rises by 10 per cent its expenditures for farm products rise by only 2.1 per cent.[14] The same condition does not hold for most other things. As people become more prosperous, they increase their spending for clothing, luxuries of various types, entertainment, and the like substantially. For example, a 10 per cent rise in personal income is typically followed by a 10 per cent rise in clothing expenditure, and a larger rise in expenditure for such things as jewelry, furniture, electrical appliances and the like.

Not only does total spending for nonfarm output tend to keep pace with changes in total personal income; the quantity of such goods and services desired tends to expand. People buy more clothing as well as better clothing; they increase their holdings of consumers' durable goods; they consume more entertainment services and the like. With regard to food, the physical quantity purchased is not greatly affected by a rise in personal income. There does seem to be an upper limit to the quantity of food that people will buy, no matter what their income. Once they have reached this limit, price reductions will not induce them to increase their total purchases perceptibly. Apparently, those of moderate means in the United States closely approach this limit. Consequently, in-

---

[14] For a review of evidence describing the relation between changes in personal incomes and sales of farm output, see Schultz, *ibid.*, pp. 60-70.

creases in their incomes primarily change the character but not the quantity of the foodstuffs they purchase.

Even when consumers increase their expenditures for food—as they do as their incomes rise—much of this increase goes to pay for things other than what the farmer produces. That is, they consume food—at higher prices—in restaurants rather than at home; they prepare food more carefully and expensively, and they purchase food of the highest quality. However, the amount of basic foodstuffs purchased is not in any great way affected beyond some point.

The reader may be puzzled by an apparent contradiction. On one hand, we said that virtually all foodstuffs grown will be purchased. That means, given a bumper crop, the nation consumes more food, a fact suggesting that purchases will expand considerably if prices decline. That implication is only partly valid. First, the lower price simply induces those who can store food to buy it when prices are low in the expectation of being better off than if they bought it later at higher prices. Second, the increase in purchases by final consumer, when it does occur, will be substantial only if prices drop drastically. In this event, the poorer classes, who will not have reached the point of the wealthier classes (who, as we explained, have little desire for additional food), will increase their food consumption. It should be noted that the purchases of food for storage do not represent increases in total purchases, but simply a shift in the time of purchase. Once these goods have been acquired, the owner will presumably reduce his subsequent purchases.

3. THE DEMAND FOR FARM OUTPUT FALLS SIGNIFICANTLY DURING DEPRESSION

There is a common mistaken notion about the demand for farm products. Many people believe that "the demand for farm products is virtually the same during depression and prosperity because people must eat, no matter whether business is good or bad." In fact, the amount that consumers will pay for food products, like all others, falls during depression. Most people are willing and able to tighten their belts somewhat when their income drops. People in this country do buy about as many food products in depression as in prosperity, simply because farmers raise as much in one time as in the other. Prices of farm products fall enough to insure that total output is consumed.

It is a well-known fact that farm prices rise substantially during periods of inflation. These price increases are interpreted as an indication of large rises in demand with expanding income. As indicated, the demand for food does vary with changes in national income but not very much. However, this kind of change in demand, combined with an unchanged output of food, gives rise to a substantial price change.

Apparently, therefore, while the sales value of farm products cannot be expanded a great deal beyond some point by even substantial increases in personal income, it can fall markedly if incomes decline. Even if farm prices were "reasonably good" during prosperity, they would probably decline to painfully low levels during depression. In actual experience, farm prices even during prosperity were too low to yield a "decent" income; during depression, the farmer was even worse off.

IV. PARTIAL SUMMARY

Up to this point, we have discussed the function of prices and criteria by which the correctness of price might be determined. The criteria advanced were

1. The price is correct when the desired output is forthcoming.

2. The price is correct when income is distributed between buyers and sellers in the manner we would favor.

3. Prices that are correct put heavy pressure on businessmen to seek out and use the most efficient methods of production.

We then examined the background of the legislation passed to raise farm prices to discover whether these prices were too low according to the three criteria listed. We learned that the main reasons given for extending special assistance to the farmer were

1. Farm prices have fallen relative to industrial prices.

2. Farm prices are determined on markets on which farmers cannot exercise market power, whereas they buy from sellers who are able to exercise this power.

3. The supply and demand conditions in agriculture are unfavorable to farmers.

V. NATURE OF AID GIVEN TO FARMERS

While these three allegations were shown to be valid, it remains to be shown that farm prices were too low. These arguments may indeed justify special help to *poor* farmers. But it is not clear that they justify assistance for all farmers. Moreover, it does not follow that the assistance should take the form of a price increase. Conceivably, farmers would be assisted by lower prices for their output. Or they might be served best by a lowering of the prices they themselves must pay. Then, again, help might be more effective if not given in the form of price change. (We say that the social consequences of markets on which sellers had market power—which is typical for industrial markets—are inferior to those on which they have none. If this market power could be eliminated, industrial prices would presumably decline and the farmer's income would then provide him with a higher level of living.)

It is clear that all arguments in favor of help to the farmer tend to return to the fact that farmers' incomes were very low. Differences in supply and demand conditions in agriculture and industry, and the greater market power exercised by industrial than by agricultural sellers help to explain the low personal incomes in agriculture. These explanations are relevant to the decision whether farmers' incomes should be raised.[15] However, they do not indicate whether the prices obtained by farmers should be increased.

Several general considerations regarding the level of farm incomes can be dealt with summarily, for there is virtually unanimous agreement on these points. First, incomes should not be equal in all occupations. Low incomes can serve the useful function of discouraging people from entering an occupation that is already overcrowded. Similarly, occupations that involve low costs for training and little training time and native skill should pay less than employments requiring expensive and long training and calling for rare skills. Pay differentials between such occupations are necessary to attract talented individuals into the more exacting occupations.

Second, agriculture is not the only employment in which incomes are very low. Other examples include personal services, clerical work, retail selling, and teaching. Any solution applied to one sector presumably should be applied to the others.

Third, to assess returns in an occupation, noneconomic as well as monetary rewards should be taken into account. Those who enter college teaching, for example, are attracted at least in part by the opportunity to spend a substantial part of the year as they wish. Moreover, even though their total hours of work may add up to the equivalent of a forty-hour week, they generally can decide when to put in most of their hours. There may be good reasons for raising teachers' incomes (presumably the test should be whether we get people in teaching whom we want to instruct the young). In deciding whether their incomes are high or low, we should take into account their considerable freedom to spend time as they wish and the congenial character of their work and associations. Similarly, the farmer's life may be considered by many persons preferable to city employment. Perhaps that preference explains why so many people remain on farms when money incomes are much higher in the city, though other reasons may be responsible.

It thus appears that we face directly conflicting objectives when we

---

[15] Not all farmers were poor; however, in giving assistance to farmers, the prosperous were helped equally with the poor. It has been suggested that the political power behind the legislation to help the farmer came principally from prosperous farmers, who justified help to themselves by taking the plight of the poor farmer as the typical case. See K. Boulding, "Economic Analysis and Agricultural Policy," *Canadian Journal of Economics and Political Science,* August, 1947, pp. 436-446.

decide whether farm prices are too high or too low, viewed from the standpoint of personal income. Almost everyone agrees that most farmers' incomes were lower than they should have been, considering the problem solely from an ethical point of view. The farmer's work is physically difficult, occupies many hours a day, involves heavy risks from weather as well as from unfavorable economic conditions, and requires a heavy capital investment. In addition, he requires considerable skill; he must use and partly maintain complex equipment, he must understand a moderate amount about horticulture and the like. One might think he was entitled to at least the income of a highly skilled industrial worker of an independent entrepreneur. In fact, however, his income was—and still is—lower than that of an unskilled worker.

On grounds of economic efficiency—that is, in trying to arrange things so that all productive factors are used where their contribution is at a maximum, the farmer apparently was receiving too high an income in the late twenties. In other words, his income was not low enough to impel him to take employment elsewhere.

A price system relies upon changes in personal incomes to adjust the numbers of productive factors to the need for them in alternative occupations. This function was not performed well in agriculture, and still does not work well. Some movement out of agriculture has occurred over the years. However, it has been slow, and sometimes it has been reversed. Without the low incomes in agriculture, it is reasonable to suppose that it would have been even slower; possibly, the change would have been in the opposite direction.

To make this point somewhat differently, a decline in farm incomes would be expected to lead farmers to accept industrial employment. For this reason, one is tempted to advocate a decline, rather than a rise, in farm prices and incomes to speed the movement out of agriculture. However, the historical record shows that relatively few farmers change occupation even when their incomes are extremely low; contrariwise, when opportunities for high earnings in industry appear, the exodus from agriculture is small. It therefore appears that a decline in farm incomes would probably not achieve the desired effect. While it would represent a pressure in the right direction, its efficacy would be too small to merit the great hardship it would impose upon all persons in agriculture.

It thus appears that one function of the price system must be repaired or supplemented, for agriculture, by some other mechanism for adjusting the supply of productive factors to the economy's need for them.

When we consider the test that a price should lead to the desired output of goods, can we conclude that farm prices were too low in the late twenties? We said earlier that the function of a low price was to reduce output, while high prices encourage an expansion of output. Can we argue that farm prices were too low in the late twenties because an increase in farm output was desired? On the contrary, farm output was, if anything, excessive. That is, it was so great that it could not be sold at a price that would afford a fair return to farmers. Higher prices presumably would encourage farmers to expand output and might possibly discourage some from taking employment in the city—the reverse of what was needed.

The prices of farm products do influence output in one important respect. They guide farmers in their planting. To the extent that farmers can produce many crops, in the light of climate, land fertility, farm equipment, and technical know-how—they are guided by price relations. A rise in public preference for one farm product usually is reflected in higher prices. This rise will encourage farmers to increase the output of that product. Thus it appears that in the 1920's price relations served a useful function in influencing the proportions of farm products, and were partly successful in this function in the early 1930's as well. However, price has not successfully regulated total farm output in a manner that contributes most to economic efficiency. Under an unregulated price system, agriculture tied up excessive productive resources, and it rewarded those engaged in agriculture less than persons in other occupations.

Thus it is clear that something was wrong with the operations of the price system in agriculture. The major defect is found primarily in the immobility of resources from agriculture to industry. Another related difficulty is the continued survival of farm enterprises that use inefficient methods and that cultivate land too poor to justify cultivation. That is to say, prices do not serve all the functions in agriculture that they are expected to perform. We must therefore adopt measures to supplement price changes in order to achieve an efficient agriculture.

Specifically, measures must be devised that will facilitate and expedite a reduction in farm population and that will improve the techniques of cultivation. We need not discuss many possible remedies in detail. It will suffice to explore the lines of approach that would seem more promising solutions than would changes in prices of farm products.

VI. REMEDIES FOR THE FARM PROBLEM

Before other approaches to the farm problem are discussed, the existing program of assistance to agriculture will be described briefly. We will then consider alternatives.

A. The Existing Farm-Assistance Program

The current farm-aid program is built around the parity-price concept. That is, the government undertakes to re-establish prices to farmers that will give individual farm products purchasing power over things that farmers buy (specifically, over commodities, interest on mortgages, real estate taxes, and hired farm labor), equal to what it was in some past (base) period. The components of the parity-price program are the "base period"; the proportion of the base-period relation to be guaranteed (farm products are now guaranteed varying proportions of the base-period relation); the mechanics of calculating parity (which concerns such questions as whether and in what way changes in farmers' costs and sales volume should influence the determination of the parity price); and, finally, measures to restrict output so that physical supply will not be far in excess of what can be sold at the price guaranteed.

When originally adopted, the parity-price program was extremely crude. The years 1909 to 1914 were used as the base, and farmers could calculate the parity price for their products by the following method. They could take the index of prices paid by farmers, calculated on a base of 1909 to 1914, and multiply it by the price of his product in the base period. For example, if the average price of corn during that period was 65 cents, and the index of prices paid by farmers was 200, then the parity price would be $1.30.

Since its adoption in 1933, the parity-price program has been refined somewhat. A more recent base period has been adopted for some products.[16] In addition, not all products are guaranteed the full base-period relation, but are entitled to varying proportions. Moreover, in calculating parity price, account was to be taken of changes in such costs as farm labor, fertilizer, feed, and agricultural equipment.

Expressed in its simplest terms, the existing farm program aims to restore a past relation between each agricultural price and the average of industrial prices. The base period is selected quite arbitrarily. It primarily reflects the balance of political forces. Farm supporters try to get a base period that is as favorable to some farmers as they can push through Congress; nonfarm groups generally favor a period as favorable to nonfarmers as is politically feasible. The period ultimately

---

[16] In 1948 and 1949, Congress set forth a new formula for calculating parity. It represents an odd mixture of the old parity formula based on 1910-1914 relations and the use of an average of prices over the last ten years. The result would be to lower the parity price for nonbasic products (all but corn, cotton, wheat, peanuts, rice, and tobacco). The basic commodities are governed by the old parity formula if it gives a higher result than the new. Use of the new formula was postponed by legislation passed in 1952.

selected—and the proportion of that base period guaranteed—hardly reflects any solid principle of equity.

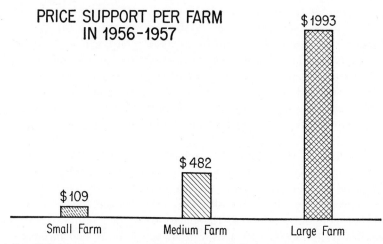

PRICE SUPPORT PER FARM IN 1956-1957

$1993

$482

$109

Small Farm   Medium Farm   Large Farm

Small farms, representing 56 per cent of all farms, receive extremely low price support payments, whereas the large farms, slightly over a quarter of all farms, are paid on the average almost 20 times as much per farm in price supports.

One should not hope to find equity in an assistance program based upon a restoration of past price relations. We have no reason to suppose that any of these were equitable, and even less to suppose that they would be equitable now.[17] If we had acceptable standards of equity, we should not need to apply them to the past, but could directly determine what any farm price should be today. We have seen that the only defensible standard for deciding what figure is fair and desirable is to be derived by recognizing the effects of price upon output, income distribution, methods of production, and pressures to produce efficiently. The parity-price program most emphatically does not make use of such criteria. It is clearly a program based upon political expediency; in the process, the workings of the price system are impaired.

B. Other Approaches to the Farm Problem

As already stressed, the basic cure for the farm problem is to be found in a reduction of resources engaged in agriculture. The decline

---

[17] The way in which the price-support program assists farmers themselves underscores the inequities inherent in this approach. Ostensibly directed at aiding those in greatest difficulties, the price-support program in 1957 allocated price supports which on the average were twenty times as great for large as for small farms. The price support per farm was $109 per small farm, $482 per medium-sized farm, and $1,993 per large farm. See *New York Times*, April 21, 1958, p. 16.

should be of such proportions that those who remain could produce enough to satisfy all demands during periods of prosperity at prices that provide a fair return to the farmer. It would seem that a reduction in farm population of at least 25 per cent is needed to achieve this objective. How can movement off the farms, now very slow, be speeded?

The purchase by the government of farm land and its retirement from use to raise crops would help the farm problem in two ways. First, it would reduce output by curtailing the amount of land under cultivation. Second, it would provide the farmer with resources that would help him finance a move to the city and a search for a job.

To increase the mobility from agriculture, an improvement in rural educational facilities is imperative. Improvement is needed at all levels, up through college. The aim must be to train farm youths so that they can compete successfully with urban youths for jobs in industry. "At present, educational facilities on the farm are much below those in town, particularly in the South."[18] A program of subsidized higher education, perhaps even covering the living costs of college students who are well-qualified, might be required to achieve the goal set; farmers—and especially poor ones—cannot afford the high nontuition costs involved in higher education.

Moreover, special efforts and expenditures must be made to acquaint those living on farms with opportunities for employment in the city. That is, improvement in the employment services rendered in rural communities would doubtless speed the movement of the poorest farmers to the city. To leave the farm to hunt for a job is a most unattractive prospect; but to leave to take a *known* position is likely to be very attractive to very poor farmers and farm youths.

There might be a federal subsidy for industrial plants to be established in the most depressed farming regions. Such measures would make it unnecessary for farmers to move to new locations; however, provisions for removing some land from cultivation would still have to be made.

Such measures attack the farm problem at its root. While they will take considerable time to achieve our objective, they at least move in the right direction. They attack the problem of excessive resources in agriculture directly, whereas higher farm prices would tend to aggravate

---

[18] G. S. Shepherd, *Agricultural Price Policy* (Ames: Iowa State College Press, 1947), p. 428. At bottom, failure of farmers to leave the farms in the desired numbers is due to their strong perference for the way of life on the farm—or perhaps a strong distaste for city life; also, these men would be completely unskilled workers in the cities and would locate jobs with great difficulty, for they would have no "contacts" or special "ins" with employers. Furthermore, even if they got jobs, their incomes would probably be low and insecure, and those with larger families would be compelled to live in the slums. Apart from these discouragements to leaving the farm, the farmer and his family would feel strangely out of place, and like social misfits because they are unfamiliar with "city ways."

the difficulty. Moreover, these measures would not weaken the function of the price system in determining which particular things should be produced.

Considerable improvement in farm technology is required in any long-range agricultural program. It has been shown that the low farm prices of the 1930's did not result in highly efficient methods of farmng. In this respect, the price system failed to realize another of its usual benefits in agriculture. Improved farm methods will call for an expansion of the already extensive work of the Department of Agriculture and the agricultural schools of the various states. Special aid to the farmer, so that he can obtain training, might be desirable.

A solution to the farm problem, as explained earlier, might be sought in the direction of removing land from cultivation. Perhaps the most direct and effective approach is to have the government actually purchase land from farmers and devote it to such uses as reforestation. This approach is costly—largely because farm houses are often involved—and faces great administrative difficulties in fixing fair values. A related approach is represented by the "soil bank" program, enacted in 1956, which pays farmers to stop raising crops on part of their land and to take measures to improve its fertility while it is not under cultivation.[19]

The foregoing measures might well be the best long-run cures for the farm problem, but they clearly would not quickly cure the low farm incomes, which were the basis for the farmer's complaint. Would Congress have been entitled to sit back and wait for the improvement in incomes that would have followed improved educational opportunities for farmers—and better employment guidance—if Congress had adopted the measures proposed? In the early thirties it was the popular view, which the author shares, that the farmer's poverty was so great that special assistance was both a moral obligation and a social necessity. It would have been inhuman to require the farmer to wait until a long-run solution to his problem was found. Some immediate relief was needed. How could the farmer have been helped?

Often the simplest answer is the best. If the objective is to raise the incomes of poor farmers, would not direct grants of money to needy farmers have been the most effective, speedy, and inexpensive method?

---

[19] The Rockefeller Report, a recent study of the United States economy, includes proposals paralleling many of those discussed above. The report's proposals include: (1) the gradual withdrawal of price supports, hand in hand with reductions in surpluses; (2) the continuation and expansion of agricultural research, soil and water conservation, self-financing crop insurance, and farm-credit programs; and (3) a constructive farm-adjustment program which (a) encourages and assists farmers wishing to enter nonfarm occupations (technical and vocational training, counseling, and help in finding employment); (b) fosters industrial development in rural areas; and (c) curtails production through lease or purchase of uneconomic farm lands. For a summary of the Rockefeller Report, see *New York Times*, April 21, 1958, pp. 16-17.

We must recognize that direct relief is complicated to administer—especially in agriculture where the recipients are so widely scattered. Yet a program of direct relief possesses great and obvious advantages over one for raising farm prices. First, it would not dissipate funds by helping farmers who do not need help. As indicated, ". . . a great deal of so-called 'aid to agriculture' is, in fact, a great political bluff engineered by the wealthier farmers who are, of course, the more politically active. They obtain general support for the policy on grounds that farmers are poor, but the assistance goes not specifically to the poor farmers, but to all. . . ." [20] Second, such a program would not attract new people to agriculture; if the payments were low enough and made contingent upon particular obligations consistent with the long-range program, movement out of agriculture would be facilitated. It would be possible to require farmers receiving direct financial assistance to send their children to schools up to an age that would greatly increase their opportunities for obtaining city employment; they could be required to accept employment in the city if suitable opportunity were turned up by the government employment service; they could be required to meet minimum standards of operating efficiency, or to take training in modern farm methods. Third, such a program could be adjusted to vary from depression to prosperity. Greater help should be given during depression, when farmers probably should not be encouraged to move to the city—where unemployment already exists.

There is no need to spell out here a system for directly supplementing the incomes of needy farmers. While such a program confronts real difficulties, these hardly seem insurmountable.

VII. CONCLUSIONS

We seem to arrive at the following conclusion in the end: farm incomes were too low during the late twenties and early thirties, but farm output was too great and too many people were engaged in farming. From every standpoint except the level of farm income, the prices of farm products would be considered too high rather than too low.

Price changes have several effects, as we have seen. We have no way of sealing off the undesirable effects of any price changes. We must take either the entire "package" of effects or none at all. Since the primary object of the farm-assistance program in the early thirties was to raise farm income, price changes were clearly inappropriate. Only where we want all or almost all of the effects of price changes that are in the "package" of effects is a change in price appropriate.

---

[20] Boulding, *loc. cit.*, p. 440.

It is not legitimate to adopt the following line of argument: the price system has worked badly in agriculture; it has distributed income poorly, and has allowed excessive resources to remain engaged in farming; therefore it is necessary for the government to step in and influence prices directly. There can be little argument with the conclusion that the price system has not resulted in efficient agriculture. As a result, we must not rely exclusively upon the free operations of the price system. Moreover, it is far from clear that what we must change is price. Indeed, the failure in agriculture shows that price alone is not an effective instrument for bringing about an effective utilization of agricultural resources. In short, we must turn to other measures to supplement the working of prices in agriculture. It has been suggested that direct-relief grants to needy farmers, contingent upon meeting certain requirements and in conjunction with a long-term program for reducing the number of persons engaged in agriculture, seems most plausible.

It must not be thought that we have discussed the entire farm problem in the United States either in the late twenties and early thirties or at present. We have been primarily interested in whether farm prices were too low. Agriculture involves many other problems that we have skipped over here.

DISCUSSION QUESTIONS

1. By what criteria would you decide whether a price is too high, too low, or just right? Apply those criteria to the price of bread, milk, teachers' services, postage rates.

2. Do you believe farmers are more entitled to preferential legislation than unskilled laborers are? What special claims can they make for special assistance that may not be made by many other groups?

3. Do all, most, or only a few farmers deserve preferential treatment? Is it practical, in your opinion, to separate the deserving from those who are not?

4. What forms of assistance do you believe to be most desirable for the deserving farmers? Direct money grants? Loans? Special training? Assistance in locating in another occupation? Special allowances for their children? Increased economic opportunity to educate themselves and their families? Higher prices for their products?

5. Would you expect the average farmer's income to be relatively stable or unstable? Why? Do you think special measures are warranted to stabilize farm prices—without increasing their average level? Should both the average level and stability of farm prices be increased? Why?

6. Should all groups with unstable and low incomes be aided? Should the price of their output be increased? Take migratory farm workers as an example, and discuss.

7. What demand conditions tend to make farm prices unstable?

8. What conditions of supply account for the relatively low price of farm commodities?

9. Discuss the possible justification for a parity-price-support program. On what basis should parity be selected?

SELECTED READINGS FOR PART 5

Adams, Walter, and Horace M. Gray. *Monopoly in America: The Government as Promoter.* New York: The Macmillan Company, 1955. Pp. xv, 221. Finding that the government is often responsible for the existence of monopoly, the authors point out what ought to be done to make our antitrust policy more meaningful. They show the effects of government policy in various areas to support their conclusions and to sound a clarion call for action.

Backman, Jules. *Price Practices and Price Policies.* New York: The Ronald Press Company, 1953. P. 674. Selected readings covering a wide area.

Bell, Daniel. *Work and Its Discontents.* Boston: The Beacon Press, 1954. Pp. viii, 56. This book is an interesting discussion of problems arising out of the increasing complexity of our economic structure. The whole concept of efficiency is viewed as a cult which is often adhered to with little serious attention to the real costs involved. In analyzing work routines, the author points up the very great loss due to the mechanization and fragmentation of work, and shows how the individual worker becomes a mere atom in a complex organization.

Benedict, Murray R. *Can We Solve the Farm Problem? An Analysis of Federal Aid to Agriculture.* New York: Twentieth Century Fund, 1955. Pp. xix, 601. This book is an extremely interesting history and analysis of the government's aid to agriculture since the Civil War. There is also included a 50-page report of the Twentieth Century Fund's Committee on Agricultural Policy, with suggestions for a revision of the price-support program.

————. *Farm Policies of the United States, 1790-1950.* New York: Twentieth Century Fund, 1953. Pp. xv, 548. A very helpful historical description of agriculture since 1790. Agricultural policies and views on agriculture over the span of the years are detailed.

————, and Oscar C. Stine. *The Agricultural Commodity Programs: Two Decades of Experience.* New York: Twentieth Century Fund, 1956. Pp. xliii, 510. A broad study of the policies and programs of the federal government set up for 11 farm commodities. These programs are evaluated in a very helpful way.

Committee for Economic Development. *Toward a Realistic Farm Program.* New York: The Committee, 1957. P. 54. This is a very useful statement by the Program Committee of the Research and Policy Committee of the CED. Its usefulness is in the clear analysis of the present farm problem, in which a program for action aimed at increasing the farmers' opportunities and reducing the public costs of farm supports is outlined. The program is based on a full study of the various types of government assistance: price supports, soil bank, etc.

Conference on Price Research. *Cost Behavior and Price Policy.* New York: National Bureau of Economic Research, Inc., 1943. Pp. xix, 356. This important study focuses attention on cost-and-price adjustments within individual firms. The findings of the study illustrate several important types of cost behavior and cost-price relations in certain important segments of the economy.

Edwards, Corwin D. *Big Business and the Policy of Competition.* Cleveland: Press of Western Reserve University, 1956. Pp. x, 180. The author deals with the problems involved in assessing the economic impact of "big business" on the economy. In addition, the author makes suggestions regarding the effective implementation of public policy.

Kaplan, A. D. H. *Big Enterprise in a Competitive System.* Washington, D.C.: Brookings Institution, 1954. Pp. xii, 269. An examination of the structure and performance of American big business in terms of the objectives of a competitive system. Attitudes toward bigness and the extent to which big business is competitive are dealt with. The author believes that big business meets the test of competitiveness; that is, it provides increasingly numerous, varied, and significant market alternatives.

Knight, Frank H. *The Ethics of Competition.* New York: Harper & Brothers, 1935. P. 363. This book is a collection of essays representative of the work of Professor Knight, an outstanding American economist at the University of Chicago. The essays cover a wide range, which includes problems of value, cost, price, marginal-utility theory, motivation in economic problems, etc. They reflect the systematic views of an outstanding proponent of the free-enterprise system.

Lilienthal, David E. *Big Business: A New Era.* New York: Harper & Brothers, 1953. P. 209. In this optimistic survey of the role played by big business in the American economy the author relates big business to a "new competition." This new competition, which is one between alternative products, involves reliance on research, industrial integration, increasingly wider geographical areas of competition, internal competition between different departments, and advertising. The positive role of big business in furthering economic progress and democracy is stressed.

Mason, Edward S. *Economic Concentration and the Monopoly Problem.* Cambridge, Mass.: Harvard University Press, 1957. Pp. xviii, 411. A review of the problems of monopoly and the large firm which covers the last fifteen or twenty years. Deals with the large firm and the structure of industrial markets, with wage problems, raw materials, security, and economic growth, and with antitrust policy.

National Industrial Conference Board. *Economic Concentration Measures: Uses and Abuses.* A Session of the 41st Annual Meeting of the Conference Board, New York City, May, 1957. Studies in Business Economics Number 57. New York: NICB, 1957. P. 57. Short papers by such contributors as M. A. Adelman, J. W. Markham, and G. R. Detlefsen on the problem of measurement.

Schickele, Rainer. *Agricultural Policy: Farm Programs and National Welfare.* New York: McGraw-Hill Book Company, Inc., 1954. Pp. x, 453. Agricultural problems are examined in relation to institutions of the United States.

The author uses both economic and sociological tools of analysis for an area where much heated policy making occurs publicly.

Stigler, George. *Five Lectures on Economic Problems*. New York: The Macmillan Company, 1950. P. 65. These lectures, delivered at the London School of Economics, deal with certain significant economic problems confronting present-day economists: income inequality, monopolistic competition, classical economic theory, mathematical method in economics, and the structure of competition in the United States. The author, an outstanding academic economist, brings his authority to bear on each problem.

————. *The Theory of Price*. New York: The Macmillan Company, 1946. Pp. vii, 340. This text on the principles of price analysis and the economics of the firm presents clearly the major problems of this area. The author makes use of numerous geometric aids in presenting the various aspects of the basic problems of the allocation of production factors.

United States. *Report of the Attorney General's National Committee to Study the Antitrust Laws*. Washington, D.C.: Government Printing Office, 1955. Pp. xiii, 393. This is an extremely valuable report analyzing the antitrust laws. It deals with the interpretations of the laws, the actual administration and enforcement of the laws, and statutory exceptions to the laws. Finally, the committee recommends changes in line with the laws' purposes.

United States Department of Agriculture. *The Soil Bank Program: How It Operates; How It Will Help Farmers*. Washington, D.C.: Government Printing Office, 1956. P. 18. This is a very useful, simple explanation of the aims and functions of the Soil Bank program. It helps to put in perspective a major project of the federal government's farm program.

Wilcox, Clair. *Public Policies toward Business*. Chicago: Richard D. Irwin, Inc., 1955. Pp. xix, 898. This is a comprehensive textbook which surveys the government's policy on competition, protection of the investor and consumer, price controls and supports, etc. It is a useful source of information on the structure of business as well as on the problems of policy in various areas of the economy.

Yamey, B. S. *The Economics of Resale Price Maintenance*. London: Pitman Publishing Corporation, 1954. P. 182. One of the very few comprehensive treatments of resale-price maintenance. It deals with the history, significance, and impacts for certain areas of England and also discusses government policy.

Part

6 Must the Economy of the United States Suffer Ups and Downs?

19 Causes and Consequences of Economic Instability

Between 1941 and 1958, the American economy maintained a very high level of activity on the whole. Total output increased substantially during this period, and a condition of approximately full employment prevailed for the most part. Even this period of unparalleled prosperity was highly unstable, however. Three recessions occurred during this seventeen-year period, one of which is just ending now; the two completed post-war recessions, which were minor, were followed immediately by surges to new peak levels of activity. In addition to the three recessions, the economy also experienced virtually uninterrupted inflation between 1941 and 1958. Apart from the recessions and inflationary periods alluded to, the nation also fought a major war for four years, a minor one in Korea, and was engaged most of the time in a cold war. Thus, even this period of unparalleled prosperity was one of substantial economic instability.

From the long-run point of view, the major worry of persons responsible for national economic policy is the threat of further inflation. Indeed, the President and his main advisers were strongly deterred from taking actions to remedy the recession starting in 1957 by the fear that it would intensify the rise in prices which, paradoxically, characterized the recession. However, there are many specialists who are fearful that the economy will be afflicted again by the horrors of economic depression. Certainly, the recession that started in 1957 reawakened such fears, and undermined the confidence of many who had held the opinion that the United States would never again experience a serious business decline.

It is supremely important that the highest national officials reach a correct judgment on the likelihood that our economy will maintain continually a very high level of employment. If the danger of depression is not past, vital and costly safeguards must be provided. Also, the generation reaching adulthood without personal experience with depression should be informed of a possible danger that could suddenly blast their lives out of their planned course.

Unfortunately, there is no reliable method of assessing the chances that there will be another depression. Certainly, we should try, among other things, to judge the probabilities by "examining the record," but if we are to judge from the record alone, it is not clear how much recent history belongs there for this purpose. If we turn back to 1929, we find an extremely severe depression, which moderated somewhat in 1935 and then became deeper again in 1937. (The 1937 decline was the sharpest on record, and most observers attribute its termination to the heavy purchases by our government and others in anticipation of military hostilities.) If we want to go deeper into history to assess the likelihood that depression will recur, we might turn back to, for instance, the late nineteenth century. We should find that the United States, United Kingdom, and other developed economies suffered marked ups and downs in output and employment at that time.

Presumably, those who think our economy is depression-proof believe that similar debacles cannot recur. They reach this conclusion because of changes that have taken place either in the nature of the economy or in the circumstances prevailing in the world at large. At best, one must consider their viewpoint controversial. There has been very little time in which to test the effect of past economic changes; moreover, some recent and possible future developments could offset favorable past changes that may have had a stabilizing effect. Then again, altogether new sources of economic instability may be arising of which no one is yet aware.

Conditions since 1941 have been decidedly conducive to a high and stable level of business activity. These conditions, or at least many of them, are clearly temporary. For example, the early part of this period was one of relatively heavy exports as nations devastated during World War II made large purchases from the United States; the cold war compelled our government to make very heavy outlays for armaments, which were stimulants to business; private industry took advantage of the large number of technological developments that had accumulated during the war but that could not then be put to use because of wartime material shortages; and heavy gifts to foreign countries raised the level of this country's foreign sales. Such conditions, or the equivalent, will not prevail indefinitely. Consequently, only a highly optimistic person, or an extremely wishful thinker, can read the record and find complete reassurance that major depressions are over for good.

Even as we must erect safeguards against depression, we live under the threat of inflation; indeed, it is a reality that has even survived a period of substantial recession. Since 1941, there have been very few years of price stability; more important, perhaps, all the movement seems to be in one direction. Prior to World War II, prices were more unstable, if anything, than they have been since. However, price movements were roughly as great in the downward as in the upward direction, if we consider periods as long as a decade or more. Persistent inflation, thus, is an active and growing concern.

It is difficult to examine the recent record of our economy and conclude confidently that it has achieved a state of perpetual prosperity and price stability. The dangers of depression and inflation are too great to ignore. But to take cognizance of dangers and to take precautionary measures must not be confused with a forecast that they will occur. Rather, it represents a policy of prudence and a humility about *anyone's* ability to forecast accurately and consistently what will happen to general business conditions.

The purpose of this section is to explain why ups and downs of business occur; to discuss their economic, political, social, and ethical implications; and, finally, to examine the potential remedies for depressions and inflations that have been advanced. It should be obvious that these problems are extremely complex as well as vital. Moreover, in order to come to grips with them, it will be necessary to digress at several points to acquaint ourselves with matters that bear on these problems. In particular, it will be necessary to examine the money and banking system to understand how it may contribute to economic instability and how it may be utilized to stabilize business activity.

I.   EFFECTS OF ECONOMIC INSTABILITY

Certainly up to World War II, the ups and downs of business caused greater personal suffering than did any other feature of the United States economy. There are other weaknesses of our economic system, such as monopoly and poverty, which are not trifling. However, depressons and inflations were far more serious.

It has already been shown that depressions have been the major cause of both national and personal poverty in the United States. When general business was prosperous, the economy produced considerably more than was needed to provide a minimum-comfort standard of living for the entire population. However, in deep depression, total output was not sufficient to provide this living standard for the population, even if income had been equally divided. In addition, severe depressions of the past caused many millions of families to lose their sources of income and forced them to depend upon charity, personal savings, or meager unemployment-insurance benefits—all of which are short-lived.

Perhaps more devastating, the ups and downs of business pose a continual threat both to those who are prosperous and to everyone else, even during periods of prosperity. This threat prevents most people from enjoying to the utmost what they do have. Economic insecurity has enormous social, psychological, and economic costs.

In the past, prolonged depressions and rapid inflations have been characterized by rapid and extreme political change. The so-called "New Deal" (during the administration of Franklin D. Roosevelt, 1933-1945) represented a break with the traditional economic philosophy of this country but captured public support during a deep depression. Hitler was a product of both a depression and an inflation. If an extreme left-wing or right-wing totalitarian philosophy were to receive strong popular support in the United States, it almost certainly would take place during a period of either acute depression or wild inflation. During such periods, many persons have "nothing to lose"—or so they think—and are willing to give extreme measures a trial. Some astute political observers believe that the nation probably would undergo an extreme change in political philosophy, and political form, if we were again to undergo a depression as severe as the one that began in 1929.

It is possible to calculate roughly the *economic* costs of severe depressions. *This cost takes the form of unproduced goods and services.* To calculate the costs of the depression that started in 1929, for example, we must estimate the output that would have been produced if business had been prosperous, and compare it with what was actually produced. For the years 1930 to 1939, the output lost was roughly $389 *billion* in 1946 prices.[1] Inasmuch as prices in 1958 were approximately 45 per cent higher than in 1946, one may put the loss in current dollars at closer to $864 billion.

The dollar cost of even minor recessions is very substantial. For example, during a later dip which started near the middle of 1953 and lasted until about the middle of 1954 (roughly twelve months), industrial production fell 10 per cent from the high point to the point of the greatest decline. Roughly speaking, we could conclude that the average loss of industrial production during this period was half of this amount —plus the amount that industrial production would have increased in the absence of the dip. Let us put the loss at 6 per cent. In the sphere of industrial production alone, then—which accounted for about one third of total national output in recent years, or about $100 billion annually during the period 1953-1955—the loss of output could hardly have been less than $6 billion.[2] Transportation, which is tied directly to the output of goods, also fell, as did residential construction. Although this estimate is very rough, the decline in output due to the minor recession be-

---

[1] Theodore Morgan, *Introduction to Economics* (New York: Prentice-Hall, Inc., 1950), pp. 509-510.

[2] U.S. Department of Commerce, *Survey of Current Business*, February, 1956, p. 13.

tween 1953 and 1954 was probably in the vicinity of $10-12 billion—a very substantial amount when compared with, say, normal expenditures of government for nonmilitary purposes. The recession which started in 1957 and apparently reached its bottom in the spring of 1958, was more severe than the 1953-1954 downswing, and its cost in lost output was substantially higher.

WHAT WAS AND MIGHT HAVE BEEN PRODUCED

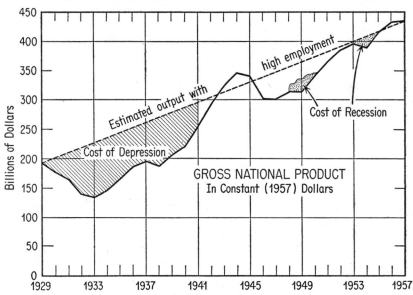

The dotted line indicates the output that could have been produced during the thirties if unemployment had been no greater than it was in 1929 and 1952. The shaded area measures roughly the "real" cost of the great depression, and of the recessions of 1949-1950 and 1953-1954. In the immediate postwar period the decline in output was the result of adjustment to peacetime levels with reduction in overtime; therefore the seeming "cost" of the readjustment is not the same as the cost of depression and recession.

Nothing is inevitable but death. (Cultivation of tax avoidance having developed into a high art, taxes are not inevitable.) Past instability is not full proof that depressions and inflations will recur. Important changes have been made in the economy since the last major depression. Our experience, however, makes it clearly imprudent to assume, merely because we know what profound suffering depressions and inflations cause, that they will never reappear. Major depressions *may* prove to be things of the past, but we'll know only on hindsight. Looking ahead, as we must, we are forced to acknowledge the danger of a major depression—and the converse danger of inflation—and take adequate measures to prevent their recurrence. The principle of insurance is well accepted in this country. It certainly has clear application to the hazards of depression and inflation.

It might be argued that we do not know how to prevent depressions; if so, we can no more criticize the government for failing to guarantee that major depressions will not recur than we can fairly criticize the medical profession for failing to prevent death. It will be demonstrated that this defense is not altogether convincing, for measures to combat major depressions have been advanced that have a reasonable prospect of success.

Inflations[3] have caused far less suffering than have depressions in the United States. Nevertheless, millions of families were seriously injured by the inflation precipitated by World War II. Between 1940 and 1950 the price of consumers' goods rose an average of 75 per cent. As a result, by 1950, savings made prior to 1940 had lost almost half of their 1940 value. The loss to individuals through depreciation in the value of savings amounted to many tens of billions of dollars.

The prospect of the immediate future—indeed, some economists expect it to become a perpetual problem—is for further inflation. Rapid mobilization of the nation on a large scale at a time when the economy is already almost fully employed could easily induce a rapid and large price rise that would lower substantially the real value of savings and of fixed incomes. A substantial rise in prices would worsen the economic position of literally millions of American families.

Inflation sometimes has resulted in drastic political change, because groups injured by inflation have taken political action to restore their economic position. These groups were primarily persons of property, and usually in the upper-middle and wealthy classes. Included among those injured by inflation also are persons of very low income, particularly aged persons, widows, disabled persons living on insurance benefits, and government employees. Combined, these groups represent a large number of voters, and also include persons who exert considerable influence; they could therefore easily alter the balance of political power in the country.

Those whose incomes are relatively fixed in amount have an obvious economic interest in stable or declining price levels. They therefore tend to favor a labor movement that is too weak to win wage increases, because increases in wages ordinarily are followed by price increases. (It should be noted that inflations also usually worsen the economic condition of workers, for wages ordinarily do not keep pace with consumers' prices. However, efforts by workers to obtain wage increases commensurate with price rises tend to extend inflations. Thus inflations tend to acti-

---

[3] Inflation is defined in a variety of ways. The term will be used here to designate rapidly rising prices, specifically, at a rate of over 5 per cent annually.

vate the antilabor political forces. Indeed, some qualified students of German and Italian history conclude that the fascist governments of those countries drew their numerical support primarily from the classes that had been nearly wiped out during the inflation following World War I.)

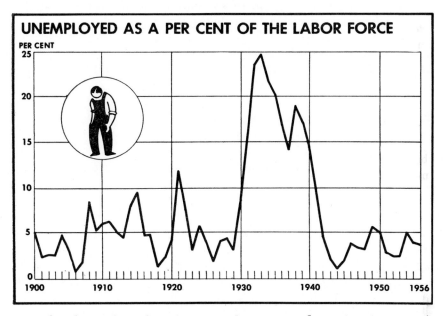

UNEMPLOYED AS A PER CENT OF THE LABOR FORCE

This chart reflects the influence of the recurrent fluctuations in economic history known as business cycles. On the economic side, depressions have meant the waste of resources that could have been used to produce goods for current consumption and for investment to make possible further growth. On the human side, they have meant demoralization for those who could not find jobs. Deep depressions are one of the hazards we must avoid if we are to provide conditions conducive to healthy economic growth in the future. Even in prosperous years, some people are temporarily out of work because they are changing jobs or just entering the labor force, or because of readjustments in individual businesses.

SOURCE: *Economic Growth in the United States: Its Past and Future* (New York: Committee for Economic Development, February, 1958), p. 35.

Little is done about inflation usually, although proved remedies do exist. Groups that profit during inflation (the incomes of some rise more than the price level) regard inflation as "too good to stop." In the political conflict between those who want to prevent further inflation and those who want it to continue unchecked, the latter almost invariably win.

Experts do not agree on the causes of depression and inflation, although there are many respected theories about the business cycle. Some persons conclude that no cures for depression are known. Many others think that since there may be dozens of possible causes for depression we must wait until we know the cause of each depression before we can apply a remedy. One would suppose that the medicine must vary with each occurrence of the disease.

Very fortunately, it appears that *no matter what the cause of business ups and downs, the remedies are much the same.*

II. CAUSES OF UPS AND DOWNS IN BUSINESS

If the individual theories of business cycles are closely examined, they boil down to the same general conclusion: that *general business conditions change whenever the total volume of spending changes substantially.* Put another way, if the total amount of spending were to remain forever the same, general business conditions would be highly stable. Let us pause for a moment to see why this should be so.

First, if a given amount of money were spent in two successive months—no matter what goods it was spent for—the total quantity of goods purchased would be roughly the same.[4] It is true that different numbers of workers are employed to make a dollar's worth of different products. However, these differences are not so great as one would suppose when the labor requirements involved in extracting raw materials, building, and servicing plant and equipment are reckoned in. (For the most part, a dollar spent by a consumer calls for a similar amount of employment, no matter what products he buys.) While this generalization may not hold for every single product, it almost certainly applies to an average of a large number of products. Accordingly, if a given amount of money were spent in two successive months, the goods purchased would require roughly equal amounts of labor.

Secondly, if an equal amount of money were spent in two successive months, then the amount of *income received* would remain unchanged. Money spent does not disappear; it ultimately gets into the hands of someone, and becomes his personal income. (Here, again, there are minor exceptions, such as money used to retire bank debt, but we can well afford to ignore these at this stage.) Consequently, when the amount of money spent remains the same, the amount of personal income will be virtually unchanged; and, in turn. the ability of individuals to spend money will also remain unaffected. Barring unusual developments, their expenditures would continue at the same level.

Conversely, a decline in total employment or production can almost certainly be traced to a decline in the amount of money spent. If expendi-

---

[4] We are assuming that prices are the same in both months. Especially if expenditure does not change, as we suppose here, constancy of prices is to be expected.

tures fall, the amount of goods that would be taken by buyers would decline. This smaller quantity of goods could be produced with fewer workers, so that businessmen presumably would discharge some workers, or at least give them less work. The decline in spending would ultimately reduce the incomes of workers and result in a further decline in expenditures.

Purchases and sales of goods that end up as inventories in the hands of businessmen can upset these relations. Increases in inventories, which may be considered production for the future, tend, as a rule, to depress future output. Conversely, reductions in inventories tend to raise the need for future output.

It might be protested that a decline in spending need not reduce the amount of goods sold. If the prices of goods and labor were reduced in proportion, the same quantity of goods might be purchased. (We have met this point before, when we considered the effect of monopoly on total employment.) There are several answers to this argument. First, and really all other arguments are superfluous, prices do not *in fact* change in direct proportion to spending. A large majority of industrial prices are slow to change, so that the amount of goods purchased actually does vary more or less directly with spending, especially immediately after expenditure changes. Similarly, wage rates and salaries do not respond directly to changes in spending. Indeed, *rates* of pay to labor show great "downward rigidity"—that is, they move up with fair alacrity, but only rarely decline. Prices and wage rates are primarily passive factors; they do not, in themselves, ordinarily initiate upswings or downswings in business. Instead, they change in response to variations in expenditure. Generally, they move in the same direction as spending, but with a lag.

The argument that output need not vary with spending because prices and wages will adjust and offset the drop in spending can be assailed on purely theoretical grounds. Only one of several basic fallacies will be cited. Consider again a decline in spending for illustrative purposes; would a decline in commodity prices that was just proportional to the decline in spending necessarily leave the quantity of goods purchased unaffected? Is it not likely that the change in prices would *itself* alter the amount of money spent? Specifically, would not many consumers and businessmen, facing declining prices, postpone their purchases in the hope of being able to buy after prices fell even more? Buyers usually hasten purchases when prices are rising—in the apparent expectation that they will rise further—and delay them when prices decline, presumably because buyers take a decline in price as an omen of further reduction. Accordingly, a drop in spending immediately followed by a decline in price might generate a further decline in spending, and a greater drop in purchases as buyers awaited further reductions in price. Consequently, even if prices fell promptly with and in proportion to total expenditures, the quantity of goods purchased might vary greatly. A greater drop in purchases than the initial decline in spending is not unlikely. The accompanying chart illustrates how variations in spending, prices, and inventories affect employment and output.

EXPENDITURE DIVIDED BY AVERAGE PRICE DETERMINES EMPLOYMENT

GRAPHICS INSTITUTE, N. Y. C.

Although expenditure changes are the most important and ordinarily the initiating cause of variations in employment, they need not affect employment directly and immediately. Other factors, in particular the level of prices and of inventories, determine the effect of a change in expenditure on employment.

Beginning with the condition set forth at the starting point, this chart works through a few examples to show the effects of changes in expenditure, average price, and inventories held. The most realistic examples are the last two, where simultaneous changes in two factors are depicted.

The causes of depressions and inflations will not be probed further at this point. It has already been demonstrated that the pivotal role in economic fluctuations is played by the volume of spending and the prices of goods. Before we can hope to understand business ups and downs, and appraise methods of eliminating them, it will be necessary to study the money and banking system, to analyze the factors determining the level of spending, and to examine the characteristic behavior of prices. To these matters we now turn.

DISCUSSION QUESTIONS

1. How would you measure the economic costs of depression? By what measures would you calculate the damage done by inflation?

2. What political threats are posed by economic instability? Trace step by

step how a major depression might bring about a fundamental change in our economic and political system.

3. Do you believe that individuals who become unemployed during depression are personally responsible for their situation? Whom would you blame? Explain.

4. Explain step by step how a drop in spending by consumers, not compensated for by increased spending by others, would lead to a drop in employment and production. Make explicit the major assumption on which your conclusion rests.

5. Explain how a rise in spending tends to increase employment and output. Under what circumstances would a rise in spending not have that effect?

6. Do you believe that the United States will ever again suffer a major depression like the one that started in 1929? Have you heard any of your family or relatives express fear of a major depression? Do you fear a major inflation? Which threat do you consider the gravest for the next ten years? Why?

20 The Money and Banking System and the Level of Spending

I. INTRODUCTORY

The expenditures that influence the level of business activity are money expenditures. The way individuals spend their time, including activities around the house or on the farm producing things for their own use, has little impact on what others do. But what individuals do with their money income does affect others, because everyone obtains his money income from the money spent by other persons. *An individual's failure to spend money therefore will reduce someone else's income.*

Money plays so dramatic a role in every individual's life, that it is difficult to recognize money for what it is. It is regarded as the root of all evil, or the path to happiness. Actually, the major economic function performed by money is quite mundane; it merely facilitates the exchange of goods. It is essentially a tool used for convenience, serving an important subsidiary function of facilitating the holding of savings.

Tools used for convenience do not seem important until they break down. Few persons, for example, recognize the extent to which our society depends upon the uniform measurement of time. A general failure of timepieces, however, would almost certainly result in near chaos until a substitute could be found. Money, likewise, underlies almost all economic life. When it operates well, little attention is paid to the role it plays. It does not alter the essence of business but only simplifies its mechanics. When money does not perform in its desired manner, it can shake the very foundation of all modern economies. Since breakdowns in the money system are becoming increasingly rare, money can be taken more and more for granted.

II. WHAT IS MONEY?

Money serves its vital functions because of one property alone: practically everyone considers money valuable. Everyone therefore is willing to trade the things he values for money. Put in reverse, money is anything that practically everyone considers valuable and will accept in exchange. Money makes willing traders out of the entire nation and offers a people the opportunity to achieve the enormous gains obtainable from specialization and division of labor.[1]

It is not simple to devise something that *everyone* will consider valuable. Try to imagine something other than money that is valuable to everyone.

How does something come to be universally regarded as valuable? Paradoxically, money is considered valuable by everyone, because everyone considers money valuable. That is, a person knows that everyone else is willing to give up valuable things in exchange for it. *Money has value because all people will give up material things they value in exchange for it.* This property of money is ordinarily termed its "general acceptability." (Of course, all persons do not value money equally, and will not give up equal amounts of it for the same product; also different persons will value their goods and services differently and will not always accept the same amount of money for identical products.)

III. HOW MUCH IS MONEY WORTH?

Like anything else, the value of money is judged by what one can get for it. We assess the value of houses and jewelry and all other things by the amount of money we can get for them. Similarly, the value of money is to be measured by the things we can obtain for it.

When some people think of what they can get for the dollar bills they have in their possession, they think of the metallic reserves, or "backing" behind the money. That is, they assume that they could get a certain quantity of silver (almost everyone not directly attached to the Treasury and the mint has long forgotten the exact amount). And, it is true, they could obtain from the Treasury a silver dollar for each silver certificate. But the value of the silver certificate is greater than the value of the silver content of the silver dollar; it is almost equal to the silver content of two silver dollars. Therefore, if a person wants silver rather than paper money he would be wise to *buy* silver instead of redeeming his silver

---

[1] A detailed analysis of these gains will be postponed until we discuss international economic relations.

certificates. Clearly, the metallic reserve or backing behind the silver certificate is not the determining factor in the buying power of the silver certificate. We must not confuse the silver dollar as a lawful coin of the country and the silver content of the dollar. By government fiat and custom the silver dollar and the silver certificate have equal purchasing power and are on a par with other forms of currency.

The unimportance of money's backing in determining its value is made all the more clear by the fact that if one were to take a $20 bill to the Treasury or to a bank and try to get its backing, he would be able to get only other paper bills. While it is true that the Treasury holds huge stocks of gold, and that this gold is technically considered backing for Federal Reserve notes (the most important type of paper money), individuals cannot obtain the gold. Despite the fact that a person can get silver for a paper dollar, no one would prefer it to a $20 bill which has not metallic backing.[2]

Thus the value of money clearly is not disclosed by what is *back* of it. Its value depends rather upon what people will put up in *front* of it. *Money is worth the amount of goods and services that will be given in exchange for it, not by what various monetary authorities put behind it.* The pack of bills in Country C, in the chart opposite, is clearly worth more than those of Country A, which have more backing.

If the value of money depends upon what a person can get for it, its value must be expressed in terms of goods and services. Since money can be exchanged for all kinds of goods—all goods have a price in terms of money—the value of money can be expressed in terms of every single product or service. For example, a dollar can be said to equal one pound of porterhouse steak, one haircut, the cleaning of one man's suit, or 10 pairs of shoelaces. To express the value of money in terms of every single product would be enormously cumbersome; moreover, it would be confusing. If measured in terms of one product, the value of money may have risen from one month to another—that is, you may be able to get more of that good for your money than in the preceding month. Measured in terms of another product, the value of money may have declined —that is, you may get less of that product for your money than before.

---

[2] It should, however, be observed that the backing for money will continue to have importance so long as many people believe the value of their money depends upon it. In times of crisis particularly, the backing of money largely determines the value it possesses, and it takes on more and more the characteristics of a commodity rather than money. Backing for money serves an important function, however, even during periods other than crisis. By tying paper money to some backing, persons responsible for determining the supply of money are prevented from issuing paper money at will. The requirement that backing must be found for all paper money discourages governments from extravagances they might practice if they could print paper money at will to pay for them. However, governments frequently have ignored or changed these laws.

For convenience, the value of money is almost always measured in terms of many commodities and is taken to vary with the amount of a selected group of products that it can purchase. More specifically, *the value of money may be said to vary inversely with the prices of a broad group of products.* (That is, as these prices rise, the value of money declines, and vice versa.) The higher the total price of a *representative* group of products, the less a person can obtain for his money *on the average;* the less he can get for his money, the less his money is worth.

GRAPHICS INSTITUTE, N. Y. C.

The value of money depends upon what can be purchased with it in the market place, rather than on what the monetary authorities hold as backing. In comparing the value of different currencies, one will sometimes find that currency with small bullion backing will buy more than an amount of another currency with greater backing in bullion.

We have thus far seen that money is a tool used for convenience that ties together individuals' economic fortunes. While its function is simply one of convenience and expediency in effecting exchanges and in storing goods for the future, the entire economy is adapted to its use. When it ceases to be a neutral tool for the convenient conduct of business, it is able to undermine the operation of the entire economy.

Money facilitates exchange because everyone will accept it in exchange for something he values. In turn, this general acceptability depends upon the very fact that it is generally acceptable to others. Only to an insignificant extent is the general acceptability of money related to its backing; indeed, the backing frequently is less valuable than the money itself. The determinants of money's value remain to be explained. Thus far we have seen only that the value of money is to be *measured* (inversely) by the prices of a broad representative group of products. Let us now attempt to explain what determines the value of money—that is, what determines the level of prices.

IV. DETERMINANTS OF THE VALUE OF MONEY

The value of money, like everything else, is determined by its *relative supply*. The term "relative" means that the size of supply is to be reckoned by a comparison with the demand for it. But this notion does not help us much, because it is quite difficult to measure the demand for money. Like most other products, it is so desirable that people would be delighted to have a huge quantity of it if they could get it free and without effort. Clearly, however, if people could have as much money as they wish, no one would be willing to give up *scarce* things of value in exchange for it. Why give up things that are scarce for things the quantity of which is unlimited?

Money is demanded for two main reasons: to facilitate the exchange of goods and services, and to hold as a store of purchasing power for future use or as a cushion against future contingencies. The demand for money holdings to make payments in the future—whether these payments are planned or unforeseen—probably varies quite closely with the volume of goods and services offered for sale. That is, as a rule, a person tends to hold his larger sums of money (1) to meet his *known* need for cash to make purchases before he receives additional income and (2) against *unforeseen* needs as he becomes adjusted to a higher level of living. Thus a person whose ordinary household expenses have risen from, say, $50 per week to $75 will require, roughly, a proportional increase in his pocket money. Accordingly, the demand for money varies more or less directly with the output of things offered for sale. As such, it typically is a passive factor that responds to developments in other spheres of the economy rather than operates as an independent and active source of economic change.

The value of money is determined primarily by its supply and the frequency with which the supply is put to use. Stated in words that are given more precise definition in the following pages, the value of money is determined primarily by variations in the supply and "velocity" of money. These factors exert their effect on the value of money, i.e., the price level, because they reflect changes in expenditure. When persons collectively purchase more goods, they make larger money payments; an increase in money payments requires either an increase in money supply that is spent with the former frequency, or a more frequent spending of the former money supply, or some increase in money supply and in the frequency with which it is spent. Just as the velocity of money rises as the population increases its purchases, it declines as people decide to reduce their spending and hold (some say "hoard") larger sums of money. Thus we see that the frequency with which money is spent is closely associated with expenditures—the demand for goods and services. Much more will be said in the following pages about why the supply and velocity of money change, and what the results of those changes are.

A. Varieties of Money

There are three major types of money: coin (hard money); currency (paper money), and bank deposits (against which one draws by check). By far the largest of these is bank deposits. To explain the supply of money it is necessary to account for the quantity of each type separately. (See Table 1.)

B. How the Quantity of Money Is Determined

1. THE SUPPLY OF COINS

The first two types of money, which together account for less than 25 per cent of all money, are issued in this country by two agencies: the Treasury and the Federal Reserve System. To expedite purchases of inexpensive things, and to permit the making of change (for slot machines and poker games, as well as for the purchase of newspapers and stamps), the Treasury purchases the required amount of metal to make up the coins that are needed. The number of coins made available is related, as closely as possible, to the apparent need for them. (With the reduced need for nickels—for subway fares, for telephone calls at public booths, and for candy confections—during the inflationary period following World War II, the number of nickels in circulation declined and the number of dimes increased.)

2. THE SUPPLY OF CURRENCY

The supply of paper money in circulation is also adjusted to the typical methods by which people make payments. As individuals request their banks to make change, or to pay out withdrawals in particular denominations, the quantity of bills of different denominations is altered by the Treasury and the Federal Reserve Banks. In both cases the supplies of currency and coin are adjusted by the monetary authorities for the convenience of the public. The mechanics by which the supply is adjusted are simple enough. If people as a whole want to hold more cash, the Treasury increases the supply of bills by purchasing the necessary types of metal for coins—or as backing for silver certificates. In making these purchases the Treasury can make payment with paper money and thereby directly increase the supply of paper money available. For example, it can buy $1 million in silver to serve as backing for silver certificates (worth about $1.25 million) by paying for them with silver certificates. The silver acquired would serve as backing for the newly issued certificates, and the "folding money" used to pay for it would increase the amount in circulation. Those who sold the silver would spend some— and it would ultimately "get around."

The method by which the supply of paper currency of large denominations is increased is more complicated but similar in principle. The laws of the land have been carefully drawn to make it simple to adjust the supply of paper money to the "needs" of the public for it. (Of course, by "need" for money, we do not mean the cost of living of individuals, but the amount of cash they hold, *given their current income.*)

**Table 1. Coin and Currency in Circulation, by Type:
1931 and 1958**

Type of Money	Quantity (millions)	
	June 30, 1931	June 30, 1958
Gold coin	$ 363	$ —
Gold certificates	997	32
Silver dollars	34	268
Silver certificates	377	2,200
Treasury notes of 1890	1	1
Subsidiary silver	273	1,346
Minor coin	117	487
United States notes	299	317
Federal reserve notes	1,708	26,342
Federal reserve bank notes	3	120
National bank notes	648	59
Total	$4,822	$29,026

SOURCES: *Treasury Bulletin,* August, 1958, p. 59; U.S. Department of Commerce, Bureau of the Census. *Statistical Abstract of the United States, 1949* (Washington, D.C.: Government Printing Office, 1949), p. 423.

3. THE SUPPLY OF BANK DEPOSITS

The most important component of the supply of money is bank deposits, which account for about 79 per cent of the total (see Table 2). The bank-deposit component of money is both the largest and the most variable; therefore it has an important influence on the level of economic activity. For a full understanding of the role the money supply plays in economic activity we must know what bank deposits are and how they expand and contract in volume.

**Table 2. Relative Importance of Currency and Demand
Deposits, Selected Years 1914-1958**

(In millions)

Mid-year	Demand deposits	Currency outside banks	Total quantity of money
1914	$ 10,082	$ 1,533	$ 11,615
1925	21,376	3,573	24,949
1929	22,540	3,639	26,179
1933	14,411	4,761	19,172
1937	25,198	5,489	30,687
1940	31,962	6,699	38,661
1946	79,476	26,561	106,037
1947	82,186	26,299	108,485
1948	82,697	25,638	108,335
1949	81,877	25,266	107,143
1950	85,040	25,185	110,225
1951	88,960	25,776	114,736
1952	94,754	26,474	121,228
1953	96,898	27,369	124,267
1954	98,132	27,093	125,225
1955	103,234	27,375	130,609
1956	104,744	28,284	133,028
1957	105,600	27,800	133,400
1958	105,700	27,800	134,400

SOURCES: *Banking and Monetary Statistics* (Washington, D.C.: Board of Governors of the Federal Reserve System, 1943), pp. 34-35. *Federal Reserve Bulletin*, December, 1948, p. 1489; December, 1949, p. 1466; December, 1951, p. 1544; August, 1953, p. 856; August, 1955, p. 896; December, 1956, p. 1329; July, 1957, p. 784; and August, 1958, p. 944.

The bank-deposit portion of the money supply differs from cash and coin in several respects. First, the government exerts less control over the supply of this type of money than over the currency supply. Second, the basis on which the supply of bank deposits is adjusted is not "convenience" alone but profitability to private bankers as well.[3]

Not all bank deposits are counted as part of the money supply. Only "demand" deposits—that is, deposits against which checks can be drawn —are included, because only those deposits are used routinely to make payments. These demand deposits are also known as "checking accounts," and are held only in *commercial* banks.[4] Since more than 90 per

---

[3] Note at the outset that there are many types of banks, and each type performs a variety of functions. This discussion will not give a complete picture of the entire banking "system." It aims instead to explain how the supply of commercial bank deposits is determined.

[4] Deposits by the U.S. Treasury, which are held in Federal Reserve Banks—not commercial banks in ordinary parlance—as well as in commercial banks are also considered part of the money supply, for they, too, can be drawn against by check.

cent of money transactions is made by check, such payment must be counted as money. Commercial banks are not to be confused with savings banks and investment banks, whose deposit accounts cannot be drawn against by check. The commercial bank is a private business organization. Although it is subject to more government regulation than are most other types of private business, it nevertheless is run primarily for profit.

The quantity of demand deposits at any time reflects in part the economic interests of commercial bank owners and in part the economic interests of businessmen and individuals who wish to borrow. A banker's ability to lend has been limited by law. That is, a bank's deposit liabilities in proportion to its holdings of particular types of assets termed "reserves" is limited. Specifically, a banker's demand deposits (which are liabilities to him, for his depositors can draw against them at will by check) cannot exceed some multiple of his "reserves." For the banks that belong to the Federal Reserve System (banks doing 85 per cent of the banking business of the country) reserves are themselves deposits. *The only bank asset that is counted as reserves, which in turn determine the amount of deposit liabilities that can be incurred, is their deposits with the Federal Reserve Banks.* To account for the supply of bank-deposit money, it is therefore necessary to understand the fundamental structure of the Federal Reserve System.

Individuals do business with two types of commercial bank in the United States—those that are members of the Federal Reserve System, already referred to, and those that are not. The latter are governed by the laws of the state in which they operate. We shall not say anything more about them, because they account for only a small fraction of all banking business and are subject to 48 different sets of rules.

The Federal Reserve System is partly a government and partly a private organization. At its head is a Board of Governors, physically located in Washington, D.C., whose seven members are appointed by the President. It has operating banks, called Federal Reserve Banks, one in each of the 12 districts into which the nation is divided. These 12 banks do for the 6,500 member banks the same kind of things that the member banks do for individual depositors. They are bankers' banks. Their dividends are limited to 6 per cent of invested capital; thus they are not motivated by profit making. In addition, they hold the deposits which determine how much individual banks can lend. More important, in an effort to alter the amount of loans that member banks make, the Federal Reserve Banks sometimes take actions that change, and are intended to change, the amount of total reserves held by these individual banks.

To lend, a bank must hold "legal reserves," which are deposits with their Federal Reserve Bank, as has already been indicated. It is, of course, possible for some banks to acquire reserves as the direct result of loss of these reserves by other banks; that would happen when deposi-

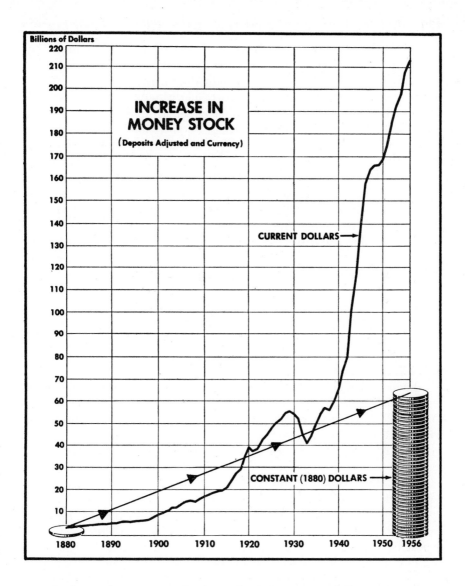

Billions of Dollars

INCREASE IN MONEY STOCK

(Deposits Adjusted and Currency)

CURRENT DOLLARS→

CONSTANT (1880) DOLLARS →

As the economy grows, a larger stock of money is needed to carry on more business transactions and to meet the desires of individuals and businesses to hold money as a provision against contingencies. In 1956, the money supply, in constant dollars, was 22 times what it was in 1880. In actual (current) dollars, the money supply was 74 times as large.

SOURCE: *Economic Growth in the United States: Its Past and Future* (New York: Committee for Economic Development, February, 1958), p. 34.

tors with the first group of banks received greater payments from depositors with other banks than they made to them. However, we are not concerned here with the situation of an individual bank, but with the banking system as a whole; and, more particularly, with the circumstances under which all banks together would either acquire deposits directly with the Federal Reserve Banks or increase their holdings of liquid resources, which could be deposited, if the banks so desired, with the Federal Reserve Banks and become the basis for additional loans. All banks together could increase their legal reserves, and therefore their loans, under the following conditions:

1. The public reduces its holdings of currency and deposits some of its currency with commercial banks.

2. Gold flows into the country from abroad or from domestic production.

3. The member banks borrow from the Federal Reserve Banks.

4. The Federal Reserve Banks purchase government bonds on the open market from individuals, businesses, and financial institutions, and the sellers of the bonds deposit the proceeds of their bond sales in commercial banks.

5. The mint increases the supply of coin and currency, some of which finds its way into the banks.

Each of these circumstances would increase commercial banks' holdings of cash or their claims on the Federal Reserve Bank. Accordingly, they would have greater resources with which to increase their deposits with the Reserve Bank.

The reverse of these five conditions would reduce member banks' reserves and lower their ability to lend. When these reverse conditions occur, member banks generally are forced to draw down their deposits with the Reserve Banks.

Regulations of the Federal Reserve Board of Governors limit the demand-deposit liabilities of member banks to some multiple of their deposits (reserves) with the Reserve Banks. In 1958, banks in small cities and towns could incur deposit liabilities of slightly over nine times their deposits with Reserve Banks (their reserves were legally required to be at least 11 per cent of their demand-deposit liabilities). Banks in Chicago and New York could incur deposit liabilities slightly over five times their reserves (they had to hold reserves not less than 18 per cent of their demand-deposit liabilities). Other banks were limited to demand-deposit liabilities about six times the size of their deposits with the Reserve Banks. The ability to incur deposit liabilities far greater than reserves is known as a "fractional reserve system." This type of banking system permits commercial banks to create money—as we have seen, by far the most important type of money in the United States—virtually out of thin air.

The ability of commercial banks to create money—exercising this power together with the government and with counterfeiters—is not obvious. Indeed, some bankers do not recognize that they possess this power and they contend that "they cannot lend more money than they have." It is a demonstrable fact that commercial banks *as a whole* take a quantity of cash and transform it into a far larger amount of bank deposits. In that way, banks create a supply of money that otherwise would not exist. (For a detailed explanation of how this comes about, see the following section, entitled "Multiple Expansion of Bank Credit.")

In the first instance, banks create money by extending loans. In exchange for customers' written promises to repay a particular sum (generally these promises are backed by "collateral," which consists of property pledged against the loan, that would pass to the lender if the loan were not repaid), the bank gives the borrower a checking account for the sum of the loan, after deducting interest and service charges. (The bank must have excess legal reserves to do this.) If the bank were loaned to the hilt, then it would require additional deposits of cash, turned into deposits with the Federal Reserve Bank, before it could extend additional loans. How would the money supply be increased by the making of a loan under these circumstances? Actually, it need not increase the money supply because, if the borrower immediately withdrew the amount put in his account or gave a check to his creditor for the full amount and he withdrew it, the money supply would not have risen. *The ability of a bank (commercial) to expand the money supply depends upon its not losing cash in consequence of its loans.*

It is not only a theoretical possibility but an established fact that when banks extend loans the amount of cash they lose as a result is a small proportion of the loans; sometimes they do not lose anything at all. If a person understands how this can be so, he will be able to explain the ability of banks to create money.

Multiple Expansion of Bank Credit

The Point

To explain how the introduction of new reserves into the banking system may spawn additional deposits and result in a manifold expansion of the money supply. (Recall that money supply includes coin and currency outside the banks and commercial bank deposits.)

Assumptions

All banks are members of the Federal Reserve System.

All banks are required to hold the same proportion of their deposits with the Federal Reserve Banks (20 per cent) as legal reserves. (Actually, this figure is a little too high, but it vastly simplifies the arithmetic.)

The banking system is "all loaned up" when additional reserves enter the system.

The Story Unfolds

1. Mr. Jones decides he need not hold so much cash "around the house" and deposits $100 in his commercial banking account. His objective is to hold the money as protection against a "rainy day"—just as he did when he kept it in a safe hiding place at home.

2. Bank A receives the deposit, crediting Mr. Jones' account with a $100 increase in his deposit. Under the law, the bank must now hold additional legal reserves—that is, it must increase its deposit with the Federal Reserve Bank in its area. We assume that it must hold $20 in additional reserves.

3. Bank A deposits the entire $100 with the Federal Reserve Bank. It now has $80 of "excess reserves" (since only $20 is legally required) and ordinarily will endeavor to use them to obtain "earning assets"—either by making loans or by purchasing securities that will yield it an income. *Recognize, however, that if Mr. Jones, were to withdraw or draw against his deposit by check, the bank would not have any funds with which to purchase securities or to make loans.*

4. Actually, no bank could identify the individuals responsible for an increase in the amount of cash deposited with it and would not attempt to guess whether those particular individuals planned to keep the funds on deposit or withdraw them. It would operate on the basis of the law of averages and draw on its past experience. That is, it generally would assume that its loss of cash or reserves would be the same on the additional deposits it received as on its other deposits. This assumption is crucial and complicated. It might turn out that the bank ordinarily does not suffer any added net cash loss. (Such losses arise from greater cash withdrawals by the bank's depositors or increased net obligations to other banks when its depositors pay out more to others who deal with different banks than they receive from depositors with other banks.) Consequently, Bank A's management might feel safe in assuming that the additional $100 cash deposit would not be "drained" out of the system.

5. Bank A would extend loans to the most deserving of the many applicants seeking to borrow. (In recent years banks almost invariably have had more requests for loans than they can fill.) For every $10 of loans extended (which initally take the form of deposits against which borrowers can draw by check) the bank must hold $2 on deposit with the Federal Reserve Bank. The bank, after depositing Mr. Jones' $100 with the F.R.B., now holds $80 more in reserves than are required by law. Its management may decide to lend out this entire amount to Mr. Abel, knowing that even if the entire amount were withdrawn, its reserve position would conform to regulations.

6. Mr. Abel draws a check against his $80 deposit with the Bank—he borrowed the money in order to use it, of course; otherwise he would not be willing to pay interest.

7. The payment(s) by Mr. Abel will go to others, many of whom may not do their banking business with Bank A. For simplicity, let us assume he makes only one payment and that it goes to someone who deals with Bank B.

The loan ultimately ends up, then, as a claim against Bank A by the person to whom Mr. Abel has made payment—say, Mr. Lary. His bank will collect it for him (through Federal Reserve Bank clearing arrangements) and credit his deposit with $80. Since both Bank A and Bank B keep deposits (reserves) at a Federal Reserve Bank, when Bank B deposits the check given it by Mr. Lary at the Federal Reserve Bank its reserves go up by $80 and those of Bank A go down by the same amount.

8. Before we go on to see what Bank B does as a result of having $80 additional cash, let us take stock of what has happened to the money supply thus far as a result of the initial deposit of $100 by Mr. Jones.

   a. The initial $100 deposit substituted a bank deposit for currency outside the banking system, so there was no change in money supply as a result of that transaction.

   b. The extension of the $80 loan added to the money supply—in the form of a bank deposit. Initially it was in the hands of the borrower, but soon its ownership was transferred to others.

   c. The bank receiving the initial deposit (Bank A) holds part of the initial deposit as legal reserves, but has "lost" the balance to other banks. (Here is one of the crucial assumptions. If the original depositor [Mr. Jones] were to withdraw his deposit, Bank A would have to dig around to find funds with which to make good. It would probably do so by temporarily reducing its reserves below the legal level and borrow from the Federal Reserve Bank [or sell some securities or fail to re-extend loans as quickly as its customers were repaying them].)

9. The story does not end there by any means. We left the $80 in the possession of Bank B and its ownership credited to Mr. Lary. Bank B now finds itself obligated to hold $16 additional deposits with the F.R.B. as legal reserve against Mr. Lary's $80 deposit (that is, 20 per cent of $80); thus, it has $64 excess reserves. These could be used as the basis for loans, on the assumption that Mr. Lary will not disturb the initial $80 deposit.

10. Let us say that Bank B lends $64 to Mr. Roberts, giving him a bank deposit of equal amount against which he draws a check for the full amount payable to Mr. Rubin, who deals with Bank C. Through the clearing machinery of the Federal Reserve System, Bank C would obtain $64 additional reserves, which would provide the basis for a repetition of the process. That is, it would make loans equivalent to its excess reserves, holding part of the additional reserves in the form of a deposit with the F.R.B.

11. There is no need to continue the process: cash deposit, addition to legal reserves, loan of the excess reserves, payment of the funds to another bank, addition to legal reserves, etc. (Table A carries it out through many more steps.) Let us now take stock of what happens in the process; let us, moreover, make very clear on what conditions this process depends—and what could call it to a halt.

   a. In each case, when the bank received an addition to its cash (or, what is equivalent, a claim against another bank, which ordinarily would be settled by the debtor bank's drawing a check in favor of the creditor bank against the debtor bank's deposit with the F.R.B.), we assumed

Table A. Multiple Expansion of Bank Loans and Deposits Seen in Schedule Form

Additional deposits received		Deposit resulting from		Legal reserve	Excess reserve	Loan made	
By bank	Amount	Cash deposit	Check deposit			Amount	To
A	$100.00	By Mr. Jones		$ 20.00	$ 80.00	$ 80.00	Mr. Abel
B	80.00		Mr. Lary	16.00	64.00	64.00	Mr. Roberts
C	64.00		Mr. Rubin	12.80	51.20	51.20	
D	51.20			10.24	40.96	40.96	
E	40.96			8.19	32.77	32.77	
F	32.77			6.55	26.21	26.21	
G	26.21			5.24	20.97	20.97	
H	20.97			4.19	16.78	16.78	
I	16.78			3.36	13.42	13.42	
J	13.42			2.68	10.74	10.74	
K	10.74			2.15	8.59	8.59	
Total, Banks A-K	$457.05			$ 91.40	$365.64	$365.64	
Other banks	42.95			8.60	34.36	34.36	
Final total	$500.00			$100.00	$400.00	$400.00	

that the owner of that deposit did not disturb it. Consequently, all of that addition, except the reserves that, legally, had to be held against it, became excess reserves.

b. We assumed that the bank made loans of the full amount of its excess reserves. We need not have serious question about the availability of desiring borrowers; however, there sometimes is a shortage of individuals and firms wishing to borrow—that is of a type which the bank's management believes to be a "good risk." *If any bank in this chain of payments did not extend a loan as a result of its increased excess reserves, the process would be cut short at that point.*

12. The most crucial point in the process of multiple expansion of bank credit has not been illustrated in the foregoing hypothetical case—the factor of simultaneous expansion of bank credit by all banks. We started by assuming that Bank A was the only bank to receive increased cash deposits and it alone expanded its loans. Let us see what would happen if all banks simultaneously were to do what Bank A did.

a. When Bank A made a loan to Mr. Abel of $80 as a consequence of Mr. Jones' deposit, we assumed that the $80 was paid over to Mr. Lary and Bank B. However, if all banks were doing what Bank A did, we should expect that even as it lost deposits it would be gaining deposits because borrowers from other banks were making payments to its own depositors. Under such circumstances, it would not lose any cash or reserves, even though it was extending loans, for its claims against other banks were offsetting their claims against it.

b. If banks never lost cash or reserves as a result of loans, they could theoretically extend an infinite volume of loans—unless there were some legal requirement that they keep some funds on hand. Legal reserve requirements thus have the effect of holding the process of multiple bank credit expansion in check—though they still permit each dollar of additional deposit to add many dollars to the money supply.

13. Thus we see that through this process of multiple-deposit expansion an increase of $100 in cash or reserves can lead to loans of $400 and new deposits of $500 for the entire banking system. As Table A demonstrates, each bank, by lending its excess reserves, contributes to this multiple expansion. For the banking system as a whole, assuming a 20 per cent reserve requirement, each $100 in additional cash or reserves makes possible new deposits five times as great as the additional cash or reserves.

If we consider what happens to a single bank loan, we should expect the borrower to use its proceeds to make payments to individuals and businesses that do their banking with another institution; also, we should expect some payments to be made to persons and businesses that would hold all or part of it in cash. As a result, the single loan presumably would cause the lending bank to lose some of its "funds" (by which we mean both vault cash or its own deposits with the Federal Reserve Bank). However, we do not see the full story if we concentrate on the consequences of a single loan; we are dealing here with something in which the whole is not equal to the sum of its parts. Loans by individual banks make it possible for other banks to make loans, because they receive funds as a consequence of the initial loans which permit them to increase their legal reserves. Banks have a financial incentive to put these additional reserves to profitable use—in other words, usually to extend loans. As a consequence of these "secondary" loans, payments will be made by borrowers to persons who bank with other institutions—including the very banks who made the loans initially.

Conceivably, banks which increase their loans would not lose any cash at all because they would receive claims against all other banks equal to the claims that other banks acquired against themselves in consequence of their loans. In other words, banks that were expanding their loans might never have to pay out any cash because they acquired claims against other banks which just offset those acquired by other banks against themselves. In these circumstances, all banks together could expand their deposits to an infinitely large amount if there were no legal requirement which limited their loans to some multiple of their reserves. Thus we see that banks can expand loans and the money supply most readily when other banks are doing likewise so that their loss of "funds" are at least partly offset by the gains from other banks that are expanding loans.

The money supply can be increased by the banking system also when the Federal Reserve Banks purchase securities and pay for them by checks drawn against themselves.

Ordinarily the funds that banks collectively spend for securities are deposited in the banking system somewhere and do not cause much net loss of cash to individual banks. The net effect is simply to increase the banking deposits of those who sold the securities to the banks, and to add to the securities in the possession of the banks.

The banking system—that is, all commercial banks, together—can expand the volume of bank deposits by roughly $6 for every dollar of reserves with the Federal Reserve Banks. Legal reserve requirements put an upper limit on the volume of deposits that banks can create. *In the absence of these requirements, they conceivably could create unlimited deposits.* The process by which the banking system creates deposits far larger than its reserves is ordinarily termed "multiple expansion of bank deposits."

The power of banks to create money in the form of commercial bank deposits can be demonstrated by reliable factual evidence. Table 3 indicates the vault cash and the deposits with the Federal Reserve Banks of all banks that are members of the Federal Reserve System. The combined total is substantially smaller than the total volume of bank deposits in those banks. As shown, in 1957, bank deposits with members of the Federal Reserve System were more than four times as large as vault cash and legal reserves combined.

Table 3. Customer Deposits, Bank-Vault Cash, and Bank Deposits with Reserve Banks,* Selected Dates 1941-1957
(In millions)

Date	Total customer deposits	Reserves with Federal Reserve Banks	Vault cash
12/31/41	$33,061	$12,396	$1,087
12/31/46	69,127	16,015	1,576
12/31/47	72,704	17,797	1,672
12/31/48	72,152	20,406	1,486
12/31/49	72,658	16,429	1,521
12/31/50	78,370	17,459	1,643
12/31/51	83,240	19,912	2,062
12/31/52	85,680	19,810	2,081
12/31/53	85,711	19,997	1,870
12/31/54	88,859	18,735	1,843
12/31/55	93,687	18,722	2,019
12/31/56	95,163	18,707	2,487
12/31/57	93,804	18,973	2,536

* For all members of the Federal Reserve System.

SOURCE: *Federal Reserve Bulletin,* November, 1950, p. 1499; December, 1951, p. 1549; December, 1954, p. 1273; April, 1956, p. 361; and August, 1958, p. 949.

4. SUMMARY TO THIS POINT

We thus have seen that the money supply is composed of three major elements and that by far the most important is bank deposits. This type of money is variable in quantity and fluctuates primarily with the number of good risks who request bank loans, and with the willingness of banks to take risks. In turn, the number of requests for loans from good risks varies directly with the activity of general business. Thus the supply of money in all three major forms usually adapts itself to variations in the amount of "money work" to be done. Much of the time, therefore, the money supply behaves passively.

To account for the value of money, another influence on its quantity must be considered. That is the frequency with which each unit of money is spent; it is generally termed the "velocity of money circulation."

C. Velocity of Money Circulation

The amount of work that can be done by a given quantity of money —that is, the amount of goods and services that can be exchanged for money at given prices—is not rigidly fixed. If each dollar is spent frequently—which also means that people on the average hold money for a short time before spending it—more business could be transacted with the same amount of money. A dollar used only once a year does only half as much work as the same dollar spent twice. Several types of money velocity have been distinguished, but the most useful one is "income velocity." [5] *Income velocity designates the average number of times annually that money received as personal income is spent for final output.* To calculate the income velocity of money for the entire nation, one need merely divide the total output of goods and services (national income) by the average quantity of money in the country. For example, if a total of $250 billion in goods and services was sold to its final users during any year, and the average quantity of money in the country during that period was $100 billion, the average income velocity would be 2.5.

Clearly, if consumers hold their income for shorter periods, so that the income velocity increases—say to 3 per year, then the total value of goods and services sold during the year *necessarily* would total $300 billion. This conclusion is simple arithmetic, and does not explain how the increased value of goods and services comes about. Possibly prices would rise, while the same quantity of goods and services was sold. Or the rise in the income velocity of money might lead to a larger output of goods and services, and prices might not change at all. Possibly both prices and output would rise somewhat. But with a money supply of $100 billion and an income velocity of 3, total national income *must* equal $300 billion.

What, then, are the major effects of a change in the total supply of money (currency and bank deposits)? Changes in money supply can be offset or neutralized by changes in the income velocity of money (note, for example, the reverse changes in money supply and income velocity in 1936, 1939, 1940, 1943, 1944, 1945, 1946, 1948, and 1954—Table 4); consequently, changes in money supply need not influence total spending, prices, or employment. Even if the volume of expenditure (money supply times income velocity) were affected, the average price of goods need not be altered. For example, national income increased between 1938 and 1939, while consumers' prices declined (Table 4). Also, between 1944 and 1946, and 1953 and 1954, prices and national income changed in opposite directions. The total output of goods might vary in direct proportion to the volume of spending. (This is more simple arithmetic.) If the quantity of goods exchanged remained the same,

---

[5] The most widely used concept is termed "transaction velocity," and means the frequency with which money is spent, no matter for what—including such things as payments to labor, payments for securities, and the like.

changes in spending would necessarily mean a rise in average prices, for *prices simply represent quantities of money exchanged for goods.*[6]

Generalizations about the relation between the quantity of money in circulation and the price level have a great many exceptions. The "quantity theory of money," which states that the price level varies directly and proportionally with changes in the supply of currency, has been repudiated by almost all economists. The effect of changes in money supply on the price level depends upon two primary circumstances: first, upon the way the velocity of circulation responds; second, upon the behavior of total output. *These circumstances do not always respond in the same way to changes in money supply,* as Table 4 clearly shows.

In the past, money supply (particularly the supply of bank deposits) has changed more than the income velocity of circulation. The income velocity of circulation is relatively stable (see Table 4), a fact which shows that spending generally, but not mechanically, varies with the money supply. Hence the quantity of money tends to fluctuate in the same direction as the general price level and with the level of output, although there have been exceptions to this usual pattern. Sometimes production and employment have increased at the same time that the quantity of money declined. For example, total money supply was lower in 1948 than in 1947 ($108.3 billion, compared with $108.5 billion); however, 1948 was a year of greater output and employment. The supply of money declined slightly, but the velocity of circulation increased somewhat.

Since the effect of changes in money supply upon prices, output, and employment varies, let us explore briefly the factors that determine what the effects will be. We should expect the effect of changes in money supply upon expenditure (and therefore upon velocity of circulation) to depend primarily upon how the change in money supply comes about. When the money supply increases, almost always it is paid out in exchange for something. Increases in money supply ordinarily come about, as we have seen, as the result of increased bank loans to businessmen. Not infrequently in the past, the money supply has risen as the banks purchased government securities, thereby enabling the government to borrow so that it might spend in excess of its revenues. The proceeds of

---

[6] This concept may be expressed in the following equation:

$$P = \frac{MV}{T},$$

where M equals the quantity of money, V indicates the transaction velocity of money, and T equals the number of transactions. The simple meaning of this equation becomes manifest when it is used to explain price in a single transaction. M, in such a case, equals the amount of money paid; V equals one, and T also equals one. Price then equals the amount of money given for the product. It holds in the same way for any number of transactions.

Table 4. Relation between Money Supply, Spending, Employment, Unemployment, and Price Levels, 1929-1956

(1)	(2)	(3)	(4)	(5)	(6)	(7)
				Index of		
			Income	consumer		
	Money	National	velocity	prices	Em-	Unem-
	supply	income	(3)	(1947–49	ployment	ployment
Year	(billions)	(billions)	(2)	=100)	(thousands)	(thousands)
1929	$ 26.2	$ 87.8	3.4	73.3	47,630	429
1930	25.1	75.7	3.0	71.4	45,480	2,896
1931	23.5	59.7	2.5	65.0	42,400	7,037
1932	20.2	42.5	2.1	58.4	38,940	11,385
1933	19.2	40.2	2.1	55.3	38,760	11,842
1934	21.4	49.0	2.3	57.2	40,890	9,761
1935	25.2	57.1	2.3	58.7	42,260	9,092
1936	29.0	64.9	2.2	59.3	44,410	7,386
1937	30.7	73.6	2.4	61.4	46,300	6,403
1938	29.7	67.6	2.3	60.3	44,220	9,796
1939	33.4	72.8	2.2	59.4	45,750	8,786
1940	38.7	81.6	2.1	59.9	47,520	8,120
1941	45.5	104.7	2.3	62.9	50,350	5,560
1942	52.8	137.7	2.6	69.7	53,750	2,660
1943	71.9	170.3	2.4	74.0	54,470	1,070
1944	80.9	182.6	2.3	75.2	53,960	670
1945	94.2	181.2	1.9	76.9	52,820	1,040
1946	106.0	180.9	1.7	83.4	55,250	2,270
1947	108.5	198.2	1.8	95.5	58,027	2,142
1948	108.3	223.5	2.1	102.8	59,378	2,064
1949	107.2	217.7	2.0	101.8	58,710	3,395
1950	110.0	241.9	2.2	102.8	59,957	3,142
1951	114.5	279.3	2.4	111.0	61,005	1,879
1952	121.8	292.2	2.4	113.5	61,293	1,673
1953	124.3	305.6	2.5	114.4	62,213	1,602
1954	125.2	301.8	2.4	114.8	61,238	3,230
1955	130.3	330.2	2.5	114.5	63,193	2,654
1956	132.5	349.4	2.6	116.2	64,979	2,551
1957	133.4	364.0	2.7	120.2	65,011	2,936

SOURCES: (2) Money Supply, from *Banking and Monetary Statistics* (Washington, D.C.: Board of Governors of Federal Reserve System, 1943), pp. 34-35; *Federal Reserve Bulletin*, December, 1948, p. 1489, July, 1957, pp. 828-829, and August, 1958, p. 944. (3) National Income, from U.S. Department of Commerce, *Survey of Current Business*, July, 1958, pp. 4-5. (5) Index of Consumer Prices, from *Economic Report of the President to Congress*, January 24, 1956, p. 208; and *Federal Reserve Bulletin*, August, 1958, p. 984. (6) Employment, from U.S. Department of Commerce, Bureau of the Census; and *Federal Reserve Bulletin*, April, 1956, p. 390, and August, 1958, p. 980. (7) Unemployment, from *Historical Statistics of the United States*, p. 65; and *Federal Reserve Bulletin*, December, 1948, p. 1514, April, 1956, p. 390, and August, 1958, p. 980.

the loans made by government have been spent in diverse ways. *To explain why and when businessmen and government borrow is therefore to explain in large part how the money supply influences both expenditure and output.* These matters will be discussed soon when we consider the factors that determine how much those in each group in the economy spend. At this point let us complete our explanation of the value of money.

Thus far, we have said that the value of money depends upon what you can get for it, and that what money will fetch is best measured by an average of many prices. The prices of many things are combined for the purpose of measuring the value of money into a price index; changes in this index are termed changes in the price level. We saw that the value of money (which rises when the price level declines, and falls when the price level rises) does not depend upon the backing of money. Like the value of most other things, it depends upon the relation between the quantity of money and the amount and prices of goods whose exchange must be effected by the money. Money, we say, consists of all things generally accepted in exchange, and in this country at the present time bank deposits are by far the most important type. Coin and currency are the other major forms of money. The effective money supply depends upon more than the volume of coin, currency, and bank deposits. Of equal importance is the frequency with which money is spent. The combined money supply times income velocity represents money expenditure. We must now investigate the connection between money expenditure and the level of prices.

D. Relation of Expenditure to Price Level

In ordinary parlance, when people spend more money, the demand for goods increases. With an increase in demand, a price rise is to be expected. This version of the influence of increased spending needs qualification. Increased spending sometimes exerts its primary effect upon output rather than upon prices. For example, if the rise in spending were to come about by government payments for relief during a period of heavy unemployment, prices probably would not rise, because wage rates ordinarily would not rise at such a time, and other business costs would tend to be stable. Since most businesses tend to set their prices primarily on the basis of their costs (some, it is true, adjust prices in accordance with changes in demand, even though costs do not change), prices might remain unchanged. Thus increased spending might simply increase output and leave prices unchanged.

Knowledge that government (or business generally) is scheduled to make heavy expenditures may lead some businessmen to increase prices even when many resources are not employed. The period 1936 through the summer of 1937 may have been an example. Appropriations by Congress for a greatly increased military establishment, for greatly increased public works, or for the payment of a large bonus to servicemen induced some businessmen to raise prices, even though costs had not changed. The rise in price can precede the increase in spending, and may even absorb it, so that the physical quantity of goods purchased may not rise at all, even though spending increases. When spending increases without output's expanding, prices must rise.

V. MONEY SUPPLY AND THE LEVEL OF SPENDING

As suggested earlier, the effect of an increase in money supply upon spending depends largely upon how the rise in money supply comes about. Obviously, monetary authorities do not create money and then scatter it about by airplane to put it into circulation. Money supply rises in response to relatively few conditions. Ordinarily it is increased by a rise in bank loans. In turn, an increase in bank loans can be traced to greater desire on the part of individuals and businesses to borrow, or to greater willingness of banks to lend. In either situation the result is to put funds into the hands of someone who wants to spend them. Bank loans thus increase the money supply and expenditure.

Money supply may rise slightly as the federal government increases its issue of coin and currency to make payments on behalf of the government. Much more important, money supply may rise as banks purchase government securities, giving the government ownership of bank deposits against which it can draw in the same way that individuals and businesses use bank loans for spending. Government security issues are almost always associated with the desire to spend (even if only to redeem outstanding securities). Consequently, an increase in money supply in response to government borrowing will also lead to spending. (If the government borrows to repay holders of existing securities, expenditures for goods and services may not be much affected.)

Accordingly, most increases in money supply result in, and make possible, increased spending. The most important exception is a change in money supply resulting from increased desires to hoard funds. During periods of political or economic crisis, the supply of coin and currency rises in response to a desire on the part of the public to hold more money in these forms. Since this money is intended for holding (hoarding), the money supply would not be accompanied by a rise in spending —indeed, there may well be a decline in the circumstances.

The bridge between the quantity of money and the level of expenditure is always to be found in the velocity of circulation. As we have seen, the velocity of circulation reflects the desire, ability, and willingness of individuals and businesses to spend. These conditions may, but need not, be affected by changes in money supply. Many other factors influence the velocity of money circulation. To account for the velocity of money and thereby for the level of spending, it will be necessary to explain the way that individuals dispose of their incomes and their accumulated savings. The following chapter will undertake this task.

VI. SUMMARY AND CONCLUSIONS

The supply of money in the United States depends largely upon the lending policies of commercial banks and the measures taken by the Federal Reserve System. Commercial banks create money, within legal restrictions, in response to requests for loans from individuals, businesses, and government. The effect of changes in the money supply upon the expenditure—which we have seen is the major determinant of the level of business activity—varies with velocity of money. *Changes in money supply need not result in increased spending.* And, even when spending rises, prices sometimes remain the same. The precise effect of a change in money supply depends primarily upon how it is brought about and the level of output at the time it occurs. If money supply rises because of business or government borrowing, spending will increase; if business were already active, prices probably would rise also. An increase in bank loans and expenditures when business is depressed might not change prices at all, though output would expand.

DISCUSSION QUESTIONS

1. For what reasons would you expect the money and banking system to affect the level of employment and output?

2. If through some catastrophe the supply of money in all forms were to be destroyed, what problems would arise before a new supply could be created? Be explicit, viewing the problem from the standpoint of housewives, businessmen, creditors, government, and savers.

3. In what major respects are coins, currency, and bank deposits different?

4. Does the supply of money determine the level of business activity, or does the level of business activity determine the supply of money? Explain.

5. Which type of money is the most passive and which the most active influence on general business conditions? Explain.

6. Give examples of the various circumstances that would influence the velocity of money circulation.

7. Which type of development would have the greater effect upon the

level of spending: a rise in the money supply; a rise in the velocity of money in circulation, or can one not tell?

8. Will a rise in spending necessarily lead to a rise in price level? Under what conditions is it likely to have this effect? When are prices likely to remain stable, despite a rise in total spending?

9. Is it likely that costs of production would decline when spending increases? Under what circumstances? Would prices ordinarily decline under these circumstances?

10. If a public announcement were made that all backing behind currency is no longer available to holders of paper money *today*, what do you think would be the consequences? Would your answer be the same if this were a period of financial crisis?

Chapter

21 Determinants of the

Level of Expenditures

As already indicated, output and employment usually vary with changes in the amount of money spent. We have seen also that a rise in the quantity of money may or may not increase the volume of expenditure, according to the response of the income velocity of money. We now will seek out the important groups of spenders and account for their behavior. In this way we shall be able to observe whether the spending of each group is strongly affected by the quantity of money in circulation. More important, we shall try to discover the major determinants of the spending by each group.

Three major types of spender may be distinguished. They are individuals, businessmen, and governmental units. These three groups in turn include important subgroups that should be differentiated. It would require more time and space than we can afford to account for the spending behavior of each of these groups in great detail. The following discussion will be general and brief. The reader should recognize that many things that might be said about the spending habits of each group will be omitted; more important, the determinants of the level of expenditure of each group are not fully understood. *To a disconcerting extent, changes in expenditure occur that are altogether unexpected and that defy confident explanation.* Nevertheless, we shall indicate the most important known influences upon expenditure.

I. DETERMINANTS OF INDIVIDUALS' EXPENDITURES

Most people adjust their spending to their income. As income rises, so too do their ability and willingness to spend. Their spending also is influenced by their ability to borrow—that is, primarily by the availability of installment credit.

Individuals spend money for two types of goods. Most of their expenditure goes for "consumers' goods." These are goods that are used up by

445

individuals within a relatively short period of time. The purchase of consumers' goods is not far removed in time from the use of the good or service purchased, and in a fairly short while nothing remains of the thing purchased. Payments for food, rent, clothing, and all kinds of services are examples of expenditures for consumers' goods.

Individuals spend part of their own funds, and funds they borrow, for things other than consumers' goods. Some of their expenditures may be termed *individual investment.* Individuals buy some important items that last for a very long time. Most important in this category are houses, automobiles, and most electrical appliances. When consumers purchase these things, they are primarily *laying aside a future store of consumers' services.* They are accumulating something that will not be consumed entirely in the near future. Purchase and full consumption are widely separated in time.

The interval between purchase and complete usage of a product varies widely from product to product. Gloves last far longer after purchase than butter does. Overcoats last longer than gloves; and lamps usually outlast all of them. There is no clear or sharp logical dividing line between consumers' goods and individual investment goods. For practical purposes, arbitrary distinctions must be made. Only individual purchases of homes and automobiles are regarded as individual investment.[1]

Expenditures by individuals in the past have been studied, and these studies reveal the following typical patterns of behavior:

1. Recipients of very low incomes on the average spend more money than they receive. They make up their deficits by drawing on savings, by borrowing, or by depending on gifts and charity. The poorest 40 per cent of the population in 1957 averaged expenditures in excess of income.[2]

2. Only 51 per cent of all spending units had net savings in 1957.[3]

3. The savings by persons with high incomes exceed those of persons with moderate incomes in both absolute amount and as a proportion of income. That is, it appears that the higher the personal income, the smaller the proportion of each added dollar of income that is spent.

4. It is not clear how consumers alter their expenditures immediately after their incomes have been changed. It might appear that there would be a lag before spending became adjusted to changes in income. On the other hand, one might suppose that many consumers would "overadjust"

---

[1] Note carefully that this term most emphatically does not refer to purchases of stocks and bonds which are not part of production. Only purchases of currently produced goods and services are included under both consumers' goods and investment goods.

[2] *Federal Reserve Bulletin,* August, 1957, p. 889.

[3] *Ibid.*

to changes in their income during the first few months following the change. That is, they will make some large expenditures on the strength of their conviction that they will be able to pay for them over the long period during which they expect to receive their increased income.

5. Total consumer spending maintains a fairly stable relation with total consumer income in general. Moderate changes do occur in consumer spending for reasons that are not explicable, however, by changes either in actual or expected consumer income.

Two major characteristics of individuals' investment expenditures have been observed:

1. Individuals' investment varies much more widely than other types of individuals' expenditures when general business conditions change. (Compare the first two columns of Table 1.)

2. Measured as a proportion of total individual expenditure, individual investment varies widely, ranging from 7.5 (1933) per cent to 15.6 (1950) per cent (see Table 1).

On the average, total individuals' expenditures represent 90 to 95 per cent of their total income. In other words, *taken together, all consumers spend significantly less than they receive* almost all the time.

It appears that we have found one possible cause for depressions. If consumers spend less for all things than they receive, they contribute toward a decline in output and employment. To offset this tendency, some other groups must persistently spend more than they receive. Otherwise, total spending will fall below total income received in the past and result in a decline in income and output.

As a rough general rule one might say that individuals' expenditures vary with their incomes. However, it would be an error to conclude that fluctuations in total expenditures rarely originate with changes in spending by individuals. Indeed, a plausible explanation for changes in economic activity in the United States following World War II can be found in economic attitudes of the public and in the effect of these attitudes upon individuals' expenditures.[4]

In accounting fully for variations in expenditures by individuals, we shall go astray unless we distinguish the many types of consumers who probably behave quite differently from one another. First, there are extravagant consumers who doubtless respond differently from economical consumers. Second, young and old consumers have different expenditure patterns; the young spend partly in anticipation of future increases in income, while the old consume largely on the basis of the resources they have accumulated over their lifetime. Of course, temperament and

---

[4] George Katona, "The Predictive Value of Data on Consumer Attitudes," in *Consumer Behavior: The Life Cycle and Consumer Behavior* (New York: New York University Press, 1955), II, 67-69.

Table 1. Analysis of Individual Spending by Broad Categories, Selected Years 1929-1957

	Billions				As per cent of total		
Year	Total personal consumption expenditure *	Durable goods †	Nondurable goods ‡	Services §	Durable goods	Non-durable goods	Services
1929	$ 79.0	$ 9.2	$ 37.7	$ 32.1	11.6%	47.7%	40.6%
1933	46.4	3.5	22.3	20.7	7.5	48.0	44.6
1937	67.3	6.9	35.2	25.1	10.3	52.3	37.3
1940	71.9	7.8	37.2	26.9	10.8	51.7	37.4
1946	147.1	15.9	84.8	46.4	10.8	57.6	31.5
1947	165.4	20.6	93.4	51.4	12.5	56.5	31.1
1948	178.3	22.7	98.7	56.9	12.7	55.4	31.9
1949	181.2	24.6	96.6	60.0	13.6	53.3	33.1
1950	195.0	30.4	99.8	64.9	15.6	51.2	33.3
1951	209.8	29.5	110.1	70.2	14.1	52.5	33.5
1952	219.8	29.1	115.1	75.6	13.2	52.4	34.4
1953	232.6	32.9	118.0	81.8	14.1	50.7	35.2
1954	238.0	32.4	119.3	86.3	13.6	50.1	36.3
1955	256.9	39.6	124.8	92.5	15.4	48.6	36.0
1956	269.4	38.4	131.4	99.6	14.3	48.8	37.0
1957	284.4	39.9	138.0	106.5	14.0	48.5	37.4

Some lines do not add to total because of rounding.

* What is here termed personal consumption expenditures includes what has been described as individual investment.

† Includes the purchase of all household furniture, appliances and utensils, as well as expenditures for user-operated transportation.

‡ Includes expenditures for clothing and accessories, meals and beverages for off-premise consumption, as well as in hotels, schools, and so forth, drug preparation, tobacco products, toilet articles, and other goods whose serviceability is limited to a period of less than three years.

§ Includes all expenditures for cleaning, repairing, storage, rentals, personal care, entertainment, and the like.

SOURCE: U.S. Department of Commerce, *Survey of Current Business,* July, 1958, pp. 4-5.

personality traits influence expenditures, but we are not trying to explain the behavior of individuals. Perhaps for some purposes it would be important to distinguish between expenditures by those whose income comes from property—primarily in the form of dividends, rent, interest, royalties, and the like—and those who receive income in the form of wages and salaries. A third group (including those whose incomes come from either property or wages or salaries) that warrants separate study is made up of those whose incomes are fairly fixed in size over substantial periods of time. As already indicated, a full explanation of total expenditure by individuals requires separate analysis of all groups whose behavior is different. For our purposes it is not necessary to discuss the behavior of individual groups of consumers further.

II. EXPENDITURES BY BUSINESS FIRMS

As with individuals, among firms there are important differences in spending characteristics. It might be desirable to study separately the expenditures of large, medium, and small businesses. And one might want to explore separately the spending behavior of firms in speculative and nonspeculative occupations. Other lines of demarcation among businesses that might be important for a full understanding of business expenditures are between firms engaged almost exclusively in domestic business and those heavily engaged in foreign trade; between old and new firms; and between agricultural and industrial businesses. The more one analyzes expenditures in detail, the greater the depth and accuracy of the understanding. However, for the purposes at hand the behavior of subgroups of business firms need not be investigated. We will be content with a brief discussion of the expenditures of all businesses lumped together.

Three major types of expenditure are made by all businesses, whether large or small, whether speculative or not, whether agricultural or industrial, whether engaged primarily in domestic or in foreign trade. These are, first, spending for raw materials and labor that are used to produce current output. When we refer to business expenditure, however, we usually consider only the next two types: expenditures for plant and equipment, and for inventories. Expenditure for plant and equipment ordinarily is described as business investment in *fixed capital*. Purchases of fixed capital to replace equipment that has been used beyond the possibility of further economical service are quite different in origin from expenditures for plant and equipment *to expand output*. Still different are expenditures for *new types of equipment*—whether to maintain the past level of output or to expand it. Presumably this type of purchase would be made to reduce a firm's cost of operation, or to obtain profits from the sale of a new type of product.

A. Purchases of Plant and Equipment

Business expenditures for plant and equipment are among the most strategic type of expenditure. Their strategic nature derives from their wide variation from year to year. Generalizations are dangerous, but it is fairly safe to say that when the output of plant and equipment is low, general business will be poor. When their output is high, the country will be prosperous. This conclusion does not mean that changes in expenditure on plant and equipment cause depressions and prosperity. Some factors account for the fluctuations in expenditures on fixed capital; these, then, would become the causes for depressions and prosperity. Whatever their cause, the wide fluctuations in plant and equipment expenditure entitle them to close scrutiny.

It is important to know whether most expenditures for plant and equipment result from increases in the output of the consumers' goods they produce, or whether they are largely independent of the output of consumers' goods. To be specific, we should ask if the demand for new factory buildings results primarily from an increased demand for consumers' goods. Or are these expenditures usually motivated by a desire to produce new products or to use improved methods of production? Can the timing of these expenditures for fixed capital be explained by the development of improved technological methods? In the technical language of economics, the distinction is between "induced investment" —purchases of plant and equipment traceable to increased output of familiar consumer goods, and "independent" or "exogenous" investment —expenditures for fixed capital that do not result from the need to increase output, but are stimulated by technological developments.

The fact of the matter is that we do not know the answer to these questions. Indeed, there probably are no single unequivocal answers, because one would expect the motives for business investment to vary from time to time—and especially from prosperity to depression.

B. Changes in Inventories

A third type of business expenditure is for inventories. At any given time all businesses together hold a huge quantity of goods. Some of these are in the form of finished products ready for sale to consumers; these goods are held by retailers and wholesalers; almost always even manufacturers hold some inventories of finished goods. In addition, large quantities of raw materials and goods in process are held. The holding of inventories is to be attributed to three major motives. First, inventories are a form of insurance against unforeseen interruptions in delivery. Manufacturers are understandably reluctant to take the risk of closing down because delivery of raw materials is slightly delayed. They therefore hold inventories to enable them to operate in spite of such delays. Distributors (wholesalers and retailers) also want to be protected against finding themselves with bare shelves in the event their orders are not delivered on time. A second motive for holding inventories is to be prepared in the event that sales are larger than expected.

A third motive for holding inventories is primarily speculative. Businessmen are sincere when they contend, as most of them do, that they try to avoid unnecessary risks, and avoid "speculation" in their business. However, almost every business speculates to a minor degree. Speculation is involved frequently in the determination of the size of inventories to hold. If the businessman believes the things he buys are certain to rise in price, he will almost certainly increase his inventories of these things. When he does this, of course, he is gambling on his forecast of future prices. Conversely, businessmen ordinarily will cut their inventories to the lowest reasonable level if they expect prices to fall. Accordingly, expectations of price increases induce the accumulation of inventories; and anticipation of price declines will result in a reduction of inventories.

The general magnitude of these business expenditures for plant and equipment and for inventories is indicated by Table 2. As this table shows, the relative proportion of each type of expenditure depends upon the stage of general business. Plant and equipment expenditures are heavy during prosperity; in depression they may be almost wholly absent. Also, inventory expenditures represent an unstable proportion of total national expenditure, and of total business expenditure. In general, spending for plant and equipment greatly exceeds expenditures for *additions* to inventories, which sometimes are negative—that is, all businesses combined reduce the amount of inventories they hold.

Many business expenditures involve purchases of things that are not quickly turned into cash. These things yield their benefits over a fairly long time. To acquire them, a business must tie up some of its funds for a time. Since most firms have fewer funds than they could use in their day-to-day operations, when they acquire plant and equipment or increase their inventories they impair their ability to purchase the raw materials and labor needed to expand output, and make it difficult to sell to new customers on credit.

Accordingly, many businesses borrow to pay for fixed capital and inventories. Funds are borrowed from a variety of financial institutions, but borrowers always pay a price for loans, in the form of "interest." In addition to repaying loans, borrowers must pay the lender an interest charge (on small loans, service charges may also bulk large). One would suppose that high interest rates would discourage businessmen from borrowing, and that low interest rates would tempt them to borrow. There is no doubt that interest rates do have this tendency *in themselves* to encourage and discourage borrowing. However, it seems that interest rates do not *strongly* influence the amount of money that businessmen borrow. Businessmen would often err by borrowing even if they did not have to pay interest. The things they bought with the borrowed money could be idle and deteriorate in value. Far more important than the interest rate (unless it were to rise to many times its present levels) are the expected level of demand, the size of cost reductions achievable, and the rate of obsolescence on new facilities. In other words, the net profit a businessman expects on an investment generally would not be greatly affected by even moderate changes in interest rates.

Table 2. Business Expenditures 1929-1957
(In billions)

Year	New construction	Producers durable equipment	Changes in business inventories	Total
1929	$ 8.7	$ 5.9	$ 1.7	$16.2
1930	6.2	4.5	0.4	10.3
1931	4.0	2.8	1.3	5.5
1932	1.9	1.6	2.6	0.9
1933	1.4	1.6	1.6	1.4
1934	1.7	2.3	1.1	2.9
1935	2.3	3.1	0.9	6.3
1936	3.3	4.2	1.0	8.4
1937	4.4	5.1	2.2	11.7
1938	4.0	3.6	0.9	6.7
1939	4.8	4.2	0.4	9.3
1940	5.5	5.5	2.2	13.2
1941	6.6	6.9	4.5	18.1
1942	3.7	4.3	1.8	9.9
1943	2.3	4.0	0.8	5.6
1944	2.7	5.4	1.0	7.1
1945	3.8	7.7	1.1	10.4
1946	11.0	10.7	6.4	28.1
1947	15.3	16.7	0.5	31.5
1948	19.5	18.9	4.7	43.1
1949	18.8	17.2	3.1	33.0
1950	24.2	18.9	6.8	50.0
1951	24.8	21.3	10.2	56.3
1952	25.5	21.3	3.1	49.9
1953	27.6	22.3	0.4	50.3
1954	29.7	20.8	1.6	48.9
1955	34.9	23.1	5.8	63.8
1956	35.7	27.0	5.4	68.2
1957	36.5	27.9	1.0	65.3

Totals may have discrepancies because of rounding.
SOURCE: U.S. Department of Commerce, *Survey of Current Business*, July, 1958, pp. 4-5.

III. GOVERNMENT EXPENDITURES

Government is a big spender, and seems to be growing even bigger; in fact, it is by far the biggest spender in the country. Not only does the federal government spend almost twice as much as state and local governments combined; it spends immensely more than any single business or any whole industry in the entire nation. In 1958, purchases of goods and services by the federal government amounted to almost one sixth of total expenditures for goods and services produced. (The chart below shows the importance of government spending.)

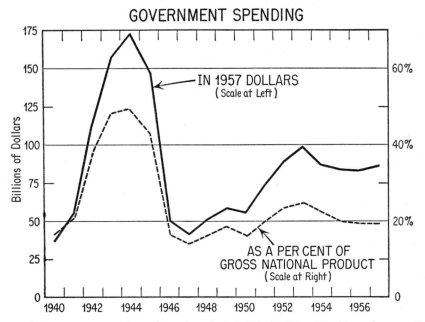

GOVERNMENT SPENDING

Government spending skyrocketed with World War II. After the war it declined sharply to less than one fifth of total expenditures. In more recent years, however, it has risen and leveled off at about one fifth of total expenditure.

Government spending is qualitatively different from the spending of consumers and businesses. Whereas fairly regular patterns of behavior have been observed in the expenditures of the latter, we know that government spending behavior is changing, and changing rapidly. Moreover, we know that government expenditures reflect—more than do the other types of expenditures—changes in attitudes toward the role of government in the economy. For this reason, it is virtually impossible to discover from past practices how government spends at present, and it is even less likely that we can learn from history how it will spend in the future. At this point only one major observation can be made about government expenditures. To many persons *the* economic issue of this generation is whether the government should plan its expenditures primarily in terms of their effects on general business conditions. That is, should the government increase its expenditures whenever the nation faces unemployment? Conversely, should it reduce the spending during

periods of labor shortage? The view that the government should increase its spending merely to increase employment seems to be growing
in popular acceptance. If this view influences the legislators, we can
expect government expenditures to rise during depressions, and to decline during prosperity.

In the past the spending policies of the federal government and
state and local governments often have been in conflict. When the
federal government was increasing its deficit to provide employment
by means of a large public works program, some state and local governments actually reduced their debts. In other words, governmental units
other than the federal government took more money from consumers in
taxes than they spent—using the difference to retire debt. This decline
partly offset the increased expenditures by the federal government
undertaken to combat depression (especially in the years 1933 to 1938).[5]
For this reason separate study of the expenditures of federal, state, and
local governments would be particularly worth while.

**Table 3. Expenditures by Federal, State, and Local
Government, Selected Fiscal Years 1913-1956**

(In billions)

Year	Federal	State	Local	Total
1913	$ 0.7	$ 0.4	$ 1.9	$ 3.0
1927	2.8	1.9	5.8	10.5
1932	4.7	2.6	5.6	12.8
1938	6.9	3.9	5.3	16.7
1940	9.2	4.5	5.8	19.5
1946	60.9	6.2	7.0	74.1
1948	33.9	9.4	10.0	53.3
1950	40.8	12.7	12.8	66.2
1952	67.9	13.3	14.9	96.2
1953	77.5	14.1	16.0	107.6
1954	71.8	15.8	17.9	105.4
1955	69.8	17.4	19.9	107.0
1956	72.6	20.0	21.6	114.2

SOURCE: The Tax Foundation, *Facts and Figures on Government Finance*, 1956-
1957 (New York, The Foundation, Inc., 1956), p. 54.

Some indication of the magnitude of expenditures by each type of
government in selected years is given in Table 3. Of course, recent outlays apply to a period of international unrest. Should some workable and
reliable resolution of the conflict among the major world powers be

---

[5] For example, while the federal government increased its debt from $21.3 to
$39.2 billion between 1932 and 1937, primarily to combat depression, local expendi-
tures dropped. State and local governments actually reduced their debt during some of
these depression years.

worked out, this picture could be drastically altered. (A war would change it even more.) In this connection, too, one finds that government expenditures depend upon factors only slightly connected with economic circumstances. They reflect primarily influences that will be quite different in the future from what they were in the past.

Receipts and expenditures of the three major groups for 1956 and 1957 are shown in Table 4. As this table indicates, individuals (designated "consumers" in the table) spent less than their disposable income, which represents personal income less taxes. The proportion of disposable income saved by all consumers combined in these two years amounted to between 6 and 7 per cent. Business, on the other hand, spent significantly more than its gross retained income (meaning business net income that was not distributed as dividends plus depreciation allowances). In 1956, for example, it spent $25 billion more than its retained receipts; in that year, consumers' incomes exceeded their expenditures by only $20 billion, showing that consumers and business combined spent $5 billion more than they received. Consequently, one would expect that employment, output, and perhaps prices would rise. Table 4, Chapter 20, confirms this view. (Government was able to operate with a surplus in that year.) In 1957, while individuals spent $19.6 billion less than they received, business spending exceeded business income by the same amount. Accordingly, during that year employment and output failed to rise as rapidly as in 1956.

Table 4. Spending Pattern of Major Economic Groups, 1956-1957

(In billions)

	1956			1957		
Spending Group	Receipts	Expenditures	Difference	Receipts	Expenditures	Difference
Consumers	$287.2	$267.2	$20.0	$300.0	$280.4	$19.6
Business	40.9	65.9	−25.0	44.0	63.6	−19.6
Government, (federal, state, and local)	85.0	80.2	4.8	88.2	86.6	1.7

SOURCE: *Economic Report of the President to the Congress*, January 20, 1958, p. 123.

The disruption that might be caused by a change in the *composition* of expenditure, unaccompanied by any change in *total* expenditure, must not be ignored. One must beware of thinking solely in terms of totals. It is possible for a shift in demand from one line of business to another to increase unemployment in the first much more than employment in the second. Output of products for which demand increases may be incapable of rapid expansion. The same total expenditure would thus provide less employment there than it had provided previously. Although in time the rise in demand for some products would lead to added output, the initial shift in expenditure might reduce total employment. While output was being expanded in the industries for which demand increased, substantial numbers of workers might remain unemployed in industries suffering a reduction in demand. As a result, their expenditures, and the total expenditures in the country, might be reduced. Thus a shift in expenditure might itself bring about a change in total expenditure.

Now that the nature of money and the determinants of spending have been discussed, it is fitting to inquire into the influence of changes

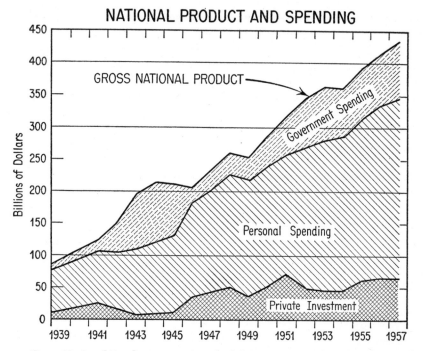

Gross National Product is composed of three major components. By far the largest of them is personal spending. While all three of these components are unstable, private investment has been most volatile during peacetime. War or the threat of war causes violent fluctuations in government spending.

in the supply of money upon expenditure. Our distinction between coin and currency and commercial bank deposits will be helpful here. As already indicated, changes in the quantity of coin and currency take place to facilitate payments, and respond to variations in the demands made by individuals, businesses, and governmental units upon the banks for coin and currency. The bank-deposit portion of the money supply is altogether different, however. The amount of credit that banks will extend strongly influences expenditures by applicants for loans. Almost invariably banks have large numbers who are anxious to borrow. Indeed, individuals and businesses often desire to borrow far more than the banks will lend but banks often have it within their power to make possible the expansion of expenditures—usually by businesses. Clearly, businessmen who request a loan to acquire inventories or equipment needed in their business will not make the expenditure if denied the loan, but will go forward with it if the loan is granted. In this way the banks become a major factor determining whether individuals and businesses will spend. Put more directly, banks do influence expenditure when they vary the level of bank deposits by making loans.

Generally speaking, however, changes in money supply seem to be more passive than changes in spending. Changes in money supply appear to be adjustments to variations in general business conditions rather than original causes of these changes. More specifically, bank loans are the major cause of changes in money supply, and these increase during prosperity and decline during depression. To explain changes in money supply, we must therefore account for changes in general business conditions.

In explaining changes in general business conditions, emphasis has been placed upon expenditure. It is possible to say exactly the same thing by casting the discussion in terms of savings rather than expenditure. Savings would be defined as income that was not used to purchase any goods or services. That is, increases in savings (corresponding to reductions in expenditure) by individuals, corporations, and government could be charged with responsibility for reductions in employment and output. The importance of saving is no greater and no less than that of expenditure, because they are opposite sides of the same shield. If consumers do not spend their income, they save it. The act of spending is an act of nonsaving. No matter how one chooses to express this phenomenon, the act itself is unchanged.

Many economists have accounted for the level of employment and output, and for changes in them, by the relation between savings and particular types of expenditure—by individuals for investment goods, and by business for all purposes. That explanation is precisely the same in substance as the one presented here. It would appear that this one is less complicated and less controversial than the other, for it rests upon changes in one phenomenon—expenditure. To account for changes in employment, one need only find what type of expenditure changed. Comparisons between savings and investment, or explanations that run in terms of savings themselves, are harder to understand. Those who wish to test their mastery of the subjects discussed here might practice by translating the foregoing explanation into the other types of explanation.

IV. SUMMARY

Let us review the ground covered thus far in this section. It was indicated at the outset that the level of employment and output depended primarily upon the level of expenditures. Expenditure that influences output and employment is in money form—that is, payments of coin and currency, and bank checks, in exchange for goods and services. Coin and currency money appears to be essentially passive in the economic process (there was a time when it was otherwise), and does not in itself influence expenditure. However, the largest proportion of the money supply—commercial bank deposits—is highly variable, and does influence the spending of both businesses and individuals. In their lending policies, bankers have the power to alter substantially total expenditures, and they exert this power when they decide how much money to lend. The primary causes of changes in total expenditure are to be found outside variations in money supply. They should be sought in the characteristic behavior of individuals, businesses, and government. Some elements of expenditure by all three groups are moderately stable; most stable are the expenditures of individuals for consumption, and of business for labor and materials to produce these consumers' goods. Far more variable are the expenditures by individuals for investment goods, and by business for plant and equipment. Government expenditure is highly erratic; it depends upon such factors as the state of international relations and the attitudes of the electorate toward the role of spending in a free-enterprise economy.

It takes little reflection to understand that when people try to spend more money, businessmen generally will give them more goods, and will ordinarily turn about and increase their orders for these goods. Conversely, when total expenditure declines, businesses producing goods whose sales have fallen will turn over fewer goods to customers, and will themselves purchase fewer goods. For the most part, it matters little who makes the expenditure. It is the spending of money that calls the tune for all participants in economic activity, and it sets in motion the ordering of goods and the employment of factors of production to fill these orders.

In this entire discussion of depression and inflation, the role of expenditures is stressed above all other factors. It is, however, dangerous to overlook the importance of other conditions that are here taken more or less for granted. Particularly, we are accepting without much discussion the observed behavior of prices, wages, and interest rates. Other writers, as will be shown presently, have singled these factors out for special attention. They are unquestionably important in determining how the economy behaves and, more particularly, in explaining conditions of depression and inflation.

Several features of the foregoing discussion of expenditure warrant special emphasis:

1. Expenditures become personal income and, when respent, become expenditures again. This condition gives rise to the concept of "the circular flow of money," a term which simply emphasizes the fact that money goes around a circle from spending to income to spending to income, etc.

2. When money is held rather than respent by the individual, business, or governmental unit that receives it as income, the incomes of others are reduced; as a result, their spending will tend to decline, a trend which, in turn, will lower the spending of others.

3. The fact that money spent ultimately tends to be respent (which is the essence of the so-called "multiplier") explains why injections of new spending tend to result in greater spending far into the future.

4. Although production takes place in advance of sale generally (that is, most businessmen produce goods—and distributors invest in inventories—before the consumer commits himself to buy), it is carried on in response to actual and expected levels of expenditure. Thus spending calls the tune and may be considered the *initiating* or *strategic* determinant of production levels.

5. Economic activity takes place on two levels—the monetary and the real. Those who *give up* real things or perform services *receive* money. As a result, one can learn about the level of productive activity from the volume of expenditure—and vice versa.

6. Not only does spending give rise to income; it is just equal to the amount of income. That is, all money spent becomes the income of some individual, business, or governmental unit.

The account here given of depression and inflation is admittedly incomplete and an oversimplification. Special attention is accorded to the factors that are most important, most active, and in the author's opinion most amenable to control.

It remains to explain in what way changes in expenditures make their influence felt on general business conditions. This having been done, we shall be able to analyze explanations for depression and inflation, and to consider a variety of proposals for correcting these conditions.

V. DETERMINANTS OF NATIONAL INCOME LEVELS RE-EXPLAINED—GRAPHIC PRESENTATION

The foregoing account of the determinants of the level of national income was quite general. Some readers may find it disappointingly imprecise. What has been said is that national income is determined by the combined spending of consumers, business, and government. This generalization may be termed a "demand theory of income determination," because it takes little account of price movements, wage rates, productivity, and costs of production. (It is possible to incorporate these last factors into the theory; indeed, they must be taken into account if we are to arrive at a full and accurate explanation.)

This explanation of income determination attempts to convey only the fundamental emphasis given to modern economic thought by the writings of the late J. M. Keynes, which represent a distinct though incomplete break with his predecessors; their discussion of income determination emphasized price, wage-rate, and interest-rate movements almost exclusively but had little to do with aggregate expenditures.

The Keynesian theory of income determination can be summarized in a few graphical illustrations. Some readers will gain considerable confidence that they understand what has already been said here if they master these essentially simple figures. Others will find the graphs instructive because they point up the many factors that are omitted from the analysis and its basically primitive character. Much more can be said, and a great deal more is known, about this problem than will be said here. However, beginners must resign themselves to starting with fundamental principles.

In the most general terms, national income is determined by the volume of spending of consumers (consumption expenditure), by the spending of businesses on durable goods and inventories, and by government spending.

To account for the level of national income, then, one must explain the size and variations in these three types of spending; the foregoing chapters have been concerned precisely with these questions. Let us, therefore, proceed to depict graphically and to review briefly what has been said. We start first with consumption expenditure: What determines its amount and variation?

In the Keynesian system, expenditures for consumers' goods depend upon one factor alone: the amount of income received by the population. Consumption expenditure is not a fixed proportion of national income but declines as a proportion of income as the level of income rises. Specifically, when national income is extremely low—as in the very depths of depression—consumer spending actually exceeds income received; at progressively higher levels of national income, the expenditures of consumers decline as a proportion of national income. At very high income levels, the proportion of the national income that is not spent for consumers goods—that is, is saved—becomes considerable. The foregoing statements about the relation between total consumption expenditure and national income can be stated in the following proposition (sometimes called the principle of the declining marginal propensity to consume): as national income rises, a progressively smaller proportion of each added dollar will be spent for consumption. Chart 1 below summarizes this relation between national income and consumption expenditure.

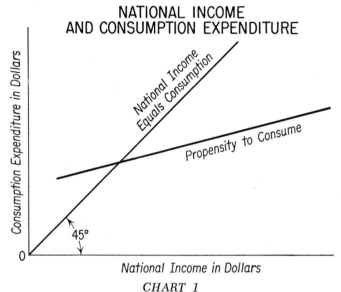

NATIONAL INCOME
AND CONSUMPTION EXPENDITURE

CHART 1

According to Keynes, the level of investment depends upon (1) the net yield on investments, i.e., on purchases of inventories, plant, and equipment, above their cost (including depreciation of the assets, if there be any), and (2) the rate of interest. The income from investment is a complex notion, involving considerations of risk, anticipations of future developments in price cost and demand, as well as technological change, and the like. Again, these questions were discussed previously, and it remains only for us here to translate this notion into graphic terms, as is done by Chart 2.

This chart shows, in the form of the line labeled *MEC* (marginal efficiency of capital) the rate of return on investment that businessmen would expect to obtain if they invested corresponding amounts of money. More specifically, the following steps are implied in the construction of the *MEC* schedule: first all investment projects that business-

men are contemplating are ranked in declining order of yield businessmen anticipate from them. Accordingly, if one businessman is considering a project involving an investment of $1 million which he believes
will yield a return, over cost, equal to $400,000 annually—and no other
projects would yield a higher return—the schedule would show that a
total investment for the entire economy of $1 million would yield a
return of 40 per cent. If there were investments aggregating $100
million that would yield a return of 35 per cent, then the next point on
the schedule would be drawn to record this fact, and so on. In Chart 2,
the *MEC* line indicates, for example, that if the best available investment projects were undertaken totaling $3 billion, the least profitable
project would yield a return of 10 per cent; if investment of $10 billion
were undertaken, the return on the least profitable (that is, on the
marginal unit of investment—or the marginal rate of return) would be
4 per cent.

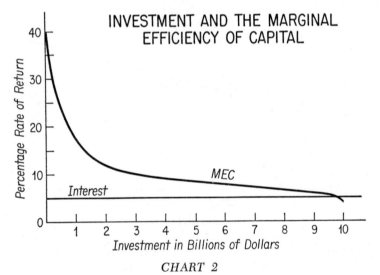

CHART 2

The rate of interest, together with the schedule of the marginal
efficiency of capital, determines the volume of investment, for fairly
obvious reasons. Because of the way the *MEC* schedule is constructed,
the only cost of undertaking investments and obtaining the yields
shown would be what the "investors" would have to pay to get use of
the funds. This cost could be an interest charge of some kind—possibly
carrying charges on a bond issue, the estimated outlays that would
result from a stock issue, payments to banks for loans, etc. If the cost of
borrowing were significantly less than the estimated return from the investment, the investments would be made, because they would contribute to a higher net profit. Conversely, interest charges above the

estimated return on an investment would actually lower net profit; presumably, such investments would not be made.

For illustrative purposes, Chart 2 includes a horizontal line indicating the prevailing rate of interest. (It should be recognized that, as a point of fact, there is no single rate of interest but a series of interest rates, which different borrowers are charged according to their credit worthiness and size, among other things. Since the purpose of the graphic explanation is to make the line of argument more vivid, such discrepancies between reality and our account of what happens should not cause concern.) The rate of interest is taken to be 5 per cent for no particular reason.

With an interest rate of 5 per cent and the schedule of marginal efficiency of capital here depicted, a volume of investment of $9.8 billion would contribute some net profit. That amount, then, would be invested under the assumed conditions. (Note that in this account of investment, nothing has been said about the level of national income; we are assuming, in effect, that the level of investment would not be influenced by the total size of the national income. In other words, we are assuming, quite unrealistically, that the volume of "induced investment" is zero. But, again since our object is to simplify and vivify the foregoing account of income determination, this omission will be overlooked here. As we delve more deeply into the matter, of course, we take these and many other factors into account.)

If we wanted to pursue the matter back one step, we could inquire into the factors that determine the rate of interest and the marginal efficiency of capital. And, in turn, we could attempt to explain these very factors themselves—and so on. We must draw a line somewhere; the author would be highly gratified if the reader would master what is said here.

To relate the foregoing paragraphs to what was said about Chart 1, we now have depicted the two private elements that determine the level of national income—consumption and investment. It is possible to construct a chart showing the combined spending for consumption and investment (see Chart 3).

Government spending is determined by a host of political, economic, and military factors that can be skipped here. In part, government spending is determined by the level of national income and, in one sense, is like private-consumption expenditure—the greater the level of national income (all other things equal), the lower will be the government's expenditure. This condition results from the growing assumption that the federal government must take measures to mitigate and lessen the suffering caused by cyclical fluctuations. Political considerations, if not compassion, would dictate that relief or other types of aid be extended to unemployed persons. Without attempting further to explain govern-

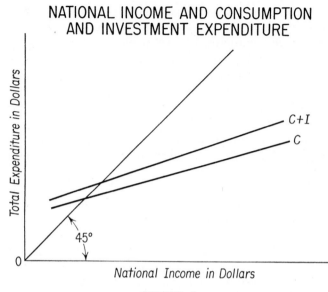

CHART 3

ment expenditures, they have been drawn in Chart 4 to show a larger expenditure (in absolute amount) when national income is low than when it is high.

Chart 5 combines these three types of spending into an aggregate-expenditure schedule. This schedule, placed in juxtaposition to a straight

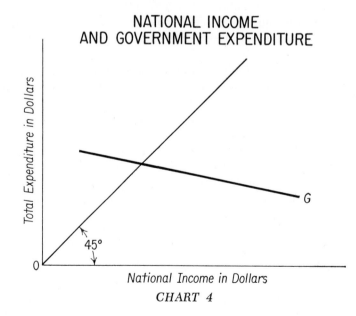

CHART 4

line which bisects the graph's vortex, can be used to explain the point at which the level of national income would settle *if the conditions depicted there remained undisturbed;* in other words, it explains what the level of national income would be if the forces implicit in the aggregate-expenditure schedule were permitted to work themselves out without disturbance. Sometimes that point is called the long-run "equilibrium level of income."

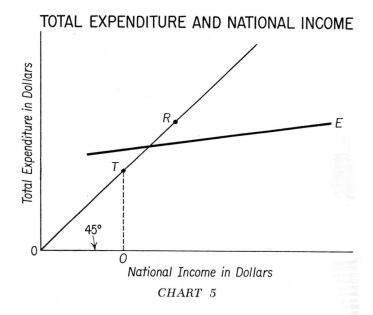

TOTAL EXPENDITURE AND NATIONAL INCOME

Total Expenditure in Dollars

National Income in Dollars

CHART 5

The 45-degree-angle line, as the straight line is sometimes called, has a simple property which facilitates explanation: lines dropped at right angles to the two axes will mark off equal distances along each; and for purposes of this type of illustration, the scales of the two axes are made equal so that at any point on the 45-degree-angle line, both national income and expenditure are equal. When the aggregate-expenditure schedule lies above the 45-degree-angle line, expenditure would exceed national income. Similarly, wherever the aggregate-expenditure schedule is below the 45-degree-angle line it represents a situation in which national income exceeds the aggregate of expenditure.

It can be explained why the level of national income must settle at the point where the aggregate-expenditure schedule (E) intersects the 45-degree-angle line. (If it intersected at more than one point, then the economy "could" settle at any of these points of intersection—but this possibility is remote, though conceivable.) Most simply, let us see why any other point would be impossible. For example, why could not national income settle at the point on the 45-degree-angle line marked *R* on Chart 5 (which is to the right of the point of intersection)? At point *R,* national income (that is, the personal income received) is greater than the amount that consumers, business, and government "decided to" spend. This is another way of saying that the volume of goods and services produced (at the prevailing prices) is greater than what all spenders taken together wanted to purchase; in consequence, inventories of goods would grow in a way that was not intended by businessmen. Put differently, when national income (which, it should be recalled, equals national output) exceeds the combined expenditure of individuals, businesses, and government, then involuntary investment in inventories occurs. When goods remain unsold, businessmen will curtail their purchases, and production will be curtailed in turn. The effect described would occur whether the point taken on the 45-degree-angle line were farther from, or closer to, the point of intersection with the aggregate-expenditure schedule.

Similarly (conversely), at point *T,* which lies below the aggregate-expenditure schedule and is to the left of the point of intersection, we have a situation that could not exist for long—if at all. At a national income of *OT,* individuals, businessmen, and government would attempt to buy more than the amount of goods and services actually produced. That is to say, they would be depleting inventories (and in that way making investment smaller than businessmen collectively had decided to hold). As a result, businessmen would increase their purchases to replace the stocks that had been depleted—causing national income to rise. Only at the point of intersection would the economy reach a position of stability from which there would be no tendency for businessmen, consumers, or government to alter their behavior. That is, the economy would be in a position of equilibrium.

Readers will get themselves into a lot of trouble if they expect miracles of the simple graphical explanation just completed for levels of national income. It is, admittedly, an oversimplification. Taken as an accurate description of reality, it can be dangerously misleading. On the other hand, many persons find this type of explanation far more convincing and memorable than the simply verbal form.

One simple rule should be understood and followed by those who grapple with graphical illustrations of economic principles: regard them as tools to clarify understanding and not as devices to prove anything. They are a substitute for words—and in many respects a poor substitute, because they generally require assumptions that are unrealistic. (Typically, they require the assumption that behavior is consistent or that certain factors are wholly without influence. By employing other forms of mathematics, we can overcome some of these limitations of geometry, but not all.)

A rule that should be followed in employing graphic explanations of economic phenomena is that you return to the beginning of the explanation and review it with one major object in mind: to collect all the assumptions made along the way that were needed because of the limitations of the geometric medium itself. In this case, the reader should have very clearly in mind that at least the following, fundamentally unrealistic, assumptions were made: that total expenditure by individuals is influenced solely by their income; that investment is unaffected by national income or fluctuations in it; that government expenditure is influenced solely by over-all economic considerations; and that prices and wage rates would not be affected by changes in "real" national income—and in turn would not affect "real" national income. To arrive at a complete and accurate explanation for the level of national income at any time, these last factors may be found to figure prominently; sometimes they may overshadow the demand factors to which attention has been directed exclusively in the foregoing explanation.

DISCUSSION QUESTIONS

1. What proportion of your family's spending is carefully planned, perhaps according to a budget, and what proportion represents a response to whim, a feeling of elation?

2. What kinds of development could induce your family to spend, say, 20 per cent more than it originally planned this year?

3. If your family's income were to decline by 20 per cent this year, how would its spending be altered? Say your family's income rose by 20 per cent, how would its spending pattern be changed?

4. Explain why the spending of business firms to pay for labor and raw materials to produce current output is considered a reflection of consumer decisions rather than of business decisions.

5. If you were a businessman, under what circumstances would you increase substantially your holding of inventories? Would your answer be the same whether you were in show business, in the liquor business, in a dairy, or working as a typewriter retailer?

6. As a businessman, would you build new factories and buy new machines after or before you found you could not fill all your customers' orders? Under what circumstances would you decide to keep your customers waiting and when would you feel that you must meet their orders promptly?

7. Do you believe the government should budget its expenditures on the same basis as you would as a private businessman? Why or why not?

8. What major factors determine the actual level of income for any period?

9. Why does each of these factors vary differently in degree? Explain in detail.

10. Using graphic techniques, show how consumption and national income are related, and how the interest rate and the marginal efficiency of capital determine the level of investment.

22   The Level of Expenditures

and General

Business Conditions

I.   HOW THE ECONOMY RESPONDS TO CHANGES IN TOTAL EXPENDITURES

A. Decline in Expenditures

Assume that individuals spend $6 billion less a year (that means that their spending drops by one-half billion dollars each month) than they did the preceding year. We need not inquire into the reasons for this decline at this point; many factors could bring this about. Possible causes will be listed later. What would happen to output and employment as a result of the decline in expenditure?

First, a drop in spending by individuals would leave businessmen with more goods than they would have had if consumers had maintained their past volume of expenditure. Businessmen, therefore, would find themselves with larger inventories than they had planned to hold. They would have invested, albeit involuntarily, in higher inventories. Not desiring to hold these, businessmen would reduce their purchases in order to return to the desired level of inventories. By reducing their purchases, presumably they would bring about a reduction in the output by their suppliers. The decline in production by these firms would spread in two directions—"backward" toward the production of raw materials, and "crosswise" to other industries.

The backward spread of a decline in production has already been illustrated. When retailers sell less, they transmit the decline in sales back to their suppliers—usually wholesalers. They in turn pass it on to the manufacturers from whom they buy, and these would lower their purchases of raw materials, equipment, and such. Firms selling to manufacturers would in turn reduce their purchases and thereby lead other firms behind them to lower output.

469

The crosswise spread of a decline in spending is not hard to understand. For example, assume that it was a drop in the purchase of consumers' durable goods (houses, cars, refrigerators, washing machines, and the like) that brought about the decline in total spending. Employees in the production of these goods will suffer a decline in personal income—due either to unemployment or to fewer hours or days of work. Almost certainly their expenditures would decline. They would reduce most their purchase of things whose acquisition could be postponed. In particular, these include durable goods that can be repaired or just "put up with" to get longer use from them. Purchases of goods from *all* industries would decline somewhat, with the result that producers and distributors of food, for example, would sell less, and they also would curtail operations, causing their employees to spend less for various things. In this way, a reduction in spending spreads and infects almost every part of the economy in time.

Only the effects on consumer spending of an initial decline in expenditure have thus far been sketched. Little has been said about business expenditures; it was indicated that purchases of finished goods would be adjusted to sales, so that inventories would not be increased after sales declined. Would not less also be spent for fixed capital than was originally planned? And, if businesses did not themselves decide to postpone projected investment expenditures, would not those on whom they depended for funds make them reconsider?

Consider separately the effects of the decline in consumer expenditure upon the various types of expenditure for fixed capital. First, consider how a drop in consumer spending would affect the purchase of equipment to replace machinery that has deteriorated beyond further economical use. When total output declines, it may be possible to meet the total demand for goods without replacing worn-out equipment. The total desired output could possibly be produced by the equipment remaining in good order. Whether some worn-out parts would have to be replaced would depend partly on the size of the decline in total sales of consumers' goods, and upon the proportion of equipment that required replacement. Thus, for example, a moderate decline in sales of consumers' goods, of, say, 15 per cent, might make it unnecessary for a firm that had contemplated a replacement of 10 per cent of its equipment to do so. (This example illustrates one aspect of the "acceleration principle," which economists sometimes adduce to explain the more violent fluctuation in output of capital goods than in output of consumers' goods. We shall not bother to discuss this principle in detail here; it should be noted, however, that the principle also explains why increases in the demand for consumers' goods will, under some conditions, result in far larger relative rises in output of capital goods.)

When businessmen fail to replace worn-out equipment, they can hardly be expected to expand their total productive capacity. A decline in a company's sales poses a danger beyond that of having idle facilities. Investment in fixed capital threatens a firm's very solvency, because it would tie up the firm's liquid financial resources at a time when its revenues declined. The business might therefore not be able to meet its obligations as they came due, and could thus become insolvent. Businessmen must be able to meet their obligations as they arise, even though their assets may exceed their liabilities; otherwise creditors could compel them to liquidate.

Like consumers, businessmen are able to postpone many forms of expenditures when business becomes bad. They will make modest expenditures to repair and maintain equipment that otherwise would be replaced; they will get along with smaller inventories, and generally will cut down research and advertising outlays.

Furthermore, business expenditures which were planned to raise the level of productivity or to make available new products might likewise be reduced when a decline in consumer expenditure has taken place. (Funds already in hand that might have been earmarked for the project might be considered a necessary reserve against the danger of a major depression.) Again, businesses contemplating such expenditures face added difficulties in obtaining the funds needed to finance the project. Financial institutions on which the business depended might become understandably reluctant to go through with the project.

Accordingly, a drop in consumer expenditures would adversely influence all types of business investment in fixed capital. An initial decline of consumer expenditures brings about secondary reductions in consumer spending, as we saw in the discussion of the backward and crosswise spread of such a decline, and reductions in business spending for both inventories and fixed capital.

Even some government expenditure might be adversely affected by a reduction in consumer spending. True, government has assumed the obligation to pay unemployment-insurance benefits in a large group of industries to workers who have lost their jobs. A decline in consumer expenditures and the consequent decline in employment will bring about a rise in government expenditures for this purpose. However, government revenues are closely tied to total output and employment. Revenue from excise, sales, and personal income and corporate profits taxes vary directly with total output. Consequently, the ability of local and state governments to spend varies closely with total output. As already indicated, these governments have tended to adjust their expenditures to their revenue, with the result that their spending has declined at the same time that consumer and business spending has dropped.

Only the federal government has shown an inclination to increase its expenditures merely because other groups have reduced their spending. But even the federal government is slow to adjust its expenditures upward when total consumer and business expenditures have dropped. The federal government's tardiness is partially attributable to the difficulty of recognizing a decline in expenditure soon after it has occurred. The time that a downswing in business started can be determined only on hindsight; at the time it is impossible to tell whether a decline is merely temporary and accidental. In addition, adjustment of government expenditures to compensate for a decline in total sales and employment requires legislation that, at best, takes considerable time to pass.

Thus we have seen that a decline in expenditures in one sector of the economy will generally spread backward and crosswise to reduce individuals' spending in other industries. A decline in consumer buying is infectious, and ultimately will reduce spending by consumers associated with all industries. Moreover, a decline in consumer expenditures ordinarily will discourage businessmen from spending as much for plant and equipment as they otherwise would. Businessmen's inventory holdings would presumably rise involuntarily under the initial impact of the decline in consumer spending, and they would thereupon try to reduce their inventories. Businessmen would also refrain from replacing worn-out equipment, and would reconsider, and often postpone, projects calling for sizable expenditures on the expansion of physical plant facilities, and for the introduction of new productive methods and new products.

Also, the drop in consumer expenditure, by reducing government revenues, is likely to reduce spending by local and state governments; for they, as a matter of policy, tend to balance expenditure with revenue. While the federal government apparently has accepted the policy of increasing its expenditures to counter a decline in employment, ordinarily a considerable interval elapses before its expenditures are increased.

It should therefore be clear that our economic system generally magnifies reductions of expenditure that take place at any single point in the economy. Reductions of expenditure, no matter where they occur, tend to cumulate. (We have dealt here only with an initial decline in expenditure by individuals; one by businessmen or government would spread in parallel fashion.) An initial minor drop in spending could result in a major over-all drop. *The tendency for changes in expenditure to become magnified accounts for the vulnerability of our economy to wide swings in general business conditions* and poses the threat that a minor decline in expenditure in one sector of the economy will snowball into a major depression.

By no means should it be concluded that *all* minor declines in expenditure grow to large proportions. The economy is often able to "absorb" minor shocks; at other times, however, it becomes particularly vulnerable, and will quickly and greatly magnify a drop in expenditure. It must be recognized that often reductions in expenditure in one sector of the economy may—for no special reason—be compensated for by increases in expenditure elsewhere. *Moreover, a decline in expenditure in some goods increases the likelihood of a rise elsewhere;* a drop in expenditures by consumers would mean that their resources available for spending on other goods would have increased correspondingly. A *net* decline in expenditure by one type of spending often will have the cumulative effects described here; the degree of cumulation will vary with a variety of circumstances.

Cumulative changes should be distinguished from those that are "self-limiting." The latter type may be considered self-correcting; they give rise to forces which reverse the initial change. For example, a sharp rise in price due to, say, a sudden increase in demand will generate strong efforts to expand production, and this expansion would ultimately reverse the initial price rise. In contrast, cumulative changes set forces in motion that accentuate rather than reverse the initial change. Cumulative changes contribute to instability, while self-limiting changes create a minimum of instability.

B. Rise in Expenditures

Let us now examine the effects of a rise in expenditure. Consider as an illustration a rise in federal government expenditures for the purpose of greatly expanding the military establishment at a time when the economy already is producing about all it can. (This situation closely approximates the condition existing at the end of 1952.) Further, make the realistic assumption that the government will not raise taxes enough to cover the total added cost of this program. Specifically, we shall assume that the increased military expenditures will be met partly from increased borrowings. (Government expenditures can be financed from three sources: taxes, borrowing, and the printing of paper money. We are assuming that the government will decline to print money to pay for its arms program, and will therefore borrow at least in part from the banks.)

The increased government spending initially will induce producers of military goods to raise output. To do so they must obtain a larger labor supply, which they will presumably acquire by increasing the hours worked by their present force, and by attracting added workers to their plants. The plants will have to bid workers away from firms in other industries. On the other hand, the rise in taxes will reduce individual spending somewhat and thereby will release some workers who may find employment in industries producing munitions. Since taxes can be assumed to rise less than expenditures for arms, the drop in individual spending will not wholly offset increased government expenditure, and the number of workers released from industries producing for individuals will not fall enough to provide all the workers needed to produce munitions. To obtain the workers they need, munition plants will have to offer higher rates of pay than were currently being received. Rates of pay will rise, therefore, in military industries, and will tend to bring about an increase in wage rates in other industries. Under the conditions assumed—near-full employment with rising rates of pay—it is to be expected that the prices of most goods will be increased. (Some industries—particularly public utilities—will not raise prices until after some time lag.) *The combination of increased pay for workers and increased prices for goods will ordinarily precipitate a general upward price movement that will feed on itself.*

The higher prices for goods will encourage consumers and businesses to increase their purchases before prices rise further. In the face of rising labor costs, businessmen will be encouraged to hire more labor and increase output before their labor costs advance further. Individuals also will increase their expenditures because of increased pay and greater security of employment. Expectation of wage and price increases will thus reinforce the rise in government expenditure which was the initial cause of the upswing in labor costs and prices. The increased purchases by business and consumers will push wages and prices up still further, and will intensify the desire of all groups to make purchases before the rise in prices proceeds still further.

At some point, output will have reached its practicable maximum, so that increases in demand will simply have the effect of raising prices and wages and will not increase output. Most individuals and firms who wished to increase their purchases and output will be frustrated. Their willingness to spend more will simply have resulted in their giving up more money for the same total quantity of goods. The demand for goods and labor may grow unendingly, even though there may be no possibility of increasing output further, because everyone will expect a further rise in prices and will try to escape its full impact.

To achieve a particular degree of military preparedness, the government must increase its appropriations for military purposes as prices increase. It will thus feed added expenditure into the economy.

Put simply, an inflation is a period of rising prices in which the value of money declines. Since those who hold money will find themselves in a far worse position, everyone makes an effort to hold goods instead of money. In the general attempt to exchange money for goods, the total volume of expenditure rises and pushes prices up further. Thus the initial price increase sets in motion a cumulative upswing in expenditures. As with the reduction of expenditure analyzed above, it does not

CHANGES IN.......

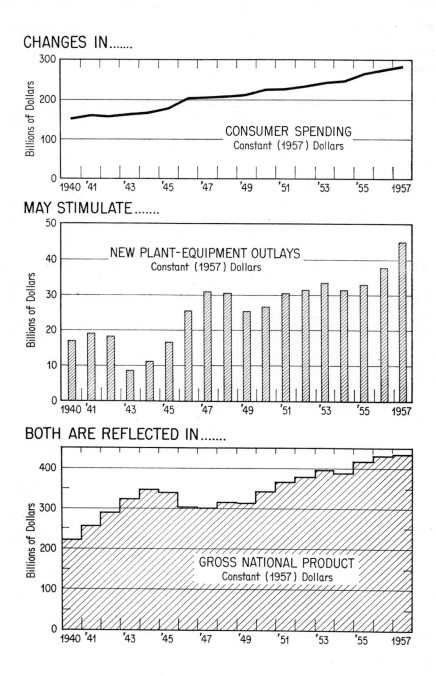

CONSUMER SPENDING
Constant (1957) Dollars

MAY STIMULATE.......

NEW PLANT-EQUIPMENT OUTLAYS
Constant (1957) Dollars

BOTH ARE REFLECTED IN.......

GROSS NATIONAL PRODUCT
Constant (1957) Dollars

matter in what sector the increase occurs initially; it will spread to almost the entire economy.[1]

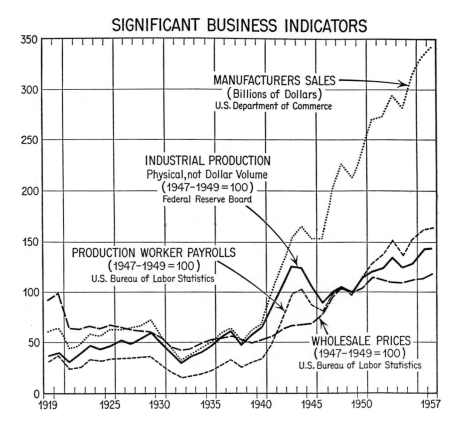

SIGNIFICANT BUSINESS INDICATORS

The foregoing account of increases and reductions in expenditure could hardly be expected to cover all possible types of changes in expenditure. Only two, but not untypical, situations were analyzed briefly. It cannot be overemphasized that *almost every business downswing and every inflationary period differs from every other one.* The economic system is constantly modified, and accordingly it responds differently to similar conditions with the passage of time. Despite these differences, important similarities are to be found among periods of depression and inflation that can be noted. Recognize that these similarities are not always found, and not found in equal degree in every instance.

---

[1] An essential characteristic of inflation that explains why it is so dreaded is the unevenness of price and income changes. Because prices change by different amounts and many incomes are slow to rise, many individuals suffer acutely during inflation. Those gain whose incomes rise faster than prices.

II. THE PROGRESSION OF ECONOMIC STATES

Business undergoes ups and downs in an orderly, some would call it a disorderly, sequence. Most business analysts and economists divide all business conditions into four phases, usually termed "prosperity," "contraction," "depression," and "expansion." (The terms used to describe the states of business vary somewhat. What will here be designated as expansion is called "revival" by some; prosperity is sometimes termed "boom"; what we call contraction often is termed "recession." Depression and "bust" are used interchangeably by some analysts.)

To understand and explain changes in business conditions, we should know what happens during all phases of business conditions. *We must know what it is that we want to explain.* Many writers have attempted to account for the ups and downs of business without bothering to study what happens to the economic system during its various stages. Little wonder that we have so many theories of the business cycle, and so little understanding of it.

The National Bureau of Economic Research in the 1920's undertook a large project to study what happens to virtually all individual economic processes as business undergoes its ups and downs. It amassed and analyzed a huge body of information that should greatly assist in the formulation of a reliable explanation of changes in general business conditions. Students who pursue their studies of economic fluctuations in more advanced courses study the behavior of individual lines of business, particularly prices, wages, and interest rates, the output of consumers' and capital goods, and the like. At this stage of our studies we shall limit our description of the four phases of business conditions to a few simple and broad generalizations.

A. *Characteristics of Periods of Low Expenditure*

As total expenditure declines, business contracts. Output in most lines and in most areas falls at such times. Ordinarily employment, prices, and wage rates decline also. During periods of contraction, most businessmen are pessimistic and pursue conservative policies. Banks reduce their outstanding loans and businessmen try to reduce inventories. The size of the decline in total expenditure generally determines the speed and magnitude of the fall in general business activity.

When the level of expenditure is low relative to the amount of spending needed to provide full employment, a condition of depression exists. Like contractions in business, depressions vary widely in severity and are characterized by a low level of output and employment. They differ from contractions in that business is not becoming worse, but has reached a low plateau. Most prices and wage rates are lower than they were during the preceding period of prosperity and contraction. The greatest reductions in output and employment occur in industries producing durable consumers' goods and capital goods. Not infrequently, the output of food is as great during depression as during prosperity. Banks are extremely reluctant to lend during depression, and consumers and businessmen tend to use their durable goods longer than they had originally planned.

B. Characteristics of Periods of High Expenditure

While total expenditures rise, business expands. Periods of expansion are characterized by upward movements in most lines of activity. Typically, prices and wage rates rise, and businessmen become hopeful and more venturesome. Inventories in the hands of both individuals and businesses are replenished during expansion. Banks lend more willingly, and good risks borrow more willingly during such periods.

When total expenditures reach so high a level that virtually all resources seeking employment are at work, business is said to be prosperous. Prosperity is usually characterized by relatively high prices, employment, wage rates, and output. Most businessmen are bold and hopeful during prosperity; some are smitten with a speculative fever. Large borrowing by businesses and consumers is characteristic of prosperity.

C. The Concept of the Business Cycle

History confirms the fact that general business conditions constantly change. Moreover, these changes usually have not been gradual and steady. Most economists think the pattern of change resembles a "cycle" —with a period of upswing to a peak, followed by a downswing which in turn gives way to another rise in general business. The term "business cycle" is firmly rooted in our vocabulary and thinking. It is desirable to make clear what is meant by a business "cycle." Another possible conception of economic change that is not cyclical in nature will be presented also.

When we speak of business cycles, we attribute three essential characteristics to the economic system. First, we imply that the economy generates reverse movements so that, for example, causes for a downturn develop during an upswing and ultimately take over, pushing business in an opposite direction. In other words, the concept of a business cycle implies the assumption that business cannot rise to a peak and remain around that peak, or fall to a very low point and remain there. Second, the concept of business cycles incorporates the notion of cumulative change—that is, that changes in business conditions usually are rapid rather than gradual. Third, to accept the existence of the business cycle is to attribute characteristics to the economic system that do not change over long periods of time. Thus, when people speak of the existence of business cycles, they imply that the economy behaves essentially the same way in the late 1950's that it did more than half a century ago, despite the enormous economic change that has occurred since then.

Rather than explore the validity of these three propositions, an alternative view of economic change will be presented that involves few assumptions and still is fully consistent with history. First, there is an inherent tendency in our economy to magnify moderate upward and downward impulses. Economic change is cumulative. Second, it is altogether possible that general business conditions will not reverse themselves for a long time. Third, a wide variety of factors could push business up and down (virtually all of them being reflected in changed expenditures); generally many opposing factors operate simultaneously, so that they partly or wholly offset one another a large part of the time.

It is not essential to choose between these two conceptions of economic change. The first is generally accepted; the second is easier to prove than the first, but it does not go so far. Whichever conception we favor, it is necessary to isolate the factors that push business up and to seek out those that depress it. Moreover, it remains important to discover what happens during the upswings and downswings of business—no matter what their cause.

III. SUMMARY AND CONCLUSIONS

Three major economic units account for almost all spending in the economy: individuals, businesses, and government. To arrive at a full and thorough understanding of why expenditure will vary and by how much, it is necessary to analyze these groups separately. To explain expenditure poses many difficult problems that are essentially psychological in character, and which have not yet been studied very thoroughly. Evidence is not lacking to demonstrate that expenditure varies considerably from time to time, however.

Once expenditure fluctuates, general business conditions are likely to be affected, though the vulnerability of the economy to changes in expenditure varies largely according to the level of business confidence. The economy of the United States shows considerable instability, cumulating modest upward and downward movements into general upswings and downswings. Cumulation of economic movements results from a backward and crosswise spread of variations in expenditure.

There is dispute about whether economic activity in the United

States must undergo cyclical changes. Periods of stability—either at high or low levels of employment or output—have been rare in the past. The economy is undeniably unstable, magnifying moderate upward and downward impulses, which may have been set in motion by a wide variety of factors. Whether past instability proves that the economic system must forever experience business cycles is a controversial issue, however.

DISCUSSION QUESTIONS

1. Explain what happens to the economy when a decline in expenditures sets in. Take into account the different types of expenditures and the factors affecting them.

2. Contrast the backward and crosswise spread of a decline in expenditures. Which of the two explains the tendency of a recession to cumulate and become more intense?

3. Trace the progressive expansion of the economy due to a rise in expenditures.

4. Do you believe that business ups and downs are inevitable? Must a period of very good business be followed by a period of very bad business?

5. Are all periods of depression and prosperity essentially the same? In what respects might they differ?

23   Depression: Causes and Possible Cures

The fundamental causes of economic instability have already been discussed in general terms. Fluctuations in total expenditures were found to be the primary cause. The main reasons for variations in spending were found to be the inherent instability of expenditures by business, especially for plant and equipment. Variations in total spending may not be very large in themselves, but they can be the initial stimulus that sets off a cumulative movement either upward or downward.

In this chapter we shall look closely at the causes for depression—the most serious, though not necessarily the most imminent, type of economic instability confronting our economy. In addition, possible remedies for, and means of prevention of, depression will be explored. Later we shall discuss the causes and possible cures for inflation in some detail.

I.   CAUSES OF DEPRESSION

To account for depression, one must explain a substantial decline in the total amount of money spent by all individuals, businesses, and governments combined. A full explanation of depression requires an explanation for failure of prices and wage and interest rates to fall sufficiently to offset the drop in expenditure. We shall concentrate on the level of expenditure, however, for it seems to be the most active influence, and also the one most amenable to control. In so doing we follow the fashion set by Keynes in 1936.

A. *The Thesis That Depressions "Cannot" Occur*

Until relatively recently, economists argued that depressions were theoretically impossible. Their optimistic conclusion, which persisted despite unmistakable ups and downs in business, rested heavily on an illuminating principle known as Say's Law of Markets, and upon the view that adjustments in prices, wages, and interest rates would correct any difficulties the economy experienced. These two general lines of argument will be reviewed briefly.

1. SAY'S LAW

Jean Baptiste Say, writing at the beginning of the nineteenth century, argued that supply creates its own demand; that is, *there would never be any shortage of purchasing power to buy back the goods that were produced at the prices that were asked for them.* The amount of money distributed as income to individuals, business, and government, according to Say, is exactly equal to the total of prices paid for goods produced. *Production gives rise both to a dollar value of goods offered for sale and to an equal dollar amount of income that could be used to repurchase them.*

Essentially this principle states the obvious but important fact that when money is paid for a product or service, it does not disappear, but becomes the personal income of someone. It also makes clear that personal and business income is not determined independently of the value of goods and services offered for sale, but that they are jointly determined and equal.[1]

We shall not criticize Say's Law in detail. Several observations must be made, however. First, it simply states, correctly, that there would be enough purchasing power distributed to repurchase the goods that have been produced. *It does not state that enough would be spent.* Second, it ignores the important sources of purchasing power that are not generated in the production process. Specifically, it neglects the possibility that changes in bank credit will alter the total volume of spending. Third, it does not state, though it implies, that the amount of money distributed as purchasing power will cover all costs and some profit for any individual businessman or for all taken together. Additional defects in Say's Law have been pointed out by others, but they need not be discussed here.

2. PRICE, WAGE, AND INTEREST-RATE ADJUSTMENTS MIGHT FORESTALL DEPRESSION

The amount of goods sold depends on more than the amount of money spent. It depends quite as much on the prices that are paid for them. Sales volume can double either by doubling expenditure or by

---

[1] This principle underlies many calculations of the output of goods and services in studies of national income. The value of services particularly cannot usually be measured directly, for this reason their value is determined by taking the incomes of those rendering the services.

cutting prices in half—or by some combination of the two. In the view of most orthodox economists up to 1930, if total spending were to decline, prices would decline correspondingly, so that the total quantity of goods produced would nevertheless be sold. The reduction in prices would be due to the pressure of competition, which would induce businessmen to lower price in an effort to win the patronage of the limited number of customers. As some businessmen lowered price, the others would have to follow, or they would not be able to sell anything. The pressure to reduce price would lead businessmen to lower price ultimately to the point where the entire output was sold.

In addition to the downward adjustment of price to be expected when total expenditure declined, orthodox theory pointed to two other more or less automatic "regulators" that would keep the economy from experiencing depression. They were adjustments in wage and interest rates. These were to combat depression by declining whenever business slackened. They were expected to decline because of competition among workers for jobs and among lenders for the business of the few good risks seeking loans. Accordingly, if unemployment existed, workers would be compelled to accept lower wages. Therefore employment would rise, ultimately, to the point where all workers were employed.

Similarly, interest rates were expected to adjust to a drop in total expenditure, and thereby increase output and employment. When business activity slackened, according to this view, interest rates would decline. Businessmen and consumers would seize the opportunity to borrow at low interest rates for the purpose of buying plant, equipment, inventories, houses, automobiles, and the like. As a result, total sales of these things would rise and restore the economy to full employment.

Theoretically at least, each of these regulators is in itself sufficient to restore the economy to full employment. The operation of all three together gave the orthodox economists confidence that business would not, save for very brief periods, perhaps, depart from full employment.

Again, we shall not discuss all the flaws in these three regulators as insurance against depression. It should suffice for our purposes to note the following limitations. First, prices and wages do not *in fact* adjust downward speedily; usually they remain for some time at prosperity levels in a substantial number of industries, even after business has become substantially worse. Likewise, interest rates are slow to adjust downward. Indeed, it becomes harder to obtain loans during periods of contraction than during prosperity, owing to the understandable fear on the part of bankers to lend when business is getting worse. Consequently, the interest rate for most of those who want to borrow becomes so high that borrowing for investment is reduced further, rather than increased, during periods of contraction. Second, *speculative motives often cause the regulators to aggravate rather than to alleviate reductions in output.* As indicated before, when prices of goods, services, labor, or borrowed funds decline, purchasers of these things are tempted to postpone their purchases in the expectation that their prices will fall further. Consequently, a drop in price may reduce rather than increase expenditures. Only when no further decline in prices is expected will price reductions increase sales for certain. Rarely will all buyers be sure that any price (wage, interest-rate) reduction is the last—even when it turns out to be so.

B. Types of Explanation for Depression

Two types of explanation for depression should be distinguished. The first is quite ambitious, and accounts for depressions as part of an explanation for all four phases of the business cycle. These explanations are "theories of the business cycle," and represent a high level of intellectual attainment and complexity. The second type is more modest, and can be reduced to a list of circumstances that might result in a reduction of business activity. More specifically, it is a list of factors that lower total expenditure.

A review of business-cycle theories would occupy considerable time and space. Moreover, to understand fully most of these theories requires sound training in economic theory. Accordingly, the major theories of the business cycle will not be reviewed here.[2]

The discussion of depression's causes presented here will be limited to a list of circumstances that might cause business to grow worse. Fundamentally, each gives a reason why some type of expenditure might decline substantially. (To explain improvements in business conditions, one need only reverse factors listed here.)

Before potential causes of depression are set forth, it is important to recognize that a "cause" or an "explanation" is a relative thing. It is possible to push one's explanation for any event far back and find the "causes for the causes of the causes," or one may be satisfied with an explanation that is less deep. For example, it is possible to account for a downswing in business by a "decline in expenditures of individuals"; this type of explanation is not unreasonable, but neither is it very helpful. We want to know why individuals' expenditures decline. One might say because they decided to save more money, but we want to know what increased their desire for savings. Perhaps the desire for savings may be attributed to increased fear of unemployment. Again, we would want to ask why individuals feared unemployment more than before. And so on. One

---

[2] Those who wish to study theories of the business cycle will find thorough and clear summaries in G. Haberler, *Prosperity and Depression,* enlarged 3d ed. (New York: United Nations, 1946), and A. Achinstein, *Introduction to Business Cycles* (New York: The Thomas Y. Crowell Company, 1950).

could stop his explanation anywhere, or could continue much further down the line.

The list that follows will go only a small way toward a complete explanation, but it should suggest the kinds of circumstances that cause economic difficulty. The explanation for depression will be divided into three categories: that involving declines in the expenditure of individuals, that accounting for depression by a drop in the spending of business, and, finally, that turning on the volume of government expenditure.

C. Major Explanations for a Reduction in Total Expenditure

A reduction in total expenditure can originate in spending by individuals, by businesses, by government, and by foreigners. The major causes for reductions in the first three types will be listed in outline form. (We shall deal with sales to foreigners at a later point. Factors accounting for reductions in the spending of individuals and business within a country also explain why both groups will spend less in other countries.)

1. DECLINE IN EXPENDITURES BY INDIVIDUALS

A. Reduction in disposable income
   1. Due to drop in general business activity
   2. Due to increased income taxes
B. Lowered desire or "need" for goods
   1. Resulting from a building up of inventories of goods to a high level—as when many consumers bring large amounts of clothing, furniture, electrical appliances—enabling them to maintain the desired level of living without further purchases for some time
   2. Resulting from a servicing of durable goods so that they are put in a state of good repair—as painting and papering a home, replacing defective wiring or plumbing, and such, overhauling the car, or servicing the electrical appliances
   3. Resulting from decline in the size of families
C. Increased apprehension concerning future income prospects
   1. Due to the publication of reports suggesting worsened general business conditions
   2. Resulting from poor crop prospects
   3. Due to expected increases in taxes
D. Expected advantage from postponing expenditures
   1. Due to an expected decline in prices
   2. Due to expected improvements in quality of goods
E. Reduced ability of individuals to spend resulting from

1. Increased difficulty of obtaining installment credit, personal loans, charge accounts, and so on, due to a credit stringency
2. Legal restrictions on consumption to release materials for defense purposes

2. DECLINES IN EXPENDITURES BY BUSINESS WHICH MAY RESULT FROM

A. Reduced income due to
   1. Increased costs
   2. Lower selling prices
   3. Increased taxes
B. Reduced desire or need for goods because
   1. Business accumulated large stocks of inventories
   2. Business put its plant and equipment in good condition, by repairs and maintenance expenditures
   3. Business expanded the stock of plant and equipment enough to produce expected increases in sales of end products
   4. Technological advance slowed down, with the result that new products and new methods of production are smaller in number
C. Increased apprehension concerning future profit prospects because
   1. The business press sounded warnings about the future for any of a multitude of reasons, including many mistaken ones
   2. Tax increases are expected
D. Expected advantages from postponing expenditures resulting from
   1. An expected rise in quality of goods
   2. Anticipated reductions in price
E. Reduced ability to spend because of
   1. Curtailment of bank loans and reduced willingness of private investors to lend
   2. Legal restrictions on investment, perhaps to release materials for armament program

3. DECLINE IN GOVERNMENT EXPENDITURES DUE TO

A. Completion of public works and provision of sufficient facilities to meet needs for some years to come
B. Expected future decline in revenues due to ominous forecasts of future business condition
C. Inability to borrow at attractive interest rates to finance expenditures
D. Legal limitations on government debt

    E. Change in economic philosophy following upon a change in administration

    F. Curtailment of military program and to increased international amity

    G. Decline in revenues of state and local governments

II. REMEDIES FOR DEPRESSIONS

Causes often suggest cures. Even as reductions in total expenditure apparently cause depression, increases in expenditure can be expected to cure it. The discussion of remedies for depression will parallel that of depression's causes in that measures for increasing the expenditures of individuals, business, and government will be treated separately. In addition, we shall consider the possibility of increasing foreigners' spending in this country and methods by which the banking system might contribute to a cure of depression.

A. Measures for Increasing Consumer Expenditures

Economists have suggested many ways of increasing consumer income and thereby of maintaining consumer expenditures when they would otherwise fall. Already widely discussed and generally understood are social insurance and relief payments. These measures need not be described in detail. Unemployment insurance supports consumer income and is an almost automatic device which goes into effect when most needed to prevent a recession from gathering momentum. Relief payments, many economists agree, should be made only as a supplement to unemployment insurance during prolonged depressions, and even then only for those who cannot be given employment on public projects.

A relatively new proposal which some economists support is an *adjustable system of personal income taxation.*[3] Some even regard it as sufficient in itself to prevent major depressions. The adjustable tax plan calls for a consolidation of most taxes into a single income tax, collected at source, which would be reduced during depression. According to this proposal, almost all government revenue (local as well as federal) would be collected by the federal government in the form of a personal and business income tax. The federal government would in turn distribute part of the proceeds to the state and local government units for expenditure.

---

[3] For a description of this proposal in greater detail, see K. Boulding, *The Economics of Peace* (Englewood Cliffs, N.J.: Prentice-Hall, Inc., 1945), pp. 161-167.

When consolidated in this way, the tax "take" of the government would constitute by far the largest single controllable influence on the amount of money available for spending. In other words, the amount of money that people have left for spending after taxes would become directly and speedily changeable by the government tax program. The plan calls for changes in tax rate to accompany changes in individuals' expenditures. When the demand for consumers' goods begins to drop, the government would reduce tax rates and thus leave consumers with more money to spend. Should inflation impend, government would increase tax rates and thereby curtail consumer expenditures.

Successful operation of an adjustable tax plan requires that decisions on tax rates be made by a skilled administrative body protected from political influences, and empowered to make speedy and large adjustments in income tax rates. It also requires that the consolidation of taxes be sufficient to make the adjustable taxes a sizable proportion of total income, and necessitates that taxes be collected frequently in order that effective counterdepression measures can be adopted with a maximum delay of a few months. These requirements suggest that much must be done before the nation can enjoy the benefits of an adjustable tax plan. They also suggest that this proposal would meet heavy political opposition.

B. Measures for Increasing Expenditures by Business

To increase expenditures for plant and equipment, some economists prescribe subsidy. Some favor low interest rates on borrowings used to finance purchase of plant and equipment. A few suggest that government not only cancel all interest charges but pay outright subsidies to induce business to invest. Many economists endorse tax remissions to firms that undertake investment during periods of bad business. Subsidizing private investment is generally favored over direct investment by the government that might put it in "competition" with private business and reduce private investment. Private investment is also favored over public investment because it is likely to be cheaper for the taxpayer —every dollar of government subsidy would lead to the investment of several private dollars—and because it probably could also be accomplished more quickly.

Less well known are proposals to encourage business spending for labor and materials by government's guaranteeing to buy what business cannot sell. These proposals rest on the fact that recessions are characterized by *extreme conservatism which restrains business from producing some goods that could probably have been sold had they been produced. But because these goods are not produced, business disbursements are lowered and, as a result, the markets for all goods shrink.*

By guaranteeing to buy the part of output that cannot be sold through normal channels, government would encourage capacity operation. High personal incomes and large markets for all goods would result. Conceivably, the guarantee could even cause markets to expand enough so that the total output would be sold through normal channels and there would be no surpluses left for the government to buy in accordance with its guarantee. Whatever surpluses do prove necessary for the government to buy must then be disposed of by the government only through channels that do not encroach on the usual markets for these goods.

In recent years the government has acquired considerable experience with market guarantees, especially for agricultural products and housing. To extend these guarantees to the entire economy, however, creates great problems to which reliable solutions have not yet been found. But guaranteed markets for specific groups of main products could counteract the depressing effects of business pessimism where it is most severe and most damaging.

C. Measures for Increasing Expenditures by Individuals and Businesses in Other Countries

In the past, most countries tried to combat unemployment by stimulating exports, and reducing imports. During periods of bad business many countries have sought to expand their domestic business at the expense of other countries. Economists refer to such actions as "exporting unemployment."

But no country wants to *import* unemployment. Almost always, devices which encroach upon the export markets of other countries evoke retaliation that cancels their effects.

Economists regard raising import restrictions as ineffective antidepression devices because other nations retaliate. However, they do not recommend lowering restrictions during depression. The case for lower tariffs is weakest during a period of depressed business, for business then needs encouragement rather than extraordinary exposure to foreign competition.

Loans made to foreign countries are a possible temporary measure for combating depressions. Foreign spending in this country also can be maintained for some time by gifts. Other than by gifts and by loans guaranteed by our government, however, little can be done to maintain or increase foreign expenditures in this country during depression. The United States probably would not be willing to take measures to increase foreign expenditure without similar attempts to increase the spending by individuals, business, and the government within the country. A similar expenditure on gifts (subsidies, and such) and loans at extralow rates would probably be a greater stimulus to domestic than to foreign spending.

D. Measures for Increasing Expenditures by Government

Most of the measures described by which the expenditures of consumers, business, and foreigners would be increased involve the government's spending[4] to stimulate others to spend. As a rough rule of thumb, if government spending is to stimulate other spending, it must be deficit spending; that is, expenditures must exceed tax receipts.[5] If the government increased taxes to finance greater expenditures, the public's spending would probably be reduced by an equal amount and the stimulation of spending would not be accomplished. Some economists urge government (and private business also) to concentrate purchases of plant and equipment during periods of dull business and thereby to benefit from lower costs, while the entire economy gains from more stable employment and output.

Probably the most important and generally acceptable government measure to correct depression is spending for "public works." Public works can be defined much more broadly than usual to include any and all public expenditures that seem justifiable during depression. In a very deep depression, they could include almost anything. In a moderate downswing, they would clearly include such things as huge irrigation and flood-control projects, technological, medical, and social research projects, road construction, and public housing which might otherwise not be undertaken for many decades—if ever.

To be an effective antidepression device, public works must be ready for speedy execution. Concrete blueprints, and careful advance planning, must lie behind these projects; they should be completed *before* a depression strikes. To keep an up-to-date portfolio of projects that could be launched quickly in the event of depression is a costly undertaking but well worth the cost. Included in such a portfolio of public works should be more than the conventional construction projects. Most

---

[4] Government policy regarding expenditures, taxes, and other receipts, and the management of the public debt, is called "fiscal policy." Fiscal policy is discussed in this section as well as in Chapters 24 and 25.

[5] Actually, there are important differences in the full impact on total spending of different government expenditures. Some expenditures, such as those for improvements in communication and transportation, and most types of military expenditures, spur additional groups to increase outlays; other types of expenditure, like those concerning government competition with private industry, may inhibit spending by these private groups.

of the people who lose their jobs during a depression will have no experience or skill, and probably are physically unfitted for construction work. Public works should include things that unemployed clerks, salesmen, accountants, and musicians could do.

One must not assume that all increases in government spending represent an equal increase in total spending. It is conceivable that government spending would inhibit an even larger amount of spending by others. Let us illustrate this type of decline in expenditure. There exists strong evidence that government expenditure for the Tennessee Valley Authority discouraged private public utility companies from carrying out heavy investment expenditures that they would have made otherwise.[6] In the Tennessee River area, and elsewhere, the TVA was regarded as government competition with private industry, and it dampened the desire of private businessmen to invest. The decline in private investment, as in that case, might, in similar cases, actually exceed the rise in spending by the government.

In assessing the effect of government spending upon total expenditure, two factors require major emphasis. First, as just shown, the net impact of government spending depends primarily upon its effect upon the willingness of other groups to spend. Second, money spent by government—like that spent by all groups—tends to be respent by those who receive it. Accordingly, an increase in government spending will affect expenditure in the future as well as in the present. For example, if the government spent $1 billion extra this month to combat depression, those who received that sum would respend at least part of it, say, next month. In turn, those who received the respent income would respend at least part of it in subsequent months. As a result, total spending resulting from the initial expenditure of $1 billion would ultimately exceed the initial billion dollars by a considerable amount. (How an increase in expenditure—particularly by the federal government—tends to add more to total spending than its initial amount is described in technical economic writings as "the multiplier.") This final conclusion, of course, holds only if government spending does not discourage private spending of equal or greater amount; for example, a rise in personal income taxes to finance greater government spending might mean that the government expenditures are simply replacing heavier spending that would have been carried on by individuals had they not been taxed. If government spending increases expenditure by other groups, which might happen if the government's spending inspired greater optimism about the future, the effect on total spending would be very great.

---

[6] T. Morgan, *Income and Employment* (Englewood Cliffs, N.J.: Prentice-Hall, Inc., 1947), 43", p. 241.

E. Can the Banking System Cure Depression?

In 1933, the government increased the powers of the Federal Reserve Board of Governors—the top policy-making and executive agency of the banking system—in the apparent hope of preventing or correcting depression. The Federal Reserve Board was given powers that many people hoped would enable it to increase and to contract bank loans. In that way, spending by individuals and business was to be influenced by the Federal Reserve System.

The powers of the Federal Reserve System that it was hoped would enable it to combat depression by stimulating bank loans were (1) the power to lower the reserve requirements that member banks must hold with the Reserve Banks behind their deposits so that it would be easier for them to make loans; (2) the ability of individual Reserve Banks to lower the rediscount rate, which represents a decline in the rate of interest that member banks pay on loans they make from the Reserve Banks; (3) "open-market operations," by means of which the Reserve Banks buy government securities on the open market, those selling the bonds ordinarily depositing the proceeds of the sale in member banks and thereby increasing their reserves. (These powers can be used in opposite ways to restrain inflation: raising reserve requirements, raising rediscount rates, and selling government securities.)

The Federal Reserve System was also given the power to control stock-market credit through its right to change the cash requirement when stocks were being purchased partially with borrowed money. This control, which is a permanent one, was supplemented by two others, which no longer are in effect—consumer-credit and real-estate-credit controls. The purpose of all such selective controls was to give the System power to ease or tighten credit. *Unquestionably, the Federal Reserve System can increase the ability of member banks to lend. However, it cannot make banks willing to lend, or safe risks willing to borrow.* During depression, the fear by banks of nonpayment of loans outweighs their desire to earn interest.

Perhaps the most important role that the banking authorities can be expected to play is to prevent a depression from starting for monetary reasons. A contraction in loans due to a shortage of bank reserves could cause major trouble if it started a cumulative downward movement. By offsetting a decline in currency holdings by the banks, the banking authorities could contribute toward economic stability when bank reserves were falling because of cash withdrawals. Downswings due to nonmonetary causes cannot ordinarily be stopped by actions of the banking authorities, who seem powerless to correct depression.

F. A Balanced Program for Combating Depression

The measures listed are not mutually exclusive. They can, and probably should, be used in combination. Virtually no one argues seriously that unemployment insurance should not be paid, at least partly to slow down the (crosswise) spread of unemployment from one industry to another. Public works, preferably projects that were carefully planned and of great value to the community, are a generally accepted element in any program for combating depression. (The costliness and effort in maintaining up-to-date blueprints and plans for public works should not be underestimated; failure to maintain a portfolio of such projects, however, means either that much time would be wasted before projects were started or that the public works undertaken probably would not be very valuable to the community.)

The adjustable tax program is gradually gaining popular favor, as was evidenced by the proposals to reduce income taxes to combat the downswing of 1949, and by the favorable response to the reduction of income and excise taxes in the contraction of 1953. Variation of tax rates as general business conditions change should, in the author's opinion, occupy a prominent place in an antidepression program. While it poses political dangers, certainly they are trifling compared to the dangers arising from a major depression.

Subsidies, in the form of preferential tax privileges on investment undertaken during depression, interest-free loans, or outright gifts for investment (in needy areas particularly), seem entitled to at least a trial. In addition, the government should make a direct appeal to businessmen, for their mutual benefit, to carry out a concerted program of investment during depression. (It should be recognized, however, that this investment during depression will come largely at the expense of investment that would otherwise take place later and that would therefore make the attainment of a state of strong prosperity more difficult.) Total spending probably would be stabilized perceptibly by guarantees of markets for such things as houses (preferably sold to consumers during depression, with low interest-rate privileges).

The particular antidepression measures applied must be selected according to the prevailing circumstances. A measure that would arrest a recession caused by one factor might be useless or even harmful under other conditions. A depression concentrated in capital-goods industries, for example, should not primarily be combated by measures to increase consumers' expenditures. Conversely, if a particular consumers'-goods industry is the source of the economic infection, measures to increase purchases of its output—like some variation of the "stamp plan," which permits low-income recipients to obtain the product at a very low price, or even free—might be tried.

Depressions are neither inevitable nor incurable. Measures capable of preventing the spread of recession—no matter what its cause—are at hand. These measures would not require any major alteration in our economic system. Those who oppose the measures listed because they somewhat modify our methods of doing business should realize that another big depression is perhaps the greatest foreseeable danger to our present economic system.

G. Major Difficulties in a Policy of Depression Prevention

To combat depression requires measures that will do two things. First, they must halt the spread of unemployment to industries not originally affected; that is, they must halt the crosswise spread of unemployment. (Little can be done about the backward spread.) Second, measures are needed to increase total expenditures so that unemployed workers will be re-employed and so that a minimum of their productive effort will be lost. Three major difficulties are confronted in pursuit of these objectives, and they will be discussed in turn.

1. DIFFICULTIES IN TAKING ACTION WITH SUFFICIENT SPEED

Business activity has both large and small ups and downs. In addition to the pronounced changes termed "depression," "expansion," "prosperity," and "contraction," business undergoes minor variations from day to day, week to week, and month to month. These variations are altogether separate from the changes associated with the weather and holidays. Businessmen are well aware of the fact that they will have "slow" weeks and months, even during prosperous periods. These minor ups and downs signify no basic change in underlying conditions, and seem really to be accidental in origin. Consequently, business may slacken for a moderately long period, although no actual downswing is under way. It therefore becomes exceedingly difficult to separate accidental fluctuations from real contractions in business. To tell them apart with confidence we must wait to see what happens. But if we do so, possibly the contraction will have proceeded too far to be corrected without extreme measures.

Some delay in adopting measures to prevent the spread of a downswing and in taking steps to increase employment is almost certain. (It is desirable that there be strong evidence that a contraction has started, lest economic controls be turned on and off with a frequency that would be disturbing to all businessmen.) If the delay is not overly long, a depression could still be prevented. Nevertheless, it is imperative to do whatever is possible to avoid any and all delays in taking remedial action when it is clear that a contraction *probably* has started—there will always be the risk of making an error. To deal with this problem of timing, the following measures and principles are particularly pertinent:

a. Make arrangements that operate "automatically" to combat business downswings

These measures would counteract drops in employment or expenditure whenever they occurred. The best example of this type of measure is unemployment insurance. It goes into effect whenever a "covered" worker loses a job (even during conditions of improving business). It therefore lessens the decline in individual expenditure and dampens the crosswise spread of reductions in total expenditure.

b. Enact provisional legislation specifying that measures are to be undertaken when designated conditions exist

For example, a law might be passed that required the federal government to undertake $3 billion of public works when official statistics showed unemployment to be in excess of 5 million. In this way, appropriate action would not be delayed by the time-consuming legislative process.

c. Delegate some of the powers now exercised directly by Congress and the President to a nonpolitical administrative agency

It is no simple matter to create such an agency, of course, one that could analyze business developments with expert knowledge, and would be empowered to take actions specified in advance by Congress, though allowing latitude for discretion.

d. Make clear in advance of any depression the types of action that the government must undertake and under what circumstances

If the principles concerning the means for combating depressions are made clear, disagreements about fundamental matters would not delay appropriate action at the proper time.

2. DANGER THAT PRICE INCREASES WILL OFFSET INCREASED EXPENDITURES

The expenditure program of government is public knowledge. Moreover, when a law calling for the government to carry out some project has been enacted, there rarely is a reversal of the decision. Thus businesses selling things needed in carrying out a project are virtually assured that the government will go ahead with its purchases, even if prices rise. Businesses possessing strong market power may seize the opportunity to raise prices for things that the government is committed to buy.

Price increases dampen the effect of increased expenditures on employment. The physical quantity of goods purchased, and the employment provided by a given amount of expenditure, declines as prices increase. This conclusion rests on simple arithmetic. A dollar will buy twice as many pencils if they cost five cents as it can buy if they cost ten cents.

The danger that prices will rise when government expenditures increase is difficult to assess. In most lines of business, market power wanes when business contracts. Contraction is generally characterized by increased difficulty of getting customers and increased efforts to capture the customers of rival firms. The danger of price increases, accordingly, is not very great. Moreover, if there were evidence that price increases were likely, the government might enact price ceilings effective at least during the period that the government made its initial disbursements.

3. DANGER THAT WORKERS WILL BE MOVED OUT OF INDUSTRIES WHERE THEY SHOULD BE KEPT AND THAT SOME WILL BE KEPT IN INDUSTRIES FROM WHICH THEY SHOULD BE INDUCED TO MOVE

Expenditures by government or by individuals, and business induced by government, provide employment; indeed, employment should be one of the primary purposes of these groups during depression. Some types of expenditure will move workers from their previous employments, in which they became unemployed, to other lines of work. For example, when the government undertakes public works as an ameliorative for depression, it usually hopes to give work to a wide variety of workers in the construction business. It is quite possible that the workers would be more productive and useful to the economy if they were to be returned to work in their prior employment. Their removal to another industry might create a difficult problem of getting them back to their original jobs when a need for them arises. Moreover, valuable skills may deteriorate in the process of shifting workers to new employments.

Conversely, some lines of business should be permitted to decline. These make products that are losing out in public favor, or produce equipment or materials that have been superseded by more efficient methods. If the government were to spend in a way that would keep workers in industries that ought to decline, they would prevent a vital economic process—albeit a painful one—from taking place. Workers in declining industries must become unemployed if they are to be transferred to occupations where their full productive contribution can be made.

As a practical matter, there is little danger that those responsible for combating depression will mistake unemployment due to a fundamental decline in a particular industry's position for a contraction of general business. However, during any contraction some workers may be unemployed because they have worked for a declining industry. So far as possible, measures to combat unemployment should not support industries that are declining in relative importance.

III. SUMMARY AND CONCLUSIONS

We saw that many circumstances may lead to a reduction in expenditure. Once total spending falls, output and employment are almost certain to follow suit, because adjustments in prices, wages, and interest rates generally are not speedy enough or sufficient to offset a decline in spending. The extent of the cumulative downswing brought about by a drop in expenditure depends upon the vulnerability of the economy when the drop in spending occurs. Strong business optimism probably is the best safeguard against a rapid and deep downswing. If spending falls when businessmen have misgivings about the future, a sharp decline is likely to result.

Downswings can be combated successfully by increasing expenditure. Crucial to the success of any program for preventing depressions is speedy action once a downswing starts. In addition, the particular types of expenditure that should be stimulated and the best way to stimulate them must be suited to the origin of the initial downswing. However, many methods of preventing a crosswise spread of reduced spending are available, and it is also possible to offset an initial decline in total expenditure. Basically, initiative for increasing spending must be taken by government, which directly or indirectly will be compelled to spend more than its income.

Speedy and wise measures to combat a downswing require the creation of an administrative agency empowered to take appropriate action. (The types of action it might take could be prescribed for it by Congress, together with the occasions when each should be taken.) We cannot afford to rely upon the slow and often inadequate measures that emerge from the usual legislative process.

It cannot be emphasized too often that the instability of capitalism is probably the single major reason why most of the world has rejected it. The United States could lose the support of many Western European nations in the "cold war" if it again suffers a major depression. Fortunately, there is no necessity for everyone to live under the threat of depression. The cures are here. We must be wise enough to employ them.

DISCUSSION QUESTIONS

1. If prices were very sensitive to changes in expenditure, falling when expenditure falls and rising when it increases, would unemployment and inflationary "overemployment" be avoided? Discuss.

2. Explain how variations in wage and interest rates were expected to forestall depression.

3. What circumstances provoke the greatest reduction in spending by individuals? What measures might be taken to counter those circumstances?

4. Is it necessary to know the original cause for a decline in consumer spending to devise a remedy for it?

5. If you were given responsibility for correcting depression or inflation, by what criteria would you decide when action should be taken and what scale of action is required?

6. Is it correct to say that spending, no matter what it is for, will correct a downswing? Give an illustration wherein a rise in spending might not have that effect.

Chapter

24 Consequences of a
Large Government Debt

Almost all the proposals for increasing consumer, business, foreign, and government spending imply that government would often operate at a deficit and that the national debt would increase. Presumably the government would be able to accumulate surpluses during periods of good business to offset its depression deficits, but the surpluses of prosperity and the deficits of depression are not necessarily equivalent. Political pressures, moreover, often dictate tax reductions when the government debt might otherwise be reduced, such tax reductions lessen the likelihood that surpluses accumulated during prosperity would fully offset the deficits of depression.

The attitude of professional economists to the national debt has changed considerably since 1929, though it remains a controversial subject. A very large debt is still considered an "evil" by almost everyone, but many believe it to be the lesser evil in many situations. A recession generally compels a choice between increased government debt and greater unemployment (and lower prices and lower profits). A large majority of economists favor increased government debt in these circumstances.

I. JUSTIFICATION FOR DEBT

Debt is widely regarded as an evil by businessmen, individuals, and government officials. Yet, debt is a commonplace of our society; more significant, debt generally increases during periods of good business, rather than during depression. Moreover, growing and successful businesses ordinarily increase rather than reduce their total debt. As income and output expand, so does debt. Table 1 shows how greatly all forms of debt have expanded.

While businessmen surely would prefer not to have any debts, they nevertheless borrow even when they do not absolutely have to do so.

499

That is, businessmen usually borrow to purchase new plant and equipment, to increase their holdings of inventories, or to increase their output, rather than to keep their creditors from shutting down their business. Borrowing is thus done voluntarily and not as the result of dire necessity. *Businessmen borrow when they believe the proceeds of the loan will give them more benefit than the debt will do them harm.* Individuals likewise borrow when they think they will be better off *on balance* after the loan than without it.

**Table 1. Total Debt Outstanding in the United States,
Selected Years 1916-1957**
(In billions)

Year	Total priv. & public	Public	Private corporate	Private noncorporate
1916	$ 82.1	$ 5.6	$ 76.5	$ 36.3
1929	190.9	29.7	88.9	72.3
1933	168.5	41.0	76.9	50.6
1941	211.6	72.6	83.4	55.6
1945	406.3	266.4	85.3	54.6
1946	397.4	243.3	93.5	60.6
1947	417.4	237.7	108.9	70.8
1948	433.6	232.7	117.8	83.1
1949	448.4	236.7	118.0	93.7
1950	490.3	239.4	142.1	108.8
1951	524.0	241.8	162.5	119.7
1952	555.2	248.7	171.0	135.5
1953	586.4	256.7	179.5	150.2
1954	611.8	263.6	182.8	165.4
1955	672.2	269.9	212.1	190.2
1956	699.8	268.1	224.2	207.5
1957	725.8	271.1	232.8	221.9

Totals will have discrepancies because of rounding.
SOURCE: U.S. Department of Commerce, *Survey of Current Business*, September, 1953, p. 14; May, 1957, p. 17; and May, 1958, p. 14.

In the case of businesses, loans do not make them worse off from an accounting standpoint. While they acquire a debt, they also gain a compensating asset—in the first instance it is cash. In turn, the cash is used to purchase some physical asset that is used in the business, presumably in ways that will add to its profitability. The gains to the business from having these assets might be (indeed, the businessmen expected they would be, or they would not have borrowed) substantially greater than the interest paid on the loan. Consequently, the financial position of the business would be improved directly as the result of the loan. Rather than a misfortune for the business, the loan is a blessing.

In the case of government borrowing, we face a curious, and unfortunate, fact. There really is nowhere a balance sheet that describes the government's financial position. (The budget, which is equivalent to a firm's profit-and-loss statement, serves quite a different purpose.) *The assets that are acquired as the result of government loans are not recorded; only the government debt figures in financial calculations.* Accordingly, whenever it borrows, the government seems to get only debts and no assets.

These appearances are deceiving. *The government, just like any business, spends the proceeds of its loans.* Presumably, the expenditures are made for "useful" purposes. An enormous number of valuable uses might be made of borrowed funds; for the most part, government has borrowed to pay for wars or for preparations for war—and these expenditures give vital assets to a nation that might be attacked. It should also be manifest that expenditures that prevent the cruel hardships, political uncertainties, and social misfortune attendant upon depression also provide valuable assets to the nation. Human beings that make up a nation are injured by depression without any apparent responsibility on their part. They are innocent bystanders of a failing of the economic system. To allow them to be injured cannot be defended on moral grounds. Moreover, on economic grounds, if unemployment is not combated, productive efficiency will be lessened and the output of these persons decreased. The asset against which government debt must be measured is the health, productive efficiency, psychological security, and morale of a large proportion of the population. Accountants have not devised acceptable measures for reducing these vital properties to dollar equivalents. Nevertheless, they are enormously valuable assets to any nation.

The measures described here to combat depression actually might keep the national debt below the level it would otherwise reach if another depression were to occur. In this country, peacetime government deficits have in fairly recent years been caused by depression. Even with only a minimum program for combating depression during 1930, 1931, and 1932, the government had an unbalanced budget. A minimum program to alleviate the suffering of another depression undoubtedly would involve the government in large deficits to meet social-insurance obligations, to compensate for the drop in tax proceeds which probably would occur, and to provide the minimum of public charity or public works needed to forestall serious political repercussions. And yet *deficits incurred pursuant to a minimum government program might greatly exceed those of a program that prevented a cumulative downswing by some of the measures listed.* This would be so if the minimum program did not stop the downswing; in other words, with a minimum program the deficit would be prolonged and might have to be increased greatly if a major depression developed.

Prejudice against government spending in excess of its tax revenues stands squarely in the way of curing depression. Many economists believe that were it not for the myths normally uttered in the name of "sound finance," major business depressions would be evils of the past. A change in the commonly held attitude toward government debt would therefore be one of the most significant economic developments of our generation.

However, a large government debt poses some risks and dangers. To these we now turn.

II. THE DANGERS AND EVILS OF A LARGE GOVERNMENT DEBT

The debt of the United States Government is owed by the American people to themselves, since practically none of the federal government bonds outstanding are owned by foreigners. The debt, now about $280 billion, involves a payment of taxes by most people to pay themselves interest or to repay principal on the debt. Specifically, the government performs two operations in paying principal and interest on the debt. First, it taxes to raise funds to pay bondholders. As a consequence of the large debt, federal taxes are higher (by about 11 per cent for fiscal year 1958) than they would be in the absence of the debt. Possibly the higher taxes result in diminished incentive to work hard, and thereby reduce total output (this possibility is discussed and largely rejected in the section dealing with income distribution). Second, the government distributes funds to bondholders as interest (which it then taxes, and uses part of the proceeds to pay interest again) and as repayments of principal.

However, the payment of interest and the repayment of the principal on the debt is not so simple or innocuous as the transfer of money from a person's right pocket to his left one. *The debt is not held in the same proportions as individuals pay taxes; consequently, when interest is paid or principal is repaid, income is redistributed.* It is generally agreed that low-income recipients pay a proportion of federal taxes that is larger than the proportion of total debt payments they receive. For example, one individual may pay $10,000 in taxes, about $1,100 of which goes to pay interest on the debt. He may himself receive $2,000 in interest on his government bonds. Others may pay $500 in taxes, $55 going for interest on the debt, while they receive only $10 per year on the bonds they hold. In this particular case, the debt would redistribute personal income toward greater inequality.

To a large extent, the government debt is, and is likely to continue to be, held by banks.[1] Government bonds represent by far the most important single asset they hold. *Consequently, government bonds are both a major source of income for banks and the fundamental determinant of their solvency.* With their income from government bonds, banks are able to make only nominal service charges to depositors for checking accounts and other services—thus redounding to the benefit of many persons not holding government bonds.

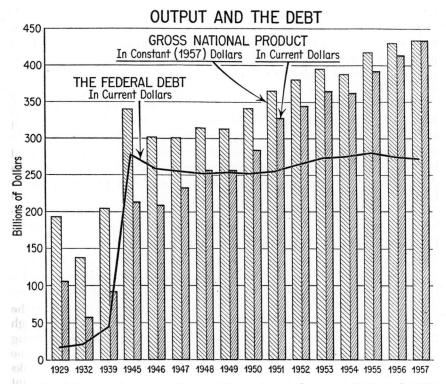

The federal debt remained virtually stationary between 1946 and 1952. During that time, total output, figured in current dollars, increased quite substantially, thereby altering markedly the relationship between national output and the federal debt. Whereas, at the end of World War II, the federal debt was considerably higher than total output, in 1957 it was substantially below. Consequently, the relative burden of the debt declined during this period.

---

[1] In 1958 the debt owed to individuals was 24 per cent; commercial banks, 21.5 per cent; federal government accounts (such as social security), 20 per cent; Federal Reserve Banks, 8.5 per cent; savings banks and insurance companies, 7.5 per cent; corporations, 6 per cent; state and local governments, 6 per cent; and miscellaneous, 6 per cent. *Federal Reserve Bulletin*, April, 1958, p. 464.

Unless the debt is paid out of taxes when it comes due, the government is under pressure to borrow funds to pay off bonds as they come due. There thus exists the possibility that investors, whether individuals, businesses, banks, or insurance companies, will not buy enough bonds to repay the debt when it falls due. The government then would be compelled to "default" on its obligations. The consequences of such default are not easy to foresee. Potentially, "confidence in the government" might collapse, with catastrophic results. The value of money and the solvency of all banks would become suspect, for the government would have been found insolvent. It must be emphasized that these results need not follow, for they basically rest upon superstition about monetary matters. Nevertheless, in the light of present misunderstanding of financial matters, they probably would happen if the government defaulted on the debts.

Default on the government debt is no more than a theoretical possibility. The government could compel the Federal Reserve Banks to buy its bonds in an emergency. It could issue paper money to pay its obligations as they come due; it could increase taxes; and it could even impose a capital levy—thereby confiscating part of the government debt. All of these measures probably would be considered preferable to default.

III. HOW HIGH A DEBT CAN WE BEAR?

It is important to distinguish two questions about the size of the government debt that are often confused. First, one might ask how high a debt it is possible for the federal government to incur "without going bankrupt." This question has been answered; we indicated that the government can continue to increase its debt as long as people or banks are willing to buy bonds. Second, it is sometimes asked at what point the government debt becomes "too large." This question is similar to asking when a headache hurts too much. It has no meaningful answer. However, there is value in probing the burden which the government debt places on the population.

The federal debt imposes a hardship on the nation in several ways. Like any debt, it requires the raising of funds to pay interest and to repay principal. The government raises its funds by either taxing or borrowing. (It could also print money, but it has refrained from doing so.) If the government taxes to pay interest and/or principal, a very large debt could possibly result in a tax rate so high that the incentives of many people would be seriously impaired. This possibility is slim, however, for the government presumably would, *under those circumstances,* pay the interest by borrowing rather than by taxation. When the government relies on borrowing to pay interest and principal, it incurs the risk of being unable to obtain sufficient funds to pay its debts as they come due. In that event, the government risks the fairly serious consequences already mentioned.

To determine the likelihood that tax rates have reached the point where they discourage incentive *because of the debt,* one test should be applied. The amount of money that must be paid as interest on the federal debt can be compared with the amount of income that individuals receive out of which this interest is paid. Specifically, the interest on the federal debt should be measured as a *percentage* of total national income. (The ability to pay interest varies with the amount of money individuals and businesses receive with which to pay it.) That calculation is offered in the Table 2 for selected years.

Table 2. Interest on National Debt as a Proportion of National Income, Selected Years 1929-1957

Year	Total national income * (billions)	Interest on federal debt † (millions)	Interest charges as per cent of national income
1929	$ 87.8	$ 657	.75
1933	40.2	742	1.85
1937	73.6	924	1.26
1941	104.7	1,218	1.16
1946	180.9	5,351	2.96
1949	217.7	5,606	2.58
1950	241.9	5,613	2.32
1951	279.3	5,740	2.06
1952	292.2	5,981	2.05
1953	305.6	6,431	2.10
1954	301.8	6,298	2.09
1955	330.2	6,387	1.93
1956	349.4	6,950	1.99
1957	364.0	7,325	2.01

* U.S. Department of Commerce, *Survey of Current Business,* July, 1958, pp. 4-5.
† U.S. Treasury Department, *Annual Report of the Secretary of the Treasury,* 1957, p. 501.

Table 2 indicates that only a very small proportion of the national income (about 2 per cent) must be taxed to pay the carrying charges on the government debt. Moreover, interest charges are only a small proportion of total government expenses—about 10 per cent. If taxes become so high that they impair incentive, the cause will be the large government expenditure for things other than interest on the debt.[2]

---

[2] It merits repetititon that even as interest charges on the debt must be paid out of personal income they also add to the incomes of holders of government bonds, including corporations and financial institutions.

One widely accepted argument against a large government debt will not stand close scrutiny. That is the view that "our children and grandchildren will be compelled to pay off the government debt." Several points need only be stated, for they are manifest. First, to the extent that our grandchildren inherit our debt, they will also inherit the bonds that are evidence of the debt. They will both make and receive payments as a result of the debt. Second, there is no more reason for our grandchildren to pay off the debt than for us to do so. The debt can be, and this author predicts will be, refinanced over the indefinite future; that is, money will be borrowed to repay the current holders of bonds. Third, the impact of the debt depends, as we have seen, on the manner in which the payment of interest is effected, and the distribution of the tax burden compares with the holdings of government bonds. A large government debt may put a burden on a later generation only if a nation borrowed from *another country* on a long-term basis, and thus took goods now for which a later generation would have to repay lenders outside the country.

There is no evidence that the nation has come close to reaching the upper limit of the government debt it could bear. Nor is it clear that it imposes an onerous burden on the taxpayer, or that it results in greatly increased income inequality. Consequently, it should be possible for the government to increase its expenditure and run a deficit whenever necessary to combat a downswing and to keep it from starting a major depression. Depressions are neither inevitable nor incurable.

IV. SUMMARY AND CONCLUSIONS

It has been shown that to combat depression effectively government deficit spending is often necessary. Such expenditures offset the declines in spending by consumers and business which usually precipitate a depression; they stimulate production and income so that consumers and business are able to spend more money. Thus the resulting increased expenditures either avert an economic contraction or raise the economy from depressed to prosperous levels.

The need for government deficit spending to forestall serious depressions has resulted in an increasingly large government debt and in many complicated problems of debt management. The fear of some people that this debt is "bad" for the economy is largely unfounded, since debt is an instrument vital to economic expansion and as such is readily used by business. Nevertheless, the extent to which government debt may affect economic activity adversely is a legitimate concern. However, so long as the economy is able to meet the costs of interest payments on the debt out of its current income, without impairing its smooth operation, the debt need not have adverse effects. Where such costs could be met only by impairing other government services or by causing increases in taxes which would dull the incentives of taxpayers and thus lead to inefficiency in the economy, the burden of the debt would be too great.

The decision to control depression thus calls for greater governmental responsibility. By increasing its expenditures, government can mitigate declines in economic activity, but only at the price of increasing its debt. To fulfill fully its responsibility of maintaining economic stability government must not only spend wisely but also manage its debt efficiently.

DISCUSSION QUESTIONS

1. When is a private corporation's debt too large? When is a government's debt too large?

2. In what major particular are the accounting procedures of government and business different? Does this difference affect the apparent size of the government debt?

3. Cannot the government escape the necessity of taxing to pay interest on the debt by borrowing to pay the interest charges? Discuss.

4. On what basis would you choose between a higher government debt and greater unemployment? How much additional debt would you be willing to have the government incur to escape 1,000,000 unemployed?

5. What dangers are potentially involved in a large public debt? Is our debt today dangerously large? How can you tell?

25 Inflation: Causes and Possible Cures

Between 1929 and the outbreak of World War II, American business was primarily beset by depression or the fear of depression. Unemployment was relatively great during the entire period, and business confidence was low. With American participation in World War II, an inflationary movement began which, with only brief interruptions, continued for over a decade. At no time in American history has the economy experienced so prolonged an inflation.

A few examples will indicate the extent of the inflation that occurred. Food that the average American purchased in 1940 for $1 cost about $2.40 in 1957; to buy the same clothing cost twice as much in 1957 as in 1940. All items in the average American family's budget cost about 100 per cent more in 1957 than in 1940.

Despite the rise in prices, most Americans were able to purchase substantially more goods in 1957 than in 1940. The average person obtained about 52 per cent more goods and services in the later year. However, owing to the sharp change in prices, some persons suffered great financial injury. Foremost among these were persons whose incomes remained much the same while prices soared, or those who depended primarily upon the savings they had accumulated.

It is dangerous to think in terms of averages. The typical American earner obtains his income from the sale of personal services. Incomes from labor more than kept pace with the rise in prices over the period as a whole. For example, factory workers averaged $25 per week in 1940; in 1957 their average weekly earnings were $82.

Large numbers of people, though a small proportion of the total population, depend upon the following sources of income: insurance annuities, life insurance and disability premiums, pensions, old-age pensions, interest on bonds, and the like. This group consists primarily of the aged, the infirm, and widows, with their children. The numbers of persons in this group have not been measured exactly, but they certainly are in the millions. The inflation since 1940 has worsened the financial condition of many who are least able to protect themselves by making added exertions.

Individuals held over $52 billion worth of liquid assets in 1940. As prices increased, the amount of goods that these assets could purchase fell. In 1957, they could purchase less than $26 billion could have bought in 1940. The loss in value of accumulated savings becomes more dramatic when one considers what happened in the period from 1945 to 1957. During that time prices in general increased by 56 per cent. By the end of 1945, Americans had accumulated $154 billion in currency, checking and savings accounts, shares in savings and loan associations, and U.S. government bonds. Consequently, in 1957 these savings could buy less than $99 billion would have purchased in 1945. Thus in these terms, Americans lost about $55 billion in savings during this period.

Americans have continued to increase their savings since the end of the war. Between 1945 and 1954 (the last year for which these data were compiled) they added approximately $158 billion to their liquid assets. However, they were worse off than the rat in a maze, for while running forward they were moving backward in the real value of their savings. The $210 billion they owned at the end of 1954 actually bought far less than the $154 billion would have bought at the end of 1945.[1]

As a result of the past inflation and the danger of future inflation, a new hazard has grown in the average American's life. He recognizes that complete economic security is a myth. One cannot simply "make a pile" and retire for life. The pile of money accumulated may become a small anthill in purchasing power by the time an individual gets around to drawing upon it. Thus, in addition to the types of real injury imposed upon those whose incomes do not keep pace with rising prices, and the loss in value of savings, inflation adds psychological damage. Fathers cannot be certain any longer that their families will be provided for in the event of their demise. Insurance has become only partial insurance.

Inflation also affects business operation. Executives no longer can make decisions on the assumption that prices will remain relatively constant over substantial periods. They must now anticipate that the things they are using up currently—mainly machinery and inventories—will cost more to replace than they cost originally; accordingly, the depreciation and obsolescence charges of these machines and equipment may prove inadequate to maintain the current level of output as the machinery and equipment require replacement. Also, decisions about what and how much to produce become far more perplexing as the level of price and the relations among individual prices change. Although inflation offers

---

[1] The statistics used in this and the foregoing discussion come from the following sources: the data on prices and weekly earnings come from the Bureau of Labor Statistics; data on personal liquid assets come from the Federal Reserve Board.

some advantages to businessmen, as shall be indicated subsequently, it also has an unstabilizing influence that must be reckoned in its cost.

These many types of injury inflicted by inflation make it a major economic problem. Whether or not the inflation abates for a while, it remains a threat. We must therefore discover its causes and devise effective cures for it. If we can do so, a major source of economic injury will have been removed from the average person's life.

I. DISTINCTION BETWEEN PROSPERITY, INFLATION, AND HYPERINFLATION

Three types of situation sometimes are confused. "Prosperity" should be distinguished from "inflation," and both should be recognized as different from "hyperinflation." All three have one thing in common: they are characterized by rising prices and very active business conditions. They differ greatly in degree and in ultimate consequences, however. *Prosperity* is a period of generally rising real income for almost everyone. Though prices ordinarily rise somewhat during prosperity, usually the increase is slow, and is far smaller than the average increase in income, so that the *average* standard of living is improved. Moreover, during prosperity almost everyone's income rises as much as prices increase. (Some prosperous periods have actually been characterized by stable prices; for example, 1924 to 1929.)

During *inflation,* the rise in prices and *average* personal income more or less keep pace with each other, but individual incomes rise very unevenly, with the result that *many* individuals suffer a drop in living standards, while others enjoy a marked increase in real income.

Hyperinflation exists when prices rise much more rapidly than during inflation—say, at the rate of 100 per cent a year or more for a year or longer. Hyperinflation is characterized by the almost universal assumption that prices will continue to rise at a very rapid rate, with the result that most individuals and businesses consciously hasten their purchases to escape the almost certain continued rise in prices. Hyperinflation is also characterized by highly uneven price changes in particular industries and for different types of income.

Prosperity, inflation, and hyperinflation differ in the length of time they continue. Prosperity generally lasts longer than the other two. While prosperity generally gives way to recession, it is conceivable that prolonged, and perpetual prosperity, could occur. Inflation generally sows the seeds of its own reversal. Hyperinflation is a wild and explosive situation that does not continue for long. It seems sure to end within a fairly short time and to create great havoc.

Although the United States has not undergone a hyperinflation, and is not likely to do so, other nations, namely, Hungary and China, have done so in very recent years; the runaway inflation in Germany following World War I is a classic example of hyperinflation. Most other countries in the world have experienced inflation to varying degrees since the outbreak of World War II.

Definitions of inflation and hyperinflation should take account of more than the rate at which prices increase, though this criterion is by far the most easily observed and measured. In particular, differences in the rate at which *individual* prices and incomes change are responsible for much of the damage wrought by inflation; if virtually all prices and incomes rise by similar proportions, inflation is far less injurious than if the rise is extremely disproportionate. In other words, the damage done by inflation arises both from a general rise in prices and from disproportionate price changes.

II. CAUSES OF INFLATION

The essential characteristic of inflation has changed in recent years. A very new phenomenon for this country is recession accompanied by inflation. The very rapid decline in business during the second half of 1957 and early 1958 was accompanied by a steady rise in the index of consumer prices. A major consequence of this change is that the fear of aggravating inflationary pressures prevents the authorities from taking quick and vigorous measures to combat recession. Specifically, during the downswing of 1957-1958, the President and his advisors delayed counter-recession measures and, indeed, never did take some of the more potent ones because of a fear that the price rise would become even greater as a result.

Until fairly recently, inflations have been pretty much of a type and have occurred when the demand for goods and services increased substantially more than the supplies of goods available. However, there are other causes for inflation. One, in particular, is receiving considerable discussion currently; this is the so-called "cost-push" type (as distinguished from the first, which is coming to be described as the "demand-pull" type), which originates in wage increases that outrun increases in labor productivity. A third type that is a constant threat in nations suffering from corrupt or unstable governments results from mistrust of the government and fear that it will print money to finance extravagances and ultimately repudiate the currency. We shall confine our discussion to the first two types of inflation, for the third type is more a political than an economic problem.

A. Inflation Resulting from Relative Increases in Demand

Fortunately, the causes of inflation are fairly obvious. Especially is this true when inflation accompanies large expenditures for war purposes or for the creation of a strong military establishment or to finance a rapid rate of economic development. The demands for goods at such times are likely to outrun by a considerable margin the ability of the nation's resources to increase output, with the result that more dollars are bid for each unit of goods and services available. Increased competition for goods will increase the prices sellers can command for them, as has already been explained. (See discussion of demand in Chapter 12.)

If the increase in demand for goods were expected to be extremely brief, the result might not be what we describe as inflation. Some sharp and erratic price changes might occur, but the levels of prices and the relation between prices and incomes, and even between individual prices and individual incomes, might quickly return to their previous levels and relations. Accordingly, important in "demand-pull" inflations is the general expectation that demands will continue at high levels and that prices will continue to rise. In other words, the expectation of further inflation generally is present during any inflation. Indeed, sometimes—as during the summer of 1950, following the outbreak of Korean hostilities—a sharp rise in prices can be induced solely by the expectation of larger government expenditures and higher prices.

Generally, inflations resulting from increases in demand can be traced to government spending. However, inflations can also start by a concurrent rise in outlays by individuals and businesses. For example, following World War II, during which backlogs of demand accumulated, all groups desired to spend well beyond their income and drew upon their accumulated savings to finance their purchases. The result was a general price inflation.

B. Inflation Resulting from Increased Costs of Production

Cost-based inflations are those in which price increases can be traced directly to increases in labor costs or to higher raw-material or rental costs. More specifically, many observers have believed that rising wage rates were the cause for higher prices in the United States during the period of, roughly, 1950 to 1957. It is easy enough to reason from an increase in costs to a rise in prices, and find inflation the outcome of general and substantial increases in wages. Without a doubt, wage increases did figure—one way or another—in the price inflation of the late 1940's and 1950's. However, there are facets of a cost-based inflation that are passed over in this rather simplified view of the matter.

In the first place, a rise in cost need not be followed by a rise in price; businessmen not infrequently find that they must absorb some cost increases. Second, increases in wages need not represent higher labor costs—they have been partly offset, and in some years more than offset, by increased productivity. Third, and most important, higher prices could result in reduced *unit* sales; indeed, unless buyers were able to spend a larger total amount of money for current output, there would necessarily be a reduction in unit purchases. (The same amount of money used to buy goods whose prices have increased would buy fewer of them.) With a decline in unit sales, the intensity of market rivalry would grow and possibly compel a reduction in prices, despite the rise in labor cost. In other words, a rise in wages *alone* would not be sufficient to increase prices unless accompanied by either increased demand or by increased unemployment.

But even the foregoing qualifications leave the question of cost-push inflation in an oversimple state. One must expect some connection between wage-rate changes and the level of demand. For one thing, the announcement of a wage increase in some supply industry is taken as a signal by its customers to increase purchases in anticipation of a price increase to follow. Therefore, wage increases tend to inspire purchases for inventory accumulation. For another thing, the rise in wages will encourage workers receiving the increase to spend more and will also lead to a general climate of opinion in which workers *in general* expect their wages to rise. The result of both would be a higher level of consumer expenditure. Finally, widespread expectation of future wage increases creates general pressure for all types of spenders (government, business, and individuals) to buy sooner rather than later, a condition which also has the effect of raising the level of expenditure at any time— the difference being made up in the distant and never-reached future. Especially with regard to major expenditures, for such things as buildings, machinery, housing, and durables is this expectation of a steady rise in wage rates likely to raise the level of purchases. In these ways, then, a steady rise in wage rates can create a pattern of price-and-expenditure reaction that may be termed a wage-push syndrome.

There is considerable agitation over the issue of whether the inflation of recent years is caused by wage increases or other factors. It is difficult to escape several conclusions on this subject: first, that some of the most vocal participants in the dispute are looking for a scapegoat and seeking to gain a public-relations advantage; second, that a high level of demand resulting at least partly from heavy expenditures by business and government has contributed significantly to the rise in prices; third, that the pattern of price change would have been substantially different during the period if wage rates had remained stable; fourth, one will not be able to discourage individual groups of workers or businessmen from seeking higher wages or prices by telling them that they are contributing to general inflation. The type of "self-restraint" sometimes called for on the part of labor (and frequently from management when it announces price increases) represents a departure from the rationale of a free-enterprise system that might actually prove more injurious than benign. These four comments do not settle the question whether recent price increases have resulted from the rise in wage rates; they simply suggest facets of the problem that one should not overlook.

The problem of "cost-push" inflations leads us to consider the thesis that the United States may face chronic inflation. This thesis revolves around the notion that labor has become very strong politically and economically. Since labor represents a majority of all voters, and an estimated 17 millions belong to unions (as of 1957),[2] we face, in the not-too-distant future, a "laboristic" society in which labor is able to get a large share of what it wants, in the way of *money*—though not *real*— wages. By the use of union bargaining power and political strength, labor will be virtually assured of increased money wage rates, according to this thesis.

A "laboristic" economy would, in addition, probably tie wage rates to the cost of living. Such an arrangement might build into the economy an upward spiral of wages and prices. Once a rise in prices started, the dependence of wage rates upon the cost of living would cause wage rates to rise. In the ordinary course of events, a rise in wage rates would justify an attempt to raise prices, with the result that an upward spiral of prices and wages would continue.

A little reflection reveals that a rise in wages that simply keeps pace with prices does not necessarily benefit labor.[3] Inasmuch as wage increases generally follow behind prices during periods of inflation, labor is in the position of "catching up" past losses. Moreover, even successful labor disputes impose heavy costs on workers as well as management. In addition, some workers can lose out because their wage increases are not so great as those won by other workers. Unless all wage rates rise equally, some workers are likely to be injured in the process. The prices they pay are likely to rise more than their wages, because of the large increases won by the strongest labor unions.

It is therefore possible that successful efforts by workers to increase their money wages would not serve their basic economic interest. How-

---

[2] Table 5, Chapter 8.

[3] From both labor's and management's standpoint cost-of-living provisions in contracts seem preferable to a renegotiation of wage terms during an inflation. It should be re-emphasized that such contracts would not cause continued inflation in themselves or compel an inflation to continue once it had started.

ever, it is not likely that most workers or their leaders will recognize this fact—if it is indeed a fact. Should the political and economic strength of unions grow and become clearly predominant, then the prediction of chronic inflation may well be proved correct. However, there are strong disagreements about the present and probable future strength of unions, and the political cohesiveness of workers in national elections.

Should the prediction of a laboristic society prove to be correct, the strength of the inflation let loose will depend upon the relation between what workers regard as a "good" wage gain and the average rise in productivity. If, for example, workers came to regard a 3 per cent rise in wages annually as "good" and their productivity increased at the same rate, then prices need not rise at all. Under such circumstances, even union contracts containing a provision that tied wage rates to prices would not result in inflation. On the other hand, if workers came to regard nothing less than 6 per cent as a good annual wage increase, though labor productivity increased by 3 per cent annually, labor costs per unit would rise. In time, higher labor costs would be reflected in higher prices. Thereupon the higher prices would lead to further wage increases under the provision tying wages to prices.

Few labor-union leaders today are willing to limit their wage demands to past productivity increases. They believe that workers are underpaid, and they want to rectify what they believe to be a long and deep injustice *as well as* obtain compensation for increases in productivity. As a result, for some time, anyhow, increases in wage rates limited to productivity increases seem to be less than most labor will accept. If labor is very strong politically and economically and feels that it is entitled to wage increases larger than growth in productivity, the threat of chronic inflation will be grave.

The foregoing argument sometimes is combined with a theory regarding the measures that a "laboristic" economy would take to combat depression. It is said that at the first signs of a downswing, a labor-dominated government would spend heavily to prevent unemployment. It will fear unemployment much more than inflation, and will therefore err in the direction of spending more than is necessary to correct the downswing. As a result, instead of depression, inflation will almost certainly result.

Several points in the thesis that we should anticipate chronic inflation are open to question. First, labor is far from a cohesive group, either economically or politically. Unions often conflict in their attempts to gain jurisdiction over the same plant or industry. Second, the economic and political strength of unions depends upon basic economic conditions to a considerable degree. A business downswing with the danger of unemployment could profoundly undermine (although it might possibly strengthen) the political and economic power of unions. Third, there have been times when "laboristic" governments have ruled a nation—

Great Britain under the Labor Government in particular—when the predictions of inflation for the reasons given do not seem to have been borne out. The failure of the prediction was caused partly by self-restraint on the part of union leaders and the rank-and-file workers, who, after a time, realized they could not forever raise wages without increasing productivity. Fourth, labor-union leadership may well behave in a fashion altogether different from now if labor gains a dominant position in society. Regarding themselves as representatives of a group that is underprivileged and politically underrepresented, union leaders understandably are concerned with serving their workers rather than the community. If a laboristic economy were to come into being, labor leaders may become more responsible, as they occupy high political office and are given the job of dealing with economic problems from the standpoint of the entire nation.

III. CURES FOR INFLATION

Clarity of cause contributes to certainty of cure. The major cures for inflation are known. However, because some politically powerful groups consider them painful, inflation is not as uncommon as one might hope.

We shall not review all possible cures for inflation; three measures will be considered in moderate detail. Measures best adapted to one situation will be of little help in another. Some seem better suited to one country than another. Certain measures deal with inflationary conditions concentrated in a few sectors of the economy, while others are unselective and general. Some are intended to correct price increases caused by rising costs or reductions in supply; others would reduce total demand. We are here concerned only with cures for general inflation resulting from rising demand when output cannot expand correspondingly. Moreover, we shall deal with measures appropriate to the United States; some of the conditions in this country do not prevail elsewhere, and our conclusions therefore will not necessarily apply to other nations.

Generalized inflation controls take three major forms: restrictions on bank credit, increased taxation, and general price control and rationing. The appropriateness of each one and its political feasibility will be discussed in turn.

A. Credit Restrictions

Commercial bank-credit expansion feeds most inflations. Bank loans generally increase substantially the quantity of goods that business and consumers can purchase during inflation, intensifying competition for scarce goods and forcing up their prices. If banks were compelled to contract their loans at such times, the demand for goods of all types would fall; such action could stop the price increase, or could even induce a downward movement. How could credit restriction be effected during an inflation under current banking arrangements?

To understand how and to what extent banking authorities can restrict bank credit, it is necessary to understand the way they can influence deposits that member banks held with the Federal Reserve Banks. As was explained earlier, each bank belonging to the Federal Reserve System cannot allow its deposit liabilities to exceed a certain multiple of legal reserves. Consequently, if the banking authorities cut down the legal reserves of commercial banks, the banks will, after some point, be compelled to cut down on their loans.

Actual and current experience shows that the Federal Reserve authorities exert considerable influence over both the volume and cost of legal reserves. They therefore can do a great deal to check an inflation, even though their ability to stimulate loans during depression is very slight.

The banking authorities can control the supply of legal reserves in three main ways. First, they have the power to alter legal-reserve requirements within prescribed limits. If they use this power to raise the amount of legal reserves that member banks must hold against their deposit liabilities, banks that have extended loans to the legal limit will be forced to reduce their loans—or to find ways of increasing their legal-reserve holdings.

This very potent technique for restricting bank loans has limited effectiveness for two main reasons: first, banks hold very large amounts of government bonds which they could sell to increase their legal reserves; second, the upper limits to which legal-reserve requirements can be pushed may be far from high enough to check loans under certain circumstances.

A second means by which banking authorities can affect the volume of commercial bank loans is to increase the cost of obtaining reserves. They can make this increase by raising the "rediscount rate"—which is the interest rate that member banks must pay on loans they make from the Reserve Banks. Banks sometimes borrow from their Federal Reserve Banks to obtain the legal reserves needed to support additional loans. An increase in the cost of borrowing reduces the attractiveness of making loans because it lowers the net return to be obtained. (If the banks try to pass along their higher costs to borrowers, it is to be expected that they will find fewer borrowers.)

The rediscount rate has also been used as a danger signal. Commercial bankers have come to interpret an increase in the discount rate as a warning to restrict credit or to face more drastic monetary action. As a result, bankers tend to be more selective in their lending and to rely less on reserves borrowed from the Reserve Banks when the rediscount rate is increased.

The third, and most effective, method by which the monetary authorities are able to influence the legal reserves of commercial banks, and thereby their ability to make loans, is through the purchase and sale of government securities. To contract credit, they will sell government securities. When the Federal Reserve Banks sell government securities, they do so on the open market. Buyers on this market are financial institutions, businesses, and individuals. There always has been a fairly active market for government securities; that is, many persons and businesses continually deal in them. As a result, the Federal Reserve authorities could readily sell large amounts of government securities—if they were willing to accept for them a price low enough to make their purchase attractive.

Purchasers of government securities ordinarily pay by check. Almost all of them hold deposits with member banks of the Federal Reserve System. Their banks would either lose cash when the reserve banks sold bonds, or suffer a reduction in their deposits with the Federal Reserve Banks. Both effects would reduce the amount of loans that the member banks could make.

Open-market selling of government securities probably restricts credit more effectively than do the two other tools. Unlike raising reserve requirements and the rediscount rate, this tool need not be used sparingly. It is best suited to day-to-day adjustments, because such sales can be used to impound small or large amounts of reserves. Thus borrowing and deposits can be curtailed with dispatch and at will, since the Reserve Banks own large quantities of government securities which they may sell without regard to price and profit.

One objection to credit control by means of purchase and sale of government securities by the Federal Reserve Banks is that it would increase the interest cost of carrying the national debt. For many decades, the federal government will not be able to pay off its obligations as they become due. Instead, it will be compelled to borrow again to retire maturing obligations. Therefore a change in policy that would allow government securities to drop in price would raise the effective interest rate at which the government debt was refunded and would thereby increase the cost of government. If only a small drop in price of government bonds (meaning a small rise in interest rate) were necessary to restrict credit, then the higher costs of carrying the government debt would be trivial. If credit contraction involved a large drop in government security prices, the interest charges on the government debt (which in 1957 ran at about $7.3 billion) would increase significantly. However, it would almost certainly be a far smaller cost to the public than continually rising prices.

A policy of credit restriction is not particularly popular with bankers or with those who want loans. It would prevent banks from expanding commercial loans at a time when attractive rates may be obtainable from borrowers with a high credit standing. Nevertheless, banker opposition to credit restriction is far from universal during inflation. In 1951, a program for voluntary credit restraint was initiated under the aegis of the Federal Reserve authorities. Although a majority of bankers supported the program, loans of commercial banks continued to rise. It is generally agreed, however, that the program did check the expansion of commercial loans somewhat.

A policy of opposing inflation by bank-credit restriction also will meet unreasoned opposition from those who fear an accounting loss in the value of government securities. Because of the many lines of objection to credit control through Federal Reserve dealings in government securities, restriction of commercial bank credit cannot be counted upon, because it is not always politically feasible. However, if undertaken, it would almost certainly go far to restrain an inflation.

B. Curbing Inflation by Taxation

Taxation has the twin purpose of raising revenue while checking inflation. If taxation were not needed to check inflation, governments would run the printing presses or borrow from banks to finance expenditures. In that way, they need not antagonize voter-taxpayers.

Taxation can be used to combat inflations caused by high government spending. It also would counteract inflations arising from greatly increased spending by individuals and businesses.

Taxes reduce the funds available to individuals and businesses, and thereby usually reduce their spending. (Some persons will reduce their current savings or even draw down past savings without cutting their spending after taxes rise, but these are the exception rather than the rule.) Inflation is not rectified by taxes alone; to fight inflation, it is necessary that tax proceeds be used in a manner that does not add to the demand for goods. If the government ran a budget surplus in an effort to combat inflation, it should hold its surpluses in the form of bank balances. If it were to reduce its outstanding debt by purchasing back on the open market its outstanding obligations, reducing thereby its interest burden, it would increase the ability of the banks, business, and individuals selling the bonds to lend and spend. To combat inflation, taxes must transfer, to the government, funds that would have been spent; the government then uses these funds in ways that do not increase spending.

Virtually all types of taxes combat inflation. Even excise taxes, which raise the prices of goods and seem to be inflationary in themselves, reduce the desire of people to purchase goods and thereby will dampen inflationary forces. Taxes are a particularly effective method of combating inflation, because they permit selectivity and flexibility in placing the burden of an inflation. General credit restriction can hit almost anyone, without respect to his income, the nature of his occupation, and so on. Income taxes, on the other hand, could be increased in a way that would exempt those of low income. It would even be possible to base the tax partly on *changes in income* from the preceding year, and in this way favor those whose incomes do not tend to keep pace with price changes. Personal exemptions could be raised for the computation of income taxes. Moreover, incomes obtained from stock or commodity speculation, which generally become sizable during inflation, might be subjected to particularly high tax rates, thus both discouraging further speculation and reducing the personal expenditures of successful speculators. In addition, income taxation is a type of inflation control with which the government has had extended experience; therefore it is likely to receive effective administration and to be put into effect more speedily than other types of anti-inflation control except credit controls.

Increases in taxes are unpopular, even during inflation. Unfortunately, inflation is similar to indirect taxation. Its effects are not fully realized by many persons; to them, inflation seems less painful than higher taxes. In addition, those with fixed incomes would be particularly hurt by higher taxes—though not necessarily more than by higher prices. These persons understandably strive to obtain reduced taxes to obtain relief from rising living costs.

Despite the many advantages of combating inflation by increasing taxes, tax increases to fight inflation are almost certain to be too little and too late. Perhaps failure to support higher taxes is due to the feeling of many persons that they cannot escape the higher taxes, but that they may be able to avoid paying higher prices. In addition, tax increases are opposed by those who feel that inflation can be dampened by increasing the supplies of goods; these persons do not want to weaken production incentives by raising tax rates to prohibitive levels lest the increased tax rates reduce output.

C. Price Control and Rationing

In retrospect, price and rationing controls in the United States during World War II were remarkably successful. Although far from perfect, their success during the war compared favorably with similar control programs of other countries, and greatly exceeded the expectations of even strong advocates of price control. During 1946, however, when price control became a political issue, weaknesses multiplied.

Thus history proves that price control can be effective even in the

United States.[4] The recent experience of Great Britain also demonstrates that a democratic country can carry out price control and rationing even in peacetime. It does not follow, however, that price control would again be successful in the United States during wartime, or that it would fail during peacetime. We can speculate about the likely success of direct controls only in the light of circumstances prevailing at the time.

It is not simple to set down standards by which to determine whether price control has been successful. All too often the effectiveness of price control is judged by the behavior of a price index. A price index may remain stationary or fall while an inflation is creating great havoc. Price controls, for example, might drastically alter the pattern of output by inducing producers to shift to the production of goods which, under inflationary conditions with price controls but not otherwise, are most profitable. Frequently they shift from basic staple items—which sell in great quantity at relatively low prices ordinarily—to luxury items, which usually carry much higher margins. In the absence of the staple items, consumers will be compelled to purchase the luxury items or go without altogether. The conventional price index would not record such a development as a rise in price.

Or price control might, through forgivable error, set ceiling prices so low that businesses would actually incur losses from making some items. Output might decline, with the result that the competition for other goods would be intensified. In such situations the index would remain firm also.

The administration of price control will scarcely be equally intelligent and zealous in all areas. Some industries will find themselves thoroughly controlled to their disadvantage, but to the gain of the nation as a whole. Others, however, will secure softer treatment from the regulatory authorities, and enforcement personnel may be quite skilled in "looking the other way." As with all broad controls, and especially with those erected in a hurry, administration of controls is likely to be imperfect, sometimes inept, and, not infrequently, downright corrupt.

For these reasons, general price and rationing controls can be successful only if an overwhelming majority of businesses and consumers believe them to be necessary. Otherwise, evasions of the law multiply by the average person's following the example of the violator. Moreover, efficient and incorruptible personnel would be needed to formulate and administer the regulations. Such administrators are always difficult to find, especially if they are offered only temporary posts with uncertain tenure. Finally, the legislation underlying price control and rationing must not be

---

[4] Many economists and politicians insist that if price controls are to work effectively there must also be wage and profit controls.

a political trap for unwary administrators, which promises more protection for business than for consumers. It is unlikely that these three minimum requirements for successful price control can be met during the usual period of peacetime inflation.

Price and rationing controls seem ideally suited to inflationary pressure that is concentrated in a few areas of the economy. These pressures might result from the diversion of raw materials or finished products to military uses. When applied to a few products, speedy action, good administration, and public support are not unlikely. However, even so, the need for direct controls is likely to spread. Inflation tends to spill over from one area into another. For example, price control and rationing of some items that become scarce leave persons who were unable to make purchases with more funds than they ordinarily wish to hold. They may try to buy other products—especially nearby substitutes. As a result, inflationary pressure builds up in these other areas. Although inflation is contagious, it can often be restricted to a narrow area where it can be held in check by direct controls.

D. Miscellaneous Inflation Controls

While we shall not discuss any other measures for controlling inflation, two will be noted. First, restrictions on the use of installment credit limit the ability of individuals to buy, and in their effects are analogous to restrictions on commercial loans. Second, widely publicized campaigns to sell government bonds to individuals could reduce personal spending. Especially if the bonds guaranteed to repay buyers in constant purchasing power, they would attract many people who would welcome a chance to protect themselves against an inflation. Most people have "no place to hide" during an inflation. It is difficult to select securities or investments that will keep pace with prices during inflation; especially is this true for the average person who has little familiarity with investment problems.

IV. SUMMARY AND CONCLUSIONS

We have seen that inflation imposes serious hardship on certain groups in the population. Recipients of fixed incomes—those who live on annuities or insurance benefits, certain types of salaried workers in particular—find their real income cut as prices outrun their incomes. A rise in prices hurts all those who have accumulated money savings, because they can buy fewer goods. Individuals holding savings suffered a loss of purchasing power due to inflation amounting to over $100 billion since 1945. The damage done by inflation tends to be underestimated because of the "money illusion." That is, people tend to judge their well-being more by their money income than by what it will buy.

Inflation may become a chronic condition in all countries where labor's political and economic power becomes dominant. Even if such a situation does not come to pass, inflations in the future cannot be considered minor hazards. War and preparations for war can give rise to profound inflations that seriously injure some classes of the population to the advantage of others.

Three types of remedies for inflation are most promising from the economic point of view; however, none of these is likely to enlist strong political support during an inflation. Credit restriction poses peculiar difficulties now that commercial banks hold large amounts of government bonds, and because effective credit control would involve a rise in interest charges in the national debt. Tax increase, the best remedy of all because of its selectivity and flexibility, is unpalatable even to those who would indirectly be most helped by it. Finally, price control and rationing are likely to be effective only under fairly unusual circumstances. During peacetime, these controls are most suited to inflations that are concentrated in a fairly narrow sector of the economy. They are most effective if supported by the other two remedies.

In viewing the prospects for inflation control, one fact stands out. In contrast to depression, where almost everyone is injured, many groups gain during inflation. Consequently, the political obstacles to the enactment of effective remedies for inflation are very great. Indeed, a person is highly optimistic if he expects them to be enacted speedily except perhaps during a war that threatens the very survival of the country.

DISCUSSION QUESTIONS

1. How do you account for the fact that the United States has never had a runaway inflation? Under what circumstances might one occur here?

2. If, by magic, every piece of currency, coin, bank deposit, check, and figure in contracts were to have a zero added to it, apart from surprise and shock, what effects would you expect?

3. Which groups are injured most by inflation? How would you measure the injury inflicted by inflation?

4. Is a little inflation a good thing? Explain. Which groups ordinarily gain from inflation?

5. Do you believe that labor-union contracts that provide for wage increases to compensate for increases in the cost of living are inflationary in themselves? Can you make a case for the thesis that such contracts reduce the injury that results from inflation?

6. In what ways does the existence of a large government debt make it difficult for the banking system to combat inflation?

7. Under what circumstances would you expect price controls to be effective? When are they most likely to fail? Would you favor them in wartime? Would you want them if the price level had increased by 10 per cent in eighteen months and you could see no unmistakable signs that the rise would soon end?

8. In what respects are higher prices and higher taxes similar? In what ways are they different?

9. Distinguish between "general inflationary controls" and "specific controls." Indicate the circumstances when each type is most appropriate.

10. Does the usual balance of political power tend to ensure the passage of adequate anti-inflation controls during inflation? Explain.

11. What are the main differences between a "cost-push" and a "demand-pull" type of inflation? Do these differences affect the manner in which the inflation is to be contained? Explain.

SELECTED READINGS FOR PART 6

Chandler, Lester V. *Inflation in the United States, 1940-1948.* New York: Harper & Brothers, 1951. Pp. xi, 402. This book deals with the major forces leading to inflation during and after World War II. Such policies as fiscal policy, wage policy, and price controls are evaluated against the background of the annals of the inflation. The effects of inflation on the distribution of income and wealth are explained.

Colm, Gerhard. *Essays in Public Finance and Fiscal Policy.* Berkeley: University of California Press, 1955. Pp. xvii, 375. This book is a collection of essays surveying the fields of public finance and fiscal policy. The essays deal with theoretical aspects of public finance, various problems of fiscal policy, government expenditures and receipts, problems of economic stability, etc.

Committee for Economic Development. *Tax Reduction and Tax Reform: When and How.* New York: The Committee, 1957. P. 40. An intelligent policy statement giving recommendations on reduction and reform of federal taxes and on budgetary expenditure control.

Fousek, Peter. *Foreign Central Banking: The Instruments of Monetary Policy.* New York: Federal Reserve Bank of New York, 1957. P. 116. This informative survey of the main instruments of monetary policy used by foreign central banks in the postwar period is a helpful guide to a broad understanding of monetary policy. The survey includes discussion of the parallel tools in use in the United States economy. Discount policy, open-market operations, reserve requirements, etc. are explained and evaluated.

Galbraith, John Kenneth. *The Affluent Society.* Boston: Houghton Mifflin Company, 1958. P. 368. This provocative analysis of the economic problems of contemporary American society questions the principle of maximum economic growth: the urgency of production is considered a myth. In fact, more and more production as a goal creates rather than solves problems. Inflation, instability, and social imbalance—starvation of public services—are traced to the drive to produce more.

Goldsmith, Raymond W. *Financial Intermediaries in the American Economy since 1900.* Princeton, N.J.: Princeton University Press, 1958. Pp. xxxv,

415. This book is another significant contribution of the author to the fund of basic information about our economy. The various dimensions of financial intermediaries—financial enterprises dealing in intangible assets and bringing savers' funds to those using them—are set forth for the period 1900-1952.

Hansen, Alvin H. *The American Economy*. New York: McGraw-Hill Book Company, Inc., 1957. Pp. xv, 199. The author examines the recent past to see how it throws light on Keynesian notions. Employment, monetary policy, fiscal policy, and the like are examined closely in the context of the Employment Act of 1946 under the various administrations since its inception. In this way the importance of Keynesian ideas is underlined.

Hawtrey, Ralph G. *The Gold Standard in Theory and Practice* (5th ed.). London: Longmans, Green & Company, Ltd., 1947. P. 280. A classic view of the gold standard's mechanisms and the theory of its operation. The author also reviews and carefully evaluates the Bretton Woods agreements.

Maxwell, James A. *Fiscal Policy: Its Techniques and Institutional Setting*. New York: Henry Holt & Company, Inc., 1955. Pp. vi, 218. This is an introduction to the problems of fiscal policy. Fiscal policy is reviewed in the framework of contracyclical control of the business cycle. Its effectiveness in the light of our technical and institutional arrangements is evaluated.

Mitchell, Wesley Clair. *Business Cycles: The Problem and Its Setting*. New York: National Bureau of Economic Research, 1957. Pp. xxii, 489. This classic presentation of the problem of the business cycle by one of the pioneering students of ups and downs defines the cycle and then proceeds to explain the dynamics of business activity at different periods of the cycle. This is a major American contribution to the understanding and control of the business cycle.

National Bureau of Economic Research. *Policies to Combat Depression*. Princeton, N.J.: Princeton University Press, 1956. Pp. x, 417. This book is made up of fourteen papers based on papers delivered at a conference on policies to combat depression held in October, 1953, and May, 1954—during a recession period. The papers deal with a variety of subjects such as fiscal policy as a stabilizing device, the effectiveness of "built-in" stabilizers, and an analysis of the 1948-1949 recession.

New York Clearing House Association. *The Federal Reserve Re-examined*. New York: New York Clearing House Association, 1953. Pp. xii, 165. A very useful critical explanation of the Federal Reserve System's aims, mechanisms, and operations.

Paul, Randolph. *Taxation in the United States*. Boston: Little, Brown & Company, 1954. Pp. xii, 830. This book treats both of the history of taxes in the United States and fiscal policies since the advent of the New Deal. Fiscal policy is dealt with at length with a view to assessing the consequences of adopted policies.

Roosa, Robert V. *Federal Reserve Operations in the Money and Government Securities Markets*. New York: Federal Reserve Bank of New York, 1956. P. 108. This is an excellent account of the role of the Federal Reserve System in carrying out its monetary policies. The role of the money market in the over-all economic picture is sketched, and then the dynamic and defensive responsibilities of the System are examined as the author traces the System's actions in the money and securities markets.

Roose, Kenneth D. *The Economics of Recession and Revival: An Interpretation of 1937-38.* New Haven, Conn.: Yale University Press, 1954. Pp. xi, 280. Business-cycle theory is put to the test in this analysis of the recession of 1937-1938 and the subsequent revival. The description of the forces at work in recession and revival is a valuable contribution to understanding ups and downs in business.

Smithies, Arthur. *The Budgetary Process in the United States.* New York: McGraw-Hill Book Company, Inc., 1955. Pp. xxi, 486. This book deals with the structure of government as related to the process of making a budget. The process is viewed both analytically and historically and related to the basic problem of economic efficiency.

———, and J. K. Butters. *Readings in Fiscal Policy.* Homewood, Ill.: Richard D. Irwin and Company, Inc., 1955. Pp. x, 596. This is Vol. VII in a series of the American Economic Association, which republishes outstanding articles on economic subjects. This volume includes more than 30 articles dealing with problems in the areas of debt management and fiscal policy as related to economic progress and cyclical stability.

United States. Board of Governors of the Federal Reserve System. *Consumer Installment Credit.* 5 vols. Washington, D.C.: Federal Reserve System, 1957. Installment credit in its many facets is discussed and measured in this important set of books. The significance and regulation of installment credit as well as its many problems are treated at length.

United States Congress, Joint Committee on the Economic Report. *Federal Tax Policy for Economic Growth and Stability.* Washington, D.C.: Government Printing Office, 1955. Pp. xii, 930. This committee publication includes 80 papers on problems relating to putting into effect a useful tax policy. The various papers, contributed by a variety of economists both academic and nonacademic, provide a fund of information and analysis on this subject.

Part

7 Should the United States Encourage Imports and Foreign Loans?

26 How Much Should We Buy from and Lend to Foreign Countries?

As a very rich and powerful nation, the United States now bears heavy and conspicuous responsibility for the state of the world. Consequently, we are a "natural" object of suspicion, jealousy, and dislike. Moreover, our relations with foreign nations have been greatly altered by the existence of the cold war, which is largely a battle for allies between the United States and the Soviet Union.

The changed political, economic, and military position of the United States in the world is profoundly affecting our foreign policy. It is clearly reflected in the growing proportion of all legislation and political debate that revolves around our relations with other nations. Whereas these questions were not long ago regarded as minor matters, they are now at the forefront of our public policy.

The policies of the United States toward the rest of the world have not crystallized firmly. Many crucial issues are still in hot dispute. However, American foreign policy seems to be evolving toward acceptance of the following principles. First, we must try to raise the living standards in the poorest countries of the world. (In this, we would act toward the rest of the world in the way that the richest individuals in our own country are expected to act toward the poorest.) Second, we must help countries that are in a desperate financial position. (These countries are not necessarily the poorest countries in the world.) We believe that totalitarianism feeds on poverty and that democracy flourishes with prosperity. For example, economic aid to Western Europe was designed partly to raise the living standards of such countries as France and Italy, where communism was thriving on widespread misery. Third, we must recognize that the economic condition of a large part of the world depends heavily upon international trade, that improvements in world living standards will require greatly expanded trade among nations, and that we must participate in it ourselves to a greater extent than heretofore. The illustration below, "A Trade View of the World," reflects the heavy

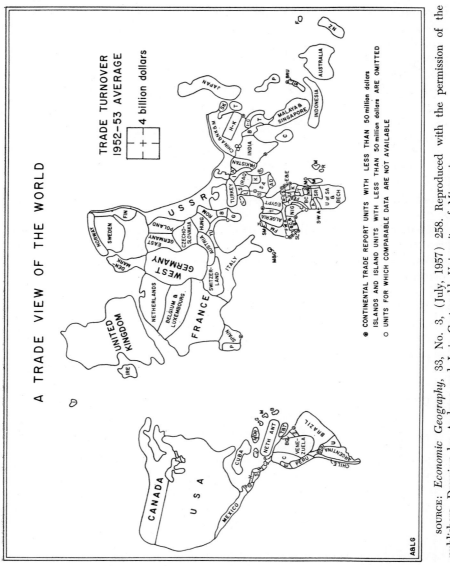

A TRADE VIEW OF THE WORLD

TRADE TURNOVER
1952–53 AVERAGE

4 billion dollars

⊛ CONTINENTAL TRADE REPORT UNITS WITH LESS THAN 50 million dollars
    ISLANDS AND ISLAND UNITS WITH LESS THAN 50 million dollars ARE OMITTED
○ UNITS FOR WHICH COMPARABLE DATA ARE NOT AVAILABLE

SOURCE: *Economic Geography*, 33, No. 3, (July, 1957) 258. Reproduced with the permission of the publishers. Drawing by Andreas and Lois Grotewold, University of Missouri.

dependence of many nations on international trade. Table 1 shows the extent of the United States' involvement in international economic relations. Fourth, we must manage our affairs in a way that will prevent major depressions, because they adversely affect most countries in the world. Fifth, we must show other nations that we are sincerely interested in their welfare and that we seek not merely our own advantage. A policy of selfishness will not develop loyal and devoted allies that will stand by us in the event of a world crisis. Powerful though we are, our very survival may depend upon whether the unpledged part of the world sides with us or with the Soviet bloc of nations.

There still remains an influential group that asserts that the United States has no foreign responsibilities. According to its view, which it generally applies in both domestic and foreign matters, everyone must stand on his own feet and look out for himself. This point of view is ordinarily termed "economic isolationism." Whether or not it is morally defensible, it is unlikely to win the support of the so-called uncommitted nations, which are likely to regard such rugged individualism as pure selfishness.[1] If these nations come to terms with the Soviets, or even if

RELATIVE IMPORTANCE OF OUR WORLD MARKETS

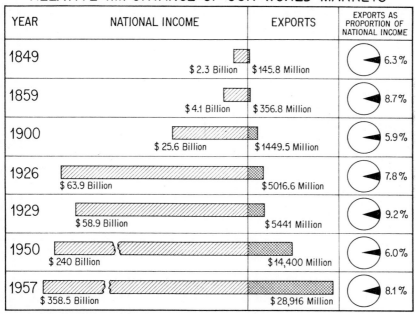

YEAR	NATIONAL INCOME	EXPORTS	EXPORTS AS PROPORTION OF NATIONAL INCOME
1849	$ 2.3 Billion	$ 145.8 Million	6.3%
1859	$ 4.1 Billion	$ 356.8 Million	8.7%
1900	$ 25.6 Billion	$ 1449.5 Million	5.9%
1926	$ 63.9 Billion	$ 5016.6 Million	7.8%
1929	$ 58.9 Billion	$ 5441 Million	9.2%
1950	$ 240 Billion	$ 14,400 Million	6.0%
1957	$ 358.5 Billion	$ 28,916 Million	8.1%

[1] Economic isolationism, like rugged individualism in general, usually is espoused by those who are very strong, talented, and lucky, and is understandably unappealing to those who need help through no fault of their own. For a more general statement on the same subject, see M. F. Millikan and W. W. Rostow, *A Proposal: Key to an Effective Foreign Policy* (New York: Harper & Brothers, 1957).

Table 1. United States Balance of International Payments, 1950-1957

(In millions)

	1950	1951	1952
Exports of goods and services, total	$ 14,427	$ 20,333	$ 20,708
Military transfers under grants	526	1,470	2,603
Other goods and services, total	13,901	18,863	18,105
Merchandise, adjusted	10,117	14,123	13,319
Transportation	1,033	1,556	1,488
Travel	419	473	550
Income on investments	1,593	1,882	1,828
Other services	739	829	920
Imports of goods and services, total	$ 12,098	$ 15,142	$ 15,760
Merchandise, adjusted	9,108	11,202	10,838
Transportation	818	974	1,115
Travel	754	757	840
Military expenditures	576	1,270	1,957
Income on investments	345	355	390
Other services	497	584	620
Balance on goods and services, total	$ 2,329	$ 5,191	$ 4,948
Net unilateral transfers [to foreign countries (—)]	$—4,533	$—4,962	$—5,108
Private remittances	— 444	— 386	— 417
Military supplies and services	— 526	—1,470	—2,603
Grants and other government transfers	—3,563	—3,106	—2,088
U.S. capital, net [outflow of funds (—)]	$—1,421	$—1,224	$—1,578
Foreign capital and gold, total [outflow of funds, gold purchases (—)]	$ 3,655	$ 525	$ 1,233
Errors and omissions	$— 30	$ 470	$ 505

* Preliminary.

SOURCE: U.S. Department of Commerce, Bureau of the Census, *Statistical Abstract of the United States, 1958* (Washington, D.C.: Government Printing Office, 1958), p. 867.

they become an independent and neutral force, our military security will be gravely weakened, and our military needs will expand greatly.

We shall examine the following problems that are involved in the foreign economic policy of the United States.

1. Do imports lower domestic employment levels?

2. Shall we gain or lose from an expansion of international trade?

1953	1954	1955	1956	1957 *
$ 21,335	$ 21,110	$ 22,328	$ 26,123	$ 28,767
4,254	3,161	2,325	2,605	2,505
17,081	17,949	20,003	23,518	26,262
12,281	12,799	14,280	17,321	19,296
1,198	1,171	1,420	1,619	1,849
574	595	654	705	769
1,910	2,227	2,444	2,658	2,862
1,118	1,157	1,205	1,215	1,486
$ 16,644	$ 16,088	$ 17,937	$ 19,810	$ 20,627
10,990	10,354	11,527	12,791	13,264
1,081	1,026	1,204	1,432	1,438
929	1,009	1,153	1,275	1,358
2,535	2,603	2,823	2,910	3,114
450	419	502	618	649
659	677	728	784	804
$ 4,691	$ 5,022	$ 4,391	$ 6,313	$ 8,140
$—6,708	$—5,423	$—4,811	$—4,937	$—4,816
— 476	— 486	— 444	— 503	— 547
—4,254	—3,161	—2,325	—2,605	—2,505
—1,978	—1,776	—2,042	—1,829	—1,764
$— 587	$—1,526	$—1,521	$—3,606	$—3,996
$ 2,308	$ 1,760	$ 1,495	$ 1,528	$— 89
$ 296	$ 167	$ 446	$ 692	$ 761

Specifically, will our living standards rise or fall if international trade expands?

3. Can we sell more to the rest of the world without buying more from them? If so, how can this be done?

4. What kinds of economic benefits, if any, accrue to us from the loans and grants we make to foreign nations?

5. What are the economic consequences of our "direct" and portfolio investments in other countries?

6. Does trade with countries whose wage levels are very low cause our own standard of living to decline?

Our special interest in discussing these topics will be the economic effects of alternative policies that the nation might pursue. However, no policies make sense in the abstract. They must be related directly to the world in which they are to be carried out. Accordingly, the following discussion must skirt close to basic questions of foreign diplomatic policy. To be acceptable, measures that are good for the country from the economic point of view must be consistent with our national military and political objectives. For example, almost every nation shelters its ship-building industry from foreign competition because of its essentiality to national defense.

In considering the economic gains from particular policies, we shall

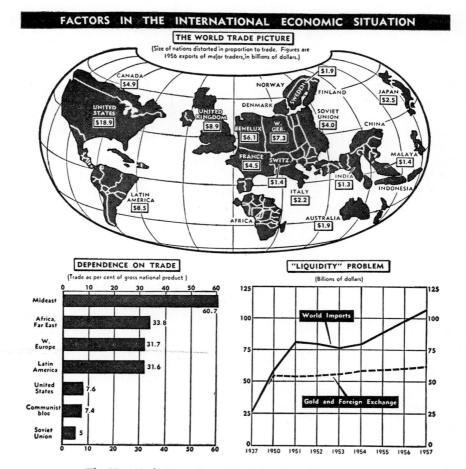

SOURCE: *The New York Times,* June 15, 1958. Map adapted from Woytinsky and Woytinsky, *World Commerce and Governments: Trends and Outlook* (New York: The Twentieth Century Fund, 1955).

evaluate international trade from the standpoint of the nation as a whole, rather than from the position of any particular group. We know that policies which enrich some individuals may harm others. It is particularly important to distinguish two interest groups: producers and consumers. Producers include two groups with opposing economic interests. One is composed of laborers, businessmen, and lenders of funds who directly or indirectly derive their incomes from domestic products that are in competition with foreign products. The other group consists of those who derive their incomes from domestic products that are or might be sold abroad. The first group obviously is interested in restricting imports, whereas the second is interested in stimulating exports. There are also two smaller groups: those who derive their incomes from the importation of foreign finished products, and those who use imported raw materials or components in the manufacture of domestic products.

Consumers include all those who buy goods for their own use and whose welfare is affected by their ability to make their purchases at low prices. Most consumers are also producers; their personal interests as producers and consumers may conflict.

It is apparent that many producers could increase their incomes at the expense of almost all consumers. They could do so by cutting off foreign competition so that domestic buyers would be compelled to pay the prices that domestic producers ask. When foreign competition is cut off, we shall place the loss to consumers above the gain to the producing group, primarily because the first group is larger. In addition, the gain that the producers would obtain in such a situation *would be smaller than the loss to the consumers;*[2] the benefits from trade would be lost to the nation.

I. VIEWS TOWARD INTERNATIONAL TRADE

Americans hold two major and conflicting views of international trade. One regards it as a means by which we can increase the sales of our products and thereby increase employment, incomes, and the level of living in this country. According to this view, trade is a battle for employment, and is essentially a struggle for exports. This line of argument holds that imports are unfortunate, for they allow foreigners to produce things that Americans would be given jobs to produce if there were no imports. We shall refer to this as the "trade-for-jobs" view of international trade.

---

[2] Domestic products that require protection from foreign competition presumably cost more to produce than similar imported goods from abroad. Consequently, domestic consumers would lose the benefits of trade, without a corresponding gain for domestic producers.

The second major view sees in imports, rather than exports, the source of gain from trade. According to this idea, trade enables everyone to buy goods and services where they can be obtained most cheaply. We will refer to this as the "trade-for-bargains" view. By enabling individuals to obtain things from elsewhere more cheaply than they would produce them for themselves, international trade would contribute toward a higher standard of living. This second view, like the first, justifies all trade on grounds of economic self-interest—the getting of things of greater value than are given up in trade.

The contradiction between the trade-for-jobs and the trade-for-bargains views is manifest. One leads to policies that restrict imports; the other encourages imports. Put in another way, the trade-for-jobs idea of trade seeks to increase work at home; the trade-for-bargains principle seeks to reduce the amount of work that must be done domestically to provide any given level of living.

Let us then explore the logic and arguments underlying these two concepts of international trade. Our purpose will be to determine whether a nation can for long periods increase employment and raise its living standards by increasing exports and restricting imports, and to understand how a nation can economize its resources and thereby raise its living standards by engaging in international trade.

II. INTERNATIONAL TRADE AND EMPLOYMENT[3]

It will be admitted at the outset that by stimulating sales to foreigners one nation can occasionally take measures that increase *total* domestic employment temporarily. Such occasions are infrequent, however, and almost invariably precipitate retaliatory action that ends these gains. Attempts to increase total domestic employment by these means result in mutual harm. No country can win an economic war, though it may conceivably win a single *battle*. *Gains in employment, as well as gains in trade, are soon lost, as will be shown.*

Before we trace the usual outcome of efforts by one country faced with unemployment to increase its employment at the expense of foreign countries, let us examine the usual and long-run effect of international trade on total employment. *Specifically, we shall ask whether a nation that greatly reduces imports would enjoy a higher level of employment than one engaging heavily in international trade.*

---

[3] In considering the influence of international trade on employment, be sure always to distinguish between total employment in the country and employment in a specific industry.

A. Long-Run Effects of International Trade on Employment

We have already seen that a nation's level of employment depends primarily upon total expenditure within the country (by domestic individuals, businesses, government, and foreigners). One would suppose that the importation of goods would lower the domestic level of expenditure, for money that might have been spent on native merchandise would instead be spent in another country. But imports are only half of the total trade picture. When an individual purchases goods from abroad, he virtually guarantees that foreigners will *spend an equal amount* of dollars here. If this can be shown to be true, then we can conclude that the total level of *domestic* expenditure is neither raised nor lowered, in the long run, by international trade. The direction, and possibly the timing, rather than the total amount of expenditure is altered by international trade.

Why should the importation of $1,000 of, say, French merchandise into the United States result in the export of $1,000 of merchandise from us to France, or to a third country? The answer to this question can be illustrated most clearly by an analogy drawn from trade among individuals. When Mr. Smith sells $1,000 more of the neckties he produces, we can say that he will tend to increase his purchases from others by an equal amount. To contend that Mr. Smith will not increase his purchases from others by $1,000 suggests that he will simply hold on to his income and not *ever* spend all of it.

People, whether in this or another country, desire revenue for the purpose of spending it eventually. True, many ordinarily save part of their income, and on balance all Americans combined save about 5 per cent of theirs. *However, money saved is at some time or another spent:* individuals usually build up their savings during the years of peak earnings and draw them down in old age and to meet emergencies. Consequently, an increase of $1,000 in Mr. Smith's income means that ultimately he will spend an added $1,000. Put in other words, when all people pay Mr. Smith $1,000 more in income, they will subsequently receive it back from him.[4]

In international trade the same condition prevails. When one country sells to another, its income rises, enabling it to respend abroad more than before. Moreover, sales to foreign countries involve payments in currencies (directly or indirectly) that are different from the currency the seller can use in his own country. For example, when Americans buy from the French, they directly or indirectly pay in American dollars, which the French can spend only in the United States. Or the French exporter may

---

[4] This discussion admittedly is an oversimplification. The conclusion reached is fundamentally valid, however.

use the dollars to pay British firms for goods, and the British in turn use these dollars to buy from us. Possibly some French exporters who receive American dollars may decide to hold on to them for a while. However, other exporters are likely to be making up for the savings of the first group by spending some of the dollars they received in the past and saved for a while. On balance, *total* spending and total income tend to be equal in the long run, even though the income and spending of *individual* exporters may be very different.

Moreover, even if in the first instance, the goods had been purchased from American rather than from French businessmen, some of the personal income resulting from the purchases would have been saved. Savings are not unique to purchases from abroad.

In short, imports provide foreigners with funds *usable only in this country*, which they ultimately use to purchase an equivalent amount of goods from us. In the long run, therefore, total domestic expenditure is not affected by international trade. In terms of total domestic expenditure, when Americans import from abroad they lower expenditures here by individuals, but they also give rise to an equal expenditure in the United States for foreigners.

An American pays for goods in dollars, whereas a Frenchman can pay only with francs. It should be understood that an American buying French goods does not simply pay over dollar bills which the Frenchman holds until he is prepared to buy something from the United States. Through the use of middlemen—banks for the most part—an American can buy francs with his dollars and a Frenchman can buy dollars with his francs. These middlemen simply buy and sell currencies in the way that others buy and sell merchandise. When the amount of dollars and francs spent are not *equivalent*, the middlemen accumulate a large amount of one currency and run out of the other. Middlemen try to keep their holdings of dollars and francs fairly constant. Thus, when middlemen obtain dollars from Americans who are paying for French imports, they want to sell these dollars to Frenchmen for francs. On both transactions they earn a commission. Middlemen take measures to reduce their holdings of a currency whose supply in their hands is becoming excessive; specifically, they reduce their purchases of it or reduce its price to dispose of their surplus.

B. Short-Run Effects of Trade on Employment

As already indicated, the equivalence of expenditures on imports and receipts from exports will exist in the long run, that is, on the average over a substantial period of time. This statement does not mean that imports and exports will be equal every day or even every month. Indeed, some nations will have a sizable net balance of imports one year and one of exports another. Over a long period, a nation's imports and exports of all goods and services must be equivalent; otherwise, it must make gifts or loans to other countries or must receive gifts or loans from them to make up the difference.

At any specific time, a nation might maintain its sales to other countries while reducing its purchases. Assume that the United States is suffering from unemployment and that some producer groups succeed in getting the enactment of *tariffs* (which are special taxes on imports) or *quotas* (which limit the quantity of goods that may enter from foreign countries), with the result that these producers are able to serve a larger proportion of the domestic market. The employment in those industries would almost certainly expand. Would there necessarily be an immediate offsetting reduction in purchases by foreigners in the United States?

As a result of the tariffs and quotas, goods of the type formerly imported by Americans would presumably remain abroad unsold. Accordingly, foreigners would now have fewer American dollars to spend. It does not follow, however, that foreigners will immediately curtail their purchases in the United States. They might not be in a position to do this, in which event the tariffs and quotas would have enabled us to increase our employment temporarily. However, the increase in *total* domestic employment is sure to be short-lived for several reasons. First, foreigners would have suffered a reduction in employment and consequently have less money to spend on all things—including imports from us. (In short, we would be hit by the crosswise spread of a reduction in expenditure, which can reach across oceans.) Second, businessmen and workers in countries injured by our tariffs and quotas would demand and almost certainly secure the enactment of similar restrictions against our goods. Nations cannot be expected to allow their own people to be injured by a foreign power that is intent only upon its own selfish advantage. Third, and this point is closely related to the first, the foreign countries could not continue for long to buy from us more than they sell to us. Nations, like individuals, do not continue long to spend abroad more than they receive from abroad.[5] Fourth, prices abroad are likely to decline somewhat, owing to the unemployment experienced. As a result, foreign countries would become more attractive sources from which to buy.

As a result of our tariff, the foreign country would take measures to prevent Americans from selling there. The particular measures and the specific American industries that would lose foreign markets cannot be foretold. The general outcome is clear, nevertheless. American industries

---

[5] In other words, if foreigners wanted to buy goods in the United States in greater quantity than we bought abroad, how would they get the dollars with which to pay us? They could force up the price for dollars—which is another way of saying that our spending of foreign funds would rise (each dollar spent abroad would buy more foreign currency).

Attempts to export unemployment generally boomerang

COUNTRY A   COUNTRY B

1. STARTING POINT—A & B'S TRADE IS UNRESTRAINED

2. A DEVELOPS UNEMPLOYMENT—TRIES TO EXPORT IT

3. WITH ITS EXPORTS SHUT OUT B SUFFERS UNEMPLOYMENT; CLOSES DOOR TO IMPORTS FROM A

4. UNEMPLOYMENT COMES HOME TO ROOST; THE BENEFITS OF TRADE ARE LOST TO BOTH A & B

GRAPHICS INSTITUTE, N. Y. C.

would suffer a loss in their foreign sales, would be compelled to curtail output, and would lower employment and reduce income payments to owners. (See Chart.)

The attempt to export unemployment thus would ordinarily have the following effects: *some industries*—those whose foreign competitors were prevented from selling in the domestic market—*would gain in sales, income, and employment. Other industries*—those that had exported before but now were kept out of foreign markets by retaliatory action—*would have lost sales, reduced the number of their employees, and lowered their income payments to owners and workers. On balance, the country ordinarily would not have increased its employment.*

Let us repeat the conclusions reached in the foregoing discussion. First, the volume a nation imports or exports does not alter the domestic level of employment over the long run. *Imports underlie exports, and trade is essentially an exchange of goods and services for other goods and services.* Accordingly, trade involves no change in total domestic expenditure, but only in its composition; with trade, part of total expenditure comes from abroad and part goes abroad. While a nation may sometimes gain employment briefly at the expense of other countries, such gains invariably provoke economic wars that are mutually harmful. These short-run gains in employment ultimately lead to a reduction in the living standards of all nations, because all are compelled to forego the gains from trade.

What are the gains from trade? How great are they? Must our workers accept low wages in order that the nation may compete successfully with countries whose workers are poorly paid?

III. GAINS FROM TRADE

Why do individuals and nations engage in trade at all? Put in reverse, why do all individuals not produce for themselves all the things that they want and need? To avoid trade altogether means that one must produce everything for himself.

No one in present-day United States produces directly all the things he needs and desires. It is taken for granted that individuals will not establish self-sufficient homesteads. Instead, they produce large surpluses of some product or service and exchange these with others who likewise rely on trading their surpluses for the things they desire. Everyone picks "an occupation"; in other words, all persons decide consciously to rely on trade rather than on producing for themselves the things they need. People rely upon trade because they recognize that in this way they will obtain a far higher standard of living, through specialization.

If even the most skilled artisan were to establish a self-sufficient homestead, he could not produce an automobile for himself. How could he hope to get most of the electrical appliances, plumbing, books, and such, that we now take almost for granted? Clearly, trade represents the means for greatly expanding living levels.

Paradoxically, while we take for granted the advantages of trade among individuals, it is commonly believed that trade among nations and even among states should be restricted. Let us examine why and in what circumstances individuals and regions within a country gain from trade, and try to see whether or not trade between nations also gives the same advantages.

Since trade is similar in its motives and consequences whether it takes place between individuals, regions within a country, or between

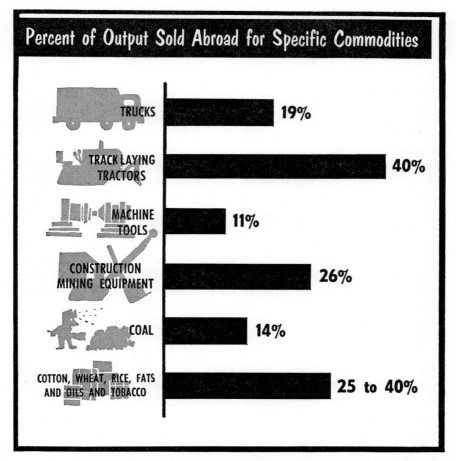

Percent of Output Sold Abroad for Specific Commodities

TRUCKS	19%
TRACK LAYING TRACTORS	40%
MACHINE TOOLS	11%
CONSTRUCTION MINING EQUIPMENT	26%
COAL	14%
COTTON, WHEAT, RICE, FATS AND OILS AND TOBACCO	25 to 40%

SOURCE: Department of Research, AFL-CIO, based on figures from U.S. Department of Commerce.

different nations, we can understand most readily many of the gains from international trade from an examination of trade among individuals. Thereupon we shall apply the principles illustrated by individual trade to that among nations. Specifically, we shall explore the conditions under which individuals would gain from trade, and shall start with the simplest case and work our way forward to more complicated ones.

A. Production Conditions Underlying Gains from Trade

CASE 1. IDENTICAL ABILITIES AND PRODUCTIVE CAPABILITIES

Take two individuals who are equally skillful in all occupations and have similar desires for goods, similar tastes in jobs, and exactly the same resources—land, machinery, and such. Would trade occur between individuals so similar in all respects? The answer is yes, for by trading each individual could specialize. By specializing each one would be able to achieve a much higher level of productivity than either could attain by producing many different things for himself. Repetition of the same tasks permits altogether ordinary persons to develop a proficiency that seems almost amazing. Moreover, it permits the use of complex equipment that would remain idle most of the time if each person were to produce many different things.

It might be helpful if we translated this example into numerical terms. To make the principles involved clear, with minimum complication, we shall make some simplifying assumptions. The conclusions reached are not contingent upon these unrealistic assumptions, it should be noted.

We shall assume that Mr. A and Mr. B live in a world where only two products compose their items of consumption. To be self-sufficient, both men would have to produce both items. We assume that they are equally efficient and that we can describe the production capabilities of both men in Table 2, which indicates that both men could produce 10 units of product 1 and 20 units of product 2—if they produced the same amounts of both products.

Table 2. Both Men Equally Productive

	Product 1	Product 2
Mr. A (output per day)	10	20
Mr. B (output per day)	10	20

If, however, each were to concentrate his efforts on one of the two products, their output would increase substantially, owing to the benefits of specialization already enumerated. Accordingly, with specialization, their production capabilities might become those shown in Table 3.

Table 3. Production Capabilities with Specialization

	Product 1	Product 2
Mr. A (output per day)	50	100
Mr. B (output per day)	50	100

The foregoing table indicates that both men would be able to produce far more if they were to specialize than if they were self-sufficient. Both could produce the same amount of either product. Whereas with a day's work applied to product 1 and another day working on product 2, each could produce 10 units of the first and 20 units of the second, the same amount of specialized work would give them 50 units of product 1 and 100 units of product 2 to divide.

In these circumstances, it would be sensible for Mr. A and Mr. B to agree to specialize and then engage in trade. (We need not concern ourselves with discovering which product each man would produce, because, since they are equally capable at both trades, the benefits of trade do not depend upon getting each man into a particular occupation.) Thus we would end with a result like that depicted in Table 4, showing Mr. A and Mr. B specializing in one of the two products. Table 4 shows Mr. A producing product 1, but it could be reversed. (Most countries can get almost all the benefits of individual specialization within their own borders and need not depend upon international trade to gain them. As we shall see, there are other types of specialization which generally do require international trade.)

Table 4. Production with Specialization

	Product 1	Product 2
Mr. A (output per day)	50	- - -
Mr. B (output per day)	- - -	100

CASE 2. DIFFERENCES IN PRODUCTIVE SKILLS: ABSOLUTE
ADVANTAGE

Assume now that Mr. A is more efficient in producing product 1 than is Mr. B, and is less efficient in producing product 2. Such a situation is generally described as a situation in which A has an absolute advantage in product 1 and B in product 2. We will measure efficiency in terms of the amount of the two products that each man can make in one day. Assume that Table 5 describes their production capabilities if they did specialize.

Table 5. Production Capabilities Illustrating Differences in Efficiency

	Product 1 With specialization	Product 2 With specialization
Mr. A (output per day)	25	50
Mr. B (output per day)	15	75

Given differences in efficiency, it would be to the combined advantage of Mr. A and Mr. B if each were to specialize in the production of the product in which he was most productive. If they followed this plan, they would get a larger combined total of products to share than if they were to produce both products for themselves. For example, if Mr. A and Mr. B were each to work two days (apiece), equally divided between the production of product 1 and product 2, the total output from the four days' work would be 40 units of product 1 and 125 units of product 2. With specialization in the output of the things they made most efficiently, the output in four days would be 50 units of product 1 and 150 units of product 2. This gain would be attributable to the fact that each man was making the product in which he possessed superior efficiency.

With the gains obtainable, one would expect Mr. A and Mr. B to agree to specialize. Both would gain, but the gains need not be divided equally. (If one man tried to take all the gains, the other presumably would refuse to specialize.) At this point we shall not consider the way the gains from trade are shared. Our purpose here is to explain why individuals gain from trade.

CASE 3. DIFFERENCES IN PRODUCTIVE RESOURCES: ABSOLUTE ADVANTAGE

Let us now assume that Mr. A and Mr. B are equally skillful, but that Mr. A owns natural resources, or is especially favored by climate and the like, so that he can produce more in one day of product 1 than Mr. B can, and Mr. B can, because he is especially favored for the production of product 2, produce more of it than Mr. A can. Put in the form of a numerical example, we could say that the production capabilities of Mr. A and Mr. B are shown again by Table 4. In other words, the effects of differences in productive skills and of differences in productive resources are the same. Accordingly, as was true for differences in productive skills, trade will offer advantages to both Mr. A and Mr. B.

CASE 4. COMPARATIVE AND ABSOLUTE ADVANTAGE

Take now the much more complicated situation in which Mr. A is more efficient than Mr. B in the production of both products, assuming each man specialized. Would trade take place under these conditions? How could Mr. A gain from trading with Mr. B?

Raw Materials Wholly or Largely Imported

PERCENT OF SUPPLY 1956

| | 0 | 50 | 100 |

- NATURAL RUBBER
- DIAMONDS
- TIN
- NICKEL
- MANGANESE
- NEWSPRINT
- ALUMINUM
- TUNGSTEN
- WOOL
- LEAD
- ZINC
- COPPER

■ IMPORTS
▒ DOMESTIC PRODUCTION

SOURCE: Department of Research, AFL-CIO, based on figures from U.S. Department of Commerce.

One might suppose that if Mr. A were to devote a day's work to either product 1 or 2, he could produce more than Mr. B and therefore would not have any reason to trade with Mr. B. While superficially reasonable, this statement is fallacious. *The factor that will determine whether Mr. A would gain from trading with Mr. B is not the relative amount each can produce in a day, but the amount it would cost Mr. A to obtain products by trade compared to the cost to him of producing them for himself.*

Table 6. One Man More Efficient Than the Other in Both Employments

	Product 1	Product 2
Mr. A (output per day)	30	90
Mr. B (output per day)	15	30

You may protest that the comparison of how much one produces in a day is exactly that—a comparison of what it costs to produce each product. That is, it would cost Mr. A one thirtieth of a day to produce one unit of product 1, and one ninetieth of a day to produce a unit of product 2, while it would cost Mr. B one fifteenth of a day to make product 1 and one thirtieth of a day to make product 2. But the question of what is to Mr. A's advantage is not solved until we discover how much he must pay to get product 1 and product 2 from Mr. B via trade. We want to know how much Mr. B would charge Mr. A for product 1 (in units of product 2) and for product 2 (in units of product 1). Then we can see whether Mr. A would find it cheaper to buy either product from Mr. B than to produce for himself. What would Mr. B charge for a unit of product 1 or product 2?

As Table 6 indicates, with one day's work Mr. B could make either 15 units of product 1 or 30 units of product 2 (that is, he must forego 30 units of product 2 in order to produce 15 units of product 1). Conversely, to obtain 30 units of product 2 he must give up 15 units of product 1. If Mr. A were willing to give Mr. B more than 15 units of product 1 for 30 units of product 2, Mr. B should be willing to engage in trade; also, he should be willing to sell a unit of product 1 for anything above 2 units of product 2. (This figure represents the ratio of 30 to 15.) These are the terms on which Mr. B would gain from trading rather than producing the product for himself. Let us see whether the efficient Mr. A would be willing to pay the prices that the much less efficient Mr. B would demand for either product.

To obtain product 1, Mr. A must give up the opportunity to make product 2. For every unit of product 1 he produces, he must forego 3 units of product 2 (ratio of 90 to 30). That is, it costs Mr. A 3 units of product 2 to get one unit of product 1 if he makes product 1 for himself. Let us check to see how much Mr. B would charge Mr. A for product 1. We said that he would gain if he sold product 1 at any price over 2 units of product 2. Under the conditions assumed, then, Mr. B would sell product 1 to Mr. A for less than it costs Mr. A to produce it for himself. And the very efficient Mr. A would be able to buy product 1 from inefficient Mr. B for less than it would cost him (in units of product 2—not in man days) to produce it for himself. Specifically, Mr. A would buy product 1 from Mr. B at a price somewhere between 2 and 3 units of product 2.

The outcome of this example seems to fly in the face of common sense. We start by stating that Mr. A is more efficient than Mr. B, and yet it seems that Mr. B is able to produce one product more cheaply than the more efficient Mr. A could produce it. The clue to this mystery is to be found in the concept of cost itself. *By cost we do not mean time involved to produce a product, but alternative products that must be given up to produce it.* It takes Mr. A fewer hours to produce product 1 than it takes Mr. B, but to produce product 1 he must give up more units of product 2 than Mr. B must give up. Hence it costs Mr. B less (and Mr. B would be willing to sell the product to Mr. A for less) than it would cost Mr. A (in units of product 2) to produce it for himself. We term this situation one of "comparative advantage"; for while Mr. A has an absolute advantage in the production of both products 1 and 2, Mr. B's costs in making product 1 are *comparatively* low.

Since the principle of comparative advantage—the technical name by which case 4 is known—is puzzling, another illustration will be cited. Take a person who is by far the most skilled business executive and also the fastest and most accurate typist in the community. Would this man work both as a business executive and a typist? That is, would he spend a substantial proportion of each day doing his own typing? Clearly, he would be able to earn more money (and would also contribute more to the output of society) if he were to occupy himself solely as a business executive and hire a typist, even though the typist could not type so rapidly as he. In effect, he would be concentrating on that occupation in which he possessed a comparative advantage, and trading for the other product. Trade emphatically is not limited to persons, regions, and nations that are productive in some employment and unproductive in others. Even nations that are unproductive in *absolute terms* can produce some products at a *relatively* low *cost*.

We have reached some far-reaching conclusions from the foregoing analysis. First, we saw that persons who were equally productive would gain from trade because of the gains from specialization. Then we saw that when they were different in productive capabilities—either because of differences in skills or in the kinds of productive resources they possess —they would also gain from trade. Indeed, even if one person were more productive than the other in making all products, there would still be gains from trade. Are there, then, any circumstances when trade would not take place among individuals?

There is one type of situation in which there would be no benefits from trade, but it certainly would be very unusual. That is where the cost of both products to both Mr. A and Mr. B is equal in terms of the other product. Such situations would exist if two individuals were able to produce exactly equal amounts of both products; or, where one individual possessed an *absolute* advantage over the other in both products but no *comparative* advantage. Table 7 indicates the latter situation.

Table 7. Absolute Advantage in Both Products with No Comparative Advantage

	Product 1	Product 2
Mr. A	10	30
Mr. B	5	15

In the hypothetical case illustrated, it costs both Mr. A and Mr. B 3 units of product 2 to make one unit of product 1. Consequently, Mr. A would not be willing to pay more than 3 units of product 2 for one unit of product 1, because he could make it for himself at that cost. Mr. B would not be willing to accept less than 3 units of product 2 for each unit of product 1, because it costs him 3 units of product 2 for each unit of product 1. Consequently, A and B would not trade for product 1. A similar situation exists for product 2. It costs both A and B one third of a unit of product 1 for each unit of product 2. Neither would give more than one third of a unit of product 1 for a unit of product 2, and neither would accept less than that amount. Each could do as well by producing the product for himself as he could hope to do by trade.

Only in the last type of situation—absolute advantage with no comparative advantage (or equal advantage in all occupations)—would neither party gain from trade. That type of situation is exceedingly unusual; it even takes some ingenuity to make up a hypothetical example. Accordingly, one would expect trade to be mutually beneficial almost all the time.

The foregoing discussion applies to trade among individuals. To what extent do the conclusions reached apply to international trade? Where many nations are involved in trade, do the gains detailed above accrue to all in the same way that they do to two individuals? Does specialization with equal productive capabilities (case 1) account for trade among nations? Do differences in productive skills (case 2), in resources, and in relative costs (case 3) lead to international trade?

Where nations, rather than individuals, are engaged in trade they gain substantially in the same way that individuals gain. That is, countries which have absolute and comparative advantages, such as in Tables 5, 6, and 7, are able to provide more goods for themselves if they trade than if they produce all goods at home. Unhampered world trade between nations, therefore, makes for the widest possible specialization with the most efficient use of resources.

International trade cannot be attributed to the benefits from specialization on individual productive tasks. Such gains from specialization generally can be achieved by a nation within its borders without international trade. Since a nation contains millions of people, it can permit its individuals to specialize on narrow tasks even while it produces a large variety of things. However, a nation that does not sell abroad generally cannot realize *fully* the gains from specialization; these gains frequently result from the emergence of entire industries to perform specialized services for other industries. The type of specialized industries referred to here include the manufacture of particular types of machinery and machine tools, specialized banking and insurance firms for certain industries, and transportation facilities that are required by only a single industry. Unless industries are very large—which they might not be unless they served a foreign as well as a domestic market—these specialized industries could not arise and endure.

Differences in productive capabilities probably underlie most international trade. It is common knowledge that nations differ in natural resources, productive skills, climate, and in various other ways. Accordingly, when each nation uses its manpower in making products for which it is especially favored, it can obtain a greater amount of other products from other nations in return for its own products than it can get by making the other things for itself. For example, if the United States raised its own coffee, or mined all of its tin requirements—which it *could* do if expense were no object—it would have to divert an enormous amount of resources from the automobile, television, machinery, and other highly efficient industries. The cost to us of a ton of coffee, if we were to raise it for ourselves, in terms of automobiles and television sets, would be very great. In countries that are favored by nature for the raising of these products, very few automobiles and television sets are given up to get a ton of coffee. Accordingly, these countries are willing to sell us coffee for relatively few automobiles and television sets.

Even though the United States may be much more efficient than many other nations[6] in making all products (that is, as in case 4), it generally still gains from trade with these nations. By buying goods from such countries, we are able to concentrate resources in occupations wherein our relative superiority is greatest. In the absence of this trade, resources that now can be used in our most efficient industries would have

---

[6] Whether or not a country is industrialized, gains from trade will occur so long as one of the four cases cited above is reflected in the country's production conditions, compared with those of other countries.

to be used in less efficient industries. Conversely, trade permits the inefficient nations to use their productive resources where they suffer the least disadvantage. When all nations concentrate their resources in their most efficient occupations and exchange their surpluses, they share a larger total quantity of goods and services than if each were to produce things which they make relatively inefficiently. The possibilities of their increasing their efficiency thus is enhanced.

At bottom, the reason why very efficient nations gain from trade with relatively inefficient nations is a paradox: the former's money costs are relatively high. And these costs are high because, in efficient nations, labor, land, and capital can be put to uses in which they are extremely productive; for this reason, resources in these nations command high money rewards. Any industry that would employ these resources would be compelled to match the high returns that extremely efficient industries can obtain. Consequently, the costs of production in industries whose efficiency is not outstandingly great would be high—and made that way by the existence of industries with the greatest efficiency. Put oversimply, the automobile and other consumers' durable-goods industries and certain parts of agriculture are so productive that workers in those industries receive high rates of pay; when similar wages are paid to workers in other industries which are not so much more efficient than foreign industries, the costs of these industries become higher than those abroad.

It need hardly be stated that trade does not occur because of comparisons of the output in different nations per man-day, of the type discussed. Economic behavior in the modern world responds to monetary rather than to "real" stimuli. Before the purchase of goods from abroad becomes advantageous, the following conditions must be met successfully: real production conditions within a country must be translated into domestic money costs. Consequently, such factors as strength of unions and the actions of governmental authorities which influence interest rates, strongly influence the outcome, since they affect final product prices in a country relative to prices abroad. Money costs need have no direct effect, but are important because they tend to set the lower limit to the price that the producers will ask for their output in their own country. Costs do not fix an upper limit, and prices might well be far above cost because of the existence of any of a variety of monopolistic restrictions. (It is also possible, of course, that conditions of excessive competition might prevail for considerable periods and make prices even lower than costs.) Finally, the price of products in the countries where they are produced must be translated into a price that foreigners must pay in their own currency.

Thus there are many possible slips between productive conditions that make possible *real gains* from trade and a relation of money prices that makes trade advantageous to both buyers and sellers.

The relation between domestic cost and price and the factors determining wage and interest rates has already been touched upon. However, to shift this discussion of international trade from the "real plane" to money terms, on which level the decisions affecting trade are actually made, it is necessary to explain the last step in the process. This step is the translation of domestic prices[7] into foreign prices, or what may be called the determination of foreign exchange rates (the explanation for the price of one currency in terms of other currencies). To this task we now turn.

B. The Determination of Foreign Exchange Rates and Monetary Gains from Trade

Foreign exchange rates are prices. Unlike conventional prices, which represent the amount of money that buyers must pay for goods and services, foreign exchange rates are prices of one money in terms of other moneys.[8] Despite their simple character, exchange rates seem complicated to almost everyone. One of the reasons for this attitude has already been indicated. We saw that if the price of a pound sterling were $3, then the price of a dollar would be one third of a pound sterling. Really, every price represents two prices: the price of both things exchanged, in each in terms of the other. If a haircut costs one dollar, one can say that the haircut is worth a dollar, and the dollar is worth (among other things) a haircut. Foreign exchange rates also seem complicated because a technical jargon has grown up around foreign exchange transactions which carries over into the press. When one has mastered the jargon, much of the mystery evaporates; for the ideas involved are not complicated. In addition, foreign exchange rates are subject to a variety of controls, and discussions often refer to restrictions that only specialists know about. The average citizen need not despair of mastering exchange rates. The fundamental ideas involved are easily within his grasp.

Let us account for the level of individual foreign exchange rates in general terms. There are two main types of exchange rate: the "pegged" —kept within a narrow range by government action—and the "free." At present, most of the important currencies in the world are of the pegged

---

[7] The most important influences on domestic prices—in comparison with foreign prices—are the money supply, wage rates, productive efficiency, and the competitiveness of markets.

[8] One must avoid the superficially appealing conclusion that a general lowering of exchange rates is desirable. Actually, it is impossible to lower all exchange rates simultaneously, because to lower the price of one currency in terms of other currencies of necessity raises the prices of the other currencies in that one currency. For example, if the dollar price of pounds sterling is lowered, the price of dollars in pound sterling is necessarily raised.

variety. For example, the currencies of the United States, the United Kingdom, France, Belgium, Russia, China, Australia, Italy, the Netherlands, and India are pegged in one way or another.

1. THE DETERMINATION OF "PEGGED" EXCHANGE RATES

The rate at which some currencies are pegged in terms of certain other currencies (no currency can be pegged in terms of all other currencies unless they too are pegged) is determined *formally* by the monetary authorities of the nation in question. That is to say, for example, that the British government determines the price at which pound sterling will sell in terms of the other major currencies of the world. However, no government can fix its exchange rates at whatever value it wishes. As indicated, exchange rates involve two currencies and are determined by transactions in other countries as well as within the borders of the country under discussion—here, England. (The price of British pounds is determined as much by what must be paid for them in New York and Paris as in London.) If two nations were determined that widely different rates of exchange ought to prevail for their currency in terms of the other, there probably would be a stalemate, not very different from the outcome of a bitter price war between two large competitors.

In the modern-day world, exchange rates are very sticky. There is strong resistance to changes in rates of exchange; it is most important that these rates remain stable, in order to minimize the hazards of international trade. (How would the reader like to be in a business where the number of dollars he gets back on sales of merchandise might vary widely, even though he had agreed on some particular amount with the purchaser?) Exchange rates do vary from time to time, it is true, but these changes occur only after consultations with other nations that would be most affected by the change—that is, nations that are important competitors, nations that serve as main sources of supply, and nations that are major markets. In addition, certain international authorities (most important being the International Monetary Fund) must be consulted, even though they have no power to prevent a nation from altering the international value of its currency.

Each nation does possess considerable influence over its own exchange rates and uses this influence to set them at a level which it believes best serves the nation's interest. Fundamentally, nations choose between two alternatives. They may elect to have high exchange rates which will give large foreign income with a relatively low *physical volume* of exports; or they may set their exchange rates at a low level to ensure a large physical volume of exports in the expectation that they will secure very large amounts of foreign income thereby. A mere statement of these alternatives makes obvious the concern that other nations, which depend upon trade with one another, have in the level at which a particular nation pegs its exchange rate. In the absence of prior consultation and negotiation, there can be—indeed there have been—currency wars in which some nations have resisted attempts of others to alter exchange rates to their disadvantage. Even if national authorities possessed full power to determine their exchange rates, the task would be extremely troublesome, for it is difficult to discover what exchange rates would yield the greatest benefit for the nation. The task essentially consists of computing thousands of monopoly prices in dozens of currencies, and then reconciling them into a single average which would give the highest net return.

Let us now take up the explanation of pegged exchange rates at the point where a nation's monetary authorities have studied the matter closely and have decided what rate would best serve their country's interest. They have completed consultations with other nations directly concerned and with the international monetary authorities they had pledged themselves to consult; in the process, which consisted largely of compromise, they will have arrived at the rates at which they will now attempt to peg the value of their currency in terms of other currencies. How can they see that these rates actually prevail in the markets where foreign exchange is sold?

In effect, they employ various measures similar to those used in domestic price control. Specifically, they can rule that purchases and sales by their citizens are illegal at any other price; they can prohibit transactions in foreign currencies except through duly constituted government agencies that would sell at the pegged price. In addition, the nation could set up a fund for the purpose of dealing in foreign exchange. This fund would be used to purchase and sell exchange in order to raise price when it was below the pegged level; and when prices were above the peg, exchange would be sold to lower its price.[9]

One form of pegged price for currency is a fixed relation between gold and the money unit. For example, $1 American is worth one thirty-fifth of an ounce of gold (or an ounce of gold is worth $35). Foreigners can therefore pay Americans $1 by shipping one thirty-fifth of an ounce of gold. This price is fixed by domestic authorities, presumably on the basis of considerations relating to the internal monetary situation in the country. However, at times international considerations will predominate and may dictate a change in the ration.

2. THE DETERMINATION OF "FREE" EXCHANGE RATES

Some exchange rates are neither pegged nor directly related to gold or any other precious metal. In such conditions, money becomes a com-

---

[9] As with domestic price control, when the imbalance of supply-and-demand factors is great, control measures break down.

modity whose value will vary with over-all conditions of supply and demand. The supply and demand for each currency vary with the efforts of individuals, businesses, and governments in each country to make foreign payments.

There are five major reasons for making payments in a foreign country, and these largely explain the demand for foreign currencies in any nation. They are

1. To pay for goods, including gold, and services that are imported;
2. To make loans abroad;
3. To pay interest and dividends on past loans or investments;
4. To give gifts to persons living abroad;
5. To permit tourists and visitors on business to make payments in foreign countries.

The relative importance of each of these five sources of demand for foreign currencies varies from country to country. For example, the United States has a heavy demand for foreign currency to accommodate its tourists abroad, whereas in most other nations tourists represent only a tiny source of demand. The following table indicates the approximate size of each of these five sources of demand for foreign money in 1957 in the United States and in a few other nations.

Table 8. United States Payments Abroad in 1957
(In billions)

1. Imported goods (including gold) and services	$18.4
2. Private and government loans abroad	4.2
3. Interest and dividend payments on past loans and investments to United States	.7
4. Gifts to persons living abroad, including government grants	4.7
5. American tourist and business visitors' expenditures abroad	1.6
Total	$29.6

SOURCE: U.S. Department of Commerce, Office of Business Economics.

Table 8, paradoxically, describes both the demand for *and supply* of individual currencies. Specifically, when Americans buy foreign money, they simultaneously offer American dollars for a foreign currency. Thus they both demand another currency and supply their own currency.

The relation between the quantity of payments that foreigners want to make in a country and the volume of payments its nationals want to make in other countries generally determines whether unpegged exchange rates will rise or fall. (Over short periods, the operations of speculators in foreign exchange will influence exchange rates for reasons that are not necessarily related to the relative desire to make payments.) For example, in the United States, when the desire of persons, businesses, and governments to make payments in another country increases, the demand here for the currency of that country will rise, and so will the price of that currency. Conversely, when the desire by foreigners to make payments in our country increases, the demand for our currency will rise and so too will its price—in nations which have not pegged the value of their currency in terms of American dollars.

To summarize, most exchange rates are not automatically determined in the present-day world. Rather, they represent both the judgment of national authorities regarding their best interest and the outcome of negotiations among interested nations and international monetary agencies. A large number of relatively unimportant currencies are "free"; they reflect variations in basic supply and demand conditions, plus the occasional strong influence of speculative activities.

We have now explained, however briefly, how money prices in one country become translated into prices in other currencies. As already implied, this process is crucial for two main reasons. First, the outcome determines whether or not trade will be advantageous to interested parties. (It is not sufficient that "real" conditions permit mutually beneficial trade.) Second, the determination of exchange rates is crucial because it is capable of being varied considerably and offers an opportunity to alter the volume and course of trade by relatively simple means.

In summary, then, *real* opportunities for mutually advantageous trade would appear to be very numerous and would be found both among countries that have reached similar stages of technological development and those at widely different stages. Opportunities are almost certain to exist between countries with different climates, dissimilar natural resources, and dissimilar human productive skills. There is serious danger that many opportunities to realize the gains from trade will be lost in translating real into money costs—especially because of the fact that exchange rates often are pegged arbitrarily and do not reflect the volume of imports and exports that people desire at the prevailing rate of exchange. The foregoing discussion leads to the conclusion that every nation should follow a policy of free trade; that is, because of the many opportunities for mutually beneficial exchange of goods, no obstacles like tariffs and quotas should be allowed to reduce the volume of international trade.[10]

---

[10] In the discussion of the gains from trade, nothing has been said about the costs of transportation involved in sending goods from one nation to another. When one is dealing with concrete cases, the costs of producing a product for export should include transportation. Sometimes it costs more to transport domestic goods from producers to consumers than to deliver foreign goods to domestic consumers; for example, it is cheaper to ship from Canada to many parts of the United States than to ship from Maine to Texas.

We also neglected to mention the obvious impossibility of exporting goods that must be consumed right "on the spot," like entertainment services, and the great difficulties in exporting highly perishable products.

C. An Alleged Loss from Trade: The So-called "Bowl of Rice" Fallacy

Many persons who accept the foregoing arguments showing trade to be mutually advantageous nevertheless find one contrary line of argument difficult to refute. This argument holds that trade by prosperous countries with poor nations endangers the formers' living standards.

The contention that international trade lowers all nations to the level of the poorest rests on the following line of reasoning. When trade is free, each seller must meet the competition of all others. If one nation pays its labor very little—as China, India, Japan, and many other countries do—its prices will be low. Products made by cheap labor will undersell those made by labor receiving higher wages. Ultimately, competition between them will compel high-paid labor to accept low wages—a bowl of rice for a day's work—like the Chinese coolie.

The argument that international trade causes poverty to spread from country to country runs exactly counter to the conclusion developed in the foregoing discussion. There it was shown that trade spreads prosperity rather than poverty from nation to nation. Both lines of argument cannot be correct; which one is in error?

If trade were free, the nation with the lowest costs in making a product would win markets for that product from nations with higher costs. It does not follow, however, that one nation can have lower costs of production for all, or nearly all, products. Indeed, the principle of comparative advantage suggests that a nation will find that some of its industries have relatively low costs, while other industries have costs that are higher than those in other nations.

Moreover, it remains to be demonstrated that low wage rates in one nation will, because of trade, drive down wage rates in nations where rates are higher. Actually, the contention that low wage rates spread rests upon a confusion of wage *rates* with wage *costs*. Labor may be very costly even though it is paid low wages. The apparent fact of the matter is that, for many products, the unit cost for labor is far higher in India, China, and Japan than in the United States—despite the fact that wage rates and living levels there are far lower than in the United States. Automobiles, television sets, refrigerators, machinery of most types, and the like are far more costly to produce in the Orient than they are to purchase in the United States. It is for this reason that these countries are so anxious to import these products from us. If the labor *costs* in those countries were low, these countries would export these goods, rather than purchase them abroad. Thus, despite their low *payments* to labor, many nations are unable to compete successfully with many American products because their labor *costs* are too high. The difference in wages among countries is smaller than the difference among them in labor efficiency in many employments.

Is it not possible for a nation to have both efficient labor and low wage rates? That is, cannot a nation have very low labor costs? First, as explained, the efficiency of labor varies from employment to employment; it is unlikely that labor in one nation will be more efficient than that in all other nations in every single use. Second, as explained by the theory of comparative advantage, even a nation with greatest efficiency in all employments (as measured by units of output per day) will have relatively higher costs than other countries in some of its occupations. *As already explained, the fact that labor is very efficient in some occupations makes it very costly to use in others.* Whereas one nation's labor may be more efficient than the labor of all other nations, it is almost inconceivable that it should also be less costly per unit of output in all uses. Consequently, efficient labor tends to be costly labor; *only in those occupations where it is most efficient will its costs be lower than in other nations.*

Third, a nation with an efficient labor force will be prosperous. By efficient labor, we mean that output by each worker is high; living levels must be high if output per person is high. Put differently, labor in China, India, and Japan *must be* inefficient because the level of living in those countries is low. Consequently, big differences between the wage rates of, say, China and the United States do not indicate corresponding differences in labor costs. The difference in wage rates may be more than offset by differences in productivity. It has already been explained that such is clearly true of the manufacture of products like automobiles, machinery, and the like.

Thus, America is prosperous because its labor is efficient,[11] that is, because labor turns out a large output each day. Because of its high efficiency, American labor earns high wages; despite high *rates* of pay, the *cost* of labor per unit is low in those occupations where we are most efficient. Conversely, those nations that are poor have a population that is relatively unproductive. At bottom, Chinese coolies receive only a bowl of rice for a day's work simply because they do not produce much more than that in a day.

Trade between prosperous and poor countries thus is not different from trade between nations of equal income. It permits each one to buy goods abroad at bargain prices, compared with what would have to be paid for goods made domestically. That is, international trade permits both poor and prosperous countries to become better off.

---

[11] Labor productivity primarily depends upon the quality of equipment used and the skill of management rather than the training and industriousness of labor itself, though that too is a factor.

IV. INTERNATIONAL CAPITAL MOVEMENTS

International economic relations take the form of borrowing and lending as well as buying and selling. Why do nations borrow and lend? Do loans increase the standard of living of the borrower nation or the lender country? Or do both nations benefit?

Almost all borrowers plan to repay their loans, and also are willing to pay interest on them. Why are loans so valuable to borrowers that they are willing to pay back more money than they borrow—i.e., the principal and interest too?

The borrower ordinarily believes that he can use the loan in a way that will increase his productivity or sales so much that he will be able to repay the loan and interest and still have some added profit for himself. Any of a large number of uses might possibly be made of borrowed funds to increase profitability, including purchase of new and improved equipment; increase in volume of output, with resulting economies of specialization; increased inventories to give customers a greater variety of choice; acquisition of an improved location; purchase of goods in advance of an expected rise in price; acquisition of the services of efficient employees; retirement of debts that involved restraints on management or that carried higher interest charges.

The borrower's motives probably are not puzzling. Why people make loans is also simple. They do so because they can get greater returns from borrowers than from using the funds themselves. Put another way, *the borrower's productivity can be raised more by increased investment in his business than that of the lender can be increased by using the funds himself.* As a result, the borrower can afford to pay as interest more than the lender could earn by using his own funds himself. The lender's gain from making loans is the amount by which his interest charges exceed the sums he could make for himself.

Thus we have suggested that both the borrower and the lender gain from loans. How is it possible for both to gain? *Because the transfer of funds permits total output to be increased, and both the borrower and the lender share in the enlarged output.*

Does the same general conclusion apply to international lending? How are payments of capital—the initial loan, interest, and repayments of principal—made between persons in different countries? Do international loans influence the level of employment? The answers to these questions will be sketched in turn.

An individual (or business) that lends abroad presumably does so to obtain a higher return than could be had by using the funds himself or by lending to someone else in his own country. Similarly, an individual or business who borrows does so in the expectation of increasing net profit;

that is, the interest (and service) charges paid are thought to be smaller than the gains obtained. Thus domestic and foreign loans are quite similar in the motive of the borrower and lender.

One type of difference between domestic and foreign capital movements should be noted. Government loans, which have figured prominently in American foreign policy since the outbreak of World War II, are inspired by motives that may have little to do with productivity. The goals sought are usually political and diplomatic. But even some domestic loans guaranteed by the government are motivated by political rather than purely economic considerations.

A. *How Funds Are Transferred between Borrower and Lender*

How are payments of international loans effected? When an American lends to, say, a Mexican, how does the Mexican obtain the proceeds of his loan? (What is said here about the transfer of funds between borrowers and lenders applies with equal force to the transfer of funds between importers and exporters.)

In the first instance, the American lender parts with dollars, for that is the only type of currency he possesses. (There are, of course, minor exceptions to this generalization.) Whether the Mexican will receive dollars or the money of his own native land (pesos) will depend upon the particular provisions of the loan. If the loan is in dollars, then the Mexican will have obtained a bank deposit in the United States against which he can draw checks. Foreign payments seem complicated only when the lender makes payment in the foreign currency.

If the Mexican were to obtain pesos and the American has only dollars to make payment, how is the apparent difficulty ironed out? In effect, the American would buy pesos from someone (a Mexican bank very likely) and pay dollars for them. (The transaction would be arranged for the lender by a bank; he would not find it necessary to seek out personally someone who would be willing to sell pesos for dollars.) Pesos would thus have been transferred from someone who sold his pesos to the American, and by him to the borrower, giving the latter funds with which he could buy goods in Mexico. Put differently, in the case examined one person (the one selling pesos to the American) gave up the power to purchase goods in Mexico, and that power was transferred to the borrower. The American gave up his power to purchase goods in the United States to persuade another person to part with his pesos. The seller of the pesos presumably would spend the dollars he received and would obtain American goods or services in exchange. *Ultimately, the loan would result in a transfer of goods from the lender's country to the borrower's, directly or indirectly.*

Sometimes loans are "tied"—that is, the borrower is *required* to spend the borrowed funds in the nation making the loan. (Sales on credit to foreigners might be considered a form of tied loan.) In loans of this sort there is no currency transaction; the loan and its expenditure are both made in the currency of the lender. As in the former illustration, the loan is followed by a movement of goods and services from the lender's country to that of the borrower.

So much for the manner in which the original loan is paid. We have reached the conclusion that "goods follow money"; that is, when you send money to a nation, you soon will back it up with goods (and get your money back). Does not the same conclusion apply to the repayment of principal and the payment of interest? Clearly, the Brazilian borrower will pay interest in his own currency initially. Even though the terms of the loan might obligate him to pay in dollars, he must first use the currency of his country to buy dollars. Ultimately pesos will be paid to someone in exchange for dollars. The dollars would be paid to the lender. Those who gave up the dollars for the borrower's pesos would obtain pesos which they would necessarily spend in Brazil. In the end, the pesos would be used to buy Brazilian goods. Interest payments and repayment of principal, therefore, also conform to the principle that goods follow money.

B. How International Capital Movements Influence the Level of Employment

What is the connection between international capital movements and the level of employment? When an American takes funds he might spend here and lends them to a foreigner, he seems to be sending expenditure out of the country. But, as has just been shown, goods follow money, indicating that the expenditure is not lost.[12] On the contrary, funds loaned abroad might not have been spent domestically in the absence of the loan. The availability of foreign borrowers willing to offer higher returns on loans than can be obtained domestically would increase the total amount of lending—and could not reduce it. Owing to the willingness of a foreigner to borrow them, idle funds might be transferred to foreigners who spend them in this country.

It follows that loans abroad ordinarily raise domestic expenditure and employment levels at the time the loans are made. What is the effect on employment of interest payments and repayments of principal? *When interest is paid, it represents at least in part an increase in total national*

---

[12] There is one important respect in which expenditures might actually be lost. There might be a delay resulting from the time involved in arranging the loan and in making the expenditure. This delay is equivalent to a drop in expenditure, and might be termed "temporary hoarding."

income. That is, had the money not been lent abroad, the interest payment (and the net increase in output in the borrowing country also) would have been smaller than the foreign lender's interest payments. Accordingly, Americans would have more money to spend as a result of the foreign loans (Americans will have acquired foreign currency when the Brazilian borrower paid interest on the loan). Because of their larger personal income, individuals presumably would increase their expenditure. Part or all of the rise in income would go to buy Brazilian goods directly or indirectly—for again goods would follow money.

One should not conclude that Americans would use interest payments on foreign loans to buy things abroad that they otherwise would have purchased at home. In the absence of the foreign loan, they would have had less to spend at home. They certainly would have received less in interest; very possibly their funds would have remained idle and they would have received nothing at all.

To assess the net effects of foreign loans on employment, it is necessary to study the borrower and the lender separately and to balance the impact of the initial loan against the effect of interest payments and the repayment of principal. When these things are done, foreign loans appear to be almost certain to increase employment levels in both the borrowing and lending countries, for one major reason. *They lead to the expenditure of funds at least some part of which would ordinarily have remained unspent otherwise.* Owing to the initial expenditure and the subsequent rise in output and productivity, income levels rise and make levels of individual expenditure higher than they would have been without these loans. To reach this conclusion, we should apply the general principle that goods follow money, and we also should recognize that the total amount of money income within both the borrowing and lending country would rise because loans increase total output.

At least in general principle, therefore, international trade and capital movements are advantageous to buying and selling countries and to borrowing and lending countries alike. In the real world, however, international economic relations involve far more than economic considerations alone. Movements of goods and services between countries and capital transactions are heavily motivated by military, diplomatic, and political considerations. Not only do many people refuse to accept free trade and unrestrained lending as a general principle, but even advocates of free trade would make a large number of exceptions to the general rule in order to realize military, diplomatic, and political gains. To base national policy on economic considerations alone would be naive; however, the economic cost of military, political, and diplomatic gains must be recognized also.

DISCUSSION QUESTIONS

1. If we tried to increase permanently the level of employment in this country by engaging in more foreign trade, is it likely that we should be paid for all of our exports? Explain your answer.

2. Under what circumstances can a nation increase its employment for a moderately long period by encouraging international trade?

3. Is domestic trade by individuals motivated by a desire to increase employment? By a desire to obtain "bargains"? Discuss.

4. Explain why a country that is very efficient in one or several lines of production is likely to have very high costs of production in all other lines.

5. Do you think it would be common or quite unlikely that neighboring nations would gain from trade with one another? Discuss.

6. Explain the parallel between a man who is both an efficient business executive and an expert typist, and a nation that has an absolute advantage in all occupations.

7. What are the main types of exchange rate in existence today? Explain the major differences between them.

8. What are the most important factors determining exchange rates? Explain how they operate.

9. Why do both the borrower and lender gain from international capital movements? What effect do international loans have upon total output and economic progress? Explain.

10. In international lending, does the borrower ordinarily receive the funds that the lender invests?

11. Explain why goods tend to follow money.

12. Do you believe international loans tend to raise, lower, or to leave unaffected the level of employment in the lending country? In the borrowing country? Explain.

13. Do you believe that exports from our country should be regulated? Should imports into our country be regulated? Under what circumstances?

Chapter

27   Difficulties Arising in

International Trade

and Lending

The preceding chapter indicated the potential gains from international trade and lending. The discussion was greatly simplified, and stressed the advantages of trade. To round out the discussion, we shall consider the kinds of difficulty in which countries may become involved if they rely heavily upon international trade and lending, and the measures that might be taken to meet these difficulties.

I.   SOURCES OF DIFFICULTY ARISING IN INTERNATIONAL ECONOMIC DEALINGS

The trade and lending of nations are beset by most of the difficulties that arise in economic relations among people. Most persons are dependent upon others for almost all their necessities; yet sometimes they cannot afford to buy as much as they need, or nearly as much as they purchased in the past. This situation usually arises if their incomes decline; declines, in turn, occur primarily when the sales of their goods or services fall—that is, when they lose their jobs or their businesses get bad.

Nations face similar difficulties. They, too, depend upon foreign sources for essential products. For this very reason, they depend upon sales in foreign markets to obtain funds with which to purchase what they need abroad. Like individuals, nations sometimes suffer sudden and drastic declines in their foreign income and, accordingly, find it necessary either to reduce their purchases or to discover ways of continuing their purchases despite the decline in income. When foreign income declines over a substantial period, a nation is required to curtail its imports. The effect of reduced imports of necessary commodities varies but is always painful.

International trade thus exposes a nation to risks and uncertainties, because the supply of goods it uses domestically becomes dependent upon conditions in foreign countries. Sometimes foreign conditions are such that the nation's exports decline. For example, when other countries experience depression, their purchases from abroad usually are curtailed. Or when other countries experience inflations, their exports cost more. Both difficulties result from conditions abroad that are largely beyond the control and influence of one's own country.

In addition to short-term changes such as depression and inflation in foreign countries, international economic dealings involve risks and difficulties of a longer and deeper kind. An industry upon which a nation depends heavily for foreign income may be displaced in the world economy by the discovery of new techniques or rich raw-material deposits in other countries. As a result, the nation may be cut off from its main sources of income. To take one example, the development of synthetic nitrates greatly reduced Chile's foreign income from the sale of its natural nitrates. Chile, which had imported many products with its income from sales of this product, was compelled to make important adjustments in its fundamental economic structure. The position of this country resembles that of a neighborhood grocer who suddenly finds a chain store operating across the street. A displaced nation, as well as a vanquished grocer, must seek some substitute source of income, or reduce its level of living.

Several risks are peculiar to international trade. One is the danger of military conflict, which can cut off both markets and sources of supply. A nation that depends upon foreign sources for vital materials—as most nations do—may be compelled to go without them because a supplier is a belligerent, or one of the belligerents interferes with its trade. In recent conflicts, many nonbelligerent countries have undergone this experience.

Another risk unique to international trade is the danger of adverse changes in foreign exchange rates. Since foreign trade generally involves several currencies, variations in exchange rates will influence the financial conditions of those holding or making payments in more than one currency.

Exchange rates may change so drastically that a borrowing nation will be compelled to default on financial obligations, even though it is willing and able to repay the amount of *domestic* currency it borrowed. If the creditor nation's money becomes scarce—because it is not importing or lending much—the price of its money in other currencies may become very high. Debtor nations will then be required to pay back far more in their own currency than they received in the original loan.

Still further difficulties beset international trade. Foreign suppliers of vital products may form cartels or commodity agreements for the purpose of substantially raising price. This type of agreement, since it occurs in foreign countries, is beyond the reach of the importing country, which is powerless to protect itself. (In domestic trade, firms sometimes form collusive arangements that raise price and compel buyers to curtail consumption also.)

Thus the many hazards besetting foreign trade can be resolved into a reduction of funds with which to obtain foreign goods, a rise in the prices that must be paid for these goods, an interruption in the supply of goods, or inability to supply goods. As indicated, similar conditions often arise in trade among individuals. Usually, it is easier for individuals than for nations to adjust to a drop in income or to higher prices. To adjust to reduced ability to obtain goods abroad, a nation will often be compelled to develop new lines of industry, to expand established industries to obtain new sources of income, or to substitute domestic output for imports. The development of new lines of activity often involves heavy costs—including at times funds to acquire equipment from abroad. Since the initial cause of the difficulty was a shortage of foreign funds, a nation will be hampered in developing new lines of industry requiring foreign goods. Individuals who have lost their jobs generally need not create any new facilities but must only find someone with available facilities who needs additional personnel.

A nation whose foreign income has fallen may be compelled to produce for itself some of the things it had been purchasing from abroad. Such a development presumably would impose a reduction in living levels, because domestic production would be less efficient than foreign production. Moreover, such changes take considerable time, during which period the country would be compelled to continue its purchases from abroad or suffer hardship. Indeed, sometimes the very maintenance of whatever foreign income the country has depends upon obtaining foreign raw materials to be processed for export.

Thus international, like domestic, trade is exposed to cyclical ups and downs and to long-range technical developments, wars, and political disturbances. To rely on trade is to accept these risks knowingly. To pursue a policy of self-sufficiency, on the other hand, is to accept lower levels of living knowingly. Confronted with this choice, almost all individuals and nations have elected to face the risks involved in trade.

It should be noted that some of the disturbances in international economic relations are unavoidable, and some are even desirable. Beneficial technological changes and the discovery of new raw-material deposits are sure to bring some painful adjustments in their wake. Others, such as fluctuations in general business conditions, are essentially harmful but are not likely to be eliminated altogether. Similarly, wars and threats of war cannot be considered things of the past. International trade can, and indeed must, adjust to such developments. What, if anything, can be done when international trade suffers from the kinds of difficulty just listed?

II. MAJOR PROBLEMS ARISING FROM INTERNATIONAL ECONOMIC DEALINGS

We shall limit our discussion to three major types of difficulty that a nation may face because of foreign trade and lending. They are

1. A nation's foreign payments and receipts may continue unequal for some time. Such a nation is said to have "balance-of-payments difficulties."

2. A nation may not be able to carry on much of the trade that would be mutually advantageous to it and to other countries, because of restrictions on trade.[1]

3. The prices of the nation's export goods, relative to the prices it pays for imports, may be unreasonably low. That is, the nation's "terms of trade" may give it only a small share of the gains from trade.

In the following discussion we shall refer from time to time to "international economic optimum." This phrase denotes a condition that is as free as possible from the three listed difficulties that sometimes beset international economic relations. A country thus has attained its international economic optimum when its foreign payments and receipts are roughly equal on the average, when its terms of trade allow it a fair share of the gains from trade, and when it takes full advantage of its opportunities for mutually advantageous trade. As defined here, the international economic optimum is achieved when all nations combined obtain the full potential benefits from international trade. This definition revolves about levels of living, terms of trade, and the international distribution of income; most national leaders, however, seem to pay far greater attention to the balance of payments than to gains from trade, and for a good reason.

There frequently are occasions when the attainment of one condition of international economic optimum requires a sacrifice of another. For example, an expansion of trade that is advantageous might aggravate a nation's balance-of-payments difficulties; a nation's leaders are confronted with difficult choices under such circumstances. Indeed, sometimes they do not even have much choice because the nation's entire monetary system may be undermined by an expansion of trade when the nation's foreign payments are unbalanced.

The preoccupation of authorities with maintaining foreign receipts in line with foreign payments probably has led many persons to neglect the other conditions of an international-economic-optimum situation. As a

---

[1] There is a fundamental difference between balance-of-payments difficulties and the other two. The first must be avoided to escape direct and immediate hardship; the others prevent a nation from enjoying to the full the benefits attainable from full, free international exchange.

result, they may overlook the fact that balance-of-payments difficulties may arise partly from the fact that a nation has foregone the gains to be attained from trade. Many authorities seem to regard foreign trade as a game of equalizing foreign income and outlay rather than as a source of the great benefits to be obtained from exchange. An optimum international economic situation must therefore be defined at least partly in terms of the basic objective of achieving these gains. Therefore, when any decision is made regarding foreign economic relations, the authorities must take account of its effects on the amount of trade, and the estimated gains to the nation resulting from it, as well as its effects on the nation's balance of payments. The "balance" a nation's authorities should strive to attain is among the various gains and difficulties that result from international economic relations.

III. CORRECTIVES FOR MAJOR PROBLEMS IN INTERNATIONAL ECONOMIC DEALINGS: MECHANISMS THAT TEND TO EQUALIZE FOREIGN RECEIPTS AND PAYMENTS

It will be useful to distinguish between two types of remedies for international-trade difficulties. Some are virtually automatic and tend to correct difficulties whenever they arise. Others are nonautomatic, and call for decision and action by the appropriate authorities. To the extent that the automatic correctives are speedy and effective, the nonautomatic measures need not be employed.

We shall first discuss balance-of-payment difficulties and shall examine the automatic mechanisms that tend to eliminate such difficulties. We shall then consider the means by which these mechanisms might be supplemented. Following this, we shall discuss the remedies for the two major difficulties besetting international economic relations. It must be emphasized at the outset that the discussion of these questions must be sketchy, and that some matters will be oversimplified for the sake of clarity.

Persons delving into problems of international economics for the first time are likely to be confused by an apparent contradiction. On one hand, they learn about the so-called "balance of payments," which, as the term implies, proves that payments to and from each nation must—in some sense—be in balance. On the other hand, they learn that nations have great difficulties sometimes in making their international receipts and payments equal. This seeming contradiction can be reconciled fairly easily.

Whenever a transaction takes place, two elements are involved.

Something is given up—generally a product or a service, though some-times a security, like a stock or bond—in exchange for money. Both are necessarily equal in value. (We are meeting here again a concept that we had seen in connection with the measurement of national output and the essence of the circular flow of money.) The same balance between payments and goods and services given in exchange for them holds for international as well as national trade. On this basis, we know that when a nation sends goods and services abroad, it receives an equal amount of goods and services, gold, or I.O.U.'s (called short-term loans) in return. By definition, the outgo and inflow of all elements that enter into foreign trade *must* balance.

On the other hand, this balance sometimes is achieved painlessly and at other times only with great difficulty. When the balance is reached by having all countries exchange only goods and services, it is likely to be quite painless. But if the balance can be achieved only by one nation's exporting its limited supply of gold or drawing down its holdings (which must be meager) of foreign currency, it can be very painful. And, more important, such a situation is almost certain to be temporary, because the country itself cannot permit it to continue for long; in fact, as shall be shown, the nations from which this country makes purchases will tend to cut short. There is a limit to the amount of business that can be done on I.O.U.'s.

We are here concerned with the very real problem of the present-day world wherein many nations experience great difficulty in obtaining foreign income equivalent to their foreign payments. (In its most acute form, this problem is known as the "dollar shortage," for some nations have difficulty obtaining the amount of dollars from their exports that they need to pay for the things they buy in the United States.) This problem has become somewhat submerged in recent years, largely because of the big loans and gifts made by the United States and the unparalleled prosperity of the United States, which has boosted imports to great heights.[2] Let us explore the mechanisms by which such painful situations tend to correct themselves *automatically*.

A. Automatic Mechanisms

Four major mechanisms operate more or less automatically to move foreign receipts and foreign payments into balance. They are efforts of individuals and businesses to balance their own spending with income, variations in foreign exchange rates, the specie-flow adjustment, and adjustment through changes in income and spending.

---

[2] See Gunnar Myrdal, *An International Economy* (New York: Harper & Brothers, 1956), pp. 76-77. The severity of the "dollar shortage" eased between 1953 and 1958.

1. INDIVIDUAL EFFORTS TO BALANCE SPENDING WITH INCOME

Why do most individuals and businesses ordinarily spend no more than their income? In part, the answer is to be found in self-restraint, prudence, and the laws of bankruptcy. Another part of the answer is that people will not sell goods to those who cannot pay for them.

Self-restraint and prudence, however, do not automatically serve to limit a nation's foreign spending to its foreign income. The inhabitants of a nation may want to spend more money abroad than has been received from abroad, without wanting to spend more than their personal income. International trade and investment are conducted by individuals and businesses rather than by governments. Those desiring to make foreign payments may well have the income or accumulated savings to do so in their own currency, even at a time when the nation lacks foreign income sufficient to allow the purchases. Consequently, self-restraint and prudence are not enough to compel a balance of foreign spending and income.

One important automatic mechanism that tends to balance foreign income and spending is the pressure from suppliers. Firms that sell abroad are well informed about currency conditions. If there is likelihood that they will not be able to receive payment in a form of currency they desire or need, they will not sell. In this way, a nation's purchases tend to be limited to what its foreign income will allow it to purchase.

2. EXCHANGE-RATE VARIATIONS

Movements of unpegged exchange rates tend to establish a balance of foreign spending and foreign income. When a nation's foreign purchases are disproportionately large, its demand for foreign currencies is high. As a result, the price of foreign exchange to it will rise—making imports more costly and therefore less advantageous. Consequently, imports would tend to decline. Conversely, nations experiencing a large demand for foreign currencies and only a low demand for their own will find the price of their currency declining. They will become more attractive sources of supply and, as a result, their exports would be stimulated by the change in foreign exchange rates. It must be emphasized that this mechanism operates only when exchange rates are free to fluctuate with conditions of supply and demand—this situation is the exception rather than the general rule.

Let us now assume that the individuals, businesses, and governmental units of a nation actually do spend considerably more money abroad than that nation has received from other countries; among other things, we are specifically assuming that the nation's exchange rates are pegged. What automatic checks operate to correct such a situation? Does anything follow from a nation's living beyond its income that would reverse such a situation? Two possible checks may come into operation. One is an effect on the level of price exerted through changes in the money supply. The second is the direct effect of unequal foreign payments and receipts upon total expenditure. Let us examine these in turn.

3. THE SPECIE-FLOW ADJUSTMENT

Countries that spend more than they receive must make up the difference. Occasionally they can borrow, but in time borrowings must be repaid, and the imbalance of payments might actually be aggravated by the loan. Sooner or later, a nation whose expenditure exceeds its income must make up the difference by paying out gold or by drawing down the stock of foreign money owned by citizens of the country.

The export of gold, particularly, is likely to have notable monetary effects. Gold represents the base on which the money and credit pyramid of many countries rests. Under the laws that govern the relation between gold, currency, and bank deposits, therefore, a decline in the supply of gold will ordinarily be followed by a drop in total money supply. Usually a loss of gold would compel banks to reduce their loans in order to re-establish the required relation between their reserves, or gold, and bank deposits. The outcome may be a drop in total money in circulation, brought about by a reduction in bank loans. The reduction in bank loans means that fewer purchases will be made, and the demand for goods will fall. In turn, a drop in the demand for goods is likely to lead to a fall in prices.

Conversely, nations whose foreign payments were lower than foreign income (if one country spends more than it receives from abroad, then other countries combined *must* receive more than they spend) will experience an increase in gold supply and bank reserves, enabling banks to increase their loans. As a result, expenditures will tend to rise and bring about an increase in price.

Divergent movement of prices in nations spending more and those spending less than their foreign income tends to bring the income and spending of individual countries back into balance. Nations whose prices fell become more attractive markets for the rest of the world to buy from, and their sales and income should rise. Similarly, the rise in prices abroad would reduce foreign purchases by their citizens and businesses. A combination of increased exports (at lower prices) and reduced imports (at higher prices) would—or so economists argued for a long time—increase the income of the country that had been living beyond its means.

This mechanism of international adjustment would operate primarily through changes in money reserves that start a chain reaction consisting of fewer loans, smaller purchases, lower prices, and lower incomes, which are followed by lower imports and higher exports. This chain of reactions has been described at some length partly because certain persons argue that this type of adjustment should be relied upon much more heavily than at present. Mostly, however, it is discussed in order to indicate the possible domestic repercussions of a balance of payments that is far out of line. *Put differently, to correct an excess of foreign spending over foreign income, it may be necessary to suffer a domestic deflation.* Since deflation is often painful and might cumulate into a major depression, a nation might prevent this mechanism of adjustment from operating.

4. BALANCE-OF-PAYMENTS ADJUSTMENT THROUGH INCOME CHANGES

Imbalance in a nation's foreign receipts and payments may be corrected automatically, without any change in prices, by the changes in income and expenditures resulting from the very imbalance. Put simply, a country that spends abroad more than it receives will suffer a decline in total domestic expenditure and in personal incomes. Conversely, incomes and expenditures would have risen in countries where receipts exceeded payments. These changes in personal incomes in countries with surpluses and deficits of foreign payments would tend to reverse the balance of payments. In the countries where incomes fell, expenditure for all things—including imports—would tend to fall. Conversely, countries spending less abroad than they received would tend to increase their expenditures, both at home and abroad. As a result, imports into deficit countries would fall and imports into surplus countries would rise, tending to correct the imbalance.

5. FAILURE OF AUTOMATIC MECHANISMS TO PREVENT BALANCE-OF-PAYMENTS DIFFICULTIES

Despite several mechanisms that operate to correct imbalances in foreign payment, they do in fact occur. Indeed, since the end of World War II, many nations have experienced severe balance-of-payments difficulties. The "dollar shortage" is a widely publicized condition of imbalance in international payments between the United States and many other countries. Clearly, the mechanisms described for automatically keeping each nation's foreign spending and foreign income in balance do not always work. Possibly they have not been allowed to do so. Some countries have been unwilling to allow their domestic price levels, for example, to be dictated primarily by considerations of foreign trade.

B. *Nonautomatic Mechanisms Which May Be Applied*

If for some reason the automatic mechanisms do not prevent balance-of-payments difficulties, or are not allowed to do so, what can a nation do to correct international payment difficulties? Several measures are at hand. First, the nation could apply direct controls over foreign spending. Second, it could alter its exchange rate. Third, it could establish and make use of agencies for international cooperation. Fourth, it could alter the structure of its economy in fundamental respects so that its ability to earn foreign income would rise or its dependence on imports would decline.

1. DIRECT CONTROLS AS A REMEDY FOR UNBALANCED FOREIGN PAYMENTS

The most widely employed direct control since World War II is known as "exchange control." In 1958 such major trading countries as the United Kingdom, France, Belgium, West Germany, India, Pakistan, Australia, New Zealand, Egypt, and Burma employed exchange controls.

Exchange control takes the form of a set of regulations dictating who can and who cannot purchase goods and invest abroad. Specifically, under a rigorous system of exchange control everyone who seeks to make a payment to another country must obtain specific permission to do so. In most actual systems, there are only a few countries to which payments are restricted (since World War II, these were primarily the United States, Canada, and several South American countries whose currency is tied specifically to the American dollar).[3]

The purposes of exchange control are both to reduce foreign spending in countries whose currency is in short supply domestically and to see that the cut in foreign spending is imposed where it will do the least damage to the economy. For example, spending of dollars by British subjects for luxuries was cut drastically, while purchases of necessary raw materials and food were not.

Through exchange control, a result equivalent to the adjustment of a private family to lowered income is sought. The purpose is to cut back spending on various products so that only the least essential materials will be foregone. In the absence of direct exchange control, the demands for foreign luxuries could use up scarce foreign currency and compel a reduction in the import of absolute necessities.

Direct foreign-exchange control is a difficult type of regulation to administer with full effectiveness. Many methods of evading the regulations exist—primarily by dealing through third and fourth countries. However, most countries have improved their exchange controls to the point where violations are the exception rather than the rule.

Some countries rely more on import restrictions than on exchange

---

[3] A currency may be tied to another in several ways. Most commonly this tying is accomplished by using another nation's currency as backing for the domestic currency, or by pegging exchange rates in terms of another currency. For example, the Philippine peso is tied to the United States dollar: two pesos equal one dollar.

controls to curb the demand for foreign exchange. Included among such restrictions are quotas and tariffs, which are discussed later in this chapter.

2. EXCHANGE-RATE VARIATION AS CORRECTIVE FOR PAYMENTS DIFFICULTIES

Under certain circumstances imbalance of foreign payments and receipts can also be corrected by variations in exchange rates. In effect, buyers of goods abroad must pay two prices. First, they must pay the price charge for foreign currency, which is called the exchange rate, and represents the price of one money in terms of other currencies. Second, importers must pay the prices prevailing in foreign countries. We have already seen how a change in the second—domestic prices prevailing in foreign countries—would influence the balance of payments. Changes in exchange rates would have a similar effect. Should a deficit country lower its exchange rates, foreigners would be able to acquire its currency more cheaply in their own currency. Therefore the price of imports in their own currency would decline. Consequently, their purchases from the deficit country would tend to rise, and frequently the deficit country's total foreign income would rise. It would be in error, however, to conclude that devaluation would necessarily lead to a rise in foreign income. For example, a nation might be in such a position that it would be compelled to lower its foreign exchange rate by 4 per cent to obtain a 2 per cent rise in the physical volume of its exports. If that were true, this nation would actually obtain less foreign income at the lower exchange rates—and be giving up more goods to boot. Such a situation is termed an "inelastic demand for exports," and a nation's foreign income is increased under such circumstances by raising rather than lowering its exchange rates. Conversely, if the demand for a nation's exports were highly "elastic"—that is, if relatively small price reductions would spur large increases in foreign sales—a drop in exchange rates would enable the country to increase its foreign income. The elasticity of demand for exports probably varies widely from country to country and is constantly changing; even more disconcerting, one cannot measure it with any accuracy in any situation.

A nation can, almost at will, decree a change in its exchange rate. (If it belongs to the International Monetary Fund, it has agreed to discuss with the Fund its intention to alter exchange rates.) As was indicated earlier, changes in exchange rates are likely to provoke retaliation by the countries that lose markets to the devaluing country. (Essentially, a decline in exchange rates is intended to shift buyers to the devaluing country from other sources of supply.) Devaluation by one nation therefore is likely to initiate competitive changes in exchange rates or other forms of retaliation, and may not help a country when it suffers balance-of-payments difficulties.

3. FINANCIAL COOPERATION AMONG MANY NATIONS

One type of arrangement that has been devised to reduce the hardship resulting from a temporary adverse balance of foreign payments is embodied in the International Monetary Fund (the IMF) and the European Payments Union (EPU). These are essentially banks for short-term loans.[4] These "banks" are unique primarily in the fact that they deal in many different currencies and are run to help their members rather than to make profit from lending to others. The logic and mechanics of the IMF will be described briefly.

All members of the IMF must invest or deposit some agreed-upon amount of their own currencies. (In 1958, the IMF had 68 members; conspicuously absent are the U.S.S.R. and its satellites; the Fund began operations with gold and dollar assets of about $3.4 billion, which, by 1958, were about $2 billion.)[5] The deposits of each member can be "loaned" (sometimes it is spoken of as being "sold") to the other nations under specified conditions. The amount any nation can borrow each year is limited partly by its contribution to the Fund. The resources of the Fund are not replaced or added to; each borrower is expected to repay its loans, thereby making these funds available again when payments become unbalanced.

Such arrangements clearly are intended to meet temporary rather than persistent balance-of-payments difficulties. The size of the fund itself shows, moreover, that it is capable of dealing only with difficulties that are not extreme. If several nations were to suffer very large balance-of-payments deficits, they would not be able to get the needed help from the IMF.

The operations of the Fund may be illustrated by a simplified example. Assume that Belgium has insufficient dollars to pay for all the purchases it wishes to make from the United States. It can apply for a loan (or ask to purchase dollars from the Fund). Its "deposit" of francs would serve as security for the loan. The administrators of the Fund, who represent many nations, will weigh the merits of Belgium's application in comparison with other applications for loans of dollars. If the loan is granted, Belgium will ordinarily be given three to five years to repay it in the currency in which it borrowed.

Arrangements such as the IMF and EPU (which is fairly similar to the Fund, but has only Western European nations as its members) rest on the assumption that over moderately long periods any nation's foreign payments and receipts would balance. If this assumption were not met,

---

[4] Transactions with the IMF are actually purchases of foreign exchange.

[5] R. F. Mikesell, *United States Economic Policy and International Relations* (New York: McGraw-Hill Book Company, Inc., 1952), p. 161, and *Federal Reserve Bulletin,* May, 1958, p. 622.

the loans of scarce currencies would not be repaid, the Fund's holding of the currencies needed to help deficit countries would be exhausted, and the Fund would cease to function.

No international agency has been established to make long-term loans to assist nations that have, or can be expected to have, persistent long-run balance-of-payments difficulties. The absence of such an agency is due in part to the generally held view that no persistent balance-of-payments difficulty is legitimate. Quite similar is the conclusion that only nations that can obtain long-term foreign loans from private sources are entitled to import persistently more than they export.

Between 1946 and 1958 the International Bank for Reconstruction and Development provided about $3.5 billion in dollars and other scarce currencies to 46 countries engaged in more than 600 projects for rebuilding or developing vital parts of their economies. This money came from the subscriptions of 68 member governments to the Bank, as well as from the Bank's own borrowings in world capital markets. Thus countries whose balance-of-payments difficulties did not permit them to obtain materials and equipment necessary to their economic well-being were assisted;[6] in this way both world trade and economic development were furthered. This type of financial aid permitted the countries receiving assistance to incur or increase a deficit "on current account."

4. ALTER THE FUNDAMENTAL STRUCTURE OF THE ECONOMY

When a nation's ability to earn foreign income is impaired more or less fundamentally, it cannot hope to meet the situation by the various automatic and nonautomatic mechanisms described. It must make a fundamental change in its economy in the direction of increasing productivity or taking on the production of new goods or services that will increase its foreign income, or in the direction of reducing its reliance upon imports. These adjustments are likely to be both painful and time-consuming, but they are really the only kinds that will be enduring, because they alone get at the root of the difficulty. A nation with persistent balance-of-payment difficulties ultimately must either raise its income-producing capabilities or accept a drop in income.

---

[6] It should be emphasized that a total of $3.5 billion loaned for reconstruction and development purposes throughout the world during a twelve-year period is an extremely limited amount of money in terms of the vast capital needs for economic development. The role of the IBRD has therefore been extremely limited, though significant, in the overall picture of economic development. See *New York Times,* October 5, 1958, Section 3, pp. 1, 7.

C. Adequacy of Nonautomatic Measures to Correct Unbalanced Foreign-Payment Situations

There can be no question that direct exchange control *could* prevent unbalanced foreign payments. However, the hardship imposed by cutting foreign expenditure has sometimes been so great that nations have suffered persistent excesses of foreign payments over income despite an effective system of direct exchange control. (In particular, this condition prevailed in the United Kingdom and in a great part of Western Europe between 1945 and 1952.) Thus, even though the measures for correcting unbalanced payments can be made adequate, dependence on trade may be so great that it is practically impossible to eliminate deficits by these measures.

A single nation can balance its foreign income and obligations by cutting its imports. However, before cutting them below some level (this level varies from nation to nation), most countries will first exhaust their savings and their ability to borrow. In the highly disturbed conditions following World War II, the automatic and nonautomatic mechanisms for correcting unbalanced foreign payments were not sufficient. However, under less extreme conditions they almost certainly would be adequate. Prior to World War II, balance-of-payments difficulties were not so grave as those that plagued the world during the first postwar years.

D. Conditions Necessary to Avert Balance-of-Payments Difficulties

The difficulties besetting international economic dealings have resulted largely from World War II and its aftermath of cold war. We must ask ourselves whether it is reasonable to expect conditions to prevail that will allow nations to depend on foreign sources for vital supplies; that is, can nations reasonably look forward to a situation in which they will earn enough foreign income to justify reliance upon foreign supplies?

A sound balance of payments among all the nations of the world will require, first, that nations have an opportunity to adjust their economies to the changed conditions now prevailing. The commodity pattern of trade and its direction have shifted substantially in the years during and following World War II, as nations built up new industries and as political alignments changed. Difficulty is almost inevitable in some countries until they adjust to these new developments.

Second, the difficulties caused by imbalances of international payments are influenced by the distribution of gold and foreign-exchange holdings. As indicated, nations can expect, and need not be much injured by, short periods of foreign deficit. These can be met by drawing upon past accumulations of gold and foreign exchange. However, the ability to sustain even temporary balance-of-payments difficulties depends upon the distribution of the gold and foreign-exchange holdings of the world. In 1958 they were very unevenly distributed, with many nations barely holding enough resources to meet the kinds of difficulties that are almost certain to arise. On the other hand, some countries (the United States particularly) held resources far out of line with any foreseeable need for them. Some redistribution of the world's gold stock would contribute substantially toward security against great hardship that might result from temporary balance-of-payments deficits. In recent years the distribution of foreign-exchange reserves has improved greatly. For example, the gold and foreign-exchange reserves of continental countries belonging to the European payments union increased from $6.9 billion in 1950 to $14.6 billion in 1957.

Third, the formation of "currency areas," or ideally (though not practically) the shift to the use of a single money the world over for the settlement of foreign obligations, would help to reduce balance-of-payments difficulties. At present, over one fourth of the world's population belongs to the "sterling area," composed of nations using sterling to make international payments, and more than one half of the world's total international payments is made in sterling. Similar, but smaller, areas composed of nations using a single currency to settle international obligations among themselves are the French-and-Belgian-franc areas.

An extension in the scope of these currency areas would greatly reduce the present hazard that, although a nation obtains enough total foreign income to meet its needs, its income is not in the type of currency needed to purchase where and what it wants. Some nations have been driven into barter relations by a shortage of suitable foreign currencies.

One fairly common method put forward to avoid balance-of-payments difficulties should be mentioned. It requires that every nation hold its dependence upon international trade to the very minimum. In this way, each country would largely avoid injury from foreign disturbances. Such a policy, we have seen, would impose a price—one that would be very heavy for many countries—in the form of giving up the gains to be achieved from trade.

No country knowingly and willingly risks its very survival by dependence on foreign trade. However, complete security is unattainable without complete self-sufficiency. In turn, complete self-sufficiency does not mean great security. A nation that is poor (because of failure to trade) will be at the mercy of the elements, with little economic "fat" on which it can draw in the event of an emergency. The amount of security a nation can possess and should try to achieve cannot be settled in the abstract. One must know what price must be paid for varying degrees of security.

In summary, then, we find that many conditions contribute toward balance of international payments, or toward the reduction of hardship caused by periods of unbalanced payments. The international conditions that would permit balanced payments for individual countries will not be achieved easily or soon. However, there is no reason to believe that they are unattainable. Because of the great disruption of trade relations in the world even thirteen years after the end of World War II, considerable adjustment of national economies, and possibly redistribution of monetary resources, may still be needed before balance-of-payments difficulties can be counted a minor problem.

We thus have discussed one of three main difficulties arising in international economic relations. There remain for discussion terms of foreign trade and restrictions on trade. These two subjects, though not necessarily less important, will be treated more briefly than the first.

IV. INAPPROPRIATENESS OF THE TERMS OF FOREIGN TRADE

International balance, as defined here, requires that the terms on which nations trade with one another be equitable. How can an appropriate relation between the prices of a nation's imports and exports be defined?

A. Possible Meanings of "Appropriate Terms of Trade"

Three standards might be applied to decide what terms of trade are appropriate. The first, which views the matter from the standpoint of a single country, is such a relation between the price of imports and exports that the particular country obtains maximum foreign net income. The appropriateness of terms of trade can be viewed from a world standpoint. That is, they can be judged according to their effect upon the total volume of international trade. The second standard would take as best whatever relation between prices of goods entering foreign trade leads to the greatest volume of trade. A third standard, also from the world viewpoint, would judge the appropriateness of the terms of trade by their effect upon the balance of foreign payments and income over the entire trading world.

Viewed from the standpoint of a single country, terms of trade resemble the prices charged by sellers who have complete market power. One level of price will be the most favorable for each country; that is, it will give that country the greatest revenue relative to the costs incurred to obtain it. That level would usually be relatively unfavorable for other countries. Accordingly, terms of trade that one country would consider appropriate would be deemed most inappropriate by other nations.

In practice, most discussions of international terms of trade resemble arguments about farm prices. A worsening in the terms of trade is often considered unfair to the injured nation and an unearned windfall to the others. That is, certain past terms of trade are accepted as fair. Or it is sometimes argued that the terms of trade in the past and present are necessarily unfavorable to poor countries and that only changes that would redistribute income in favor of poor countries are fair. As we have already seen, neither of these conclusions is necessarily valid.[7]

A compromise position with reference to the terms of trade might consider as appropriate a relation between the prices of imports and exports for any country that divided equally the gains from trade. Unfortunately, these gains are virtually unmeasurable. Moreover, one might hold that the poorest countries should get more than half of the gains from trade. It would thus appear that little progress is made by defining the appropriateness of the terms of trade from the standpoint of individual countries.

In applying the two standards of appropriateness of the terms of trade from the world standpoint, we find that they sometimes conflict. Equality of foreign payments and receipts may be easier to attain with a low than with a high level of total international trade. This possible conflict actually confronts some countries and poses a dilemma. If, as a practical matter, they insisted on balancing their foreign income and payments, they would be compelled to import less. In consequence, both the volume of trade and the gains of trade would decline. One certain way of attaining equality of foreign payments and receipts is to discontinue foreign trade and lending altogether.

As a practical matter, many nations elect to suffer some imbalance in their financial position rather than forego the gains from trade. Especially is this true of nations highly dependent upon international trade. *From their individual standpoints, inequality of foreign payments is a far smaller evil than—a reduction in imports.* Presumably, the choice from the standpoint of the world as a whole would be the same. More specifically, appropriate terms of trade are those that foster a high level of trade, even if they involve minor and temporary imbalances of payments.

The foregoing definitions should help clarify thinking about terms of trade, even though their application in concrete instances requires enormous information and a large dose of genius. In assessing changes in terms of trade, one must distinguish the self-interest of individual countries from the good of the entire trading community. Even from the standpoint of the entire world, distinction must be made between problems of financial balance and total trade volume. In practice, however, no one and no agency is entrusted with the task of establishing appropriate

---

[7] See discussion in Chapter 18.

terms of trade. As was indicated previously, exchange rates—which underlie the terms of trade—are determined primarily by unilateral action taken by individual nations in pursuit of their self-interest.

In short, nations possessing the strongest bargaining power and strategic position presumably will obtain the lion's share of the gains from trade. As it happens, ". . . because of their poverty, the precariousness of their narrow exchange margins, and their desperate need of continuing large exports in order to be able to import both essential consumer goods and capital goods for their economic development, the bargaining power of underdeveloped countries has been, and remains, relatively very weak." [8] Thus the terms of trade have moved in a manner that has tended to increase the inequality among nations. In much the same way that the Congress of the United States has endeavored to alter the terms of trade between agriculture and industry within one country, the General Assembly of the United Nations, in December, 1952, adopted a resolution calling for an investigation of the terms of trade, particularly of nations producing "primary commodities," and an exploring of measures for keeping these prices in an adequate, just, and equitable relation to the prices of capital goods and other manufactured articles.[9] Although no action will be taken as a result of this or similar resolutions, their existence suggests the importance of the terms of trade to the welfare of individual nations, and indicates the misgivings of many about the "fairness" of the terms of trade prevailing at the present time.

B. How Terms of Trade Actually Are Determined

Terms of trade have two primary elements: domestic prices in nations trading with one another, and their foreign exchange rates. Both of these matters were discussed earlier in broad and general terms. They need not be reviewed here, but the implications of what had been said may gain new significance in this context.

In our discussion of depression and inflation, considerable emphasis was attached to the fact that monetary and fiscal measures could and should be taken to avert painful economic fluctuations. These measures frequently would affect price levels as well as the volume of employment and production. Whatever affects domestic prices of a nation also affects the prices that foreigners must pay for goods. Thus, the terms among nations are influenced by measures taken domestically to mitigate inflations and depressions.

Similarly, terms of trade are strongly influenced by government measures taken to influence exchange rates. As explained, governments

---

[8] Myrdal, *op. cit.*, p. 233.
[9] *Ibid.*, p. 236.

have the power to vary their exchange rates, within limits, and their actions will influence the terms of trade. Consequently, both domestic price levels and the prices of currencies in terms of one another reflect the arbitrary actions of government authorities. The terms of trade accordingly cannot be considered the resultant of free market forces—determining price levels within each nation and the price of each currency in terms of all others. One can well understand how Dr. Mikesell reached the conclusion that "world trade is directed by a monstrously complex network of trade and payments arrangements which has minimized the role of market forces in determining what nations will produce and what they will sell to one another." [10] One might add, "and the terms on which they will sell to one another."

V. LOSSES FROM RESTRICTIONS ON TRADE

In this section we shall discuss the third ingredient of an international economic optimum situation, namely, that there be a maximum of mutually advantageous trade. To do so, we shall examine restrictions on international trade—and particularly those that currently affect the trade of the United States. It should be emphasized that some restrictions on trade might be required, in order to avoid serious imbalances in international payments or inequitable terms of trade. Consequently, one cannot oppose *all* restrictions on trade; the total economic situation of a nation must be considered if we are to determine whether the limitations on trade are necessary.

Reference has already been made at several points to restrictions on international trade. These do not arise automatically, but are imposed mainly by individual governments, generally in response to domestic political pressures. As this text is being written, more restrictions afflict international trade than at almost any other peacetime period in recent history. Strong efforts toward freer trade are being made by several governments working through agencies of the United Nations, but progress has been slow.

Among the most important forms of trade restriction today are direct exchange control, tariffs, quotas, and bilateral trade agreements. Each of these will be discussed briefly in turn.

A. Direct Controls

Certain regulations require that persons engaging in international trade obtain a license either to import and export goods, or to purchase

---

[10] R. F. Mikesell, *Foreign Exchange in the Post-War World* (New York: The Twentieth Century Fund, 1954), p. 523.

foreign currencies in order to pay for imports. Direct exchange control is an unusual type of trade restriction for the United States. It is most commonly invoked by nations suffering an acute shortage of foreign exchange; even in 1958, direct exchange controls were to be found in such nations as Australia, Burma, Colombia, France, Greece, India, Indonesia, Japan, Pakistan, Turkey, and Uruguay. Direct controls have been applied in the United States to trade, in a long list of strategic items, with nations behind the Iron Curtain. As a consequence of these controls, trade between the United States and Russia, Poland, Czechoslovakia, Hungary, China, and Rumania has fallen to a small fraction of its former volume. These United States controls differ from most restrictions on international trade in that their objectives are political and military rather than economic.

B. Tariffs

Tariffs are the most common form of trade restriction applied in the United States. A tariff is a tax on imports paid upon entry into the country imposing the tariff. The rate of the tariff is determined by the importing nation according to its own legislative processes. Tariff rates are stated either as a percentage of the imported commodity's value (so-called *ad valorem* tariffs, which create rather delicate problems of determining the value of the imported merchandise) or as a specific duty per unit.

Tariffs are not necessarily imposed for the purpose of restricting trade; sometimes they are simply revenue-raising measures. In the United States, however, their main object is to exclude foreign merchandise or to put it at a competitive disadvantage with domestic goods.

The number of tariff duties on goods entering the United States runs into the thousands. It is difficult to summarize this large number of individual tariff duties. Some apply to goods of no great importance in our total volume of trade; others go virtually unpaid, because the duties are so high that no goods are imported. (The truly effective tariff is rarely collected, because the tariff makes the domestic sale of the imported product almost impossible.) Other tariffs are of little significance, because the goods in question would not be imported in any quantity even in the absence of the tariff. Nevertheless, some understanding of the number of tariff restrictions on the trade of the United States can be obtained from an examination of Table 1, which lists some of the more significant and interesting tariffs in effect in the United States through 1957.

The following characteristics of United States tariff duties should be noted particularly. First, they even apply to some products in whose production this country enjoys unusually great advantage—like automobiles, which carry a 20 per cent duty. Second, the amount of the duty imposed on individual products varies very widely, sometimes reaching very great heights and being quite insignificant in the case of others.

Table 1. Various Measures of the Importance and Size of United States Tariffs, 1901-1957

Year	Per cent of value of imports nondutiable	Ratio of duties to value of imports		Duties per capita *
		Total	Dutiable	
1901–1910	45.7%	24.6%	45.3%	$3.32
1911–1915	56.9	16.7	38.7	2.91
1916–1920	68.8	6.9	22.1	2.17
1921–1925	61.0	14.0	35.9	4.22
1926–1930	65.8	13.7	40.1	4.52
1931–1935	63.1	18.5	50.0	2.46
1936–1940	60.5	15.0	37.9	2.76
1941–1945	66.0	10.9	32.1	2.72
1946–1950	58.4	6.7	16.0	2.94
1951	55.4	5.5	12.3	3.76
1952	58.2	5.3	12.7	3.56
1953	54.9	5.4	12.0	3.59
1954	55.3	5.2	11.6	3.20
1955	53.2	5.6	12.0	3.76
1956	49.8	5.7	11.3	4.14
1957	46.5	5.8	10.8	4.28

* Beginning 1940, based on estimated population, including Armed Forces Overseas.

SOURCE: U.S. Department of Commerce, Bureau of the Census, *Statistical Abstract of the United States, 1958* (Washington, D.C.: Government Printing Office, 1958), p. 900.

Tariffs probably are higher now than they were at any time prior to the passage of the Hawley-Smoot Act in 1930. This bill, passed partly because of the effects of the depression that had started the year before, was so obnoxious to foreign countries that communications of protest were received and published from 24 nations while the bill was being debated in the Senate.[11] However, United States duties on imports have been lowered somewhat under the Reciprocal Trade Agreements Program[12] initiated in 1933 and kept in force ever since. The extent to which tariffs on imports into the United States have been reduced since 1933 can be observed from Table 2, which sums up the most recent changes in tariffs.

---

[11] Mikesell, *United States Economic Policy and International Relations*, p. 62.

[12] In 1958, once again, a sharp political struggle arose over the Eisenhower administration's attempts to extend the RTA Program; nevertheless, it was extended, with some modifications, for four years.

HOW A RECIPROCAL TRADE AGREEMENT IS MADE

After preliminary study by experts, State Department recommends to President that we try to negotiate reciprocal-trade-agreement with Country X.

If President approves, a list of items that each country wants concessions on, is drawn up for study and discussion.

Secretary of State publishes lists. Spokesmen for agriculture, industry, labor, consumers, exporters, importers present views at public hearing.

At same time, government economic experts study competitive position of U. S. industries, and tariff cuts which can be made by U. S. and Country X.

All information from experts and public hearings is reviewed and schedule of concessions to be made and asked is drawn up.

After approval of schedule by President, negotiations begin. By law, U. S. rates cannot be cut more than 50% below level of Jan. 1, 1945.

U. S. negotiators must get O. K. of experts and President before making any concessions in excess of approved schedule.

Agreement is approved and goes into operation. Any concessions made are extended to all other nations which are not found to discriminate against U. S. trade.

Committee for reciprocity information receives any complaints about economic results of the agreement

Agreement clause allows U. S. and Country X, after discussion, to withdraw or modify concessions on any item in order to protect domestic producers.

Table 2. Per Cent of Imports of Merchandise Free of Duty,*
by Economic Class, 1926-1957

Year	Crude materials	Crude food-stuffs and food animals	Manufactured foodstuffs	Semi-manufactures	Finished manu-factures
1926–1930	82.8	80.4	18.5	71.3	39.0
1931–1935	77.4	83.2	30.6	68.2	44.5
1936–1940	77.7	74.6	21.3	66.1	43.6
1941–1945	67.8	76.4	32.5	70.2	69.8
1946–1950	63.4	83.4	15.6	55.9	52.3
1951–1955	59.7	87.2	14.1	51.7	44.1
1956	59.6	89.3	2.7	47.9	36.8
1957	52.0	86.6	2.6	46.9	34.2

* Based on dollar values of general imports before 1934; imports for consumption thereafter.

SOURCE: U.S. Department of Commerce, Bureau of the Census, *Statistical Abstract of the United States, 1958* (Washington, D.C.: Government Printing Office, 1958), p. 902.

Thus it is quite clear that tariffs imposed on imports into the United States reflect strong efforts to curtail imports. These tariffs affect a very long list of commodities, many of which are in common use.

Before we leave the question of tariffs, one common error should be dispelled. That is the notion that tariffs are paid by foreigners, so "why worry about them." The fact of the matter is quite the reverse, of course. Tariffs are passed along to consumers of the product; if goods imported into this country could not be sold at prices high enough to cover their cost plus the duty, importers would not deal in them.

Indeed, it is not unlikely that consumers pay tariffs indirectly even when they buy certain domestic merchandise. They would do so under the following circumstances: the tariff is so high that little foreign merchandise enters the country; the exclusion of imports permits domestic producers to command a higher price for their merchandise. In such circumstances the tariff will have raised the price of domestic goods. It may well be that this second effect of tariffs is the more common one.

C. Quotas

Quotas limit the physical quantity of specified products that may be imported from all or particular nations. These regulations, applying primarily to sugar, petroleum, rubber, and nitrates, are of only moderate importance in the United States.

Quotas limit foreign imports to some predetermined share of the domestic market. In this way they insure domestic producers of some share—generally by far the larger share—of the domestic market. By limiting imports, quotas also permit prices to be higher than they would be in the absence of quota restrictions. (Quotas have been employed in connection with the Reciprocal Trade Agreements Program to limit the amount of imports to which reduced duties apply.)

D. Bilateralism

"Some trade is better than no trade at all" is a pretty safe generalization. It was on this assumption that, during the 1930's (when almost all countries were erecting high barriers against imports in the somewhat mistaken belief that they could provide jobs for their own workers in this way), the United States and other countries sought to unshackle their international trade. There resulted a large number of agreements between *pairs* of countries which facilitated trade between them. (Hitler's Germany was one of the first and perhaps the most active nation in carrying out such a program.)

These agreements were *bilateral* in nature, because they affected trade between only two parties; they had a mixed effect. On one hand, they did give rise to trade that would not have taken place in their absence, and represented a first step toward a *general* loosening of trade restrictions. On the other hand, they created artificial trade relations that could not endure when the worst restrictions on trade were removed. Bilateral trade involves participating nations in serious risks, because they become heavily dependent upon particular trade partners, tend to develop inefficient industries—and because it may lull them into neglecting to reduce trade restrictions that would contribute to freer multilateral trade.

Trade restrictions are contagious. As indicated, if one nation restricts imports from another nation—no matter by what means—the latter frequently will retaliate. Restrictions arise from another source. Domestic producing groups generally advocate curtailments of the things they sell in order to avoid foreign competition. Consequently, when foreign sources increase their sales in the United States or threaten to do so, domestic producers—generally allied with labor representatives—press for "protection" against foreign competitors. A striking example in post-World War II is that of the Danish cheese industry, which consciously aimed to increase its dollar earnings by concentrating on exports to the United States. When it succeeded in expanding these, the domestic cheese producers were able to erect barriers against them, and cheese imports from Denmark virtually stopped.[13]

There can be little question that *in practice,* no matter what the

---

[13] It should be remarked that the United States has been an exception. When the rest of the world restricted imports from us for balance-of-payments reasons, the United States has not retaliated.

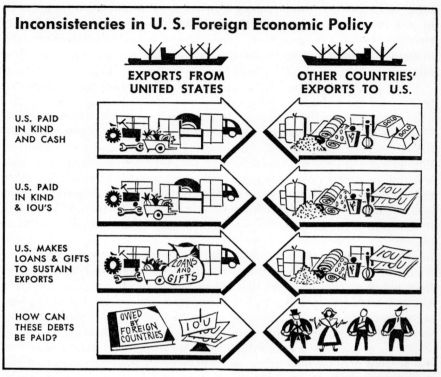

Inconsistencies in U. S. Foreign Economic Policy

EXPORTS FROM UNITED STATES **OTHER COUNTRIES' EXPORTS TO U.S.**

U.S. PAID IN KIND AND CASH

U.S. PAID IN KIND & IOU'S

U.S. MAKES LOANS & GIFTS TO SUSTAIN EXPORTS

HOW CAN THESE DEBTS BE PAID?

Chart by GRAPHICS INSTITUTE

YOU CAN'T COLLECT IF YOU WONT ACCEPT PAYMENTS

Political pressure from producer-labor groups within the United States is weighted heavily in favor of a policy of curtailing imports in order to protect domestic industries. Consequently, we have experienced a persistent export surplus, and are likely to do so in the future, despite recent efforts to adopt a policy of "trade not aid" for our foreign allies.

Past export surpluses have been made possible both by a drawing down of other nations' stocks of gold and foreign exchange and by large loans from the United States. If loans are curtailed to foreign countries that have import surpluses, they must either reduce their imports or increase exports. Even if further loans are extended, their repayment depends upon our willingness to accept payment in the form of goods and services, for few nations have, or are likely to accumulate, gold and foreign exchange balances that would permit them to discharge their indebtedness by making direct money payments.

If a "trade not aid" policy is to be adopted, it will either be necessary to overcome the strong political pressures that oppose such a policy, or to devise measures to compensate domestic industries for the losses they sustain when foreign competition is increased.

principles espoused, United States regulations of international trade result in persistently greater exports than imports. These regulations arise, as already explained, because of the opposition of domestic producing groups to an expansion of imports, while other producing groups seek to increase exports.

A brief digression on the connection between American commercial policy and the balance of payments of the world is appropriate at this point. If one nation persistently obtains foreign income substantially in excess of foreign payments, then other nations *must* be running deficits; the United States surplus must be paid for by some country or countries. Put differently, American commercial policy is incompatible with balanced payments in the rest of the world unless the United States is willing to lend the surplus balance back to these countries. And even this proviso is not sufficient; we must also be willing to accept repayment of our loans if we succeed in our policy of lending to make up the payments deficits of other countries. But if payment is to be accepted on foreign loans, it must take the form of imports into this country sufficient to allow foreign countries to pay both for our exports and for interest and dividends on their borrowings—unless we are willing constantly to increase our loans to cover both deficits from trade and interest and principal payments on loans. Thus the commercial policy of the United States is, in itself, sufficient to cause balance-of-payments difficulties in the rest of the world.

Two major conclusions follow from the foregoing discussion. First, the foreign commercial policy of the United States contributes to the world's international trade difficulties. Second, the remedy for this situation—apart from a change in American commercial policy—is a program of foreign gifts. Much as many spokesmen may try to avoid this conclusion, there is no escape from it. Foreign nations have already long since reached this conclusion and take a sardonic view of our solemn and pontifical preachments in favor of free trade.

VI. SUMMARY AND CONCLUSIONS

Trade is confronted with numerous difficulties. Many nations, through their dependence upon foreign supplies of important products, run the risk of serious hardship for their foreign income may decline sharply because of circumstances beyond their control. The uneven distribution of gold holdings and the small foreign exchange holdings of most countries mean that these countries will not be able to finance even brief periods of difficulty from accumulated resources. Many automatic and nonautomatic measures operate, or could be put into operation, to correct payment deficits, but when foreign trade is highly disturbed—as it has been since the end of World War II—these measures do not suffice.

All nations gain from foreign trade, but the sharing of the gains is not necessarily equitable. Each nation, especially in setting its foreign exchange rates, pursues a policy based wholly on national interest, paying no heed to the loss that it may impose on other nations. There is nothing to be found in the determination of the rates of exchange that indicates that the terms of trade are equitable. Moreover, the difficulty of defining standards of equity in sharing the terms of trade and in measuring these gains in each country makes it unlikely that equitable terms of trade will be established.

The foregoing discussion of the difficulties involved in international trade illustrates many things. Foremost among them is the possible contradiction between what may be good for an individual group and what is best for the nation and the world as a whole. Restrictions on imports usually help particular groups at the expense of other groups in the same country and to the detriment of foreign nations.

Finally, countries of the world apparently engage in only a fraction of the trade that would be mutually beneficial. Every nation restricts both exports and imports. Trade between countries of the "East" and the "West" has been sharply curtailed for political reasons. Long before such restrictions, heavy tariffs, quota restrictions, and direct exchange control limited trade between nations. Little hope for a substantial freeing of trade can be held out as long as producing groups can so easily secure the enactment of tariffs and quotas against foreign imports. Moreover, these restrictions, when imposed by a major nation like the United States in an effort to maintain a consistent exports surplus, impose a balance-of-payments problem on many other countries of the world. In the absence of willingness on the part of the United States to elect a conscious policy of making foreign gifts and grants in aid, other nations may be plagued constantly by balance-of-payments difficulties.

DISCUSSION QUESTIONS

1. Under what circumstances do individuals suffer the equivalent of an imbalance of foreign receipts and payments?

2. In what sense are certain "mechanisms" automatic? Illustrate by the manner in which adjustments in income levels tend to equalize foreign receipts and payments.

3. Can a government have a domestic surplus while the nation is suffering an international deficit? Can you think of any examples?

4. If every individual within a country spends no more than his total income, could the nation run a foreign payments deficit? Explain.

5. Explain why the flow of gold from a nation that is a net importer was expected to put an end to the excess of imports over exports.

6. Does the United States employ direct controls over imports? Are they employed to counteract balance-of-payments difficulties? Give examples.

7. Is there necessarily some exchange rate that would correct a nation's balance-of-payments difficulties? Explain.

8. The determination of a nation's exchange rate may be likened to the determination of price by a monopolist. Explain the similarity between them.

9. Explain the basic principle on which the International Monetary Fund and the European Payments Union operate. Are these organizations suited to meeting long-term balance-of-payments difficulties? Explain.

10. What two elements enter into the terms of trade between two countries? How are they determined?

11. Are foreign exchange rates determined by relatively free forces of supply and demand for currencies? Explain.

12. What factors account for the wide differences in the relative dependence of individual countries upon international trade?

13. Is the absolute amount of a nation's foreign trade increased or reduced by increases in its domestic output? Explain. Is the proportion of its national income that is purchased from abroad likely to rise or fall with increases in its domestic output? Explain.

14. Do you expect the United States to support actively and cooperate in a world-wide movement to reduce restrictions on international trade? Explain your answer.

SELECTED READINGS FOR PART 7

Allen, R. G. D., and J. E. Ely (eds.). *International Trade Statistics.* New York: John Wiley & Sons, Inc., 1953. P. 460. This book deals with the standards, methods, and practices involved in the gathering and presentation of statistics on international trade. The book provides a very useful guide for treating the problems of international measurement.

American Economic Association. *Readings in the Theory of International Trade.* New York: Blakiston Division—McGraw-Hill Book Company, Inc., 1949. P. 637. A collection of articles appearing in the various scholarly journals covering different aspects of international economic problems. The articles, selected by a committee of the American Economic Association, are among the most important written on this subject by experts in the field.

Behrman, Jack N., and Wilson E. Schmidt. *International Economics: Theory, Practice, Policy.* New York: Rinehart & Company, Inc., 1957. P. 561. Following a brief and clear introduction to the theory of international economic relations, including the arguments for and against free trade, this book presents a short historical survey. Most of the book is devoted to an analysis of actual policies relating to overseas trade, aid, and finance.

Bidwell, Percy W. *What the Tariff Means to American Industries.* New York: Harper & Brothers, 1956. Pp. xvi, 304. This is an extremely interesting and useful evaluation of the protective tariff in eight American industries ranging from the watch industry to the iron and steel industries. The impact of tariff reductions in each industry is assessed.

Buchanan, Norman S., and Friederich A. Lutz. *Rebuilding the World Economy: America's Role in Foreign Trade and Investment.* New York: Twentieth Century Fund, 1947. P. 434. The problems of the world economy after World War II are sifted vis-à-vis the United States economy. In addition, the book offers outlines of world economy before the war.

Elliott, William Y. *The Political Economy of American Foreign Policy.* New York: Henry Holt and Company, Inc., 1955. Pp. xv, 414. In this book the outgrowth of foreign economic policy is explored in the context of dynamic social and political forces shaping different interest groups within a country. Problems of trading with different areas of the world, especially under-developed areas, are dealt with.

Ellsworth, Paul T. *The International Economy: Its Structure and Operation.* New York: The Macmillan Company, 1950. P. 922. An outstanding text on international economic problems in their historical and institutional setting. It provides the basic information and mechanisms necessary to an understanding of the international economy.

Graham, Frank D. *The Theory of International Values.* Princeton, N.J.: Princeton University Press, 1948. P. 349. The author explains in theoretical terms the mechanism of international exchange. His approach represents a critique of the classical theory of international exchange.

Humphrey, Don D. *American Imports.* New York: Twentieth Century Fund, 1955. Pp. xviii, 546. The volume and composition of American imports are analyzed, with attention given to their long-run and cyclical patterns. Trade restrictions and efforts to reduce them are discussed, together with the impact of our imports on domestic industry.

International Monetary Fund. *The First Ten Years of the International Monetary Fund.* Washington, D.C.: The Fund, 1956. P. 47. This is a very useful review of the operations, achievements, and aims of the IMF since its inception. It helps to put the IMF in a clear perspective for the layman.

Kindleberger, Charles P. *International Economics.* Homewood, Ill.: Richard D. Irwin, Inc., 1953. P. 543. This is a general approach to the international economy. It includes the more recent additions to international economic theory in a well-integrated work.

Klopstock, Fred H. *The International Status of the Dollar.* Princeton, N.J.: International Financial Section, Princeton University, 1957. P. 26. This is a very useful survey of the dollar's changing status since World War I in which the author touches on many aspects of the dollar shortage and the economic implications of the dollar's present status.

Lekachman, Robert (ed.). *National Policy for Economic Welfare at Home and Abroad.* Garden City, N.Y.: Doubleday & Company, Inc., 1955. Pp. xii, 366. A collection of essays dealing with economic welfare, freedom, the theory of economic growth, international economic integration, etc. Included among the contributors are Arthur F. Burns, J. M. Clark, S. Kuznets, and G. Myrdal.

MacDougall, Donald. *The World Dollar Problem.* New York: St. Martin's Press, Inc., 1957. P. 622. The author examines the world dollar shortage in the context of the world imbalance in trade. Both the effects of these conditions on the world economy and the ways open to mitigate the adverse effects are dealt with.

Mikesell, Raymond F. *Foreign Exchange in the Postwar World*. New York: Twentieth Century Fund, 1954. Pp. xv, 658. A very valuable survey of postwar foreign-exchange and currency problems. Different areas and nations are discussed, and the controlling devices used in their payments mechanisms are analyzed.

Myrdal, Gunnar. *An International Economy*. New York: Harper & Brothers, 1956. Pp. xi, 381. This book is an examination of international economic relations outside the Russian orbit. The author discusses the possibilities of effecting a higher level of economic integration for this international economy.

National Industrial Conference Board, Inc. *Convertibility and Foreign Trade*. New York: The Board, 1954. P. 159. A general treatment of the major factors involved in the problem of currency convertibility. In addition, there are appropriate statistical series brought to bear on the problem at hand.

Ohlin, Bertil. *Interregional and International Trade*. Cambridge, Mass.: Harvard University Press, 1935. P. 617. A classic work in the theory of international economic relations in which the author presents his original approach. It is a significant work used as standard equipment in this area.

United Nations. *The International Flow of Private Capital, 1946-1952*. New York: United Nations, 1954. Pp. iii, 61. A very useful survey of the flows of private capital, with an analysis of their nature and the limiting factors involved. The statistics deal with the amounts and kinds of flows.

Viner, Jacob. *Studies in the Theory of International Trade*. New York: Harper & Brothers, 1937. P. 650. Studies bearing on the history of economic thought in the context of international trade and finance. This, too, is a standard work used in approaching the problems of the international economy.

Williams, John B. *International Trade under Flexible Exchange Rates*. Amsterdam: North-Holland Publishing Company, 1954. Pp. xiv, 332. The operation of international trade under flexible exchange rates, rather than the traditional gold standard, is analyzed in detail. In the postwar institutional setup this book provides a valuable assortment of tools and benchmarks for problems of current trade and exchange.

Woytinsky, W. S., and E. S. Woytinsky. *World Commerce and Governments: Trends and Outlook*. New York: Twentieth Century Fund, 1955. Pp. lii, 907. This is a valuable comprehensive reference book with statistics on foreign trade and governments. Most of the nations of the world are covered, from the nineteenth century to the present.

Conclusions

The present-day American economy is not accurately described by the terms that are customarily used for this purpose. It can scarcely be described as a "free-enterprise" economy, for example, because the restraints upon entrepreneurs' freedom of choice are substantial. These come from government, from labor unions, and from the demonstrated need of corporate officials to show concern with the public welfare. Executives of some large and influential corporations have been moving slowly in the direction of acting like self-appointed public-utility officials rather than private businessmen, with consequences that are not yet clear. The consequences may in fact not be beneficial, even though businessmen's concern for the social implications of their actions is undoubtedly greater than ever.

The American economy of the 1960's surely will have little in common with the world lived in and described by Adam Smith, John Stuart Mill, and Alfred Marshall. Indeed, it bears only slight resemblance to the economies excogitated by Edward Chamberlin, Joan Robinson, and John M. Keynes. Although reality has always deviated from traditional economic models, the deviation may have become intolerably great and may require new theoretical formulations. Professor Galbraith's two recent books, *American Capitalism: The Concept of Countervailing Power* and *The Affluent Society,* are notable efforts in this direction and perhaps contain the elements of a body of new economic principles applicable to our present economic arrangements. One might say that, at present, we are almost without a useful body of economic theory to explain important facets of the American economy. Few economists are trying to see the economy "whole," if one can judge by their current writings. They seem concerned mainly with containing inflation and with the nature of economic development, when they do not concentrate upon adding embellishments to traditional economic theory.

Public officials, teachers, and students run the serious risk of applying concepts and principles that are quite inapplicable—or, at least, misleading. As the economy departs more and more from the stereotype of a free-enterprise economy, the need for using cautiously—and perhaps discarding—some traditional economic principles becomes more essential. We are not likely to reach correct solutions for our economic problems for the wrong reasons.

Even though it may be impossible to see the main forces that govern the emerging economy, one cannot assume that they are the same as those that dominated the old. Efforts to develop a new body of economic principles that fits prevailing circumstances will not be made, however, until those principles applied currently that no longer serve have been frankly disavowed.

One method of assessing the usefulness of each individual economic principle is to face up to the main economic problems of the present day and to assess the help it gives in diagnosing and in finding cures for difficulties. That approach is likely to reveal where fresh concepts and insights are needed and where added information may fill in present voids in our understanding. That approach has been employed in this book and has led to the conclusion that traditional economic principles remain valuable in the analysis of some problems, though a half-baked understanding of them will almost always be more misleading than helpful. In other words, those who can parrot but have not mastered economic theory are more likely to reach wrong conclusions than correct ones. Also, in many vital areas of public concern, one is likely to make more progress and achieve deeper and more useful understanding from an empirical analysis of the problem and the application of *ad hoc* common sense and logic than by starting with the relevant theoretical principles.

Economic theory is in need of an overhaul. Beyond that, there is the added need to set down the central principles that govern the American economy in particular, for they are likely to be different from those that apply almost anywhere else in the world. A great difference probably will prove to exist between the economic principles that were appropriate to the United States economy of the 1920's and 1930's and those principles that will be taught and applied in the 1960's. If so, then we must guard against misapplication of the economic principles discussed here and elsewhere. The unique features of our economy should inspire many to take the challenge and search out and make clear the main forces that underlie the rapidly changing and perplexing United States economy. The new body of economic theory must do more than take account of the hydrogen bomb, missiles, earth and moon satellites, and the intense competition between the Iron Curtain countries and the Western World. It must pay attention to the enormous concern of businessmen with taxes and public relations; it must give heavy weight to the nature and power of seller persuasion (*The Hidden Persuaders* and all that); it must take account of the changed political power of various groups—particularly labor and small business. Most of all, the new economics must reckon with the fact that most people work and consume for reasons only remotely connected with the gratification of stable and basic needs. Although this book deals with the world of the present and the issues of the moment, it certainly has not presented a blueprint of the new economic order. Hopefully, it has provided at least a blurred picture of what may have been altogether formless before, and raised questions and stimulated interest that will induce others to make the picture more clear and accurate.

Author Index

Subject Index

Author Index

Subject Index